Why Do You Need This New Edition?

6 good reasons why you should buy this new edition of *The Heritage of World Civilizations,* Brief Fifth Edition

1. This edition is tied more closely than ever to the innovative website, MyHistoryLab, which helps you save time and improve results as you study history (www.myhistorylab.com). Improved MyHistoryLab icons appear in the textbook, alerting you to important connections between the textbook and MyHistoryLab resources. At the end of each chapter you will find a *MyHistoryLab Connections* table. These tables provide a checklist of the most important *MyHistoryLab* resources related to the chapter, facilitating the integrated study of the textbook and the website.

2. Each chapter includes a new feature called "A Closer Look," which provides in-depth commentary on visual sources in world history. This feature teaches you to view photos, paintings, and other illustrations as historical documents. Each feature concludes with questions that encourage you to focus on important issues raised within the feature.

3. Chapter 11 features expanded coverage of the Byzantine Empire, including discussions of Byzantine imperial power in the 10th century, the importance of Constantinople, and Byzantium's impact on Islam.

4. In Chapter 13, coverage of Mesoamerica has been expanded significantly, including extensive new discussions of Mesoamerican ballgames, Olmec culture and civilization, Teotihuacán, and the Maya. Coverage of the Aztecs, the Moche, and the Inca Empire has also been greatly expanded.

5. Coverage of early Korean and Vietnamese history, which was spread between two chapters in the Brief Fourth Edition (Chapters 9 and 19), has been consolidated in Chapter 18 of the Brief Fifth Edition in order to create a more logical text flow. Chapter 9 now focuses exclusively on early Japanese history.

6. The last three chapters (Chapters 31, 32, and 33) carry the narrative through important recent events in Europe, Asia, Latin America, Africa, and the Middle East.

PEARSON

VOLUME 1: To 1700

The Heritage of World Civilizations

Brief Fifth Edition

ALBERT M. CRAIG
Harvard University

WILLIAM A. GRAHAM
Harvard University

DONALD KAGAN
Yale University

STEVEN OZMENT
Harvard University

FRANK M. TURNER
Yale University

Prentice Hall
Boston   Columbus   Indianapolis   New York   San Francisco   Upper Saddle River
Amsterdam   Cape Town   Dubai   London   Madrid   Milan   Munich   Paris   Montréal   Toronto
Delhi   Mexico City   São Paulo   Sydney   Hong Kong   Seoul   Singapore   Taipei   Tokyo

Editorial Director: Craig Campanella
Executive Editor: Jeff Lasser
Editorial Project Manager: Rob DeGeorge
Editorial Assistant: Julia Feltus
Director of Marketing: Brandy Dawson
Senior Marketing Manager: Maureen E. Prado Roberts
Marketing Assistant: Samantha Bennett
Senior Managing Editor: Ann Marie McCarthy
Project Manager: Cheryl Keenan
Senior Manufacturing and Operations Manager for Arts & Sciences: Nick Sklitsis
Operations Specialist: Christina Amato
Brief Edition Editor: Katie Janssen
Manager, Visual Research and Permissions: Beth Brenzel
Senior Art Director: Maria Lange

Cover Designer: Bruce Killmer
Cover Art: Erich Lessing/Art Resource, NY/Harpist playing and singing to Anhour Khaou, chief builder at Thebes, and to his wife. Wall painting in Anhour Khaou's tomb, carved 10 m below ground level, in the cemetery of Deir el-Medina, Tombs of the Nobles, Thebes, Egypt.
AV Project Manager: Mirella Signoretto
Media Director: Brian Hyland
Media Project Manager: Tina Rudowski
Digital Media Editor: Alison Lorber
Composition and Full-Service Project Management: Linda Ruggeri, Prepare, Inc.
Printer/Binder: Webcrafters, Inc.
Cover Printer: Lehigh Phoenix Color
Text Font: 10/13 Goudy

Library of Congress Cataloging-in-Publication Data

The heritage of world civilizations / Albert M. Craig ... [et al.]. -- Brief 5th ed.
   p. cm.
Includes bibliographical references and index.
ISBN 978-0-205-83549-2 (combined edition : alk. paper)
ISBN 978-0-205-83548-5 (volume 1 : alk. paper)
ISBN 978-0-205-83547-8 (volume 2 : alk. paper)
1. Civilization--History--Textbooks. I. Craig, Albert M. II. Title.

CB69.H45 2011
909--dc22
                                       2011005330

10 9 8 7 6 5 4 3 2 1

Combined Volume
ISBN-10: 0-205-83549-X
ISBN-13: 978-0-205-83549-2

Exam Copy
ISBN-10: 0-205-05254-1
ISBN-13: 978-0-205-05254-7

Volume 1
ISBN-10: 0-205-83548-1
ISBN-13: 978-0-205-83548-5

Volume 1 a la Carte
ISBN-10: 0-205-05226-6
ISBN-13: 978-0-205-05226-4

Volume 2
ISBN-10: 0-205-83547-3
ISBN-13: 978-0-205-83547-8

Volume 2 a la Carte
ISBN: 0-205-05256-8
ISBN: 978-0-205-05256-1

Prentice Hall
is an imprint of

www.pearsonhighered.com

Brief Contents

Contents

Documents

Maps

Preface

The global financial crisis that commenced in 2008 has painfully sparked for this generation a new sense of the connectedness of international economic events and financial forces. The banking crisis in the United States, the burgeoning Chinese economy, the debt upheaval within the European Union, the rise and fall of commodity prices, and the entanglement of the flows of capital from one part of the developed world to another have painfully demonstrated how events and decisions in one nation or upon one continent can impact millions of people living far from the centers of those decisions. The economic crisis has followed fast upon a decade during which the military forces of the United States and Europe have invaded nations of the Middle East in response to terrorist attacks. Environmental crises, whether in the form of oceanic oil spills or volcanic eruption, can interfere with trade, commerce, and tourism, as can changes in the price and availability of oil on which the United States, Europe, Japan, China, and India—to mention only the largest industrial economies—are dependent from sources outside their borders and regions.

Economic and military interaction and environmental crises upon the global scene are the most dramatic and disruptive signs of the impact of globalization. However, more quietly but not less dramatically, for the past two decades, the steady growth of the Internet has created in a less dramatic and far more peaceful fashion a sense of world wide cultural and commercial interconnectedness. Whereas once undergraduates in American universities might have gone to a larger newspaper room in their college or university library to read newspapers from other countries several days or even weeks after they had been published, today's students can follow the press of countries around the world from smart phones, computers, and other electronic reading devices. The Internet permits students to view museum collections located on every continent. Books of great rarity and value once reserved for students in a few elite universities are now available electronically in all parts of the world. United States colleges and universities to an extent previously unimagined are establishing branches far beyond North America. Whereas American students as recently as the 1970s found almost half the world closed to travel, now they can travel globally with almost no barriers.

Today, the interconnectedness of cultures and peoples as well as of economies is inescapable. We certainly dwell in an era in which no active citizen or educated person can escape the necessity of understanding the past in global terms. Both the historical experience and the moral, political, and religious values of the different world civilizations now demand our attention and our understanding. It is our hope that in these new, challenging times *The Heritage of World Civilizations* will provide one path to such knowledge.

THE ROOTS OF GLOBALIZATION

Globalization—that is, the increasing interaction and interdependency of the various regions of the world—has resulted from two major historical developments: the closing of the European era of world history and the rise of technology.

From approximately 1500 C.E. to the middle of the twentieth century, Europeans, later followed by the United States, gradually came to dominate the world through colonization (most particularly in North and South America), state-building, economic productivity, and military power. That era of European dominance ended during the third quarter of the twentieth century after Europe had brought unprecedented destruction on itself during World War II, as the United States eventually confronted limitations in its post-war influence, and as the nations of Asia, the Near East, and Africa achieved new positions on the world scene. Their new political independence, their control over strategic natural resources, the expansion of their economies (especially those of the nations of the Pacific rim of Asia), and in some cases their access to nuclear weapons have changed the shape of world affairs.

Further changing the world political and social situation has been a growing discrepancy in the economic development of different regions that is often portrayed as a problem between the northern and southern hemispheres. Beyond the emergence of this economic disparity has been the remarkable advance of radical political Islamism during the past forty years. In the midst of all these developments, as a result of the political collapse of the former Soviet Union, the United States has emerged as the single major world power, though its position has been increasingly challenged by China, whose economic might now rivals that of the United States and whose military has embarked on a rapid buildup of its forces in Asia.

The second historical development that continues to fuel the pace of globalization is the advance of technology, associated most importantly with transportation, military weapons, and electronic communication. The advances in transportation over the past two centuries, including ships, railways, and airplanes, have made more parts of the world and its resources accessible to more people in ever shorter spans of time. Over the past century and a half, military weapons of increasingly destructive power enabled Europeans and then later the United States to dominate other regions of the globe. Now, the spread of these weapons means that any nation with sophisticated military technology can threaten other nations, no matter how far away. Furthermore, technologies that originated in the West from the early twentieth century to the present have been turned against the West. More recently, as already noted, the electronic revolution associated with computer technology and most particularly the Internet has sparked unprecedented speed and complexity in global communications. It is astonishing to recall that personal computers have been generally available for less than thirty-five years and the rapid personal communication associated with them has existed for less than twenty years.

Why not, then, focus only on new factors in the modern world, such as the impact of technology and the end of the European era? To do so would ignore the very deep roots that these developments have in the past. More important, the events of recent years demonstrate, as the authors of this book have long contended, that the major religious traditions continue to shape and drive the modern world as well as the world of the past. The religious traditions link today's civilizations to their most ancient roots. We believe this emphasis on the great religious traditions recognizes not only a factor that has shaped the past, but one that is profoundly and dynamically alive in our world today.

STRENGTHS OF THE TEXT

BALANCED AND FLEXIBLE PRESENTATION
In this edition, as in past editions, we have sought to present world history fairly, accurately, and in a way that does justice to its great variety. History has many facets, no one of which can account for the others. Any attempt to tell the story of civilization from a single perspective, no matter how timely, is bound to neglect or suppress some important part of that story.

Historians have recently brought a vast array of new tools and concepts to bear on the study of history. Our coverage introduces students to various aspects of social and intellectual history as well as to the more traditional political, diplomatic, and military coverage. We firmly believe that only through an appreciation of all pathways to understanding of the past can the real heritage of world civilizations be claimed.

The Heritage of World Civilizations, Brief Fifth Edition, is designed to accommodate a variety of approaches to a course in world history, allowing teachers to stress what is most important to them. Some teachers will ask students to read all the chapters. Others will select among them to reinforce assigned readings and lectures.

CLARITY AND ACCESSIBILITY
The Heritage of World Civilizations, Brief Fifth Edition, provides a powerful but concise narrative enriched by abundant illustrations, focused study tools, and critical-thinking questions that make the past come alive. Good narrative history requires clear, vigorous prose. Our goal has been to make our presentation fully accessible to students without compromising on vocabulary or conceptual level. We hope this effort will benefit both teachers and students.

CURRENT SCHOLARSHIP
As in previous editions, changes in this edition reflect our determination to incorporate the most recent developments in historical scholarship and the expanding concerns of professional historians. To better highlight the dynamic processes of world history, significant new and expanded coverage of the Byzantine Empire and the early civilizations of the Americas—particularly the civilizations of Mesoamerica and the Andes during the pre-colonial period—has been added to the Brief Fifth Edition.

CONTENT AND ORGANIZATION
The many changes in content and organization in this edition of *The Heritage of World Civilizations* reflect our ongoing effort to present a truly global survey of world civilizations that at the same time gives a rich picture of the history of individual regions:

- **Global Approach.** The Brief Fifth Edition continues to explicitly highlight the connections and parallels in global history among regions of the world. Each chapter begins with a "Global Perspective" essay that succinctly places in a wider, global framework the regions and topics that are to be discussed with an emphasis on the connections, parallels, and comparisons between and among different cultures.

- **Improved Organization.** Some chapters have been reorganized to improve narrative flow and to highlight important topics more clearly. At the suggestion of reviewers, Chapter 4 (Iran, India, and Inner Asia to 200 C.E.) and Chapter 10 (Iran and South Asia, 200 C.E.–1000 C.E.) in the Brief Fourth Edition have been consolidated into a single chapter in the Brief Fifth Edition: Chapter 4 (West Asia, Inner Asia, and South Asia to 1000 C.E.). Coverage of early Korean and Vietnamese history has been moved from Chapter 9 to Chapter 18, leaving Chapter 9 solely devoted to early Japan. Coverage of Korea and Vietnam has been consolidated in Chapter 18 with a far greater sense of continuity and a more effective and concise presentation.

- **New Design and Photo Program.** The entire text has been set in a crisp and engaging new design. Each of the 33 chapters includes photos never before included in previous editions of the text.

PEDAGOGICAL FEATURES

This edition retains many of the pedagogical features of previous editions, while providing increased assessment opportunities.

- **Global Perspective Essays** introduce the key problems of each chapter and place them in a global and historical context. Focus Questions prompt students to consider the causes, connections, and consequences of the topics they will encounter in the main narrative.

- **A Closer Look**—Each chapter includes this **new** feature, which provides in-depth commentary on visual sources in world civilization. This feature engages student visually with the textbook and encourages them to look at visuals as documents, not just as pictures. Each feature concludes with questions that encourage students to focus on important issues raised by the feature.

- **Religions of the World** essays examine the historical impact of each of the world's great religious traditions: Judaism, Christianity, Islam, Buddhism, and Hinduism.

- **Focus Questions,** organized by key subtopics, open each chapter and help students think about important topics for study and review. The focus questions are repeated at the appropriate sections in each chapter.

- **Overview Tables** summarize key concepts and reinforce material presented in the main narrative.

- **Chronologies** within each chapter help students situate key events in time.

- **Quick Reviews,** found at key places in the margins of each chapter, encourage students to review important concepts.

- **Documents,** including selections from sacred books, poems, philosophical tracts, political manifestos, letters, and travel accounts, expose students to the raw material of history, providing an intimate contact with peoples of the past. Questions accompanying the source documents direct students toward important, thought-provoking issues and help them relate the documents to the main narrative.

- **Visual Analysis Questions** ask students to consider photographs, fine art, and other illustrations as visual evidence.

- **Key Terms** are boldfaced in the text and are defined in the margin of the page.

- **Interactive Maps,** called "Map Explorations," prompt students to explore the relationship between geography and history in a dynamic fashion. There is at least one interactive map per chapter and all interactive maps can be found at *www.myhistorylab.com*

- **Chapter Summaries** conclude each chapter, organized by subtopic, and recap important points.

- **Chapter Review Questions,** organized by key subtopics, help students interpret the broad themes of each chapter.

NEW TO THIS EDITION

There is a new feature in the Brief Fifth Edition:

    A Closer Look—*Each* chapter includes a new feature called "A Closer Look," which provides in-depth commentary on visual sources in world history. This feature teaches students to view photos, paintings, and other illustrations as historical documents. Each feature concludes with questions that encourage students to focus on important issues raised within the feature. See the Contents on page vi for the title of each of these new features.

    Here are just some of the changes that can be found in the Brief Fifth Edition of *The Heritage of World Civilizations*:

Chapter 3, Greek and Hellenistic Civilization:
- A new document has been added: "The Delian League Becomes the Athenian Empire."

Chapter 4, West Asia, Inner Asia, and South Asia to 1000 C.E.:
- At the suggestion of reviewers, Chapter 4 (Iran, India, and Inner Asia to 200 C.E.) and Chapter 10 (Iran and South Asia, 200 C.E.–1000 C.E.) in the Brief Fourth Edition have been consolidated into a single chapter in the Brief Fifth Edition: Chapter 4 (West Asia, Inner Asia, and South Asia to 1000 C.E.).
- The Global Perspective feature is new.
- There is a new document, an excerpted letter from Tansar about the Shahanshah, titled "Tansar's Defense of His King, Ardashir I."
- Consolidation of the two chapters involved considerable rearranging, with coverage of Iran and Central Asia located in the first section of the consolidated chapter and coverage of India in the second section. These sections have been renamed as follows: "West and Inner Asia" and "South Asia."
- Coverage of caste has been improved.

Chapter 5, Africa: Early History to 1000 C.E.:
- Coverage of historians' and anthropologists' methods and crossovers has been expanded.

Chapter 6, Republican and Imperial Rome:
- A new document has been added on the ruin of the Roman family farm and the Gracchan reforms.

Chapter 8, Imperial China, 589–1368:
- Coverage of Empress Wu has been updated to reflect new biographical scholarship.

Chapter 9, Early Japanese History:
- Global Perspective feature has been rewritten.
- Coverage of early Korean and Vietnamese history has been moved from this chapter to Chapter 18, leaving Chapter 9 solely devoted to early Japan.
- Japanese Origins section and Jōmon subsection have been updated.
- Yayoi section has been updated with a discussion of new DNA findings.
- There is new coverage of Shōtoku and Kamatari in the section on Nara and Heian Japan.

[*Note*: Brief Fourth Edition Chapters 4 and 10 have been combined in the Brief Fifth Edition, causing all chapters that follow—Chapters 11 – 34 in the Brief Fourth Edition—to be renumbered in the Brief Fifth Edition.]

Chapter 11, The Byzantine Empire and Western Europe to 1000:

- Coverage of Byzantium has been greatly expanded, with new sections on Byzantine imperial power in the 10th century, Byzantium's impact on Islam, and the city of Constantinople.
- A new document has been added in response to reviewer suggestions: The Nicene Creed

Chapter 13, Ancient Civilizations of the Americas:

- Coverage of the Paleolithic and Archaic periods in the Americas has been greatly expanded.
- There is a more detailed discussion on the influence of the European perspective on how the history of the Americas in the pre-Columbian period has been written.
- Coverage of Mesoamerica has been expanded significantly, including extensive new discussions of Mesoamerican ballgames, Olmec culture and civilization, Teotihuacán, and the Maya.
- Coverage of the Aztecs, the Moche, and the Inca Empire has been greatly expanded.

Chapter 17, Conquest and Exploitation: The Development of the Transatlantic Economy:

- There is new coverage of the Indian Wars in the 17th century North American British colonies.
- There is new coverage of the alleged slave conspiracy in 1741 in New York City.

A NOTE ON DATES AND TRANSLITERATION

We have used B.C.E. (before the common era) and C.E. (common era) instead of B.C. (before Christ) and A.D. (anno domini, the year of our Lord) to designate dates.

Until recently, most scholarship on China used the Wade-Giles system of romanization for Chinese names and terms. China today, however, uses another system known as pinyin. Virtually all Western newspapers have adopted it. In order that students may move easily from the present text to the existing body of advanced scholarship on Chinese history, we now use the pinyin system throughout the text.

Also, we have followed the currently accepted English transliterations of Arabic words. For example, today Koran is being replaced by the more accurate Qur'an; similarly Muhammad is preferable to Mohammed and Muslim to Moslem. We have not tried to distinguish the letters *'ayn* and *hamza*; both are rendered by a simple apostrophe (') as in Shi'ite. With regard to Sanskritic transliteration, we have not distinguished linguals and dentals, and both palatal and lingual *s* are rendered *sh*, as in Shiva and Upanishad.

| **SUPPLEMENTS FOR QUALIFIED COLLEGE ADOPTERS** | **SUPPLEMENTS FOR STUDENTS** |

MyHistoryLab (www.myhistorylab.com) *Save Time. Improve Results.* MyHistoryLab is a dynamic website that provides a wealth of resources geared to meet the diverse teaching and learning needs of today's instructors and students. MyHistoryLab's many accessible tools will encourage students to read their text and help them improve their grade in their course.

Instructor's Resource Manual   Available at the Instructor's Resource Center, at **www.pearsonhighered.com/irc**, the Instructor's Resource Manual includes chapter outlines, overviews, key concepts, discussion questions, and suggestions for useful audiovisual resources.

Test Bank   Available at the Instructor's Resource Center, at **www.pearsonhighered.com/irc**, the Test Bank includes approximately 1,500 test items (essay, multiple choice, true/false, and matching).

Instructor's Resource Center (www.pearsonhighered.com/irc) Text-specific materials, such as the Instructor's Resource Manual, Test Bank, map files, and PowerPoint™ presentations, are available for downloading by adopters.

MyTest   Available at **www.pearsonmytest.com**, MyTest is a powerful assessment generation program that helps instructors easily create and print quizzes and exams. Questions and tests can be authored online, allowing instructors ultimate flexibility and the ability to efficiently manage assessment anytime, anywhere! Instructors can easily access existing questions and edit, create, and store using simple drag-and-drop and Word-like controls.

MyHistoryLab (www.myhistorylab.com) *Save Time. Improve Results.*   MyHistoryLab is a dynamic website that provides a wealth of resources geared to meet the diverse teaching and learning needs of today's instructors and students. MyHistoryLab's many accessible tools will encourage you to read your text and help you improve your grade in your course.

CourseSmart www.coursesmart.com   CourseSmart is an exciting new choice for students looking to save money. As an alternative to purchasing the printed textbook, students can purchase an electronic version of the same content. With a CourseSmart eTextbook, students can search the text, make notes online, print out reading assignments that incorporate lecture notes, and bookmark important passages for later review. For more information, or to purchase access to the CourseSmart eTextbook, visit **www.coursesmart.com**

Books à la Carte   Books à la Carte editions feature the exact same content as the traditional printed text in a convenient, three-hole-punched, loose-leaf version at a discounted price—allowing you to take only what you need to class. You'll **save 35% over the net price** of the traditional book.

Primary Source: Documents in Global History **DVD** is an immense collection of textual and visual documents in world history and an indispensable tool for working with sources. Extensively developed with the guidance of historians and teachers, the DVD includes over 800 sources in world history—from cave art to satellite images of the Earth from space. More sources from Africa, Latin America, and Southeast Asia have been added to the latest version of the DVD. All sources are accompanied by head notes, focus questions, and are searchable by topic, region, or time period. The DVD can be bundled with *The Heritage of World Civilizations*, Brief Fifth Edition, at no charge. Please contact your Pearson representative for ordering information. (ISBN 0-13-178938-4)

 Titles from the renowned **Penguin Classics** series can be bundled with *The Heritage of World Civilizations*, Brief Fifth Edition, for a nominal charge. Please contact your Pearson sales representative for details.

(continued)

Library of World Biography Series
www.pearsonhighered.com/educator/series/Library-of-World-
Biography/10492.page   Each interpretive biography in the
Library of World Biography Series focuses on a person whose
actions and ideas either significantly influenced world events or
whose life reflects important themes and developments in global
history. Titles from the series can be bundled with *The Heritage of
World Civilizations*, Brief Fifth Edition, for a nominal charge.
Please contact your Pearson sales representative for details.

 **The Prentice Hall Atlas of World History, Second
Edition**   Produced in collaboration with Dorling
Kindersley, the leader in cartographic publishing, the
updated second edition of *The Prentice Hall Atlas of World History*
applies the most innovative cartographic techniques to present
world history in all of its complexity and diversity. Copies of the
atlas can be bundled with *The Heritage of World Civilizations*, Brief
Fifth Edition, for a nominal charge. Contact your Pearson sales
representative for details. (ISBN 0-13-604247-3)

Longman Atlas of World History   This atlas features carefully
selected historical maps that provide comprehensive coverage of
the major historical periods. Contact your Pearson sales representative for details. (ISBN 0-321-20998-2)

*A Guide to Your History Course: What Every Student Needs to
Know*   Written by Vincent A. Clark, this concise, spiral-bound
guidebook orients students to the issues and problems they will
face in the history classroom. Available at a discount when bundled with *The Heritage of World Civilizations*, Brief Fifth Edition.
(ISBN 0-13-185087-3)

A Short Guide to Writing about History, Seventh Edition
Written by Richard Marius, late of Harvard University, and
Melvin E. Page, Eastern Tennessee State University, this engaging
and practical text helps students get beyond merely compiling
dates and facts. Covering both brief essays and the documented
resource paper, the text explores the writing and researching
processes, identifies different modes of historical writing, including argument, and concludes with guidelines for improving style.
(ISBN 0-13-205-67370-8)

PEARSON
myhistorylab™

FOR INSTRUCTORS AND STUDENTS

Save TIME. Improve Results.

MyHistoryLab is a dynamic website that provides a wealth of resources geared to meet the diverse teaching and learning needs of today's instructors and students. MyHistoryLab's many accessible tools will encourage students to read their text and help them improve their grade in their course.

Features of MyHistoryLab

- **Pearson eText**—An e-book version of *The Heritage of World Civilizations* is included in MyHistoryLab. Just like the printed text, students can highlight and add their own notes as they read the book online.
- **Audio Files**—Full audio of the entire text is included to suit the varied learning styles of today's students. In addition there are audio clips of speeches, readings, and music that provide another engaging way to experience history.
- **Pre-tests, Post-tests, and Chapter Reviews**—Students can take quizzes to test their knowledge of chapter content and to review for exams.
- **Text and Visual Documents**—A wealth of primary source documents, images, and maps are available organized by chapter in the text. Primary source documents are also available in the MyHistoryLibrary and can be searched by author, title, theme, and topic. Many of these documents include critical thinking questions.
- **History Bookshelf**—Students may read, download, or print 100 of the most commonly assigned history works like Homer's *The Iliad* or Machiavelli's *The Prince*.
- **Lecture and Archival Videos**—Lectures by leading scholars on provocative topics give students a critical look at key points in history. Videos of speeches, news footage, key historical events, and other archival videos take students back to the moment in history.
- **MySearchLab**—This website provides students access to a number of reliable sources for online research, as well as clear guidance on the research and writing process.

- **Gradebook**—Students can follow their own progress and instructors can monitor the work of the entire class. Automated grading of quizzes and assignments helps both instructors and students save time and monitor their results throughout the course.

NEW In-text References to MyHistoryLab Resources

Read, View, See, Watch, Hear, and **Study and Review Icons** integrated in the text connect resources on MyHistoryLab to specific topics within the chapters. The icons are not exhaustive; many more resources are available than those highlighted in the book, but the icons draw attention to some of the most high-interest resources available on MyHistoryLab.

Read the Document Primary and secondary source documents on compelling topics such as *Excerpts from Sundiata: An Epic of Old Mali, 1235* and *Tang Daizong on the Art of Government* enhance topics discussed in each chapter.

View the Image Photographs, fine art, and artifacts provide students with a visual perspective on topics within the chapters, underscoring the role of visuals in understanding the past.

See the Map Atlas and interactive maps present both a broad overview and a detailed examination of historical developments.

Watch the Video Video lectures highlight topics ranging from Agriculture in Africa, to Witch Hunts, to the Columbian Exchange, engaging students on both historical and contemporary topics. Also included are archival videos, such as *The Silk Road: 5,000 Miles and 1,500 Years of Cultural Interchange* and *Teotihuacán Ruins in Mexico*.

Hear the Audio For each chapter there are audio files of the text, speeches, readings, and other audio material that will enrich students' experience of social and cultural history.

Study and Review MyHistoryLab provides a wealth of practice quizzes, tests, flashcards, and other study resources available to students online.

NEW MyHistoryLab Connections

At the end of each chapter, a new section, MyHistoryLab Connections, provides a list of the references within the chapter and additional documents, maps, videos, or additional resources that relate to the content of the chapter.

ACKNOWLEDGMENTS

We are grateful to the many scholars and teachers whose thoughtful and often detailed comments helped shape this as well as previous editions of *The Heritage of World Civilizations*. The advice and guidance provided by Katie Janssen on the coverage of African history and Thomas M. Ricks on the coverage of Islam and the Middle East are especially appreciated. Steven Ozment would like to thank Ammanuel Gashaw Gebeyehu and Ece G. Turnator for their contributions to Chapter 11. Much of the coverage of the Byzantine Empire that is new to the Brief Fifth Edition was written by these two fine scholars.

REVIEWERS OF THIS EDITION
Wayne Ackerson, *Salisbury University*
Heather Barry, *St. Joseph's College*
Eric Martin, *Lewis-Clark State College*
Gary Paul Ritter, *Central Piedmont Community College*
Anthony R. Santoro, *Christopher Newport University*
Gilmar Visoni, *Queensborough Community College*
Kristen Post Walton, *Salisbury University*
William Zogby, *Mohawk Valley Community College*

REVIEWERS OF PREVIOUS EDITIONS
W. Nathan Alexander, *Troy University*
Jack Martin Balcer, *Ohio State University*
Charmarie J. Blaisdell, *Northeastern University*
Deborah Buffton, *University of Wisconsin at La Crosse*
Loretta Burns, *Mankato State University*
Gayle K. Brunelle, *California State University, Fullerton*
Douglas Chambers, *University of Southern Mississippi*
Chun-shu Chang, *University of Michigan, Ann Arbor*
Mark Chavalas, *University of Wisconsin at La Crosse*
Anthony Cheeseboro, *Southern Illinois University at Edwardsville*
William J. Courteney, *University of Wisconsin*
Samuel Willard Crompton, *Holyoke Community College*
James B. Crowley, *Yale University*
Bruce Cummings, *The University of Chicago*
Stephen F. Dale, *Ohio State University, Columbus*
Clarence B. Davis, *Marian College*
Raymond Van Dam, *University of Michigan, Ann Arbor*
Bill Donovan, *Loyola University of Maryland*
Wayne Farris, *University of Tennessee*
Anita Fisher, *Clark College*
Suzanne Gay, *Oberlin College*
Katrina A. Glass, *United States Military Academy*
Robert Gerlich, *Loyola University*
Samuel Robert Goldberger, *Capital Community-Technical College*
Andrew Gow, *University of Alberta*
Katheryn L. Green, *University of Wisconsin, Madison*
David Griffiths, *University of North Carolina, Chapel Hill*
Louis Haas, *Duquesne University*
Joseph T. Hapak, *Moraine Valley Community College*
Hue-Tam Ho Tai, *Harvard University*
David Kieft, *University of Minnesota*
Don Knox, *Wayland Baptist University*
Frederick Krome, *Northern Kentucky University*

Lisa M. Lane, *Mira Costa College*
Richard Law, *Washington State University*
David Lelyveld, *Columbia University*
Jan Lewis, *Rutgers University, Newark*
James C. Livingston, *College of William and Mary*
Garth Montgomery, *Radford University*
Richard L. Moore Jr., *St. Augustine's College*
Beth Nachison, *Southern Connecticut State University*
Robin S. Oggins, *Binghamton University*
George S. Pabis, *Georgia Perimeter College*
Louis A. Perez Jr., *University of South Florida*
Jonathan Perry, *University of South Florida*
Cora Ann Presley, *Tulane University*
Norman Raiford, *Greenville Technical College*
Norman Ravitch, *University of California, Riverside*
Thomas M. Ricks, *University of Pennsylvania*
Philip F. Riley, *James Madison University*
Thomas Robisheaux, *Duke University*
William S. Rodner, *Tidewater Community College*
David Ruffley, *United States Air Force Academy*
Dankwart A. Rustow, *The City University of New York*
James J. Sack, *University of Illinois at Chicago*
William Schell, *Murray State University*
Marvin Slind, *Washington State University*
Daniel Scavone, *University of Southern Indiana*
Linda B. Scherr, *Mercer County Community College*
Roger Schlesinger, *Washington State University*
Charles C. Stewart, *University of Illinois*
Nancy L. Stockdale, *University of Central Florida*
Carson Tavenner, *United States Air Force Academy*
Truong-bu Lam, *University of Hawaii*
Deborah Vess, *Georgia College and State University*
Harry L. Watson, *Loyola College of Maryland*
William B. Whisenhunt, *College of DuPage*
Paul Varley, *Columbia University*

Finally, we would like to thank the dedicated people who helped produce this revision: our editor, Jeff Lasser; editorial project manager Rob DeGeorge; Maria Lange, who created the handsome new design for this edition; Cheryl Keenan, our project manager; Christina Amato, our operations specialist, and Linda Ruggeri from Prepare, Inc, our production editor. We also owe a special thanks to Katie Janssen for her invaluable help in preparing this brief edition.

A.M.C

W.A.G

D.K

S.O

F.M.T

About the Authors

Albert M. Craig is the Harvard-Yenching Research Professor of History Emeritus at Harvard University, where he has taught since 1959. A graduate of Northwestern University, he received his Ph.D. at Harvard University. He has studied at Strasbourg University and at Kyoto, Keio, and Tokyo universities in Japan. He is the author of *Choshu in the Meiji Restoration* (1961), *The Heritage of Chinese Civilization*, Third Edition (2011), *The Heritage of Japanese Civilization*, Second Edition (2011), and, with others, of *East Asia: Tradition and Transformation* (1989). He is the editor of *Japan: A Comparative View* (1973) and co-editor of *Personality in Japanese History* (1970). At present he is engaged in research on the thought of Fukuzawa Yukichi. For eleven years (1976–1987) he was the director of the Harvard-Yenching Institute. He has also been a visiting professor at Kyoto and Tokyo universities. He has received Guggenheim, Fulbright, and Japan Foundation Fellowships. In 1988 he was awarded the Order of the Rising Sun by the Japanese government.

William A. Graham is Albertson Professor of Middle Eastern Studies in the Faculty of Arts and Sciences and O'Brian Professor and Dean of the Faculty of Divinity at Harvard University, where he has taught since 1973. He has directed the Center for Middle Eastern Studies and chaired Near Eastern Languages and Civilizations and the Study of Religion. He received his B.A. from the University of North Carolina, Chapel Hill, and the A.M. and Ph.D. from Harvard. He also studied in Göttingen, Tübingen, Lebanon, and London. He has chaired the (N. American) Council on Graduate Studies in Religion. In 2000 he received the quinquennial Award for Excellence in Research in Islamic History and Culture from the Research Centre for Islamic History, Art and Culture of the Organisation of the Islamic Conference. He has held Guggenheim and vòn Humboldt research fellowships and is a fellow of the American Academy of Arts and Sciences. He is the author of *Divine Word and Prophetic Word in Early Islam* (1977—ACLS History of Religions Prize, 1978), *Beyond the Written Word: Oral Aspects of Scripture in the History of Religion* (1987), *Islamic and Comparative Religious Studies* (2010), and, with others, of *Three Faiths, One God* (2003).

Donald Kagan is Sterling Professor of History and Classics at Yale University, where he has taught since 1969. He received the A.B. degree in history from Brooklyn College, the M.A. in classics from Brown University, and the Ph.D. in history from Ohio State University. During 1958–1959 he studied at the American School of Classical Studies as a Fulbright Scholar. He has received three awards for undergraduate teaching at Cornell and Yale. He is the author of a history of Greek political thought, *The Great Dialogue* (1965); a four-volume history of the Peloponnesian war, *The Origins of the Peloponnesian War* (1969); *The Archidamian War* (1974); *The Peace of Nicias and the Sicilian Expedition* (1981); *The Fall of the Athenian Empire* (1987); a biography of Pericles, *Pericles of Athens and the Birth of Democracy* (1991); *On the Origins of War* (1995); and *The Peloponnesian War* (2003). He is coauthor, with Frederick W. Kagan, of *While America Sleeps* (2000). With Brian Tierney and L. Pearce Williams, he is the editor of *Great Issues in Western Civilization*, a collection of readings. And with Gregory F. Viggiano, he is the editor of *Problems in the History of Ancient Greece: Sources and Interpretation* (2010). He was awarded the National Humanities Medal for 2002.

Steven Ozment is McLean Professor of Ancient and Modern History at Harvard University. He has taught Western Civilization at Yale, Stanford, and Harvard. He is the author of nine books. *The Age of Reform, 1250–1550* (1980), won the Schaff Prize, and was nominated for the 1981 National Book Award. Five of his books have been selections of the History Book Club: *Magdalena and Balthasar: An Intimate Portrait of Life in Sixteenth Century Europe* (1986), *Three Behaim Boys: Growing Up in Early Modern Germany* (1990), *Protestants: The Birth of A Revolution* (1992), *The Burgermeister's Daughter: Scandal in a Sixteenth Century German Town* (1996), and *Flesh and Spirit: Private Life in Early Modern Germany* (1999). Recent books include *Ancestors: The Loving Family of Old Europe* (2001), *A Mighty Fortress: A New History of the German People* (2004), and *The Serpent and the Lamb: When Lucas Cranach, the Elder Met Martin Luther* (2012).

Frank M. Turner was John Hay Whitney Professor of History at Yale University and Director of the Beinecke Rare Book and Manuscript Library at Yale University, where he served as University Provost from 1988 to 1992. He received his B.A. degree from the College of William and Mary and his Ph.D. from Yale. He received the Yale College Award for Distinguished Undergraduate Teaching. He directed a National Endowment for the Humanities Summer Institute. His scholarly research received the support of fellowships from the National Endowment for the Humanities, the Guggenheim Foundation, and the Woodrow Wilson Center. He is the author of *Between Science and Religion: The Reaction to Scientific Naturalism in Late Victorian England* (1974); *The Greek Heritage in Victorian Britain* (1981), which received the British Council Prize of the Conference on British Studies and the Yale Press Governors Award; *Contesting Cultural Authority: Essays in Victorian Intellectual Life* (1993); and *John Henry Newman: The Challenge to Evangelical Religion* (2002). He also contributed numerous articles to journals and served on the editorial advisory boards of *The Journal of Modern History*, *Isis*, and *Victorian Studies*. He edited *The Idea of a University*, by John Henry Newman (1996), *Reflections on the Revolution in France by Edmund Burke* (2003), and *Apologia Pro Vita Sua and Six Sermons* by John Henry Newman (2008). He served as a Trustee of Connecticut College from 1996–2006. In 2003, Professor Turner was appointed Director of the Beinecke Rare Book and Manuscript Library at Yale University.

1

The Birth of Civilization

Mohenjo-Daro Figure. Scholars believe this limestone statue from about 2500 B.C.E. depicts a king or a priest from Mohenjo-Daro in the Indus valley in present-day Pakistan.

Does this figure seem to emphasize the features of a particular person or the attributes of a particular role?

he earliest humans lived by hunting, fishing, and collecting wild plants. Around 10,000 years ago, they learned to cultivate plants, herd animals, and make airtight pottery for storage. These discoveries transformed them from gatherers to producers, allowing them to grow in number and to lead a settled life. Beginning about 5,000 years ago, a far more complex way of life began to appear in some parts of the world. In these places humans learned how to increase harvests through irrigation and other methods. Much larger populations came together in towns, cities, and other centers, where they erected impressive structures and where industry and commerce flourished. They developed writing, enabling them to keep inventories of food and other resources. Specialized occupations emerged, complex religions took form, and social divisions increased. These changes marked the birth of civilization. ■

culture
The ways of living built up by a group and passed on from one generation to another.

EARLY HUMANS AND THEIR CULTURE

Humans are cultural beings. **Culture** is the sum total of the ways of living built up by a group and passed on from one generation to another. Culture includes behavior such as courtship or child-rearing practices; material things such as tools, clothing, and shelter; and ideas, institutions, and beliefs. Language, apparently a uniquely human trait, lies

WHY IS "culture" considered a defining trait of human beings?

GLOBAL PERSPECTIVE

CIVILIZATIONS

The way of life of prehistoric cave dwellers differed immensely from that of humans today. Yet the few millennia in which we have been civilized are but a tiny fraction of the long span of human existence. Especially during recent millennia, changes in our culture—our way of life—have far outpaced changes in our bodies. We retain the emotional makeup and motor reflexes of prehistoric men and women while living highly organized and often sedentary lives.

We might best view the early civilizations by asking how they fit into the sweep of history. One notable feature of human history is the acceleration in the pace of change. From the time that modern humans first appeared 100,000 years ago until 7000 B.C.E., few changes occurred. Humans migrated from Africa to other parts of the world and adapted to new climes. All lived by hunting, fishing, and gathering. The chief advance in technology during this longest span of human existence was from rough to smooth stone weapons and tools.

Then, from about 7000 B.C.E., innovations began. Humans learned to till the soil, domesticate animals, and make pots for the storage of food. A few millennia later, bronze was discovered and the so-called river valley civilizations formed along the Nile, the Tigris-Euphrates, the Indus, and the Yellow rivers. Cities rose. Writing was invented. Societies divided into classes or castes: Most members engaged in farming, a few traded, and others assumed military, priestly, or governmental roles. As these civilizations expanded, they became richer, more populous, and more powerful.

The last millennium B.C.E. witnessed two major developments. One was the emergence, during 600–300 B.C.E., of the religious and philosophical revolutions that would indelibly mark their respective civilizations: monotheistic Judaism from which would later develop the world religions of Christianity and Islam; Hinduism and Buddhism in southern Asia; the philosophies of Greece and China. The second development was the rise of the Iron Age empires—the Roman, the Mauryan along the Ganges, the Han in China—during the centuries straddling the end of the millennium.

After the fall of these early empires, swift changes occurred. For a millennium, Europe and Byzantium fell behind, while China and the Middle East led in technology and the arts of government. But by 1500 Europe had caught up, and after 1700, it led. India had invented Arabic numerals, and Arab thinkers inspired

behind our ability to create ideas and institutions and to transmit culture from one generation to another. Our flexible and dexterous hands enable us to hold and make tools and so to create the material artifacts of culture. Because culture is learned and not inherited, it permits rapid adaptation to changing conditions, making possible the spread of humanity to almost all lands of the globe.

THE PALEOLITHIC AGE

Anthropologists designate early human cultures by their tools. The earliest period— the **Paleolithic Age** (from the Greek, "old stone")—dates from the earliest use of stone tools some 1 million years ago to about 10,000 B.C.E. During this immensely long period, people were hunters, fishers, and gatherers, but not producers, of food.

Paleolithic people learned to make increasingly sophisticated tools and to control fire, and they acquired language.

Evidence of religious faith and practice, as well as of magic, goes as far back as archaeology can take us.

Fear or awe, exultation, gratitude, and empathy with the natural world are reflected in the cave art and in the ritual practices, such as burial, found at the Paleolithic. The sense that there is more to the world than meets the eye—in other words, the religious response to the world—seems to be as old as humankind.

Paleolithic culture could support only a sparsely settled society. If hunters were too numerous, game would not suffice. Since labor appears to have been divided according to sex, it was probably women, gathering food, who discovered how to plant and care for seeds. This knowledge eventually led to agriculture and the Neolithic Revolution.

Paleolithic Age
The earliest period when stone tools were used, from about 1,000,000 to 10,000 B.C.E. From the Greek meaning "old stone."

•••—Read the Document
From Hunter-gatherers to Food-producers-
Overcoming Obstacles
at **myhistorylab.com**

•••—Read the Document
The Development of Religion
at **myhistorylab.com**

•••—Read the Document
The Toolmaker (3300 B.C.E.)
at **myhistorylab.com**

the Renaissance, but it was Europe that produced Copernicus and Newton.

The nineteenth century saw the invention of the steam engine, the steamship, the locomotive, the telegraph and telephone, and the automobile. After those inventions came electric lights, the radio, and, in the century that followed, the airplane.

In the twentieth century, invention and scientific discovery became institutionalized in university, corporate, and government laboratories. Ever increasing resources were committed to research. By the beginning of the twenty-first century man had walked on the moon, deciphered the human genome, and unlocked the power of the atom. Today, as discoveries occur ever more rapidly, we cannot imagine the science of a hundred years into the future.

If this process of accelerating change had its origins in 7000 B.C.E., what was the original impetus? Does the logic of nature dictate that once agriculture develops, cities will rise in alluvial valleys favorable to cultivation? Was it inevitable that the firing of clay to produce pots would produce metals from metallic oxides and lead to the discovery of smelting? Did the formation of aristocratic and priestly classes automatically lead to record keeping

and writing? If so, it is not at all surprising that parallel and independent developments should have occurred in regions as widely separated as China and the Middle East.

Or was the almost simultaneous rise of the ancient Eurasian civilizations the result of **diffusion**? Did migrating peoples carry seeds, new tools, and metals over long distances? The available evidence provides no definitive answer. Understanding the origins of the early civilizations and the lives of the men and women who lived in them from what is left of their material culture is like reconstructing a dinosaur from a broken tooth and a fragment of jawbone.

Focus Questions

◆ What were the processes behind the creation of early civilizations?

◆ What are the similarities and differences among the world's earliest civilizations?

◆ Why has the pace of change accelerated with time?

THE NEOLITHIC AGE

Anthropologists and archaeologists disagree as to why and how it happened, but around 10,000 years ago some groups in what we now call the Middle East began to change from a nomadic hunter-gatherer culture to a more settled agricultural one.

The shift to agriculture coincided with advances in stone tool technology, so this period is called the Neolithic Age (from the Greek, "new stone"). Productive animals, such as sheep and goats, were domesticated, as were food crops including wheat and barley.

Domestication allowed people to settle new areas. The invention of pottery enabled people to store, transport, and cook foods and liquids. People made cloth from flax and wool.

Because crops required constant care from planting to harvest, Neolithic farmers built permanent dwellings. Houses in a Neolithic village were normally all the same size, suggesting that most Neolithic villagers had about the same level of wealth and social status. Stones and shells were traded long distance, but Neolithic villages tended to be self-sufficient.

Two larger Neolithic settlements do not fit this village pattern. Çatal Hüyük, in a fertile agricultural region of present-day Turkey, was a large town with astonishingly diversified agriculture, arts, and crafts.

At an oasis near the Dead Sea, the town of Jericho was surrounded by a massive stone wall with at least one tower against the inner face. No other Neolithic settlement has been found with fortifications. These two sites show that the economies and settlement patterns of the Neolithic period may have been more complicated than scholars previously thought.

◉ See the Map
The Beginnings of Food Production
at **myhistorylab.com**

(((•— Hear the Audio
at **myhistorylab.com**

•◦•— Read the Document
Redefining Self—From Tribe to Village to
City 1500 B.C.E. at **myhistorylab.com**

Çatal Hüyük. The illustration reconstructs part of Çatal Hüyük on the basis of archaeological findings.

What impression does this image give you of life in Çatal Hüyük?

●●●[Read the Document
The Neolithic Village
at **myhistorylab.com**

Throughout the Paleolithic Age, the human population had been small and relatively stable. Over time, in the regions where agriculture and animal husbandry appeared, the number of human beings grew at an unprecedented rate. Farmers usually had larger families than hunters, and their children matured at a younger age than the children of hunters. But farmers had to work harder and longer than hunters did, and they had to stay in one place. Some scholars refer to the dramatic changes in subsistence, settlement, technology, and population of this time as the **Neolithic Revolution**. The earliest Neolithic societies appeared in the Middle East in about 8000 B.C.E., based on the cultivation of wheat and barley. In China, Neolithic agriculture based on millet and rice emerged around 4000 B.C.E. The Neolithic period began about 3600 B.C.E. in India, and Neolithic agriculture based on corn developed in Mesoamerica several millennia later.

THE BRONZE AGE AND THE BIRTH OF CIVILIZATION

Another major shift occurred first in the plains along the Tigris and Euphrates rivers in the region the Greeks and Romans called **Mesopotamia** (modern Iraq), later in the valley of the Nile River in Egypt, and somewhat later in India and the Yellow River basin in China. Towns grew alongside villages, and some towns then grew into much larger urban centers. The urban centers, or cities, usually had monumental buildings, such as temples and fortifications. These could be built only by the sustained effort of hundreds and even thousands of people over many years. Elaborate representational artwork appeared, sometimes made of rare and imported materials. New technologies, such as smelting and the manufacture of metal tools and weapons, were characteristic of urban life. Commodities such as pottery and textiles that had been made in individual houses in villages were mass-produced in cities, which also were characterized by social stratification—that is, different classes of people based on factors such as control of resources, family, religious or political authority, and personal wealth. The earliest writing is also associated with the growth of cities. Writing, like representational art, was a powerful means of communicating over space and time and was probably invented to deal with urban problems of management and record keeping. These attributes— urbanism; technological, industrial, and social change; long-distance trade; and new methods of symbolic communication—are defining characteristics of the form of human culture called **civilization**. At about the time the earliest civilizations were emerging, someone discovered how to combine tin and copper to make a stronger and more useful material—bronze. Archaeologists coined the term **Bronze Age** to refer to the period 3100–1200 B.C.E. in the Near East and eastern Mediterranean.

civilization

A form of human culture marked by urbanism, technological adaptation, social complexity, long-distance trade, and symbolic communication.

Bronze Age

The name given to the earliest civilized era, ca. 3100 to 1200 B.C.E. The term reflects the importance of the metal bronze, a mixture of tin and copper, for the peoples of this age for use as weapons and tools.

EARLY CIVILIZATIONS IN THE MIDDLE EAST TO ABOUT 1000 B.C.E.

By 4000 B.C.E., people had settled in large numbers in the river-watered lowlands of Mesopotamia and Egypt. By about 3000 B.C.E., when the invention of writing gave birth to history, urban life and the organization of society into centralized states were well established in the valleys of the Tigris and Euphrates rivers in Mesopotamia and the Nile River in Egypt.

Urban life is possible only when farmers and stockbreeders produce a substantial surplus beyond their own needs, so that city dwellers can eat. Water also has to be controlled. Mesopotamians had to build dikes to keep rivers from flooding their fields in the spring, and they had to store water for use in the autumn. In Egypt the Nile River flooded at the right moment for cultivation, so irrigation was simply a matter of directing the water to the fields. (water channeling)

HOW DID control over water resources influence early Middle Eastern civilizations?

●●●⌐Read the **Document**
Geography and Civilization: Egypt and Mesopotamia-Impact of Agriculture
at **myhistorylab.com**

MESOPOTAMIAN CIVILIZATION

Mesopotamia is divided into two ecological zones, Assyria (roughly north of modern Baghdad) and Babylonia to the south. The oldest Mesopotamian cities seem to have been founded by the Sumerians during the fourth millennium B.C.E. in southern Babylonia. By 3000 B.C.E., the Sumerian city of Uruk was the largest city in the world (see Map 1–1 on page 6).

From about 2800 to 2370 B.C.E., during the Early Dynastic period, Sumerian city-states formed leagues among themselves that apparently had both political and religious significance. Quarrels over water and agricultural land led to incessant warfare, and in time, stronger towns and leagues formed kingdoms.

The people who occupied northern Mesopotamia and Syria spoke mostly Semitic languages (that is, languages in the same family as Arabic and Hebrew). Many of these Semitic peoples absorbed aspects of Sumerian culture, especially writing. The Mesopotamians believed that the large city of Kish, in northern Babylonia, had history's first kings.

In the east, a people known as the Akkadians established their own kingdom at a capital city called Akkad, under their first king, Sargon. The Akkadians conquered all the Sumerian city-states and invaded southwestern Iran and northern Syria. This was history's first empire, having a heartland, provinces, and an absolute ruler. It included numerous peoples, cities, languages, and cultures, as well as different ecological zones. Sargon's name became legendary as the first great conqueror of history. His grandson, Naram-Sin, ruled from the Persian Gulf to the Mediterranean Sea, with a standardized administration, vast wealth and power, and a grand style. Naram-Sin even declared himself a god. External attack and internal weakness destroyed the Akkadian Empire, but several smaller states survived independently.

●●●⌐Read the **Document**
Sumerian Law Code
at **myhistorylab.com**

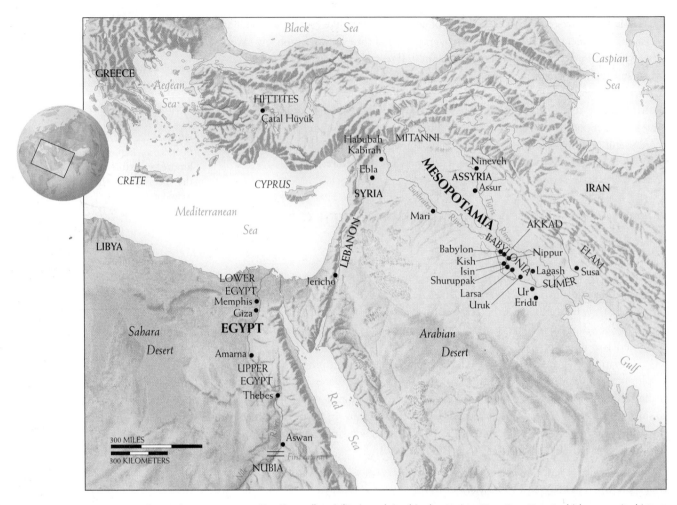

MAP 1–1. **The Ancient Near East.** Two river valley civilizations thrived in the Ancient Near East: Egypt, which was united into a single state, and Mesopotamia, which was long divided into a number of city-states.

What Factors in local geography might help explain the different political histories of Egypt and Mesopotamia?

◆◆◆Read the Document
Two Accounts of an Egyptian Famine 2600s
B.C.E.: at **myhistorylab.com**

●◆View the Image
Hammurabi Receives His Law Code
from the Gods
at **myhistorylab.com**

cuneiform
A writing system invented by the Sumerians that used a wedge-shaped stylus, or pointed tool, to write on wet clay tablets that were then baked or dried (*cuneus* means "wedge" in Latin). The writing was also cut into stone.

chattel slavery
A form of slavery in which humans are owned as goods; the slave has no legal standing as a person and few, if any, rights.

In about 2125 B.C.E. the Sumerian city of Ur rose to dominance. Sumerian culture and literature flourished. Epic poems glorified the deeds of the ancestors of the kings of Ur. A highly centralized administration kept detailed records. After little more than a century, the Third Dynasty of Ur disintegrated in the face of famine and invasion. Elamites attacked from the east and captured the king. The Semitic-speaking Amorites invaded from the north and west, settling around the Sumerian cities and eventually founding their own dynasties. The Sumerians gradually disappeared as an identifiable group. The Sumerian language survived only in writing as the learned language of Babylonia taught in schools and used by priests and scholars.

The Amorite kings of Isin maintained relative peace until they were challenged by another Amorite dynasty at the city of Larsa, and a period of warfare began. A powerful new dynasty at Babylon defeated Isin, Larsa, and other rivals and dominated Mesopotamia for nearly 300 years. Its high point was the reign of its most famous king, Hammurabi (r. ca. 1792–1750 B.C.E.), best known today for the collection of laws that bears his name.

The Sumerians invented the writing system now known as **cuneiform** (from the Latin *cuneus*, meaning "wedge") because of the wedge-shaped marks they made by writing on clay tablets with a cut-reed stylus. The Sumerian writing system was hard to learn. It used several thousand characters, some of which stood for words and some for sounds. Literacy was restricted to an elite who could afford to go to school.

The Sumerians also began the development of mathematics. Before around 3000 B.C.E., people had not conceptualized the idea of numbers independently of counting specific things. Once an independent concept of number was established, mathematics developed rapidly. The Sumerian system was based on the number 60 (sexagesimal) rather than the number 10 (decimal). Sumerian counting survives in the modern 60-minute hour and the circle of 360 degrees. By the time of Hammurabi, the Mesopotamians were expert in many types of mathematics, including mathematical astronomy.

The Sumerians and their successors worshiped many gods and goddesses. These took human forms but differed from humans in their greater power, sublime position in the universe, and immortality. The Mesopotamians believed that the human race was created to serve the gods. The gods were considered universal but also as residing in specific places, usually one important god or goddess in each city. Mesopotamian temples were run like great households where the gods were fed lavish meals, entertained with music, and honored with devotion and ritual. The Mesopotamians were religiously tolerant and readily accepted the possibility that different people might have different gods.

The Mesopotamians had a vague and gloomy picture of the afterworld. The winged spirits of the dead were recognizable as individuals. They were confined to a dusty, dark netherworld, doomed to perpetual hunger and thirst unless someone offered them food and drink. There was no preferential treatment in the afterlife for those who had led religious or virtuous lives—everyone was in equal misery. Mesopotamian religion focused on problems of this world and how to lead a good life before dying.

The Mesopotamian peoples who came after the Sumerians believed that the gods revealed a person's destiny to those who could understand the omens, or indications of what was going to happen. The Babylonians therefore developed an elaborate science of divination based on chance observations, such as a cat walking in the street, and on ritual procedures, such as asking a question of the gods and then slaughtering a sheep to examine its liver and entrails for certain marks and features. Illness was blamed on witchcraft.

Religion played a large part in the literature and art of Mesopotamia. Epic poems told of the deeds of the gods, such as how the world was created and organized, of a great flood the gods sent to wipe out the human race, and of the hero-king Gilgamesh, who tried to escape death by going on a fantastic journey to find the sole survivor of the great flood.

The most imposing religious structure was the *ziggurat*, a tower in stages, sometimes with a small chamber on top. The terraces may have been planted with trees to resemble a mountain. Their precise purpose is not known. Through the Bible, they have entered Western tradition as the Tower of Babel.

Hundreds of thousands of cuneiform texts—royal letters, administrative records, and numerous documents belonging to private families—reveal how peoples in ancient Mesopotamia conducted their lives. Many of Hammurabi's laws deal with commerce, land tenure, and land rights. The subject that is most highly regulated in Hammurabi's code is the maintenance and protection of family, including marriage, inheritance, and adoption. Parents usually arranged marriages, and the bride usually left her own family to join her husband's. A marriage started out monogamous, but a husband whose wife was childless or sickly could take a second wife. Women could own property and conduct business independently.

There were two main types of slavery in Mesopotamia: **chattel slavery** and debt slavery. Chattel slaves were bought like any other piece of property and had no legal rights. They were often non-Mesopotamians bought from slave merchants

Akkadian Victory Stele.   The victory stele of Naram-Sin, king of Akkad, over the mountain-dwelling Lullubi, Mesopotamian, Akkadian period, ca. 2230 B.C.E. (pink sandstone). The king, wearing the horned helmet denoting divine power, strides forward at the head of his army. This is one of the finest sculptures to survive from the Akkadian period.

Louvre, Paris, France. The Bridgeman Art Library International Ltd.

How does this glorify the king? What makes him seem especially important?

QUICK REVIEW

Mesopotamian Religion

- Sumerians worshiped gods with human forms
- Babylonians sought evidence of divine action in movements of heavenly bodies
- Religion played an important part in Mesopotamian art and literature

Read the Document
The Development of Religion in Primitive Cultures at **myhistorylab.com**

Read the Document
Excerpts from *The Epic of Gilgamesh* at **myhistorylab.com**

A Closer Look

Babylonian World Map

Cartography was among the many intellectual achievements of the Babylonians. The map illustrated here was inscribed on a clay tablet in about 600 B.C.E., and appears to be the earliest surviving map of the world.

The Babylonians did not intend this map to be a precise or literal picture of the universe or even of the land on which human beings lived, for they omitted any representation of such important and numerous peoples as the Egyptians and Persians whom they knew very well.

There is a text written in cuneiform script above the picture and on the back of the tablet that helps make its identification as a map secure.

All the lands are encircled by a "Bitter River". Beyond that are seven islands arranged to form a seven-pointed star.

The tablet shows the world from a Babylonian point of view as flat and round, with Babylon sitting at its center on the Euphrates River.

Surrounding Babylon are cities and lands, including Armenia and Assyria.

Courtesy of the Trustees of the British Museum. © The British Museum.

Questions

1. What can we learn from this map about how the Babylonians saw the world around them and their own place in it?

2. Why do you think this map locates some of the Babylonians' neighbors but ignores other important neighboring cultures?

3. Why has cartography remained so important throughout the ages?

4. Is the subjectivity reflected here confined to this map, or is it a general characteristic of cartography throughout history?

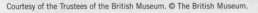

myhistorylab   To examine this image in an interactive fashion, please go to **www.myhistorylab.com**

and were used in domestic service rather than in production. Chattel slaves were expensive luxuries. True chattel slavery did not become common until the Neo-Babylonian period (612–539 B.C.E.).

Debt slavery was more common. Rates of interest were high, as much as 33 $\frac{1}{3}$ percent, so people often defaulted on loans. If debtors had pledged themselves or members of their families as surety for a loan, they became the slave of the creditor; their labor went to pay the interest on the loan. Debt slaves could not be sold but could redeem their freedom by paying off the loan. Slaves and masters often labored side by side; little separated them except the misfortune of indebtedness.

CHRONOLOGY

KEY EVENTS AND PEOPLE IN MESOPOTAMIAN HISTORY

ca. 3500 B.C.E.	Development of Sumerian cities, especially Uruk
ca. 2800–2370 B.C.E.	Early Dynastic period of Sumerian city-states
ca. 2370 B.C.E.	Sargon establishes Akkadian Dynasty and Empire
ca. 2125–2027 B.C.E.	Third Dynasty of Ur
ca. 2000–1800 B.C.E.	Establishment of Amorites in Mesopotamia
ca. 1792–1750 B.C.E.	Reign of Hammurabi
ca. 1550 B.C.E.	Establishment of Kassite Dynasty at Babylon

EGYPTIAN CIVILIZATION

From its sources in Lake Victoria and the Ethiopian highlands, the Nile flows north some 4,000 miles to the Mediterranean. Ancient Egypt included the 750-mile stretch of smooth, navigable river from Aswan to the sea. South of Aswan the river's course is interrupted by several cataracts—rocky areas of rapids and whirlpools.

The Egyptians recognized two sets of geographical divisions in their country. Upper (southern) Egypt consisted of the narrow valley of the Nile. Lower (northern) Egypt referred to the broad triangular area, named by the Greeks after their letter *delta*, formed by the Nile as it branches out to empty into the Mediterranean. They also made a distinction between what they termed the "black land," the dark fertile fields along the Nile, and the "red land," the desert cliffs and plateaus bordering the valley.

The Nile alone made agriculture possible in Egypt's desert environment. Each year the rains of central Africa caused the river to rise over its floodplain. When the floodwaters receded, they left a rich layer of organically fertile silt. The construction and maintenance of canals, dams, and irrigation ditches to control the river's water, together with careful planning and organization of planting and harvesting, produced agricultural prosperity unmatched in the ancient world.

The Nile served as the major highway connecting Upper and Lower Egypt (see Map 1–2 on page 10). The cataracts, the desert, and the sea made Egypt relatively isolated. Egypt's security, along with the predictable flood calendar, gave its civilization a more optimistic outlook than that of Mesopotamia.

The 3,000-year span of ancient Egyptian history is traditionally divided into thirty-one royal dynasties, clustered into eight periods. During three so-called Intermediate periods, Egypt experienced political and social disintegration, and rival dynasties often set up separate power bases in Upper and Lower Egypt until a strong leader reunified the land. The unification of Egypt was vital, for it meant that the entire Nile valley could benefit from an unimpeded distribution of resources.

During the more than 400 years of the Old Kingdom (2700–2200 B.C.E.), Egypt enjoyed internal stability and great prosperity. The ruler, later given the title **pharaoh**, was a king who was also a god (the term comes from the Egyptian for "great house," much as we use "White House" to refer to the president). From his capital at Memphis, the god-king ruled Egypt according to principles that included *maat*, an ideal of order, justice, and truth.

In return for the king's building and maintaining temples, the gods preserved the equilibrium of the state and ensured the king's continuing power, which was absolute. Because the king was obligated to act infallibly in a benign and beneficent manner, the welfare of the people of Egypt was automatically guaranteed and safeguarded.

pharaoh
The god-kings of ancient Egypt. The term originally meant "great house" or palace.

Read the **Document**
Workings of Ma'at: "The Tale of the Eloquent Peasant" at **myhistorylab.com**

MAP EXPLORATION

To explore this map further, go to **http://www.myhistorylab.com**

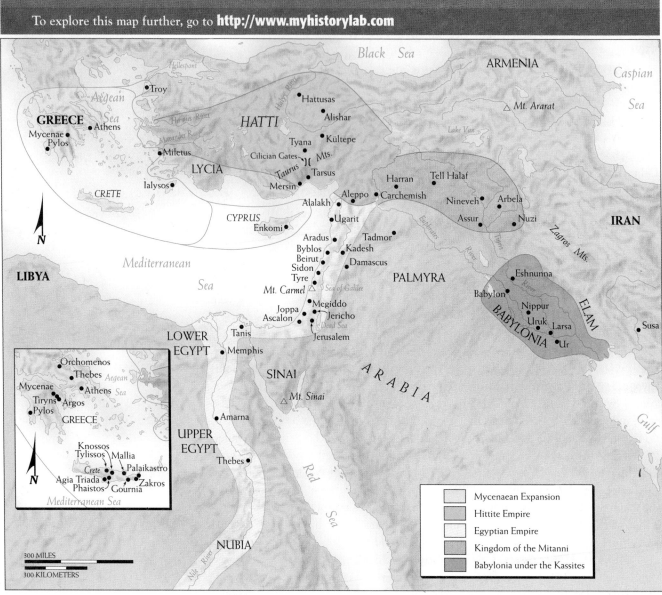

MAP 1–2.   The Near East and Greece, ca. 1400 B.C.E.

About 1400 B.C.E., the Near East was divided among four empires. Egypt extended south to Nubia and north through Palestine and Phoenicia. Kassites ruled in Mesopotamia, Hittites in Asia Minor, and the Mitannians in Assyrian lands. In the Aegean, the Mycenaean kingdoms were at their height.

Do Certain empires seem more geographically "natural" to you than others? Besides coastal access and rivers, what physical factors might help unify some of these empires?

QUICK REVIEW

Egyptian Kingship

- Egyptian kings were considered gods
- Kings were the direct source of law and justice
- Egyptian government was an aspect of religion

Nothing better illustrates the nature of Old Kingdom royal power than the pyramids built as pharaonic tombs. Beginning in the Early Dynastic period, kings constructed increasingly elaborate burial complexes in Upper Egypt. Djoser, a Third Dynasty king, was the first to erect a monumental six-step pyramid of hard stone. Subsequent pharaohs built other stepped pyramids until Snefru, the founder of the Fourth Dynasty, converted a stepped pyramid to a true pyramid over the course of putting up three monuments.

Djoser's son Khufu (Cheops in the Greek version of his name) chose the desert plateau of Giza, south of Memphis, as the site for the largest pyramid ever constructed. Its dimensions are prodigious: 481 feet high, 756 feet long on each side, and its base covering 13.1 acres. The pyramid is made of 2.3 million stone blocks averaging 2.5 tons each. It is also a geometrical wonder, barely deviating from absolutely level and square.

Khufu's successors, Khafre (Chephren) and Menkaure (Mycerinus), built equally perfect pyramids at Giza, and together the three constitute one of the most extraordinary achievements in human history. Khafre also built the huge composite creature, part lion and part human, which the Greeks named the Sphinx. Recent research has shown that the Sphinx played a crucial role in the solar cult aspects of the pyramid complex.

The pyramids are remarkable not only for the great technical skill they demonstrate, but also for the concentration of resources they represent. They are evidence that the pharaohs controlled vast wealth and had the power to focus and organize enormous human effort over the years it took to build each pyramid. They also provide a visible indication of the nature of the Egyptian state: The pyramids, like the pharaohs, tower above the land, while the low tombs at their base, like the officials buried there, seem to huddle in relative unimportance.

In about 2200 B.C.E. the Old Kingdom collapsed and gave way to the decentralization and disorder of the First Intermediate period (2200–2025 B.C.E.). Later, Middle Kingdom (2025–1630 B.C.E.) pharaohs sought to evoke the past by building pyramid complexes like those of the later Old Kingdom rulers. Yet the events of the First Intermediate period had irrevocably changed the nature of Egyptian kingship. Gone was the absolute, distant god-king; the king was now more directly concerned with his people. In art, instead of the supremely confident faces of the Old Kingdom pharaohs, the Middle Kingdom rulers seem thoughtful, careworn, and brooding.

Egypt's relations with its neighbors became more aggressive during the Middle Kingdom. To the south, royal fortresses were built to control Nubia and the growing trade in African resources. To the north and east, Syria and Palestine increasingly came under Egyptian influence, even as fortifications sought to prevent settlers from the Levant from moving into the Delta.

The western Delta established an independent dynasty, ushering in the Second Intermediate period (1630–1550 B.C.E.). The eastern Delta came under the control of the Hyksos. Much later sources describe the Hyksos as ruthless invaders from parts unknown, but they were almost certainly Amorites from the Levant, part of the gradual infiltration of the Delta during the Middle Kingdom. After nearly a century of rule, the Hyksos were expelled, and the New Kingdom (1550–1075 B.C.E.) was established. During the Eighteenth Dynasty, Egypt pursued foreign expansion with renewed vigor. Military expeditions reached as far north as the Euphrates in Syria with frequent campaigns in the Levant. To the south, major Egyptian temples were built in the Sudan. Egypt's economic and political power was at its height.

Egypt's position was reflected in the unprecedented luxury and cosmopolitanism of the royal court and in the ambitious palace and temple projects undertaken throughout the country. The Eighteenth Dynasty pharaohs were the first to cut their tombs deep into the rock cliffs of a desolate valley in Thebes, known today as the Valley of the Kings. To date, only one intact royal tomb has been discovered there, that of the young Eighteenth Dynasty king Tutankhamun, and even it had been disturbed shortly after his death. The thousands of goods buried with him, many of them marvels of craftsmanship, give a glimpse of Egypt's material wealth during this period.

Following the premature death of Tutankhamun in 1323 B.C.E., a military commander named Horemheb assumed the kingship, which passed in turn to his own army

Making Bread. A hallmark of the early river civilizations was the development of techniques to increase harvests. This statue from the Old Kingdom in Egypt (ca. 2700–2200 B.C.E.) shows a woman kneading dough for bread.

What clues does this sculpture offer about this woman's quality of life?

View the Image
The Pyramids at Giza
at **myhistorylab.com**

View the Image
The Sphinx at **myhistorylab.com**

See the Map
Egypt in the Middle Kingdom
at **myhistorylab.com**

Pyramids at Giza. The three largest pyramids of Egypt, located at Giza, near Cairo, are the colossal tombs of pharaohs of the Fourth Dynasty (ca. 2640–2510 B.C.E.): Khufu (right), Chafre (center), and Menkaure (left). The small pyramids and tombs at their bases were those of the pharaohs' queens and officials.

What does the relative size of these pyramids suggest about the distribution of power in ancient Egypt?

⊙ View the Image
at **myhistorylab.com**

⊙ View the Image
Great Temple of Abu Simbel
at **myhistorylab.com**

⊙ See the Map
Egypt in the New Kingdom
at **myhistorylab.com**

hieroglyphs
The complicated writing script of ancient Egypt. It combined picture writing with pictographs and sound signs. Hieroglyph means "sacred carvings" in Greek.

commander, Ramses I. The Ramessides of Dynasty 19 undertook numerous monumental projects, among them Ramses II's rock-cut temples at Abu Simbel, south of the First Cataract, which had to be moved to a higher location when the Aswan High Dam was built in the 1960s. There and elsewhere, Ramses II left textual and pictorial accounts of his battle in 1285 B.C.E. against the Hittites at Kadesh on the Orontes in Syria. Sixteen years later, the Egyptians and Hittites signed a formal peace treaty, forging an alliance against an increasingly volatile political situation in the Middle East and the eastern Mediterranean during the thirteenth century B.C.E.

Merneptah, one of the hundred offspring of Ramses II, held off a hostile Libyan attack, as well as incursions by the Sea Peoples, a loose coalition of Mediterranean raiders who seem to have provoked and taken advantage of unsettled conditions. One of Merneptah's inscriptions commemorating his military triumphs contains the first known mention of Israel.

Despite Merneptah's efforts, by the end of the Twentieth Dynasty, Egypt's period of imperial glory had passed. The next thousand years witnessed a Third Intermediate period, a Saite renaissance, Persian domination, conquest by Alexander the Great, the Ptolemaic period, and finally, defeat at the hands of the Roman emperor Octavian in 30 B.C.E.

Writing first appears in Egypt about 3000 B.C.E. The writing system, dubbed **hieroglyphs** ("sacred carvings") by the Greeks, was highly sophisticated, involving hundreds of picture signs that remained relatively constant in the way they were rendered for over 3,000 years. Texts were usually written horizontally from right to left but could be written from left to right, as well as vertically from top to bottom in both horizontal directions. Egyptian literature includes narratives, myths, books of instruction in wisdom, letters, religious texts, and poetry, written on papyri, limestone flakes, and potsherds. The Egyptian language, part of the Afro-Asiatic (or Hamito-Semitic) family, evolved through several stages—Old, Middle, and Late Egyptian, Demotic, and Coptic—and has a history of continuous recorded use well into the medieval period.

The Egyptian gods, or pantheon, defy neat categorization, in part because of the common tendency to combine the character and function of one or more

CHRONOLOGY

MAJOR PERIODS IN ANCIENT EGYPTIAN HISTORY (DYNASTIES IN ROMAN NUMERALS)

3100–2700 B.C.E.	Early Dynastic period (I–II)
2700–2200 B.C.E.	Old Kingdom (III–VI)
2200–2025 B.C.E.	First Intermediate period (VII–XI)
2025–1630 B.C.E.	Middle Kingdom (XII–XIII)
1630–1550 B.C.E.	Second Intermediate period (XIV–XVII)
1550–1075 B.C.E.	New Kingdom (XVIII–XX)

gods. Amun, one of the eight entities in the Hermopolitan cosmogony, provides a good example. Thebes, Amun's cult center, rose to prominence in the Middle Kingdom. In the New Kingdom, Amun was elevated above his seven cohorts and took on aspects of the sun god Re to become Amun-Re.

Not surprisingly in a nearly rainless land, solar cults and mythologies were highly developed. Much thought was devoted to conceptualizing what happened as the sun god made his perilous way through the underworld in the night hours between sunset and sunrise. Three long texts trace Re's journey as he vanquishes immense snakes and other foes.

The Eighteenth Dynasty was one of several periods during which solar cults were in ascendancy. Early in his reign, Amunhotep IV promoted a single, previously minor aspect of the sun, the Aten ("disc") above Re himself and the rest of the gods. He declared that the Aten was the creator god who brought life to humankind and all living beings, with himself and his queen Nefertiti the sole mediators between the Aten and the people. He went further, changing his name to Akhenaten ("the effective spirit of the Aten"), building a new capital called Akhetaten ("the horizon of the Aten") near Amarna north of Thebes and chiseling out the name of Amun from inscriptions everywhere. Shortly after his death, Amarna was abandoned and partially razed. A large diplomatic archive of tablets written in Akkadian was left at the site, which give us a vivid, if one-sided, picture of the political correspondence of the day. During the reigns of Akhenaten's successors, Tutankhamun (born Tutankhaten) and Horemheb, Amun was restored to his former position, and Akhenaten's monuments were defaced and even demolished.

In representations, Egyptian gods have human bodies, possess human or animal heads, and wear crowns, celestial discs, or thorns. The lone exception is the Aten, made nearly abstract by Akhenaten, who altered its image to a plain disc with solar rays ending in small hands holding the hieroglyphic sign for life to the nostrils of Akhenaten and Nefertiti. The gods were thought to reside in their cult centers, where, from the New Kingdom on, increasingly ostentatious temples were built and staffed by full-time priests. At Thebes, for instance, for over 2,000 years successive kings enlarged the great Karnak temple complex dedicated to Amun.

Though the ordinary person could not enter a temple precinct, great festivals took place for all to see. During Amun's major festival of Opet, the statue of the god traveled in a divine boat along the Nile, whose banks were thronged with spectators.

The Egyptians thought that the afterlife was full of dangers, which could be overcome by magical means, among them the spells in the *Book of the Dead*.

The goals were to join and be identified with the gods, especially Osiris, or to sail in the "boat of millions." Originally only the king could hope to enjoy immortality with the gods, but gradually this became available to all. Since the Egyptians believed that the preservation of the body was essential for continued existence in the afterlife, early on they developed mummification, a process that by the New Kingdom took seventy days.

It is difficult to assess the position of women in Egyptian society because our pictorial and textual evidence comes almost entirely from male sources. Women's prime roles were connected with the management of the household. They could not hold office, go to scribal schools, or become artisans. Nevertheless, women could own and control property, sue for divorce, and, at least in theory, enjoy equal legal protection. Royal women often wielded considerable influence. The most remarkable was Hatshepsut, who ruled as pharaoh for nearly twenty years.

Seated Egyptian Scribe. One of the hallmarks of the early river valley civilizations was the development of writing. Ancient Egyptian scribes had to undergo rigorous training but were rewarded with a position of respect and privilege. This statue from the Fifth Dynasty (ca. 2510–2460 B.C.E.) is of painted limestone and measures 21 inches (53 cm) in height.

Musée du Louvre, Paris, © Giraudon/ Art Resource, New York.

What clues does this sculpture offer about this man's quality of life?

Watch the **Video**
The Temple of Karnak
at **myhistorylab.com**

Read the **Document**
Papyrus of Ani, The Egyptian Book of the Dead c. 1200 B.C.E. at **myhistorylab.com**

View the **Image**
Scene from the Egyptian Afterlife
at **myhistorylab.com**

Scene from the *Book of the Dead.* The Egyptians believed in the possibility of life after death through the god Osiris. Before the person could be presented to Osiris, forty-two assessor-gods tested aspects of the person's life. In this scene from a papyrus manuscript of the *Book of the Dead*, the deceased and his wife (on the left) watch the scales of justice weighing his heart (on the left side of the scales) against the feather of truth. The jackal-headed god Anubis also watches the scales, while the ibis-headed god Thoth keeps the record.

What does the presence of so many gods at a person's judgment ceremony suggest about the Egyptians' sense of an individual's significance?

View the Image
Egyptian Relief of Anubis
at **myhistorylab.com**

Watch the Video
Ramses II's Abu Simbel
at **myhistorylab.com**

QUICK REVIEW

Women in Ancient Egypt
- Household management was women's responsibility
- In theory women had legal rights equal to men's
- Royal women could hold great power

In art, both royal and nonroyal women are conventionally shown smaller than their husbands or sons, yet it is probably of greater significance that they are so frequently depicted in such a wide variety of contexts. Much care was lavished on details of their gestures, clothing, and hairstyles. With their husbands, they attend banquets, boat in the papyrus marshes, make and receive offerings, and supervise the myriad affairs of daily life.

Slaves did not become numerous in Egypt until the growth of Egyptian imperial power in the Middle Kingdom and the imperial expansion of the New Kingdom. Black Africans from Nubia to the south and Asians from the east were captured in war, branded, and brought back to Egypt as slaves. Sometimes an entire people were enslaved, as the Hebrews were, according to the Bible. Slaves in Egypt performed many tasks. Egyptian slaves could be freed, although manumission seems to have been rare. Nonetheless, former slaves were not set apart and could expect to be assimilated into the mass of the population.

ANCIENT NEAR EASTERN EMPIRES

HOW DID conquest and trade shape early empires in the Near East?

In the time of the Eighteenth Dynasty in Egypt, new groups of peoples had established themselves in the Near East: the Kassites in Babylonia, the Hittites in Asia Minor, and the Mitannians in northern Syria and Mesopotamia (see Map 1–2). The Kassites and Mitannians were warrior peoples who ruled as a minority over more civilized folk and absorbed their culture. The Hittites established a kingdom of their own and forged an empire that lasted some 200 years.

THE HITTITES

The Hittites were an Indo-European people, speaking a language related to Greek and Sanskrit. By about 1500 B.C.E., the Hittites had established a strong, centralized government with a capital near Ankara, the capital of modern Turkey. Between 1400 and 1200 B.C.E., they contested Egypt's control of Palestine and Syria. They played an important role in transmitting the ancient cultures of Mesopotamia and Egypt to the Greeks, who lived on their western frontier. The government of the Hittites was different from that of Mesopotamia in that Hittite kings did not claim to be divine or even to be the chosen representatives of the gods. In the early period, a council of nobles limited the king's power, and the assembled army had to ratify his succession to the throne.

Read the Document
Hittite Law Code: excerpts from *The Code of the Nesilim* at **myhistorylab.com**

By 1200 B.C.E., the Hittite Kingdom disappeared, swept away in invasions and the collapse of Middle Eastern nation-states at that time. Successors to the empire, called the Neo-Hittite states, flourished in southern Asia Minor and northern Syria until the Assyrians destroyed them in the first millennium B.C.E.

An important technological change took place in northern Anatolia, somewhat earlier than the creation of the Hittite Kingdom, but perhaps within its region. This was the discovery of how to smelt iron and the decision to use it rather than copper or bronze to manufacture weapons and tools. Archaeologists refer to the period after 1100 B.C.E. as the Iron Age.

THE KASSITES

The Kassites were a people of unknown origin who spoke their own language and who established at Babylon a dynasty that ruled for nearly 500 years. The Kassites were organized into large tribal families and carved out great domains for themselves in Babylonia. They promoted Babylonian culture, and many of the most important works of Babylonian literature were written during their rule. They supported a military aristocracy based on horses and chariots, the prestige weaponry of the age.

THE MITANNIANS

The Mitannians belonged to a large group of people called the Hurrians, some of whom had been living in Mesopotamia and Syria in the time of the kings of Akkad and Ur. Their language is imperfectly understood, and the location of their capital city, Washukanni, is uncertain. The Hurrians were important mediators of Mesopotamian culture to Syria and Anatolia. They developed the art of chariot warfare and horse training to a high degree and created a large state that reached from the Euphrates to the foothills of Iran. The Hittites destroyed their kingdom, and the Assyrian Empire eventually incorporated what was left of it.

THE ASSYRIANS

The Assyrians were originally a people living in Assur, a city in northern Mesopotamia on the Tigris River. They spoke a Semitic language closely related to Babylonian. They had a proud, independent culture heavily influenced by Babylonia. Assur had been an early center for trade but emerged as a political power during the fourteenth century B.C.E., after the decline of Mitanni. The first Assyrian Empire spread north and west against the neo-Hittite states but was brought to an end in the general collapse of Near Eastern states at the end of the second millennium. A people called the Arameans, a Semitic nomadic and agricultural people originally from northern Syria who spoke a language called Aramaic, invaded Assyria. Aramaic is still used in parts of the Near East and is one of the languages of medieval Jewish and Middle Eastern Christian culture.

THE SECOND ASSYRIAN EMPIRE

After 1000 B.C.E., the Assyrians began a second period of expansion, and by 665 B.C.E. they controlled all of Mesopotamia, much of southern Asia Minor, Syria, Palestine, and Egypt to its southern frontier.

They succeeded thanks to a large, well-disciplined army and a society that valued military skills. Some Assyrian kings boasted of their atrocities, so that their names inspired terror throughout the Near East. They constructed magnificent palaces at Nineveh and Nimrud (near modern Mosul, Iraq), surrounded by parks and gardens.

Assyrian Palace Relief. This eighth-century B.C.E. relief of a hero gripping a lion formed part of the decoration of an Assyrian palace. The immense size of the figure and his powerful limbs and muscles may well have suggested the might of the Assyrian king.

Gilgamesh. Relief from the Temple of Saragon II, Khorsabad. Assyrian, 8th century B.C.E. Giraudon/Art Resource, New York.

What else besides size and muscles suggests the power of this king?

•••⌐Read the Document
Empire of Assiria, ca. 1800 B.C.E.
at **myhistorylab.com**

CHRONOLOGY

KEY EVENTS IN THE HISTORY OF ANCIENT NEAR EASTERN EMPIRES

ca. 1400–1200 B.C.E.	Hittite Empire
ca. 1100 B.C.E.	Rise of Assyrian power
732–722 B.C.E.	Assyrian conquest of Syria–Palestine
671 B.C.E.	Assyrian conquest of Egypt
612 B.C.E.	Destruction of Assyrian capital at Nineveh
612–539 B.C.E.	Neo-Babylonian (Chaldean) Empire

The Assyrians systematically exploited their empire. They used various methods of control, collecting tribute from some regions, stationing garrisons in others, and sometimes pacifying districts by deporting and scattering their inhabitants.

The empire became too large to govern efficiently. The last years of Assyria are obscure, but civil war apparently divided the country. The Medes, a powerful people from western and central Iran, had been expanding across the Iranian plateau. They were feared for their cavalry and archers, against which traditional Middle Eastern armies were ineffective. The Medes attacked Assyria and were joined by the Babylonians, who had always been restive under Assyrian rule, under the leadership of a general named Nebuchadnezzar. In 612 B.C.E., they so thoroughly destroyed the Assyrian cities, including Nineveh, that Assyria never recovered. The ruins of the great Assyrian palaces lay untouched until archaeologists began to explore them in the nineteenth century.

THE NEO-BABYLONIANS

See the Map
The Neo-Babylonian Empire, ca. 580 B.C.E.
at **myhistorylab.com**

The Medes did not follow up on their conquests, so Nebuchadnezzar took over much of the Assyrian Empire. Under him and his successors, Babylon grew into one of the greatest cities of the world.

The Greek traveler Herodotus described its wonders, including its great temples, fortification walls, boulevards, parks, and palaces, to a Greek readership that had never seen the like. Babylon prospered as a center of world trade, linking Egypt, India, Iran, and Syria–Palestine by land and sea routes. For centuries, an astronomical center at Babylon kept detailed records of observations that were the longest running chronicle of the ancient world. Nebuchadnezzar's dynasty did not last long, and the government passed to various men in rapid succession. The last independent king of Babylon set up a second capital in the Arabian Desert and tried to force the Babylonians to honor the moon god above all other gods. He allowed dishonest or incompetent speculators to lease huge areas of temple land for their personal profit. These policies proved unpopular—some said that the king was insane—and many Babylonians may have welcomed the Persian conquest that came in 539 B.C.E. After that, Babylonia began another, even more prosperous phase of its history as one of the most important provinces of another great Eastern empire, that of the Persians. We shall return to the Persians in Chapter 4.

EARLY INDIAN CIVILIZATION

WHAT INFLUENCES did the first Indus valley civilization have on later Indian religious and social practices?

To the east of Mesopotamia, beyond the Iranian plateau and the mountains of Baluchistan, the Asian continent bends sharply southward below the Himalayan mountain barrier to form the Indian subcontinent (see Map 1–3 on page 17). Several sizable rivers flow west and south out of the Himalayas in Kashmir and the Punjab (*Panjab*, "five rivers"), merging into the single stream of the Indus River in Sind before emptying into the Indian Ocean. The headwaters of South Asia's other great river system—the Ganges and its tributaries—are also in the Himalayas but flow south and east to the Bay of Bengal on the opposite side of the subcontinent.

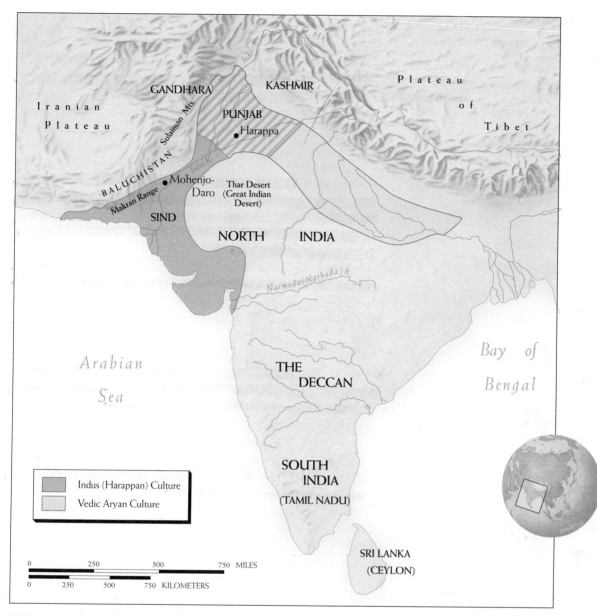

MAP 1–3.   Indus and Vedic Aryan Cultures.
Indus culture likely influenced the Vedic Aryans, although the influence cannot be proved. Some scholars surmise, for example, that the fortified Aryan city of Hariyupiya, mentioned in later texts, may have been the same site as the older Indus city of Harappa.

What Geographical features appear to have influenced the size and shape of regions dominated by different cultures?

The subcontinent's earliest literate, urban civilization arose in the valley of the Indus River sometime after 2600 B.C.E. and by about 2300 B.C.E. was trading with Mesopotamia. Known as the **Harappan** or Indus civilization, it lasted only a few centuries. The region's second identifiable civilization dates to about 1500 B.C.E. and is known as the Vedic Aryan civilization—after the nomadic Indo-European immigrant people, or **Aryans,** who founded it, and their holy texts, or **Vedas.** This civilization endured for nearly 1,000 years without cities or writing, but its religious and social traditions commingled with older traditions in the subcontinent to form the Indian civilization as it has developed over the past 2,500 years.

Harappan
Term used to describe the first civilization of the Indus valley.

Aryans
The Indo-European speakers who invaded India and Iran in the second and first millennia B.C.E.

Vedas
The sacred texts of the ancient Aryan invaders of India. The Rig-Vedas are the oldest materials in the Vedas.

THE INDUS CIVILIZATION

Archaeologists discovered the existence of the Indus culture at the site of Harappa in the 1920s. Since then, some seventy cities, the largest being Harappa and Mohenjo-Daro, have been identified. This urban civilization had bronze tools, writing, covered drainage systems, and a diversified social and economic organization. Because its writing is still undeciphered, it remains the least understood of the early river valley civilizations. Archaeological evidence and inferences from later Indian life, however, allow us to reconstruct something of its highly developed and once thriving culture.

The Indus culture covered a huge area, yet it was remarkably homogeneous. City layouts, building construction, weights and measures, seal inscriptions, patterned pottery and figurines, and even the burnt brick used for buildings and flood walls are unusually uniform in all Indus towns, suggesting an integrated economic system and good internal communications.

Indus culture was also remarkably constant over time. Because the main cities and towns lay in river lowlands subject to flooding, they were rebuilt often, with each reconstruction closely following the previous pattern. Similarly, the Indus script, known from more than 2,000 stamp seals and apparently using both pictographic and phonetic symbols, shows no evidence of change over time. This evidence of stability, regularity, and traditionalism has led scholars to speculate that a centralized government, perhaps a conservative (priestly) theocracy, controlled this far-flung society.

Both Harappa and Mohenjo-Daro apparently had populations of more than 35,000 and were meticulously designed on a similar plan. To the west of each town stood a large, walled citadel on a raised rectangular platform. The town proper was laid out on a grid of main avenues, some as wide as 30 feet. The "blocks" formed by the main avenues were crisscrossed by small, less rigidly planned lanes, off which opened private houses, sometimes of more than one story. The typical house was built around a central courtyard and presented only blank walls to the lanes or streets outside, an arrangement still common in many Near Eastern and South Asian cities.

Ancient Mohenjo-Daro. Like most cities of the Indus valley civilization, Mohenjo-Daro was built principally of mud brick. The structures are laid on straight lines; streets cross each other at right angles. The impression is one of order, prosperity, and civic discipline.

Borromeo/Art Resource, New York.

How do the uniformity and regular placement of bricks influence your reaction to this site?

Perhaps the most striking feature of these cities was a complex system of covered drains and sewers. Private houses were serviced by wells, bathrooms, and latrines, and the great bath at Mohenjo-Daro was filled from its own large well. The drainage system that served these facilities was an engineering feat unrivaled until the time of the Romans, nearly 2,000 years later.

The economy of the Indus state or states was based on agriculture. Wheat and barley were the main crops. The Indus valley people wove cloth from cotton, made metal tools, and used the potter's wheel. Evidence points to trade between the Indus culture and Mesopotamia. Metals and semiprecious stones were apparently imported into the Indus region from present-day Iran and Afghanistan, as well as from Central Asia, from farther south on the Indian peninsula, and perhaps from Arabia. Similarities in artistic styles suggest that trade contacts resulted in cultural borrowings.

Among the most striking accomplishments of the Indus culture are fine bronze and stone sculptures. Other evidence of the skill of Indus artisans includes copper and bronze tools and vessels, black-on-red painted pottery, dressed stonework, stone and terra-cotta figurines and toys, silver vessels and ornaments, gold jewelry, and dyed woven fabric.

The elaborate bath facilities suggest that ritual bathing and water purification rites were important, as they still are in India today. The stone images from the so-called temples of Mohenjo-Daro and the more common terra-cotta figurines from other sites also suggest links to later Indian religious practices and symbols. The many images of male animals such as the humped bull might be symbols of power and fertility or might indicate animal worship. A recurring image of a male figure with leafy headdress and horns, often seated in a posture associated later in India with yogic meditation, has been likened to the Vedic Aryan "Lord of All Creatures." Terra-cotta figurines of females, often pregnant or carrying a child, are similar to female images in several prehistoric cultures. As possible precursors of Shiva's consort, they too may represent an element of pre-Aryan religion that reemerged later to figure in "Hindu" culture. Other aspects of Indus religion—burial customs, for example—are not clearly related to later Indian practices.

Sometime between 1800 and 1700 B.C.E., Indus civilization disappeared. Aryan invaders, changes in the course of the Indus, or a long period of dessication might have contributed to the Indus culture's demise. This civilization remains too shadowy for us to measure its influence, but Harappan predecessors of the Aryans likely contributed to later life in the subcontinent in ways that we have yet to discover.

THE VEDIC ARYAN CIVILIZATION

We know more about the Aryan culture that effectively "refounded" Indian civilization around 1500 B.C.E. Yet unlike Indus civilization, it was not urban and left neither city ruins nor substantial artifacts beyond tools, weapons, and pottery. Virtually our only source of knowledge about ancient Aryan life are the words of the Vedas, the Aryan sacred texts—hence we know the culture as "Vedic." Although the latest Vedic texts date from perhaps 500 B.C.E., the earliest may go back to 1700 B.C.E. Transmitted orally through the centuries, the Vedas were not written down until writing was reintroduced to India sometime after 700 B.C.E. The Vedas are priestly works, not histories; they reveal little about events but do offer insight into the religion, society, values, and thought of early Aryan India.

Veda, which means "knowledge," is the collective term for the texts still recognized today by most Indians as the holiest sources of their tradition. For Hindus, Veda is the eternal wisdom of primordial seers preserved for thousands of years in an unbroken oral tradition. The Vedas are the four major compilations of Vedic ritual, explanatory, and speculative texts. The collection of 1,028 religious hymns known as the *Rig-Veda* represents the oldest materials of the Vedas. The latest of these hymns date from about 1000 B.C.E., the oldest from perhaps 1700–1200 B.C.E., when the Aryans spread across the northern plains to the upper reaches of the Ganges.

Aryan is a different kind of term. The second-millennium invaders of northern India called themselves *Aryas* as opposed to the peoples whom they conquered. Vedic Sanskrit, the language of the invaders, gave this word to later Sanskrit as a term for "noble" or "free-born" (*arya*). The word is found also in old Iranian, or Persian, texts, and even the term *Iran* is derived from the Old Persian equivalent of *arya*. The peoples who came to India are more precisely designated Indo-Aryans, or Vedic Aryans.

In the nineteenth century, *Aryan* was the term applied to the widespread language group known today as **Indo-European**. This family includes Greek, Latin, the Romance and Germanic languages, the Slavic tongues, and the Indo-Iranian languages, including Persian and Sanskrit and their derivatives. The Nazis perversely misused "Aryan" to refer to a white "master race." Today most scholars use *Aryan* only to

Indus Stamp Seal. Note the familiar humped bull of India on this stone stamp seal.

© Scala/Art Resource, New York.

What impression does the level of detail in this depiction give you?

Indo-European

A widely distributed language group that includes most of the languages spoken in Europe, Persian, Sanskrit, and their derivatives.

identify the Indo-European speakers who invaded India and the Iranian plateau in the second millennium B.C.E. and the Indo-Iranian languages.

The Vedic Aryans were seminomadic warriors who reached India in small tribal groups through the mountain passes of the Hindu Kush. They were horsemen and cattle herders rather than farmers and city builders. They left their mark not in material culture but in the changes that their conquests brought to the regions they overran: a new language, social organization, techniques of warfare, and religious forms and ideas.

The early Aryans penetrated first into the Punjab and the Indus valley around 1800–1500 B.C.E., presumably in search of grazing lands for their livestock. Their horses, chariots, and copper-bronze weapons likely gave them military superiority over the Indus peoples or their successors. Rig-Vedic hymns echo these early conflicts. One late hymn praises the king of the *Bharatas*, giving us the Indian name for modern India, *Bharat*, "land of the Bharatas."

During the Rig-Vedic age (ca. 1700–1000 B.C.E.), the newcomers settled in the Punjab and beyond, where they took up agriculture and stockbreeding. Then, between about 1000 and 500 B.C.E., the *Late Vedic Age*, these Aryan Indians spread across the plain between the Yamuna and the Ganges and eastward. They cleared (probably by burning) the heavy forests that covered this region and then settled there. They also moved farther northeast to the Himalayan foothills and southeast along the Ganges, in what was to be the cradle of subsequent Indian civilization. The late Vedic period is also called the Brahmanic Age because it was dominated by the priestly religion of the Brahman class, as evidenced in commentaries called the *Brahmanas* (ca. 1000–800 or 600 B.C.E.). It is also sometimes called the Epic Age because it provided the setting for India's two classical epics, the **Mahabharata** and the **Ramayana**.

Both epics reflect the complex cultural and social mixing of Aryan and other earlier subcontinent peoples.

By about 200 CE, this mixing produced a distinctive new "Indian" civilization over most of the subcontinent. Its basis was clearly Aryan, but its language, society, and religion incorporated many non-Aryan elements. Harappan culture vanished, but both it and other regional cultures contributed to the formation of Indian culture as we know it.

Aryan society was apparently patrilineal—with succession and inheritance in the male line—and its gods were likewise predominantly male. Marriage appears to have been monogamous, and widows could remarry. Related families formed larger kin groups. The largest social grouping was the tribe, ruled by a chieftain or **raja** ("king" in Sanskrit), who shared power with a tribal council. In early Vedic days the ruler was chosen for his prowess; his chief responsibility was to lead in battle, and he had no priestly function or sacred authority. A chief priest looked after the sacrifices on which religious life centered. By the Brahmanic age the king, with the help of priests, had assumed the role of judge in legal matters and become a hereditary ruler claiming divine qualities. The power of the priestly class had also increased.

Although there were probably subgroups of warriors and priests, Aryan society seems originally to have had only two basic divisions: noble and common. The Dasas—the darker, conquered peoples—came to form a third group (together with those who intermarried with them) of the socially excluded. Over time, a more rigid scheme of four social classes (excluding the non-Aryan Dasas) evolved. By the late Rig-Vedic period, religious theory explicitly sanctioned these four divisions, or *varnas*—the priestly (*Brahman*), the warrior/noble (*Kshatriya*), the peasant/tradesman (*Vaishya*), and the servant (*Shudra*). Only the members of the three upper classes participated fully in social, political, and religious life. This scheme underlies the rigid caste system that later became fundamental to Indian society.

Mahabharata and **Ramayana**
The two classical Indian epics.

••◦─[Read the **Document**
Excerpt from Mahábhárata
(1000–600 B.C.E.) at **myhistorylab.com**

raja
An Indian king.

OVERVIEW   The First Civilizations

Civilization is a form of human culture usually marked by the development of cities, the ability to make and use metal tools and instruments, and the invention of a system of writing. The first civilizations appeared in the Middle East between 4000 and 3000 B.C.E., and by the second millennium B.C.E., there were civilized societies in Eurasia, China, and the Americas.

Mesopotamia	Sumerians arrive in the Tigris-Eurphrates River valley, ca. 3500 B.C.E., and establish the first city-states, ca. 2800 B.C.E.
Egypt	Egyptian civilization develops along the Nile River, ca. 3100 B.C.E. Egypt becomes a unified state, ca. 2700 B.C.E.
Indus Valley	Flourishing urban civilization develops in northern India along the Indus River, ca. 2250 B.C.E.
China	City-states appear in the Yellow River basin, ca. 1766 B.C.E.
Americas	Agricultural surplus gives rise to the first cities in Mesoamerica, ca. 1500 B.C.E., and to the first Andean civilization in South America, ca. 2750 B.C.E.

The early seminomadic Aryans lived simply in wood-and-thatch or, later, mud-walled dwellings. They measured wealth in cattle and were accomplished at carpentry and bronze working (iron probably was not known in India before 1000 B.C.E.). They used gold for ornamentation and produced woolen textiles. They also cultivated some crops, especially grains, and were familiar with intoxicating drinks, including soma, used in religious rites, and a kind of mead. Music and gambling with dice appear to have been popular.

The Brahmanic Age left few material remains. Urban culture remained undeveloped, although mud-brick towns appeared as new lands were cleared for cultivation. Established kingdoms with fixed capitals now existed. Trade grew, especially along the Ganges, although there is no evidence of a coinage system. Later texts mention specialized artisans, including goldsmiths, basket makers, weavers, potters, and entertainers. Writing had been reintroduced to India around 700 B.C.E., perhaps from Mesopotamia along with traded goods.

Vedic India's main identifiable contributions to later history were religious. The central Vedic cult—controlled by priests serving a military aristocracy—remained dominant until the middle of the first millennium B.C.E. By that time other, perhaps older, religious forms were evidently asserting themselves among the populace. The increasing ritual formalism of Brahmanic religion provoked challenges both in popular practice and in religious thought that culminated in Buddhist, Jain, and Hindu traditions of piety and practice (see Chapter 2).

The earliest Indo-Aryans seem to have worshiped numerous gods, most of whom embodied or were associated with powers of nature. (See Document, "Hymn to Indra" on page 22.) The Rig-Vedic hymns are addressed to anthropomorphic deities linked to natural phenomena such as the sky, the clouds, and the sun. These gods are comparable to those of ancient Greece (see Chapter 3) and are apparently distantly related to them through the Indo-European heritage the Greeks and Aryans shared. The name of the Aryan father-god Dyaus, for example, is linguistically related to the Greek Zeus. The Vedic hymns praise each god they address as possessing almost all powers, including those associated with other gods.

Ritual sacrifice was the central focus of Vedic religion, its goal apparently being to invoke the presence of the gods to whom an offering was made rather than to expiate sins or express thanksgiving. Drinking soma juice was part of the ritual. A recurring

DOCUMENT

Hymn to Indra

This hymn celebrates the greatest deed ascribed to Indra, the slaying of the dragon Vritra to release the waters needed by people and livestock (which is also heralded at one point in the hymn as the act of creation itself). These waters are apparently those of the dammed-up rivers, but possibly also the rains as well. This victory also symbolizes the victory of the Aryans over the dark-skinned Dasas. Note the sexual as well as water imagery. The kadrukas may be the bowls used for soma in the sacrifice. The vajra is Indra's thunderbolt; the name Dasa for the lord of the waters is also that used for the peoples defeated by the Aryans and for all enemies of Indra, of whom the Pani tribe is one.

- **WHAT** are the main kinds of imagery used for Indra and his actions in the hymn? What divine acts does the hymn ascribe to Indra?

Indra's heroic deeds, indeed, will I proclaim, the first ones which the wielder of the vajra accomplished. He killed the dragon, released the waters, and split open the sides of the mountains.

He killed the dragon lying spread out on the mountain; for him Tvashtar fashioned the roaring vajra. Like bellowing cows, the waters, gliding, have gone down straightway to the ocean.

Showing off his virile power he chose soma; from the three kadrukas he drank of the extracted soma. The bounteous god took up the missile, the vajra; he killed the first-born among the dragons.

When you, O Indra, killed the first-born among the dragons and further overpowered the wily tricks (maya) of the tricksters, bringing forth, at that very moment, the sun, the heaven and the dawn—since then, indeed, have you not come across another enemy. Indra killed Vritra, the greater enemy, the shoulderless one, with his mighty and fatal weapon, the vajra. Like branches of a tree lopped off with an axe, the dragon lies prostrate upon the earth. . . .

Over him, who lay in that manner like a shattered reed flowed the waters for the sake of man. At the feet of the very waters, which Vritra had [once] enclosed with his might, the dragon [now] lay [prostrate]. . . .

With the Dasa as their lord and with the dragon as their warder, the waters remained imprisoned, like cows held by the Pani. Having killed Vritra, [Indra] threw open the cleft of waters which had been closed.

You became the hair of a horse's tail, O Indra, when he [Vritra] struck at your sharp-pointed vajra—the one god [eka deva] though you were. You won the cows, O brave one, you won soma; you released the seven rivers, so that they should flow. . . .

Indra, who wields the vajra in his hand, is the lord of what moves and what remains rested, of what is peaceful and what is horned. He alone rules over the tribes as their king; he encloses them as does a rim the spokes.

—*Rig-Veda 1.32*

Source: From Sources of Indian Tradition by William Theodore de Bary. Copyright © 1988 by Columbia University Press. Reprinted with permission of the publisher.

---

theme of the Vedic hymns that accompanied the rituals is the desire for prosperity, health, and victory. The late Vedic texts emphasize magical and cosmic aspects of ritual and sacrifice. Indeed, some of the *Brahmanas* maintain that only exacting performance of the sacrifice can maintain the world order.

The word *Brahman*, originally used to designate the ritual utterance or word of power, came to refer also to the generalized divine power present in the sacrifice. In the **Upanishads**, some of the latest Vedic texts and the ones most concerned with speculation about the universe, *Brahman* was extended to refer to the Absolute, the transcendent principle of reality. As the guardian of ritual and the master of the sacred word, the priest was known throughout the Vedic Aryan period by a related word, *Brahmana*, for which the English is *Brahman*. Echoes of these associations were to lend force in later Hindu tradition to the special status of the Brahman caste groups as the highest social class (see Chapter 4).

Upanishads

The Upanishads, which date to about the seventh century B.C.E., have been perennial sources of spiritual knowledge for Hindus. The word *upanishad* means "secret and sacred knowledge." This word occurs in the Upanishads themselves in more than a dozen places in this sense. The word also means "texts incorporating such knowledge." There are ten principal Upanishads.

CHRONOLOGY

ANCIENT INDIA

ca. 2250–1750 (2500–1500?) B.C.E.	Indus (Harappan) civilization (written script still undeciphered)
ca. 1800–1500 B.C.E.	Aryan peoples invade northwestern India
ca. 1500–1000 B.C.E.	Rig-Vedic period: composition of Rig-Vedic hymns; Punjab as center of Indo-Aryan civilization
ca. 1000–500 B.C.E.	Late Vedic period: Doab as center of Indo-Aryan civilization
ca. 1000–800/600 B.C.E.	Composition of Brahmanas and other Vedic texts
ca. 800–500 B.C.E.	Composition of major Upanishads
ca. 700–500 B.C.E.	Probable reintroduction of writing
ca. 400 B.C.E.–**200** C.E.	Composition of great epics, the *Mahabharata* and Ramayana

EARLY CHINESE CIVILIZATION

NEOLITHIC ORIGINS IN THE YELLOW RIVER VALLEY

Agriculture began in China in about 4000 B.C.E. in the basin of the southern bend of the Yellow River. This is the northernmost of eastern Asia's four great river systems, all of which drain eastward into the Pacific Ocean. In recent millennia, the Yellow River has flowed through a deforested plain, cold in winter and subject to periodic droughts. But in 4000 B.C.E., its climate was warmer, with forested highlands in the west and swampy marshes to the east.

The chief crop of China's agricultural revolution was millet. A second agricultural development focusing on rice may have occurred on the Huai River. In time, wheat entered China from the west. The early Chinese cleared land and burned its cover to plant millet and cabbage and, later, rice and soybeans. When the soil became exhausted, fields were abandoned, and sometimes early villages were abandoned, too. Pigs, sheep, cattle, dogs, and chickens were domesticated, but hunting continued to be important to the village economy. Grain was stored in pottery, and stone tools included axes, hoes, spades, and sickle-shaped knives.

The earliest cultivators lived in wattle-and-daub pit dwellings with wooden support posts and sunken, plastered floors. Their villages were located in isolated clearings along slopes of river valleys. Archaeological finds of weapons and remains of earthen walls suggest tribal warfare between villages. Little is known of the religion of these people, although some evidence suggests the worship of ancestral spirits. They practiced divination by applying heat to a hole drilled in the shoulder bone of a steer or the under-shell of a tortoise and then interpreting the resulting cracks in the bone. They buried their dead in cemeteries with jars of food. Tribal leaders wore rings and beads of jade.

EARLY BRONZE AGE: THE SHANG

The traditional history of China tells of three ancient dynasties: Xia (2205–1766 B.C.E.), Shang (1766–1050 B.C.E.), and Zhou (1050–256 B.C.E.).

WHY DID large territorial states arise in ancient China?

See the **Map**
Ancient China at **myhistorylab.com**

Hear the **Audio**
at **myhistorylab.com**

◉⎯See the **Map**
The Shang Kingdom
at **myhistorylab.com**

◉⎯View the **Image**
An Inscribed Oracle Bone
at **myhistorylab.com**

Until early in the twentieth century, historians thought the first two were legendary. Then, in the 1920s, archaeological excavations near present-day Anyang uncovered the ruins of a walled city that had been a late Shang capital.

Other Shang cities have been discovered more recently. The ruins contained the archives of the department of divination of the Shang court, with thousands upon thousands of "oracle bones" incised with archaic Chinese writing.

The names of kings on the bones fit almost perfectly those of the traditional historical record. This evidence that the Shang actually existed has led historians to suggest that the Xia may also have been an actual dynasty.

The characteristic political institution of Bronze Age China was the city-state. The largest was the Shang capital, which, frequently moved, lacked the monumental architecture of Egypt or Mesopotamia. The walled city contained public buildings, altars, and the residences of the aristocracy; it was surrounded by a sea of Neolithic tribal villages. The military aristocracy went to war in chariots, supported by levies of foot soldiers. The Shang fought against barbarian tribes and, occasionally, against other city-states in rebellion against Shang rule. Captured prisoners were enslaved.

The three most notable features of Shang China were writing, bronzes, and the appearance of social classes. Scribes at the Shang court kept records on strips of bamboo, but these have not survived. What have survived are inscriptions on bronze artifacts and the oracle bones. Some bones contain the question put to the oracle, the answer, and the outcome of the matter. Representative questions were: Which ancestor is causing the king's earache? If the king goes hunting at Qi, will there be a disaster? Will the king's child be a son? If the king sends his army to attack an enemy, will the deity help him? Was a sacrifice acceptable to ancestral deities?

What we know of Shang religion is based on the bones. The Shang believed in a supreme "Deity Above," who had authority over the human world. Also serving at the court of the Deity Above were lesser natural deities—the sun, moon, earth, rain, wind, and the six clouds. Even the Shang king sacrificed not to the Deity Above but to his ancestors, who interceded with the Deity Above on the king's behalf. Kings, while alive at least, were not considered divine but were the high priests of the state.

In Shang times, as later, religion in China was closely associated with cosmology. The Shang people observed the movements of the planets and stars and reported eclipses. Celestial happenings were seen as omens from the gods. The chief cosmologists also recorded events at the court. The Shang calendar had a month of 30 days and a year of 360 days. Adjustments were made periodically by adding an extra month. The king used the calendar to tell his people when to sow and when to reap.

Bronze appeared in China in about 2000 B.C.E., 1,000 years later than in Mesopotamia and 500 years later than in India. Because Shang casting methods were more advanced than those of Mesopotamia and because the designs on Shang bronzes continued those of the preceding black pottery culture, the Shang probably developed its bronze technology independently.

Among the Shang, as with other early river valley civilizations, the increasing control of nature through agriculture and metallurgy was accompanied by the emergence of a rigidly stratified society in which the many were compelled to serve the few. A monopoly of bronze weapons enabled aristocrats to exploit other groups. Nowhere was the gulf between the royal lineage and the baseborn more apparent than it was in the Shang institution of human sacrifice. When a king died, hundreds of slaves or prisoners of war, sometimes together with those who had served the king during his lifetime, might be buried with him. Sacrifices also were made when a palace or an altar was built.

Oracle Bone. Inscribed oracle bone from the Shang Dynasty city of Anyang.

Does the quality of the inscriptions on this bone make you think the bone is more a symbolic object or a tool?

LATE BRONZE AGE: THE WESTERN ZHOU

To the west of the area of Shang rule, in the valley of the Wei River, lived the warlike Zhou people. The last Shang kings were weak, cruel, and tyrannical. By 1050 B.C.E., they had been debilitated by campaigns against nomads in the north and rebellious tribes in the east. Taking advantage of this opportunity, the Zhou made alliances with disaffected city-states and swept in, conquering the Shang.

In most respects, the Zhou continued the Shang pattern of life and rule. The agrarian-based city-state continued to be the basic unit of society, and the Zhou social hierarchy was similar to that of the Shang. The Zhou assimilated Shang culture, continuing without interruption the development of China's ideographic writing. The Zhou also maintained the practice of casting bronze ceremonial vessels, but their vessels lacked the fineness that set the Shang above the rest of the Bronze Age world.

The Zhou kept their capital in the west but set up a secondary capital at Luoyang, along the southern bend of the Yellow River. They appointed their kinsmen or other aristocratic allies to rule in other city-states. Blood or lineage ties were essential to the Zhou pattern of rule.

One difference between the Shang and the Zhou was in the nature of the political legitimacy each claimed. The Shang kings, descended from shamanistic (priestly) rulers, had a built-in religious authority and needed no theory to justify their rule. But the Zhou, having conquered the Shang, needed a rationale for why they were now the rightful rulers. Their argument was that Heaven (the name for the supreme being that gradually replaced the Deity Above during the early Zhou), appalled by the wickedness of the last Shang king, had withdrawn its mandate to rule from the Shang, awarding it instead to the Zhou. This concept of the **Mandate of Heaven** was subsequently invoked by every dynasty in China down to the twenty-first century.

IRON AGE: THE EASTERN ZHOU

In 771 B.C.E. the Wei valley capital of the Western Zhou was overrun by barbarians. The heir to the throne, with some members of the court, escaped to the secondary capital at Luoyang, 200 miles to the east and just south of the bend in the Yellow River, beginning the Eastern Zhou period.

The first phase of the Eastern Zhou lasted until 481 B.C.E. The Zhou kings at Luoyang were unable to reestablish their old authority. By the early seventh century B.C.E., Luoyang's political power was nominal, although it remained a center of culture and ritual observances. During the seventh and sixth centuries B.C.E., the political configuration was an equilibrium of many small principalities on the north-central plain surrounded by larger, wholly autonomous territorial states along the borders of the plain (see Map 1–4 on page 26). The larger states consolidated the areas within their borders, absorbed tribal peoples, and expanded by conquering states on their periphery.

The second phase of the Eastern Zhou is known as the Warring States period, after a chronicle of the same name treating the years from 401 to 256 B.C.E. By the fifth century B.C.E., all defensive alliances had collapsed. Strong states swallowed their weaker neighbors. The border states grew in size and power. Interstate stability disappeared. By the fourth century B.C.E., only eight or nine great territorial states remained as contenders. The only question was which one would defeat the others and go on to unify China.

CHRONOLOGY

EARLY CHINA

4000 B.C.E.	Neolithic agricultural villages
1766 B.C.E.	Bronze Age city-states, aristocratic charioteers, pictographic writing
771 B.C.E.	Iron Age territorial states
500 B.C.E.	Age of philosophers
221 B.C.E.	Unification of China

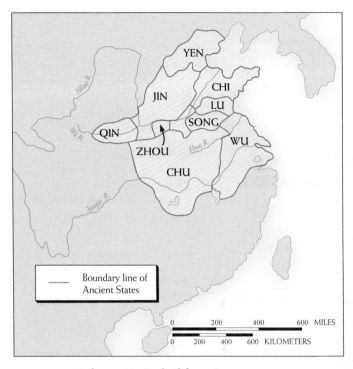

MAP 1-4. Early Iron Age Territorial States in China during the Sixth Century B.C.E..

After the fall of the Western Zhou in China in 771 B.C.E., large territorial states formed that became increasingly independent of the later Zhou kings.

Which States appear strongest in this period?

Three basic changes in Chinese society contributed to the rise of large territorial states. One was the expansion of population and agricultural lands. The walled cities of the Shang and Western Zhou had been like oases in the wilds, bounded by plains, marshes, and forests. But as population grew, wilds began to disappear, and the economy became almost entirely agricultural. Friction arose over boundaries as states began to abut. After the start of the Iron Age, farmers used iron tools to clear new lands and plow deeper, raising yields and increasing agricultural surpluses. Irrigation and drainage canals became important for the first time. Serfs gave way to independent farmers, who bought and sold land. By the third century B.C.E., China had about 20 million people, making it the most populous country in the world, a distinction it has never lost.

A second development was the rise of commerce. Roads built for war were used by merchants. Copper coins joined bolts of silk and precious metals as media of exchange. Rich merchants rivaled in lifestyle than landowning lower nobility. Bronze bells and mirrors, clay figurines, lacquer boxes, and musical instruments found in late Zhou tombs show that China's material and artistic culture leaped ahead during this period.

A third change that doomed the city-state was the rise of a new kind of army. The war chariots of the old aristocracy, practical only on level terrain, gave way to cavalry armed with crossbows. Most of the fighting was done by conscript foot soldiers. Armies numbered in the hundreds of thousands. The old nobility gave way to professional commanders. The old aristocratic etiquette, which governed behavior even in battle, gave way to military tactics that were bloody and ruthless. Prisoners were often massacred.

Change also affected government. Lords of the new territorial states began to style themselves as kings, taking the title that previously only Zhou royalty had enjoyed. To survive, new states had to transform their agricultural and commercial wealth into military strength. To collect taxes, conscript soldiers, and administer the affairs of state required records and literate officials. Academies were established to fill the need. Beneath the ministers, a literate bureaucracy developed. Its members were referred to as *shi*, a term that had once meant "warrior" but gradually came to mean "scholar-bureaucrat." The *shi* were of mixed social origins, including petty nobility, literate members of the old warrior class, landlords, merchants, and rising commoners. From this class, as we will see in Chapter 2, came the philosophers who created the "one hundred schools" and transformed the culture of China.

Bronze Vessel from the Shang Dynasty.
The little elephant on top forms the handle of the lid. Wine was poured through the spout formed by the big elephant's trunk.

What do you observe about the craftsmanship with which this vessel was created? What does this suggest about the situations in which it might have been used?

THE RISE OF CIVILIZATION IN THE AMERICAS

During the last Ice Age, the Bering region between Siberia and Alaska was dry land. Humans crossed this land bridge from Asia to the Americas, probably in several migrations, and moved south and east over many centuries. From these peoples a wide variety of original American cultures and many hundreds of languages arose.

The earliest immigrants to the Americas, like all Paleolithic peoples, lived by hunting, fishing, and gathering. At the time of the initial migrations, herds of large game animals were plentiful. By the end of the Ice Age, however, mammoths and many other forms of game had become extinct in the Americas. Where fishing or small game was insufficient, people had to rely on protein from vegetable sources. American production of plants providing protein far outpaced that of European agriculture. One of the most important early developments was the cultivation of maize (corn). The cultivation of maize appears to have been in place in Mexico by approximately 4000 B.C.E. Other important foods were potatoes (developed in the Andes), manioc, squash, beans, peppers, and tomatoes. Many of these foods entered the diet of Europeans, Asians, and other peoples after the European conquest of the Americas in the sixteenth century C.E.

Eventually four areas of relatively dense settlement emerged in the Americas. One of these, in the Pacific Northwest in the area around Puget Sound, depended on the region's extraordinary abundance of fish rather than on agriculture; this area did not develop urbanized states. Another was the Mississippi valley, where, based on maize agriculture, the inhabitants developed a high level of social and political integration that had collapsed several centuries before European contact. The other two, Mesoamerica and the Andean region of South America, saw the emergence of strong, long-lasting states. In other regions with maize agriculture and settled village life—notably the North American Southwest—food supplies might have been too insecure to support the development of states.

Mesoamerica, which extends from the central part of modern Mexico into Central America, is a region of great geographical diversity, ranging from tropical rain forest to semiarid mountains (see Map 1–5 on page 28). Archaeologists traditionally divide its preconquest history into three broad periods: pre-classic or formative (2000 B.C.E.– 150 C.E.), classic (150–900 C.E.), and post-classic (900–1521). The earliest Mesoamerican civilization, that of the Olmecs, arose during the pre-classic period on the Gulf Coast beginning approximately 1500 B.C.E. The Olmec centers at San Lorenzo (ca. 1200–ca. 900 B.C.E.) and La Venta (ca. 900–ca. 400 B.C.E.) exhibit many of the characteristics of later Mesoamerican cities, including the symmetrical arrangement of large platforms, plazas, and other monumental structures along a central axis and possibly courts for the ritual ball game played throughout Mesoamerica at the time of the Spanish conquest. Writing developed in Mesoamerica during the late formative period. As we will see in Chapter 14, succeeding civilizations—including the classic period civilization of Teotihuacán, the post-classic civilizations of the Toltecs and Aztecs, and the classic and post-classic civilization of the Mayas—created large cities, developed sophisticated calendar systems, and were organized in complex social and political structures.

The Andean region is one of dramatic contrasts. Along its western edge, the narrow coastal plain is one of the driest deserts in the world. The

HOW DID agriculture influence the development of civilizations in Mesoamerica?

((••─Hear the Audio
at **myhistorylab.com**

Mesoamerica
The part of North America that extends from the central part of modern Mexico to Central America.

CHRONOLOGY

EARLY CIVILIZATIONS OF MESOAMERICA

1500–400 B.C.E.	The Olmecs
200–750 C.E.	The Classic period in central Mexico. Dominance of Teotihuacán in the Valley of Mexico and Monte Alban in the Valley of Oaxaca
150–900 C.E.	The Classic period of Mayan civilization in the Yucatán and Guatemala

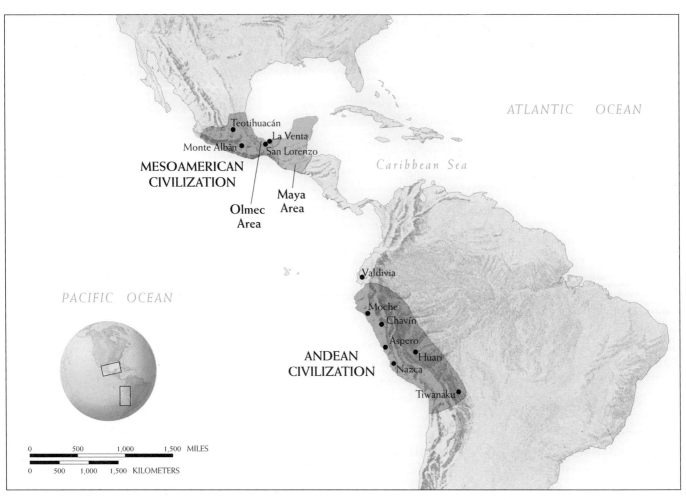

MAP 1–5. Civilization in Mesoamerica and the Andes.
Both Mesoamerica and the Andean region of South America saw the development of a series of civilizations beginning between 1500 and 1000 B.C.E.

What Geographical features do these civilizations have in common? How do they differ?

Olmec Head. This colossal Olmec head, now in the Museo Nacional de Antropologia in Mexico City, was excavated at San Lorenzo. Carved of basalt, it may be a portrait of an Olmec ruler. Olmec civilization thrived between 1500 and 800 B.C.E.

Compare this head to the statue from Mohenjo-Daro at the beginning of this chapter. How does this head's projection of power differ from the other statue's?

Andes rise abruptly from the coastal plain and then descend gradually into the Amazon basin to the east. Agriculture is possible on the coast only in the valleys of the many rivers that flow from the Andes into the Pacific. The earliest monumental architecture in the Andean region, built on the coast at the site of Aspero by people who depended on a combination of agriculture and the Pacific's rich marine resources, dates to about 2750 B.C.E., contemporary with the Great Pyramids of Egypt's Old Kingdom.

From 800 to 200 B.C.E. a civilization associated with the site of Chavín de Huantar in the highlands of Peru exerted great influence in the Andes. Artifacts in the distinctive Chavín style can be found over a large area dating to this period, which archaeologists call the Early Horizon. In many areas, this was a time of technical innovation, including pottery, textiles, and metallurgy. Whether the spread of the Chavín style represents actual political integration or the influence of a strong religious center is not known. The period following the decline of Chavín, which archaeologists call the Early Intermediate period, saw the development of distinc-

CHRONOLOGY

EARLY CIVILIZATION OF THE ANDES

ca. 2750 B.C.E.?	Monumental architecture at Aspero
800–200 B.C.E.?	Chavín (Early Horizon)
200 B.C.E.–600 C.E.	Early Intermediate period (Moche on the northern coast of Peru, Nazca on the southern coast)

tive cultures in several regions. Notable among these are the Moche culture on the northern coast of Peru and the Nazca culture on the southern coast. A second period of transregional integration—called the Middle Horizon—occurred around 600 C.E., this time probably associated with empires centered on the highland sites of Huari and Tiahuanaco. The succeeding Late Intermediate period was dominated on the northern coast of Peru by the Chimu successors of the Moche state. This period ended with the founding of the vast, tightly controlled empire of the Incas in the fourteenth and fifteenth centuries C.E.

SUMMARY

 WHY IS "culture" considered a defining trait of human beings?

Early Humans and Their Culture. Language facilitates the transmission of culture—the lifeways of a group—from one generation to the next. Cultural adaptation has allowed humans to spread around the globe. Beginning in 10,000 B.C.E., human beings shifted from a hunter-gatherer way of life to one marked by settled agriculture and the domestication of animals—a shift known as the Neolithic Revolution. Between 4000 and 3000 B.C.E., civilization began to appear in the Tigris and Euphrates valleys in Mesopotamia, then along the Nile River in Egypt, and somewhat later in the Indus valley in India and the Yellow River basin in China. Each of these early civilizations developed urban centers, monumental architecture, a hierarchical society, and a system of writing. The period is known as the Bronze Age because it coincided with the discovery of the technique for making bronze tools and weapons. *page 1*

HOW DID control over water resources influence early Middle Eastern civilizations?

Early Civilizations in the Middle East to about 1000 B.C.E. The Sumerians founded the oldest Mesopotamian cities around 3000 B.C.E. Beginning around 2370 B.C.E., the Sumerian city-states were conquered and absorbed in turn by the Akkadian, Babylonian, and Assyrian empires. The Sumerians passed much of their civilization down to their successors: a system of writing on clay tablets called *cuneiform*, the worship of gods based on natural forces, semidivine kings, and a highly developed bureaucracy. Watered by the Nile River and protected by deserts and the sea, Egyptian civilization was more secure and peaceful than that of Mesopotamia. Egypt became a unified kingdom around 2700 B.C.E. Religion dominated Egyptian life. The kings, or pharaohs, were considered gods on whom the lives and prosperity of their people depended. Egyptian history is divided into three main periods: Old Kingdom (2700–2200 B.C.E.), Middle Kingdom (2025–1630 B.C.E.), and New Kingdom (1550–1075 B,C.E.). Under the New Kingdom, Egypt contended for mastery of the Near East with the Hittite Empire. *page 5*

HOW DID conquest and trade shape early empires in the Near East?

Ancient Near Eastern Empires. The Hittites, based in what is now Turkey between 1400 B.C.E. and 1200 B.C.E., helped transmit Mesopotamian and

Egyptian culture to the Greeks. They were also early smelters of iron. The Kassites, with their military aristocracy, helped preserve Babylonian culture. The Mitannians were horse-based warriors. The Assyrians were significantly influenced by Babylonian culture. By 665 B.C.E., thanks to military conquest, they controlled a vast territory. The Assyrian Empire fell to Nebuchadnezzar in 612 B.C.E., and the neo-Babylonians built their empire on trade. *page 14*

 WHAT INFLUENCES did the first Indus valley civilization have on later Indian religious and social practices?

Early Indian Civilization. By 2300 B.C.E. at least seventy Indus cities, the largest being Harappa and Mohenjo-Daro, had developed a sophisticated urban culture. Between 1800 and 1700 B.C.E., Indus civilization disappeared for unknown reasons. In its place, Indo-European (or Aryan) invaders established the Vedic culture, named after the ritual writings known as the Vedas. In turn, Vedic culture evolved into a "new" Indian civilization that spread over the whole subcontinent. *page 16*

WHY DID territorial states arise in ancient China?

Early Chinese Civilization. The Shang Dynasty (1766–1050 B.C.E.) founded the earliest known Bronze Age civilization in China. The Shang and their successors, the Zhou (1050–256 B.C.E.), ruled as warrior aristocrats from city-states that fought outsiders and each other. By the fourth century B.C.E., as population and commerce expanded, rulers needed bigger armies to defend their states and trained bureaucrats to administer them. The result was the consolidation of many petty states into a few large territorial units. *page 23*

 HOW DID agriculture influence the development of civilizations in Mesoamerica?

The Rise of Civilization in the Americas. The first civilizations in the Americas arose in places that produced an agricultural surplus. In Mesoamerica (central Mexico and Central America) this was based on the cultivation of maize (corn). In the Andes valleys, it was based on a combination of agriculture and the rich marine resources of the Pacific. The Olmecs (1500–400 B.C.E.) established the first civilization in Mesoamerica, whereas the first monumental architecture appeared in the Andes region around 2750 B.C.E. *page 27*

KEY TERMS

Aryans (AIR-ee-uhns) (p. 17)
Bronze Age (p. 5)
chattel slavery (SHAT-1) (p. 7)
civilization (p. 5)
culture (p. 1)
cuneiform (koo-NAY-form) (p. 6)
diffusion (p. 3)
Harappan (huh-RAHP-uhn) (p. 17)
hieroglyphs (p. 12)
Indo-European (p. 19)
Mahabharata **(muh-HAH-BAHR-uh-tuh)** and *Ramayana* **(RAH-MAH-yuh-nuh)** (p. 20)

Mandate of Heaven (p. 25)
Mesoamerica (p. 27)
Mesopotamia (p. 4)
Neolithic Revolution (p. 4)
Paleolithic Age (p. 2)
pharaoh (p. 9)
raja (rah-JAH) (p. 20)
Upanishads (oo-PAHN-ee-shahdz) (p. 22)
Vedas (vay-DAHZ) (p. 17)

REVIEW QUESTIONS

1. How was life during the Paleolithic Age different from that in the Neolithic Age? What advances in agriculture and human development had taken place by the end of the Neolithic era? Is it valid to speak of a "Neolithic Revolution"?

2. What defines civilization? What are the similarities and differences among the world's earliest civilizations?

3. What general conclusions can you draw about the differences in the political and intellectual outlooks of the civilizations of Egypt and Mesopotamia?

4. Why were the Assyrians so successful in establishing their Near Eastern empire? How did their empire differ from that of the Hittites or Egyptians? In what ways did this empire benefit the Near East? Why did the Assyrian Empire ultimately fail to survive?

5. How does the early history of Indian civilization differ from that of the river valley civilizations of China, Mesopotamia, and Egypt? What does the evidence suggest were the social, economic, and political differences between the Indus civilization and the Vedic Aryan civilization?

6. What were the stages of early Chinese history? What led each to evolve toward the next?

7. What does the story of the appearance of civilization in the Americas tell us about the development of civilization generally? In what ways did the development of Mesoamerican civilizations follow patterns similar to those of early civilizations in the Middle East, the Near East, India, or China? In what ways did it differ?

Note: To learn more about the topics in this chapter, please turn to the Suggested Readings at the end of the book. For additional sources related to this chapter please see www.myhistorylab.com

PEARSON
myhistorylab Connections

Reinforce what you learned in this chapter by studying the many documents, images, maps, review tools, and videos available at **www.myhistorylab.com**

Read and Review

✓•⌐ **Study** and **Review**   Chapter 1

•❖•⌐ Read the Document *From Hunter-gatherers to Food-producers–Overcoming Obstacles, p. 2*
The Development of Religion, p. 2
The Toolmaker (3300 B.C.E.), p. 2
Redefining Self—From Tribe to Village to City 1500 B.C.E., p. 3
The Neolithic Village, p. 4
Sumerian Law Code: The Code of Lipit-Ishtar, p. 5
Geography and Civilization: Egypt and Mesopotamia–Impact of Agriculture, p. 5
Two Accounts of an Egyptian Famine 2600s B.C.E., p. 6
The Development of Religion in Primitive Cultures, p. 7
Excerpts from The Epic of Gilgamesh, p. 7
Workings of Ma'at: "The Tale of the Eloquent Peasant", p. 9
The Report of Wenamun
Papyrus of Ani, The Egyptian Book of the Dead c. 1200 B.C.E., p. 13
Hittite Law Code: excerpts from The Code of the Nesilim, p. 14
Excerpt from Mahábhárata (1000-600 B.C.E.), p. 20
"Hou-Shih, from the Shih-Ching," p. 25

◉⌐ See the Map *The Beginnings of Food Production, p. 3*
Egypt in the Middle Kingdom, p. 11
Egypt in the New Kingdom, p. 12
Empire of Assiria, ca. 1800 B.C.E., p. 15
The Neo-Babylonian Empire, ca. 580 B.C.E., p. 16
The Shang Kingdom, p. 24

◉⌐ View the Image *Hammurabi Receives His Law Code from the Gods, p. 6*
The Pyramids at Giza, p. 11

The Sphinx, p. 11
Egyptian Throne of Tutankhamun, 1333–1323 B.C.E.
Great Temple of Abu Simbel, p. 12
Scene from the Egyptian Afterlife, p. 13
Egyptian Relief of Anubis, p. 14
An Inscribed Oracle Bone, p. 24

◉⌐ Watch the Video *The Temple of Karnak, p. 13*
Ramses II's Abu Simbel, p. 14

Research and Explore

◉⌐ See the Map *Prehistoric Human Migration Patterns: From 1 million to 15,000 years ago*

◉⌐ See the Map *Ancient China on page 23*

((•⌐ **Hear** the **Audio**

Hear the audio file for Chapter 1
at **www.myhistorylab.com**

2

Four Great Revolutions in Thought and Religion

The Way. Detail from a twelfth-century Daoist scroll, showing the feats of the "Eight Immortals," the most famous characters in Daoist folklore. **How does this landscape evoke the ineffability and mystery of Dao, or "the way"?**

ll human cultures develop religious or philosophical systems. Some scientists have even debated whether humans are biologically "hard-wired" for religious beliefs. Certainly religion and philosophy meet profound human psychological needs, offering explanations of life's meaning. ■

COMPARING THE FOUR GREAT REVOLUTIONS

The most straightforward case is that of China. Both geographically and culturally, its philosophical breakthrough grew directly out of the earlier river valley civilization. No such continuity existed elsewhere in the world. In India, for example, the great tradition of Indian thought and religion emerged after 600 B.C.E. out of the Ganges civilization of Indo-Aryan warriors who had swept in from the northwest. Absorbing many particulars from the earlier Indus civilization, which had collapsed, the Aryans built a new civilization on the plains farther east along the mighty Ganges River. The transition was even more complex along the shores of the Mediterranean. No direct line of development can be traced from the Nile civilization of ancient Egypt or the civilizations of the Tigris-Euphrates River valley to Greek philosophy or to Judaic monotheism. Rather, the ancient river valley civilizations evolved into a complex amalgam that included diverse older religious, mythical, and cosmological traditions, as well as newer mystery cults. Judaic monotheism and Greek philosophy—representing different

WHAT ARE the fundamental beliefs or worldviews that were expressed in the four great revolutions in thought that occurred between 800 B.C.E.?

33

PHILOSOPHY AND RELIGION

Between 800 and 300 B.C.E, four philosophical or religious revolutions shaped the subsequent history of the world. The names of many of the figures involved in these revolutions are world-famous—Confucius, the Buddha, Abraham, Socrates, Plato, and Aristotle. All the revolutions occurred in or near the four heartland areas in which the river valley civilizations (described in Chapter 1) had appeared fifteen hundred or more years earlier. The transition from the early river valley civilizations to the intellectual and spiritual breakthroughs of the middle of the first millennium B.C.E. is schematized in Figure 2–1 on page 48.

Before considering each of the original breakthroughs that occurred between 800 and 300 B.C.E., we might ask whether they have anything in common. Five points are worth noting.

1. All the philosophical or religious revolutions occurred in or near the original river valley civilizations. These areas contained the most advanced cultures of the ancient world. They had sophisticated agriculture, cities with many literate inhabitants, and specialized trades and professions. In short, they had the material preconditions for breakthroughs in religion and thought.

2. Each of the revolutions in thought and ethos was born of a crisis in the ancient world. The appearance of iron meant better tools and weapons and, by extension, greater riches and more powerful armies. Old societies began to change and then to disintegrate. Old aristocratic and priestly codes of behavior broke down, producing a demand for more universalized rules of behavior, in other words, for ethics. The very relation of humans to nature or to the universe seemed to be changing. This predicament led to new visions of social and political order. The similarity between the Jewish Messiah, the Chinese sage-king, and Plato's philosopher-king is more than accidental. Each was a response to a crisis in a society of the ancient world. Each would reconnect ethics to history and restore order to a troubled society.

3. The number of philosophical and religious revolutions can be counted on the fingers of one hand. The reason is not that humans' creativity dried up after 300 B.C.E., but that subsequent breakthroughs and advances tended to occur within the original traditions, which, absorbing new energies, continued to evolve.

outgrowths of this amalgam—were each important in their own right. But their greatest influence occurred centuries later when they helped shape first Christianity and then Islam. (See Overview Figure 2–1 on page 48.)

PHILOSOPHY IN CHINA

WHY WAS the revolution in Chinese thought more similar to that in Greek thought than to Indian religion or Judaic monotheism?

Of the four great revolutions in thought of the first millennium B.C.E., the Chinese was closer to the Greek than to the Indian religious transformations or to Judaic monotheism. Just as Greece had a gamut of philosophies, so in China there were the "one hundred schools." But whereas Greek thought was speculative and concerned with the world of nature, Chinese thought was sociopolitical and practical. The background of the philosophical revolution in China was the disintegration of the old Zhou society (see Chapter 1). Thinkers searched for new principles by which to re-create a peaceful society. Even the Daoist sages, who were inherently apolitical, found it necessary to offer a political philosophy. Chinese thought also had far greater staying power than Greek thought, which only a few centuries after the glory of Athens was submerged by Christianity and did not reemerge as an independent force until the Renaissance. Chinese philosophy, though challenged by Buddhism, remained dominant until the early twentieth century. How were these early philosophies able to maintain such a grip on China when the cultures of every other part of the world fell under the sway of religions?

Part of the answer is that most Chinese philosophy had a religious dimension. But it was a religion with assumptions different from those with Judaic roots. In the Christian or Islamic worldview, there is a God who, however concerned with humankind, is not of this world. This worldview leads to dualism, the distinction between an otherworld, which is supernatural, and this world, which is natural.

•◦•─ Read the Document
Origins of the Chinese Civilization –
Confucianism, Daoism or Legalism?
at **myhistorylab.com**

4. After the first- and second-stage transformations, much of the cultural history of the world involves the spread of cultures derived from these original heartlands to ever-wider spheres. Christianity spread to northern and eastern Europe, the Americas, and parts of Asia and Africa; Buddhism to central, southeastern, and eastern Asia; Confucianism to Korea, Vietnam, and Japan; and Islam to Africa, southeastern Europe, and southern, central, and southeastern Asia. Sometimes the spread was the result of movements of people; other areas were like dry grasslands needing only the spark of the new ideas to be ignited. Typically, the process spread out over centuries.

5. Once a cultural pattern was set, it usually endured. Each major culture was resistant to the others and was only rarely displaced. Even in modern times, although the culture of modern science, and the learning associated with it, has penetrated every cultural zone, it has reshaped—and is reshaping, not displacing—the major cultures. Only Confucianism, the most secular of the traditional cultures, crumbled at the touch of science, and even its ethos remains a potent force in East Asian societies. These major cultures endured because they were not only responses to particular crises, but also attempts to answer universal questions concerning the human condition: What are human beings? What is our relation to the universe? How should we relate to others?

Focus Questions

◆ Why do you think so many revolutionary philosophical and religious ideas emerged at about the same time in many different regions? Do these ideas share any fundamental concerns?

◆ Why is this period in Eurasian history sometimes referred to as the "axial age"?

In the Chinese worldview, the two spheres are not separate: The cosmos is single, continuous, and nondualistic. It includes heaven, earth, and humanity. Heaven is above; earth is below. Humans, ideally guided by a wise and virtuous ruler, stand in between and regulate or harmonize the cosmological forces of heaven and earth through virtue and ritual sacrifices.

CONFUCIANISM

Confucius was born in 551 B.C.E. in a minor state in northeastern China. He probably belonged to the lower nobility or the knightly class, because he received an education in writing, music, and rituals. His father died when Confucius was young, so he may have known privation. He made his living by teaching. He traveled with his disciples from state to state, seeking a ruler who would put his ideas into practice. Although he may once have held a minor position, his ideas were rejected as impractical. He died in 479 B.C.E., honored as a teacher and scholar but having failed to find a ruler to advise. The name *Confucius* is the Latinized form of *Kong Fuzi*, or *Master Kong*, as he is known in China.

We know of Confucius only through the *Analects*—sayings collected by his disciples. They are mostly in the form of "The Master said," followed by his words. The picture that emerges is of a man of moderation, propriety, optimism, good sense, and wisdom. In an age of cruelty and superstition, he was humane, rational, and upright, demanding much of others and more of himself. Asked about death, he replied, "You do not understand even life. How can you understand death?"[1]

---

[1] All quotations from Confucius in this passage are from Confucius, *The Analects*, trans. by D. C. Lau (Penguin Books, 1979).

●◆●⎯Read the **Document**
Confucius, selections from the Analects
at **myhistorylab.com**

QUICK REVIEW

Confucius

● Born in 551 B.C.E. in northeastern China

● Probably belonged to the lower nobility or knightly class

● Made his living as a teacher and a scholar

•◆•⟩Read the Document
Confucianism: Government and the
Superior (551–479 B.C.E.)
at **myhistorylab.com**

•◆•⟩Read the Document
Confucian Political Philosophy:
An Excerpt from Mencius
at **myhistorylab.com**

Confucius. The master is shown here wearing the robes of a scholar of a later age.

Collection of the National Palace Museum, Taipei, Taiwan.

What clues does this image offer about the personality of Confucius?

CHRONOLOGY

CHINA

551–479 B.C.E.	Confucius
370–290 B.C.E.	Mencius
Fourth century B.C.E.	Laozi
221 B.C.E.	Qin unifies China

Confucius described himself as a conservator and transmitter of tradition. He idealized the early Shang and Zhou kings as paragons of virtue and particularly saw early Zhou society as a golden age. He sought the secrets of this golden age in its writings. Some of these writings, along with later texts, became the Confucian classics, which through most of Chinese history had an authority not unlike Scripture in the West.

Confucius proposed to resolve the turmoil of his own age by a return to the good old ways. When asked about government, he said, "Let the ruler be a ruler, the subject a subject, the father a father, the son a son." (The five Confucian relationships were ruler–subject, father–son, husband–wife, older brother–younger brother, and friend–friend.) If everyone fulfilled the duties of his or her status, then harmony would prevail. Confucius understood that the well-being of a society depends on the morality of its members.

But China was undergoing a dynamic transition, and it was not enough to stress basic human relationships. The genius of Confucius was to transform the old aristocratic code into a new ethic that any educated Chinese could practice. His reinterpretation of tradition can be seen in the concept of the *junzi*. This term literally meant "the son of the ruler" (or the aristocrat). Confucius redefined it to mean one of noble behavior, a person with the inner virtues of humanity, integrity, righteousness, altruism, and loyalty, and an outward demeanor and propriety to match. This redefinition was not unlike the change in the meaning of *gentleman* in England, from "one who is gentle-born" to "one who is gentle-behaved." But whereas *gentleman* remained a fairly superficial category in the West, in China *junzi* went deeper. Confucius saw ethics as grounded in nature. The true gentleman was in tune with the cosmic order.

Good government for Confucius depended on the appointment to office of good men, who would serve as examples for the multitude: "Just desire the good yourself and the common people will be good. The virtue of the gentleman is like wind; the virtue of the small man is like grass. Let the wind blow over the grass and it is sure to bend." Beyond the gentleman was the sage-king, who possessed an almost mystical virtue and power.

Confucianism was not adopted as the official philosophy of China until the Han Dynasty (202 B.C.E.–9 C.E.; see Chapter 7). But two other important Confucian philosophers had appeared in the meantime. Mencius (370–290 B.C.E.) represents the idealistic extension of Confucius's thought. He is famous for his argument that humans tend toward the good just as water runs downward. The role of education is to uncover and cultivate that innate goodness. Moreover, just as humans tend toward the good, so does Heaven possess a moral will. The will of Heaven is that a government should see to the education and well-being of its people. The rebellion of people against a government is the primary evidence that Heaven has withdrawn its mandate. At times in Chinese history, concern for the people was given only lip service. In fact, rebellions occurred more often against weak governments than against harsh ones. But the idea that government ought to care for the people became an intrinsic part of the Confucian tradition.

The other influential Confucian philosopher was Xunzi (300–237 B.C.E.), who represents a tough-minded extension of Confucius's thought. Xunzi felt Heaven was amoral, indifferent to whether China was ruled by a tyrant or a sage. He believed that human desires and emotions, if unchecked and unrefined, led to social conflict. So he emphasized etiquette and education as restraints on an unruly human nature, and good institutions, including punishments and rewards, as a means for shaping behavior. These ideas influenced the thinkers of the Legalist school.

DAOISM

It is often said that the Chinese have been Confucian while in office and Daoist in their private lives. Daoism offered a refuge from the burden of social responsibilities. The classics of the school are the *Laozi*, dating from the fourth century B.C.E., and the *Zhuangzi*, dating from about a century later.

The central concept of Daoism is the *Dao*, or Way. It is mysterious, ineffable, and cannot be named. It is the creator of the universe, the sustainer of the universe, and the process or flux of the universe. The *Dao* functions on a cosmic, not a human, scale. As the *Laozi* put it, "Heaven and Earth are ruthless, and treat the myriad creatures as straw dogs; the sage (in accord with the *Dao*) is ruthless, and treats the people as straw dogs."[2]

A sage joins the rhythms of nature by regaining an original simplicity. Various similes describe this state: "to return to the infinite," "to return to being a babe," or "to return to being the uncarved block." To attain this state, one must "learn to be without learning." Knowledge creates distinctions and interferes with participation in the *Dao*. One must also learn to be without desires beyond the immediate and simple needs of nature: "The nameless uncarved block is but freedom from desire." The sage acts without acting, and "when his task is accomplished and his work is done, the people will say, 'It happened to us naturally.'"

Beyond becoming one with the *Dao* are two other assumptions or principles. One is that any action pushed to an extreme will initiate a reaction to the opposite extreme. The other is that too much government, even good government, can become oppressive by its very weight. As the *Laozi* put it, "Govern a large state as you would cook small fish," that is, without too much stirring.

LEGALISM

A third great current in classical Chinese thought, and the most influential in its own age, was Legalism. Legalists were also concerned with ending the wars that plagued China. True peace, they believed, required a united country and a strong state. The Legalists did not seek a model in the distant past; different conditions require new principles of government. Nor did the Legalists model their state on a heavenly order of values. Human nature is selfish, argued both of the leading Legalists, Han Feizi (d. 233 B.C.E.) and Li Si (d. 208 B.C.E.). It is human to like rewards or pleasure and to dislike punishments or pain. If laws are severe and impartial, if what strengthens the state is rewarded and what weakens the state is punished, then a strong state and a good society will ensue.

Legalism was the philosophy of the state of Qin, which destroyed the Zhou in 256 B.C.E. and unified China in 221 B.C.E. Because Qin laws were cruel and severe, and because Legalism put human laws above an ethic modeled on Heaven, later generations of Chinese have denounced its doctrines. Yet its legacy of administrative and criminal laws became a vital part of subsequent dynastic China.

Laozi. The founder of Daoism, as imagined by a later artist.

Courtesy of the Freer Gallery of Art, Smithsonian Institution, Washington, DC (72.1).

What might be the significance of showing Laozi in the middle of a large, apparently empty space?

Daoism
A Chinese philosophy that teaches that wisdom lies in becoming one with the Dao, the "way," which is the creative principle of the universe.

Legalism
The Chinese philosophical school that argued that a strong state was necessary in order to have a good society.

●●●─Read the Document
Laozi, excerpt from Tao Te Ching, "The Unvarying Way" at **myhistorylab.com**

●●●─Read the Document
Daoism: The Classic of the Way and Virtue (500s-400s B.C.E.) at **myhistorylab.com**

●●●─Read the Document
The Way of the State (475-221 B.C.E.) Legalism at **myhistorylab.com**

●●●─Read the Document
Li Si and the Legalist Policies of Qin Shihuang (280-208 B.C.E.) at **myhistorylab.com**

---

[2] All quotations from the Laozi are from *Tao Te Ching*, trans. by D. C. Lau (Penguin Books, 1963).

WHAT FUNDAMENTAL institutions and ideas form the basis of Indian religion?

Hindu
Term applied to the diverse social, racial, linguistic, and religious groups of India.

Brahmanas
Texts dealing with the ritual application of the Vedas.

QUICK REVIEW

Sacred Texts

◆ Latest Vedic texts were a reaction against excessive emphasis on ritual and sacrifice

◆ *Brahmanas* dealt with ritual application of Vedic texts

◆ Upanishads were an extended reflection on meaning of ritual and nature of *Brahman*

RELIGION IN INDIA

By 400 B.C.E., new social and religious forms took shape on the Indian subcontinent. This tradition took its classical "Indian" shape in the early first millennium C.E. Despite staggering internal diversity and divisions, and long periods of foreign rule, this Indian culture has survived for over 2,000 years.

"HINDU" AND "INDIAN"

Indian culture and tradition include more than what the word **Hindu** commonly implies today. Earlier, *Hindu* simply meant "Indian." Outsiders used "Hindu" to characterize religious and social institutions of India as a whole, such as the concept of transmigration, the sacredness of the Vedas and the cow, worship of Shiva and Vishnu, and caste distinctions. *Hindu* is not a term for any single or uniform religious community.

Indian, on the other hand, commonly refers today to all native inhabitants of the subcontinent, whatever their beliefs. In this book we shall generally use the term *Indian* in this inclusive sense. For the period before the arrival of Muslim culture (ca. 1000 C.E.), we will use *Indian* also to refer to the tradition of thought and culture that began around the middle of the first millennium B.C.E. and achieved its classical formulation in the Hindu society and religion of the first millennium C.E.

HISTORICAL BACKGROUND

Chapter 1 showed how, in the late Vedic or Brahmanic period, a priest-centered cult dominated the upper classes of Aryanized northern Indian society. By the sixth century B.C.E., this had become an elite, esoteric cult. Elaborate animal sacrifices on behalf of Aryan rulers were an economic burden on the peasants, whose livestock provided the victims. During the seventh and sixth centuries B.C.E., skepticism in religious matters accompanied social and political upheavals.

The latest Vedic texts themselves reflected a reaction against excessive emphasis on the power of sacrifice and ritual, accumulation of worldly wealth and power, and hope for an afterlife in a paradise. The treatises of the **Brahmanas** (ca. 1000–800 B.C.E.) dealt with the ritual application of the old Vedic texts, the explanation of Vedic rites and mythology, and the theory of the sacrifice. Early on they focused on controlling the sacred power (*Brahman*) of the sacrificial ritual, but they gradually stressed acquiring this power through knowledge instead of ritual.

This tendency became central in the Upanishads (ca. 800–500 B.C.E.). The Upanishadic sages and the early Jains and Buddhists (fifth century B.C.E.) shared certain revolutionary ideas and concerns. Their thinking and piety influenced all later Indian intellectual thought and also, through the spread of the Buddhist tradition, much of the intellectual and religious life of East and Southeast Asia as well. Thus, the middle centuries of the first millennium B.C.E. in India began a religious and philosophical revolution that ranks as a turning point in the history of civilization.

THE UPANISHADIC WORLDVIEW

The Upanishads emphasize knowledge over ritual and stress immortality in terms of escape from existence itself. These ideas were already evident in two sentences from the prayer of an early Upanishadic thinker who said, "From the unreal lead me to the Real. . . . From death lead me to immortality." The first sentence points to knowledge, not the sacred word or act, as the ultimate source of power. The second sentence reflects a new concern with life after death. The old Vedic ideal of living a full and upright life so as to attain an afterlife among the gods no longer appears adequate. Immortality is now interpreted in terms of escape from mundane existence in any form. These two Upanishadic emphases changed the shape of Indian thought forever and provide the key to its basic worldview.

The quest for knowledge by the Upanishadic sages focused on the nature of the individual self (*atman*) and its relation to ultimate reality (*Brahman*). The gods are now merely part of the total scheme of things, subject to the laws of existence, and not to be put on the same plane with the transcendent Absolute. Prayer and sacrifice to particular gods for their help continue, but the higher goal is realization of *Brahman* through mental action alone, not ritual performance.

The culmination of Upanishadic speculation is the recognition that the way to the Absolute is through the self. Through contemplation, **atman-Brahman** is recognized not as a deity but as the principle of reality itself: the unborn, unmade, unitary, unchanging infinite. Of this reality, all that can be said is that it is "neither this nor that," because the ultimate cannot be conceptualized or described in finite terms. Beneath the impermanence of ordinary reality is the changeless *Brahman*, to which every being's immortal self belongs and of which it partakes. The difficulty is recognizing this self, and with it the Absolute, while one is enmeshed in mortal existence.

A second, related focus of Upanishadic inquiry was the nature of "normal" existence. The realm of life is impermanent, ever changing. What seem to be "solid" things—the physical world, our bodies and personalities, worldly success—are revealed in the Upanishads as insubstantial. Even happiness is transient. Existence is neither satisfying nor lasting. Only *Brahman* is eternal and unchanging. This perception prefigures the Buddhist emphasis on impermanence and suffering as the fundamental facts of existence.

The Upanishadic conception of existence as a ceaseless cycle, a never-ending alternation between life and death, became the basic assumption of all Indian thought and religious life. The endless cycle of existence, or **samsara**, is the key to understanding reality. The terrifying prospect of endless "redeath" as the normal lot of all beings in this world, whether animals, plants, humans, or gods, is the fundamental problem for all later Indian thought.

The Indian tradition developed two approaches to the problem of *samsara*. These two characteristic Indian responses to the problem posed by *samsara* underlie the fundamental forms of Indian thought and piety that took shape in the middle to late first millennium B.C.E. Both depend on **karma**, which in Sanskrit literally means "work" or "action." *Karma* is the concept that every action has its inevitable effects; as long as there is action of mind or body, there is continued effect and hence continued existence.

The first strategy for dealing with *samsara* has been characterized as the "ordinary norm," life lived according to *dharma*. Although **dharma** has many meanings, it most commonly means "the right (order of things)," "moral law," "right conduct," or even "duty." It includes the cosmic order (compare the Chinese *Dao*) as well as right action and individual moral responsibility. For the masses of Hindus, Buddhists, and Jains—those we might call the laity, as distinguished from monks and ascetics—life according to *dharma* demands acceptance of the responsibilities appropriate to one's sex, class and caste group, stage in life, and other life circumstances. It also allows for legitimate self-interest: one's duty is to do things that acquire merit for one's eternal *atman* and to avoid those that bring evil consequences. Rebirth in paradise is the highest goal attainable through the life of *dharma*, but all achievement in the world of *dharma* is ultimately impermanent and subject to change. (See Document, "The 'Turning of the Wheel of the Dharma': Basic Teachings of the Buddha" on page 40.)

The "extraordinary norm" is a more radical solution, seeking "liberation" (*moksha*) from existence: escaping all karmic effects by escaping action itself. Nonaction

atman-Brahman The unchanging, infinite principle of reality in Indian religion.

samsara
The endless cycle of existence, of birth and rebirth.

karma
The Indian belief that every action has an inevitable effect. Good deeds bring good results; evil deeds have evil consequences.

dharma
Moral law or duty.

DOCUMENT

The "Turning of the Wheel of the Dharma": Basic Teachings of the Buddha

Following are selections from the sermon said to have been the first preached by the Buddha. It was directed at five former companions with whom he had practiced extreme austerities. When he abandoned asceticism to meditate under the Bodh tree, they had become disillusioned and left him. This sermon is said to have made them the first to follow him. Because it set in motion the Buddha's teaching, or Dharma, on earth, it is usually described as "setting in motion the wheel of Dharma." The text is from the Dhammacakkappavattanasutta.

- **WHAT** extremes does the Middle Path try to avoid? What emotion drives the chain of suffering? How does the "knowledge" that brings salvation compare to the knowledge sought in the Hindu tradition?

Thus have I heard. The Blessed One was once living in the Deer Park at Isipatana (the Resort of Seers) near Baranasi (Benares). There he addressed the group of five *bhikkhus.*

"Bhikkhus, these two extremes ought not to be practiced by one who has gone forth from the household life. What are the two? There is devotion to the indulgence of sense-pleasures, which is low, common, the way of ordinary people, unworthy and unprofitable; and there is devotion to self-mortification, which is painful, unworthy and unprofitable.

"Avoiding both these extremes, the Tathagata has realized the Middle Path: it gives vision, it gives knowledge, and it leads to calm, to insight, to enlightenment, to Nibbana. And what is that Middle Path? It is simply the Noble Eightfold Path, namely, right view, right thought, right speech, right action, right livelihood, right effort, right mindfulness, right concentration. This is the Middle Path realized by the Tathagata, which gives vision, which gives knowledge, and which leads to calm, to insight, to enlightenment, to Nibbana. . . .

"The Noble Truth of suffering (*Dukkha*) is this: Birth is suffering; aging is suffering; sickness is suffering; death is suffering; sorrow and lamentation, pain, grief and despair are suffering; association with the unpleasant is suffering; dissociation from the pleasant is suffering; not to get what one wants is suffering—in brief, the five aggregates of attachment are suffering.

"The Noble Truth of the origin of suffering is this: It is this thirst (craving) which produces re-existence and re-becoming, bound up with passionate greed. It finds fresh delight now here and now there, namely, thirst for nonexistence (self-annihilation)."

"The Noble Truth of the Cessation of suffering is this: It is the complete cessation of that very thirst, giving it up, renouncing it, emancipating oneself from it, detaching oneself from it."

"The Noble Truth of the Path leading to the Cessation of suffering is this: It is simply the Noble Eightfold Path. . . ."

" 'This is the Noble Truth of Suffering (*Dukkha*)': such was the vision, the knowledge, the wisdom, the science, the light, that arose in me with regard to things not heard before. 'This suffering, as a noble truth, should be fully understood.' "

" 'This is the Noble Truth of the Cessation of suffering': such was the vision, 'This Cessation of suffering, as a noble truth, should be realized.' "

" 'This is the Noble Truth of the Path leading to the Cessation of suffering': such was the vision, 'This Path leading to the Cessation of suffering, as a noble truth, has been followed (cultivated).' "

"As long as my vision of true knowledge was not fully clear regarding the Four Noble Truths, I did not claim to have realized the perfect Enlightenment that is supreme in the world with its gods, in this world with its recluses and brahmanas, with its princes and men. But when my vision of true knowledge was fully clear regarding the Four Noble Truths, then I claimed to have realized the perfect Enlightenment that is supreme in the world with its gods, in this world with its recluses and brahmanas, with its princes and men. And a vision of true knowledge arose in me thus: My heart's deliverance is unassailable. This is the last birth. Now there is no more re-becoming (rebirth)."

This the Blessed One said. The group of five bhikkhus was glad, and they rejoiced at his words.

—Samyutta-nikaya, LVI, II

is achieved only by withdrawal from "normal" existence. The person seeking release has to move beyond the usual responsibilities of family and society. Most often, this involves becoming a "renouncer" (*sannyasi*)—whether a Hindu hermit, yogi, or wanderer, or a Jain or Buddhist monk. The highest goal is not rebirth in heaven but permanent liberation (*moksha*) from all rebirth and redeath. The ideas that led individuals to seek the extraordinary norm were first fully elaborated in the Upanishads. Increasing numbers of people abandoned both the ritualistic religious practices and the society of class distinctions and material concerns around them. Many of these seekers were of warrior-noble (*Kshatriya*), not Brahmanic, birth. They took up the wandering or hermitic existence of the ascetic, seeking spiritual powers in yogic meditation and self-denial or even self-torture. Such seekers wanted to transcend bodily existence to realize the Absolute.

In the sixth century B.C.E., teachers of new ideas appeared, especially in the lower Ganges basin, in the area of Magadha (modern Bihar). Most of them rejected traditional religious practices as well as the authority of the Vedas in favor of ascetic discipline as the true spiritual path. The ideas and practices of two of these teachers became the foundations of new and lasting traditions of piety and faith, those of the Jains and the Buddhists.

MAHAVIRA AND THE JAIN TRADITION

The **Jains** are an Indian community that traces its tradition to Vardhamana, known as Mahavira ("the great hero"), who is traditionally believed to have lived from about 540 to 468 B.C.E. The Jains consider Mahavira as the final *Jina* ("victor" over *samsara*) or *Tirthankara* ("ford maker," one who finds a way across the waters of existence), in a line of twenty-four great teachers. The Jains (or *Jainas*, "adherents of the *Jina*") see in Mahavira not a god, but a human teacher who found and taught the way to extricate the soul from the bonds of the material world and its karmic accretions.

In the Jain view, there is no beginning or end to phenomenal existence, only ceaseless cycles of generation and degeneration. The universe is alive from end to end with an infinite number of souls, all immortal, omniscient, and pure in their essence. But all are trapped in *samsara*, whether as animals, gods, humans, plants, or even inanimate stones or fire. *Karma* here takes on a quasi-material form: Any thought, word, or deed attracts karmic matter that clings to and encumbers the soul. The greatest amounts come from evil acts, especially those done out of hate, greed, or cruelty.

Mahavira's path to release focused on eliminating evil thoughts and acts, especially those harmful to others. His radical ascetic practice aimed at destroying karmic defilements and, ultimately, all actions leading to further karmic bondage. At the age of 30, Mahavira began practicing the radical self-denial of a wandering ascetic, eventually even giving up clothing. After twelve years of self-deprivation and yogic meditation, he attained enlightenment. Then, for some thirty years, he went about teaching his discipline to others. At the age of 72 he chose to fast to death to burn out the last karmic residues, an action that some of the most advanced Jain ascetics have emulated down to the present day.

It would, however, be wrong to think of the Jain tradition in terms only of the extreme ascetic practices of some Jain mendicants. Jain monks are bound basically by the five great vows they share with other monastic traditions like the Buddhist and the Christian: not to kill, steal, lie, engage in sexual activity, or own anything.

Most Jains are not monks. Today there is a thriving lay community of perhaps 3 million Jains, most in western India. Laypersons have close ties to the monks and nuns, whom they support with gifts and food. Many Jain laypersons spend periods of their lives in retreat with monks or nuns. They are vegetarians and regard *ahimsa* ("noninjury") to any being as paramount. Compassion is the great virtue

Jains
An Indian religious community that teaches compassion for all beings.

⬩●⬩⎡Read the **Document**
Selections from the Rig Veda
at **myhistorylab.com**

⬩●⬩⎡Read the **Document**
Jainism: Selections from The Book of Sermons and The Book of Good Conduct 6th century B.C.E.-5th century C.E.
at **myhistorylab.com**

CHRONOLOGY

INDIA

ca. 800–500 B.C.E.	The Upanishads
540–ca. 468 B.C.E.	Mahavira, the Jina/Vardamana
ca. 566–ca. 486 B.C.E.	Siddhartha Gautama, the Buddha

Jain Nuns. Jain pilgrims attend the Mahamastak Abhisheka ceremony in Shravanabelagola, India. During this ceremony, which takes place once every twelve years, the statue of Jain sage Gomateswara is bathed with milk, yogurt, saffron, gold coins, and religious items. This statue is thought to be the world's largest monolith.

What is noteworthy about these women's clothing? What questions would you like to ask them?

View the **Image**
Buddhist Religious Site
at **myhistorylab.com**

Read the **Document**
Rise of Buddhism–Forces for Social Change? at **myhistorylab.com**

Read the **Document**
Siddhartha Gautama
at **myhistorylab.com**

Read the **Document**
Buddha's Sermon at Benares - The Edicts of Ashoka (530 B.C.E., 268-233 B.C.E.)
at **myhistorylab.com**

Read the **Document**
Vardhamana Mahariva, selections from Akaranga-sutra, "Jain Doctrines and Practices of Nonviolence."
at **myhistorylab.com**

QUICK REVIEW

Siddhartha Gautama

- Great Renunciation: at age 29 left home to seek answers to eternal questions
- Unsatisfied with study with renowned teachers
- Achieved status as the Buddha through yogic meditation

for them, as for Buddhists. The merit of serving the extraordinary-norm seekers who adopt the mendicant life and of living a life according to the high standards of the community provides a goal even for those who as laypersons are following the ordinary norm.

THE BUDDHA'S MIDDLE PATH

It can be argued that India's greatest contribution to world civilization was the Buddhist tradition. It ultimately faded out in India, but it left its mark on Hindu and Jain religion and culture. Like the two other great universalist traditions, Christianity and Islam, it traces its origins to a single figure who for centuries has loomed larger than life for the faithful.

This figure is Siddhartha Gautama, known as the Buddha, or "Enlightened/ Awakened One." A contemporary of Mahavira, Gautama was also born (ca. 566 B.C.E.) in comfortable circumstances. At the age of 29, Gautama first perceived the reality of aging, sickness, and death as the human lot. He abandoned his home and family to seek an answer to the dilemma of the endless cycle of mortal existence. After this Great Renunciation, he studied with renowned teachers and later took up extreme ascetic disciplines of penance and self-mortification. He turned finally to intense yogic meditation under a Bodhi tree in the place known as Gaya. In one historic night, he moved through different levels of trance, during which he realized all of his past lives, the reality of the cycle of existence of all beings, and how to stop the karmic outflows that fuel suffering. Thus he became the Buddha; that is, he achieved full enlightenment—the omniscient consciousness of reality as it truly is. He pledged himself to achieving release for all beings.

Gautama devoted himself to teaching others his Middle Path between asceticism and indulgence. This path has been the core of Buddhist faith and practice ever since. It begins with realizing the Four Noble Truths: (1) All life is *dukkha*, or suffering; (2) the source of suffering is desiring; (3) the cessation of desiring is the way to end suffering; and (4) the path to this end is eightfold: Right Understanding, Right Thought, Right Speech, Right Action, Right Livelihood, Right Effort, Right Mindfulness, and Right Concentration. The key idea of the Buddha's teaching, or *dharma*, is that everything in the world of existence is causally linked. The essential fact of existence is *dukkha*: No pleasure—however great—is permanent (here we see the Buddhist variation on the central Indian theme of *samsara*).

Thus, Buddhist discipline focuses on the moral Eightfold Path, and the cardinal virtue of compassion for all beings, as the way to eliminate the selfish desiring that is the root of *samsara* and its unavoidable suffering. The Buddha himself had attained this goal; when he died (ca. 486 B.C.E.) after a life of teaching others how to master desiring, he passed from the round of existence forever. In Buddhist terminology, he attained nirvana, the extinguishing of karmic bondage. This attainment became the starting point for the growth and eventual spread of the Buddhist *dharma*, which was to assume new and diverse forms in its long history.

Buddhist tradition, like that of the Jains, encompassed from the outset seekers of both the extraordinary and the ordinary norms in their present lives. This dual community has remained characteristic of all forms of Buddhism wherever it is practiced. The fundamental vision has persisted of a humanly attainable wisdom that leads to compassion and release.

The later emergence of "Hindu" tradition drew on all three of these revolutionary strands in Indian thought—Upanishadic, Jain, and Buddhist—and integrated parts of their fundamental ideas about the universe, human life, morality, and society into the cultic and mythic strands of both Brahmanic and popular Indian practice.

A Closer Look

Statue of Siddhartha Gotama as Fasting Ascetic (Second Century C.E.)

This Gandharan statue represents Siddhartha Gotama before his enlightenment and achievement of Buddhahood, when he spent six years practicing ascetic austerities of extreme fasting and self-denial—an experience that he abandoned for what became his "Middle Path" teaching and practice. The Kushan Dynasty (first to seventh century C.E.) of NW India and modern Pakistan and Afghanistan (see Chapter 4) patronized art and architecture that seem to have had their formative patronage from the Buddhist Kushan king, Kanishka, in the early second century C.E. in the region of Gandhara (in present-day Pakistan). Gandharan art developed from the Kushana's employment of foreign artisans trained in Roman styles, leading to an art that fused Greco-Roman with Indian and Central Asian styles to produce one of the great cross-cultural traditions of art history. In its heyday, down to roughly the early third century C.E., Gandhara produced some of the most remarkable Buddhist art ever, influencing not only Buddhist but also Indian art long after.

Note the highly realistic depiction of bone structure and sinew on the emaciated ascetic figure. Not only is the Gandharan School credited with the first anthropomorphic depictions of the Buddha, but these depictions were done in highly realistic style, likely influenced by Roman realism.

The drapery style of the Gandharan figures is clearly derived from Roman style of the Imperial Period, which derives in turn from Greek styles.

The proportions of the body have a 1:5 relation of head-to-body height (more evident in standing statues), which is exactly that of late Roman and early Christian sculptures. Note the nimbus behind the realistic head; this motif may have originated in Central Asia and diffused east to China and west to the Mediterranean, but the earliest evidence for Buddhist use is in Kushan sculpture from the late first and second centuries.

Borromeo, EPA/Art Resource, New York.

Question

1. What might the various indications of Greco-Roman influence in this south-central Asian Buddhist sculpture suggest about the permeability of political and cultural boundaries from the Mediterranean to South and Central Asia in the early centuries C.E.?

2. The nimbus or halo of light behind the head here is widely attested in various forms across Asia as well as in the Mediterranean, in Hellenistic, Greek, Roman, Christian, Buddhist, and Hindu art. Why might this be so attractive, and what particular purposes would

you think it serves in this or other figures in various traditions?

3. Most religious traditions have strands of piety within them that emphasize ascetic renunciation of worldly things, often involving extreme renunciation involving fasting (even to death in a few cases), sexual and other kinds of abstinence, and refusal to have any "possessions." In the Buddha's teaching, why is extreme renunciation and asceticism rejected? Can you compare these ideas to those in another tradition with which you are familiar?

THE RELIGION OF THE ISRAELITES

HOW WAS the Hebrew concept of God and religion distinctive?

The ancient Near East was a **polytheistic** world; its people worshiped many gods. Local or regional gods and goddesses were represented largely as capricious, amoral beings, unaffected by the actions of humans. The major traditions of religious thought in Egypt and Mesopotamia did not offer comprehensive interpretations that linked humans to a transcendent realm.

Out of this pluralistic and religiously fragmented world came the great tradition of monotheistic faith represented historically in the Jewish, Christian, and Islamic communities. This tradition traces its origin to the small nation of the Israelites, or Hebrews. **Monotheism**, faith in a single, all-powerful God as the sole creator, sustainer, and ruler of the universe, may be older than the Hebrews, but its first clear historical manifestation was with them. It was among the Hebrew tribes that emphasis on the moral demands and responsibilities that the one God placed on individual and community was first definitively linked to human history itself, and history in turn was linked to a divine plan. This is the tradition of ethical monotheism.

FROM HEBREW NOMADS TO THE ISRAELITE NATION

The history of the Hebrews, later known as Israelites, must be pieced together from various sources, including the Hebrew Bible (the "Old Testament" in Christian terminology). Scholars once tended to disregard the Bible as a historical source, but the trend today is to take it seriously while using it cautiously.

According to tradition, Abraham came from Ur in southern Mesopotamia and wandered west with his Hebrew clan to tend his flocks in the land later known as Palestine. Such a movement would be in accord with what we know of a general westward migration of seminomadic tribes from Mesopotamia after about 1950 B.C.E. Some of Abraham's people settled in the Palestinian region, but others apparently wandered farther into Egypt. By about 1400 B.C.E., they had become a settled but subjected, even enslaved, people there. Under Moses, some of the Egyptian Israelites fled Egypt to find a new homeland to the east. They may then have wandered in the Sinai Desert and elsewhere for several decades before reaching Canaan, the province of Palestine that is described in the Bible as their promised homeland. This experience is the key event in biblical Israel's history: the forging of the covenant, or mutual pact, between God, or Yahweh, and his people. The Israelites emerged from the Exodus as a nation, a people with a sense of community and common faith.

The nation reached its peak as a kingdom under David (r. ca. 1000–961 B.C.E.) and Solomon (r. ca. 961–922 B.C.E.). But in the ninth century B.C.E., the kingdom split into two parts: Israel in the north and Judah, with its capital at Jerusalem, in the south (see Map 2–1). The rise of great empires around them brought disaster to the Israelites. The

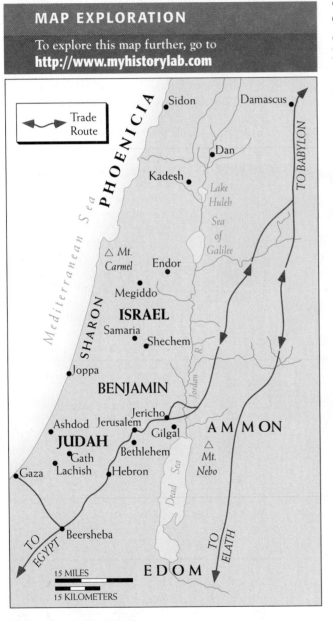

MAP EXPLORATION

To explore this map further, go to
http://www.myhistorylab.com

MAP 2–1.   Ancient Palestine.

The Hebrews established a unified kingdom under Kings David and Solomon in the tenth century B.C.E. After Solomon, the kingdom was divided into Israel in the north and Judah, with its capital, Jerusalem, in the south. North of Israel were the great commercial cities of Phoenicia.

How might the proximity of trade routes have influenced the development of Hebrew culture and belief?

Northern Kingdom fell to the Assyrians in 722 B.C.E.; its people were scattered and, according to tradition, lost forever—the so-called ten lost tribes. Only the kingdom of Judah, with its seat at Jerusalem, remained, and after that we may call the Israelites Jews. In 586 B.C.E., Judah was defeated by the Neo-Babylonian king Nebuchadnezzar II (d. 562 B.C.E.). He destroyed the great Temple built by Solomon and sent the Jewish nation into exile in Babylon. There, in the "Babylonian captivity," the Jews clung to their traditions and faith. After the Achaemenids defeated the Babylonians in 539 B.C.E., the Jews were allowed to return to their homeland. By about 516 B.C.E. they erected a second temple in a restored Jerusalem.

The new Judaic state was dominated for centuries by foreign peoples, but it maintained its religious and national identity. It was again destroyed and its people dispersed after the Romans' destruction of Jerusalem in 70 C.E., and yet again in 132 C.E. By this era, however, the Jews had developed a religious worldview that would long outlive any Judaic national state.

THE MONOTHEISTIC REVOLUTION

This small nation developed a tradition of faith that amounted to a revolution in ways of thinking about the human condition, the meaning of life and history, and the nature of the Divine. The revolutionary character of this interpretation lay in its uniquely moralistic understanding of human life and history and the uncompromising monotheism on which it was based.

At the root of this monotheistic tradition stands the figure of Abraham. Jews, Christians, and Muslims all look to him as the symbolic founder of their monotheistic faith. Abraham probably conceived of his Lord simply as his chosen deity among the many divinities who might be worshiped. Yet for the strength of his faith in his God, the biblical account recognizes him as the "Father of the Faithful," the first of the Hebrew patriarchs to make a **covenant** with the God who would become unique and supreme. In this, Abraham promised to serve only him, and his God promised to bless his descendants and guide them as his special people.

After Abraham, the next major step came with Moses. It is difficult to say how much the Mosaic covenant at Sinai actually marked the achievement of an exclusively monotheistic faith. Certainly, the covenant event was decisive in uniting the Israelites as a people with a special relationship to God. At Sinai, they received both God's holy Law (the Torah) and his promise of protection and guidance as long as they kept the Law. This was the pivotal moment in the monotheistic revolution.

After the bipartite division of the Israelite kingdom in 922 B.C.E., the *prophets* arose. These men and women believed they were messengers inspired by God to call their people back from immorality and the worship of false gods. The activity of the prophets was closely linked to the saga of Israelite national success, exile, and return in the mid-first millennium B.C.E. In the biblical interpretation of these events, we can see the progressive consolidation of the Judaic religion. The prophets' concern with purifying Jewish faith and with morality focused in particular on two ideas that proved central to Judaic monotheism. The first was the significance of history in the divine plan. Calling on the Jews' awareness of the Sinai covenant, the prophets saw in Israel's past and present

polytheistic
The worship of many gods.

monotheism
The worship of one universal God.

covenant
A solemn and formal pledge between two or more parties, usually to perform particular actions.

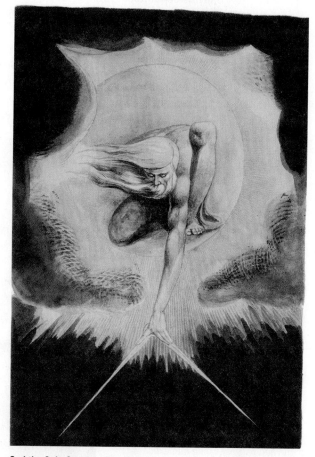

God the Sole Creator. The British poet and artist William Blake (1757–1827) envisions God.

What makes this God seem powerful? What relationship, if any, does this God seem to have with the human realm?

CHRONOLOGY

THE ISRAELITES

ca. 1000–961 B.C.E.	Reign of King David
ca. 961–922 B.C.E.	Reign of King Solomon
722 B.C.E.	Assyrian conquest of Israel (Northern Kingdom)
586 B.C.E.	Destruction of Jerusalem; fall of Judah (Southern Kingdom); Babylonian captivity
539 B.C.E.	Restoration of Temple; return of exiles

troubles God's punishment for failing in their covenant duties. The prophets saw Israel as the "suffering servant" among the nations, the people who would purify other nations and bring them ultimately to God. Here the nationalistic, particularistic focus of previous Israelite religion gave way to a universalist monotheism: Yahweh was now God of all, even the Babylonians or Assyrians. The second central idea emphasized the nature of Yahweh. The prophets saw in him the transcendent ideal of justice and goodness. God was a righteous God who expected righteousness from human beings. A corollary of God's goodness was his love for his people. However much he might have to punish them for their sins, God would finally lead them back to his favor.

The crux of the breakthrough to ethical monotheism lay in linking the Lord of the Universe to history and morality. The Almighty Creator was seen as actively concerned with the actions and fates of his human creatures as exemplified in Israel. God's involvement in history took on transcendent meaning; humankind was involved in the fulfillment of God's divine purpose.

Even after the exile, however, the realization of the prophesied days of peace and blessedness under God's rule clearly still had not come. This led to the concept that history's culmination would come in a future Messianic age; later, the idea that a Day of Judgment would cap the golden age of the **Messiah**, the redeemer who Jews believed would establish the kingdom of God on earth, became popular. Some of these ideas might have come from the Jews' encounter with Zoroastrian traditions during the exile, and they later influenced Christian and Muslim beliefs.

Another key element in the monotheistic revolution of the Jews was the Law itself. The Law is embodied in the five books of the Torah (the Pentateuch, or "five

⊙ See the **Map**
Israel and Judah, Eighth Century B.C.E.
at **myhistorylab.com**

Watch the **Video**
The Old City of Jerusalem
at **myhistorylab.com**

Messiah
The redeemer whose coming Jews believed would establish the kingdom of God on earth. Christians consider Jesus to be the Messiah (*Christ* means "Messiah" in Greek).

Exile of the Israelites. In 722 B.C.E. the northern part of Jewish Palestine, the kingdom of Israel, was conquered by the Assyrians. Its people were driven from their homeland and exiled all over the vast Assyrian Empire. This wall carving in low relief comes from the palace of the Assyrian king Sennacherib at Nineveh. It shows the Jews with their cattle and baggage going into exile.

Erich Lessing/Art Resource, New York.

What seems to be important to these people as they go into exile?

books": Genesis, Exodus, Leviticus, Numbers, and Deuteronomy). Observation of the Torah allowed Jews to keep their faith even while in exile or without a temple. A holy, authoritative, divinely revealed scripture as an element of Judaic monotheism had revolutionary consequences, not only for Jews but also for Christians and Muslims.

For the first time, a nation defined itself not primarily by dynastic, linguistic, or geographic considerations but by shared religious faith and practice. Ethical monotheism was later to have still greater effects when not only Judaic but also Christian and Muslim traditions would change the face of much of the world.

GREEK PHILOSOPHY

Greek ideas had much in common with the ideas of earlier peoples. The Greek gods had most of the characteristics of the Mesopotamian deities; magic and incantations played a part in Greek lives, and their law was usually connected with divinity. But surprisingly, some Greeks developed ideas that were strikingly different and, in so doing, set a part of humankind on an entirely new path. As early as the sixth century B.C.E., Greeks living in the Ionian cities of Asia Minor raised questions and suggested answers about nature that produced an intellectual revolution. Their speculations about the nature of the world and its origin were completely naturalistic and included no reference to supernatural powers. One historian of Greek thought, discussing the views of Thales (624–545 B.C.E.), the first Greek philosopher, put the case particularly well:

> *In one of the Babylonian legends it says: "All the lands were sea. Marduk bound a rush mat upon the face of the waters, he made dirt and piled it beside the rush mat." What Thales did was to leave Marduk out. He, too, said that everything was once water. But he thought that earth and everything else had been formed out of water by a natural process, like the silting up of the Delta of the Nile. It is an admirable beginning, the whole point of which is that it gathers together into a coherent picture a number of observed facts without letting Marduk in.[3]*

By putting the question of the world's origin in a naturalistic form, Thales may have initiated both Western philosophy and Western science. This rational approach was applied even to the gods themselves. In the same century as Thales, Xenophanes of Colophon expressed the opinion that humans think of the gods as resembling themselves. Thus, Africans believed in flat-nosed, black-faced gods, and the Thracians in gods with blue eyes and red hair.[4] In the fifth century B.C.E. Protagoras of Abdera (ca. 490–420 B.C.E.) went so far in the direction of agnosticism as to say, "About the gods I can have no knowledge either that they are or that they are not or what is their nature."[5]

Rationalism and skepticism carried over into practical matters as well. The school of medicine led by Hippocrates of Cos (ca. 400 B.C.E.) attempted to understand, diagnose, and cure disease without recourse to supernatural forces or beings. One of the Hippocratics wrote of the mysterious disease epilepsy:

The Fall. The German artist Albrecht Dürer (1471–1528) engraved this image of the biblical first humans whose creation and fall are recounted in Genesis. God's covenant with humankind is central to his divine plan. However much he might punish people for their sins, God would finally lead them back to his favor.

How does Dürer's depiction highlight the special status of humans in God's creation?

WHY DID Greek thinkers, beginning in the sixth century B.C.E., produce an intellectual revolution?

[3] Benjamin Farrington, *Greek Science* (London: Penguin Books, 1953), p. 37.
[4] Frankfort et al., *Before Philosophy* (1949), pp. 14–16.
[5] Hermann Diels, *Fragmente der Vorsokratiker*, 5th ed., ed. by Walther Kranz (Berlin: Weidmann, 1934–1938), Frg. 4.
[6] Ibid., Frgs. 14–16.

OVERVIEW   Four Great Systems of Thought and Religion

In the accompanying flowchart, note the river valleys in which the original civilizations arose. Each was characterized by cities, writing systems, agriculture, and so on. (The Mississippi, Amazon, and Congo lacked such developments.) During the axial age from 500 to 200 B.C.E., the same areas saw the birth of the world religions of Hinduism, Buddhism, and Judaism, and the world philosophies of China and Greece. Each continued to develop, and in the Middle East, by a combination of Judaic and Greek elements, there occurred the rise of Christianity and Islam.

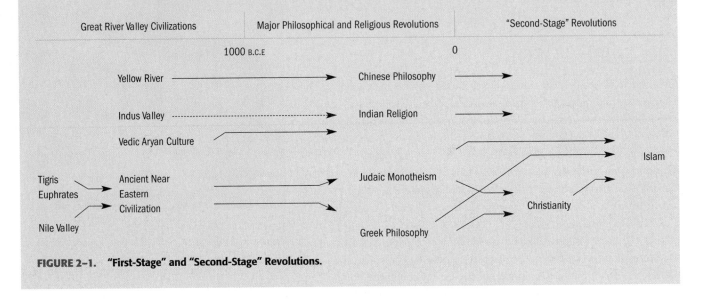

FIGURE 2–1.   "First-Stage" and "Second-Stage" Revolutions.

It seems to me that the disease is no more divine than any other. It has a natural cause, just as other diseases have. Men think it divine merely because they do not understand it. But if they called everything divine which they do not understand, why, there would be no end of divine things.[6]

By the fifth century B.C.E., the historian Thucydides (ca. 460–400 B.C.E.) was analyzing and explaining the behavior of humans in society completely in terms of human nature and chance, leaving no place for the gods or supernatural forces. The relative unimportance of divine or supernatural forces also characterized Greek views of law and justice. Most Greeks, especially in the democratic states, understood that laws were made by humans and should be obeyed because they represented the expressed consent of the citizens.

These ideas are different from any that came before, and they are still relevant to major concerns in the modern world: What is the nature of the universe and how can it be controlled? Are there divine powers, and if so, what is humanity's relationship to them? Are law and justice human, divine, or both? What is the place in human society of freedom, obedience, and reverence?

REASON AND THE SCIENTIFIC SPIRIT

The rational spirit characteristic of Greek culture blossomed in the sixth century B.C.E. into what we call *philosophy*. The first steps were taken in Ionia on the coast of Asia Minor, on the fringe of the Greek world and in touch with the learning of the East (see

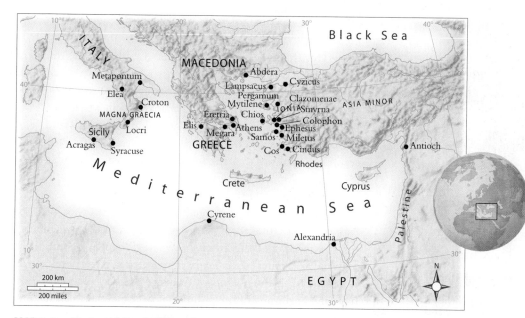

MAP 2–2. **Centers of Greek Philosophy.**

Why are many centers of Greek philosophy located on the periphery of the Greek civilization?

Map 2–2). The Ionians were among the first to recognize that the Greek account of how the world was created and maintained and of the place of humans in it was not universally accepted. Perhaps this realization helped spark the first attempts at disciplined philosophical inquiry.

Thales of Miletus believed that the earth floated on water and that water was the primary substance. Thales observed that water has many forms: liquid, solid, and gaseous. He saw that it could "create" land by alluvial deposit and that it was necessary for all life. He used reason to organize these observations into a single explanation that accounted for many phenomena without any need for the supernatural. Thales of Miletus thus set the tone for future investigations: Greek philosophers assumed that the world was knowable, rational, and simple.

Another Milesian, Anaximander (ca. 611–546 B.C.E.), imagined that the basic element was something undefined, "unlimited." The world emerged from this basic element as the result of an interaction of opposite forces—wet and dry, hot and cold. Anaximander pictured the universe in eternal motion. Heraclitus of Ephesus, who lived near the end of the sixth century B.C.E., carried the dialogue further. He famously claimed, "All is motion." Yet Heraclitus also believed that the world order had a guiding principle, the *Logos*, and that though phenomena changed, the *Logos* did not. *Logos* has several meanings, among them "word," "language," "speech," and "reason." So when Heraclitus said that the physical world was governed by *Logos*, he implied that it could be explained by reason. Speculations about the physical world, what we would call natural science, thus led to even more difficult philosophical speculations about language, human thought, and knowledge itself.

In opposition to Heraclitus, the fifth century B.C.E. philosopher Parmenides of Elea and his pupil Zeno argued that change was only an illusion. Reason and reflection showed that reality was fixed and unchanging because it seemed evident that nothing could be created out of nothingness. Empedocles of Acragas (flourished [fl.] ca. 450 B.C.E.) spoke of four basic elements: fire, water, earth, and air. Like Parmenides, he thought reality was permanent but not immobile, for the four elements were moved by two

"The School of Athens." In this painting, the great Italian Renaissance painter Raphael portrayed the ancient Greek philosopher Plato and his student, Aristotle, engaged in debate. Plato, who points to the heavens, believed in a set of ideal truths that exist in their own realm distinct from the earth. Aristotle urged that all philosophy must be in touch with lived reality and confirms this position by pointing to the earth.

Does Raphael seem to endorse the position of either Plato or Aristotle, or does he seem to respect the ideas of each one equally?

atomists
School of ancient Greek philosophy founded in the fifth century B.C.E. by Leucippus of Miletus and Democritus of Abdera. It held that the world consists of innumerable, tiny, solid, indivisible, and unchangeable particles called atoms.

Sophists
Professional teachers who emerged in Greece in the mid-fifth century B.C.E. who were paid to teach techniques of rhetoric, dialectic, and argumentation.

polis
The basic Greek political unit, usually, but incompletely, translated as "city-state." The Greeks thought of the *polis* as a community of citizens theoretically descended from a common ancestor.

primary forces, Love and Strife, or, as we might say, attraction and repulsion.

This theory was a step on the road to the atomic theory of Leucippus of Miletus (fl. fifth century B.C.E.) and Democritus of Abdera (ca. 460–370 B.C.E.). They believed that the world consisted of innumerable tiny, solid particles (atoms) that could not be divided or modified and that moved about in the void. The size of the atoms and the ways they were arranged produced the secondary qualities that the senses could perceive, such as color and shape. Anaxagoras of Clazomenae (ca. 500–428 B.C.E.) had previously spoken of tiny fundamental particles called *seeds* that were put together on a rational basis by a force called *nous*, or "mind." Thus, Anaxagoras suggested a distinction between matter and mind. But the **atomists** regarded "soul," or "mind," as material and believed that everything was guided by purely physical laws. In the arguments of Anaxagoras and the atomists, we have the beginning of the philosophical debate between materialism and idealism that has continued through the ages. (See Document, "The Atomists' Account of the Origin of the World Order.")

POLITICAL AND MORAL PHILOSOPHY

Most Greeks were suspicious of metaphysical speculations. A far more influential debate was begun by a group of professional teachers who emerged in the mid-fifth century B.C.E. Called **Sophists**, they traveled about and received pay for teaching practical techniques of persuasion, such as rhetoric, which were highly valued in democracies like Athens. Some claimed to teach wisdom and even virtue. They applied reasoned analysis to human beliefs and institutions. They analyzed the tension and even the contradiction between nature and custom, or law. The more traditional among them argued that law itself was in accord with nature, and this view fortified the traditional beliefs about the *polis*, the Greek city-state (see Chapter 3). Others argued that laws were merely the result of an agreement among people, a way to prevent people from harming each other. The most extreme Sophists argued that law was contrary to nature, a trick whereby the weak controlled the strong. Critias (ca. 460–403 B.C.E.) went so far as to say that the gods themselves had been invented by some clever man to deter people from doing what they wished. Such ideas attacked the theoretical foundations of the *polis*.

The Greek concern with ethical, political, and religious issues is expressed brilliantly in the philosophical tradition that began with Socrates in the latter half of the fifth century B.C.E. That tradition continued with Socrates' pupil Plato and with Plato's pupil Aristotle. Aristotle also made great contributions to the scientific understanding of the physical world, but he is perhaps more important for his impact on later Western and Islamic metaphysics.

The starting point for the three giants of Hellenic moral and political philosophy was the social and political reality of the Greek city-state, or *polis*. The greatest crisis for the *polis* was the Great Peloponnesian War (435–404 B.C.E.), which is discussed in Chapter 3. Probably the most complicated response to this crisis may be found in the life and teachings of Socrates (469–399 B.C.E.). He wrote nothing, so our knowledge of him comes from his disciples Plato and Xenophon (ca. 435–354 B.C.E.) and from later tradition.

DOCUMENT

The Atomists' Account of the Origin of the World Order

Leucippus and Democritus were Greek thinkers of the fifth century B.C.E. who originated the theory that the world is entirely material, made up of atoms and the void, moving through space without external guidance. As these selections show, they provided a fundamental explanation of things that was purely natural, without divine or mythical intervention. Their view was passed on and later influenced such Renaissance scientists as Galileo.

- Compare the atomists' explanation of the origins of the world with that presented in the box entitled "Hymn to Indra" in Chapter 1. How do these explanations of the nature of things and how they got that way differ from those offered by different civilizations and by the Greeks before the sixth century B.C.E.? What are the consequences and significance of this new way of looking at the universe?

1. The world-orders arise in this way. Many bodies of all sorts of shapes "split off" from the infinite into a great void where, being gathered together, they give rise to a single vortex, in which, colliding and circling in all sorts of ways, they begin to separate apart, like to like. Being unable to circle in equilibrium any longer because of their congestion, the light bodies go off into the outer void like chaff, while the rest "remain together" and, becoming entangled, unite their motions and produce first a spherical structure. This stands apart like a "membrane," containing in itself all sorts of bodies; and, because of the resistance of the middle, as these revolve the surrounding membrane becomes thin as contiguous bodies continually flow together because of contact with the vortex. And in this way the earth arose, the bodies which were carried to the middle remaining together. Again, the surrounding membrane increases because of the acquisition of bodies from without; and as it moves with the vortex, whatever it touches it adds to itself. Certain of these, becoming entangled, form a structure at first very watery and muddy; but afterward they dry out, being carried about with the rotation of the whole, and ignite to form the substance of the heavenly bodies.

2. Certainly the atoms did not arrange themselves in order by design or intelligence, nor did they propound what movements each should make. But rather myriad atoms, swept along through infinite time or myriad paths by blows and their own weight, have come together in every possible way and tried out every combination that they could possibly create. So it happens that, after roaming the world for aeons of time in making trial of every combination and movement, at length they come together—those atoms whose sudden coincidence often becomes the origin of mighty things: of earth and sea and sky and the species of living things.

Source: The first selection is from Diogenes Laertius 9.31; the second is from Lucretius, De Rerum Naturae 5.419–431. Both selections from John Mansley Robinson, An Introduction to Early Greek Philosophy. Copyright © 1968 by John Mansley Robinson. Used with permission of the author.

Socrates was committed to the search for truth and for the knowledge about human affairs that he believed reason could reveal. His method was to question and cross-examine fellow Greeks. The result was always the same: Those he questioned might have technical information and skills but seldom had any knowledge of the fundamental principles of human behavior. Unlike the Sophists, Socrates did not accept pay for his teaching; he professed ignorance and denied that he taught at all. His individualism, moreover, was unlike the worldly hedonism of some of the Sophists. It was not wealth or pleasure or power that he urged people to seek, but "the greatest improvement of the soul." Contrary to the more radical Sophists, he thought that the *polis* and its laws had a legitimate claim on the citizen. But he was contemptuous of democracy, which seemingly relied on ignorant amateurs to make important political

QUICK REVIEW

Socrates and Athens

- Socrates distrusted democracy
- Athenians thought Socrates undermined the *polis*
- An Athenian jury sentenced Socrates to death

Read the Document

Aristotle, excerpts from Physics and Posterior Analytics at **myhistorylab.com**

QUICK REVIEW

Plato and the *Polis*

- Plato hoped to reform the *polis*
- The *polis* could mold good men
- A philosopher-king would be the ideal ruler

decisions without any certain knowledge. Athenians thought Socrates was undermining the beliefs and values of the *polis*, and his dialectical inquiries had angered many important people. Socrates' insistence on the primacy of his own individualism and his determination to pursue philosophy even against the wishes of his fellow citizens created hostility. In 399 B.C.E., Socrates was condemned to death by an Athenian jury on the charges of bringing new gods into the city and of corrupting its youth. He was given a chance to escape, but in Plato's *Crito* we are told of his refusal to do so because of his veneration of the laws.

Socrates' career set the stage for later responses to the travail of the *polis*. Socratic beliefs were distorted almost beyond recognition by the Cynic school. The most famous Cynic was Diogenes of Sinope (ca. 400–325 B.C.E.). Socrates disparaged wealth and worldly comfort, so Diogenes wore rags and lived in a tub. As Plato said, Diogenes was Socrates gone mad. The Cynics moved even further from Socrates by abandoning the concept of the *polis* entirely. When Diogenes was asked about his citizenship, he answered that he was *kosmopolites*, a citizen of the world.

Plato (429–347 B.C.E.), the most important of Socrates' associates, is a perfect example of the pupil who becomes greater than his master. He was a writer of genius, leaving us twenty-six philosophical discussions, mostly in the form of dialogues. In 386 B.C.E., Plato founded the Academy, a center of philosophical investigation and a school for training statesmen and citizens that had a powerful impact on Greek thought and endured until the sixth century C.E.

Like Socrates, Plato firmly believed in the *polis* and its virtues of order, harmony, and justice. Unlike the radical Sophists, Plato thought that the *polis* was in accord with nature, and that one of its main objects was to produce good people. He accepted Socrates' doctrine of the identity of virtue and knowledge, or *episteme*, a body of true and unchanging wisdom. Only the few philosophers whose training, character, and intellect allowed them to see reality were qualified to rule; they themselves would prefer the life of pure contemplation but would accept their responsibility and take their turn as philosopher-kings. According to Plato's definition of justice, each man should do only that one thing to which his nature was best suited. The individual was subordinated to the community.

Plato understood that the *polis* of his day suffered from terrible internal stress, class struggle, and factional divisions. Redemption of the *polis* was at the heart of Plato's system of philosophy. He began by asking the traditional questions: What is a good man, and how is he made? Because goodness depended on knowledge of the good, it required a theory of knowledge. Even when the philosopher knew the good, the question remained of how the state could bring that knowledge to its citizens. That answer required a theory of education. Even purely logical and metaphysical questions, therefore, were subordinate to the overriding political questions. Plato's need to find a satisfactory foundation for the beleaguered *polis* thus contributed to the birth of systematic philosophy.

Aristotle (384–322 B.C.E.) was a pupil of Plato, but his different experience and cast of mind led him in new directions. As a young man, he came to study at the Academy, where he stayed until Plato's death. Later, he carried on research in marine biology, and biological interests played a large part in all his thoughts. In 342 B.C.E., Philip, the king of Macedon, appointed him tutor to his son, the young Alexander (see Chapter 3). In 336 B.C.E. he returned to Athens, where he founded his own school, the Lyceum. On the death of Alexander in 323 B.C.E., the Athenians rebelled against Macedonian rule, and Aristotle found it wise to leave Athens. He died the following year.

Aristotle studied an astonishing range of subjects including logic, physics, astronomy, biology, ethics, rhetoric, literary criticism, and politics. In each field, his method was the same. Aristotle began with observation of the empirical evidence, whether it was physical or common opinion. He applied reason and discovered inconsistencies or difficulties, then introduced metaphysical principles to explain the problems or to reconcile the inconsistencies. His view on all subjects, like Plato's, was teleological; that is, he recognized purposes apart from and greater than the will of the individual human being. Plato's purposes, however, were contained in the Ideas, or Forms—transcendental concepts outside the experience of most people. For Aristotle, the purposes of most things were easily inferred by observing their behavior in the world.

Aristotle's most striking characteristics are his moderation and common sense. His epistemology finds room for both reason and experience; his metaphysics gives meaning and reality to both mind and body; his ethics aims at the good life, which is the contemplative life, but recognizes the necessity for moderate wealth, comfort, and pleasure.

All these qualities are evident in Aristotle's political thought. Like Plato, he opposed the Sophists' assertion that the *polis* was the result of mere convention. Aristotle applied to politics the teleology that he saw in all nature. The *polis* made individuals self-sufficient and allowed them to realize their potential. It was therefore natural. It was also the highest point in the evolution of the social institutions: marriage, household, village, and finally, *polis*. For Aristotle, the purpose of the *polis* was neither economic nor military but moral: "The end of the state is the good life," the life lived "for the sake of noble actions," a life of virtue and morality.[7]

Characteristically, Aristotle was less interested in the best state—the utopia that required philosophers to rule it—than in the best state practically possible, one that would combine justice with stability. The constitution for that state was not the best constitution, but the next best, the one most possible for most states. Its quality was moderation, and it naturally gave power to neither the rich nor the poor but to the middle class, which also had to be the most numerous. The middle class possessed many virtues: It was free of the arrogance of the rich and the malice of the poor. One of its main objects was to produce good people. It was also the most stable class. The stability of the constitution came from being a mixed constitution, blending in some way the laws of democracy and those of oligarchy. Aristotle's scheme was unique because of its realism and the breadth of its vision.

All the political thinkers of the fourth century B.C.E. recognized that the *polis* was in danger and hoped to save it. All recognized the economic and social troubles that threatened it. It is ironic that the ablest defense of the *polis* came soon before its demise.

---

[7]Aristotle, *Politics*, 1280b, 1281a.

CHRONOLOGY

MAJOR GREEK PHILOSOPHERS

469–399 B.C.E.	Socrates
429–347 B.C.E.	Plato
384–322 B.C.E.	Aristotle

QUICK REVIEW

Aristotle and Moderation

- Aristotle balanced idealism and practicality
- The middle class was virtuous
- A mixed constitution fostered stability

SUMMARY

WHAT ARE the fundamental beliefs or worldviews that were expressed in the four great revolutions in thought that occurred between 800 and 300 B.C.E.?

Comparing the Four Great Revolutions. Between 800 and 300 B.C.E., four philosophical and religious revolutions occurred. Chinese philosophy, Indian religion, Hebrew monotheism, and Greek philosophy have shaped world history ever since they emerged. *page 33*

WHY WAS the revolution in Chinese thought more similar to that in Greek thought than to Indian religion or Judaic monotheism?

Philosophy in China. Traditional Chinese philosophical thought, which took shape with the teachings of Confucius in the sixth century B.C.E., remained dominant in China until the early twentieth century. It was concerned with social and political issues and sought to teach human beings how to live harmoniously and ethically under Heaven by prescribing correct relationships between people. Confucianism became China's official philosophy in the second century B.C.E. Other Chinese philosophies were Daoism and Legalism. As in Greece, there were many competing schools of thought in China. *page 34*

 WHAT FUNDAMENTAL institutions and ideas form the basis of Indian religion?

Religion in India. Hinduism, the dominant Indian religious tradition, took shape by 400 B.C.E. In Indian religion, existence was an endless alternation between life and death (*samsara*). The escape from this dilemma lay in the concept of *karma*, the idea that good actions (*dharma*) could lead to rebirth as a higher being, even a god, or to escape the cycle entirely and cease to exist entirely (*moksha*). Other religious traditions that originated during this period in India include Jainism and Buddhism. *page 38*

HOW WAS the Hebrew concept of God and religion distinctive?

The Religion of the Israelites. Monotheism is the faith in a single, all-powerful God as the sole creator, sustainer, and ruler of the universe. The Hebrews were the first people to emphasize the moral demands that the one God, Yahweh, placed on the individual and the community and to see history as the unfolding of a divine plan. The Hebrews, or Jews, were also the first people in history to be defined by shared religious faith and practice. Through the Christian and Muslim traditions, Judaic monotheism would change the face of much of the world. *page 44*

WHY DID Greek thinkers, beginning in the sixth century B.C.E., produce an intellectual revolution?

Greek Philosophy. The Greeks were the first to initiate the unreservedly rational investigation of the universe. They are the forerunners of Western philosophy and science. In the sixth and fifth centuries B.C.E., Greek thinkers sought to explain natural phenomena without recourse to divine intervention. In the later fifth century and the fourth century B.C.E., Socrates, Plato, Aristotle, and others applied the same rational, inquisitive approach to the study of moral and political issues in the life of the Greek city-state, or *polis*. *page 46*

KEY TERMS

atman-Brahman (AHT-muhn BRAH-mahn) (p. 39)
atomists (p. 50)
Brahmanas (p. 38)
covenant (p. 45)
Daoism (daow-ihzm) (p. 37)
dharma **(DAHR-muh)** (p. 39)
Hindu (p. 38)
Jains (p. 41)
karma (KAHR-muh) (p. 39)
Legalism (p. 37)
Messiah (p. 46)
monotheism (MAH-nah-THEE-iz-im) (p. 44)
polis **(POH-lihs)** (p. 50)
polytheistic (p. 44)
samsara **(suhm-SAHR-ah)** (p. 39)
Sophists (p. 50)

REVIEW QUESTIONS

1. Is your own outlook on life closer to Confucianism, Daoism, or Legalism? What specifically makes you favor one over the others?

2. Which fundamental assumptions about the world, the individual, and reality do the Jain, Hindu, and Buddhist traditions share? How do these assumptions compare with those that underlie Chinese philosophy, Jewish religious thought, and Greek philosophy?

3. In what sense is Buddhism the "Middle Path"? Buddha filled his own life with extreme asceticism; do you think this distorted his perspective on human suffering, or did it allow him to gain a true understanding of suffering?

4. What makes the monotheism of the Hebrews unique? To what extent did their faith bind the Jews politically? Why was the concept of monotheism so radical for Near Eastern civilization?

5. Describe the covenant between Jews and God. Could a polytheistic people have a covenant with one or more of their gods?

6. In what ways did the ideas of the Greeks differ from those of other ancient peoples? How do Aristotle's political and ethical ideas compare with those of Confucius? What were Socrates' contributions to the development of philosophy?

Note: To learn more about the topics in this chapter, please turn to the Suggested Readings at the end of the book. For additional sources related to this chapter please see www.myhistorylab.com

myhistorylab Connections

Reinforce what you learned in this chapter by studying the many documents, images, maps, review tools, and videos available at **www.myhistorylab.com**

Read and Review

Research and Explore

((•— Hear the Audio

Hear the audio file for Chapter 2
at **www.myhistorylab.com**

RELIGIONS OF THE WORLD

JUDAISM

Monotheism, the belief in a unique God who is the creator of the universe and its all-powerful ruler, first became a central and lasting element in religion among the Hebrews, later called Israelites and also Jews. Their religion, more than the many forms of polytheistic worship that characterized the ancient world, demanded moral rectitude and placed ethical responsibilities both on individuals and on the community as a whole. Their God had a divine plan for human history, which was linked to the behavior of his chosen people. This vision of the exclusive worship of the true God, obedience to the laws governing the community that derive from him, and a strong ethical responsibility was connected to humanity's historical experience in this world. Ultimately it gave rise to three great universal monotheistic religions: Judaism, Christianity, and Islam.

At the beginning of this tradition stands Abraham, whom all three religions recognize as the founder. According to the Torah (the first five books of the Hebrew Bible; the Christian Old Testament), Abraham entered into a covenant with God in which he promised to worship only this God, who in turn promised to make Abraham's descendants his own chosen people—chosen to worship him, to obey his Laws, and to undertake a special set of moral responsibilities. God renewed the covenant with Moses at Mount Sinai when he freed the Israelites from Egyptian bondage. He promised them the land of Canaan (later called Palestine and part of which is now the state of Israel) and gave them the Law (the Torah), including the Ten Commandments, by which they were to

"In the Beginning." The Hebrew word *Beresheet*, which means "in the beginning," opens the Book of Genesis. The Jews are people of the Book, and foremost among their sacred writings is the Hebrew Bible.

How does the design of this page reflect the role of the Book in Jewish faith?

guide their lives. As long as they lived by his Law, God would give them his guidance and protection.

In time the Israelites formed themselves into a kingdom that remained unified from about 1000 to 922 B.C.E. In the period after its division, prophets emerged. Thought to be inspired by God, they chastised the Israelites for their lapses into idolatry and immorality. Even as the kingdom was disintegrating and the Israelites were falling under the control of alien empires, the prophets preached social reform and a return to God's laws. The prophets saw Israel's misfortune as punishment for failing to keep the covenant and predicted disaster if the Israelites did not change their ways. When disasters came—the Jewish kingdoms captured, the people enslaved and exiled—the prophets interpreted Israel's status as a chosen people to mean that their sufferings would make them "a light unto the nations," leading other nations to the true worship of one God.

The prophets also preached that God was righteous and demanded righteousness from his people. But he was also a God of justice; although he might need to punish his people for their sins, he would one day reward them with divine favor. Traditional Jewish belief expects that the Messiah, or Anointed One, will someday come and establish God's kingdom on earth. He will introduce an age of universal brotherhood in which all nations will acknowledge the one true God.

The Jews are people of the Book, and foremost among their sacred writings is the Hebrew Bible, consisting of the Five Books of Moses (the Torah), the books of the prophets, and other writings. The Torah is the source of Jewish Law. Over the centuries, new experiences required new interpretation of the Law, which was accomplished by the oral Law, no less sacred than the written Law. Compilations of interpretation and commentary by rabbis (wise and learned teachers) were brought together to form the Talmud.

The destruction of their temple in Jerusalem by the Romans in 70 C.E. hastened the scattering of the Jews throughout the empire. Thereafter almost all Jews lived in the Diaspora (dispersion), without a homeland, a political community, or a national or religious center. In the fifth and sixth centuries the decline of the Sassanid Empire in Iran and the collapse of the Western Roman Empire undermined the institutions in which the Jews had found a stable way of life. In the seventh and eighth centuries the missionary zeal of the Christian church also brought hard times for the Jews in western Europe and in the Byzantine East. In the West, their condition improved in the ninth century under Charlemagne and his successors.

Persecution of the Jews. This 1900 painting, *After the Pogrom*, by the Polish painter Maurycy Minkowski, shows a group of women and children in the aftermath of a pogrom, an organized persecution of Jews that was once common in eastern Europe and Russia. Pogroms often became massacres. Encouraged by the Russian government, pogroms were particularly brutal in the late nineteenth and early twentieth centuries.

What seems to have happened to these people as a result of a pogrom?

Gift of Mr. and Mrs. Lester Klien. Jewish Museum/Art Resource, New York.

Under Islam, Jews, like Christians, were tolerated as people of the Book. Jewish settlements flourished throughout the Islamic world. After the Islamic conquest of Spain in 711, the Jews there enjoyed an almost 300-year-long golden age. During this period of extraordinary intellectual and cultural accomplishment, Jews practiced their religion openly and flourished economically.

The beginning of the Crusades in the eleventh century brought renewed persecution of the Jews in both the Christian and Islamic worlds. In the wake of the Christian reconquest of Spain, Jews were persecuted, killed, forced to convert, and finally expelled in 1492.

By the Middle Ages, Jews had divided into two distinct branches: those who lived in Christian Europe, called *Ashkenazim,* and those in the Muslim world, particularly Spain, called *Sephardim.* The Sephardim, with greater opportunities, developed a more secular life. Their language, Ladino, combined Hebrew and Spanish elements. The Ashkenazim, scattered in tiny communities, were forced to turn inward. Centered in German lands, they developed Yiddish, a combination of Hebrew and German. In time Yiddish became the language of most Jews in northern Europe, although the Torah was always read and studied in Hebrew.

Two of the dominant influences on modern Judaism have been Zionism—the effort to found a Jewish nation—and the death of some 6 million Jews in the Holocaust of World War II. Bolstered by the determination of Jews never again to find themselves victimized by the forces of anti-Semitism, the Zionist movement culminated in the founding of the state of Israel in 1948.

The adherents of Judaism are divided into several groups—Reform, Reconstruction, Conservative, and Orthodox—each holding significantly different views about the place of tradition and the traditional law in the modern world. All, however, would give assent to the saying of Hillel, the great Talmudic teacher of the first century B.C.E.: "What is distasteful to you do not to your fellow man. This is the Law, all the rest is commentary. Now go and study."

◆ In what ways did Judaism differ from the polytheistic religions?

◆ What elements of the religion helped it persist through the ages?

3

Greek and Hellenistic Civilization

((•—Hear the Audio for Chapter 3 at www.myhistorylab.com

Bronze Statue. This striking bronze statue of Poseidon, created ca. 460 B.C.E. by the Greek sculptor Calamis, was found off the coast of Cape Artemision, Greece.

Is there anything about this statue that suggests it might have had a religious use?

bout 2000 B.C.E., *Greek-speaking peoples settled the lands surrounding the Aegean Sea, where they came into contact with the advanced civilizations of the Near East. The Greeks forged their own way of life, forming a set of ideas, values, and institutions that would spread far beyond their homeland. The foundation of this way of life was the independent city-state, or polis.*

Early in the fifth century B.C.E., *the great Persian Empire (see Chapter 4) threatened to extinguish Greek independence. Led by the city-states of Sparta and Athens, the Greeks won a remarkable victory over the Persians, securing a period of freedom and autonomy during which they realized their greatest political and cultural achievements. Athens developed an extraordinarily democratic constitution, but fears and jealousies created a split in the Greek world that led to a series of wars.*

In 338 B.C.E., *Philip of Macedon conquered the Greek states, ending the age of the polis. The conquests of Philip's son, Alexander, spread Greek culture far from its homeland. Preserved and adapted by the Romans, Greek culture influenced western Europe and the Byzantine Empire in the Middle Ages. In time the civilization emerging from the Greek and Roman experience crossed the Atlantic to the Western Hemisphere.* ■

See the **Map**
The Greek World at **myhistorylab.com**

THE ACHIEVEMENTS OF GREEK AND HELLENISTIC CIVILIZATION

Hellenic civilization lies at the root of Western civilization, and it has powerfully influenced the modern world. It emerged from the collapse of the Bronze Age Mycenaean civilization. However, it had little in common with Mycenaean civilization and the Bronze Age civilization of Crete or with other early civilizations—in Mesopotamia, Palestine-Syria, China, India, and elsewhere. These civilizations were characterized by strong, centralized monarchical governments ruling through tightly organized, large bureaucracies; hierarchical social systems; professional standing armies; and a regular system of taxation to support it all. To varying degrees, they all tended to cultural stability and uniformity. Hellenic civilization departed sharply from this pattern of development.

The crucial unit of the Greek way of life—forged in poverty and isolation following the Mycenaean collapse—was the *polis*, the Hellenic city-state. There were hundreds of *poleis*, ranging in size from a few thousand inhabitants to hundreds of thousands. Each evoked a kind of loyalty and attachment in its citizens that

made it unthinkable for them to allow it to be part of a larger political unit. The result was a dynamic, many-faceted, competitive, sometimes chaotic society in which rivalry for excellence and victory had the highest value. This competitiveness led to almost constant warfare, but it also inspired the Greeks' extraordinary achievements in literature and art.

In the Classical Age, which followed the Greeks' defeat of the powerful Persian Empire in the early sixth century B.C.E., while the rest of the world's civilizations remained monarchical, hierarchical, command societies, Athens, the seat of an Aegean empire, developed democratic government to an extent not seen again until modern times. Athenian citizenship—though limited to adult males of native parentage—granted full and active participation in every decision of the state without regard to wealth or class.

Despite the unique aspects of its culture, Greece was also deeply influenced by its neighbors, especially in its earliest stages. The influences of Egyptian art, for example, on early Greek sculpture are evident in the style and stance of statues, jewelry, and fig-

---

MINOANS, MYCENAEANS, AND THE GREEK "MIDDLE AGES" TO ca. 750 B.C.E.

WHAT WERE the defining qualities of Minoan, Mycenaean, and Homeric Greek society?

The large island of Crete was a cultural bridge between the older civilizations of Egypt and Asia and the new one of the Greeks.

THE MINOANS

In the third and second millennia B.C.E., a Bronze Age civilization arose on Crete that influenced the islands of the Aegean and the mainland of Greece (see Map 3–1 on page 62). This civilization is called **Minoan**, after Crete's legendary King Minos. Scholars have divided Minoan history into three major periods, Early, Middle, and Late Minoan. Dates for Bronze Age settlements on the Greek mainland, for which the term *Helladic* is used, are derived from the same chronological scheme.

The civilization of the Middle and Late Minoan periods in eastern and central Crete centered on several great palaces, the most important of which is Cnossus. The distinctive and striking art and architecture of these palaces reflect regional influences but are uniquely Cretan. Minoan cities lacked strong defensive walls, suggesting that they were not built for defense.

Along with palaces, paintings, pottery, and jewelry, excavations at Minoan sites have revealed clay writing tablets like those found in Mesopotamia. These tablets have three distinct kinds of writing on them, one of which is an early form of Greek. The tablets reveal a king who was supported by an extensive bureaucracy that kept remarkably detailed records. This sort of organization is typical of early civilizations in the Near East but, as we shall see, is nothing like that of the Greeks after the Bronze Age. The fact that some inventories were written in a form of Greek raises questions about the relationship between Crete and the Greek mainland during the Bronze Age.

Minoan

The Bronze Age civilization that arose in Crete in the third and second millennia B.C.E.

View the Image

The Toreador Fresco, Knossos, ca. 1500 B.C.E. Archeological Museum, Herakleion at **myhistorylab.com**

urines. The Greeks adopted the Phoenician alphabet as the basis for their own. Nonetheless, as in the case of political development and the unique *polis*-centered way of life, the Greeks adapted and made uniquely their own the artistic styles, alphabet, and intellectual ideas they borrowed from their neighbors.

Even more significant, however, was the influence of Greek culture in world history. The culture of democratic yet imperial Athens gave rise to the greatest artistic, literary, and philosophical achievements of the Greek classical period, achievements that became integral to Roman culture and, via the Greco-Roman cultural synthesis, a pillar of European civilization. The conquests of Alexander and the Hellenistic states that followed in their wake spread Greek culture over a remarkably wide area and made a significant and lasting impression on the conquered societies and their neighbors. The Seleucid Dynasty ruled some parts of the Persian Empire for almost two centuries. As we will see in Chapter 4, a group of Greeks who broke away from the Seleucids carried Hellenistic culture even farther east, to the

Indus valley in northwest India, creating the Indo-Greek Bactrian society. In art, Hellenistic influence reached even as far away as China. In the West, of course, the legacy of Hellenism was more substantial and enduring, powerfully shaping the culture of the Roman Empire that ultimately dominated the entire Mediterranean world.

Focus Questions

◆ Why are the achievements of Greek culture so fundamental to the development of Western civilization?

◆ In what ways was Greece influenced by neighboring civilizations? Which civilizations had the most influence on Greek culture, and why?

◆ How did the Hellenistic era differ from the Hellenic? What made Hellenistic culture more cosmopolitan than Hellenic culture?

THE MYCENAEANS

In the third millennium B.C.E., most of the Greek mainland was settled by people who used metal, built some impressive houses, and traded with Crete and the islands of the Aegean. They were not Greeks, and they spoke a language that was not Indo-European (the language family to which Greek belongs). The Late Helladic period began soon after 2000 B.C.E., when many of the Early Helladic sites show signs of invasion. These invasions probably signal the arrival of the Greeks.

Shaft graves cut into the rock at the royal palace-fortress of Mycenae show that by the Late Helladic period the conquerors had prospered. The whole mainland culture of the Late Helladic period goes by the name **Mycenaean**. Greek invaders also established themselves in a still flourishing Crete, making it part of the Mycenaean world. Mycenaean culture was very different from Minoan. Mycenaean cities were built on hills in positions commanding the neighboring territory. The Mycenaean people were

Mycenaean
The Bronze Age civilization of mainland Greece that was centered at Mycenae.

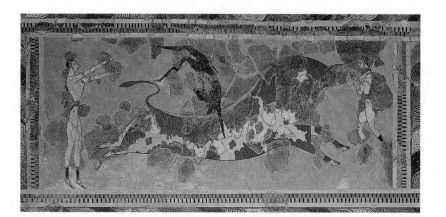

A Minoan Fresco. Acrobats leaping over a charging bull, from the east wing of the Minoan-period palace at Cnossus on the island of Crete. It is not known whether such acrobatic displays were for entertainment or were part of some religious ritual.

Scala/Art Resource, New York.

Why do you think the bull's power and size are emphasized in this image?

MAP 3–1.   The Aegean Area in the Bronze Age.   The Bronze Age in the Aegean area lasted from ca. 1900 to ca. 1100 B.C.E. Its culture on Crete is called Minoan and was at its height about 1900–1400 B.C.E. Bronze Age Helladic culture on the mainland flourished from ca. 1600 to 1200 B.C.E.

What geographic features of this area seem noteworthy to you?

warriors, led by strong kings who lived in palaces protected by defensive walls. Mycenaean palaces were adorned with murals, but instead of the peaceful scenery and games depicted on the Cretan murals, the Mycenaean murals depicted scenes of war and boar hunting.

About 1500 B.C.E. *tholos* tombs—large, beehivelike chambers cut into hillsides—replaced the earlier shaft graves. The *tholos* tombs, built of enormous, well-cut, fitted stones, were approached through an unroofed passage cut horizontally into the side of the hill. Only a strong king whose wealth was great, whose power was unquestioned, and who commanded the labor of many could undertake such a project.

The Mycenaean world was made up of a number of independent, powerful, and well-organized monarchies. At the height of their power (1400–1200 B.C.E.),

View the Image
Tomb Mask, Mycenaen
at **myhistorylab.com**

the Mycenaeans were prosperous and active traders. They are mentioned in the archives of the Hittite kings of Asia Minor and are named as marauders in Egyptian records. Sometime about 1250 B.C.E. they probably sacked Troy on the coast of northwestern Asia Minor, giving rise to the epic poems of Homer, the *Iliad* and the *Odyssey* (see Map 3–1). Around the year 1200 B.C.E., however, the Mycenaean world showed signs of great trouble; by 1100 B.C.E. it was gone. Its palaces were destroyed; many of its cities abandoned; and its art, its pattern of life, its system of writing buried and forgotten.

The reasons for the collapse of Mycenaean civilization are not known. Greek legends attribute it to the Dorians, a rude new wave of Greek speakers who invaded the Greek mainland from the north. Greece entered a dark "middle age" about which little is known. The Dorians, after occupying most of the Peloponnesus, swept south across the Aegean. Another group, known as the Ionians, spread east to what became Ionia.

These migrations made the Aegean a Greek lake. Trade, however, had ended with the fall of the region's advanced civilizations. Each Greek community was left largely to its own devices. The Near East was also in disarray at this time, so the Greeks had time to recover from their disaster and to create their unique style of life.

THE AGE OF HOMER

Homer provides the best picture of society in these "dark ages." His epic poems, the *Iliad* and the *Odyssey*, emerged from a tradition of oral poetry whose roots reached back to the Mycenaean Age. Through the centuries bards had sung tales of the heroes who had fought at Troy, preserving very old material by using verse arranged in rhythmic formulas to aid the memory. In the eighth century B.C.E., the oral poetry was reworked as the poems attributed to Homer. Although the poems tell of the deeds of Mycenaean heroes, the world they describe resembles that of the tenth and ninth centuries B.C.E.

See the **Map**
Mycenean Trade and Contacts at **myhistorylab.com**

The *Iliad* and the *Odyssey*
The epic poems by Homer about the "dark age" heroes of Greece who fought at Troy. The poems were written down in the eighth century B.C.E. after centuries of being sung by bards.

Read the **Document**
Homer, Debate Among the Greeks, from The Odyssey at **myhistorylab.com**

The Trojan Horse, Depicted on a Seventh-Century B.C.E. Greek Vase. According to legend, the Greeks finally defeated Troy by pretending to abandon their siege of the city, leaving behind a giant wooden horse. Soldiers hidden in the horse opened the gates of the city to their compatriots after the Trojans had brought it within their walls. Note the wheels on the horse and the Greek soldiers who are hiding inside it holding weapons and armor.

What is the general meaning of the metaphor "a Trojan horse"? Can you think of an example?

Kings in the Homeric poems have much less power than Mycenaean rulers had. Homeric kings were expected to consult their followers on important decisions. The right to speak in council was limited to noblemen, but common people could not be ignored. If a king planned a major change of policy, he would call the common soldiers to an assembly. They could not take part in debate, but they could express their feelings by acclamation. Homer shows that even in these early times Greeks practiced a form of constitutional government.

Homeric society was aristocratic. Noble status was hereditary and usually associated with wealth. Below the nobles were two other classes: *thetes* and slaves. Thetes were landless laborers, who endured the worst conditions in Homeric society. In a world where membership in a settled group provided the only security, free laborers were desperately vulnerable. Slaves—mostly women who served as maids and concubines—were attached to family households, so they were at least protected and fed. Throughout Greek history, agriculture mostly utilized free labor.

Homer's poems became the schoolbooks of the Greeks, who memorized his texts and emulated the behavior displayed in them. The values of the Homeric poems—physical prowess, courage, and fierce protection of family, friends, and property—reflected an aristocratic code that influenced all future Greek thought. Defense of personal honor and reputation was of supreme importance. The great hero of the *Iliad*, Achilles, withdraws from the field of battle at Troy and allows his fellow Greeks to be almost defeated when Agamemnon wounds his honor. He returns to the army not out of a sense of duty but to avenge the death of his friend Patroclus.

The highest virtue in Homeric society was *arete*: manliness, the excellence proper to a hero. Arete was best demonstrated by competing in a contest, an *agon*. Homeric battles are primarily individual matches between champions, and the major entertainment for Homer's heroes are athletic contests. The central ethical idea in Homer's epics is found in the instructions that fathers give their hero-sons: "Always be the best and distinguished above others"; "Do not bring shame on the family of your fathers." The chief aristocratic values of Homer's world—to vie for individual supremacy in *arete* and to defend and increase the honor of the family—would remain prominent Greek values long after Homeric society was only a memory.

THE *POLIS* IN THE EXPANDING GREEK WORLD

WHY WAS the *polis* the most characteristic Greek institution?

The characteristic Greek institution was the *polis*. The common translation of that word as "city-state" says both too much and too little. All Greek *poleis* began as agricultural villages or towns, and many stayed that way, so the word *city* is inappropriate. They were states, in the sense of being independent political units, but they were much more than that. The *polis* was thought of as a community of relatives; all its citizens, who were theoretically descended from a common ancestor, belonged to subgroups such as fighting brotherhoods (*phratries*), clans, and tribes. They worshiped the gods in common ceremonies.

Aristotle (see Chapter 2) argued that the *polis* was a natural growth and that the human being is by nature "an animal who lives in a *polis*." Humans alone have the power of speech and from it derive the ability to distinguish good from bad and right from wrong. Without law and justice, humans are the worst and most dangerous of the animals. With them they can be the best, and justice exists only in the *polis*.

DEVELOPMENT OF THE POLIS

Originally the word *polis* referred to a citadel, an elevated, defensible rock to which the farmers of the neighboring area could retreat when attacked. The **Acropolis** in Athens is an example. Gradually and without planning, towns grew up around these fortresses. For centuries they had no walls. The availability of farmland and of natural defenses determined where *poleis* sprang up. They were usually situated far enough away from the sea to avoid raids by pirates. Only later did an *agora*—a marketplace and civic center—appear within the *polis*. The *agora* became the heart of the Greeks' remarkable social life, distinguished by conversation and argument carried on in the open air.

All the colonies established by the Greeks after 750 B.C.E. took the form of *poleis*; true monarchy disappeared. The original form of the *polis* was an aristocratic republic dominated by a council of nobles, who also monopolized political offices.

THE HOPLITE PHALANX

Crucial to the development of the *polis* was a new military technique. In earlier times the brunt of fighting had been carried on by small troops of cavalry and individual "champions" who first threw their spears and then came to close quarters with swords. Toward the end of the eighth century B.C.E., however, the **hoplite phalanx** came into being and remained the basis of Greek warfare thereafter.

A hoplite was a heavily armed infantryman who fought with a spear and a large shield. Hoplites were closely arrayed in a phalanx that was at least eight ranks deep. The success of a hoplite army depended on the discipline and courage of its individual soldiers: If they maintained formation, they were almost impossible to defeat, but if they broke ranks they were easily routed. Until the Roman legion appeared, the hoplite phalanx was the dominant military force in the Mediterranean.

The usual hoplite battle in Greece involved the armies of two *poleis* quarreling over a piece of land. One army invaded the territory of the other when its crops were almost ready for harvest. The defending army had to protect the fields. The farmer-soldier-citizen, who defended the *polis*, usually hoped to settle a dispute quickly by a single decisive battle and then get back to work. It was to the advantage of an agriculturally based society to keep wars short and limit their cost. Service in the phalanx created bonds between the aristocrats and the family farmers who fought side by side. This may explain why class conflicts were slow to develop, but it also meant that aristocratic monopolies of political power would eventually be challenged.

GREEK COLONIES

Between the eighth and the sixth century B.C.E., the Greeks vastly expanded the territory they controlled as well as their wealth and their contacts with other peoples. A burst of colonizing activity placed *poleis* from Spain to the Black Sea.

The Greeks settled the sparsely populated southern coast of Macedonia and the Chalcidian peninsula (see Map 3–2 on page 66). There were so many Greek colonies in Italy and Sicily that the Romans called the whole region **Magna Graecia** ("Great Greece"). The Greeks also put colonies in Spain and southern France. In the seventh century B.C.E. the Greeks had outposts throughout the Mediterranean world. Most colonies, though independent, were friendly with their mother cities. Each might ask the other for aid in time of trouble and expect to receive a friendly hearing, although neither was obliged to help.

Colonization had a powerful influence on Greek life. By relieving the pressure and land hunger of a growing population, it provided a safety valve that allowed the *poleis* to escape civil wars. Colonization also gave the Greeks a sense of cultural identity

Acropolis
The religious and civic center of Athens. It is the site of the Parthenon.

agora
The Greek marketplace and civic center. It was the heart of the social life of the *polis*.

hoplite phalanx
The basic unit of Greek warfare in which infantrymen fought in close order, shield to shield, usually eight ranks deep.

QUICK REVIEW

Greeks in Battle
◆ Hoplite: heavily armed infantryman
◆ Phalanx: close formation of hoplites at least eight ranks deep
◆ Most hoplite battles in Greece were between two *poleis* fighting over a piece of land

Magna Graecia Meaning "Great Greece" in Latin, it was the name given by the Romans to southern Italy and Sicily because there were so many Greek colonies in the region.

⊙ See the **Map**
Greece in the Archaic and Classical Ages, ca. 750–350 B.C.E. at **myhistorylab.com**

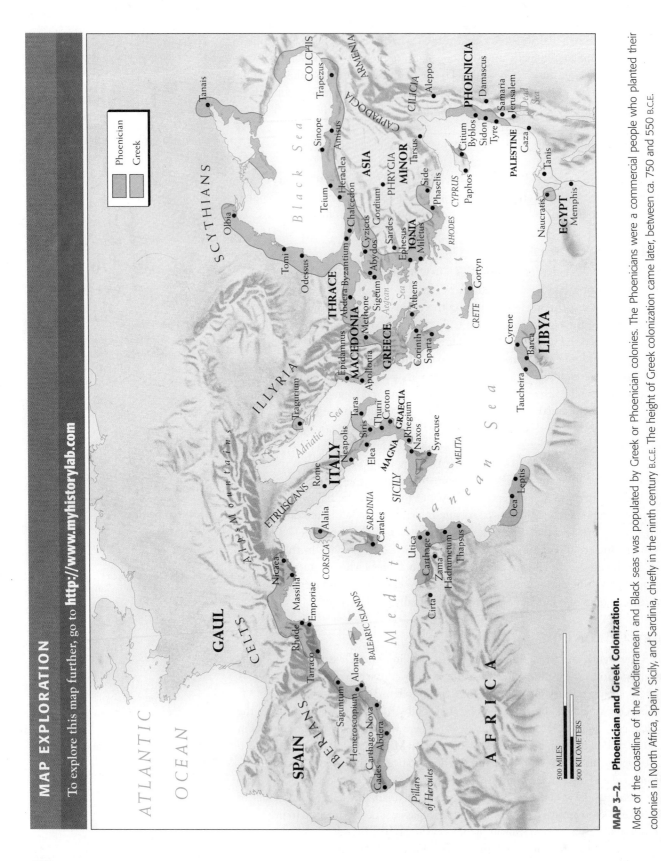

MAP 3–2. Phoenician and Greek Colonization.

Most of the coastline of the Mediterranean and Black seas was populated by Greek or Phoenician colonies. The Phoenicians were a commercial people who planted their colonies in North Africa, Spain, Sicily, and Sardinia, chiefly in the ninth century B.C.E. The height of Greek colonization came later, between ca. 750 and 550 B.C.E.

What impact did colonization have on Phoenician and Greek societies?

and fostered a **Panhellenic** ("all-Greek") spirit that led to the establishment of a number of religious festivals.

Colonization also encouraged trade and industry. The influx of new wealth and the increased demand for goods stimulated a more intensive use of the land and an emphasis on crops for export, chiefly the olive and the wine grape. The manufacture of pottery, tools, weapons, fine metalwork, and perfumed oil was encouraged. The newly wealthy were not always aristocrats, and they resented their exclusion from political power, religious privileges, and social acceptance. In many states the resulting crises culminated, between 700 and 500 B.C.E., in the establishment of tyrannies.

Panhellenic ("all-Greek")
The sense of cultural identity that all Greeks felt in common with each other.

THE TYRANTS (CA. 700–500 B.C.E.)

A tyrant was a monarch who had gained power in an unorthodox way and who exercised a strong one-man rule that might well be beneficent and popular. The founding tyrant, usually an aristocrat, typically sought the support of disgruntled elements within the *polis*: the politically powerless, newly wealthy, and poor farmers. He often expelled his aristocratic opponents and divided their land among his supporters. Tyrants presided over a period of population growth in the Greek world, and to maintain popular support they fostered trade and colonization. They sponsored programs of public works, founded new festivals, and provided patronage for the arts.

Tyranny, however, could turn oppressive, and it was inimical to the idea of the *polis*. The notion of the *polis* as a community for which each of its members was responsible, the connection of justice with that community, and the aristocratic hatred of monarchy all made tyranny seem alien and offensive to the Greeks. By the end of the sixth century B.C.E., tyranny had disappeared, and the last tyrants were remembered with bitterness. The tyrants had, however, helped secure the prosperity of Greece and had cultivated technology, the arts, and literature. Most importantly, they had broken the grip of the aristocracy on Greek society.

CHRONOLOGY	
RISE OF GREECE	
ca. 2900–1150 B.C.E.	Minoan period
ca. 1900 B.C.E.	Probable date of the arrival of the Greeks on the mainland
ca. 1600–1150 B.C.E.	Mycenaean period
ca. 1250 B.C.E.	Sack of Troy (?)
ca. 1200–1150 B.C.E.	Destruction of Mycenaean centers in Greece
ca. 1100–750 B.C.E.	Dark ages
ca. 750–500 B.C.E.	Major period of Greek colonization
ca. 725 B.C.E.	Probable date of Homer
ca. 700 B.C.E.	Probable date of Hesiod
ca. 700–500 B.C.E.	Major period of Greek tyranny

LIFE IN ARCHAIC GREECE

As the dark ages came to an end, the features that would distinguish Greek society took shape.

WHAT FEATURES distinguished Archaic Greek society?

SOCIETY

Most people farmed the land, but the role of the artisan and the merchant grew increasingly important. Aristocrats led privileged lives.

Works and Days by the poet Hesiod (ca. 700 B.C.E.) gives a glimpse of a Greek farmer's life. His crops included grain (chiefly barley but some wheat), grapes for wine, olives for oil (used for cooking, lighting, and washing), green vegetables, and fruit. Sheep and goats provided milk and cheese, but farmers usually ate meat only when animals were sacrificed at religious festivals. Life was continual toil under the burning sun and in the freezing cold, and pleasures were few.

Attic Jar. From late in the sixth century B.C.E. this jar shows how olives, one of Athens's most important crops, were harvested.

Why would olive harvesting be considered a suitable subject for illustrating a vase?

Most aristocrats employed hired laborers, sharecroppers, and sometimes slaves to work their lands. This gave them leisure for other activities. Aristocratic social life revolved around the drinking party, or **symposion**, a carefully organized activity for men only. Symposium guests might play games, enjoy professional entertainment, or amuse themselves with songs, poetry, or even philosophical disputes. Often their activities took the form of contests. Aristocratic values emphasized competition, the need to excel, and the desire to be recognized for one's achievements.

Athletic contests became especially popular in the sixth century B.C.E. The games included running events, boxing, wrestling, and the chariot race. Only the rich could afford racehorses, so the chariot race was a special preserve of aristocracy. Wrestling, however, was also favored by the nobility, and the *palaestra* where wrestlers practiced became an important social center. The contrast between the hard, drab life of the peasant and the leisured and lively one of the aristocrat could hardly be greater.

RELIGION

Like most ancient peoples, the Greeks were polytheists. A great part of Greek art and literature was closely connected with religion, as was the life of the *polis* in general. The Greek pantheon consisted of the following twelve gods who lived on Mount Olympus.

- Zeus, the father of the gods

- Hera, his wife

- Zeus's siblings:
  Poseidon, his brother, god of the seas and earthquakes
  Hestia, his sister, goddess of the hearth
  Demeter, his sister, goddess of agriculture and marriage

- Zeus's children:
  Aphrodite, goddess of love and beauty
  Apollo, god of the sun, music, poetry, and prophecy
  Ares, god of war
  Artemis, goddess of the moon and the hunt
  Athena, goddess of wisdom and the arts
  Hephaestus, god of fire and metallurgy
  Hermes, messenger of the gods, connected with commerce and cunning

The gods were assumed to behave like humans, from whom they differed primarily in strength and immortality. Like humans, the Olympians were believed to be subordinate to the Fates. Zeus was a defender of justice. Each *polis* honored one of the Olympians as its guardian deity, but all the gods were Panhellenic—they were worshiped throughout Greece. In the eighth and seventh centuries B.C.E., shrines were established at Olympia for the worship of Zeus, at Delphi for Apollo, and at Corinth for Poseidon. Each shrine held athletic contests in honor of its deity, to which all Greeks were invited and for which a sacred truce was declared.

The worship of the Olympian deities did not inspire intense emotion. Most Greeks seem to have thought that civic virtue consisted of worshiping the state deities in the traditional way, performing required public services, and fighting in defense of the state. Private ethics required only that one do good to one's friends and harm to one's enemies.

symposion
The carefully organized drinking party that was the center of Greek aristocratic social life. It featured games, songs, poetry, and even philosophical disputation.

In the sixth century B.C.E., the cult and oracle of Apollo at Delphi began to exercise great influence. The priests of Apollo urged self-control and warned that arrogance (*hubris*) caused moral blindness and invited divine vengeance. Famous mottos summed up their advice: "Know thyself," and "Nothing in excess."

Later, Greeks turned to deities who were worshiped with more emotional rites. Of these, the most popular was Dionysus, a god of nature and fertility, of the grape and drunkenness, and of ecstasy and sexual abandon.

THE ALPHABET

Early Greek traders in Syria had learned craft techniques and much more from the older civilizations of the Near East. About 750 B.C.E. they borrowed a writing system from one of the Semitic scripts and added vowels to create the first true alphabet. The new Greek alphabet was easier to learn than any earlier writing system, and Greece became a widely literate society.

POETRY

Changes in sixth-century B.C.E. Greek society were reflected in a new genre of poetry, the lyric. Sappho of Lesbos, Anacreon of Teos, and Simonides of Cous wrote on personal themes, often describing the pleasure and agony of love. The most interesting poet from a political point of view was Theognis of Megara, the spokesman for the old, defeated aristocracy of birth. He divided Greeks into two classes—the noble and the base. Only nobles could aspire to virtue, for he said that only they possessed critical moral and intellectual qualities. These prejudices remained strong in aristocratic circles throughout the next century and greatly influenced later thinkers, including Plato.

The God Dionysus Dances with Two Female Followers. The vase was painted in the sixth century B.C.E.

What do the women here appear to be doing?

THE *POLEIS* AND THE PERSIAN WARS

Each *polis* developed in unique ways. Sparta and Athens, which became the two most powerful Greek states, had particularly unusual histories. The Persian Wars of the sixth century B.C.E. brought an end to the fortunate isolation and freedom of the Greek cities on the coast of Asia Minor.

HOW WERE the Greeks able to defeat the Persians?

DEVELOPMENT OF SPARTA

About 725 B.C.E., population pressure and land hunger led the Spartans to conquer their western neighbor, Messenia. The Spartans won as much land as they would ever need. Because they reduced the Messenians to serfs, or **Helots**, they no longer had to work this land themselves. About 650 B.C.E., the Helots rebelled, and the Spartans faced a turning point. To keep down the Helots, who outnumbered them perhaps ten to one, they turned their city into a permanent military academy and camp.

The new system was designed to subordinate the natural feelings of devotion to family to a more powerful commitment to the *polis*. Privacy and comfort were sacrificed to produce the best soldiers in the world. Spartan officials decided which infants, male and female, were allowed to survive. At age 7, the Spartan boy was taken from his mother and trained in athletics and the military arts. He was enrolled in the army at age 20 and lived in barracks until he was 30. He could marry but could visit his wife only by stealth. At age 30 he became a full citizen and was allowed to live in his own

Read the **Document**
Education and the Family in Sparta, ca. 100 C.E. at **myhistorylab.com**

Helots
Hereditary Spartan serfs.

QUICK REVIEW

Spartan Society

- Spartan system controlled Spartan life from birth
- At age 7 Spartan boys began military training
- Spartan girls were also indoctrinated with idea of service to the state

Spartan Warrior. A bronze statuette from Corinth showing a warrior holding a Boeotian Shield ca. 500 B.C.E.

What is emphasized in this depiction of a warrior?

Read the Document
Plutarch on Life in Sparta (1st c. B.C.E.)
at **myhistorylab.com**

See the Map
Greece and Greek Colonies of the World, ca. 431 B.C.E. at **myhistorylab.com**

Areopagus
The governing council of Athens, originally open only to the nobility. It was named after the hill on which it met.

house with his wife, although he took his meals at a public mess in the company of fifteen comrades. His simple food was provided by his own plot of land, worked for him by Helots. Only when he reached age 60 could the Spartan retire from military service.

Spartan girls were permitted greater freedom than other Greek females. Like their brothers, they were indoctrinated with the idea of service to Sparta. Nothing that might turn the mind away from duty was permitted.

Sparta was governed by two kings, a council of elders, and an assembly. The power of the kings was limited. The council of elders—twenty-eight men over age 60 who were elected for life—was consulted before any proposal was put before the assembly. The assembly, which consisted of all males over age 30, could only ratify, not debate, the decisions of magistrates, elders, and kings. Sparta also had a board of ephors, five men elected annually by the assembly. The ephors controlled foreign policy, oversaw the generalship of the kings, presided at the assembly, and guarded against rebellion by the Helots.

Suppression of the Helots required all the Spartans' effort and energy. They did not try to expand their borders, but they did force their neighbors to follow their lead in foreign affairs and supply them with troops. These alliances grew into the powerful Peloponnesian League led by Sparta. By 500 B.C.E., the Greeks had a force capable of facing mighty threats from abroad.

DEVELOPMENT OF ATHENS

In the seventh century B.C.E., Athens and the region of Attica constituted a typical aristocratic *polis*. The state was governed by the **Areopagus**, a council of nobles. Each year the council elected nine magistrates, called *archons*, who became members of the Areopagus after their year in office. A broad-based citizens' assembly represented the four tribes into which Attica's inhabitants were traditionally divided. The Areopagus, however, was the true master of the state.

Quarrels within the nobility and the beginnings of an agrarian crisis created pressure for socioeconomic change. A shift to more intensive agricultural techniques forced the less successful farmers to borrow from wealthy neighbors. Many defaulted and were enslaved for their debts. Some were sold abroad. The poor began to demand the abolition of debt and a redistribution of the land.

According to tradition, the Athenians elected the reformer Solon (ca. 639–559 B.C.E.) in 594 B.C.E. Solon immediately canceled debts, forbade debt slavery, and brought back Athenians enslaved abroad. He forbade the export of wheat, a food staple, but encouraged production of olive oil and wine for sale abroad. This nudged the Athenians toward a commercially based economy that utilized their land most efficiently for cash crops, such as olives and grapes. Solon changed the way Athens was governed. He expanded citizenship to include immigrant artisans and merchants and divided the citizenry into four classes on the basis of wealth. Only men of the wealthiest two classes could be *archons* and sit on the Areopagus. Men of the third class could be hoplites and serve on a council of 400 chosen by the assembly of all male citizens. The fourth class, the *thetes*, voted in the assembly and also sat on a new court of appeals.

Pisistratus (605?–527 B.C.E.) seized power in 546 B.C.E. and made himself the city's first tyrant. Pisistratus sought to increase the power of the central government at the expense of the nobles. He made no formal change in the institutions of government but saw to it that his supporters filled key offices. The unintended effect was to

CHRONOLOGY

KEY EVENTS IN THE EARLY HISTORY OF SPARTA AND ATHENS

ca. 725–710 B.C.E.	First Messenian War
ca. 650–625 B.C.E.	Second Messenian War
ca. 600–590 B.C.E.	Solon initiates reforms at Athens
ca. 560–550 B.C.E.	Sparta defeats Tegea: beginning of Peloponnesian League
546–527 B.C.E.	Pisistratus reigns as tyrant at Athens (main period)
510 B.C.E.	Hippias, son of Pisistratus, deposed as tyrant of Athens
ca. 508–501 B.C.E.	Clisthenes institutes reforms at Athens

give more Athenians a taste for participatory government. The tyranny ended with Pisistratus's son, Hippias (r. 527–510 B.C.E.). When his rule became harsh and unpopular, his aristocratic opponents, with Sparta's help, rallied and drove him into exile (510 B.C.E.).

Some Athenian aristocrats tried to restore the dominance they had enjoyed before Solon. Their plans were upset by Clisthenes, an aristocrat whose program won the backing of the masses. Clisthenes replaced Attica's traditional four tribes with ten new tribes composed of units drawn from all parts of Attica. The new organization increased devotion to the *polis* by weakening regional loyalties; it also deprived the nobility of their traditional power base. Clisthenes vested final authority in the assembly of all adult male Athenian citizens. Debate in the assembly was free and open; any Athenian could submit legislation, offer amendments, or argue the merits of any question.

Solon, Pisistratus, and Clisthenes put a more centralized and united Athens well on the way to prosperity and democracy by the beginning of the fifth century B.C.E.

Read the Document
Aristotle, The Creation of the Democracy in Athens at **myhistorylab.com**

THE PERSIAN WARS

Greek cities on the coast of Asia Minor came under the control first of King Croesus of Lydia (r. ca. 560–546 B.C.E.), and then in 546 B.C.E. of the powerful Persian Empire (see Chapter 4). At first, the cities of Ionia prospered under Persian rule. An ambitious tyrant of Miletus named Aristagoras, however, ended this calm. Aristagoras had urged a Persian expedition against the island of Naxos. When it failed, he tried to avoid punishment from Persia by raising a rebellion in Ionia (499 B.C.E.). He turned to the mainland Greeks for help. In 498 B.C.E., the Athenians and their allies burned Sardis, the seat of the Persian governor. But after the Athenians withdrew, the Persians reimposed their will. In 494 B.C.E. they wiped out Miletus and put down the Ionian rebellion.

WAR COMES TO GREECE

In 490 B.C.E. the Persian king, Darius (r. 521–486 B.C.E.), sent an expedition to punish Athens. Miltiades (d. 489 B.C.E.) led the Athenian army to a confrontation with the invaders at Marathon, a plain north of Athens, and won a decisive victory. For the Persians, however, Marathon was only a temporary defeat. In 481 B.C.E., Darius's successor, Xerxes (r. 486–465 B.C.E.), gathered an army of at least 150,000 men and a navy of more than 600 ships for the conquest of Greece. By then, Themistocles (ca. 525–462 B.C.E.) had become Athens's leading politician. His policies were aimed at making

A Closer Look

The Trireme

The Greeks of the Classical Period owed their prosperity and their freedom to the control of the seas that surrounded their lands, for without the navies that defeated the Persian invaders in 480–479 B.C.E. their cities would have been conquered and their distinctive civilization smothered before it had reached its peak. The key to their naval supremacy was their dominant warship, the trireme. The trireme was the combat vessel that dominated naval warfare in the Mediterranean in the fifth and fourth centuries B.C.E. The naval battles of the Persian Wars and the Peloponnesian War were fought between fleets of triremes—light, fast, and maneuverable ships powered by oars. This is a picture of the *Olympias*, a modern reconstruction of an ancient trireme, commissioned by the Greek navy.

The mast supported a sail that could help propel the ship when the wind was favorable. During battle, however, the mast was taken down, and the trireme maneuvered by oars alone.

The principal armament of the trireme was a bronze-clad ram, which extended from the keel at or below the waterline and was designed to pierce the light hulls of enemy warships. The ship also carried spearmen and bowmen who sometimes attacked enemy crews and could be landed like today's marines to fight on shore.

The trireme was propelled by 170 rowers, usually free citizens of the lower classes, in three tiers along each side of the vessel: 31 in the top tier, 27 in the middle, and 27 in the bottom. It was about 120 feet long and 18 feet wide, with a hull that was made of a thin shell of planks joined edge-to-edge and then stiffened by a keel and light transverse ribs.

Questions

1. What advantages do you think the trireme had over other kinds of warships? What disadvantages can you think of?

2. What is the significance, military and political, of having these ships rowed by free citizens?

Athens a major naval power, and by 480 B.C.E., when Xerxes invaded, Athens had more than 200 ships. It was the Athenian navy that defeated the Persians.

Darius had launched a naval attack on the Greek mainland, but Xerxes invaded by land. His huge army had to keep in touch with its fleet for supplies. Themistocles reasoned that if the Greeks could defeat the Persian navy, the Persian army would have to retreat. His strategy was to try to delay the advance of the Persian army until he could fight the kind of naval battle he might hope to win.

The Spartans led a Greek army that made a famous, but futile, attempt to block the Persian invasion at a place called Thermopylae. The fate of Greece was subsequently decided by the Athenians in a sea battle in the narrow straits to the east of the island of Salamis. When they destroyed more than half of Xerxes' fleet, he retreated to Asia with a good part of his army.

The Persian general Mardonius was left behind to continue the fight. The Spartan regent, Pausanias (d. ca. 470 B.C.E.), amassed the largest army of Greek allies yet assembled. In the summer of 479 B.C.E., the army killed Mardonius and routed the remaining Persian forces. Meanwhile, the Ionian Greeks urged King Leotychidas, the Spartan commander of the fleet, to fight the Persian fleet. At Mycale, near Samos, he destroyed the Persian camp and fleet, and the Persians withdrew from the Aegean and Ionia.

CHRONOLOGY

GREEK WARS AGAINST PERSIA

ca. 560–546 B.C.E.	Greek cities of Asia Minor conquered by Croesus of Lydia
546 B.C.E.	Cyrus of Persia conquers Lydia and gains control of Greek cities
499–494 B.C.E.	Greek cities rebel (Ionian rebellion)
490 B.C.E.	Battle of Marathon
480–479 B.C.E.	Xerxes' invasion of Greece
480 B.C.E.	Battles of Thermopylae, Artemisium, and Salamis
479 B.C.E.	Battles of Plataea and Mycale

CLASSICAL GREECE

The repulse of the Persians marked the beginning of the Classical period in Greece, 150 years of intense cultural achievement that has rarely, if ever, been matched anywhere since (see Map 3–3 on page 74). The Classical period was also a time of destructive conflicts among the *poleis* that in the end left them weakened and vulnerable.

WHAT WERE the main cultural achievements of Classical Greece?

●•●–|Read the **Document**
Herodotus, Histories (400 B.C.E.)
at **myhistorylab.com**

THE DELIAN LEAGUE

Greek unity was short-lived. Within two years of the Persian retreat, two spheres of influence emerged, one dominated by Sparta, the other by Athens. Athens, as Greece's largest naval power, was best equipped to protect the Ionian Greeks and make sure that the Persians did not return to the Aegean.

In the winter of 478–477 B.C.E., Aegean islanders, Greeks from the coast of Asia Minor, and some from other Greek cities met with Athenians on the sacred island of Delos to swear a permanent alliance under Athenian leadership. This **Delian League** kept the Persians at bay and cleared the Aegean of pirates. To create a workable system, some Greek states were forced into the league, and some that wished to resign were prevented from doing so. (See Document, "The Delian League Becomes the Athenian Empire" on page 75.) The Delian League and Athens were led at this time by a statesman and soldier named Cimon (d. 449 B.C.E.). His policy was to aggressively attack Persia while maintaining friendly relations with Sparta. He worked within the constraints of the popular democratic constitution that Clisthenes had given Athens.

Delian League
An alliance of Greek states under the leadership of Athens that was formed in 478–477 B.C.E. to resist the Persians.

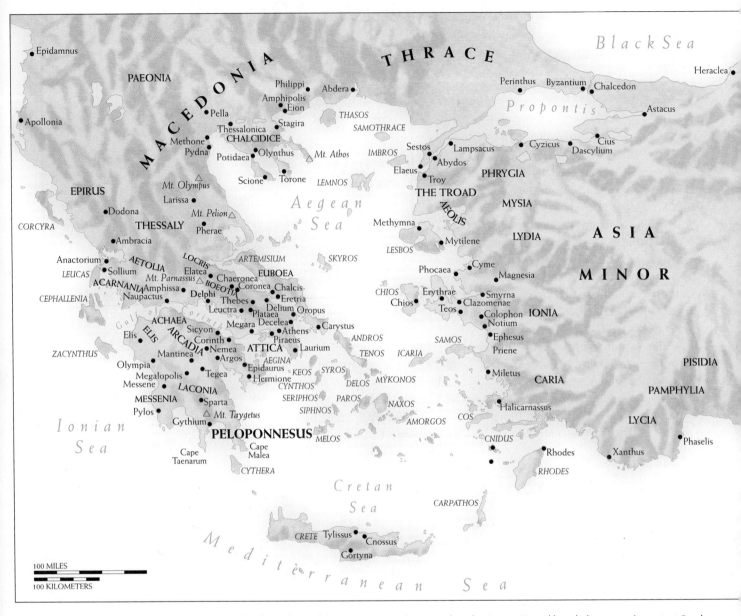

MAP 3–3. **Classical Greece.** Greece in the Classical period (ca. 480–338 B.C.E.) centered on the Aegean Sea. Although there were important Greek settlements in Italy, Sicily, and all around the Black Sea, the area shown in this general reference map embraced the vast majority of Greek states.

Why were most Greek cities located close to the sea?

THE FIRST PELOPONNESIAN WAR

In 465 B.C.E., the island of Thasos rebelled against the league. Cimon's suppression of this rebellion began the transformation of the league into an Athenian empire. Despite his success abroad, at home Cimon faced challenges from a faction that included Pericles (ca. 495–429 B.C.E.). Although Pericles was a member of a distinguished Athenian family, he wanted to increase the power of ordinary Athenians and break with the Spartans, traditional allies of some Athenian aristocrats.

In 461 B.C.E. Cimon's opponents engineered his exile, and Athens allied with Argos, Sparta's enemy in the Peloponnese. Almost overnight, Cimon's domestic and foreign policies were overturned. The policies of Athens's new regime helped incite a

DOCUMENT

The Delian League Becomes the Athenian Empire

In the years after its foundation in the winter of 478-477 B.C.E., the Delian League gradually underwent changes that finally justified calling it the Athenian Empire. In the following selection, the historian Thucydides explains why the organization changed its character.

- **WHY** did some allies choose to pay money rather than supply ships and men? Since membership in the league was originally voluntary, why did the allies refuse to meet their obligations? Who was responsible for converting a voluntary league of allies into the Athenian Empire?

The causes which led to the defections of the allies were of different kinds, the principal being their neglect to pay the tribute or to furnish ships, and, in some cases, failure of military service. For the Athenians were exacting and oppressive, using coercive measures towards men who were neither willing nor accustomed to work hard. And for various reasons they soon began to prove less agreeable leaders than at first. They no longer fought upon an equality with the rest of the confederates, and they had no difficulty in reducing them when they revolted. Now the allies brought all this upon themselves; for the majority of them disliked military service and absence from home, and so they agreed to contribute a regular sum of money instead of ships. Whereby the Athenian navy was proportionally increased, while they themselves were always untrained and unprepared for war when they revolted.

Source: Thucydides, *The Peloponnesian War*, Vol. 1, trans, by Benjamin Jowett, in *The Greek Historians*, ed. by F. R. B. Godolphin (New York: Random House, 1942), p. 609.

---

conflict with Sparta known as the First **Peloponnesian War**. The Athenians made great gains during the war's early years. They seemed invulnerable, winning control of some neighboring states and dominating the sea.

In 454 B.C.E., however, the tide turned. An Athenian fleet, which was dispatched to help the Egyptians rebel against Persia, was destroyed, and revolts broke out within the Delian League. Athens agreed to a peace of thirty years with Sparta. Greece was divided into two blocs: Sparta and its allies on the mainland, and Athens and what had become its empire in the Aegean.

THE ATHENIAN EMPIRE AND DEMOCRACY

The Athenians moved the Delian League's treasury from Delos to Athens and began to keep one-sixtieth of the league's annual revenues for themselves. Athens gave up the pretext of being the leader of a free alliance; the league was now the Athenian Empire, the key to Athens's prosperity and security.

While the Athenians tightened their control over their subjects, they expanded democracy for themselves at home. Under the leadership of Pericles, they evolved the freest government the world had yet seen. Property qualifications for offices were removed, opening all offices to all adult male citizens. Pericles introduced pay for jury service, which

Peloponnesian Wars

The protracted struggle between Athens and Sparta to dominate Greece between 465 and Athens's final defeat in 404 B.C.E.

CHRONOLOGY

KEY EVENTS IN ATHENIAN HISTORY BETWEEN THE PERSIAN WAR AND THE GREAT PELOPONNESIAN WAR

478–477 B.C.E.	Delian League founded
ca. 474–462 B.C.E.	Cimon leading politician
467 B.C.E.	Victory over Persians at Eurymedon River
465–463 B.C.E.	Rebellion of Thasos
462 B.C.E.	Ephialtes murdered; Pericles rises to leadership
461 B.C.E.	Cimon ostracized
461 B.C.E.	Reform of Areopagus
ca. 460 B.C.E.	First Peloponnesian War begins
454 B.C.E.	Athens defeated in Egypt; crisis in the Delian League
449 B.C.E.	Peace with Persia
445 B.C.E.	Thirty Years' Peace ends First Peloponnesian War

allowed the poor to take time off from work to serve. Judges traveled circuits to provide swift impartial justice for the poor who were living in the countryside. As the privileges of Athenian citizenship grew, however, access to citizenship was sharply restricted. Only those who had two citizen parents could claim what had become a valuable commodity.

Athens was governed as a direct democracy. Every political decision had to be approved by the popular assembly—the people themselves, not their representatives. Every judicial decision was subject to appeal to a popular court chosen from the Athenian male population. Many officials were selected by lot, which made class irrelevant. Elected officials generally continued to be members of noble families and were almost always rich men, but the people were free to choose whomever they wanted. All public officials could be removed from office and were held to a compulsory accounting at the end of their terms. There was no standing army; no police force; and no way to coerce the people.

Pericles was elected to the generalship (a military office with important political influence) fifteen years in a row and thirty times in all. After the First Peloponnesian War, he instituted a conservative policy designed to preserve the empire in the Aegean and peace with Sparta.

WOMEN OF ATHENS

Greek society was dominated by men, and Athenian democracy did nothing to change that. Women were excluded from most aspects of public life. They could not vote, take part in political assemblies, or hold office. Their only public function—an important one—was participation in certain rituals and festivals of the state religion.

In private life, women were always under the control of a male guardian—a father, husband, or relative. Women married young, usually between the ages of 12 and 18, whereas men typically did not marry until the age of 30. Marriages were arranged. To obtain a divorce, a woman needed the approval of a male relative.

The main function of an Athenian woman of a citizen family was to produce male heirs for her husband's household (*oikos*). Because the pure and legitimate lineage of offspring was important for ensuring transmission of rights to citizenship, women were segregated from men outside the family and confined to women's quarters in their homes. Men spent most of their time outside the home and were free to seek whatever sexual gratification they wanted.

The role played by Athenian women may have been more complex than their legal status suggests, for myths, pictorial art, and the tragedies and comedies performed at Athenian religious festivals often feature women as central characters and powerful figures in both the public and the private spheres.

THE GREAT PELOPONNESIAN WAR

The Thirty Years' Peace of 445 B.C.E. only lasted ten years. About 435 B.C.E., Athens and Sparta plunged back into conflict. This new war, long and disastrous, shook the foundations of Greek civilization.

The Spartan strategy was traditional: to invade the enemy's country and threaten the crops, forcing the enemy to defend them in a hoplite battle. The Athenian strategy was to retreat to their impregnable city, allow the devastation of their land, and raid the Peloponnesian coast to put pressure on Sparta by harassing its allies. The

QUICK REVIEW

Athenian Women

- Greek society was dominated by men
- Women were always under control of a male guardian
- Main function of Athenian women was to produce male heirs

CHRONOLOGY

THE GREAT PELOPONNESIAN WAR

435 B.C.E.	Civil war at Epidamnus
432 B.C.E.	Sparta declares war on Athens
431 B.C.E.	Peloponnesian invasion of Athens
421 B.C.E.	Peace of Nicias
415–413 B.C.E.	Athenian invasion of Sicily
405 B.C.E.	Battle of Aegospotami
404 B.C.E.	Athens surrenders

●◆●─ Read the Document
The Peloponnesian War
at **myhistorylab.com**

OVERVIEW Greek Civilization

Historians divide ancient Greek civilization into periods marked by different forms of social and political organizations and by significant cultural achievements.

Minoan Based on the island of Crete, ca. 2900–1150 B.C.E., sea-based power, probably ruled by kings. Palace architecture, vivid frescoes.

Mycenaean Mainland Greece, ca. 1600–1150 B.C.E., city-states ruled by powerful kings assisted by an elaborate bureaucracy. Monumental architecture, gold- and bronzework.

Archaic Colonization from Greece to Asia Minor, southern Italy, and the coasts of the Black Sea, 700–500 B.C.E. Characteristic form of government was the *polis*, a city-state dominated by landholding aristocrats or ruled by tyrants. Lyric poetry, natural philosophy.

Classical Golden age of Athenian civilization, fifth century B.C.E. Athens and other *poleis* became much more democratic. Drama, sculpture in marble and bronze, architecture (the Acropolis), philosophy, history.

Hellenistic Conquests of Alexander the Great (356–323 B.C.E.) spread Greek culture to Egypt and as far east as the Indus Valley. Decline of the *polis*. Domination of the Greek world by large monarchical states. Stoic and Epicurean philosophy, realistic sculpture, advances in mathematics and science.

Athenian plan required restraint, which was abandoned after Pericles died in 429 B.C.E. After ten years of fruitless fighting, the war ended in stalemate.

In 415 B.C.E., Alcibiades (ca. 450–404 B.C.E.), a young and ambitious kinsman of Pericles, persuaded the Athenians to invade Sicily. When the entire expedition was destroyed, Athens's power and prestige were greatly diminished. Subjects of Athens's empire rebelled, and Sparta reopened the war—with Persian aid.

The Athenians fought on and won several important victories at sea, but their resources steadily diminished. When their fleet was destroyed at Aegospotami in 405 B.C.E., they could not rebuild it. The Spartans, under Lysander (d. 395 B.C.E.), blockaded Athens and cut off its food supply. In 404 B.C.E., Athens surrendered unconditionally.

STRUGGLE FOR GREEK LEADERSHIP

The collapse of the Athenian Empire opened the way for Spartan dominance of the Aegean. Lysander installed boards of ten local oligarchs loyal to him and supported by Spartan garrisons in most of the cities along the European coast and the islands of the Aegean. These tributaries brought Sparta almost as much revenue as the Athenians had collected.

Some of Sparta's allies, especially Thebes and Corinth, were alienated by Sparta's increasingly arrogant policies. The oligarchic government that Lysander installed in Athens in 404 B.C.E. came to be called the "Thirty Tyrants" by Athenians who resented its heavy-handed policies. When supporters of democracy fled to Thebes and Corinth and recruited an army to challenge the oligarchs' hold on Athens, Sparta's conservative king, Pausanias, arranged a peaceful settlement and the restoration of democracy. Thereafter, Athenian foreign policy remained under Spartan control, but otherwise Athens was free.

In 405 B.C.E. Greek mercenaries recruited with Spartan help intervened in Persia on behalf of Cyrus the Younger, who was contesting the accession to the Persian throne of his brother Artaxerxes II (r. 404–358 B.C.E.). The Greeks marched inland to

((•—[**Hear** the **Audio**

The Persian and Peloponnesian War 492–404 B.C.E. at **myhistorylab.com**

((•—[**Hear** the **Audio**
at **myhistorylab.com**

View the Image
The Parthenon at **myhistorylab.com**

Read the Document
Greece and Persia: The Treaty of
Antalcides, 387 B.C.E.
at **myhistorylab.com**

Study and Review
Comparing Athens and Sparta
(5th century B.C.E.) at **myhistorylab.com**

Mesopotamia, defeating the Persians at Cunaxa in 401 B.C.E. Cyrus was killed, however, and the Greeks marched back to the Black Sea and safety. Their success revealed the potential weakness of the Persian Empire.

The Greeks of Asia Minor had supported Cyrus and were now afraid of Artaxerxes' revenge. The Spartans accepted their request for aid and sent an army into Asia, attracted by the prospect of prestige, power, and money. In 396 B.C.E. the command of this army was given to Sparta's new king, Agesilaus (444–360 B.C.E.), whose aggressive policy was to dominate Sparta until his death.

The Persians responded to Agesilaus's plundering army by seeking assistance among Greek states disaffected with Spartan domination, offering them money and other support. Thebes forged an alliance with Argos, Corinth, and Athens and engaged Sparta in the Corinthian War (395–387 B.C.E.), ending Sparta's Asian adventure. In 394 B.C.E. the Persian fleet destroyed Sparta's maritime empire. Athens, meanwhile, had rebuilt its walls, resurrected its navy, and recovered some of its lost empire. The Persians, who dictated the terms of the peace that ended the Corinthian War to the exhausted Greeks, were alarmed by this Athenian recovery and turned the management of Greece over to Sparta.

Sparta's actions grew increasingly arrogant and lawless. Agesilaus broke up all alliances except the Peloponnesian League and put friends in power in several Greek cities. In 382 B.C.E. Sparta seized Thebes during peacetime without warning or pretext. In 379 B.C.E. a Spartan army made a similar attempt on Athens. That action persuaded the Athenians to join with Thebes, which had rebelled from Sparta a few months earlier. In 371 B.C.E. the Thebans defeated the Spartans at Leuctra. They then encouraged the Arcadian cities of the central Peloponnesus to form a federal league and freed the Helots, helping them found a city of their own. Sparta's population had been shrinking so that it could field an army of fewer than 2,000 men at Leuctra. Now, hemmed in by hostile neighbors, deprived of much of its farmland and of the slaves who had worked it, Sparta ceased to be a first-rank power. Its aggressive policies had led to ruin.

For a short time, Thebes held power, thanks to its democratic constitution, its control over Boeotia, and two outstanding generals, Pelopidas (d. 364 B.C.E.) and Epaminondas (d. 362 B.C.E.). Under their leadership Thebes challenged the reborn Athenian Empire in the Aegean. But by 362 B.C.E. Thebes faced a Peloponnesian coalition as well as Athens. When Epaminondas was killed in battle, Theban dominance came to an end.

In 378 B.C.E. Athens organized a second confederation aimed at resisting Spartan aggression in the Aegean. The collapse of Sparta and Thebes removed the rationale for membership, so Athens's allies revolted. By 355 B.C.E. Athens had to abandon most of the empire. After two centuries of almost constant warfare, the Greeks returned to the chaotic disorganization that had characterized the era before the founding of the Peloponnesian League.

CLASSICAL CULTURE

The term *classical* often suggests calm and serenity, but the word that best describes Greek life, thought, art, and literature during the Classical period is *tension*. Among the achievements of this era (discussed in Chapter 2) were the philosophical works

CHRONOLOGY

SPARTAN AND THEBAN HEGEMONIES

404–403 B.C.E.	Thirty Tyrants rule at Athens
401 B.C.E.	Expedition of Cyrus, rebellious prince of Persia; Battle of Cunaxa
400–387 B.C.E.	Spartan War against Persia
398–360 B.C.E.	Reign of Agesilaus at Sparta
395–387 B.C.E.	Corinthian War
382 B.C.E.	Sparta seizes Thebes
378 B.C.E.	Second Athenian Confederation founded
371 B.C.E.	Thebans defeat Sparta at Leuctra; end of Spartan hegemony
362 B.C.E.	Battle of Mantinea; end of Theban hegemony

The Acropolis. It was both the religious and civic center of Athens. In its final form it is the work of Pericles and his successors in the late fifth century B.C.E. This photograph shows the Parthenon and, to its left, the Erechtheum.
Meredith Pillon, Greek National Tourism Organization.

What other buildings in the world do the buildings pictured here remind you of? Why do you think there is a resemblance?

of Socrates (469–399 B.C.E.), Plato (ca. 427–347 B.C.E.), and Aristotle (384–322 B.C.E.). The same curiosity about the nature and place in the universe of human beings that motivated the philosophers also animated the arts of the period.

Two sources of tension contributed to the artistic outpouring of fifth century B.C.E. Greece. One was the conflict between the Greeks' pride in their accomplishments and their concern that overreaching would bring retribution. The second was the conflict between the hopes and achievements of individuals and the claims and limits put on them by their fellow citizens in the *polis*. These tensions were felt throughout Greece. They had the most spectacular consequences, however, in Athens in its Golden Age between the Persian and Peloponnesian wars.

Nothing reflects these concerns better than Attic (Athenian) tragedy, which emerged in the fifth century B.C.E. The tragedies were selected in a contest and presented in a large theater as part of public religious observations in honor of the god Dionysus. Most Attic tragedy was based on mythological subjects and dealt solemnly with religion, politics, ethics, or morality. The plays of the dramatists Aeschylus (525–456 B.C.E.) and Sophocles (ca. 496–406 B.C.E.) follow this pattern. The later plays of Euripides (ca. 480–406 B.C.E.) are more concerned with individual psychology.

Comedy was introduced into the Dionysian festival early in the fifth century B.C.E. The great master of the genre called Old Comedy, Aristophanes (ca. 450–385 B.C.E.), wrote political comedies filled with scathing invective and political satire.

Beginning in 448 B.C.E., Pericles undertook a great building program on the Acropolis with funds from the empire. The new buildings visually projected Athenian greatness, emphasizing the city's intellectual and artistic achievements and providing tangible proof that Athens was the intellectual center of Greece.

The first prose history ever written was a description of the Persian War by Herodotus (ca. 484–ca. 425 B.C.E.), "the father of history." His account attempts to explain human actions and draw instruction from them. He claimed that the Greek *polis* inspired voluntary obedience to the law in its citizen soldiers, whereas fear of punishment motivated the Persians.

Thucydides, the historian of the Peloponnesian War, was born about 460 B.C.E. and died about 400 B.C.E. He believed that human nature was essentially unchanging, so that a wise person, equipped with an understanding of history, might foresee events and guide them.

As the power of the *poleis* waned after the Great Peloponnesian War, some Greeks tried to shore up its weakening institutions. Others looked for radical alternatives; and still others turned their back on public life altogether. All these attitudes are reflected in the literature, philosophy, and art of the period.

View the Image
The Athenian Acropolis at **myhistorylab.com**

Read the Document
Antigone (442 B.C.E.) and Drama: Antigone, by Sophocles, ca. 441 B.C.E. and Sophocles, from Antigone at **myhistorylab.com**

The tendency to forsake the public for the private sphere is clear in a new genre that emerged in the fourth century B.C.E.: Middle Comedy. Old Comedy had dealt amusingly with serious subjects, but the themes of Middle Comedy were ordinary daily life, intrigue, and domestic satire. This tendency was magnified in New Comedy, which focused entirely on domestic scenes, the foibles of ordinary people, and the travails of lovers. The art of tragedy declined, but the great works of the previous century were revived, and Euripides, who had explored the psyches of individual characters, found his most appreciative audiences.

Fourth-century sculpture reflects the same movement away from the grand, the ideal, and the general toward the ordinary, the real, and the individual.

EMERGENCE OF THE HELLENISTIC WORLD

WHY DID Alexander the Great become an almost mythological figure?

The term *Hellenistic* was coined in the nineteenth century to describe a period of three centuries during which Greek culture spread from its homeland to Egypt and far into Asia. The result was a new civilization that combined Greek and Asian elements. The Hellenistic world was larger than the world of classical Greece, and its major political units were much larger than the *poleis*, although these endured in modified forms. Hellenistic civilization had its roots in the rise to power of a dynasty in Macedonia whose armies conquered Greece and the Persian Empire in the space of two generations.

MACEDONIAN CONQUEST

The kingdom of Macedon, north of Thessaly, had long served as a buffer between the Greek states and barbarian tribes farther to the north. The Macedonians were of the same stock as the Greeks and spoke a Greek dialect. By Greek standards, however, Macedon was semibarbaric. Constant internal conflict prevented Macedon from playing much of a part in Greek affairs up to the fourth century B.C.E., but once Macedon was unified under a strong king, that changed.

Philip II of Macedon (r. 359–336 B.C.E.), like many of his predecessors, admired Greek culture. He was talented in war and diplomacy and had boundless ambition. After he won control of a lucrative gold and silver mining region, he used his resources to turn his army into the finest fighting force in the world.

In 340 B.C.E., Philip besieged Perinthus and Byzantium, the lifeline of Athenian commerce. The Athenian fleet saved both cities, so Philip instead marched directly into Greece, and in 338 B.C.E., he defeated Athens and Thebes in Boeotia. Freedom and autonomy ended for the Greek *polis*. *Poleis* retained their institutions and control over their internal affairs for some time, but new political realities began to chart Greece's future.

ALEXANDER'S CONQUESTS

Philip was assassinated in 336 B.C.E., as he prepared to invade Persia. Philip's son, Alexander III (356–323 B.C.E.), later called Alexander the Great, succeeded his father at the age of 20 and inherited his plans for the conquest of Persia.

CHRONOLOGY

RISE OF MACEDON

359–336 B.C.E.	Reign of Philip II
338 B.C.E.	Battle of Chaeronea; Philip conquers Greece; founding of League of Corinth
336–323 B.C.E.	Reign of Alexander III, the Great
334 B.C.E.	Alexander invades Asia
333 B.C.E.	Battle of Issus
331 B.C.E.	Battle of Gaugamela
330 B.C.E.	Fall of Persepolis
327 B.C.E.	Alexander reaches Indus valley
323 B.C.E.	Death of Alexander

The usurper Cyrus and his Greek mercenaries had shown the vast and wealthy Persian Empire to be vulnerable when they penetrated deep into its interior early in the fourth century B.C.E. In 334 B.C.E. Alexander crossed the Hellespont into Asia. His army consisted of about 30,000 infantry and 5,000 cavalry; he had no navy and little money. Consequently he sought quick and decisive battles to gain money and supplies from the conquered territory. To neutralize the Persian navy he moved along the coast, depriving it of ports.

Alexander met the Persian forces of Asia Minor at the Granicus River (see Map 3–4 on page 82), where he won a smashing victory in characteristic style: He led a cavalry charge across the river into the teeth of the enemy on the opposite bank, almost losing his life in the process and winning the devotion of his soldiers. With the coast of Asia Minor now open, Alexander captured the coastal cities, denying them to the Persian fleet.

In 333 B.C.E. Alexander marched inland to Syria, meeting the main Persian army under King Darius III (r. 336–330 B.C.E.) at Issus. Alexander himself led the cavalry charge that broke the Persian line and sent Darius fleeing to the east. Alexander continued along the coast and captured previously impregnable Tyre after a long and ingenious siege, putting an end to the threat of the Persian navy. He took Egypt with little trouble and was greeted as liberator, pharaoh, and son of the Egyptian god Re. While Alexander was at Tyre, Darius offered him his daughter and his entire empire west of the Euphrates River in exchange for an alliance and an end to the invasion. But Alexander wanted the whole empire and probably whatever lay beyond that.

In the spring of 331 B.C.E. Alexander marched into Mesopotamia. At Gaugamela, near the ancient Assyrian city of Nineveh, he met Darius, ready for a last stand. Once again, Alexander's tactical genius and personal leadership carried the day. The Persians were broken and Darius fled once more. Alexander entered Babylon, again hailed as liberator and king. In January of 330 B.C.E. he came to Persepolis, the Persian capital, which held splendid palaces and the royal treasury. This bonanza ended his financial troubles and put a vast sum of money into circulation, with economic consequences that lasted for centuries. After a stay of several months, Alexander burned Persepolis to dramatize the destruction of the native Persian Dynasty and the completion of Hellenic revenge for the earlier Persian invasion of Greece.

Setting off after Darius, Alexander found him, dead, just south of the Caspian Sea. He had been murdered and replaced by his relative Bessus, with the support of the Persian nobility. Alexander soon captured Bessus. This pursuit, and his own great curiosity and desire to see the most distant places, took Alexander to the frontier of India.

Near Samarkand, in the land of the Scythians, he founded the city of Alexandria Eschate ("Furthest Alexandria"), one of the many cities bearing his name that he founded as he traveled. As a part of his grand scheme of amalgamation and conquest, he married the Bactrian princess Roxane and enrolled 30,000 young Bactrians to be trained for his army.

In 327 B.C.E. Alexander took his army through the Khyber Pass to conquer the lands around the Indus River (modern Pakistan). Reducing the region's king, Porus, to

Alexander and Darius. King Darius III looks back in distress as Alexander advances against his vanguard during the battle of Issus, as depicted in a Roman mosaic from the first century B.C.E.

Do you think a Persian king with a different personality could have resisted Alexander?

•••⟊ **Read** the **Document**

Plutarch on Alexander the Great (1st century B.C.E.) at **myhistorylab.com**

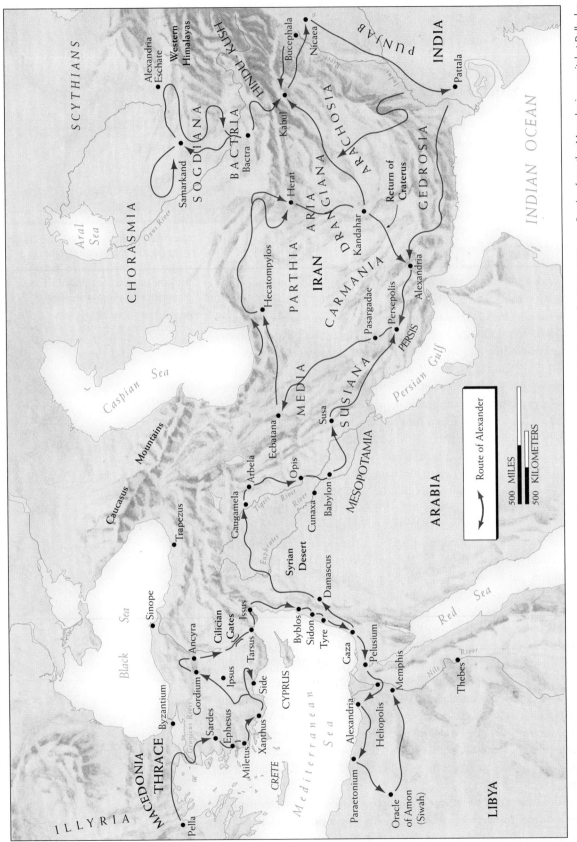

MAP 3–4. Alexander's Campaigns. The route taken by Alexander the Great in his conquest of the Persian Empire, 334–323 B.C.E. Starting from the Macedonian capital at Pella, he reached the Indus valley before being turned back by his own restive troops. He died of fever in Mesopotamia.

What are some factors that contributed to the breaking up of Alexander's empire after his death?

vassalage, he pushed on in the hope of reaching the river called Ocean that the Greeks believed encircled the world. Finally his weary men refused to go on. By the spring of 324 B.C.E. the army was back at the Persian Gulf, celebrating Macedonian style with a wild spree of drinking.

DEATH OF ALEXANDER

Alexander had great plans for the future: for the consolidation and organization of his empire; for geographic exploration; for new cities, roads, and harbors; perhaps even for further conquests in the West. There is some evidence that he asked to be deified and worshiped as a god. But in June 323 B.C.E. he got sick and died in Babylon at the age of 33. He quickly entered myth and legend, and a debate began about his goals, his personality, and his achievements that has continued to the present day.

Alexander was childless, and he made no arrangements for a successor. After prolonged warfare, three of his generals founded dynasties that continued the spread of Hellenistic culture:

- Ptolemy I, ca. 367–283 B.C.E.; founder of the Thirty-First Dynasty in Egypt, the Ptolemies, of whom Cleopatra, who died in 30 B.C.E., was the last
- Seleucus I, ca. 358–280 B.C.E.; founder of the Seleucid Dynasty in Mesopotamia
- Antigonus I, 382–301 B.C.E.; founder of the Antigonid Dynasty in Asia Minor and Macedon

For seventy-five years or so, the world ruled by Alexander's successors enjoyed prosperity. The vast sums of money he and they had put into circulation increased economic activity. The opening of vast new territories to Greek trade and the increased demand for Greek products helped stimulate commerce. The new prosperity, however, was not evenly distributed. The urban Greeks, the Macedonians, and the Hellenized natives who made up the upper and middle classes lived in comfort and even luxury, but native peasants did not.

Eventually, war and inflation produced economic crises. The kings bore down heavily, but the middle classes skillfully avoided their exactions, and peasants and city laborers reacted by slowing work and striking. In Greece, economic pressures led to civil wars. These internal difficulties made the Hellenistic kingdoms vulnerable to attack, and by the middle of the second century B.C.E. Rome had absorbed all of them except for Egypt. The two centuries of Hellenistic rule had, however, promoted economic and cultural cohesion throughout the eastern Mediterranean coast, Greece, Egypt, Mesopotamia, and the old Persian Empire.

HELLENISTIC CULTURE

Alexander's conquests and the establishment of the successor kingdoms, by ending the central role of the *polis* in Greek life and thought, marked a significant turning point in Greek literature, philosophy, religion, and art.

Deprived of control of their foreign affairs, their important internal arrangements determined by a foreign monarch, the postclassical cities lost the kind of political freedom that was basic to the old outlook. They were cities, but not *poleis*. As time passed they lost their sovereignty, becoming municipalities within military empires. For the most part, the Greeks after Alexander turned inward, away from politics, to address their hopes and fears. The confident, sometimes arrogant, humanism of the fifth century B.C.E. gave way to a kind of resignation to fate, a recognition of helplessness before forces too great for humans to manage.

QUICK REVIEW

Alexander's Leadership

- Alexander displayed tactical genius in military conflict
- Alexander's charisma attracted followers
- Marriage to a Bactrian princess exemplified Alexander's policies for integrating conquered peoples
- Alexander died without an heir or a plan for his successor

•→ Read the Document
Descriptions of Alexandria, Egypt (1st century C.E.) at **myhistorylab.com**

⊙→ See the Map
The Conquests of Alexander the Great at **myhistorylab.com**

HOW DID the Hellenistic world influence Western culture?

PHILOSOPHY

These developments are noticeable in the changes that overtook the established schools of philosophy as well as in the emergence of two new and influential groups of philosophers, the Epicureans and the Stoics.

Plato's Academy and Aristotle's Lyceum (see Chapter 2) continued to operate, reinforcing Athens's position as the center of philosophical studies. The Lyceum turned gradually away from Aristotle's universal investigations to become a center of literary and historical studies. The Academy turned even further from its founder's tradition, adopting the philosophical approach known as skepticism, established by Pyrrho of Elis (ca. 365–275 B.C.E.). The Skeptics thought that nothing could be known and so consoled themselves by suggesting that nothing mattered. It was easy for them, therefore, to accept conventional morality and the world as it was. The Cynics continued to denounce convention and to advocate a crude life in accordance with nature. Neither of these views had much appeal to the middle-class city dweller of the third century B.C.E., who sought some basis for choosing a way of life now that the *polis* no longer provided one ready-made.

Epicurus of Athens (342–271 B.C.E.), who founded a school in that city in 306 B.C.E., formulated a philosophy in keeping with the new mood. The goal of this philosophy was not knowledge but happiness, which Epicurus believed could be achieved through a life based on reason. Accepting the description of the physical universe proposed by the atomists Democritus and Leucippus (see Chapter 2), the **Epicureans** took sense perception to be the basis of all human knowledge. According to Epicurus, atoms were continually falling through the void and giving off images in direct contact with the senses. These falling atoms could swerve in an arbitrary, unpredictable way to produce the combinations seen in the world. When a person died, the atoms that composed the body dispersed so that the person had no further existence or perception and therefore nothing to fear after death. The gods, according to Epicurus, took no interest in human affairs. This belief amounted to a practical atheism, and the Epicureans were often thought to be atheists.

The purpose of Epicurean physics was to liberate people from the fear of death, the gods, and the supernatural. Epicurean ethics were hedonistic, identifying happiness with pleasure. But *pleasure* for Epicurus was chiefly negative: the absence of pain and trouble. The goal of the Epicureans was *ataraxia*, the condition of being undisturbed, without trouble, pain, or responsibility. To achieve it, one should ideally have sufficient means to withdraw from worldly affairs; Epicurus even advised against marriage and children. He preached a life of genteel, restrained selfishness, which might appeal to intellectuals of means but was not calculated to be widely attractive.

The Stoic school, established by Zeno of Citium (335–263 B.C.E.) soon after Epicurus began teaching, took its name from the Stoa Poikile, or Painted Portico, in the Athenian Agora, where Zeno and his disciples met. Like the Epicureans, the **Stoics** sought the happiness of the individual; but unlike Epicurean philosophy, Stoic philosophy was almost indistinguishable from religion. The Stoics believed that god and nature are the same and that humans must live in harmony within themselves and with nature. The guiding principle in nature is divine reason, (**logos**), or fire. Every human has a spark of this divinity, and after death it returns to the eternal Divine

One of the Masterpieces of Hellenistic Sculpture, the *Laocoön.* This is a Roman copy. According to legend, Laocoön was a priest who warned the Trojans not to take the Greeks' wooden horse within their city. This sculpture depicts his punishment. Great serpents sent by the goddess Athena, who was on the side of the Greeks, devoured Laocoön and his sons before the horrified people of Troy.

Laocoön, Vatican Museums, Vatican State. Copyright Giraudon/Art Resource, New York.

What message do you think a viewer was meant to take from looking at this statue?

Epicureans
School of philosophy founded by Epicurus of Athens (342–271 B.C.E.). It sought to liberate people from fear of death and the supernatural by teaching that the gods took no interest in human affairs and that true happiness consisted in pleasure, which was defined as the absence of pain.

Stoics
A philosophical school founded by Zeno of Citium (335–263 B.C.E.) that taught that humans could be happy only with natural law.

logos Divine reason, or fire, which according to the Stoics, was the guiding principle in nature.

Spirit. From time to time the world is destroyed by fire, from the ashes of which a new world arises.

Human happiness, according to the Stoics, lies in the virtuous life, lived in accordance with natural law, in which "all actions promote the harmony of the spirit dwelling in the individual man with the will of him who orders the universe."

Only the wise—who know what is good, what is evil, and what is "indifferent"—can live such a life. Good and evil are dispositions of the mind or soul. Thus prudence, justice, courage, and temperance are good, whereas folly, injustice, and cowardice are evil. Life, health, pleasure, beauty, strength, wealth, and so on are neutral—morally "indifferent." The source of misery is passion, a disease of the soul and an irrational mental contraction that arises from morally indifferent things. The goal of the wise is *apatheia*, or freedom from passion.

With their striving for inner harmony and a life lived in accordance with the Divine Will, their fatalistic attitude, and their goal a form of apathy, the Stoics fit the post-Alexandrian world well. The spread of Stoicism eased the creation of a new political system that relied on the docile submission, not the active participation, of the governed.

LITERATURE

The literary center of the Hellenistic world in the third and second centuries B.C.E. was Alexandria, Egypt. There, Egypt's Hellenistic rulers, the Ptolemies, had founded a museum—a great research institute where royal funds supported scientists and scholars—and a library with almost half a million books. The library housed much of the great body of past Greek literature, most of which has since been lost. Alexandrian scholars had what they judged to be the best works copied, editing and criticizing them from the point of view of language, form, and content, and writing biographies of the authors. It is to this work that we owe the preservation of most of what remains to us of ancient literature.

The scholarly atmosphere of Alexandria stimulated the study of history and its ancillary discipline, chronology. Eratosthenes (ca. 275–195 B.C.E.) developed a chronology of important events since the Trojan War, and others undertook similar tasks. Contemporaries of Alexander, such as Ptolemy I (d. 284 B.C.E.), Aristobulus, and Nearchus, wrote apparently sober, factual accounts of his career. The fragments we have of the work of most Hellenistic historians suggest that they emphasized sensational and biographical detail over the rigorous, impersonal analysis characteristic of Thucydides.

ARCHITECTURE AND SCULPTURE

The Hellenistic monarchies greatly increased the opportunities open to architects and sculptors. Money was plentiful, rulers sought outlets for conspicuous display, new cities needed to be built and beautified, and the well-to-do created an increasing demand for objects of art. New cities were usually laid out on the grid plan introduced in the fifth century B.C.E. by Hippodamus of Miletus. Temples were built on the classical model, and the covered portico, or *stoa*, became a very popular addition to Hellenistic agoras.

Reflecting the cosmopolitan nature of the Hellenistic world, leading sculptors accepted commissions wherever they were attractive. The result was a certain uniformity, although Alexandria, Rhodes, and the kingdom of Pergamum in Asia Minor developed distinctive styles. In general, Hellenistic sculpture continued the trend that emerged in the fourth century B.C.E. toward the sentimental, emotional, and realistic

●◦●—[Read the Document

The Conquests of Alexander the Great (1st century B.C.E.) at **myhistorylab.com**

A Page from *On Floating Bodies*.
Archimedes' work was covered by a tenth-century manuscript, but ultraviolet radiation reveals the original text and drawings underneath.

What scientific documents from our time do you think will be preserved?

and away from the balanced tension and idealism of the fifth century B.C.E. The characteristics of Hellenistic sculpture are readily apparent in the *Laocoön*, carved at Rhodes in the second century B.C.E.

MATHEMATICS AND SCIENCE

Among the most spectacular intellectual accomplishments of the Hellenistic Age were those in mathematics and science. Indeed, Alexandrian scholars were responsible for most of the scientific knowledge available to the West until the scientific revolution of the sixteenth and seventeenth centuries C.E.

Euclid's *Elements* (written early in the third century B.C.E.) is still the foundation for courses in plane and solid geometry. Archimedes of Syracuse (ca. 287–212 B.C.E.), who also made advances in geometry, established the theory of the lever in mechanics and invented hydrostatics.

Advances in mathematics, when applied to Babylonian astronomical tables available to Hellenistic scholars, spurred great progress in astronomy. As early as the fourth century B.C.E. Heraclides of Pontus (ca. 390–310 B.C.E.) had argued that Mercury and Venus circulate around the sun and not the Earth. He appears to have made other suggestions leading in the direction of a **heliocentric theory** of the universe. Aristarchus of Samos (ca. 310–230 B.C.E.) asserted that the sun, along with the other fixed stars, did not move and that the Earth revolved around the sun in a circular orbit and rotated on its axis while doing so. The heliocentric theory, however, did not take hold. Hipparchus of Nicaea (b. ca. 190 B.C.E.) constructed an ingenious and complicated geocentric model of the universe that did a good job of accounting for the movements of the sun, the moon, and the planets. Ptolemy of Alexandria (second century C.E.) adopted Hipparchus's system with a few improvements, and it remained dominant until the work of Copernicus, in the sixteenth century C.E.

Hellenistic scientists made progress in mapping the Earth as well as the sky. Eratosthenes of Cyrene (ca. 275–195 B.C.E.) accurately calculated the circumference of the Earth and wrote a treatise on geography based on mathematical and physical reasoning and the reports of travelers. Eratosthenes' map was in many ways more accurate than a later one, created by Ptolemy, which became standard during the Middle Ages.

heliocentric theory

The theory, now universally accepted, that the Earth and the other planets revolve around the sun. First proposed by Aristarchos of Samos (310–230 B.C.E.).

SUMMARY

WHAT WERE the defining qualities of Minoan, Mycenaean, and Homeric Greek society?

Minoans, Mycenaeans, and Greek "Middle Age" to ca. 750 B.C.E. In the Minoan and Mycenaean periods, the Greek states were ruled by powerful kings supported by elaborate bureaucracies. The Mycenaean culture was militaristic, in contrast to that of the Minoans. Invaders

from the north destroyed Mycenaean civilization around 1150 B.C.E. Homer's epic poems describe a society that emphasized honor. *page 60*

WHY WAS the *polis* the most characteristic Greek institution?

The *Polis* in the Expanding Greek World. By 750 B.C.E., during the Archaic period, Greek society took its characteristic form: the *polid* (plural *poleis*), a self-governing city-state. The Greek innovations that continue to influence our world, including democracy and Greek philosophy, developed in the *poleis*. The most important *poleis* were Athens and Sparta. At first governed by landowning aristocrats, then by tyrants, many *poleis* evolved more democratic forms of government by 500 B.C.E. In an effort to avoid the pressures of overpopulation and land hunger, the Greeks established colonies around the shores of the Mediterranean and Black seas. *page 64*

 WHAT FEATURES distinguished Archaic Greek society?

Life in Archaic Greece. Most Greeks were hardworking farmers, a way of life described by Hesiod. The Greeks were polytheists who worshiped a pantheon of twelve gods. Cults gained importance. Literacy and poetry were important elements of Archaic culture. *page 67*

 HOW WERE the Greeks able to defeat the Persians?

Sparta and Athens. The policies and conflicts of Greece's two most significant *poleis*, Sparta and Athens, shaped Greek history. Alliances and military actions—the Persian War, the Peloponnesian Wars, and other conflicts—interacted with the internal politics and the social development of Greek states. Naval battles were decisive in defeating the Persians. *page 69*

 WHAT WERE the main cultural achievements of Classical Greece?

Classical Greece. After defeating two Persian attempts to conquer them in the early fifth century B.C.E., the Greeks entered their Golden Age. Among the accomplishments of Greek artists, writers, and thinkers were tragedy and comedy, secular history, and systematic logic, all of which still influence Western art and thought. *page 73*

 WHY DID Alexander the Great become an almost mythological figure?

Emergence of the Hellenistic World. Macedon under Philip II (r. 359–336 B.C.E.) and Alexander the Great (r. 336–323 B.C.E.) came to dominate first Greece and then all the Near East from Asia Minor to northern India. Daring and dashing, Alexander conquered vast territories. He died while he was still formulating plans for how to administer his empire, leaving his legacy open to interpretation. *page 80*

 HOW DID the Hellenistic world influence Western culture?

Hellenistic Culture. Alexander's conquests spread Greek culture over a wide area and ushered in the Hellenistic era. Hellenistic scholars made Greek literature and science available to many different peoples who adopted it as their own. The Romans spread Hellenistic culture across the Mediterranean world and transmitted it to later generations in the West. *page 84*

KEY TERMS

Acropolis (uh-KRAH-puh-liss) (p. 65)
agora **(AG-ehr-uh)** (p. 65)
Areopagus (are-ee-OH-pag-uhs) (p. 70)
Delian (DEEL-yuhn) League (p. 73)
Epicureans (ehp-ih-KYOOR-ee-uhns) (p. 84)
heliocentric theory (p. 86)
Helots (HEH-lohtz) (p. 69)
hoplite phalanx (HOP-lahyt FAY-langks) (p. 65)
the *Iliad* (ILL-ee-uhd) and the *Odyssey* (p. 63)
logos (LOW-gos) (p. 84)
Magna Graecia (MAHG-nuh GREE-shuh) (p. 65)
Minoan (mih-NOH-uhn) (p. 60)
Mycenaean (mahy-sin-NEE-uhn) (p. 61)
Panhellenic (*PAN-huh-LAYN-ick*) (p. 67)
Peloponnesian (PEL-uh-puh-NEE-zhun) War (p. 75)
Stoics (*STOW-icks*) (p. 84)
symposion (sihm-POE-see-ON) (p. 68)

REVIEW QUESTIONS

1. Describe the Minoan civilization of Crete. How did the later Bronze Age Mycenaean civilization differ from the Minoan civilization in political organization, art motifs, and military posture? How valuable are the Homeric epics as sources of early Greek history?

2. Define the concept of *polis*. What role did geography play in its development, and why did the Greeks consider it a unique and valuable institution?

3. Compare the fundamental political, social, and economic institutions of Athens and Sparta about 500 B.C.E. Why did Sparta develop its unique form of government? What were the main stages in the transformation of Athens from an aristocratic state to a democracy between 600 and 500 B.C.E.?

4. Why did the Greeks and Persians go to war in 490 and 480 B.C.E.? What benefit could the Persians have derived from conquering Greece? Why were the Greeks able to defeat the Persians, and how did they benefit from the victory?

5. How was the Delian League transformed into the Athenian Empire during the fifth century B.C.E.? Did the empire offer any advantages to its subjects? Why was there such resistance to Athenian efforts to unify the Greek world in the fifth and fourth centuries B.C.E.?

6. Why did Athens and Sparta come to blows in the Great Peloponnesian War? What was each side's strategy for victory? Why did Sparta win the war?

7. Using examples from art, literature, and philosophy, explain the tension that characterized Greek life and thought in the Classical period.

8. Between 431 and 362 B.C.E. Athens, Sparta, and Thebes each tried to impose hegemony over the city-states of Greece, but none succeeded for long. Why did each state fail? How was Philip II of Macedon able to conquer Greece? Does more of the credit for Philip's success lie in Macedon's strength or in the weakness of the Greek city-states? What does your analysis reveal about the components of successful rule?

9. What were the major consequences of Alexander's death? Assess the achievements of Alexander. Was he a conscious promoter of Greek civilization or just an egomaniac drunk with a lust for conquest?

Note: To learn more about the topics in this chapter, please turn to the Suggested Readings at the end of the book. For additional sources related to this chapter please see www.myhistorylab.com

PEARSON
myhistorylab Connections

Reinforce what you learned in this chapter by studying the many documents,
images, maps, review tools, and videos available at **www.myhistorylab.com**

Read and Review

Research and Explore

((•⌐**Hear** the **Audio**

Hear the audio file for Chapter 3
at **www.myhistorylab.com**

4

West Asia, Inner Asia, and South Asia to 1000 C.E.

((••—Hear the **Audio** for Chapter 4 at www.myhistorylab.com

The Bodhisattva Avalokiteshvara. Detail of a Buddhist wall painting from the cave shrines at Ajanta (Maharashtra, India), Gupta period, ca. 475 C.E. Avalokiteshvara (known in China as Kwan-yin and in Japan as Kannon) is the bodhisattva of infinite mercy.

Why were *bodhisattvas* important to Mahayana Buddhists?

WEST AND INNER ASIA

SOUTH ASIA

 rom the Mediterranean to China, the period from about 600 B.C.E. to the rise of Islam in the seventh century C.E. saw centralized empires flourish on an unprecedented scale—a development in which Iran and India preceded both China and the Roman West. Starting in the third millennium B.C.E., the Elamites (ca. 2700–639 B.C.E.), Achaemenids (ca. 539–330 B.C.E.), Seleucids (312–125 B.C.E.), Arsacids (c. 247 B.C.E.–233 C.E.), and Sasanids (224–651 C.E.) incorporated the Iranian plateau in their domains. Farther east, the Mauryas founded the first great Indian Empire (ca. 321–185 B.C.E.), followed by the Guptas (ca. 320–550 C.E.). Many of these empires built sophisticated bureaucracies, professional armies, and strong communication systems; they also facilitated or contributed to new cultural, political, and religious developments in their domains.

INDO-IRANIAN ROLES IN THE EURASIAN WORLD BEFORE ISLAM

The period of more than a millennium before the rise of Islam in the central lands of the Eurasian world is often thought of as dominated by the great empires of the Roman-Byzantine world and Han China. In global perspective, however, they had worthy counterparts in four empires in the Indo-Iranian world of West, Inner (Central), and South Asia between the Mediterranean and East Asia. In their heydays, the Achaemenids and Sasanids in Iran and the Mauryas and Guptas in India displayed the cultural vibrancy, economic prosperity, and wide dominion historically characteristic of all powerful imperial dynasties. They also built impressive road systems and played important roles in both linking the Roman, Byzantine, and African worlds with those of East and Southeast Asia, and in spreading Manichaean, Nestorian Christian, and, most importantly, Buddhist traditions across Asia.

In the West, Roman civilization had, by the third century C.E., its chief locus in regions east and south of Rome, while in Europe it endured more as a legacy coexisting uneasily with traditions of Germanic invaders. Roman imperial power had shifted east to Byzantium, where political and cultural traditions were under marked influences from Africa and West Asia. Alexandria, at the mouth of the Nile, was long the center of Hellenistic civilization, and the major Christian doctrinal councils were held in Asia. The post-Alexander states of West and Inner Asia and northwest India were important cultural melting pots and loci of contacts with the Greco-Roman "West," the Mesopotamian-Iranian world, the rest of India, and the Chinese "East." Other developments of major global importance also had their origin or locus in the Indo-Iranian world in these centuries: the Sasanid revival of imperial power and Zoroastrian religion, the rise and spread from North Africa to western China of the Manichaean movement, the completion of world masterpieces in the Sanskrit epics of the *Mahabharata* and *Ramayana*, Gandharan and then Guptan art, Indian religious, literary, mathematical, and scientific thought, and the spread of Mahayana Buddhist traditions over Tibet and Central Asia, and to China and ultimately Japan.

In Asia this was also an era in which influential, lasting religious traditions came of age. Some spread and took root far from their regions of origin—the Christian, Buddhist, and Confucian, as well as Judaic and Hindu traditions, for example. Others, such as Zoroastrianism, never attracted a wide following outside of their homelands. Zoroastrianism, however, was especially attractive to merchants, who carried it throughout Central Asia in their travels along the old Silk Road. It won converts among other merchants from elsewhere in Asia, and, more importantly, it influenced

Three noteworthy developments characterize this period. First, the era saw sustained contact among the major centers of culture from the Mediterranean to China. Trade drove much of the contact: large-scale empires created new markets for diverse goods, both material and human (such as slaves, soldiers, and artisans).

Alexander the Great's conquest (334–323 B.C.E.) of the Persian Empire and the regions eastward to North India provided the impetus for the era's second characteristic— dramatically increased contact among diverse cultures, races, and religious traditions. Although Alexander's empire was ephemeral, his conquests ended the Achaemenid Dynasty and allowed the rising Maurya power to extend across North India. The Hellenes and steppe peoples of northeastern Iran and Central (Inner) Asia, who ruled first post-Alexandrine Iran and then post-Maurya India down to the third century C.E., inherited a much wider world than those of their original homelands.

A third characteristic of this period was the rise of major religious traditions that would influence history from Africa to China. Judaism, Christianity, Hellenistic cults, Han Confucianism and classical Daoist thought, Zoroastrianism, the Hindu tradition, and Buddhism all developed in significant ways during this period. ■

WEST AND INNER ASIA

"Iran" designates the massive expanse of Southwest Asia bounded to the north by the Caspian and Aral seas and Jaxartes (Syr Darya) River, east by the Indus valley, south by the Arabian Sea and Persian Gulf, and west by the Tigris-Euphrates

Judaism through Babylonia (where the major recension of the Talmud was codified) and in varying degree other religious traditions of Asia and the Middle East, including the Christian, Islamic, and Buddhist.

All of these developments should indicate that the notion of the "rise of the West" as a keynote of history only holds at most for the past six centuries, not for the past three millennia. When we consider the expansion of lands, luxuries, and trade under the several Persian, Byzantine, and Indian, let alone the subsequent Islamic, empires, the European world in these centuries did not promise much as a future global center of political or cultural life. Progress and culture seemed best embodied either in Achaemenid, Maurya, Sasanid, Gupta, and Byzantine culture in West and South Asia, in China under the Han, Sui, and Tang dynasties, or in Japan in Nara and Heian times.

A more impartial perspective on these centuries identifies important centers of cultural, religious, economic, and political vitality around the globe—in West, South, and East Asia, and in Rome, Byzantium, and Aksumite Ethiopia. Societies in each of these regions, themselves products of a syncretic blending of multiple cultural traditions, were dynamic enough to influence neighboring peoples and in some cases to export their religious and cultural traditions far afield. Merchants and missionaries alike braved hazardous land and sea travel, carrying ideas as well as goods to remote lands. Wares and religious ideas passed from hand to hand and mouth to mouth on the roads and sea routes from Byzantium to China, and Africa and West Asia to India and Southeast Asia, as centers of civilization in Africa and Asia flourished.

Yet with the rise of the last monotheistic world religious tradition, Islam, Indo-Iranian lands soon faced far-reaching changes that would later come to North and East Africa and Central, South, and Southeast Asia. In the time of Chosroes Anoshirvan in the sixth century C.E., who could have suspected that within a few hundred years Persian culture would eventually be recast in Islamic forms?

Focus Questions

◆ Why is a European perspective not helpful for understanding the world in the first millennium C.E.? How does a global perspective offer a better understanding of the development of civilizations in this era?

◆ Why did this period see a significant increase in cross-cultural contacts? How were these contacts manifested? Who participated in these increased contacts?

---

basin and Armenia. The heart of this region is the vast Iranian plateau, bounded on all sides by great mountain ranges, and containing two large, uninhabitable salt deserts.

People clustered wherever rainfall or groundwater was plentiful and communication easiest, notably the slopes and lowlands between the Zagros, Persis (Pars, Persia), Media, Hyrcania, and Parthia. The great Asian trade routes put Iran at the heart of east–west interchange.

ANCIENT BACKGROUND AND THE FIRST PERSIAN EMPIRE IN THE IRANIAN PLATEAU (550–330 B.C.E.)

THE ELAMITES

The Elamites were a non-Semitic-speaking people who built a flourishing civilization on the eastern frontier of Mesopotamia. They were repeatedly at war with the Sumerians, Babylonians, and Assyrians from around 2700 B.C.E. until their destruction by the Assyrian emperor Asshurbanipal in 639 B.C.E., when their cities were ransacked and their soil sown with salt. Although we have tablets, monumental inscriptions, and brick imprints from Elamite remains, scholars have not determined the language group to which Elamite belongs. It did, however, long outlive the Elamite state and was one of the three official languages of the Persian Empire.

WHAT WERE the main teachings of Zoroaster, and how did Zoroastrianism influence other traditions?

Ahura Mazda

Supreme god in ancient Iranian religion, especially in the religious system of the Iranian prophet Zoroaster. Ahura Mazda was worshiped by the Persian king Darius I (reigned 522 B.C.E.–486 B.C.E.) and his successors as the greatest of all gods and protector of the just king.

Zoroastrian priests hold hands around a devotional flame during a religious New Year's celebration in London in 1999.

What is the importance of fire in the Zoroastrian faith?

THE IRANIAN PEOPLES

The forefathers of the Iranian dynasts were Aryans. The oldest texts in ancient Persian dialects show that Aryan peoples settled on the Iranian plateau around 1100 B.C.E. Like their Vedic or Indo-Aryan relations in North India, these peoples were pastoralists—horse breeders—from the Eurasian or Central Asian steppes. The most prominent of these ancient Iranians were the Medes and the Persians. By the eighth century B.C.E., they had spread around the deserts of the plateau to settle and control its western and southwestern reaches, to which they gave their names, Media and Persis (Pars, and later Fars).

The Medes developed a tribal confederacy in western Iran and were the predecessors of today's Kurds. By 612 B.C.E., they and the Neo-Babylonians had defeated the mighty Assyrians and broken their hold on the Fertile Crescent. Persian power increased under the Achaemenid clan, starting in the seventh century B.C.E. Median supremacy on the Iranian plateau was over by the time of the Achaemenid ruler Cyrus the Great, around 550 B.C.E. Many of the institutions that developed in the ensuing empire were apparently based on Median practices; the Medes, in turn, had often drawn from Babylonian and Assyrian models. Part of the genius of the Achaemenids' unparalleled imperial success lay in their ability to use existing institutions to build their own state and to administer their far-flung dominions well.

ANCIENT IRANIAN RELIGION

Pre-Achaemenid texts suggest that old Iranian culture and religion were similar to those of the Vedic Aryans. The importance of water, fire, sacrifice, and the cow, as well as the names and traits of major divine beings and religious concepts, all have counterparts in Vedic texts. The emphasis was on moral order, or the "Right." The supreme heavenly deity was **Ahura Mazda**, the "Wise Lord."

ZOROASTER AND THE ZOROASTRIAN TRADITION

The first person who stands out in Iranian history was not Cyrus, the famous founder of the Achaemenid Empire, but the great prophet-reformer of Iranian religion, Zarathustra, commonly known in the West by the Greek version of his name, Zoroaster. Zoroaster probably lived in northeastern Iran, no later than 1000 B.C.E. Like the Hebrew prophets, the Buddha, and Confucius, Zoroaster presented a message of moral reform in an age of materialism, political opportunism, and ethical indifference.

Zoroaster was evidently trained as a priest in the old Iranian tradition, but his hymns, or *Gathas*, reflect his new religious vision. In these hymns we glimpse the values of a peasant-pastoralist society that was growing up alongside early urban trade centers in northeastern Iran. Zoroaster's personal experience of Ahura Mazda as the supreme deity led him to reinterpret the old sacrificial fire as Ahura's symbol. He called on people to abandon worship of all lesser deities, whom he identified as demons. He warned of a "final reckoning," when the good would be rewarded with "future glory" but the wicked with "long-lasting darkness, ill food, and wailing."

Zoroaster's preaching probably did not become an official "state" creed during his lifetime. But by the mid-fourth century B.C.E., the Zoroastrian reform had spread into western as well as eastern Iran. The quasi-monotheistic worship of Ahura Mazda, the Wise Lord, was rapidly accommodated to the veneration of older Iranian gods by the interpretation of these deities as secondary gods or even manifestations of the Wise Lord himself. The old Iranian priestly clan of the **Magi** may have integrated Zoroastrian ideas and texts into their older polytheistic tradition. Certainly the name "magi" was later used for the priests of the tradition that we call "Zoroastrian."

Zoroastrianism probably influenced not only Jewish, Christian, and Muslim ideas of angels, devils, messiah, last judgment, and afterlife, but also Buddhist concepts as well. Zoroastrianism was wiped out as a major force in Iran by the spread of Islam from the seventh and eighth centuries C.E. However, its tradition continues in the faith and practice of the Parsis, a community today of perhaps 100,000 people, most of them in western India.

THE ACHAEMENIDS

In October 1971 C.E., the Iranian monarch Muhammad Reza Shah (r. 1941–1979) hosted a lavish pageant amid the ruins of the ancient Persian capital, Persepolis, to commemorate the 2,500-year anniversary of the beginning, under Cyrus the Great, of "the imperial glory of Iran." The shah felt his modern secularist regime had re-created traditional Iranian glory. Although the Iranian revolution of 1978 ended his heavy-handed dictatorship, modern Iran does have a dual heritage: that of the rich Iranian Islamic culture and that of the far older, Indo-Iranian, Zoroastrian, and imperial culture of pre-Islamic Iran. The latter began with the Persian Achaemenid Dynasty.

Achaemenid rule in southwestern Iran (Persis) went back at least to Cyrus I (d. 600 B.C.E.), but the rise of Iran as a major imperial civilization is usually dated from the reign of his grandson, Cyrus the Great (559–530 B.C.E.). Cyrus defeated the last Median king about 550 B.C.E., and the last Babylonian king in 539 B.C.E. This victory marks the beginning of the Achaemenid Empire, for it joined Mesopotamia and the Iranian plateau for the first time under one rule—a unity that would last for centuries (see Map 4-1 on page 96). One result was the end of the Babylonian Exile of the Jews, for Cyrus allowed the Jews to return to their Holy Land and rebuild their Jerusalem temple (see Chapter 2). His most notable legacy to his heirs was not only his conquests, but also his model of rule through local elites and institutions rather than imperial administrative superstructures.

Early in his career, Cyrus had moved his capital from Susa to the old Median capital of Ecbatana (later Hamadan). He and his successors adopted Median administrative practice, and many Medes served the new state. Thus the Bible and other sources refer to Achaemenids as "Medes and Persians."

The new Persian Empire became the most extensive the world had ever seen. Cyrus's successor, Cambyses (r. 529–522 B.C.E.) added Egypt to the Achaemenid dominions. Darius I (r. 521–486 B.C.E.) enjoyed a prosperous reign in which the empire reached its greatest extent—from Egypt northeast to southern Russia and Sogdiana (Transoxiana) and east to the Indus valley.

Magi

A tribe from ancient Media, who, prior to the conquest of the Medes by the Achaemenid Empire in 550 B.C.E., were responsible for religious and funerary practices. The best known Magi were the "Wise Men from the East" in the Bible.

Zoroastrianism

A quasi-monotheistic Iranian religion founded by Zoroaster, who preached a message of moral reform and exhorted his followers to worship only Ahura Mazda, the Wise Lord.

((•─[Hear the Audio
at **myhistorylab.com**

CHRONOLOGY

IRAN TO THE THIRD CENTURY C.E.

ca. 2000–1000 B.C.E.	Indo-Iranian (Aryan) tribes move south into the Iranian plateau and the Punjab of India
Between 1400 and 1000 B.C.E.	Probable range of dates within which Zarathushtra (Zoroaster) lived, likely in eastern/northeastern Iran (perhaps originally in Herat?)
ca. 628–551 B.C.E.	Traditional dating of the life of Zoroaster
559–530 B.C.E.	Reign of Cyrus the Great, Persian Achaemenid ruler
539–330 B.C.E.	Achaemenid Empire
331–330 B.C.E.	Alexander the Great (d. 323 B.C.E.) conquers Achaemenid Empire
312–63 B.C.E.	Seleucids rule in eastern territories of Achaemenid realm
ca. 248 B.C.E.–224 C.E.	Parthian Empire of the Arsacids in Iran, Babylonia

MAP EXPLORATION

To explore this map further, go to **http://www.myhistorylab.com**

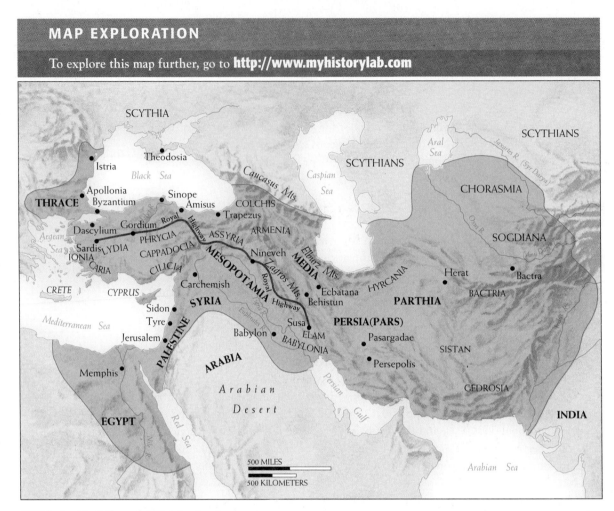

MAP 4–1. The Achaemenid Persian Empire.

The empire created by Cyrus had reached its fullest extent under Darius when Persia attacked Greece in 490 B.C.E. It extended from the subcontinent of India to the Aegean Sea, and even into Europe, encompassing the lands formerly ruled by Egyptians, Hittites, Babylonians, and Assyrians.

Why were the Persians able to govern such a large empire for so long?

The next five rulers (486–359 B.C.E.) fared less well, and after 478 B.C.E., the Persians found themselves militarily inferior to the Greeks. Although they kept the divided Greeks at bay by clever diplomacy, Greek cultural influence grew in Asia Minor. Egyptian rebellions, succession struggles, conflict with Scythian steppe tribes, and poor leadership plagued Achaemenid rule, which was ended by Alexander the Great (see Chapter 3).

THE ACHAEMENID STATE

Shahanshah

"King of kings," the title of the Persian ruler.

Perhaps the Achaemenids' greatest achievement was the relative stability of their rule. To justify their sovereignty—and the title of **Shahanshah**, "king of kings"—they claimed that Ahura Mazda had entrusted them with universal sovereignty, which they earned through justice and uprightness. The ruler became priest and sacrificer in the court rituals; a royal fire that burned throughout his reign symbolized his role as cosmic ruler. The success of the early Achaemenids strengthened their claim to divinely sanctioned royal status.

The Achaemenids were tolerant of other cultural and religious traditions in ways earlier empires had not been. In part, the sheer size of their realms demanded it, but the contrast to later Roman imperial practice is striking. Even Darius's emphasis on Zoroastrian ritual and theology did not bring forced conformity or conversion to the "state cult," as his leniency toward the Jews shows (see Chapter 2).

The Achaemenids built a powerful army, but much of their success lay in their administrative abilities and willingness to borrow from predecessors. Most of their leaders were adept at conciliation and worked to establish their special *pax Achaemenica*. They maintained continuity as their state evolved from a tribal confederation into a sophisticated monarchy. Cyrus's state, with its largely Iranian troops and tribute system of revenue, was replaced by a monarchy supported by a noble class, professional armies (led by Persian elite troops), an administrative system of provinces ruled by governors called *satraps*, and fixed levies of revenue.

The excellence of Achaemenid administration can be seen in their communication and propaganda systems. Couriers linked imperial outposts with the heartlands over well-kept highways, which also facilitated rapid troop deployment. Herodotus called the greatest of these, from Sardis to Susa, "the King's Road" (see Map 4-1). A network of observers and royal inspectors kept the court abreast of activities outside the capital. An efficient chancery with large archives and numerous scribes served administrative needs. The Achaemenid bureaucracy's adoption of Aramaic, which had become the common language of the Near East under the Assyrians, helped link East and West. The Achaemenids never had a single fixed capital; they moved the court as needed. Although *satraps* were powerful princes in their own right, the power of the "king of kings" held together the diverse *satrapies* and tributary states.

satraps
Governors of provinces in the Persian Empire.

See the **Map**
The Persian Empire at Its Greatest Extent at **myhistorylab.com**

THE ACHAEMENID ECONOMY

Economic life from Greece to India profited substantially from Achaemenid success. Although Croesus had introduced a coin-based monetary system in Lydia (sixth century B.C.E.), the Achaemenids greatly expanded on this. Coinage was used to pay part of the workers' wages in the construction of Persepolis and displaced in-kind payment altogether under Darius. Coinage stimulated banking operations, which had declined since the heyday of Mesopotamian rule in the previous millennium. The Achaemenids taxed diverse sources of income—estates, livestock, mines, trade, and production. They regulated wages and established money-goods equivalences (thus a sheep might be set at three shekels).

Agriculture remained the basic industry and normal occupation of free men. Serfs and slaves, both chattel and domestic, formed most of the labor force. Work animals were bred, bees colonized, and grapes, wheat, barley, and olives cultivated widely. Where water was scarce, the government dug irrigation canals. Rulers such as Darius mandated the transfer of fruit trees and other plants to different parts of the empire; thus from the east pistachio cultivation came to Aleppo, rice to Mesopotamia, and sesame to Egypt.

Fishing, timbering, and mining were fundamental to the economy. Some industries, such as those producing clothing, shoes, and furniture, developed alongside the older luxury crafts for the wealthy. The unprecedented volume of trade in Achaemenid times included large quantities of everyday household products that were now widely exchanged where earlier only luxury goods had been traded over long distances. Goods from India crossed paths with those of the Rhine valley; it was a prosperous era, marked by expanding markets—into southern Europe especially—and increased foreign travel, exploration, and investment.

The empire's stability laid the cosmopolitan basis for the coming Hellenic influences in western Asia in the wake of Alexander's conquests.

Daric. A gold coin first minted under Darius I of Persia, fourth century B.C.E.

© Ashmollean Museum, Oxford, England, UK.

What are some important features of the Achaemenid economy?

SUCCESSOR STATES AND STEPPE PEOPLES

HOW DID the steppe peoples act as vehicles for cultural exchange?

THE SELEUCID SUCCESSORS TO ALEXANDER IN THE EAST (ca. 312–63 B.C.E.)

Alexander's successors in Achaemenid lands, the Greek general Seleucus and his heirs (see Chapter 3) ruled much of the former Achaemenid realm from Babylon between about 312 and 246 B.C.E. They lost Babylonia to the Iranian Parthians in 140 B.C.E. Their capital moved from Babylon to Antioch during their long decline, until Pompey finally ended the much-reduced Seleucid kingdom in 63 B.C.E.

Alexander's policies of Hellenic-Persian fusion—the appointment of Iranians and Greeks as *satraps*, as well as large-scale Greek and Persian intermarriage—helped make Seleucid rule viable in many eastern areas. As a foreign minority, the Seleucids had to maintain control with mercenary troops. Always at war, neither Seleucus (r. 311–281 B.C.E.; see Chapter 3) nor the greatest of his successors, Antiochus the Great (r. 223–187 B.C.E.), ever matched the sustained power and scale of Achaemenid rule.

In the end, Alexander's policy of linking Hellenes with Iranians in political power, marriage, and culture bore fruit more lasting than empire. The Seleucid emphasis on building Greek-style cities stimulated the Hellenization process. During the second century B.C.E., Hellenistic culture and law became new ideals among Seleucid elites. The Seleucids welcomed into the ruling classes those non-Hellenes willing to become Hellenized. Aramaic, though declining in eastern Iran, remained the common tongue from Syria to the Hindu Kush. Greek culture penetrated but did not displace local social and cultural forms.

Zoroastrian religious tradition declined with the loss of its imperial-cult status. Syncretic cults of the Mediterranean Hellenistic world made inroads even in the East in Seleucid and, later, Parthian times (see below). Mystery and savior cults were becoming more popular in East and West. Hellenistic urban centers provided an environment in which the individual was less rooted in established traditions. This may have enhanced the attraction of the individual salvation promised by some Hellenistic cults and the emerging Christian, Mahayana Buddhist, Manichaean, and Hindu traditions.

QUICK REVIEW

Alexander's Successors in Achaemenid Lands

- General Seleucus and his heirs ruled most of the Achaemenid realm
- Alexander's "new" cities served as bases for Seleucid control
- Seleucids maintained control with mercenary troops

Parthian Warrior. The Parthians were superb fighters and were particularly noted for the "Parthian shot," firing arrows backward while mounted on a galloping horse.

How would you imagine foot soldiers reacting to swift and mobile cavalry fighters like this?

steppe peoples
Nomadic tribespeople who dwelled on the Eurasian plains from eastern Europe to the borders of China and Iran. They frequently traded with or invaded more settled cultures.

THE PARTHIAN ARSACID EMPIRE (ca. 247 B.C.E.–223 C.E.)

The history of the Iranian plateau (and North India) was dominated from about 250 B.C.E. to 300 C.E. by incursions of Iranian tribal peoples originally from the Central Asian steppes. These were neither the first nor last such invasions from the steppe. Commonly ignored, these pastoral **steppe peoples** have been a major force in Eurasian history.

The Parni, said to be related to the Scythians, were probably the major group of Iranian steppe peoples who first settled the area south of the Aral Sea and Oxus. In late Achaemenid times, they moved south into Parthia and adopted its dialect; thereafter we call them Parthians. Stating around 247 B.C.E., the dynastic family of the Arsacids controlled first Parthia, and then expanding portions of the Iranian plateau. Under Mithradates I (ca. 171–138 B.C.E.) they emerged as a new Eurasian imperial force and true Achaemenid successors who were able to extinguish Seleucid power east of the Euphrates by 129 B.C.E.

Under the Parthians, trade apparently increased, especially north over the Caucasus, on the "Silk Road" to China, and along the Indian Ocean coast. Culturally, the Parthians were oriented toward the Hellenistic world of their Seleucid predecessors until the mid-first century C.E., after which they seem to have experienced a kind of Iranian revival that laid the groundwork for the nationalistic emphases of subsequent centuries. Despite their religious tolerance, the Parthians upheld such Zoroastrian traditions as maintenance of a royal sacred fire. The increasing popularity of Christianity and Buddhism in border areas may have stimulated Parthian attempts to collect the largely oral Zoroastrian textual heritage.

The Parthian Arsacids' imperial borders varied, but from their victory over the Romans at Carrhae in 53 B.C.E. (see Chapter 6) until their fall in 224 C.E., they were the major Eurasian power alongside Rome. Eventually the constant Roman wars of their last century and the pressure of the Kushan Empire in the east weakened them sufficiently for a new Persian dynasty, the Sasanids, to replace them.

THE INDO-GREEKS

The farthest reach of Hellenization in the East came with the **Indo-Greek** rulers of Bactria. About 246 B.C.E., Bactria's Greek *satrap* broke away from the Seleucids. His successors controlled territory that expanded into northern India. Most of the Indo-Greeks were Indian in language, culture, and religion, as their coins and inscriptions show. Before their demise at the hands of invading steppe peoples (ca. 130–100 B.C.E.), these Indo-Greeks left their mark on civilization in all the areas around their Bactrian center. Bactria was a major source of the later Greco-Buddhist art of Gandhara, one of history's remarkable examples of cross-cultural influence. The Indo-Greeks also probably helped spread Buddhism from India to Central Asia. The most famous of the Bactrian rulers, Menander, or Milinda (r. ca. 155–130 B.C.E.), is depicted as a Buddhist convert in a later Buddhist text, *The Questions of King Milinda*.

SCYTHIANS AND KUSHANS

The successors of the Indo-Greeks were steppe peoples who reflect the cosmopolitan nature of the world of Central Asia, eastern Iran, and northwestern India at this time.

Beginning about 130 B.C.E., Scythian, or Saka, tribes from beyond the Jaxartes (Syr Darya) overran northeastern Iran, taking Sogdiana's Hellenic cities and then Bactria. One group of Scythians extended their domain from Bactria into North India. Another went southwest into Herat and Sistan, where they encroached on Parthian territories. In northwestern India the Sakas were defeated by invading Iranians known as the Pahlavas, who went on to rule in northwestern India in the first century C.E. Still, Saka dynasties continued to rule in parts of northwestern and western India through the fourth century C.E.

The Sakas had been displaced earlier in Sogdiana by another steppe people, known from Chinese sources as the Yuezhi, from western China. These peoples, led by the Kushan tribe, drove the Sakas out of Bactria in the mid-first century B.C.E. About 100 years later, they swept over the mountains into northwestern India, ending Pahlava rule. The Kushans founded a long-lived Indian dynasty that controlled a relatively stable empire from the upper Oxus regions through Bactria, Gandhara, Arachosia, the Punjab, and over the Ganges plains as far as Varanasi (Banaras).

Indo-Greeks
Bactrian rulers who broke away from the Seleucid Empire to found a state that combined elements of Greek and Indian civilizations.

Greco-Buddhist Art. A sculpted head of the Buddha, second century B.C.E. Hellenistic influences are evident in the realistic modeling and sculptural plasticity.

Sculpted head of Buddha, from Gandhara, second century B.C. Paris, Musee Guimet. RMN: Reunion Musees Nationaux/Art Resource.

In what ways does this sculpture seem to be a portrayal of a real person? In what ways does it seem to be an idealized representation?

The Kushan kingdom of India was—along with Rome, China, and the weakened Parthian Empire of Iran—one of four major centers of civilization in Eurasia around 100 C.E. Its greatest ruler, Kanishka, was a great patron of Buddhism, and Kushan power in Central Asia facilitated the missionary activity that carried Buddhism across the steppes into China. The Kushan rulers had diplomatic contacts with Han China, Iran, and Rome. Greco-Buddhist art was fostered in Gandhara by Kanishka and his successors.

THE SASANID EMPIRE (224–651 C.E.)

HOW DID the Sasanids build a strong state?

See the **Map**
Arabia Before the Prophet, ca. 250–600 C.E.
at **myhistorylab.com**

Sasanid victory. Cliff-cut tombs at Nagsh-i Rustam, Iran. Stone relief depicts Philip the Arab in Roman dress kneeling before the third-century Persian King Shapur I on horseback wearing royal armor and crown, who grasps with his right hand the uplifted arms of the Byzantine Emperor Valerian. Located at the tombs of the Achaemenids, in Istakhr, Iran.

What major empires were in conflict during the Sasanid period?

THE SASANIDS

The Sasanids were a Persian dynasty who claimed to be the rightful Achaemenid heirs. They championed Iranian legitimacy and tried to brand their predecessor Parthians as outside invaders. The first Sasanid king, Ardashir (r. 224–ca. 239 C.E.), was a Persian warrior noble. He and his son, Shapur I (r. ca. 239–272), built a strong internal administration. Under Shapur's long rule, the Persian Empire grew. Shapur defeated three Roman emperors, even capturing one of them, Valerian (r. 253–260). Thus he could justifiably claim to be a restorer of Iranian glory and a "king of kings," or *shahanshah*. He also centralized and rationalized taxation, the civil ministries, and the military, although neither he nor his successors could fully contain the growing power of the nobility.

With the shift of the Roman Empire east to Byzantium in the early fourth century C.E., the West Asian stage was set for the next 350 years of conflict between the Byzantines based in Constantinople on the Bosphorus, and the Sasanids based in Ctesiphon on the Tigris. These two imperial centers were home to the two mightiest thrones of Eurasia until the coming of the Arabs. Each side won victories over the other and championed a different religious orthodoxy, but neither could completely subdue the other. In the sixth century each produced its greatest emperor: the Byzantine Justinian (r. 527–565) and the Sasanid Chosroes Anosharvan ("Chosroes of the Immortal Soul," r. 531–579). Yet, less than a century after their deaths, the new Arab power to the south reduced one empire dramatically and destroyed the other. Byzantium survived with the loss of most of its territory for another 800 years, but the Sasanid imperial order was swept away entirely in 651. Memory of the Sasanids did not, however, die. Chosroes became a legendary model of greatness for Persians and a symbol of imperial splendor among the Arabs. The Pahlavi monarchy in twentieth-century Iran attempted to use the historical memory of the Sasanids to legitimize its rule.

SOCIETY AND ECONOMY

Sasanid society was largely like that of earlier times. The extended family was the basic social unit. Zoroastrian orthodoxy recognized four classes: priests, warriors, scribes, and peasants. However, a great divide separated the royal house, the priesthood, and the warrior nobility from the common people (artisans, traders, and the rural peasantry).

The basis of the economy remained agriculture, but land became increasingly concentrated in the hands of an ever-richer minority of the royalty, nobility, and Zoroastrian priesthood. The burden of land taxation, like that of conscript labor and army duty, hit hardest those least able to afford it. This eventually produced a popular reaction, as shown by the Mazdakite movement discussed below.

The Sasanids taxed the lucrative caravan and sea trade in their territory (see Map 4-2). The empire's many urban centers and its foreign trade relied on a money system. It was from Jewish bankers in Babylonia and their Persian counterparts that Europe got the use of bills of exchange (the term *check* comes from a Pahlavi word).

Sasanid aristocratic culture drew on diverse traditions. The Sasanid heyday was the reign of Chosroes. Indian influences—not only religious, as in the case of Buddhist ideas, but also artistic and scientific—were especially strong. Indian medicine and mathematics were notably in demand and transmitted west by way of the Persian Gulf and Indian Ocean maritime routes. Hellenistic culture was also revived in the academy at Jundishapur, where Nestorian Christian scholars fleeing Byzantine persecution brought many Greco-Roman philosophical, scientific, and literary texts with them.

QUICK REVIEW

Sasanid Economy

◆ Based on agriculture

◆ Four classes, according to Zoroastrian orthodoxy

◆ Increasing gap between the rich and the poor

◆ Heavy taxes on trade

◆ Money system, including checks

MAP EXPLORATION

To explore this map further, go to **http://www.myhistorylab.com**

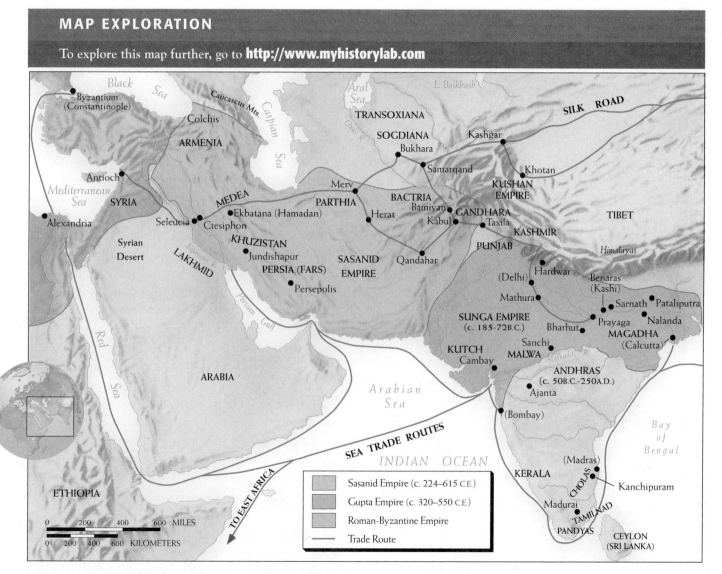

MAP 4-2. **International Trade Routes in Gupta and Sasanid Times.**

This map shows the Gupta and Sasanid empires and the trade routes that linked them to each other and to other areas of the world.

How did the Indian Ocean facilitate trade between different regions?

RELIGION

The Sasanids institutionalized Zoroastrian ritual and theology as state orthodoxy. The first chief priest (*mobad*) of the empire, Tansar (or Tosar) began to compile an authoritative, written scriptural canon known as the *Avesta*; these texts include the hymns and sayings of Zarathushtra. He may also have instituted a calendar reform and replaced all images in the temples with the sacred altar fires of Zoroastrian tradition. (See Document, "Tansar's Defense of His King, Ardashir I.")

The most influential figure in Sasanid religious history was Tansar's successor, Kartir (or Kirdir) (ca. 239–293). After the death of the religiously tolerant Shapur, Kartir tried to convert not only pagans, but also Christians, Buddhists, and others. His

DOCUMENT

Tansar's Defense of His King, Ardashir I

The following is a brief excerpt from what is probably at base an actual letter of the Zoroastrian high priest, Tansar (third century C.E.*) to a conquered vassal of the Sasanid Shahanshah, Ardashir I, which was revised in the sixth century for Sasanid propaganda purposes. The letter argues in general that religious norms had been restored by Ardashir after their collapse in Arsacid times. The text comes from a thirteenth-century Muslim history of Tabaristan in a Persian translation of an Arabic translation of the original.*

- **WHY** might Tansar be an apologist for Anushirvan I? What can be inferred about the relationship between religious and imperial authority under the Sasanids?

The chief herbad, Tansar, has received the letter of Gushnasp, prince and king of Tabaristan and Parishwar.... You declared: "There is much talk about the blood shed by the king and people are dismayed." The answer is that there are many kings who have put few to death, yet have slain immoderately if they have killed but ten; and there are many who if they put men to death in their thousands would slay still more, being driven to it at the time by their people.... Punishments, you must know, are for three kinds of transgressions; first that of the creature against his God... when he turns from the faith and introduces a heresy into religion.... For (this) the King of kings has established a law far better than that of the ancients. For in former days any man who turned from the faith was swiftly... put to death.... The King of kings has ordered that such a man should be imprisoned, and that for the space of a year

learned men should summon him at frequent intervals and advise him and lay arguments before him and destroy his doubts. If he become penitent and contrite and seek pardon of God, he is set free. If obstinacy and pride hold him back, then he is put to death. Next for what you said, that the King of kings has taken away fires from the fire temples, extinguished them and blotted them out, and that no one has ever before presumed so far against religion; know that the case is not so grievous but has been wrongly reported to you. The truth is that after Darius (III) each of [the Parthians' vassal kings] built his own [dynastic] fire temple. This was pure innovation, introduced by them without the authority of kings of old. The King of kings has razed the temples, and confiscated the endowments, and had the fires carried back to their places of origin.... Then you said: "He has exacted money from men of wealth and merchants".... The idea that the king of the day should seek help for the common people from the superfluity of the wealthy is a religious principle and clearly justified in reason.... The King of kings has cast the shadow of his majesty over all who have acknowledged his pre-eminence and service and have sent him tribute.... In the space of fourteen years, he thus brought it about that he made water flow in every desert and established towns and created groups of villages.... Good order in the affairs of the people affects him more than the welfare of his own body and soul....

Source: From Mary Boyce, ed. and trans., *Textual Sources for the Study of Zoroastrianism* (Manchester, England: Manchester University Press, 1984), pp. 109–110.

chief opponents were the Manichaeans, whom he considered Zoroastrian heretics, much as Christian groups, such as the Nestorians, saw them as Christian heretics.

The founder of the faith that bears his name, Mani (216–277 C.E.) preached a message both similar to and sharply divergent from its Zoroastrian, Judaic, and Christian forerunners. **Manichaeism** centered on a radically dualistic and moralistic view of reality in which good and evil, spirit and matter, always warred. These ideas are now commonplace in the major monotheistic religions. He sought to convert others to his views, which he presented as the culmination and restoration of the original unity of Zoroastrian, Christian, and Buddhist teachings. Mani may have been the first person in history to consciously "found" a new religious tradition or to seek to create a "scripture" for his followers.

Kartir eventually had Mani executed as a heretic in 277, but Mani's movement had great consequences. It spread westward to challenge the Christian church and eastward along the Silk Road to Central Asia and China to vie with Buddhist and Nestorian Christian traditions. Its ideas figured even centuries later in both Christian and Islamic heresies. Its adherents probably carried the Western planetary calendar to China, where in some areas it was used for centuries.

Despite the persistence of challenges such as Mani's, Kirdir had firmly grounded Zoroastrian orthodoxy, which became the backbone of Sasanid culture. Throughout Sasanid times, the priesthood increased its power as the jurists and legal interpreters of the land. With increasing endowments of new fire temples, the church establishment also eventually controlled much of Iran's wealth.

Nestorius (ca. 386–ca. 451), the Patriarch of Constantinople, had taught that the human and divine natures of Jesus Christ were distinct and separate, not unified in one person. Nestorius was condemned as a heretic at the Council of Ephesus in 431. The Sasanid kings, who were at war with the Byzantines, saw an opportunity: They supported the Nestorian Christians and opened schools to Nestorian scholars. Indeed, the Nestorian Church flourished in Persia, producing many missionaries who preached throughout Persia and Central and East Asia in the seventh and eighth centuries, reaching China in 635.

LATER SASANID DEVELOPMENTS

Despite the high Zoroastrian moral intent of many of their rulers, the Sasanid ideal of justice did not include equal distribution of the empire's bounty. The radical inequalities between the aristocracy and the masses erupted at least once in conflict with the Mazdakite movement at the end of the fifth century. Its leader, Mazdak, preached ideas drawn

CHRONOLOGY

SASANID IRAN

216–277 C.E.	Mani
223–224	Ardashir (r. 224–ca. 239) defeats the last Arsacid ruler, becomes *shahanshah* of Iran
ca. 225–ca. 239	Tansar chief priest (*mobad*) of the realm
239–272	Reign of Shapur I; expansion of the empire east and west
ca. 239–293	Kartir chief priest of the realm
ca. 307–379	Reign of Shapur II
488–531	Reign of Kavad I; height of Mazdakite movement
528	Mazdak and many of his followers massacred
531–579	Reign of Chosroes Anosharvan at Ctesiphon
651	Death of last Sasanid; Arabs conquer Persian Empire

Manichaeism
One of the major dualistic religions in ancient Persia, in which good and evil were constantly at odds with one another.

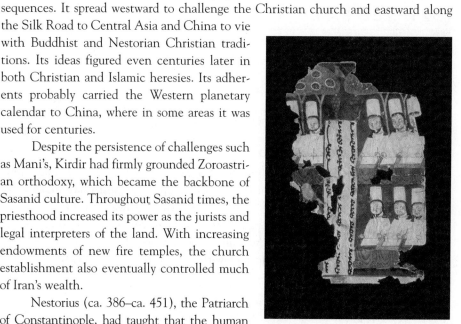

Manichaean Priests. This leaf from a Manichaean book (ca. eighth–ninth century C.E.) shows priests in white robes and tall hats kneeling in front of low desks. Each has a sheet of white paper, and some hold pens. Works such as this are an important source for our knowledge of Manichaean communities.

A leaf from a Manchurian book, Roko, Templek (MIK III 6368), eighth–ninth century, a manuscript painting 17.2 × 11.2 cm. Bildarchiv Preussischer Kulturbesitz/Art Resource, New York.

What are the basic beliefs of Manichaeism?

QUICK REVIEW

Mani (216–277 C.E.)

- Born of a noble Parthian family
- Mani's message similar to Zoroastrian, Judaic, and Christian forerunners
- Executed as a heretic in 277

ultimately from Manichaeism and the need for a more equal distribution of society's goods. This appealed primarily to the oppressed classes, although even one Sasanid ruler, Kavad I (r. 488–531), was sympathetic for a time. In 528 Kavad's son, the future Chosroes Anosharvan, massacred Mazdak and his followers. Although this finished the Mazdakites, the name was still used later, in Islamic times, for various Iranian popular revolts.

SOUTH ASIA

Large-scale imperial expansion came much later to the South Asian, or Indian, subcontinent than to the Iranian plateau. A cultural and religious heritage going back to the Aryan invaders of North India influenced the subsequent history of the vast and diverse subcontinent. Political unity has been rare. Today's division into India, Pakistan, and Bangladesh is merely the most recent. Only four times has much of the whole come under one rule: in the Maurya, Gupta, Mughal, and British imperial epochs. We look now at the first two of these.

THE FIRST INDIAN EMPIRE: THE MAURYAS (321–185 B.C.E.)

HOW WAS the Maurya Empire created?

Alexander the Great conquered the Achaemenids' northwest Indian provinces of Gandhara and the Indus valley in 327 B.C.E. The conquest had little or no impact on the Indian subcontinent except in Gandhara, where Greek and Indian cultural interpenetration increased. Only with the Mauryas was much of North India and the Deccan incorporated into the first true Indian Empire.

POLITICAL BACKGROUND

The basis for empire in North India was the rise of regional states and commercial towns between the seventh and fourth centuries B.C.E. The most powerful of these were the monarchies of the Ganges plains. North and northwest, in the Himalayan foothills and in the Punjab, tribal republics were more common. The Buddha and Mahavira came from two of these republics (see Chapter 2), although both spent much of their lives in the two most powerful Gangetic monarchies, Kosala and Magadha.

THE MAURYAS

Chandragupta Maurya (r. ca. 321–297 B.C.E.), an adventurer who seized Magadha and the Ganges basin in about 324 B.C.E., established the first true Indian Empire (see Map 4-3). Marching westward into the vacuum created by Alexander's departure (326 B.C.E.), he brought the Indus region and much of west-central India under his control. A treaty with the invading Seleucus added Gandhara and Arachosia to his empire and led to much Seleucid–Maurya contact thereafter.

Chandragupta's fame as the first Indian empire builder is rivaled by that of his Brahman minister, Kautilya, who may have been the actual architect of Maurya rule. However, even though it is ascribed to him, he probably did not write the *Arthashastra*, the most famous Indian treatise on the arts of governing. Chandragupta's son and successor, Bindusara (r. ca. 297–272 B.C.E.), conquered the Deccan, the great plateau that covers central India.

•••[Read the **Document**
Kautilya, from Arthashastra, "The Duties of Government Superintendents" at **myhistorylab.com**

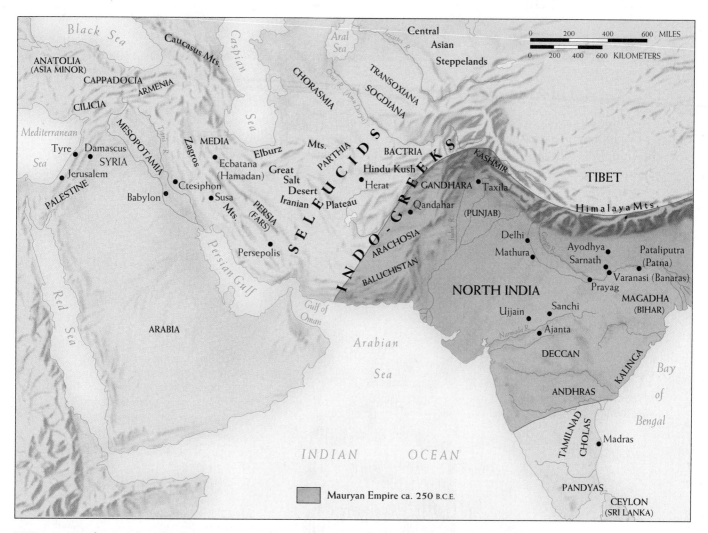

MAP 4–3.   Southwest Asia and India ca. 250 B.C.E.   This map shows not only the major cities and regions of the Iranian lands and the Indian subcontinent, but also the neighboring eastern Mediterranean world. Although the Mediterranean was closely tied to the Iranian plateau from Achaemenid times onward, its contacts with India in the wake of the conquests of Alexander the Great were many and varied.

Which states helped spread Greek culture from the Mediterranean to northern India?

The third and greatest Maurya, Ashoka (r. ca. 272–232 B.C.E.), left us numerous rock inscriptions. From Ashoka's edicts, we can piece together much of his reign and glimpse his character. In his first years as king, he conquered Kalinga, thus extending Maurya control over all the subcontinent except the far south.

Apparently revolted by the bloody Kalinga war, Ashoka underwent a religious conversion. Thereafter he pursued the Buddhist Middle Path as his ideal in both personal and state relations. He did not abandon all warfare, but he did eschew aggression in favor of "conquest by righteousness (*dharma*)." His edicts show that he pursued the laity's norm of the Buddhist *dharma*, striving to attain heaven by the merit of good actions. Ashoka eased some burdens imposed on the populace by earlier governments, and he instituted many beneficial public works. Ashoka provided the model of the ideal king for later Hindu and Buddhist thought—the *chakravartin*, or universal monarch who rules with righteousness, justice, and wisdom. He is a symbol of enlightened rule with few equals in history.

See the Map

Ashoka's Empire
at **myhistorylab.com**

QUICK REVIEW

Ashoka

♦ Considered a model ruler

♦ Rock inscriptions of his edicts are oldest deciphered Indian writings

♦ Converted to Buddhism after Kalinga war

♦ Appointed "*dharma* officials"

A Closer Look

Lion Capital of Ashoka at Sarnath

This sculpture, carved from a single sandstone block, sat originally (c. 250 B.C.E.) atop the Ashoka pillar or column at Sarnath, close by Varanasi (Banares) in present-day Uttar Pradesh, India. The base of the column is still in its original place (where it commemorated the Buddha's first sermon), but the lion capital resides in Sarnath Museum. The heads of the four Asiatic lions on the Ashoka column are said to have originally carried a large *dharmachakra* (now lost) above them. Used by Ashoka as the emblem of his rule, it was also adopted in 1950 as the Indian national emblem or seal and set, minus the lotus, over Sanskrit words from the Mundaka Upanishad, "Truth alone triumphs."

The *chakra*, or (chariot) wheel, was originally the prime Buddhist symbol, the "wheel of the Dharma" (*dharmachakra*), signifying the Buddha's teaching (*dharma*), often with eight spokes for the eightfold path, but here with twenty-four said to symbolize the Buddhist twelve laws of dependent origination and twelve of dependent cessation. Today the *dharmachakra*, or *ashokachakra*, is also the central emblem on the flag of India, representing the eternal wheel of cosmic law (Dharma).

The three visible and fourth (unseen here) lions sit on an abacus of circular *chakra* shape, on which an encircling frieze is emblazoned with four *chakras* alternating with four animals that may have represented four periods of the Buddha's life. The Indian national emblem interprets them as guardians of the four directions: the lion (north), elephant (east), horse (south), and bull (west). Some have seen Achaemenid Persian influence on these figures and the lions above.

The Ashoka capital rests on a bell-shaped lotus blossom in bloom, associated with purity in ancient Hindu and Buddhist lore, and sometimes said to represent the fountainhead of life and creativity.

The Great Stupa at Sanchi. This is an outstanding example of early Buddhist relic mounds. The mound, seated on an Ashokan foundation, was added to over the centuries. Magnificent carvings adorn its stone railing and gateways, one of which is shown in the left foreground. Sanchi is located in north-central India.

How does the worship of relics reflect Hindu influence on Buddhist practice?

Questions

1. Why might Ashoka have chosen the elements used in this capital as emblematic of his rule? Draw on what you know of his reign and life.

2. Why might independent India have decided on this royal emblem of an ancient Buddhist ruler as its national emblem? How does its symbolism transcend its possible original Buddhist symbolism?

3. How can the *chakra* be an apposite symbol both in Ashokan usage and in modern Indian usage?

By the end of Ashoka's reign, however, the empire's size hampered effective administration, and under his successors, Maurya rule disintegrated. Neither Ashoka's Buddhism nor his rejection of aggression was the cause of decline; more likely factors were economic strains and increased bureaucratic corruption, as well as his heirs' inability to claim the personal allegiances he had maintained. After his death local dynasties seized power in many areas.

In its heyday, Maurya bureaucracy was marked by centralization, standardization, and efficiency in long-distance communications; civil and military organization; tax collection; and information gathering. The fundamental unit of government was the village. Groups of villages formed districts within the larger provincial unit. Governors sent from the capital controlled most provinces.

The administration of the empire depended primarily on the king himself. Each of the three great Maurya kings was associated with one of the "new" religious movements of the age: Chandragupta with the Jains (see Chapter 2), his son with an ascetic tradition known as that of the Ajivikas, and Ashoka with the Buddhists. Such links must have strengthened Maurya claims to righteous leadership.

Revenues in the Maurya Empire came primarily from taxing the produce of the land, which was regarded as the king's property. Urban trade and production were also taxed heavily. The Maurya economic system also involved slavery, although most of it was domestic labor, often a kind of temporary indentured service.

Cities thrived across the empire. They were centers for arts, crafts, industry, literature, and education. Ashokan stone buildings and sculpture reflect sophisticated aesthetics and technique, as well as strong Persian and Greek influence.

An imperial ideal, a strengthened Buddhist movement, and strong central administration were among the Mauryas' gifts to Indian culture. They also left behind new cosmopolitan traditions of external relations and internal communication. Their many contacts with the West reflect their international perspective. The edicts suggest that writing and reading had become common. The Mauryas' excellent road system would later serve as routes for Buddhism's spread to Central Asia and China, as well as corridors for successive invaders moving in the opposite direction.

QUICK REVIEW

The Maurya State

- Government was centralized, standardized, and efficient
- The fundamental unit of government was the village
- Administration depended on the king

✓●─[Study and **Review**
at **myhistorylab.com**

◉─[See the Map
India at the Time of Ashoka, ca. 268–237 B.C.E. at **myhistorylab.com**

CHRONOLOGY

INDIA FROM THE SIXTH CENTURY B.C.E. to the End of Maurya Rule

ca. 600–400 B.C.E.	Late Upanishadic age: local/regional kingdoms and tribal republics along the Ganges and in Himalayan foothills, the Punjab, and northwestern India
ca. 550–324 B.C.E.	Regional empire of Maghadan kings
ca. 540–ca. 468 B.C.E.	Vardhamana Mahavira, Jain founder
ca. 537–ca. 486 B.C.E.	Siddhartha Gautama, the Buddha
330–325 B.C.E.	Alexander campaigns in Indus valley, Sogdiana, Bactria, and Punjab
324–ca. 185 B.C.E.	Maurya Empire controls most of northern India and the Deccan
ca. 272–232 B.C.E.	Reign of the Maurya emperor Ashoka

THE CONSOLIDATION OF INDIAN CIVILIZATION (ca. 200 B.C.E.–300 C.E.)

WHAT ROLES did Buddhism play in post-Maurya Indian culture?

In the post-Maurya period, the history of North India was dominated by the influx of various foreign peoples. In the rest of the subcontinent, indigenous Indian dynasties held sway, establishing a general pattern of regional and local political autonomy. Religiously and culturally, however, the centuries between the Mauryas and the Gupta Dynasty saw the consolidation of transregional patterns that permanently shaped Indian and, through the diffusion of Buddhism, Asian civilization.

THE ECONOMIC BASE

Although agriculture remained the basis of the post-Maurya economy, India's merchant classes prospered. The fine Maurya road system facilitated trade throughout India. India became a center of world trade largely because of Chinese and Roman demand for Indian luxury goods—jewels, semiprecious stones, sandalwood, teak, spices, cotton and silk textiles, exotic animals, and slaves. Within India, guild organizations flourished and provided technical education in skilled crafts. Coin minting increased after Maurya times, and banking flourished.

HIGH CULTURE

The great achievements of the post-Maurya arts were primarily Buddhist in inspiration. The Gandharan school of Buddhist art emerged in northwestern India. In Gandharan sculpture, Hellenistic naturalism of form joined with the more recent Indian tradition of Buddha images, producing sculptural figures with flowing draped garments through which the muscular lines of the human body are discernible. In central India as early as the first century B.C.E., artists were producing stone-relief sculpture with the naturalistic, yet flowing, human and animal forms that would become earmarks of the "classical" style of Indian art. The finest surviving examples are at the great Buddhist *stupas* (shrines) of Bharhut and Sanchi.

✓•—[Study and Review
at **myhistorylab.com**

Language and literature during this period rested on the sophisticated Sanskrit grammar of Panini (ca. 300 B.C.E.?), which remains standard even today. Two Sanskrit masterpieces, the epics of the *Mahabharata* and the *Ramayana*, probably took shape by 200 C.E. The first is a composite work concerned largely with the nature of *Dharma* (the moral and cosmic Law; see Chapter 2). Included in its earlier, narrative portions are systematic treatments of *Dharma*, such as the Bhagavad Gita, or "Song of the Blessed Lord," the most influential of all Indian religious texts.

RELIGION AND SOCIETY

Brahmans continued to dominate Vedic learning and ritual. The major developments shaping "Hindu" tradition were (1) the consolidation of the caste system, Brahman ascendancy, and the "high" culture of Sanskrit learning; (2) the increasing dominance of theistic devotionalism (especially the cults of Vishnu and Shiva); and (3) the intellectual reconciliation of these developments with the older ascetic and speculative traditions deriving from the Upanishadic age. These social and religious developments would continue and solidify in the Gupta era and beyond.

Indian Buddhist monastic communities prospered under mercantile and royal patronage, especially in or near urban centers. Buddhist lay devotion figured prominently in Indian religious life. It was, however, a different tradition from the Buddhism of the theological texts, which focuses on the quest for *nirvana* and the "extraordinary norm" (see Chapter 2). The Buddha and Buddhist saints were naturally identified with popular Indian deities, and Buddhist worship easily assimilated to common Indian patterns of theistic piety. One reason that Buddhist tradition remained only one among many Indian religious paths was its absorption into the religious variety that then and now typifies the Hindu religious scene.

THE GOLDEN AGE OF THE GUPTAS (ca. 320–550 C.E.)

Indians have always considered the Gupta era a golden age of civilization in the subcontinent. Historians have seen it as the source of "classical" norms for Hindu religion and Indian culture—the symbolic equivalent of Periclean Athens, Augustan Rome, Sasanid Persia, or Han China. Most of the Guptas's reign was marked by relative peace and stability.

GUPTA RULE

The first Gupta king was Chandragupta (r. 320–ca. 330 C.E.), who became prominent in the whole Ganges basin after he married Princess Kumaradevi, daughter of a powerful tribal leader. Their son, Samudragupta (r. ca. 330–375), and especially their grandson, Chandragupta II (r. 375–415), turned kingdom into empire (see Map 4-2). Gupta splendor and power had no rival. Under Chandragupta II, India was arguably the most civilized and peaceful country in the world.

By about 500 a new wave of steppe nomads, the Huns, had overrun western India. This contributed to the collapse of the Gupta Empire in about 550.

GUPTA CULTURE

The Gupta era's claim to being India's golden age of culture could be sustained solely by its magnificent sculpture, the wall paintings of the Ajanta caves, and Kalidasa's matchless

WHY IS the Gupta Empire considered a high point of Indian civilization?

●•●─┤**Read** the **Document**
Excerpt from Kama Sutra (1883)
Vatsayayana at **myhistorylab.com**

Gupta Sculpture. Fifth-century C.E. statue of Lokanatha from Sarnath, which, despite damage, shows the fine sculptural work of the important school of Gupta artists at Sarnath and the influence on them of both Greco-Roman antecedents and native Indian traditions and conventions.

What are some of the details visible in this sculpture?

CHRONOLOGY

INDIA FROM THE GUPTA AGE TO ca. 1000 C.E.

320–550 C.E.	Gupta period
320–330	Reign of Chandragupta, first Gupta king
376–454	Reigns of Chandragupta II and Kumaragupta: Kalidasa flourishes; heyday of Gupta culture
399–414	Chinese Buddhist monk Faxien travels in India
ca. 440-500	Hun invasions from Central Asia into North India; Gupta decline, especially after Skandagupta's death in 467
550–ca. 1000	Regional Indian kingdoms in north and south; major Puranas composed; age of first great Vaishnava and Shaivite devotional poets in southern India
616–657	Reign of Harsha; revival of Gupta splendor and power
820	Death of Shankara, Vedantin philosopher-theologian

QUICK REVIEW

"Golden" Gupta Culture

- Kalidasa, the "Shakespeare" of Sanskrit letters
- Sarnath sculpture
- Ajanta cave-shrine

View the Image
Closer Look Ch. 4
at **myhistorylab.com**

dharma
Moral law or duty.

varnas
The four main classes that form the basis for Hindu caste relations.

jatis
The many subgroups that make up the Hindu caste system.

drama and verse. The "Shakespeare" of Sanskrit letters, Kalidasa flourished in the time of Chandragupta II and his successor.

We can see the depth of Gupta culture in its emphasis on education. In addition to religious texts, typical subjects included rhetoric, prose and poetic composition, grammar, logic, medicine, and metaphysics. Using an older Indian number system that the Arabs transmitted to Europe as "Arabic numerals," Gupta scholars cultivated mathematics especially.

Even in handwork and luxury crafts, Gupta products achieved new levels of quality and were in great demand abroad: silks, muslin, linen, ivory and other carvings, bronze metalwork, gold and silver work, and cut stones, among others.

RELIGION AND SOCIETY

The hierarchical character of Hindu/Indian society was formalized. The oldest manual of legal and ethical theory, the *Dharmashastra* of Manu, dates from about 200 C.E. Based on Vedic tradition, it treats the **dharma** appropriate to one's class and stage of life, rules for rites and study of the Veda, pollution and purification measures, dietary restrictions, royal duties and prerogatives, and other legal and moral questions.

In the *Dharmashastra* we find the classic statement of the four-class theory of social hierarchy. This traditional construct rests on the principle that every person is born into a particular station in life (as a result of *karma* from earlier lives), and every station has its particular *dharma*, or appropriate duties and responsibilities, from the lowest servant to the highest prince or Brahman. The Brahmans' ancient division of Aryans into the four **varnas**, or classes, of *Brahman* (priest), *Kshatriya* (noble/warrior/ruler), *Vaishya* (tradesperson/merchant etc.), and *Shudra* (servant/worker) provides a schematic structure. Although class distinctions had already hardened before 500 B.C.E., the classes were, in practice, somewhat fluid.

Much smaller and far more numerous subgroups, or **jatis**, are the units to which our English term *caste* best refers. These divisions (most representing originally occupational groups) were already the primary units of social distinction in Gupta times. *Jati* groupings are hereditary and distinguished essentially on principles of purity and pollution, which are expressed in three kinds of regulation: (1) commensality (one may take food only from or with persons of the same or a higher group); (2) endogamy (one may marry only within the group); and (3) trade or craft limitation (one must practice only the trade of one's group).

The caste system has been the basis of Indian social organization for at least two millennia. It enabled Hindus to accommodate foreign cultural, racial, and religious communities within Indian society by treating them as new caste groups. It permitted everyone to tell by dress and other marks how to relate to another person or group, thus giving stability and security to the individual and to society. It also represented the logical extension of the doctrine of *karma* into society—whether as justification, result, or partial cause of the system itself (see Chapter 2).

The Guptas' support of Brahmanic traditions and Vaishnava devotionalism reflected the waning of Buddhist traditions in the mainstream of Indian religious life. Devotional cults continued to grow in popularity. After Vishnu (especially in his form as the hero-savior Krishna) and Shiva (originally a fertility god), the chief focus of devotion came to be the Goddess in one of her many forms, such as Parvati, Shakti, Durga, or Kali.

Indian reverence for all forms of life and stress on *ahimsa*, or "noninjury" to living beings (see Chapter 2), are most vivid in the sacredness of the cow, a mainstay of life in India. In the development of Hindu piety and practice, a major strand was the tradition

The Buddhist temple of Borobodur, with tiers of stupas looking out over the island of Java. Built out of a half million blocks of stone, it represents a schema of the Buddhist cosmos. Construction began late in the eighth century; the temple was intended originally to be a Hindu sanctuary.
What is the relationship between Hinduism and Buddhism?

of ardent theism known as *bhakti*, or "loving devotion." *Bhakti* was already evident in the Bhagavad Gita's treatment of Krishna. Gupta and later times saw the rise, especially in the Tamil-speaking south, of schools of bhakti poetry and worship. Also of major importance to devotional piety was the development in this era of the Puranas—epic, mythological, and devotional texts. They are still the functional sacred scriptures of grass-roots Hindu religious life, the Vedic texts remaining the special preserve of the Brahmans.

Whatever god or goddess a Hindu worships, it is usual to also pay homage on proper occasions to other appropriate deities. Most Hindus view one deity as their Supreme Lord but see others as manifestations of the Ultimate at lower levels. Hindu polytheism vividly affirms the infinite forms that transcendence takes in this world. The sense of the presence of the Divine everywhere is evident in the importance attached to sacred places.

The intellectual articulation of Hindu polytheism and relativism found its finest expression in post-Gupta formulations of Vedanta ("the end of the Veda"). The major Vedantin thinker, Shankara (d. 820), stressed a strict "nonduality" of the Ultimate, teaching that Brahman was the only Reality behind the "illusion" (*maya*) of the world of sense experience. Yet he accepted the worship of a lesser deity as appropriate for those who could not follow his extraordinary norm—the intellectual realization of the formless Absolute beyond all "name and form."

QUICK REVIEW

Bhakti

- *Bhakti*, or loving devotion, evident in the Bhagavad Gita's treatment of Krishna
- Derives in part from Tamil and other vernacular poets
- Through *bhakti*, pre-Aryan religious sensibilities reasserted themselves

Mahayana
The "Great Vehicle" for salvation in Buddhism. It emphasized the Buddha's infinite compassion for all beings.

Theravada
The "Way of the Elders." A school of Buddhism that emphasized the monastic ideal.

bodhisattva
A "Buddha to be" who postpones his own nirvana until he has helped all other beings become enlightened.

Within the Buddhist tradition, the major developments of these centuries were (1) the solidification of the two main strands of Buddhist tradition, the **Mahayana** and the **Theravada**, and (2) the spread of Buddhism abroad from its Indian homeland. The Mahayana ("Great Vehicle [of salvation]") arose in the first century B.C.E. Its proponents differentiated it sharply from the older, more conservative traditions of monk-oriented piety, which they labeled the Hinayana ("Little Vehicle"). In Mahayana speculation Buddhas were seen as manifestations of a single principle of "Ultimate" Reality, and Siddhartha Gautama was held to be only one Buddha among many. The Mahayana stressed the model of the Buddha's infinite compassion for all beings. The highest goal was not a *nirvana* of "selfish" extinction but the status of a **bodhisattva**, or "Buddha-to-be," who postpones his own nirvana until he has helped all other beings become enlightened.

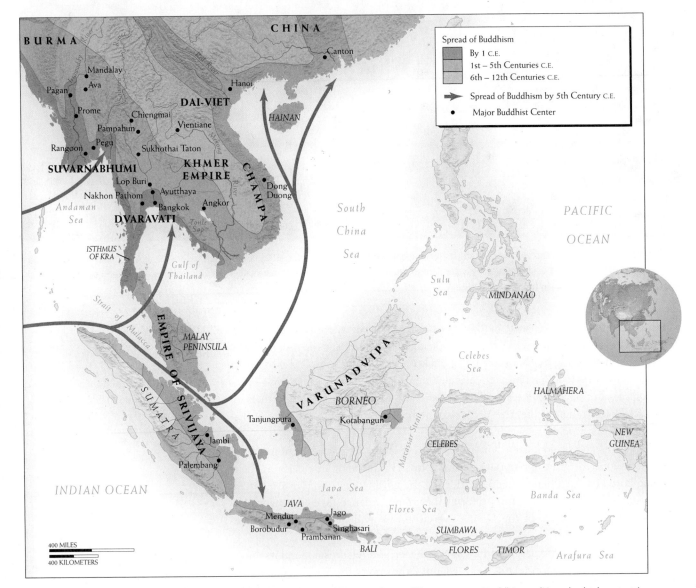

MAP 4-4.   Spread of Buddhist Traditions throughout Southeast Asia.   By the twelfth century C.E., Buddhist traditions had taken root in many parts of Southeast Asia, often blending with local customs, as well as Hindu traditions that had been introduced earlier.

How did the spread of Buddhism in Southeast Asia replicate the earlier spread of Hindu traditions? Were there differences in the ways Hindu traditions spread and the ways Buddhism spread?

The *bodhisattva* can offer this aid because his long career of self-sacrifice has gained him infinite merit. Salvation becomes possible not only through individual merit, but also through devotion to the Buddhas and *bodhisattvas*. At the popular level, this idea translated into devotional cults of transcendent Buddhas and *bodhisattvas* conceived as cosmic beings. One of the most important of these beings was the Buddha Amitabha, who personifies infinite compassion. Amitabha presides over a Western Paradise, or Pure Land, to which all who have faith in him have access. (See Chapter 9 on Pure Land Buddhism in Japan.)

The older, more conservative "Way of the Elders" (Theravada) always focused on the monastic community but taught that service and gifts to the monks were a major source of merit for the laity. It emphasized gaining merit for a better rebirth through righteous conduct, lay devotion to the Buddha, and pilgrimage to his relics at various shrines, or **stupas**. The basis of Theravada piety and practice was the scriptural collection of traditional teachings ascribed to the Buddha, as reported by his disciples.

stupa
A Buddhist shrine.

Indian culture experienced little new outside influence from the Gupta era until Islamic times (after about 1000 C.E.). India's chief contacts were now with Southeast Asia and China, and most of the cultural transmission was from India eastward, not vice versa. India gave Theravada Buddhism to Ceylon, Burma, and parts of Southeast Asia (see Map 4-4). Mahayana Buddhism predominated in Central Asia and China, from which it spread in the fifth through eighth centuries to Korea and Japan. Tantric Buddhism, an esoteric Mahayana tradition heavily influenced by Hinduism, entered Tibet from North India in the seventh century and became the dominant tradition there.

SUMMARY

 WHAT WERE the main teachings of Zoroaster, and how did Zoroastrianism influence other traditions?

Ancient Background and the First Persian Empire in the Iranian Plateau (550–330 B.C.E.). Ancient Iranian traditions had much in common with Vedic Aryan beliefs. Zarathustra (known in Greek as Zoroaster) spread a message of moral reform and emphasized a single supreme deity, Ahura Mazda. Zoroaster's teachings influenced later monotheistic religions, as well as Buddhism. The Persian Achaemenid Empire, based in Iran, established two centuries of tolerant, stable, prosperous rule from Egypt to the borders of India. Although the Achaemenid regime was tolerant of diverse religious traditions, the rulers practiced Zoroastrianism. *page 93*

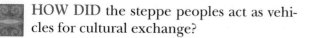 **HOW DID** the steppe peoples act as vehicles for cultural exchange?

Successor States and Steppe Peoples. The Hellenic Empire of the Seleucids, starting around 312 B.C.E., permitted trade and culture to flourish from the Mediterranean to India. Seleucid rule fostered Greek culture in Western Asia. The Parthians (247 B.C.E.–223 C.E.) continued many Achaemenid traditions. They were religiously tolerant but supported Zoroastrianism, and laid much of the groundwork for later Persian nationalism. The Indo-Greeks of Bactria helped spread Greek ideas and aesthetics, while also helping Buddhism spread beyond India. Steppe peoples—particularly the Scythians and Kushans—fostered cross-cultural contact throughout the Iranian and Indian realms. *page 98*

HOW DID the Sasanids build a strong state?

The Sasanid Empire. The Sasanids sought to restore the glory of the ancient Achaemenid Persian Empire and promoted native Persian culture. They based their rule on orthodox Zoroastrianism and suppressed the Manichaeans as heretics. Although foreign trade flourished, Sasanid rulers favored the landed aristocracy at the expense of the peasantry, who were heavily taxed. Long wars with Rome and Byzantium ultimately sapped Sasanid strength and left the empire vulnerable to Islamic Arab invasion in the seventh century. *page 100*

HOW WAS the Maurya Empire created?

The First Indian Empire: The Mauryas (321–185 B.C.E.). The Mauryas created the first true empire in India, starting around 321 B.C.E., using conquest, treaties, and possibly marriage to gain territory. The third Maurya ruler, Ashoka, has served as a universal model of enlightened rule. The strong and cosmopolitan Maurya Empire absorbed cultural influences from the Persians and the Greeks, among others. Buddhism flourished. *page 104*

WHAT ROLES did Buddhism play in post-Maurya Indian culture?

The Consolidation of Indian Civilization (ca. 200 B.C.E.–300 C.E.). Trade was important in post-Mauryan India. Both Buddhist and Hindu devotional cults gained popularity. The arts were heavily influenced by Buddhism. *page 108*

WHY IS the Gupta Empire considered a high point of Indian civilization?

Golden Age of the Guptas. The Gupta period (320–467 C.E.) is considered one of the highlights of Indian civilization. Indian civilization took on its enduring "Hindu" social, religious, and cultural shape. The fundamentally hierarchic nature of the caste system solidified. Hindu piety emphasized devotional cults to deities, especially Vishnu and Shiva. Indian Buddhism developed two main schools, the Mahayana and the Theravada, which spread to other parts of Asia. *page 109*

KEY TERMS

Ahura Mazda (ah-HOO-rah MAHZ-dah) (p. 94)
bodhisattva (p. 112)
dharma (p. 110)
Indo-Greeks (p. 99)
jatis (p. 110)
Magi **(MEY-jeye)** (p. 95)
Mahayana (p. 112)

Manichaeism (p. 103)
satrap **(sah-TRAP)** (p. 97)
Shahanshah (p. 96)
steppe peoples (p. 98)
stupa (p. 113)
Theravada (p. 112)
varna (p. 110)
Zoroastrianism (p. 95)

REVIEW QUESTIONS

1. Why was the Achaemenid Empire successful for so long? What was the political basis for Achaemenid power?

2. How was the Maurya Empire created? What role did Greeks play in its creation? How did Ashoka develop Maurya power and prestige?

3. How did the role of religion in the Achaemenid Empire compare to its role in the Maurya Empire?

4. Compare the historical importance of the Achaemenid and the Maurya empires. How does each compare to the empires of Rome and Han China?

5. Compare the major features of the Hindu and Buddhist traditions. Why do you think Buddhism and not Hinduism spread to much of Asia?

6. How did the Kushans, Scythians, and other inner Asian groups play important roles in world history?

7. What are the key elements of Manichaean religion? How was it related to Christian and Zoroastrian traditions?

8. How did the Sasanid Empire develop after the fall of the Parthians? What were the principal economic bases of the Sasanid state?

9. What were the major religious issues in the Sasanid Empire? What role did Zoroastrian "orthodoxy" play in Sasanid affairs?

10. How did new religious ideas come to Central Asia and China in these centuries?

11. In what sense can the high Gupta period (ca. 320–450 C.E.) be considered a "golden age"? What was the extent of the empire? Why did it collapse?

12. What factors in Persia and India in the seventh century might have made the Arab invasions possible?

13. What major affinities and differences do you see between the classical Buddhist and Hindu traditions that had crystallized by 500 C.E.?

Note: To learn more about the topics in this chapter, please turn to the Suggested Readings at the end of the book. For additional sources related to this chapter please see www.myhistorylab.com

PEARSON
myhistorylab Connections

Reinforce what you learned in this chapter by studying the many documents, images, maps, review tools, and videos available at **www.myhistorylab.com**

Read and Review

✓• Study and Review   Chapter 4

•• Read the Document   *Kautilya, from Arthashastra, "The Duties of Government Superintendents," p. 104*
Excerpt from Kama Sutra (1883) Vatsayayana, p. 109

◉• See the Map   *Ashoka's Empire, p. 105*
Arabia Before the Prophet, ca. 250–600 C.E, p. 100
India at the Time of Ashoka, ca. 268–237 B.C.E., p. 107

•• View the Image   *Closer Look, p. 106*

Research and Explore

◉• See the Map   *The Persian Empire at Its Greatest Extent, p. 97*

◉• Watch the Video   *The Aryans in India*

— ((• Hear the **Audio** —

Hear the audio file for Chapter 4
at **www.myhistorylab.com**

HINDUISM

The term *Hinduism* is our modern word for the whole of the diverse religious traditions of India. Until the word was coined in the nineteenth century, it (like *Buddhism*) was not even a concept in the West, let alone in India. In contemporary usage, it has become a catchall term for all the Indian religious communities that look upon the texts of the Vedas (see Chapter 1) as eternal, perfect truth.

The historical beginnings of the varied Hindu traditions can be traced to the ancient Aryan migrations into southern Asia in the second millennium B.C.E. During this era the Vedic hymns were composed. They describe a pantheon of gods not unlike that among the Greeks, the Romans, the Iranians, and other Indo-European peoples. Centered on a sacrificial cult of these gods, Vedic religion increasingly became the preserve of the Brahman priestly class of early Indian society. The Brahmans gradually elaborated a cult characterized by sacrificial rituals, purificatory rules, and fixed distinctions of birth on which India's later caste system was based (see Chapter 4). These developments are mirrored in the later Vedic, or Brahmanical, texts (ca. 1000–500 B.C.E.) that provide commentary on and instructions for ritual use of the Vedic hymns.

After about 700 B.C.E. new developments emerged. North India produced a series of religious reformers, some of whom broke with Vedic tradition and championed knowledge and ascetic discipline over purity and ritual action. Of these, the most famous were Siddhartha Gautama (the Buddha, b. ca. 563 B.C.E.) and Mahavira Vardhamana (founder of the Jain tradition, b. ca. 550 B.C.E.). Other religious leaders reinterpreted the older sacrifice as an inner activity and deepened its spiritual dimensions. Their thinking is represented especially in the Upanishads, which many Hindus consider the most sublime philosophical texts in the Indian tradition.

Developed so long ago, such notions have been part of the complex vision of existence that lies behind the myriad forms of religious life known to us as Hinduism. In this vision the immortal part of each human being, the *atman*, is enmeshed in existence, but not ultimately of it. The nature of existence is *samsara*, a

Dancing Shiva. A magnificent South Indian bronze of Shiva. The fluid, balanced image depicts the so-called dancing Shiva engaged in his dance of simultaneous destruction and creation of the universe, an artistic-mythical rendering of the eternal flux of all worldly existence (13th century; bronze; 33.5 × 24.8 cm).

© The Nelson-Atkins Museum of Art, Kansas City, MO. (Purchase: Nelson Trust) 50-20.

In what ways is the circle an appropriate symbol for Hindu beliefs?

ceaseless round of cause and effect determined by the inescapable consequences of *karma*, or "action." The doctrine of *karma* is a moral as well as physical economy in which every act has unavoidable results; as long as mental or physical action occurs, life and change go on repeatedly. Birth determines one's place and duties in the traditional Indian caste system. Caste is the most visible and concrete reminder of the pervasiveness of the Hindu concept of absolute causality that keeps us enmeshed in existence. The final goal is to transcend this cycle, or *samsara*, in which we are all caught. The only way out of this otherwise endless becoming and rebirth is *moksha*, which may be gained through knowledge, action, or devotion.

On the popular level, the period after about 500 B.C.E. is most notable in Indian religious life for two developments. Both took place alongside the ever deeper entrenchment in society of caste distinctions and a supporting ethic of obligations and privileges. The first was the elaboration of ascetic traditions of inner quest and self-realization, such as that of yoga. The second was the rise of devotional worship of specific gods and goddesses who were seen by their worshipers as identical with the Ultimate—in other words, as supreme deities for those who served them. The latter development was of particular importance for popular religion in India. Evident in the famous and beloved Hindu devotional text, the Bhagavad Gita, it reached its highest level after 500 B.C.E. in the myriad movements of fervent, loving devotionalism, or *bhakti*, many of which remain important today. A striking aspect of Hindu piety has been its willingness to accommodate the focus on one "chosen deity" who is worshiped as supreme to a worldview that holds that the Divine can and does take many forms. Thus most Hindus worship one deity, but they do so in the awareness that faith in other deities can also lead one to the Ultimate.

The period between about 500 B.C.E. and 1000 C.E. saw the rise to special prominence of two gods, Vishnu and Shiva, as the primary forms in which the Supreme Lord was worshiped. Along with the mother-goddess figure, who takes various names and forms (Kali and Durga, for example), Vishnu and Shiva have remained the most important manifestations of the Divine in

Purification rituals in the waters of the holy Ganges. Purification rituals are part of the obligatory daily rituals of all "twice-born" Hindus. The morning purificatory-bathing rituals performed by the women here in the Ganges include greeting the sun with recitation and prayer.

Can you think of similar water-based rituals in other faiths?

India. Their followers are known as Vaishnavas and Shaivas, respectively. A few recurring phenomena and ideas can suggest something of Indian religiousness in practice.

Hindu practice is characterized especially by temple worship (*puja*), in which worshipers bring offerings of flowers, food, and the like. They especially seek out temple images for the blessing that the sight of these images brings. Another important part of Hindu devotionalism is the recitation of sacred texts, many of which are vernacular hymns of praise to a particular deity. *Mantras*, or special recitative texts from the Vedas, are thought to have extraordinary power and are used by many Hindus in their original Sanskrit form. Pilgrimage to sacred sites, especially rivers, mountains, and famous shrines, is a prominent part of Hindu religious life. India's landscape is filled with sacred sites and sacred pilgrim routes, both local and national in reputation. A prominent feature of Hindu life is preoccupation with purity and pollution, most evident in the food taboos associated with caste groupings.

The ascetic tendency in India is also highly developed. Although only a tiny minority of Indians take up a life of full renunciation, they are influential. Ascetic worshipers do not settle in one place, acquire possessions, or perform regular worship. Rather, they wander about in search of teachers and devote themselves to meditation and self-realization. Even though most Hindus have families and work at their salvation through *puja* and moral living, the ascetic ideal has an important place in the overall Indian worldview. It stands as a constant reminder of the deeper reality beyond the everyday world and any individual life.

◆ Compared to other faiths that have expanded globally, such as Christianity and Islam, why has Hinduism been largely confined to India?

◆ How has Hinduism accommodated and absorbed different beliefs and value systems?

5

Africa: Early History to 1000 C.E.

Rock Art from Tassili n'Ajjer National Park in Algeria, a UNESCO World Heritage Site. This painting might represent women gathering grain. It is one of a large group of works created between approximately 8000 B.C.E. and the early part of the Common Era. Now part of the Sahara Desert, at the time this area was much wetter and supported populations of large animals (other paintings show giraffes, elephants, and other animals) and humans.

Henri Lhote Collection. Musée de l'Homme, Paris, France/© Erich Lessing/Art Resource, New York.

How did changes in the climate of the Sahara influence settlement patterns and trade?

We now turn from the ancient societies that emerged in the Persian, Greek, and Hellenistic worlds to the world's second-largest continent—Africa. East Africa was the original home for the human species. In the ancient world, pharaonic Egypt, the Kushite kingdoms of Napata and Meroe, and the Ethiopian state of Aksum were all major powers with highly complex cultures in regular interchange with other civilizations from Rome to India and beyond. The Bantu expansion is one of the epic migrations of human history. The myriad ways Africans have adapted to various challenging environments provide invaluable information about human societies. Finally, the difficulties of writing African history have encouraged scholars to cross traditional disciplinary boundaries, bringing important new perspectives and tools to the repertoire of all historians.

GLOBAL PERSPECTIVE

"TRADITIONAL" PEOPLES AND NONTRADITIONAL HISTORIES

People in early African societies, like people everywhere, had definite ideas about what was important in their past—they had histories. What most of them did not have was writing, and historians have built their craft around interpretation of written records. African histories were generally transmitted in performance: in songs, poems, dances, rituals, and other activities that symbolically reenacted events from the past. Before the twentieth century, such performances and the artifacts they left behind (such as masks and costumes, rock paintings, ceremonial sites) lay outside historians' purview. Growing discontent with the privileging of the affairs and interests of societal elites—emphasis on ruling dynasties, wars, exploration, and invention, at the expense of the lives of ordinary people—eventually led historians to experiment with different types of source material and to subject traditional documentary sources to new types of analysis.

Historians of Africa arguably have to work harder than specialists in other regions to gather the information they need, but they also have unusually rich opportunities to collaborate with scholars in other disciplines. They often call themselves "Africanists" or "African Studies" scholars, to reflect their necessary expertise in fields such as paleontology, archaeology, anthropology, linguistics, demography, and oral literature. In their typically cross-disciplinary work, they are similar to Classicists, whose training may incorporate history, ancient languages, archaeology, art history, and other fields, or Environmental Historians, who highlight the role of nature in historical narratives, and whose backgrounds might include study in history, climatology, geography, biology, and other fields.

Academic research in African history is still an amazingly recent phenomenon. In the academic year 1958–1959, of 1,735 history graduate students in the United States, precisely one was concentrating on African history.[1] Within the past century,

---

[1]Steven Feierman, "African Histories and the Dissolution of World History," in R. Bates et al., eds., *Africa and the Disciplines* (Chicago: University of Chicago Press, 1993), p. 168.

ISSUES OF INTERPRETATION, SOURCES, AND DISCIPLINES

WHAT ARE the sources and techniques used for studying African history?

THE QUESTION OF "CIVILIZATION"

In Chapter 1 we defined "civilization" in terms of a cluster of attributes that relate to social complexity and technological development. In that sense the term identifies some common characteristics of the ancient societies that emerged in the valleys of the Nile, Mesopotamia, the Indus and Ganges, and China, and also of more recent societies. The term *civilization* is also associated more broadly with the sophistication of a people's intellectual, cultural, and artistic traditions. Too often we assume that societies that lack writing, cities, or a state bureaucracy are "uncivilized." Most historical African societies—indeed, most societies anywhere for most of history—may not have been civilizations in the narrow sense, but they were civilized in the broader sense. Like other continents, Africa has been home to both "civilizations"—large-scale states with writing, cities, and technology—and "civilized" societies that relied on rich traditions for their identities while adapting to changing circumstances and shaping their own histories.

SOURCE ISSUES

African history has matured in recent decades, but there is still much we do not know. Written documents, the evidence historians are most comfortable using, are minimal for much of sub-Saharan African history. Local oral traditions provide one valuable source of information (see Document, "Origins of the Gikuyu" on page 122). But oral traditions can give us access only to relatively recent history. Another source for African history is archaeology. The tropical climate that prevails in much of sub-Saharan Africa unfortunately destroys many types of artifacts that survive in drier regions. Nonetheless, archaeological scholarship has brought to light many formerly unknown

intellectuals in Europe and America (not coincidentally, the same parts of the world where governments held colonies and legislated race-based discrimination) widely considered Africans to be "primitives" whose lives were governed by ancestral traditions and whose cultures were static, largely untouched by historical processes. Twentieth-century events—most visibly the wave of decolonization that swept Africa after World War II—demonstrated that Africans had a role in world history. The development of African universities and the internationalization of Western academia have created a small cadre of Africanists. These scholars have done important work, some of which has influenced historical study of other parts of the world; still, many questions in African history remain unanswered. Fifty years ago textbooks like this one insisted that "civilization" required not only population density, political organization, and writing, but also the plow. In the intervening decades, researchers in Africa and elsewhere have proven that in many places, plows quickly destroy the soil; some peoples' use of hoes instead of plows does not signal technological backwardness, but intelligent adaptation to local conditions. Consequently, this and other textbooks now consider metallurgy, not the use of plows, a hallmark of civilization. Some historians—including Africanists, as well as many who study women, peasants, and other groups whose members were generally illiterate—now question whether even writing is a necessary attribute of civilization.

Focus Questions

◆ What are the advantages and disadvantages of using written texts as primary sources for history?

◆ Think about the histories of other regions you have studied. Have you noticed historians using sources other than documents in these histories? If so, what kinds of sources?

◆ For histories of what other regions, peoples, or topics (e.g., history of science, art history, history of religion) can scholars make good use of nonwritten sources?

cultures. The Nok and Zimbabwean cultures, for example, left impressive but hard-to-decipher remains. Reports from outside observers are another source. It is only after about 950 C.E., however, that Islamic (and later, European) historians, geographers, and travelers provide detailed descriptions of the vast reaches of Africa beyond Egypt, Ethiopia, and North Africa. These outside records are of mixed value, since most authors brought strong biases to their assessments of this vast, diverse continent.

HISTORY AND DISCIPLINARY BOUNDARIES

History as we know it came of age in tandem with European nation-states. As the modern university emerged—with knowledge departmentalized into disciplines—Europe's global technological and economic dominance was immense. Around the time of the nineteenth-century European "Scramble for Africa" (see Chapter 26), racism combined with colonial self-interest caused many Western intellectuals to assume that Africans (and other "primitive" peoples) lived outside of historical time: Their lives were the same as their ancestors' lives, no matter how many generations into the past one looked—they had no history. According to European nationalism, one of the criteria for nationhood was that a people have a shared history (see Chapter 23). Conveniently, Africans and others who lacked history were incapable of forming their own nations.

There were interesting features of these peoples' lives, however, and academics who wanted to study them. Thus was born the discipline of anthropology. Anthropology has changed considerably over the past century, but in the nineteenth and early twentieth centuries it strove to give formal structure to observations of the "Other," people whose lives were imagined as utterly different from—and fundamentally unconnected to—those of contemporary Westerners.[2]

---

[2]See Sally Falk Moore, "Changing Perspectives on a Changing Africa: The Work of Anthropology," in Bates et al., *Africa and the Disciplines*.

DOCUMENT

Origins of the Gikuyu

This version of the creation story of the Gikuyu in Kenya was published by Jomo Kenyatta in 1938. Kenyatta was a Gikuyu (nowadays more frequently written as "Kikuyu") who studied in London under one of the foremost anthropologists of the day, Bronislaw Malinowski. Kenyatta was a leader in political organizations opposed to British colonial rule in Kenya. When Kenya became independent in 1963, Kenyatta was the first prime minister, and he led the country until his death in 1978.

- **DOES** anything in the style or content of this written document suggest that it is based on an oral tradition?

- In what ways might authoring this text have elevated Kenyatta's stature within Kenya? Can you imagine any potentially negative consequences for Kenyatta's authorship of this text?

- Do you notice similarities to other creation stories?

. . . According to the tribal legend, we are told that in the beginning of things, when mankind started to populate earth, the man Gikuyu, the founder of the tribe, was called by the Mogai (the Divider of the Universe), and was given as his share the land with ravines, the rivers, the forests, the game, and all the gifts that the Lord of Nature (Mogai) bestowed on mankind. At the same time Mogai made a big mountain which he called Kere-Nyage (Mount Kenya). . . . He then took the man Gikuyu to the top of the mountain of mystery, and . . . pointed out to the Gikuyu a spot full of fig trees (*mikoyo*), right in the centre of the country. [T]he Mogai . . . commanded him to descend and establish his homestead on the selected place. . . .

Gikuyu did as was commanded by the Mogai, and when he reached the spot, he found that the Mogai had provided him with a beautiful wife whom Gikuyu named Moombi (creator or moulder). Both lived happily, and had nine daughters and no sons.

Gikuyu was very disturbed at not having a male heir. In his despair he called upon the Mogai, [who] told Gikuyu not to be perturbed. . . . He then commanded him, saying, "Go and take one lamb and one kid from your flock. Kill them under the big fig tree (*mokoyo*) [then] burn the meat as a sacrifice to me, your benefactor. When you have done this, take home your wife and daughters. After that go back to the sacred tree, and there you will find nine handsome young men who are willing to marry your daughters under any condition that will please you and your family."

Gikuyu did as he was directed. . . . [W]hen Gikuyu returned to the sacred tree, there he found the promised nine young men who greeted him warmly. . . . [H]e took the nine youths to his homestead and introduced them to his family.

The strangers were entertained and hospitably treated according to the social custom. A ram was killed and a millet gruel prepared for their food. While this was being made ready, the youths were taken to a stream nearby to wash their tired limbs. After this, they had their meal, and conversed merrily with the family and then went to bed.

Early the next morning Gikuyu rose and woke the young men to have their morning meal with him. When they finished eating, the question of marriage was discussed. Gikuyu told the young men that if they wished to marry his daughters he could give his consent only if they agreed to live in his homestead under a matriarchal system.

The young men agreed to this condition, for they could not resist the beauty of the Gikuyu daughters, nor the kindness which the family had showed them. . . . [A]fter a short time all of them were married, and soon established their own family sets. . . . Thus the nine principal Gikuyu *meherega* clans were founded.

Source: From *Facing Mountain Kenya*, by Jomo Kenyatta, Vintage Books copyright © 1965. Published by William Heinemann Ltd., a division of Random House, Inc. Used by permisson of Alfred A. Knopf, a division of Random House, Inc.

While historians have traditionally concentrated on the use of documentary sources, anthropologists developed techniques for analyzing cultures based on either archaeological study of past societies or direct observation of present societies. In recent decades, however, historians and anthropologists have increasingly shared each others' concerns and techniques. In attempting to understand Africans and their histories, historians have moved beyond colonial-era paradigms, often collaborating with anthropologists and scholars in other disciplines.

PHYSICAL DESCRIPTION OF THE CONTINENT

Africa is three and a half times the size of the continental United States and second only to Asia in total area (see Map 5–1 on page 124). Because steep escarpments surmount most of its narrow coasts, Africa has few natural harbors, and communication between the coast and the interior is difficult. Of Africa's major rivers (the Niger, Congo, Nile, Zambezi, and Orange), only the Nile has a relatively long navigable reach below its **cataracts** in upper Egypt. The continent's vast size and sharp physical variations, from high mountains to swamplands, tropical forests, and deserts, have channeled long-distance communication and movement along certain corridors including the Rift Valley of East Africa, the coastal reaches of East or North Africa, the Niger or Zambezi River valley, and the sahelian savannahs bordering the great equatorial forest.

The characteristics of different regions derive largely from Africa's position astride the equator. As a whole, its climate is unusually hot. Climate bands north and south of the equator roughly mirror each other. Along the equator, dense rain forests dominate a west–east band of tropical woodland. North and south of this band, the lush rain forests give way to **savannah**—open woodlands and grassy plains. Savannah in turn passes into steppe, semidesert, and finally true desert as one moves farther from the equator. In the north, the semidesert is known as the **Sahel**. The adjoining **Sahara** ("the Desert"; Arabic *al-Sahrá*) is the world's largest desert. In southwestern Africa the **Kalahari** Desert partially cuts off the southern plateau and coastal regions from central Africa.

Other natural factors are important to Africa's history. Soils across Africa are typically tropical in character: They are low in hummus and are not highly productive for

WHICH CHARACTERISTICS of Africa's physical geography have influenced human history on the continent?

cataract
A waterfall or steep rapids. Major cataracts on the Nile River are numbered.

savannah
An area of open woodlands and grassy plains.

Sahel
An area of steppe and semidesert that borders the Sahara.

Sahara
The world's largest desert. It extends across Africa from the Atlantic to the eastern Sudan. Historically, the Sahara has hindered contact between the Mediterranean and sub-Saharan Africa.

Kalahari
A large desert in southwestern Africa that partially isolates southern Africa from the rest of the continent.

Great Rift Valley. A Samburu warrior stands before the eastern scarp of the Great Rift Valley in northern Kenya. This is believed to be the region where modern humans originated sometime before 100,000 B.C.E.

What are the noteworthy features of African geography?

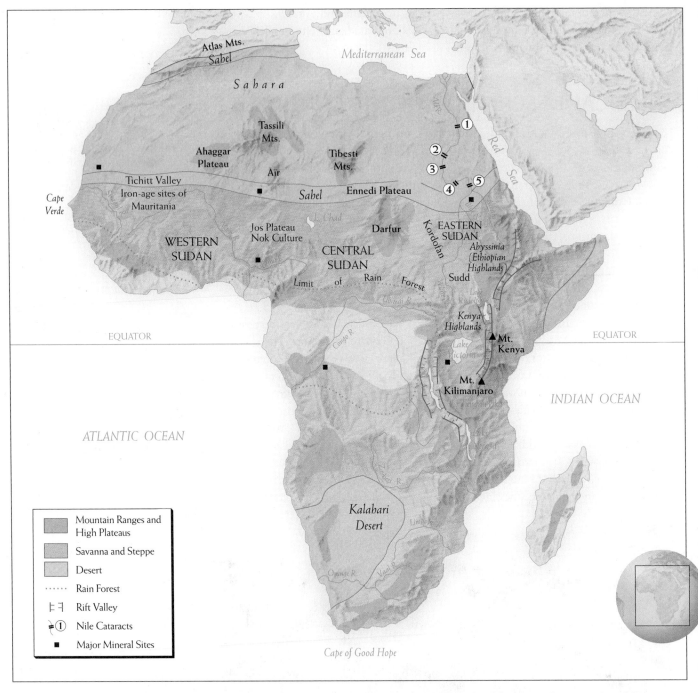

MAP 5–1.   Africa: Physical Features and Early Sites.   This map shows the major physical features of the continent and Iron Age sites of the western and central Sudan.

What patterns can you identify in Africa's physical features? Consider comparisons and contrasts north and south of the equator and between the eastern and western portions of the continent.

long. Water is scarce in most of Africa. Crop pests and insects such as the tsetse fly, mosquito, and locust have hampered farming and pastoralism in Africa. Still, abundant animal life has made hunting and fishing important means of survival in most of Africa. Africa also has great mineral wealth. Salt, iron, copper, and gold have been major trade goods from ancient times.

Africa is often discussed in terms of seven major regions: *North Africa*, the Mediterranean coastal regions from modern Morocco through Libya and including the northern Sahara; **Nilotic Africa**, roughly comprising the modern states of Egypt and Sudan; the **Sudan**, the broad belt of Sahel and savannah below the Sahara, stretching across the entire continent; *West Africa*, including the woodland coastal regions from Cape Verde to Cameroon and the western desert, Sahel, and savannah as far east as the Lake Chad basin; *East Africa*, from the Ethiopian highlands (a high, fertile plateau with steppe, Sahel, and desert to north and south) south over modern Kenya and Tanzania, an area split north to south by the Great Rift Valley; *central Africa*, the region north of the Kalahari, from the Chad basin across the Congo basin and southeast to Lake Tanganyika and south to the Zambezi River; and *southern Africa*, from the Kalahari Desert and Zambezi south to the Cape of Good Hope.

QUICK REVIEW

Regions in Africa

- North Africa: Mediterranean coast, Sahara
- Nilotic Africa: lands surrounding Nile River
- The Sudan: Sahel/savannah band south of Sahara
- West Africa: coast, desert, Sahel, and savannah of the western Sudan
- East Africa: Ethiopian highlands, south to Tanzania
- Central Africa: Chad basin, Zaïre basin, south to Zambezi River
- Southern Africa: Cape of Good Hope, north to Kalahari Desert and Zambezi River

AFRICAN PEOPLES

AFRICA AND EARLY HUMAN CULTURE

Paleontological research indicates that our hominid ancestors evolved in the Great Rift Valley of highland East Africa at least 1.5 million years ago. Sometime before 100,000 B.C.E., modern humans—the species *Homo sapiens* (*sapiens*)—appeared and moved out to populate the world.

Archaeology documents substantial internal movements of peoples—and hence languages, cultures, and technologies—both north–south and east–west within the continent in ancient times. African goods circulated through Indian Ocean as well as Mediterranean trade. Nilotic Egypt served as a bridge between the rest of Africa and the Mediterranean and Near East. Well before the Common Era, the peoples of the upper Nile, Ethiopian highlands, and coastal areas of East Africa maintained contacts with Egypt, south Arabia, and probably India and Indonesia, via the Indian Ocean. Like Egypt, the North African coast engaged in Mediterranean trade throughout antiquity. Africa's Mediterranean littoral was a place where Berber speakers mixed with other Mediterraneans such as the Phoenicians. Here the powerful Carthaginian Punic state arose in the mid-first millennium, only to fall prey to Rome (see Chapter 6).

DIFFUSION OF LANGUAGES AND PEOPLES

Cultural and linguistic diffusion shows that, despite the continent's natural barriers, Africans have moved extensively. Between 1,000 and 3,000 languages are found in Africa, depending on how one distinguishes languages from dialects. They can be roughly divided into four major indigenous families (the Afro-Asiatic, the Nilo-Saharan, the Niger-Kongo, and the Khoisan), plus two later arrivals (the **Austronesian** language of Madagascar, and Indo-European languages from western Europe).

The Africanist scholar Roland Oliver has linked the development of language families to population growth that brought larger communities and extended movements of peoples.[3] After about 8000 B.C.E., **Afro-Asiatic** languages from the Jordan and Nile valleys spread to Arabia and across North Africa. Two southward extensions of these languages, from North Africa across the Sahara to the Chad basin, and from Egypt into the Ethiopian highlands and the Horn, likely occurred after 4000 B.C.E., possibly through the movement of sheep and cattle herders.

WHY ARE ideas about race not useful in understanding the histories of different groups in Africa?

Nilotic Africa
The lands along the Nile River.

Sudan
The broad band of Sahel and savannah that crosses the African continent south of the Sahara.

Austronesian
A widely dispersed language family with origins in the Pacific. Malagasy, spoken in Madagascar, is an Austronesian language.

Afro-Asiatic
A language family that includes Semitic languages, Kushitic, and others.

---

[3]For the discussion of language here and below, we rely on the summary and analysis of R. Oliver, *The African Experience* (Boulder, CO: Westview Press, 1991), pp. 38–50, and of E. Gilbert and J. Reynolds, *Africa in World History* (Upper Saddle River, NJ: Pearson Prentice Hall, 2008), especially Chapters 2 and 3.

Nilo-Saharan

A language family concentrated in the band between the Nile and Rift highlands of Morocco.

Niger-Congo

A language family that originated in the savannah and woodlands of west and south-central Africa.

Bantu

A large subgroup of the Niger-Congo language family; also, the people who speak Bantu languages.

Khoisan

The language group spoken by the Khoikhoi, the San, and other peoples; also, the Khoikhoi and San peoples.

San Hunters, Southern Africa. There are many groups in Africa with different typical physiologies, skin pigmentation, and lifeways. As with all humans, however, there are more genetic differences between individuals than between groups.

Has race been a helpful concept for historians trying to understand African cultures?

The **Nilo-Saharan** languages may have originated among fishing and cereal-growing societies in the Nubian region of the Nile and spread before 5000 B.C.E. west into the Sahara. Later they were largely displaced there by the southward extension of Afro-Asiatic languages into the Sahara through their pastoralist carriers. Nilo-Saharan languages must also have spread southeast with fisherman-farmers as far as the lakes region of the Great Rift Valley, where they were later partially displaced by Kushitic-speaking pastoralists or farmers.

The **Niger-Kongo** family had its homeland in the woodland savannah and equatorial forests of West and central Africa. Spoken by fisherfolk who may also have turned to farming, this group spread to the Atlantic coast from the Senegal River to the Cameroon mountains. Its largest subgroup, the **Bantu** speakers, later spread southward into the equatorial forestlands (largely as agriculturalists) and around the rain forests of central Africa (as herders and farmers) until they entered the eastern and southern savannahs (see Map 5–2).

The fourth language family, nowadays called **Khoisan**, apparently covered most of the southern half of the African continent by late Neolithic times but was largely displaced by the migration of Niger-Kongo Bantu speakers. The varied peoples who were ancestors of today's Khoisan speakers were probably primarily hunter-gatherers at this time. Eventually, most of these peoples adopted the languages of the immigrant Bantu-speaking agriculturalists and pastoralists.

The development of the complex language map of present-day Africa can thus be seen in terms of ancient developments in food production and movement of peoples within the continent.

"RACE" AND PHYSIOLOGICAL VARIATION

As recently as the late twentieth century, some interpreters attempted to link color or racial differences to the development of everything—from language and food production, to ironworking and state building—in Africa. None of these theories is tenable, however, because race itself is such a problematic concept, both historically and biologically. In the 1990s, there was a running dispute about whether ancient Egyptians were more "black" or "white," an argument in which skin pigmentation was meant to signal other attributes. (If Egyptians were black, they were assumed to be somehow more African than they already were simply by being in Africa, whereas white Egyptians would somehow have been more Mediterranean than African.) In reality, ancient Egypt was a multiethnic society, and ancient Egyptians seem to have been a people of many hues.

The Greeks called all the dark-skinned peoples they were aware of in Africa *Ethiopians*, "those with burnt skins." The Arabs termed all of Africa south of the Sahara and Egypt *Bilad al-Sudan*, "Land of the Blacks" (from this we get the term *Sudan*). Although ancient writers observed variations in skin tone, it is important to avoid assuming that we understand what they meant in their observations. As with all historical records, these documents need to be read with attention to the authors' contexts and intentions.

MAP EXPLORATION

To explore this map further, go to **http://www.myhistorylab.com**

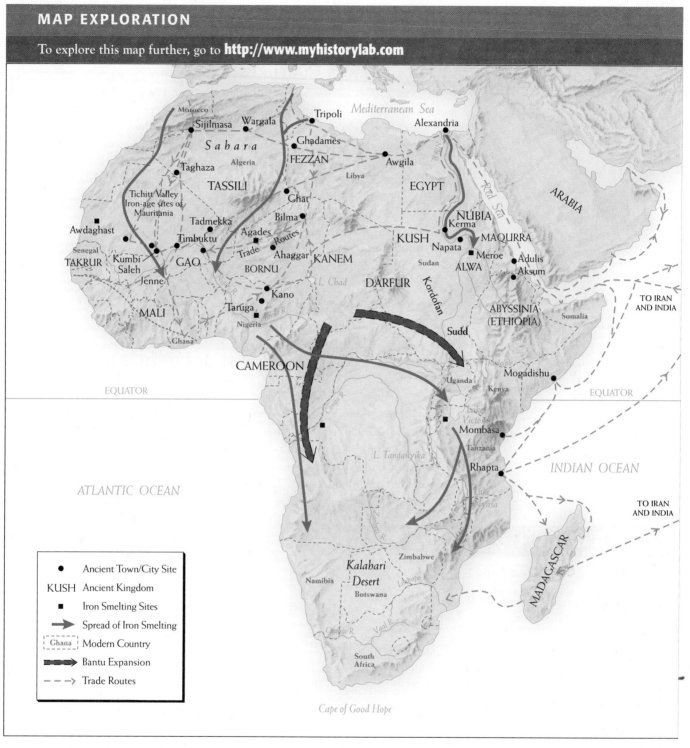

MAP 5–2. **Ancient African Kingdoms and Empires.**

What effect did the migrations of people and the spread of technology have on early African history?

Meanwhile, although skin color and other physiological characteristics are partially determined by genes, current research has found no genetic basis for the racial categories that humans have invented. There are more genetic differences between individuals than between groups.[4]

---

[4]See Gilbert and Reynolds, *Africa in World History,* Chapters 1–4.

THE SAHARA AND THE SUDAN TO THE BEGINNING OF THE COMMON ERA

WHAT EVIDENCE is there that early African cultures were in contact with each other?

EARLY SAHARAN CULTURES

Until about 2500 B.C.E. the Sahara was arable land with lakes and rivers, trees, grasses, and a reasonable climate. Animal, fowl, reptile, and fish populations allowed riparian (river- and lakeside) communities of considerable size to live with ease off the land. Then, from about 2500 B.C.E., climatic changes caused the Sahara to undergo a relatively rapid dessication, and the riparian communities of this vast territory disappeared.[5] By 1000 B.C.E., the dessication process had rendered the Sahara an immense, largely uninhabitable desert separating most of Africa from its Mediterranean coastal rim and the Near Eastern centers of early civilization. Even then, however, regular contacts between sub-Saharan Africa and the Mediterranean continued. Various north–south routes across the western and central Sahara were traversed by horses and carts or chariots and by migrating peoples long before the coming of the camel.

NEOLITHIC SUDANIC CULTURES

From the first millennium B.C.E., preliterate but complex agricultural communities of Neolithic and Early Iron Age culture dotted the central and western reaches of the sub-Saharan Sudan. These peoples may have once been spread farther north, in the then-arable Saharan lands they would have shared with ancestors of the Berber-speaking peoples of contemporary west-Saharan and North Africa.

This hypothesis has been bolstered by the excavation of town cultures from the mid-fifth millennium B.C.E. in Mali and Mauritania. In inland Mauritania, remains of an ancient but later agricultural civilization with as many as 200 towns have also been found. These reflect the transition from a hunting and fishing to a herding and rudimentary agricultural society. The progressive dessication of the second millennium B.C.E. may have forced these peoples farther south. These migrants carried with them both languages and techniques of settled agriculture. They domesticated new crops using their old techniques. Assisted by knowledge of ironworking, they effected an agricultural revolution. This meant considerable population growth in the more fertile Sudanic regions, especially near the Niger and Senegal rivers and Lake Chad. (A similar spread of agricultural techniques and cattle- and sheep-raising seems to have occurred down the Rift Valley of the East African highlands.) This agricultural revolution, completed during the first millennium B.C.E., enabled new cultural centers to develop in the sub-Saharan regions.

In the first millennium B.C.E. the Sudanic peoples carried their agricultural techniques and their languages eastward through the savannahs and southward, largely along the rivers, into the tropical rain forests of central and West Africa.

CHRONOLOGY

EARLY AFRICAN CIVILIZATIONS

ca. 7500–2500 B.C.E.	"Wet Holocene" period
ca. 2500 B.C.E.	Rapid dessication of Saharan region begins
ca. 2000–1000 B.C.E.	Increasing Egyptian influence in Nubia
ca. 1000–900 B.C.E.	Kushite kingdom with capital at Napata becomes independent of Egypt
751–663 B.C.E.	Kushite kings Piankhi and Taharqa rule all Egypt
ca. 600–500 B.C.E.	Meroe becomes new Kushite capital
ca. 500 B.C.E.–330 C.E.	Meroitic kingdom of Kush (height of Meroitic Kushite power ca. 250 B.C.E.–50 C.E.)
ca. 500 B.C.E.–500 C.E.?	Nok culture flourishes on Jos plateau in western Sudan (modern central Nigeria)

---

[5]Oliver, *The African Experience*, pp. 31–37.

This changed the face of sub-Saharan Africa, where previously small groups of hunter-gatherers had predominated. With the advent of iron smelting, these settled peoples were able to develop larger, more complex societies than their predecessors.

THE EARLY IRON AGE AND THE NOK CULTURE

Features of iron-smelting furnaces from widely scattered sites from the seventh century B.C.E. to the fourth century C.E. suggest that smelting was both introduced to Africa from the Near East, via Egypt, and independently invented within the continent, probably in the Great Lakes region. Thence it likely spread southward into western, central, and eastern parts of the continent.

Some of the most significant Iron Age sites have been found in what is today northeastern Nigeria on the Jos plateau. Here archaeological digs have yielded evidence of an early Iron Age people labeled the **Nok** culture (see Map 5–1). Excavations at Nok sites have yielded stone tools, iron implements, and sophisticated terra-cotta sculptures dating from about 900 B.C.E. to 200 C.E. Scholars date the introduction of iron smelting there to about the sixth century B.C.E. The Nok people cleared substantial woodlands from the plateau and combined agriculture with cattle herding. The continuities between the Nok culture's extraordinary sculptural art—especially magnificent burial or ritual masks—and later West African sculptural traditions suggest that this culture influenced later central and West African life. Ancient communities laid a foundation on which later and better-known Sudanic civilizations may have built.

A Terra-Cotta Head. This is from the Iron Age Nok culture, which occupied what is today northeastern Nigeria from about 900 B.C.E. to about 200 C.E.

© Werner Forman Archive/Art Resource, New York/Jos Museum, Nigeria.

What is the significance of continuities between Nok culture and later Sudanic civilizations?

Nok

A West African Iron Age culture renowned for its artistry.

NILOTIC AFRICA AND THE ETHIOPIAN HIGHLANDS

THE KINGDOM OF KUSH

The lower Nubian land of **Kush** lies in the upper Nile basin, just above the first cataract (see Map 5–2). There an Egyptianized segment of Nilo-Saharan-speaking Nubians built the second (after pharaonic Egypt) literate and politically unified civilization in Africa. As early as the fourth millennium B.C.E., the Old Kingdom pharaohs had subjugated and colonized Nubia. In the early second millennium B.C.E., however, an independent kingdom arose in Kush in the broad floodplain just above the third cataract of the Nile. As early as 2000 B.C.E., its capital, Kerma, had been a major trading outpost for Middle Kingdom Egypt, sending building materials, ivory, slaves, mercenaries, and gold north down the Nile.

The early Kushite kingdom achieved its greatest wealth and prosperity between the Middle and New Kingdoms of Egypt (ca. 1700–1500 B.C.E.). Finds in the royal palace fortress ruins and tombs suggest that its kings may have taken the gold mines of lower Nubia from the weakened Egyptian state in the Intermediate period. After the Hyksos invasions, with Egypt's recovery (from about 1500 B.C.E.), Kush came once more under Egyptian colonial rule and stronger Egyptian cultural influence. Then, sometime after 1000 B.C.E., as Egypt's New Kingdom floundered, a new Kushite state reasserted itself and by about 900 B.C.E. conquered both lower and upper Nubia, regaining independence and wealth from the Nubian gold mines.

HOW DID Egyptian civilization and the various Nilotic civilizations—Kush, Meroe, and Aksum— influence each other?

Kush

An ancient Nubian kingdom that in some periods dominated, and in others was dominated by, pharaonic Egypt.

QUICK REVIEW

The Early Kushite Kingdom

- Located just above first cataract of the Nile
- Capital Kerma was a major trading outpost as early as 2000 B.C.E.
- It reached its zenith between 1700 and 1500 B.C.E.

THE NAPATAN EMPIRE

This new Kushite Empire was centered first at Napata, just below the fourth Nile cataract. The royal line that ruled at Napata saw themselves as Egyptian. They practiced the pharaonic custom of marrying their sisters, a practice known in many kingship institutions around the world. They buried their royalty embalmed in traditional Egyptian-style pyramids. In the eighth century B.C.E., they conquered Egypt and ruled it for about a century as the Twenty-fifth pharaonic dynasty. This Kushite Dynasty was driven out of Egypt proper by Assyria around 650 B.C.E.

THE MEROITIC EMPIRE

Forced back above the lower cataracts of the Nile by the Assyrians and kept there by the Persians, the Napatan kingdom became increasingly isolated and developed in its own distinctive ways. When an Egyptian army sacked Napata in 591 B.C.E., the capital was relocated farther south in the prosperous city of **Meroe**, bringing the seat of rule closer to the geographic center of the Kushite domains. Meroe was the center of a flourishing iron industry, from which iron smelting may have spread south and west. The Meroitic state was built on a staggeringly wide network of internal African and intercontinental trade. Its empire lasted until it was defeated and divided in the fourth century C.E. by Nuba peoples from west of the upper Nile.

In its heyday, from the mid-third century B.C.E. to the first century C.E., the Meroitic kingdom was "middleman" for varied African goods in demand in the Mediterranean and Near East: animal skins, ebony and ivory, gold, oils and perfumes, and slaves. The Kushites traded with the Hellenistic-Roman world, southern Arabia, and India. They shipped quality iron to Aksum and the Red Sea, and the Kushite lands between the Nile and the Red Sea were a major source of gold for Egypt and the Mediterranean world. Cattle breeding, cotton cultivation, and other agriculture were their economic mainstays.

This was an era of prosperity. Many monuments were built, including royal pyramids and the storied palace and walls of the capital. Fine pottery and jewelry were produced. Meroitic culture is especially renowned for its two kinds of pottery. The first, turned on wheels, was the product of an all-male industry attuned apparently to market demands; the second, made exclusively by hand by women, was largely for domestic use.

The political system of the Meroitic Empire had several features that distinguished it from its Egyptian models. The king seems to have ruled strictly by customary law, presumably as interpreted by whatever clerics served the state's needs. According to Greek accounts, firm taboos limited his actions; kings who violated those taboos could be forced to commit suicide. There was also a royal election system. The priests apparently considered the king a living god, an idea found in both ancient Egypt and many other African societies. Royal succession was often through the maternal rather than the paternal line (matrilineal succession was widespread in ancient Africa). The role of the queen mother in the election appears to have been crucial—another practice found elsewhere in Africa as well. By the second century B.C.E. a woman had become sole monarch, initiating a long line of queens, or "Candaces" (*Kandake*, from the Meroitic word for "queen mother"). The monarch seems to have presided over a central administration run by numerous high officials. The provinces were delegated to princes who must have enjoyed considerable autonomy, given the slow communications.

Beyond the ruling class, the few records available mention slaves, both female domestics and male laborers drawn largely from prisoners of war. Cattle breeders, farmers, traders, artisans, and minor government functionaries probably formed an

Meroe

The capital city of the ancient Napatan Empire, which at one time rivaled Aksum.

Meroitic Culture. The people of Meroe produced many examples of fine pottery. This fired clay jar is decorated with giraffes and serpents.

What were the two types of Meroitic pottery?

intermediate class between the slaves and the rulers. Kushite religious practices followed Egyptian traditions for centuries. By the third century B.C.E., however, gods unknown to Egypt became prominent. Most notable was Apedemak, a warrior god with a lion's head. The many lion temples associated with him (forty-six have been identified) reflect his importance. Such gods likely represented local deities who gradually took their places alongside the highest Egyptian gods.

THE AKSUMITE EMPIRE

A highland people who had developed their own commercially powerful trading state finished off the weakened Kushite Empire around 330 C.E. This was the newly Christianized state of **Aksum**, centered in the northern Ethiopian, or Abyssinian, highlands where the Blue Nile rises.

The peoples of Aksum descended from African Kushitic speakers and Semitic speakers from Yemenite southern Arabia. This mixing gave Aksum, and later Ethiopia, Semitic speech and script closely related to South Arabian. Greek and Roman sources tell of an Aksumite kingdom from at least the first century C.E.

In the first two centuries C.E., the kingdom's chief port of Adulis on the Red Sea made Aksum a strategic site on the increasingly important Indian Ocean trade routes that linked India and the East Indies, Iran, Arabia, and the East African coast with the Roman Mediterranean. Aksum also controlled trade between the African interior and the extra-African world, from Rome to Southeast Asia—notably exports of ivory, but also of elephants, obsidian, slaves, gold dust, and other inland products.

By the third century C.E., Aksum was one of the most impressive states of its age. A work attributed to the prophet Mani (ca. 216–277 C.E.) describes Aksum as one of the four greatest empires in the world. The Aksumites often held tributary territories across the Red Sea in southern Arabia. They also controlled northern Ethiopia and conquered Meroitic Kush. Thus they dominated some of the most fertile cultivated regions of the ancient world: their own plateau, the rich Yemenite highlands of southern Arabia, and much of the eastern Sudan across the upper Nile as far as the Sahara.

A king of kings in Aksum ruled this empire through tribute-paying vassal kings in the other subject states. By the sixth century the Aksumite king was even appointing southern Arabian kings himself. Aksum's gold, silver, and copper coins symbolized both its political and economic power. The Aksumites enjoyed a long-lived economic prosperity.

In religion, the pre-Christian paganism of Aksum resembled the pre-Islamic paganism of southern Arabia, with various gods and goddesses closely tied to natural phenomena. Jewish, Meroitic, and even Buddhist minorities lived in the major cities of Aksum—an index of the cosmopolitanism of the society and its involvement with the larger worlds beyond the Red Sea.

An inscription of the powerful fourth-century King Ezana tells of his conversion to Christianity, which led to the Christianizing of the kingdom as a whole. Subsequently, under Alexandrian influence, the Ethiopian church became **Monophysite** (that is, it adhered to the dogma of the single, unitary nature of Christ). In the fifth century C.E., the native Semitic language, Ge'ez, began to replace Greek in the liturgy, which proved a major step in the unique development of the Ethiopic or Abyssinian Christian church over the succeeding centuries.

A Giant Stela at Aksum. Dating probably from the first century C.E., this giant carved monolith is the only one remaining of seven giant stelae—the tallest of which reached a height of 33 meters—that once stood in Aksum amidst numerous smaller monoliths. Although the exact purpose of the stelae is not known, the generally accepted explanation is that they were commemorative funerary monuments. Erecting them required engineering of great sophistication.

What does this stela suggest to you about Aksumite beliefs regarding death?

Aksum

A powerful Christianized trading state in the Ethiopian highlands.

Monophysite

Adhering to the dogma of the single, unitary nature of Christ (in opposition to the orthodox doctrine that Christ had two natures: human and divine).

ISOLATION OF CHRISTIAN ETHIOPIA

Aksumite trade continued to thrive through the sixth century. Aksumite power was eclipsed in the end by Arab Islamic power. Nevertheless, the Aksumite state continued to exist. Having sheltered a refugee group of Muhammad's earliest Meccan converts, the Aksumites enjoyed relatively cordial relations with Islamic domains. But Aksum became increasingly isolated. Its center of gravity shifted to the more rugged parts of the plateau, where a Monophysite Christian, Ge'ez-speaking culture emerged in the region of modern Ethiopia and lasted in relative isolation until modern times. Ultimately the whole Nubian region was Islamized, leaving Ethiopia the sole predominantly Christian state in Africa.

THE WESTERN AND CENTRAL SUDAN

WHAT ROLE did trade play in the rise of large political entities in the western and central Sudan?

AGRICULTURE, TRADE, AND THE RISE OF URBAN CENTERS

As Neolithic peoples moved southward, they discovered that Africa's equatorial rain forests were inhospitable to cows and horses, largely because of the animals' inability to survive the sleeping sickness (**trypanosomiasis**) carried by the tsetse fly. But the agriculturalists who brought their cereal grains and stone tools south found particularly good conditions in the savannah just north of the West African forests. By the first or second century C.E., settled agriculture, augmented by iron tools, had become the way of life of most inhabitants of the western Sudan; it had even progressed in the forest regions farther south. The savannah areas seem to have experienced a population explosion in the first few centuries C.E., especially around the Senegal River, the great northern bend in the Niger River, and Lake Chad. Villages, and chiefdoms of several villages, were the largest political units. As time went on, larger towns and political units developed in the western Sudan.

Trypanosomiasis

Sleeping sickness, a parasitic disease that is transmitted by tsetse flies. If untreated, it is fatal both to humans and animals.

Regional and interregional trade networks in the western and central Sudan date to ancient times; trans-Saharan trading routes were maintained throughout the first millennium B.C.E. Urban settlements—such as Gao, Kumbi (or Kumbi Saleh), and Jenne—emerged in the western Sahel. Excavations at Jenne in the upper Niger indicate that it dates from 250 B.C.E. and had a population of more than 10,000 by the late first millennium C.E.[6]

These and other early urbanized areas combined farming with fishing and hunting, and all developed in oasis or river regions rich enough to support dense populations and trade. The existence of relatively autonomous settlements made possible loose confederations or even imperial networks as time went on.

The introduction of the domesticated camel (the one-humped Arabian camel, or dromedary) from the East around the beginning of the Common Era increased trans-Saharan trade. By the early centuries C.E., the West African settled communities had developed important trading centers on their northern peripheries, in the Sahel near the edge of the true desert. The salt of the desert, needed in the settled savannah, and the gold of West Africa, coveted

A Camel Caravan Crossing the Sahara.
Use of the camel as a beast of burden from the first century C.E. onward greatly increased trans-Saharan trade.

Why was the camel important to trade in Africa?

[6]S. K. and R. J. McIntosh, *Prehistoric Investigations in the Region of Jenne, Mali* (Oxford: Oxford University Press, 1980), pp. 41–59, 434–461; and Oliver, *The African Experience*, p. 90. The ensuing discussion of West African urban settlement is taken primarily from Oliver's excellent summary, ibid., pp. 90–101.

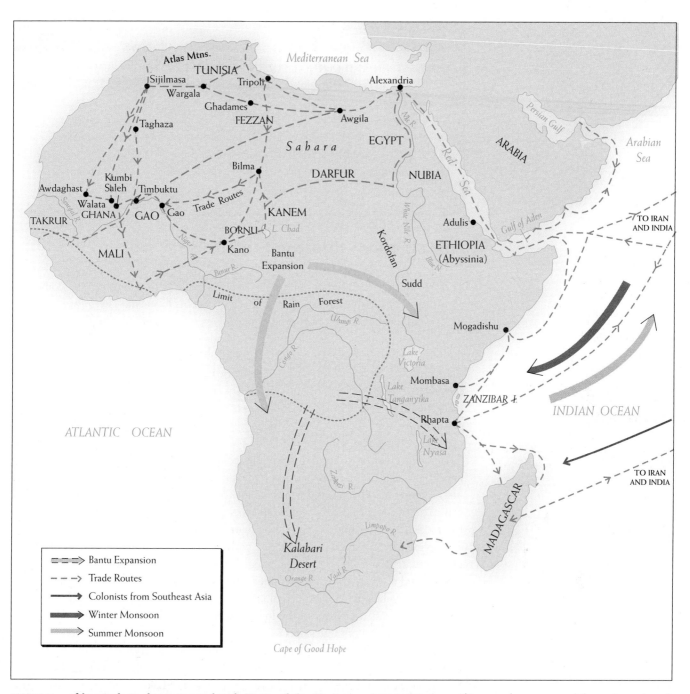

MAP 5–3. Africa: Early Trade Routes and Early States of the Western and Central Sudan. This map shows some of the major routes of north–south trans-Saharan caravan trade and their links with Egypt and with Sudanic and forest regions of West Africa.

How did Africa's geography help determine its trade routes?

in the north, were prime trade commodities. Other items were also traded, including cola nuts, slaves, dates, and gum from West Africa, and horses, cattle, millet, leather, cloth, and weapons from the north. Towns such as Awdaghast, Walata, Timbuktu, Gao, Tadmekka, and Agades were the most famous southern terminals for this trade (see Map 5–3). These centers allowed the largely Berber middlemen who plied the desert routes to cross the perilous Sahara via oasis stations en route to the North African coasts or even Egypt. This was not an easy means of transporting goods; a typical crossing could take two to three months.

QUICK REVIEW

Trade

♦ Trade contributed to rise of larger political entities

♦ Regional and interregional trade networks date to ancient times

♦ Trade routes connected western and central Sudan with Egypt

CHRONOLOGY

THE WESTERN AND CENTRAL SUDAN: PROBABLE DATES FOR FOUNDING OF REGIONAL KINGDOMS

ca. 400 C.E.	Takrur (Senegal River valley) or earlier
400–600 C.E.	Ghana (in Sahel between great northern bends of the Senegal and Niger rivers)
ca. 700–800 C.E.	Gao (on the Niger River or before southeast of great bend)
ca. 700–900 C.E.	Kanem (northeast of Lake Chad)

FORMATION OF SUDANIC KINGDOMS IN THE FIRST MILLENNIUM

The growth of settled agricultural populations and the expansion of trade coincided with the rise of sizable states in the western and central Sudan. The most important states were located in Takrur on the Senegal River, from perhaps the fifth century, if not earlier; Ghana, between the northern bends of the Senegal and the Niger, from the fifth or sixth century; Gao, on the Niger southeast of the great bend, from before the eighth century; and Kanem, northeast of Lake Chad, from the eighth or ninth century. Although the origins of the major states in these areas are obscure, each represents the first of a series of large political entities in its region. All continued to figure prominently in subsequent West African history (see Chapter 14).

The states developed by the Fulbe people of Takrur and the Soninke people of Ghana depended on their ability to draw gold from the savannah region west of the upper Senegal into the trans-Saharan trade. Of all the sub-Saharan kingdoms of the late first millennium, Ghana was the most famous outside of the region, largely because of its control of the gold trade. Its people built a large regional empire centered at its capital, Kumbi Saleh. Inheriting his throne by matrilineal descent, the ruler was treated as a semidivine personage whose interaction with his subjects was mediated by a hierarchy of government ministers. He commanded a sizable army, including horsemen and archers, and was buried with his retainers under a dome of earth and wood. In contrast, the Songhai rulers of Gao had no gold trade until the fourteenth century. Gao was oriented in its forest trade toward the lower Niger basin and in its Saharan trade toward eastern Algeria. All of these states were based on agriculture and settled populations.

The power of Kanem originated with a nomadic federation of tribal peoples that merged to form a single people, the Kanuri. They took over the sedentary societies of Kanem, just east of Lake Chad, and later, Bornu, west of Lake Chad. By the thirteenth century the Kanuri had themselves become sedentary. Their kingdom controlled the southern terminus of perhaps the best trans-Saharan route—that running north via good watering stations to the oasis region of Fezzan in modern central Libya and thence to the Mediterranean. (We shall return to the later development of Kanem and the western Sudanic states in Chapter 14.)

QUICK REVIEW

Ghana and Gold

◆ The people of Ghana depended on gold for Saharan trade

◆ Ghana was famous outside the region for control of gold

◆ Ruler of region inherited throne through matrilineal descent

CENTRAL, SOUTHERN, AND EAST AFRICA

WHY DID the coastal and inland regions of East Africa have different histories?

The African subcontinent is that part of central, southern, and East Africa that lies south of a line from roughly the Niger Delta and Cameroon to southern Somalia on the east coast.

BANTU EXPANSION AND DIFFUSION

In the southern subcontinent, most people speak one of more than 400 languages that belong to a single language group, Bantu, a subgroup of the Niger-Congo family. All Bantu languages are as closely related as are the Romance tongues of Europe. The proto-Bantu language probably arose south of the Benue River, in eastern Nigeria and modern Cameroon. Thence, during the latter centuries B.C.E. and the first century C.E., Bantu-speaking peoples apparently migrated in two basic directions: (1) south into the lower Congo basin and ultimately to the southern edge of the equatorial forest in present-day northern Katanga; and (2) east around the equatorial forests into the lakes of highland East Africa (see Map 5–3).

In all these regions, Bantu tongues developed and multiplied in contact with other languages. Likewise, Bantu speakers intermixed and adapted. Further migrations, from the first to as late as the eleventh century C.E., dispersed Bantu peoples more widely, into south-central Africa, coastal East Africa, and southern Africa. This dispersion led to the early civilization of "Great Zimbabwe" and Mapungubwe in the upper Limpopo region (treated in Chapter 14).

How the Bantu peoples managed to impose their languages on the earlier cultures of these regions, or intermix to produce hybrid-language cultures such as the Bantu-Arab Swahili (see Chapter 14), remains unexplained. The proto-Bantu had apparently been fishermen and hunters who also cultivated yams, date palms, and cereals. They raised goats and possibly sheep and cattle, but they did not bring cattle along in their migrations. Most of those migrating seem to have been cereal farmers whose basic political and social unit was the village. Perhaps they had unusually strong social cohesion, which allowed them to absorb other peoples; they were apparently not military conquerors. Possibly they simply had sufficient numbers to become dominant, or they may have brought diseases with them against which the aboriginals of the forests and southern savannah had no immunities. Bantu cultures became so fully interwoven with those of the peoples among whom they settled that we may never know the full story.

Bantu Languages and Group Distribution.
A Bantu-speaking mother with her child, photographed in South Africa around 1925. There are many distinct languages within the Bantu family distributed throughout Africa. Scholars use the relationships between these languages to trace the great Bantu migrations.

What kinds of factors might cause a group to develop a new dialect or new language?

Cave Painting from Namibia from at least 15,000 B.C.E., depicting rhinoceroses, giraffes, antelope, and zebra.

What do these images suggest to you about the importance of animals to the artist?

THE KHOISAN AND TWA PEOPLES

Alongside the Bantu-speaking majority in southern Africa is a minority who speak "Khoisan." The main two peoples that constitute the Khoisan speakers are the San and the Khoikhoi. (Westerners once referred to them as "Bushmen" and "Hottentots," names now considered offensive.) Formerly, observers believed the Khoikhoi and San could be distinguished from each other largely by their livelihood, the Khoikhoi labeled as herdsmen and the San as hunter-gatherers.[7] Both were seen as surviving representatives of a "primitive" stage of cultural evolution. More recent research has challenged these notions, and scholars now reject the very notion of cultural evolution. Much of the common wisdom about these peoples results from colonialist and postcolonial prejudice, which also accounts for the Khoisan's low socioeconomic status in contemporary Africa.

The San are likely the descendants of Neolithic and Early Iron Age peoples who created the striking prehistoric rock paintings of southern Africa. Today they are linguistically and culturally diverse subgroups throughout southern Africa who survive most prominently in the Kalahari region. The more homogeneous Khoikhoi were generally sheep- and cattle-herding pastoralists scattered across the south, yet speaking closely related Khoisan tongues. Their ancestors probably originated in northern Botswana. They were hunters who adopted animal herding from their Bantu-speaking neighbors, likely between 700 and 1000 C.E. They flourished as far south as the Cape of Good Hope as pastoralist clans, until their encounter with invading Dutch colonists in the mid-seventeenth century resulted in their demise as a distinct people.

In the central African rain forests, the Twa people commonly referred to in the West as "Pygmies" speak Bantu languages, but show other links to the Khoisan. Sandwe, a Khoisan language, is spoken by foraging groups in Tanzania, and small foraging groups in Kenya speak similar languages. They too are probably descendants of a population that preceded the Bantu migration.

EAST AFRICA

The history of pre-Islamic coastal East Africa differed from that of the inland highlands. Long-distance travel was easy and common along the seashore but less so inland. The coast was in contact with India, Arabia, and the Mediterranean via the Indian Ocean and Red Sea trade routes from at least the second century B.C.E. By contrast, we know little about the long-distance contacts of inland regions with the coastal areas until after 1000 C.E. Nonetheless, regional inland and coastal trade must also be ancient. Both coastal and overseas trade remained important and interdependent over the centuries because the Indian Ocean trade depended on the monsoon winds and could use only the northernmost coastal trading harbors of East Africa for round-trip voyages in the same year. The monsoon winds blow from the northeast December to March and thus can carry sailing ships south from Iran, Arabia, and India only during those months; they blow from the southwest April to August, so ships can sail from Africa northeast during those months. Local coastal shipping thus had to haul cargoes from south of Zanzibar and then transfer them to other ships for the annual round-trip voyages to Arabia and beyond.

---

[7]On distinctions between San and Khoikhoi, see Richard Elphick, *Kraal and Castle: Khoikhoi and the Founding of White South Africa* (New Haven, CT: Yale University Press, 1977), pp. xxi–xxii, 3–42; on the "construction" of their respective identities and for a summary of research on their antiquity and history, see E. N. Wilmsen, *Land Filled with Flies* (Chicago: University of Chicago Press, 1989). Note also that the once widely held notion that the Bantu and the Khoikhoi arrived in southern Africa at about the same time as the first European settlers was a fabrication to justify apartheid (see Chapter 34).

A Closer Look

Four Rock Art Paintings from Tassili n-Ajjer (4000–2000 B.C.E.)

These rock paintings from the central Saharan plateau of Tassili n-Ajjer in Algeria are four of hundreds of such paintings preserved from the late Neolithic period in Africa; on this plateau, paintings have been dated to the period 9000–1000 B.C.E. In the 4000–2000 B.C.E. period to which all four paintings here are dated, the art often depicts the cattle herded by pastoral nomads who spent the dry season largely sedentary on the plateau with their cattle, but it also depicts the animals hunted for food by the same peoples. Remember that this period coincided with the end of the long wet Neolithic or Holocene wet period (ca. 9000–2500 B.C.E.), when the Sahara had lakes and plains and dunes covered in places with grassland and populated by herds of elephants, giraffes, antelopes of various kinds, and other animals, such as the hippopotamus, that could not survive in the dessicated periods in the Sahara such as that which has prevailed since the late third millennium B.C.E. down to the present. These artists' keen observation of domesticated animals as well as varied wild animals is evident in these paintings, as is their ability to create striking and dramatic renderings of the human figure.

The magnificent artistry of this drawing of hippopotamuses reflects a keen aesthetic sensibility as well as a sharp observational capacity for the creatures these people encountered.

Here two antelopes are shown, again in highly artistic naturalistic rendering.

Both cattle and human figures are depicted here, without apparent linkage between the two. Note the elegant yet realistic rendering of both human and animal bodies and limbs.

Hunter with bow. Note the combination in the same figure of fidelity to life in the proportions and body parts of the hunter with the artistic rendering of motion and athletic grace that the figure displays.

Questions

1. Scholars have offered many differing interpretations—from magical efficacy of the images, to teaching images for youth, to simply rendering artistically scenes from daily life. What do you think might have been likely motivations for Neolithic nomadic peoples to create figural art on the rock walls near their dry-season camps?

2. Can you compare the relative simplicity or sophistication of these paintings with other examples of art in this book or with art that you know from other sources? How do these renderings change or reinforce your previous ideas about "prehistoric" African civilization or culture?

CHRONOLOGY

MOVEMENT AND CONTACT OF PEOPLES IN CENTRAL, SOUTHERN, AND EAST AFRICA

ca. 1300–1000 B.C.E.	Kushitic-speaking peoples migrate from Ethiopian plateau south along Rift Valley
ca. 400 B.C.E.–400 C.E.	Probable era of major Bantu migrations into central, East, and southeastern Africa
200–100 B.C.E.	East African coast becomes involved in Indian Ocean trade
ca. 100 B.C.E.	Probable time of first Indonesian immigration to East African coast
ca. 100–1500 C.E.	Nilotic-speaking peoples spread over upper Nile valley; Nilotic peoples spread over Rift Valley region

Long-distance trade came into its own in Islamic times—about the ninth century—as an Arab monopoly. Arab traders had settled in East African coastal towns for centuries. We can document Greco-Roman contact with East African trading centers as early as the first century C.E. Malagasy, the Austronesian language of Madagascar, points to the antiquity of contact with the East Indies. Southeast Asian crops including bananas and coconut palms spread across Africa as staple foods. East Africa also imported such items as Persian Gulf pottery, Chinese porcelain, and cotton cloth. The major African export around which east coast trade revolved was ivory, which was in perennial demand from Greece to India and even China. The slave trade was important, with African slaves exported to the Arab and Persian world, as well as to India or China. Gold became important in external trade only in Islamic times, from about the tenth century (see Chapter 14). With all this trade, ethnic and cultural mixing has long been the

Manyatta. Aerial view of a contemporary Maasai settlement, or *manyatta*, in Kenya.

What differentiates the Maasai from other groups living in the same region?

rule for the East African coast; even today, its linguistic and cultural traditions are rich and varied (see Chapter 14).

The history of inland East Africa south of Ethiopia is more difficult to trace, because of the absence of written sources. Linguistic and other clues indicate some key developments in the eastern highlands. These regions had seen an early infusion of peoples from the north, and over the centuries small groups continued to arrive. First came peoples speaking Kushitic languages of the Afro-Asiatic family, likely cattle herders and grain cultivators. Perhaps as early as 2000 B.C.E., they pushed from their homeland on the Ethiopian plateau down the Rift Valley as far as the southern end of Lake Tanganyika. They apparently displaced Neolithic hunter-gatherers possibly related to the Khoisan minorities of modern East and southern Africa.

Later, Nilotic-Saharan speakers moved from southwest of the Ethiopian plateau over the upper Nile valley by about 1000 C.E. Then they pushed east and south, following older Kushite paths, to spread over the Rift Valley and supplant the Kushites by the fifteenth century and subsequently cover much of the East African highlands in today's Uganda, Kenya, and Tanzania. Among these Nilotic peoples were the Luo and the Maasai. The Luo spread over a 900-mile-long swath of modern Uganda and parts of southern Sudan and western Kenya, adapting wherever they went. The Maasai, on the other hand, were and still are cattle pastoralists proud of their language, way of life, and cultural traditions. These distinguish them from the farmers or hunters whose settlements abut their pastures at the top of the southern Rift Valley in modern Kenya and Tanzania. Here the Maasai have concentrated and remained.

These migrations and those of the Bantu, who entered the eastern highlands over many centuries, have made the highlands a melting pot of Kushitic, Nilotic, Bantu, and Khoisan groups. Today's populations here represent an immense linguistic and cultural diversity. Here as well as anywhere we see the myriad African peoples and cultures mirrored in a single region.

SUMMARY

WHAT ARE the sources and techniques used for studying African history?

Issues of Interpretation, Sources, and Disciplines. Historians are challenged in their study of Africa by the paucity of written sources and by the European prejudices that have traditionally devalued African contributions to world culture. Africanists use cross-disciplinary methods and innovative scholarship to understand Africa's past. *page 120*

WHICH CHARACTERISTICS of Africa's physical geography have influenced human history on the continent?

Physical Description of the Continent. Africa is large; much of it is at high elevation, and generally hot. Climate is very roughly symmetrical north and south of the equator. Communications and migrations are easiest in a few channels. African soils must be nurtured to retain productivity. *page 123*

WHY ARE ideas about race not useful in understanding the histories of different groups in Africa?

African Peoples. The human species, *Homo sapiens* (*sapiens*) originated in Africa. Archaeology reveals that there were extensive migrations of peoples across the continent from the earliest days of African history with widespread cross-cultural influences. Although many types of physiologies are visible in Africa, the concept of race does not help historians understand different groups. Migrations and cultural exchanges are not dependent on skin coloration, but many historical sources are distorted by discredited ideas about human characteristics. *page 125*

WHAT EVIDENCE is there that early African cultures were in contact with each other?

The Sahara and the Sudan. Neolithic agriculturalists spread south of the Sahara, bringing the agricultural revolution with them. Pottery styles and iron-smelting technologies spread between groups. The early Iron Age Nok culture is renowned for sophisticated sculpture. *page 128*

 HOW DID Egyptian civilization and the various Nilotic civilizations—Kush, Meroe, and Aksum—influence each other?

Nilotic Africa and the Ethiopian Highlands. Egypt had extensive interaction with the Nubian peoples to the south. Nubian kingdoms—Kush, Napata, Meroe, and Aksum (Ethiopia)—adopted many features of Egyptian civilization and sometimes dominated Egypt itself. Aksum adopted Christianity in the fourth century C.E. *page 129*

 WHAT ROLE did trade play in the rise of political entities in the western and central Sudan?

The Western and Central Sudan. Extensive trade across the Sahara between North Africa and the western and central Sudan enabled products and ideas from the Mediterranean to reach the African interior in exchange for African products, such as gold, ivory, and salt. Large, settled populations facilitated the development of states. *page 132*

WHY DID the coastal and inland regions of East Africa have different histories?

Central, Southern, and East Africa. The dominance of the Bantu language across the African subcontinent reflects ancient migration patterns. On the coast of East Africa, trade across the Red Sea and the Indian Ocean with Arabia and East Asia fostered a distinctive and sophisticated culture. *page 134*

KEY TERMS

Afro-Asiatic (p. 125)
Aksum (AHK-suhm) (p. 131)
Austronesian (p. 125)
Bantu (BAN-tu)
  (pp. 126)
cataract (p. 123)
Kalahari (p. 123)
Khoisan (KOI-sahn) (p. 126)
Kush (koosh) (p. 129)
Meroe (MEH-roh-ee)
  (p. 130)

Monophysite (moh-NOH-
  fiss-it) (p. 131)
Niger-Kongo (p. 126)
Nilo-Saharan (p. 126)
Nilotic Africa (p. 125)
Nok (p. 129)
Sahara (p. 123)
Sahel (p. 123)
savannah (p. 123)
Sudan (p. 125)
trypanosomiasis (p. 132)

REVIEW QUESTIONS

1. Why have historians generally paid more attention to pharaonic Egypt than to the societies of sub-Saharan Africa?

2. Summarize the argument for including writing among the necessary attributes of a "civilization." Summarize the argument against the writing requirement. Which argument do you find more compelling?

3. Discuss the strengths and weaknesses of the various sources and tools available to scholars of early African history.

4. What does the diffusion of peoples and languages in Africa tell us about early African history?

5. How does the political system of the Meroitic Empire compare to that of Egypt?

6. How did Aksum become a Christian state?

7. What were the most important goods for African internal trade? Which products were traded abroad? What can we learn from these trade patterns?

8. What was the role of geography in early African history? What about the specific case of Ghana? Of North Africa? Of the East African littoral? Of southern Africa?

9. Is the role of geography different in Africa than in the Near East or other regions you have studied? Explain.

10. What information presented in this chapter was most surprising to you, and why?

Note: To learn more about the topics in this chapter, please turn to the Suggested Readings at the end of the book. For additional sources related to this chapter please see www.myhistorylab.com

PEARSON myhist☉rylab Connections

Reinforce what you learned in this chapter by studying the many documents, images, maps, review tools, and videos available at **www.myhistorylab.com**

Read and Review

✓●—[Study and Review Chapter 5

👁●—[See the Map *Kingdoms of the Upper Nile, p. 161*

Research and Explore

🎬●—[Watch the Video *Agriculture in Africa*
African Maps
Who were the Ancient Egyptians?
Ironworks in Africa

🎬●—[Watch the Video *West African States*

((●●—[Hear the Audio

Hear the audio file for Chapter 5
at **www.myhistorylab.com**

6

Republican and Imperial Rome

((•▢Hear the Audio for Chapter 6 at www.myhistorylab.com

Lady Playing the Cithara. This wall painting from the first century B.C.E. comes from the villa of Publius Fannius Synistor at Pompeii and shows a woman playing a cithara, a type of lyre. Behind her a child, presumably her daughter, provides support.

Roman. Paintings. Pompeian, Boscoreale. 1st Century B.C. "Lady playing the cithara." Wall painting from the east wall of large room in the villa of Publius Fannius Synistor. Fresco on lime plaster. H. 6 ft. 1/2 in. (187 × 187 cm.) The Metropolitan Museum of Art, Rogers Fund, 1903 (03.14.5) Photograph © 1986 The Metropolitan Museum of Art.

What were women's most important roles in ancient Rome?

T he ancient Romans were responsible for one of the most remarkable achievements in history. From their city in central Italy, they conquered most of the Near East and much of Europe. They brought peace, prosperity, and unity to this vast region, a feat that has never been repeated.

Rome's legacy is more than military prowess and superb political organization. The Romans transformed the intellectual and cultural achievements of the Greeks, creating the Greco-Roman tradition in literature, philosophy, and art. This tradition remains the heart of Western civilization. ∎

REPUBLICAN AND IMPERIAL ROME

Despite the nearly continuous warfare that marked Roman history, including a long-lasting rivalry with the Sasanid Empire, it was primarily through trade that Romans came into contact with peoples beyond the borders of their empire.

Nonetheless, most Romans focused their energies on internal Roman territory, which expanded considerably during the late republic and the early empire to include much of the former Hellenistic kingdoms. Rome was a multicultural empire, encompassing territory and cultures in Africa and the Middle East, as well as northern and central Europe. Rome profited enormously from the territories it conquered in terms of material wealth, including foodstuffs, as Egypt quickly became the "breadbasket" of

the empire. It also realized cultural benefits, especially the blending of Greek and Asian culture that characterized the Hellenistic world. But the infusion of new ideas caused tension among Romans, as many conservative Romans objected to what they viewed as corrupting Asian influences from even the much admired, and copied, Greeks, which threatened to undermine traditional Roman values and strengths.

The conquest of a vast empire had moved the Romans away from their unusual historical traditions toward the more familiar path of empire trodden by rulers in Egypt, Mesopotamia, China, India, and Iran. It is especially instructive to look at Rome from the perspective of historians who discern a "dynastic cycle" in

ITALY BEFORE ROME

WHO WERE the early peoples of Italy?

In about 1000 B.C.E. bands of warlike peoples speaking a set of closely related languages we call Italic began to infiltrate Italy. By 800 B.C.E. they had occupied the highland pastures of the Apennines and soon challenged the earlier settlers for control of the western plains. The Romans would emerge from descendants of these tough mountain people.

Others who shaped the future of Italy included the Etruscans, the Greeks who colonized Sicily and southern Italy, and the Celts. Etruscan civilization, which was to have a powerful influence on the Romans, arose about 800 B.C.E. In the seventh and sixth centuries B.C.E. the Etruscans conquered Latium (which included Rome) and Campania, where they became neighbors of the Greeks of Naples. But after 500 B.C.E. Etruscan power rapidly declined. The Celts drove them from the Po valley about 400 B.C.E., and soon thereafter they lost control of their Etrurian heartland to an expanding Rome.

ROYAL ROME

WHAT PATTERNS of Roman governance were set in the royal period?

In the sixth century B.C.E. the town of Rome in Latium came under Etruscan control. Although it had been of little importance, it was a natural center for communication and trade. Led by Etruscan kings, the Roman army conquered most of Latium.

GOVERNMENT

imperium

"The power to command." The right of Roman kings to issue commands and to enforce them by fines, arrests, and physical punishment.

Roman kings had the awesome power of **imperium**—the right to issue commands and to enforce them by fines, arrests, and physical punishment, including execution. Although it tended to remain in families, kingship was elective. The Roman Senate approved the candidate for the office, and the Roman people, voting in assembly, formally granted the *imperium*. This procedure—the granting of great power to executive officers contingent on the approval of the Senate and ultimately the people—would remain a basic characteristic of Roman government.

The Senate met only when summoned by the king and then only to advise him. In reality its authority was great, for the senators, like the king, served for life. The Senate

((•─ Hear the Audio
at **myhistorylab.com**

China (see Chapter 7). The development of the Roman Empire, though by no means the same as the Chinese, fits the pattern fairly well. Like the former Han Dynasty in China, the Roman Empire in the West fell, leaving in its wake disunity, insecurity, disorder, and poverty. Like other similar empires in the ancient world, it had been unable to sustain what historian Edward Gibbon termed its "immoderate greatness."

◆ What was it about the period from the second century B.C.E. through the third century C.E. that allowed the opening of new routes by land and sea linking Europe to Central Asia, India, and China?

◆ Why did the Roman Empire decline in the West? Which of the problems that Rome faced were internal, and which were external? How were the two connected?

Focus Questions

◆ Why might we describe the Roman Empire as "multicultural"? What cultures most influenced Roman culture, and why?

---

had continuity and experience, and it was composed of the most powerful men in the state. It could not be ignored.

The third branch of government, the curiate assembly, was made up of all citizens and divided into thirty groups. The assembly also met only when summoned by the king. Voting was not by head but by group; a majority within each group determined its vote, and the decisions were made by majority vote of the groups. Group voting would be typical of all future forms of Roman assembly.

FAMILY

The center of Roman life was the family. At its head stood the father, whose power and authority resembled those of the king within the state. Over his children he held broad powers analogous to *imperium*; he could sell his children into slavery and might even kill them. Over his wife he had less power; he could not sell or kill her. In practice his

●●●—[Read the Document
Excerpt from *The Life of Cato the Elder* (2 C.E.) Plutarch at **myhistorylab.com**

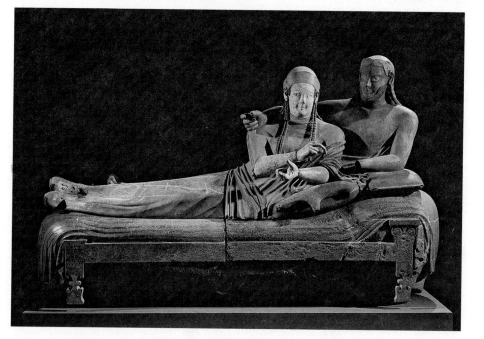

Sarcophagus of an Etruscan Couple. Much of what we know of the Etruscans comes from their funerary art. This sculpture of an Etruscan couple is part of a sarcophagus.

© Erich Lessing/Art Resource, New York.

What continuities were there between Etruscan and Roman history?

power to dispose of his children was limited by other family members, by public opinion, and, most of all, by tradition. A wife could be divorced only for serious offenses. The Roman woman had a respected position and the main responsibility for managing the household. The father was the chief priest of the family, leading it in daily prayers to the dead that reflected the ancestor worship central to Roman culture.

CLIENTAGE

Clientage was one of Rome's most important institutions. The client was "an inferior entrusted, by custom or by himself, to the protection of a stranger more powerful than he, and rendering certain services and observances in return for this protection."[1] The client was said to be in the *fides*, or trust, of his patron, giving the relationship a moral dimension. The patron provided his client with physical and legal protection and economic support. In return the client would fight for his patron, work his land, and support him politically.

PATRICIANS AND PLEBEIANS

In the royal period Roman society was divided into two classes based on birth. The wealthy **patrician** upper class held a monopoly of power and influence. Its members alone could conduct state religious ceremonies, sit in the Senate, or hold office. They formed a closed caste by forbidding marriage outside their own group.

The **plebeian** lower class must have consisted originally of poor, dependent small farmers, laborers, and artisans, the clients of the nobility. As Rome grew, nonpatrician families acquired wealth. From early times, therefore, there were rich plebeians and patrician families that fell into poverty from incompetence or bad luck. The line between the classes and the monopoly of privileges nevertheless remained firm.

patricians
The hereditary upper class of early Republican Rome.

plebeians
The hereditary lower class of early Republican Rome.

THE REPUBLIC

WHAT CULTURES most influenced Roman culture, and why?

According to Roman tradition, the outrageous behavior of the last kings provoked the noble families to revolt in 509 B.C.E., leading to the creation of the republic.

CONSTITUTION

The Roman constitution was an unwritten accumulation of laws and customs. The Twelve Tables, the first attempt to codify Rome's harsh customs, was not published until 450 B.C.E.

The Romans granted consuls, their chief magistrates, the power of *imperium* that kings had exercised. Like the kings, the consuls led the army, had religious duties, and served as judges. But the power of the consul was kept in check in two ways. Two men held consulships simultaneously, and each could overrule the other. Both were limited to a term of only one year. Their *imperium* was also limited. Although the consuls had full powers of life and death in the field with the army, within the city of Rome, citizens could appeal to the popular assembly any cases involving capital punishment. Each consul also knew that, after one year in that role, he would spend the rest of his life as a member of the Senate, so only a reckless consul would ignore its advice. In serious crises, the consuls could, with the advice of the Senate, appoint a single *dictator*, who would hold *imperium* not subject to appeal both inside and outside the city for six months.

Read the Document
Livy: The Rape of Lucretia and the Origins of the Republic, ca. 10 B.C.E.
at **myhistorylab.com**

[1]E. Badian, *Foreign Clientelae (264–70 B.C.E.)* (Oxford: Oxford University Press, 1958), p. 1.

A Closer Look

Lictors

The lictors were attendants of the Roman magistrates who held the power of *imperium*, the right to command. In republican times these magistrates were the consuls, praetors, and proconsuls. The lictors were men from the lower classes—some were even former slaves. They constantly attended the magistrates when the latter appeared in public. The lictors cleared a magistrate's way in crowds, and summoned, arrested, and punished offenders for him. They also served as their magistrate's house guard.

After the establishment of the Roman Republic, the lictor and his fasces and axe were the symbols of those magistrates that held *imperium*, which means that they had the right to command. Twelve lictors accompanied each *consul* and a *praetor* had six. When a *dictator* was appointed during a crisis, he had an escort of twenty-four lictors to show that he was more powerful than both consuls.

The axe carried by the man on the left is a symbol of the magistrate's power, when he was acting as a military commander outside the city, to put a Roman citizen to death.

The bundle of sticks, called fasces, the other two lictors carry indicates the magistrate's right to employ corporal punishment, but their bindings symbolize the right of citizens not on military duty not to be punished without a trial.

The traditional dress of a lictor was a toga when in Rome, and a red coat called a *sagum* when outside the city or when taking part in a triumph.

Questions

1. Why do you think the Roman magistrates required such bodyguards?

2. What does their presence indicate about the nature of early Roman public life?

3. How does the presence of lictors suggest a different attitude toward public officials between the Roman and classical Athenian republics?

In 325 B.C.E. the Romans created the office of proconsul, which permitted a consul in the field to retain command during a long campaign. Another new office, that of praetor, was primarily judicial, but praetors also had *imperium* and served as generals. After the middle of the fifth century B.C.E., the job of identifying citizens and classifying them according to age and property was delegated to another new office, that of censor, a position that grew in power and prestige.

The Senate, composed of leading patricians, gained power when the monarchy ended. As the only ongoing deliberative body in the Roman state, it soon controlled finances and foreign policy.

The *centuriate assemble,* the early republic's most important popular assembly, was in a sense the Roman army acting in a political capacity. Its basic unit was the century, theoretically 100 fighting men who fought with the same kind of equipment. Because each man equipped himself, this organization divided the assembly into classes according to wealth.

THE STRUGGLE OF THE ORDERS

Patricians monopolized power in the early republic. Plebeians, however, made up much of the Roman army, and this gave them great political leverage. Their fight for political, legal, and social equality, the "struggle of the orders," lasted 200 years. They won the right to a plebeian tribal assembly led by elected officials called tribunes. A tribune could veto any action of a magistrate or any bill proposed in a Roman assembly or by the Senate. In 445 B.C.E. plebeians won the right to marry patricians, though not until 367 B.C.E. could they serve as consul. Gradually other offices, including the dictatorship and the censorship, opened to them. In 300 B.C.E. they were admitted to the most important priesthoods. In 287 B.C.E., plebeians secured the passage of a law making the decisions of the plebeian assembly binding on all Romans without the approval of the Senate.

The victory of the plebeians in the "struggle of the orders" primarily benefited wealthy plebeian families by allowing them to share the political privileges of the patrician aristocracy. The *nobiles*—a small group of wealthy families, both patrician and plebeian—dominated the Senate and controlled the highest offices of the state.

CONQUEST OF ITALY

By the beginning of the fourth century B.C.E., the Romans had become the chief power in central Italy. The city's Latin neighbors, the Latin League, sought to curtail Rome's expansion, but in 338 B.C.E. the Romans defeated the league and dissolved it.

The Romans did not destroy any conquered Latin cities. To some near Rome they granted full citizenship. To others farther away they granted municipal status, which included the right to local self-government and the right to trade and intermarry with Romans. Still other states became allies of Rome. The Romans established permanent colonies of veteran soldiers in conquered lands. The colonists remained Roman citizens and deterred rebellion. A network of durable roads—some still in use—connected the colonies to Rome.

Rome divided its enemies and extended its influence through military force and diplomatic skill. Rebels were punished harshly, but Rome was generous to those who submitted. Loyal allies could even gain full Roman citizenship. This policy gave allies a stake in Rome's future, and most remained loyal.

ROME AND CARTHAGE

In the ninth century B.C.E., the Phoenician city of Tyre had established the North African coastal colony of Carthage. In the sixth century B.C.E., Carthage became independent and expanded west and east. Carthage claimed an absolute monopoly on trade in the western Mediterranean (see Map 6–1).

censor
A Roman official who counted the populace and drew up the citizen roles, thereby fixing taxation and status.

tribunes
Roman officials who had to be plebeians and were elected by the plebeian assembly to protect plebeians from the arbitrary power of the magistrates.

Punic Wars
Three wars between Rome and Carthage for dominance of the western Mediterranean that were fought from 264 B.C.E. to 146 B.C.E.

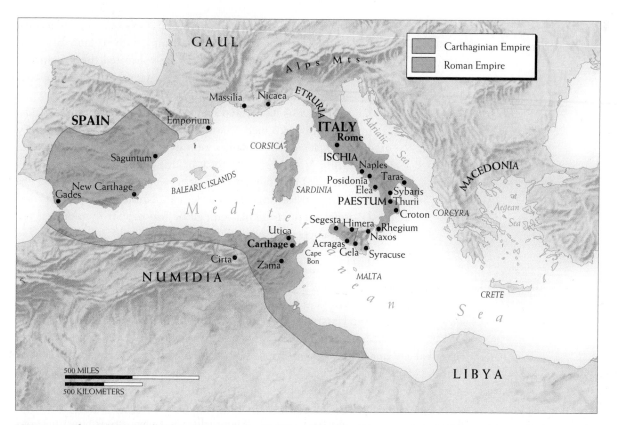

MAP 6–1. The Western Mediterranean Area during the Rise of Rome.   This map covers the theater of the conflict between the growing Roman dominions and those of Carthage in the third century B.C.E. The Carthaginian Empire stretched westward from Carthage along the North African coast and into southern Spain.

Why did Rome repeatedly come into conflict with Carthage?

Sicily was strategically important to both Carthage and Rome. There, in 264 B.C.E., the two expanding powers first came to blows. Because the Romans called the Carthaginians Poeni or Puni (meaning "Phoenician"), the conflicts between them are called the **Punic Wars**.

Rome's strength was its army and Carthage's power was its navy, so at first neither side could make much progress against the other in the First Punic War. Once the Romans built a fleet, they were able to blockade the Carthaginian ports in Sicily. Carthage capitulated in 241 B.C.E., giving up Sicily and agreeing to pay a war indemnity. Neither side was to attack the allies of the other.

These terms were fair, but Rome broke them almost immediately. In 238 B.C.E., Rome seized Sardinia and Corsica, demanding an additional indemnity from Carthage. Carthage, meanwhile, was building a rich empire in Spain. In 221 B.C.E., Hannibal (247–182 B.C.E.) took command of Carthaginian forces in Spain. A few years earlier, Rome had received an offer of alliance from the Spanish town of Saguntum. The Romans accepted, and the Saguntines began to stir up Spanish tribes allied with Hannibal. Hannibal retaliated by seizing

A Roman Warship. Rome became a naval power late in its history, in the course of the First Punic War. Roman sailors initially lacked the skill and experience in sea warfare of their Carthaginian opponents, who could maneuver their oared ships to ram the enemy. To compensate for this disadvantage, the Romans sought to make a sea battle more like an encounter on land by devising ways to grapple enemy ships and board them with armed troops. In time they also mastered the skillful use of the ram. This picture shows a Roman ship, propelled by oars, with both ram and soldiers, ready for either kind of fight.

How did war with Carthage shape Roman history?

CHRONOLOGY

THE PUNIC WARS

264–241 B.C.E.	First Punic War
238 B.C.E.	Rome seizes Sardinia and Corsica
221 B.C.E.	Hannibal takes command of Punic army in Spain
218–202 B.C.E.	Second Punic War
216 B.C.E.	Battle of Cannae
202 B.C.E.	Battle of Zama
149–146 B.C.E.	Third Punic War
146 B.C.E.	Destruction of Carthage

Saguntum. Rome declared war in 218 B.C.E., but Hannibal struck first, marching overland from Spain to launch a swift and daring invasion of Italy. His army defeated the Romans in three battles, but his hopes for final victory depended on persuading Rome's allies to switch sides.

In 216 B.C.E., at Cannae, Hannibal destroyed a Roman army of 80,000 men. It was the worst defeat in Roman history, and many of Rome's allies went over to Hannibal. In 215 B.C.E., Philip V (r. 221–179 B.C.E.), king of Macedon, allied with Hannibal and launched a war to recover his influence on the Adriatic. For more than a decade Hannibal was free to roam Italy and do as he pleased, but he had neither the numbers nor the supplies to besiege the city of Rome itself.

The turning point in the conflict came when the Romans appointed Publius Cornelius Scipio (237–183 B.C.E.), later called Scipio Africanus, to the command in Spain. He was almost as talented as Hannibal. Within a few years Scipio had conquered all Spain and deprived Hannibal of help from that region. In 204 B.C.E., Scipio invaded Africa, forcing Hannibal to return to protect Carthage. In 202 B.C.E., Scipio defeated Hannibal at Zama. Carthage was stripped of its empire, and Rome emerged dominant over the Mediterranean from Italy westward.

Even so, some Romans refused to abandon their hatred of Carthage. Cato is said to have ended all his speeches in the Senate with the same sentence, "Besides, I think that Carthage must be destroyed." Eventually, the Romans took advantage of a technical breach of the peace to plow up the city's land, even putting salt in the furrows to ensure abandonment of the site. The Romans incorporated Carthage as the province of Africa.

The Roman conquest of overseas territory presented a new problem. The old practice of extending citizenship to defeated opponents stopped at the borders of Italy. The Romans made Sicily, Sardinia, and Corsica provinces. The governors of these provinces exercised an *imperium* free of the limits put on the power of officials in Rome. The natives of provinces became tribute-paying subjects of a Roman empire. Rome collected taxes by "farming them out," that is, by auctioning the right to collect taxes to the man who made the highest bid. The treasury got a guaranteed sum, and the tax collector made a profit by exploiting the provincials. Provincial government spread so much corruption that it threatened to destabilize the republic.

THE REPUBLIC'S CONQUEST OF THE HELLENISTIC WORLD

By the middle of the third century B.C.E., the eastern Mediterranean had reached a stable balance of power. That equilibrium was threatened by two aggressive monarchs, Philip V of Macedon and the Seleucid Antiochus III (223–187 B.C.E.). Philip and Antiochus moved swiftly, Antiochus against Syria and Palestine, Philip against Greek cities.

The threat that a more powerful Macedon might pose to Rome's friends, and perhaps even to Italy, persuaded the Romans to intervene. In 197 B.C.E., with Greek support, they defeated Philip in Thessaly. The Greek cities taken from Philip were made autonomous and declared free.

Soon after, Antiochus landed an army on the Greek mainland. The Romans drove him from Greece, and in 189 B.C.E. they crushed his army at Magnesia in Asia Minor. The Romans left Greek cities free, but they regarded Greece and Asia Minor as protectorates in which they could intervene as they chose.

QUICK REVIEW

Rome Conquers Greece

- Romans forbid interference in Greek cities by Macedonia
- Rome sees Greek cities as a kind of protectorate
- Rome responds with force to signs of anti-Roman feeling in Greek cities

A Master among His Students. This carved relief from the second century C.E. shows a schoolmaster and his pupils. The one at the right is arriving late.

Rheinisches Landesmuseum, Triern, Germany/Alinari/Art Resource, New York.

What elements of Greek culture influenced Roman education?

In 179 B.C.E., Perseus (r. 179–168 B.C.E.) succeeded Philip V as king of Macedon. He tried to gain popularity in Greece by favoring the democratic and revolutionary forces in the cities. The Romans defeated him in 168 B.C.E. and divided Macedon into four separate republics. The new plan reflected a stern, businesslike policy promoted by the conservative censor Cato (234–149 B.C.E.). Leaders of anti-Roman factions in the Greek cities were punished severely, and in 146 B.C.E., the city of Corinth was destroyed. The Roman treasury benefited so much from these wars that Rome abolished direct property taxes on its citizens. Romans were learning that foreign campaigns could bring profit to the state, rewards to soldiers, and wealth, fame, and power to their generals.

See the Map
The Roman Conquest of the Mediterranean During the Republic
at **myhistorylab.com**

GREEK CULTURAL INFLUENCE

Among the most important effects of Rome's expansion overseas were changes in the Roman style of life and thought. Roman aristocrats surrounded themselves with Greek intellectuals. Even conservatives, such as Cato, who spoke contemptuously of "Greek-lings," learned Greek and absorbed Greek culture.

Almost from the beginning, the Romans identified their gods with Greek equivalents and incorporated Greek mythology into their own. In the third century B.C.E. important new cults were introduced from the East: the worship of Cybele, the Great Mother goddess from Asia Minor, and of Dionysus, or Bacchus. Interest in Babylonian astrology also grew.

Education was entirely the responsibility of the Roman family. It is not clear whether girls received any education in early Rome, although they did later on. Boys' education aimed at making them moral, pious, patriotic, law-abiding, and respectful of tradition. Contact with the Greeks of southern Italy produced momentous changes in Roman curricula. Greek teachers introduced the study of language, literature, and philosophy, as well as the idea of a liberal education, or what the Romans called *humanitas*—the root of our concept of the humanities.

The first need was to learn Greek, for Rome did not yet have a literature of its own. Schools were established in which the teacher, called a *grammaticus*, taught his students the Greek language and its literature, particularly the works of Homer. Thereafter, educated Romans were expected to be bilingual. Roman boys of the upper classes then studied rhetoric—the art of speaking and writing well—with Greeks who were expert in it. The Greeks considered rhetoric less important than philosophy. But the more practical Romans took to it avidly, for it was of great use in legal disputes and was becoming ever more valuable in political life. By the last century of the Roman Republic, the new Hellenized education had become dominant. Latin literature formed part of the course of study, but much of it was modeled after Greek examples. The number of educated people grew, extending beyond the senatorial class and outside the city of Rome.

Girls of the upper classes were educated similarly to boys. They were probably taught by tutors at home, although they were usually married by the age when men were pursuing higher education. Still, some women became prose writers or poets.

Read the Document
Issue of the Day: Religion and Philosophy in the Roman Empire-Stoicism and Christianity? at **myhistorylab.com**

humanitas
The Roman name for a liberal arts education.

QUICK REVIEW

Roman Education

- Traditional Roman education was the responsibility of family
- Encounters with Greece changed form and content of education
- Schools established to teach Greek and Latin literature

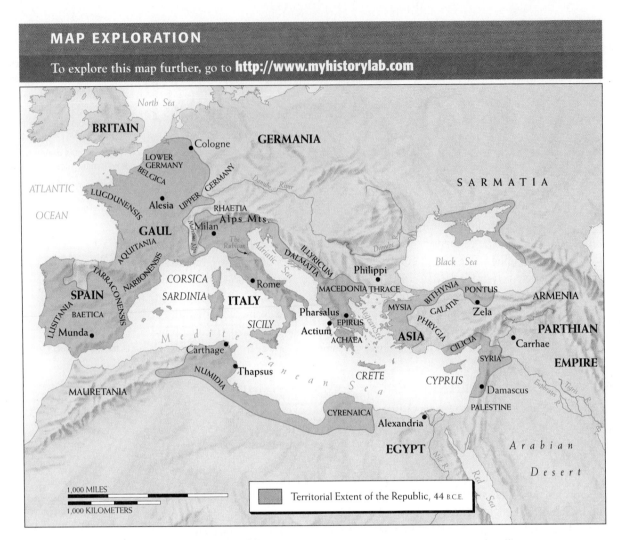

MAP EXPLORATION

To explore this map further, go to **http://www.myhistorylab.com**

MAP 6–2.   Roman Dominions of the Late Republic.

This map shows the extent of the territory controlled by Rome at the time of Caesar's death in 44 B.C.E.

How did Rome's geographic location influence its growth?

A rich, socially ambitious Roman might support a Greek philosopher in his own home, so that through conversation his son could acquire the learning and polished thought necessary for the fully cultured gentleman. Some, like the great orator Cicero (106–43 B.C.E.), traveled to Greece to study with great teachers of rhetoric and philosophy. Education made the Romans part of the culture of the Hellenistic world, a world they dominated and, therefore, needed to understand.

ROMAN IMPERIALISM

WHY DID a growing gap between the wealthy and everyone else contribute to political instability?

Rome's expansion in Italy and overseas was accomplished without a plan. It brought the Romans an empire, and with it, power, wealth, and responsibilities (see Map 6–2).

AFTERMATH OF CONQUEST

War and expansion changed the economic, social, and political life of Italy. The Second Punic War damaged Italian farmland, and many veterans were unable to go back to their farms. Most became tenant farmers or hired hands. Often the land they abandoned was acquired by the wealthy, who converted these farms, later called *latifundia*, into large plantations.

Land was inexpensive, and slaves conquered in war provided cheap labor. By fair means and foul, large landholders obtained sizable quantities of public land and forced small farmers off it. These changes separated the people of Rome and Italy more sharply into rich and poor, the landed and the landless. The result was conflict that threatened the republic.

THE GRACCHI

By the middle of the second century B.C.E., the unintended consequences of Rome's rapid expansion troubled perceptive Roman nobles. The fall in status of the peasant farmers made it harder to recruit soldiers, and the patron's traditional control over his clients was weakened by their flight from their land.

Tiberius Gracchus (168–133 B.C.E.) became tribune in 133 B.C.E. on a program of land reform. (See Document, "The Ruin of the Roman Family Farm and the Gracchan Reforms" on page 154.) He had popular support but encountered political hostility. When another tribune twice vetoed his land reform bill, Tiberius had the offending tribune removed from office—in violation of the constitution. Tiberius then proposed and passed a bill that was even harsher than the first and more appealing to the people. Because no tribune dared to oppose him, he got his way. But the cost was the destruction of the Roman constitution.

Tiberius understood the danger to himself and to prospects for implementing his reforms once his term as tribune came to an end, so he announced his candidacy for a second successive term. This violated the term limits posed by the Roman constitution. Having no legal recourse, a mob of senators and their clients resorted to violence. They killed Tiberius and some 300 of his followers and threw their bodies into the Tiber River.

The Senate had put down the threat to its rule but at the price of the first internal bloodshed in Roman political history. Roman politics was changed irrevocably. Tiberius had demonstrated how to build a political career based on pressure from the people, not on aristocratic influence. In the last century of the republic, such politicians were called *populares*, whereas those who supported the traditional role of the Senate were called *optimates* ("the best men").

The tribunate of Gaius Gracchus (ca. 159–121 B.C.E.), brother of Tiberius, posed a greater threat to the Senate than that of Tiberius because all the tribunes supported Gaius. There would be no veto, and tribunes could now retain power through reelection. Gaius courted popularity by establishing colonies for landless veterans and passing a law stabilizing the price of grain in Rome. He also divided the wealthy by winning the backing of the equestrian order in his struggles with the Senate. The equestrians were rich men who supplied goods and services to the Roman state and collected taxes in the provinces. When Pergamum became the Roman province of Asia in 129 B.C.E., Gaius gave them the right to collect taxes there.

Gaius easily won reelection as tribune for 122 B.C.E., but then he made a misstep. He proposed giving citizenship to Italian allies, but the common people did not want to share the advantages of their Roman citizenship. Gaius lost his reelection campaign in 121 B.C.E., and a hostile consul provoked an incident that led to violence. Gaius was killed, and 3,000 of his followers were put to death without trial.

MARIUS AND SULLA

Before long the senatorial oligarchy faced a stronger opponent who got his start in a war with Jugurtha (d. 104 B.C.E.), king of Numidia. When the war dragged on, the people elected Gaius Marius (157–86 B.C.E.) to the consulship for 107 B.C.E. Later, when Rome faced threats from barbarians to the north, Marius served five consecutive terms

latifundia
Large plantations for growing cash crops owned by wealthy Romans.

populares
Roman politicians who sought to pursue a political career based on the support of the people rather than just the aristocracy.

equestrians
Literally "cavalrymen" or "knights." In the earliest years of the Roman Republic, those who could afford to serve as mounted warriors.

DOCUMENT

The Ruin of the Roman Family Farm and the Gracchan Reforms

The independent family farm was the backbone both of the Greek polis and of the early Roman Republic. Rome's conquests, the long wars that kept the citizen-soldier away from his farm, and the availability of great numbers of slaves at a low price, however, badly undercut the traditional way of farming and with it the foundations of republican society. In the following passage, Plutarch describes the process of agricultural change and the response to it of the reformer Tiberius Gracchus, tribune in 133 B.C.E.

- **WHY** did Roman farmers face troubles? What were the social and political consequences of the changes in agricultural life? What solution did Tiberius Gracchus propose? Why, besides selfishness and greed, did people oppose his plan?

Of the territory which the Romans won in war from their neighbours, a part they sold, and a part they made common land, and assigned it for occupation to the poor and indigent among the citizens, on payment of a small rent into the public treasury. And when the rich began to offer larger rents and drove out the poor, a law was enacted forbidding the holding by one person of more than five hundred [iugera] of land. For a short time this enactment gave a check to the rapacity of the rich, and was of assistance to the poor, who remained in their places on the land which they had rented and occupied the allotment which each had held from the outset. But later on the neighbouring rich men, by means of fictitious personages, transferred these rentals to themselves, and finally held most of the land openly in their own names. Then the poor, who had been ejected from their land, no longer showed themselves eager for military service, and neglected the bringing up of children, so that soon all Italy was conscious of a dearth of freemen, and was filled with gangs of foreign slaves, by whose aid the rich cultivated their estates, from which they had driven away the free citizens.

And it is thought that a law dealing with injustice and rapacity so great was never drawn up in milder and gentler terms. For men who ought to have been punished for their disobedience and to have surrendered with payment of a fine the land which they were illegally enjoying, these men it merely ordered to abandon their injust acquisitions upon being paid their value, and to admit into ownership of them such citizens as needed assistance. But although the rectification of the wrong was so considerate, the people were satisfied to let bygones be bygones if they could be secure from such wrong in the future; the men of wealth and substance, however, were led by their greed to hate the law, and by their wrath and contentiousness to hate the lawgiver, and tried to dissuade the people by alleging that Tiberius was introducing a redistribution of land for the confusion of the body politic, and was stirring up a general revolution.

Source: From Plutarch, "Tiberius Gracchus," in *Lives* 8–9, Vol. 10, trans. by Bernadotte Perrin and William Heinemann (London: G. P. Putnam's Sons, 1921), pp. 159-167.

from 104 B.C.E. until 100 B.C.E. He was a *novus homo* ("new man"), a political outsider, the first man from his family to win a consulship. He promised the voters that popular military reforms would lead to speedy victory. He eliminated the traditional property qualification for military service and opened the ranks to volunteers, mostly dispossessed farmers and rural proletarians. They enlisted for long terms of service, looked on the army as a career, and expected land as a bonus when they retired. They became semiprofessional clients of their general and backed the politician who seemed most likely to get them what they wanted. Marius had to obtain grants from the Senate to maintain his power and reputation. But with a large, loyal army behind him, he could frighten the Senate into doing his bidding. Marius's innovation created both the opportunity and the necessity for military leaders to challenge the authority of civilian government.

Marius quickly routed Jugurtha, but a guerrilla war dragged on. Finally, Marius's subordinate, Lucius Cornelius Sulla (138–78 B.C.E.), captured Jugurtha and ended the war. Marius, however, took the credit, leaving Sulla to plot his revenge.

WAR AGAINST THE ITALIAN ALLIES (90–88 B.C.E.)

For a decade Rome ignored Italian discontent. In frustration, the Italians revolted. The Romans immediately offered citizenship to those cities that remained loyal and soon made the same offer to the rebels if they laid down their arms. By 88 B.C.E. the war against the allies was over. All the Italians became Roman citizens, but they retained local self-government. Time blurred the distinction between Romans and Italians and forged them into a single nation.

SULLA'S DICTATORSHIP

Sulla was elected consul for 88 B.C.E. He backed the Senate in a war against Marius and his supporters, and following its victorious conclusion, he had himself appointed dictator. He used his power to restore the traditional Roman constitution and the power of the Senate. He could not, however, undo the effect of his example. Sulla had taken possession of Rome with its own army and led Romans in slaughtering Romans. Others soon followed suit.

ARTS AND LETTERS OF THE LATE REPUBLIC

The high point of Roman culture began in the last century of the republic, when art and writing show uniquely Roman qualities in spirit and sometimes in form.

The late republic's towering literary figure, Cicero (106–43 B.C.E.), is most famous for his orations. Together with his private letters, the speeches give us a clearer and fuller insight into his mind than the works of any other figure in antiquity. We see the political life of his period largely through his eyes. He also wrote treatises on rhetoric, ethics, and politics that put Greek philosophical ideas into Latin terminology, changing them to suit Roman conditions and values. Cicero believed in a world governed by divine and natural law that human reason could perceive. He looked to law, custom, and tradition to produce stability and liberty. His literary style, as well as his values and ideas, created an important legacy for the Middle Ages and, reinterpreted, for the Renaissance.

The period from the Gracchi to the fall of the republic was important for the development of Roman law. The edicts of the magistrates who dealt with foreigners developed the idea of a comprehensive *jus gentium*, or "law of peoples," as opposed to a law based strictly on Roman custom. In the first century B.C.E., under the influence of the Greeks, the *jus gentium* was equated with the *jus naturale*, or "natural law," taught by the Stoics.

Two of Rome's greatest poets, Lucretius and Catullus, were citizens of the late republic. The Hellenistic literary theorists believed that poetry should educate as well as entertain, a task Lucretius (ca. 99–ca. 55 B.C.E.) undertook in his epic poem *De Rerum Natura* (*On the Nature of Things*). It explained and advocated the scientific and philosophical theories of Epicurus and Democritus, which Lucretius believed would liberate people from superstition and the fear of death. Catullus's (ca. 84–ca. 54 B.C.E.) poems were personal. He wrote of the joys and pains of love and amused himself composing witty poetic exchanges. He illustrates the mind-set of the proud, independent, pleasure-seeking, late republican nobility.

Bust of Julius Caesar
What impression does this sculpture give you of Julius Caesar's personality?

THE FALL OF THE REPUBLIC AND THE AUGUSTAN PRINCIPATE

WHAT WERE the central features of Octavian rule?

POMPEY, CRASSUS, AND CAESAR

Marcus Licinius Crassus (115–53 B.C.E.) and Cnaeus Pompey (106–48 B.C.E.) won election to the consulship for the year 70 B.C.E. and repealed most of Sulla's laws. In 67 B.C.E., a special law gave Pompey *imperium* for three years over the entire Mediterranean and coastal lands to rid the area of pirates. When he returned to Rome in 62 B.C.E., he had more power, prestige, and popular support than any Roman in history. Crassus, though rich and influential, did not have a firm political base of his own or the kind of military glory needed to rival Pompey. During the 60s B.C.E., therefore, he allied himself with various popular leaders, the ablest of whom was Gaius Julius Caesar (100–44 B.C.E.).

FIRST TRIUMVIRATE AND THE DICTATORSHIP OF JULIUS CAESAR

To general surprise, Pompey disbanded his army and returned to Italy as a private citizen. But when the fearful Senate decided to try to turn his veterans against him by refusing to grant them land, he forged an alliance with Crassus and Caesar called the First Triumvirate.

Caesar was elected consul for 59 B.C.E. and enacted the Triumvirate's program. Caesar raised a great army for the conquest of Gaul, Crassus got a similar military command in the Middle East, and Pompey got land for his veterans and confirmation of his treaties from the Senate. By the time Caesar had conquered Gaul and was ready to return to Rome, the Triumvirate had dissolved. Crassus's invasion of Parthia had ended with his death at Carrhae in 53 B.C.E., and Pompey had allied with the Senate against Caesar.

Early in January of 49 B.C.E. the more extreme faction in the Senate ordered Pompey to defend the state and Caesar to lay down his command. For Caesar this meant exile or death, so he ordered his legions to cross the Rubicon River, the boundary of his province. This action was the first act of a civil war that ended in 45 B.C.E., when Caesar defeated forces under Pompey's sons.

Caesar made few changes in the government of Rome, but his monopoly of military power made a sham of the republic. His senatorial enemies conspired against him, and on March 15, 44 B.C.E., they stabbed him to death at a meeting of the Senate. The assassins expected his death to restore the republic, but instead thirteen more years of civil war eviscerated what was left of the republic.

SECOND TRIUMVIRATE AND THE EMERGENCE OF OCTAVIAN

Caesar's heir was his grandnephew, Octavian (63 B.C.E.–14 C.E.). Marcus Antonius (Mark Antony) (ca. 83–30 B.C.E.) and Lepidus (d. 13 B.C.E.), two of Caesar's officers, joined Octavian in forming the Second Triumvirate, an alliance dedicated to punishing Caesar's assassins. The triumvirs defeated their enemy in 42 B.C.E. but soon quarreled among themselves. Octavian gained control of the western

•••⫶**Read** the **Document**
Excerpt from Life of Caesar (2nd century C.E.), Plutarch at **myhistorylab.com**

◉⫶**See** the **Map**
The Career of Julius Caesar at **myhistorylab.com**

CHRONOLOGY

THE FALL OF THE ROMAN REPUBLIC

133 B.C.E.	Tribunate of Tiberius Gracchus
123–122 B.C.E.	Tribunate of Gaius Gracchus
111–105 B.C.E.	Jugurthine War
104–100 B.C.E.	Consecutive consulships of Marius
90–88 B.C.E.	War against the Italian allies
70 B.C.E.	Consulship of Crassus and Pompey
60 B.C.E.	Formation of First Triumvirate
58–50 B.C.E.	Caesar in Gaul
53 B.C.E.	Crassus killed in Battle of Carrhae
49 B.C.E.	Caesar crosses Rubicon; civil war begins
46–44 B.C.E.	Caesar's dictatorship
45 B.C.E.	End of civil war
43 B.C.E.	Formation of Second Triumvirate
42 B.C.E.	Battle of Philippi
31 B.C.E.	Octavian defeats Antony at Actium

part of the empire. Antonius, together with Egypt's Queen Cleopatra (r. 51–30 B.C.E.), ruled the East. In 31 B.C.E., Octavian crushed the fleet and army of Antony and Cleopatra at Actium and ended the civil war. Octavian emerged in control of the Mediterranean world but faced the daunting challenge of restoring peace, prosperity, and confidence without making the mistake that had cost Caesar his life: He had to exercise the power of a king without appearing to threaten the republican traditions to which his fellow Romans were passionately attached.

THE AUGUSTAN PRINCIPATE

Octavian's constitutional solution was to drape a monarchy in republican trappings by apparently sharing authority with the Senate. All real power, however, lay with the ruler, whether he was called by the unofficial title of "first citizen" (*princeps*) like Octavian, or "emperor" (*imperator*) like those who followed. The outline of his plan emerged in 27 B.C.E.: He was to rule the provinces of Spain, Gaul, and Syria with proconsular power for military command and retain a consulship in Rome. The Senate would govern the other provinces. Twenty of Rome's twenty-six legions were stationed in Octavian's provinces, giving him effective control of the empire. The Senate, however, was grateful to him for establishing peace after Rome's long civil war, and it voted him many honors, including the semireligious title "**Augustus**," which connoted veneration, majesty, and holiness. Historians refer to Octavian in his role as Rome's first emperor as Augustus and characterize his regime as the Principate, a government that tried to conceal the naked power on which it rested.

AUGUSTAN ADMINISTRATION, ARMY, AND DEFENSE

Augustus made important administrative changes to reduce inefficiency and corruption, to eliminate the threat to peace and order by ambitious individuals, and to reduce the distinction between Romans and Italians, senators and equestrians. Augustus controlled the elections and saw to it that promising young men, whatever their origin, served the state. Equestrians and Italians who had no connection with the Roman aristocracy were admitted to the Senate, which Augustus treated with respect and honor.

The economy prospered, stimulated by wealth from newly conquered Egypt, by a general peace that stimulated commerce and industry, by a vast program of public works, and by a revival of small farming on the lands granted to Augustus's veterans.

Rome's soldiers became true professionals under Augustus. Enlistment was for twenty years, the pay was good, and there were bonuses and a pension on retirement. The citizen legions, together with auxiliary units staffed by provincials, stationed about 300,000 men on the empire's frontiers—barely enough to hold the line. The army in the provinces brought Roman culture to the natives. The soldiers spread their language and customs, often marrying local women and settling down there. They attracted merchants, who became the nuclei of new towns that became centers of Roman civilization. As time passed, the provincials on the frontiers became Roman citizens and helped strengthen Rome's defenses against the barbarians.

RELIGION AND MORALITY

A century of political strife and civil war had undermined traditional Roman society. Augustus undertook to preserve and restore family life by curbing adultery and divorce and encouraging early marriage and the procreation of legitimate children. He restored the dignity of formal Roman religion by building temples and reviving cults. Like Julius Caesar, he was deified after his death, and a state cult was dedicated to his worship.

Emperor Augustus (r. 27 B.C.E.–14 C.E.). This statue, now in the Vatican, stood in the villa of Augustus's wife Livia. The figures on the elaborate breastplate are all of symbolic significance. At the top, for example, Dawn in her chariot brings in a new day under the protective mantle of the sky god; in the center, Tiberius, Augustus's successor, accepts the return of captured Roman army standards from a barbarian prince; and at the bottom, Mother Earth offers a horn of plenty.

Why was symbolism particularly important to Augustus?

◆◆—**Read** the **Document**
Augustus on His Accomplishments
(1st century C.E.) at **myhistorylab.com**

imperator
Under the Roman Republic, it was the title given to a victorious general. Under Augustus and his successors, it became the title of the ruler of Rome, meaning "emperor."

Augustus
The title given to Octavian in 27 B.C.E. and borne thereafter by all Roman emperors.

◉—**See** the **Map**
Rome in the Age of Augustus, 31 B.C–A.D. 14 at **myhistorylab.com**

QUICK REVIEW

The Army under Augustus

- Augustus professionalized army
- 20-year enlistment with good pay and pension
- 300,000 men formed frontier army

•••—Read the Document
Augustus's Moral Legislation: Family Values,
18 B.C.E. at **myhistorylab.com**

•••—Read the Document
Horace, "Dulce et Decorum Est Pro Patria
Mori" at **myhistorylab.com**

THE GOLDEN AGE OF ROMAN LITERATURE

Augustus replaced the complexity of republican patronage with a simple scheme in which all patronage flowed from the *princeps*. Two of the major poets of this time, Virgil and Horace, had lost their property during the civil wars. The patronage of the *princeps* allowed them the leisure and the security to write poetry and also made them dependent on him and limited their freedom of expression.

Virgil (70–19 B.C.E.) was the most important Augustan poet. His greatest work is the *Aeneid*, a long epic that linked the history of Rome with the Homeric tradition of the Greeks. Its hero, the Trojan Aeneas, personifies the ideal Roman qualities of duty, responsibility, serious purpose, and patriotism. Virgil celebrated the peace and prosperity Augustus established for the empire and supported Augustus's program for the revival of traditional Roman virtues.

The great skills of the lyric poet Horace (65–8 B.C.E.) are best revealed in his *Odes*. Many of them glorify the new Augustan order, the imperial family, and the empire. Ovid (43 B.C.E.–18 C.E.) wrote entertaining love elegies that reveal the sophistication and the loose sexual conduct of the Roman aristocracy. His most popular work is *Metamorphoses*, a graceful, lively poem of epic length that retells Greek myths as charming stories. Ovid was exiled because his poetry did not conform to Augustan values.

The most important and influential prose writer of the time was Livy (59 B.C.E.–17 C.E.). His *History of Rome* traced the period from Rome's legendary origins until 9 B.C.E. Only one-fourth of his work survives. Livy's great achievement was the creation of a continuous, impressive narrative encompassing the full sweep of Roman history. Its purpose was to promote traditional morality and patriotism. He glorified Rome's greatness and, like Augustus, grounded it in Rome's hardy virtues.

Augustus was also a great patron of the visual arts. Augustus embarked on a building program that beautified Rome, glorified his reign, contributed to the general prosperity, and enhanced his popularity. The greatest sculptural monument of the age is the Altar of Peace (*Ara Pacis*), dedicated in 9 B.C.E. Its walls show a procession in which Augustus and his family appear to move forward, followed by the magistrates, the Senate, and the people of Rome. There is no better symbol of the new order.

PEACE AND PROSPERITY: IMPERIAL ROME

WHAT ROLE did cities play in the Roman Empire?

Augustus tried to cloak the monarchical nature of his government, but his successors soon abandoned all pretense. The rulers came to be called *imperator*—root of our word *emperor*—as well as *Caesar*. Augustus designated his heirs by giving them a share in the imperial power and responsibility (see Map 6–3). Tiberius (emperor

A Panel from the Ara Pacis (Altar of Peace). The altar was dedicated in 9 B.C.E. It was part of a propaganda campaign—involving poetry, architecture, myth, and history—that Augustus undertook to promote himself as the savior of Rome and the restorer of peace. This panel shows the goddess Earth and her children with cattle, sheep, and other symbols of agricultural wealth.

Saturnia, Tellus, Goddess of Earth, Air and Water. Panel from the Ara Pacis. 13–9 B.C.E. Museum of the Ara Pacis, Rome. Nimatallah/Art Resource, New York.

Why would agricultural products make good symbols of peace?

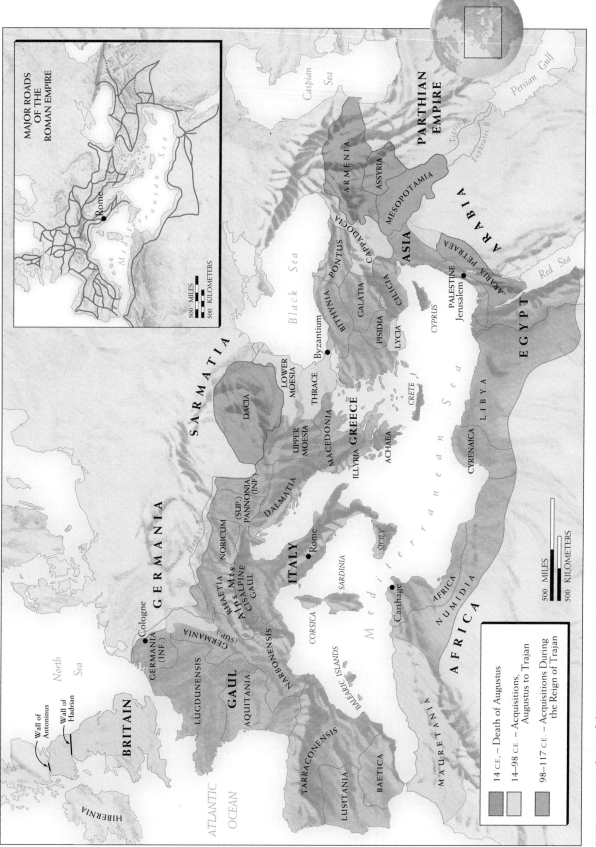

MAP 6–3. **Provinces of the Roman Empire to 117 C.E.** The growth of the empire to its greatest extent is shown in three stages—at the death of Augustus in 14 B.C.E., at the death of Nerva in 98 C.E., and at the death of Trajan in 117 C.E. The division into provinces is also indicated. The inset outlines the main roads that tied the far-flung empire.

What trends can you observe in Roman expansion over time?

Relief from the Arch of Titus. Spoils from the Temple in Jerusalem were carried in triumphal procession by Roman troops. This relief from Titus's Arch of Victory in the Roman Forum celebrates his capture of Jerusalem in 70 C.E. after a two-year siege. The Jews found it difficult to reconcile their religion with Roman rule and frequently rebelled.

What are the most noticeable elements in this image? Why?

•••┤Read the Document

Marcus Aurelius, *The Meditations*, Book Two (167 C.E.) at **myhistorylab.com**

⊙┤See the Map

The Roman Empire at Its Greatest Extent at **myhistorylab.com**

CHRONOLOGY

RULERS OF THE EARLY EMPIRE

27 B.C.E.–14 C.E.	Augustus
The Julio-Claudian Dynasty	
14–37 C.E.	Tiberius
37–41 C.E.	Gaius (Caligula)
41–54 C.E.	Claudius
54–68 C.E.	Nero
69 C.E.	Year of the four emperors
The Flavian Dynasty	
69–79 C.E.	Vespasian
79–81 C.E.	Titus
81–96 C.E.	Domitian
The "Good Emperors"	
96–98 C.E.	Nerva
98–117 C.E.	Trajan
117–138 C.E.	Hadrian
138–161 C.E.	Antoninus Pius
161–180 C.E.	Marcus Aurelius

14–37 C.E.), Gaius (Caligula, 37–41 C.E.), Claudius (41–54 C.E.), and Nero (54–68 C.E.) descended from Augustus's family. After their line died out in 68 C.E., various Roman armies marched on Italy and elevated four men in rapid succession to the throne. Vespasian (69–79 C.E.), the first emperor who did not come from the old Roman nobility, emerged victorious from the chaos, and his sons, Titus (79–81 C.E.) and Domitian (81–96 C.E.), carried forward the Flavian Dynasty.

The Flavian Dynasty ended with the assassination of Domitian. The Senate appointed Nerva (96–98 C.E.) emperor, and he became the first of the five "good emperors"; the others were Trajan (98–117 C.E.), Hadrian (117–138 C.E.), Antoninus Pius (138–161 C.E.), and Marcus Aurelius (161–180 C.E.). Until Marcus Aurelius, none of these men had sons, so they were each free to choose an able successor. The result was almost a century of excellent administration. This ended when Marcus Aurelius's incompetent son Commodus (180–192 C.E.) succeeded him.

ADMINISTRATION OF THE EMPIRE

The empire was a collection of cities and towns. Roman policy during the Principate was to raise urban centers to the status of Roman municipalities. The upper classes of the provinces were enlisted in the governments of their regions. This spread Roman culture and won the loyalty of influential people. As the imperial bureaucracy grew and became more efficient, however, the central administration took a greater role in local affairs and the municipalities lost autonomy. Efficient centralized control was obtained at the cost of the vitality of the cities.

Unlike most conquered peoples, the Jews found accommodation to Roman rule difficult. Their first rebellion was crushed by Vespasian's son, the future emperor Titus, in 70 C.E. At that time the Temple in Jerusalem was destroyed. A second revolt was put down in 117 C.E. Finally, when Hadrian ordered a Roman colony placed on the site of Jerusalem, Simon led a last uprising from 132 to 135 that was brutally suppressed.

Augustus and his successors had not tried to expand the empire, but Trajan launched a sustained offensive into neighboring territory. Between 101 and 106 C.E., he established the new province of Dacia north of the Danube. His intent was probably to defend the empire by driving wedges into enemy territory. The same strategy led him to invade the Parthian Empire in the East (113–117 C.E.). Hadrian kept Dacia but abandoned Trajan's eastern conquests. The Roman defense became rigid, and initiative passed to the barbarians. Marcus Aurelius spent most of his reign resisting attacks in the East and on the Danube frontier, and these attacks put enormous pressure on the empire's resources.

CULTURE OF THE EARLY EMPIRE

The prosperity and relative stability of the first two centuries of imperial Rome brought Roman architecture to full flower. Roman contributions to the building arts were largely advances in engineering that made huge structures feasible. To the basic post-and-lintel construction used by the Greeks, the Romans added the semicircular arch, borrowed from the Etruscans. When used internally in the form of vaults and domes, the arch permitted great buildings like the Roman baths. Romans also made good use of concrete, a building material first used by the Hellenistic Greeks. The Colosseum, an arena in Rome built by the Flavian emperors, is an excellent example of Roman architecture. The only major Roman temple to survive intact is the Pantheon, a building roofed by a great dome. Roman engineers also spread impressive bridges, roads, and aqueducts throughout the empire.

In Latin literature, the years between the death of Augustus and Marcus Aurelius are known as the Silver Age. Writers were gloomy, negative, and pessimistic, prone to criticism and satire. Historians of the era wrote about remote periods to avoid the risk of offending an emperor's sensibilities. Scholarship was encouraged, but we hear little of poetry. Romances written in Greek became popular as an escape from contemporary realities.

LIFE IN IMPERIAL ROME: THE APARTMENT HOUSE

The civilization of the Roman Empire was the product of the vitality of its cities. The typical city had about 20,000 inhabitants; Rome probably had in excess of half a million. Most of its residents were squeezed into tall apartment buildings, which the Romans called *insulae* ("islands"). The buildings, which were five or more stories tall, were uncomfortable and dangerous. Built cheaply, they were prone to collapse, and they were easily set on fire by the many torches, candles, oil lamps, and braziers their inhabitants used. They had no running water or other conveniences. Not surprisingly, Romans spent most of their time out of doors.

Pompeiian Woman. The Roman provincial city of Pompeii, near the Bay of Naples, was buried by an eruption of Mount Vesuvius in 79 C.E. As a result, the town, together with its private houses and their contents, was remarkably well preserved until recovery in the eighteenth century. Among the discoveries were a number of works of art, including pictorial mosaics and paintings. This depiction of a young woman, on a round panel from a house in Pompeii, is part of a larger painting that includes her husband holding a volume of Plato's writings. The woman is holding a stylus and a booklet of wax tablets and is evidently in the process of writing. Her gold earrings and hair net show that she is a fashionable person of some means.

Late first century C.E. Diameter 14 ⅜ inches. Sappho, idealized portrait of a girl posing as a poetess. Fresco from Pompeii, Insula occidentale. Museo Archeologico Nazionale, Naples, Italy, © Erich Lessing/Art Resource, New York.

What does this image suggest about the lives of well-to-do Roman women?

View the Image
Hadrian's Wall at **myhistorylab.com**

View the Image
Roman Coliseum at **myhistorylab.com**

View the Image
The Interior of the Dome of the Pantheon, Rome at **myhistorylab.com**

View the Image
Roman aqueduct at **myhistorylab.com**

A Roman Apartment House. This is a reconstruction of a typical Roman apartment house found at Ostia, Rome's port. The ground floor contained shops, and the stories above it held many apartments.

Gismondi (20th C). Museo della Civiltà Romana, Rome, Italy/© Scala/Art Resource, New York.

How do these buildings compare with the dwellings of other civilizations of this era?

THE RISE OF CHRISTIANITY

HOW DID Paul resolve the central dilemma of the relationship between Judaism and early Christianity?

"mystery" religions
The cults of Isis, Mithras, and Osiris, which promised salvation to those initiated into the secret or "mystery" of their rites.

✓•─⌐Study and Review
The Roman and Christian Views of the Good Life at **myhistorylab.com**

•••─⌐Read the Document
Excerpt from The Gospel According to Luke (1st century C.E.) at **myhistorylab.com**

•••─⌐Read the Document
Excerpt from The Gospel According to Matthew (1st century C.E.) at **myhistorylab.com**

•••─⌐Read the Document
The Acts of the Apostles: Paul Pronounces the "Good News" in Greece, ca. 100 at **myhistorylab.com**

Pharisees
The group that was most strict in its adherence to Jewish law.

The story of how Christianity ultimately conquered the Roman Empire is one of the most remarkable in history. Christianity was opposed by the established religious institutions of its native Judaea and had to compete not only against the official cults of Rome and the sophisticated philosophies of the educated classes but also against **"mystery" religions** such as the cults of Mithra, Isis, and Osiris. Christians were also at times officially persecuted by the state. Despite all this, Christianity became the official religion of the empire.

JESUS OF NAZARETH

An attempt to understand the triumph of Christianity must begin with Jesus of Nazareth. The Gospel authors believed that Jesus was the son of God who came to redeem humanity and bring immortality to those who followed his teachings.

Jesus was born in Judaea in the time of Augustus and was an effective teacher in the tradition of the Jewish prophets. This tradition promised the coming of a Messiah (in Greek, *christos—Jesus Christ* means "Jesus the Messiah"), a redeemer who would make Israel triumph over its enemies and establish the kingdom of God on Earth. Jesus seems to have insisted that the Messiah would not establish an earthly kingdom but, at the Day of Judgment, God would reward the righteous and condemn the wicked. Until that day, which his followers believed would come soon, Jesus taught the faithful to abandon sin and worldly concerns; to follow the moral code described in the Sermon on the Mount, which preached love, charity, and humility; and to believe in him and his divine mission.

Jesus won a following, especially among the poor. This provoked the hostility of Jerusalem's religious leaders, who convinced the Roman governor that Jesus and his followers might be dangerous revolutionaries. Jesus was put to death in Jerusalem by the cruel and degrading method of crucifixion, probably in 30 C.E. His followers believed that he was resurrected on the third day after his death, and that belief became a critical element in their religion.

Although faith in Jesus as the Christ spread to some Jewish communities in Syria and Asia Minor, without Saint Paul it might have remained a small, heretical cult within Judaism.

PAUL OF TARSUS

Paul (?5–67 C.E.), whose Hebrew name was Saul, was born in Tarsus in Asia Minor. He had an excellent Hellenistic education and held Roman citizenship. He was also a **Pharisee**, a strict adherent of the Jewish law. He persecuted the early Christians until his own sudden conversion while traveling to Damascus about 35 C.E. The great problem facing the early Christians, like Paul, was their relationship to Judaism. If the new faith was a version of Judaism, then it must adhere to the Jewish law and seek converts only among Jews. James, called the brother of Jesus, held that view, whereas Hellenist Jews tended to see Christianity as a new and universal religion.

Paul supported the position of the Hellenists and soon won many converts among the gentiles. He believed that the followers of Jesus were called to be evangelists ("messengers") and to spread the gospel ("good news") of salvation during the short time that remained before Jesus returned for the Day of Judgment. Faith in Jesus as the Christ was necessary for salvation, but salvation was a gift of God's grace, not something earned by good works.

ORGANIZATION

The new religion had its greatest success in the cities and among the poor and uneducated. The rites of the early Christians appear to have been simple and few. Baptism by water removed original sin and permitted participation in the community and its activities. The central ritual was a common meal called the *agape* ("love feast"), followed by the ceremony of the *Eucharist* ("thanksgiving"), a celebration of the Lord's Supper in which unleavened bread was eaten and unfermented wine drunk. There were also prayers, hymns, and readings from works that eventually became the Christian scriptures.

At first the churches had little formal organization, but by the second century C.E., most cities had leaders called bishops. The doctrine of Apostolic Succession asserted that the message and authority Jesus had entrusted to his original disciples were passed on from bishop to bishop by the rite of ordination. The bishops maintained discipline within their churches and dealt with the civil authorities. In time they began meeting in councils to settle difficult questions, define orthodox belief, and expel those who would not accept it. Christianity could probably not have survived without such strong internal organization and government.

PERSECUTION OF CHRISTIANS

The new faith soon incurred the distrust of the pagan world and of the imperial government. The Christians' refusal to demonstrate their patriotism by worshiping the emperor was considered treason. By the end of the first century, membership in the Christian community had become a crime. Most persecutions during this period, however, were instituted not by the government but by mobs.

EMERGENCE OF CATHOLICISM

Most Christians held to traditional, simple, conservative beliefs. This body of majority opinion and the church that enshrined it came to be called **Catholic**, which means "universal." Its doctrines were deemed **orthodox**; those holding contrary opinions were called **heretics.**

By the end of the second century, an orthodox scriptural canon had emerged that included the Old Testament, the Gospels, and the Epistles of Paul. The orthodox drew up creeds, brief statements of faith to which true Christians should adhere. By the end of the second century, an orthodox Christian—that is, a member of the Catholic Church—had to accept its creed, its canon of holy writings, and the authority of the bishops.

ROME AS A CENTER OF THE EARLY CHURCH

The church in the city of Rome acquired special prominence. Rome benefited from the tradition that Jesus' apostles Peter and Paul were martyred there. Peter was thought to be the first bishop of Rome, and the Gospel of Matthew (16:18) reported Jesus saying to Peter, "Thou art Peter [in Greek, *Petros*] and upon this rock [in Greek, *petra*] I will build my church." Subsequent bishops of Rome claimed supremacy over the Catholic Church as heirs to the role Jesus granted to Peter.

Christian Martyr. Thrown to the lions in 275 C.E. by the Romans for refusing to recant his Christian beliefs, St. Mamai is an important martyr in the iconography of Georgia, a Caucasian kingdom that embraced Christianity early in the fourth century. This gilded silver medallion, made in Georgia in the eleventh century, depicts the saint astride a lion while he bears a cross in one hand, symbolizing his triumphant victory over death and ignorance.

agape
Meaning "love feast." A common meal that was part of the central ritual of early Christian worship.

Eucharist
Meaning "thanksgiving." The celebration of the Lord's Supper. Considered the central ritual of worship by most Christians. Also called Holy Communion.

See the **Map**
The Spread of Christianity
at **myhistorylab.com**

View the **Image**
Early Christian Symbols
at **myhistorylab.com**

Catholic
Meaning "universal." The body of belief held by most Christians enshrined within the church.

orthodox
Meaning "holding the right opinions." Applied to the doctrines of the Catholic Church.

heretics People who publicly dissent from officially accepted dogma.

QUICK REVIEW

Early Christian Rites

- Baptism by water to remove original sin, enter community
- *Agape*, a shared meal or "love feast"
- *Eucharist*, a thanksgiving celebration featuring unleavened bread and unfermented wine

THE THIRD AND FOURTH CENTURIES: CRISIS AND LATE EMPIRE

WHY DID the capital of the empire move from Rome to Constantinople, and what was the significance of this shift?

The prosperity created in Augustus's day by the end of the civil war and the influx of wealth from the East could not be sustained. Population seems to have declined. The cost of government, however, kept rising. Pressure on Rome's frontiers, meanwhile, reached massive proportions. In the East, by 224 C.E., a new Iranian dynasty, the Sasanids, reinvigorated Persia (see Chapter 4), recovered Mesopotamia, and raided deep into Roman territory. Germans, especially the Goths, threatened Rome's northern and western frontiers.

MILITARY REORGANIZATION

●●●─┤Read the Document
Jordanes, The Origin and Deeds of the Goths, Book twenty-six, at **myhistorylab.com**

Septimius Severus (r. 193–211 C.E.) and his successors transformed the character of the Roman army. Septimius was a military usurper who owed everything to the support of his soldiers. He was prepared to make Rome into an undisguised military monarchy. Septimius drew recruits for the army increasingly from peasants of the less civilized provinces, and the result was a barbarization of Rome's military forces.

ECONOMIC, SOCIAL, AND POLITICAL COSTS OF DEFENSE

Inflation had forced Commodus (r. 180–192 C.E.) to raise the soldiers' pay, but the Severan emperors had to double it to keep up with prices, which increased the imperial budget by as much as 25 percent. The emperors invented new taxes, debased the coinage, and even sold the palace furniture to raise money. Still, it was hard to recruit troops.

As external threats distracted the emperors, they were less able to preserve domestic peace. Piracy, brigandage, and the neglect of roads and harbors hampered trade. So, too, did inflation. As the money supply deteriorated, the government began to demand payment in food, supplies, and labor. Rebellions erupted in some provinces, and peasants and even town administrators fled to escape their burdens. The result was further weakening of the Roman economy.

The new conditions caused important changes in the social order. The state began to take on a military appearance. People's clothing became a kind of uniform that indicated their status. Titles were assigned to ranks in civilian society as to ranks in the army. The most important distinction was the one formally established by Septimius Severus between the *honestiores* (senators, equestrians, municipal aristocracy, and soldiers) and the lower classes, or *humiliores*. Septimius granted the *honestiores* legal privileges: lighter punishments, exemption from torture, and right of appeal to the emperor. It became more difficult to move from the lower order to the higher. Freedom and private initiative were suppressed as the state's needs forced it steadily to increase its control over its citizens.

By the mid-third century the empire seemed on the point of collapse, but two able soldiers, Claudius II Gothicus (r. 268–270 C.E.) and Aurelian (r. 270–275 C.E.), drove back the barbarians and stamped out disorder. Later emperors built defensive walls around Rome and other cities and hired Germanic mercenaries whose officers gave personal loyalty to the emperor rather than to the empire. These officers became a foreign, hereditary caste of aristocrats that increasingly supplied high administrators and even emperors. In effect, the Roman people succumbed to an army of mercenaries they themselves had hired.

PRESERVATION OF CLASSICAL CULTURE

The new ruling class thought of itself as effecting a great restoration, not a revolution. The new aristocracy sought order and stability—ethical, literary, and artistic—in the classical tradition. The great classical authors were reproduced in many copies, and their works were transferred from perishable and inconvenient papyrus rolls to sturdier codices, bound volumes that were as easy to use as modern books. Scholars digested long works like Livy's *History of Rome* into shorter versions and wrote learned commentaries and compiled grammars.

THE LATE EMPIRE: DIOCLETIAN TO CONSTANTINE

The period from Diocletian (r. 284–305 C.E.) to Constantine (r. 306–337 C.E.) was one of reconstruction and reorganization. The emperor Diocletian was a man of undistinguished birth who rose to the throne through the army. He concluded that the job of defending and governing the entire empire was too great for one man. He devised a new administrative system, a **tetrarchy**, to divide territorial responsibility for the empire among four men: two emperors and two assistants who were designated as their successors. This system seemed to promise orderly, peaceful transitions instead of assassinations, chaos, and civil war.

In 305 Diocletian retired and compelled his co-emperor to do the same. But his plan for a smooth succession failed. In 310 there were five competing emperors. Out of this chaos Constantine emerged as sole emperor in 324; he reigned until 337.

The emperor had now become almost unapproachable. Those admitted to his presence had to prostrate themselves before him and kiss the hem of his robe. He was addressed as *dominus* ("lord"), and he claimed a divine right to rule.

Constantine erected the new city of Constantinople on the site of ancient Byzantium on the Bosporus, which leads to both the Aegean and the Black seas, and made it the new capital of the empire. Its strategic location was excellent for protecting the eastern and Danubian frontiers, and, surrounded on three sides by water, it was easily defended.

The autocratic emperors governed through a civilian bureaucracy, which was kept separate from the army to divide power and reduce the temptation an official might have to challenge the emperor. The system was kept under surveillance by a network of spies and secret police, but they failed to eliminate corruption and inefficiency.

The cost of maintaining a 400,000-man army, a vast civilian bureaucracy, and an expensive imperial court strained an already weak economy. Peasants unable to pay their taxes and officials unable to collect them fled their posts. Wealthy individuals moved from cities to their rural estates, and many peasants sought protection from the government's tax collectors by becoming tenant farmers on these estates. They were tied to the land, as were their descendants, as a caste system hardened.

The peace and unity established by Constantine did not last. The Germans in the west attacked along the Rhine, but even greater trouble was brewing along the Danube where the Visigoths had been driven from their home in the Ukraine by the Huns. The Emperor Valentinian (r. 364–375) saw that he could not defend the empire alone and appointed his brother Valens (r. 364–378) as co-ruler in the East. The empire was again divided in two, and the cultures of the Latin West and the Greek East grew increasingly distinct. In 376, the Goths began to plunder the Balkan provinces. In 378, Valens met them in battle at Adrianople in Thrace, and he was cut down with most of the eastern army. Theodosius (r. 379–395), an able and experienced general, unified the empire, but at his death in 395 it was divided between his sons and never reunited again.

tetrarchy

Diocletian's (r. 284–305 C.E.) system for ruling the Roman Empire by four men with power divided territorially.

QUICK REVIEW

Constantinople

♦ Built on site of ancient Byzantium

♦ Established by Constantine

♦ On a peninsula, easily defended

♦ Access to Asia

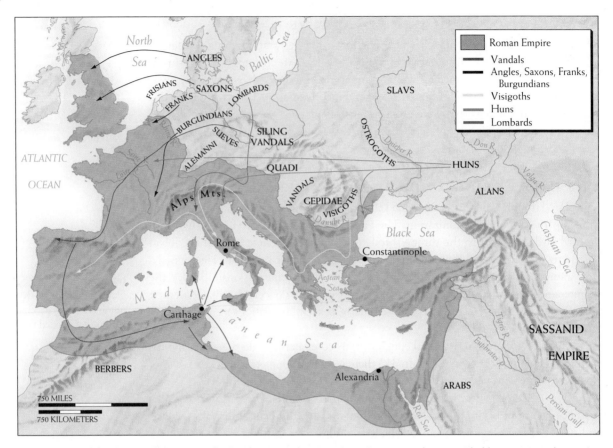

MAP 6–4. The Empire's Neighbors. In the fourth century the Roman Empire was nearly surrounded by ever-more threatening neighbors. The map shows where these so-called barbarians lived and the invasion routes many of them took in the fourth and fifth centuries.

How did barbarian invasions transform the Roman world?

The West became increasingly rural as barbarian invasions grew (see Map 6–4). The villa, a fortified country estate, became the basic unit of society. *Coloni* (tenant farmers) served local magnates in return for economic assistance and protection. Cities were depopulated and shrank to tiny walled fortresses ruled by military commanders and bishops. The upper classes left the cities and moved to the country to escape the imperial authorities. The inability of the central authority to maintain and police roads curtailed trade and communications, and living conditions became increasingly primitive. By the fifth century, the West was devolving into rural enclaves ruled by independent aristocrats and worked by a dependent labor force. The only unifying institution was the Christian church. The pattern of life that was to prevail in the West during the early Middle Ages had been generally established.

The East was different. The Roman Empire, in altered form, persisted. Constantinople flourished as the "New Rome." Although its people continued to call themselves "Romans," their lifestyles were so different from those of ancient Rome that historians refer to them as subjects of the medieval *Byzantine* Empire. Constantinople's defensible location, the services of some skillful emperors, and the resources of its base in Asia Minor enabled the eastern empire to deflect and repulse barbarian attacks. A strong Byzantine navy allowed commerce to flourish and cities to prosper. Emperors generally kept the upper hand in dealing with restive aristocratic elements. Byzantine civilization was a unique combination of classical culture, Christian religion, Roman law, and eastern artistic influences. When historians speak of the decline and fall of the Roman Empire in the fourth and fifth centuries, they reference only the West. A form of classical culture persisted in Byzantium for another thousand years.

TRIUMPH OF CHRISTIANITY

In the troubled fourth and fifth centuries people sought the help of powerful, personal deities. It was by no means unusual for people to worship new deities alongside traditional ones and to intertwine features of several gods to create new ones, a phenomenon called **syncretism.** Christianity bore some resemblance to other new faiths of the period, but none of them developed its universal appeal.

In 303, Diocletian had launched the most serious persecution inflicted on the Christians in the Roman Empire. It failed to stem the Christian tide. Ancient states could not carry out a program of terror with the thoroughness of modern totalitarian governments, and the witness of Christian martyrs may have strengthened the faith. In short order, Christians witnessed a miraculous reversal of fortune.

The conversion of Diocletian's ultimate successor, Constantine, and his ascent as sole ruler of the empire transformed Christianity's prospects. Constantine provided lavish patronage for the church and encouraged widespread conversion. In 394, the emperor Theodosius forbade the celebration of pagan cults, and by the time he died, Christianity had become the official religion of the Roman Empire (see Map 6–5 on page 168).

Temptations of power and privilege constituted new threats to some Christians. State support for the faith threatened to subordinate the church to the state. In the East, that was generally the church's fate, but in the West, the weakness of emperors permitted church leaders to exercise independence. In 390, when Ambrose

Read the Document
Eusebius on the Vision and Victory of Constantine I (The Great) (312)
at **myhistorylab.com**

syncretism
Blending or fusion of different systems of religious or philosophical beliefs.

CHRONOLOGY

THE TRIUMPH OF CHRISTIANITY

ca. 4 B.C.E.	Jesus of Nazareth born
ca. 30 C.E.	Crucifixion of Jesus
64 C.E.	Fire at Rome: persecution by Nero
ca. 70–100 C.E.	Gospels written
ca. 250–260 C.E.	Major persecutions by Decius and Valerian
303 C.E.	Persecution by Diocletian
311 C.E.	Galerius issues Edict of Toleration
312 C.E.	Battle of Milvian Bridge; conversion of Constantine to Christianity
325 C.E.	Council of Nicaea
ca. 330 C.E.	Georgia and Armenia become first Christian kingdoms
395 C.E.	Christianity becomes official religion of Roman Empire

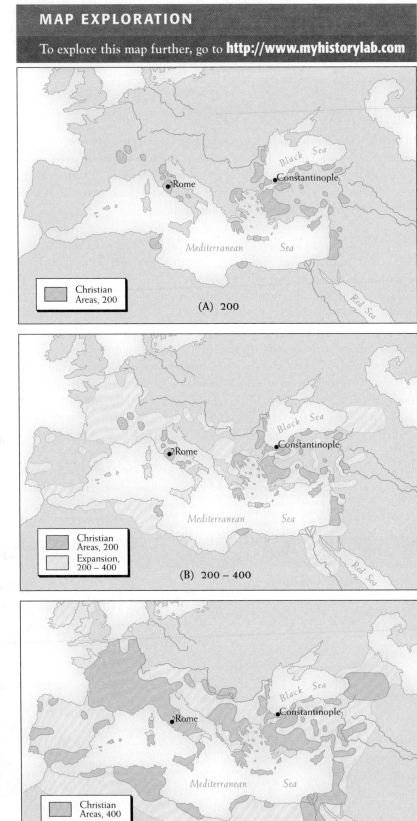

MAP EXPLORATION

To explore this map further, go to **http://www.myhistorylab.com**

MAP 6–5. The Spread of Christianity.

Christianity grew swiftly in the third, fourth, fifth, and sixth centuries—especially after the conversion of the emperors in the fourth century. By 600, on the eve of the birth of the new religion of Islam, Christianity was dominant throughout the Mediterranean world and most of western Europe.

Which areas remained largely non-Christian at the end of the seventh century?

(ca. 339–397), bishop of Milan, excommunicated Emperor Theodosius, the emperor submitted to his authority and did penance. This set an important precedent for future assertions of the church's autonomy and authority.

The Christian emperors hoped to unify their increasingly decentralized realms by imposing Christianity as the only religion, but Christianity divided society in new ways. Safe from persecution, Christians engaged in doctrinal disputes among themselves, causing serious disturbances as Christians sought to distinguish orthodoxy from heresy. The most important controversy concerned **Arianism**, a debate begun by a priest named Arius of Alexandria (ca. 280–336). Arius's view that Jesus was not co-equal and co-eternal with God the Father was dismissed by his orthodox opponents, who argued that it undercut Jesus' power as savior. In 325, Constantine summoned the Council of Nicaea to settle the issue. The **Nicene Creed** issued by the council endorsed the doctrine of the Trinity: the belief that God is three persons (Father, Son, and Holy Spirit) who share one substance. Arianism, however, survived and spread and continued to create political difficulties for generations.

Arianism
The belief formulated by Arius of Alexandria (ca. 280–336 C.E.) that Jesus was a created being, neither fully man nor fully God, but something in between.

Nicene Creed
A statement of Christian belief, formulated by the council of Christian bishops at Nicaea in 324 C.E., that rejected Arianism in favor of the doctrine that Christ is both fully human and fully divine.

OVERVIEW The Fall of the Roman Empire in the West

For centuries historians and social scientists have speculated why the ancient world collapsed. By contrast, the great English historian Edward Gibbon (1737–1794) wrote in his classic work *The Decline and Fall of the Roman Empire* that we should really ask not why Rome fell but why so vast an empire survived for so long. The following are some of the causes and explanations scholars have proposed for the fall of Rome. They range from the plausible to the ridiculous.

CAUSE	EXPLANATION
Climate change	A gradual drying and cooling climate destroyed the productivity of ancient agriculture on which the empire depended.
Soil exhaustion	Depleted soil around the Mediterranean no longer produced enough food to feed the population, which weakened and declined.
Lead poisoning	The use of lead pipes for drinking and cooking water led to widespread lead poisoning and sterility, especially among the upper classes who had the most access to running water.
Racial pollution	Eastern immigrants to Rome—Syrians, Greeks, and Jews—sapped the vitality of the Romans and destroyed their ability to rule and defend themselves.
Slavery	The prevalence of slavery made the Romans lazy and undercut free labor.
Intellectual stagnation	The failure to make advances in science and technology—to achieve a scientific revolution—led the empire to an intellectual and economic dead end.
Social disorder	The destruction of the middle class through civil war, invasion, and overtaxation wiped out the most productive and culturally aware part of the Roman population. Third-century emperors encouraged the rural poor to plunder the middle and upper classes.
Excessive government	Government exactions and regulations destroyed the operation of a market economy, which was the basis for prosperity.
Christianity	The adoption of Christianity as the official religion of the empire in the fourth century weakened the Roman state, diverted scarce resources to building and staffing churches and monasteries, and led large segments of the population to embrace pacifism.
Immorality	Gluttony, sloth, and sexual depravity replaced the old Roman virtues that had enabled Rome to conquer its empire.

CHRISTIAN WRITERS

Christianity inspired scholars who did important original work. Jerome (348–420), a Christian who had superb classical education, used his linguistic skills to create the Vulgate, a revised version of the Bible in Latin. It became the official version of the Bible used by the medieval Catholic Church.

In the East, Eusebius of Caesarea (ca. 260–ca. 340) attempted to develop a Christian theory of history as a working out of God's will in his *Ecclesiastical History*. All of history, he claimed, had divine significance and direction. Constantine's victory and the subsequent unity of empire and church was its culmination.

The closeness and complexity of the relationship between classical pagan culture and the Christianity of the late empire are exemplified in the career and writings of Augustine (354–430), bishop of Hippo in North Africa. His skill in pagan rhetoric and philosophy made him peerless among his contemporaries as a defender of Christianity and a theologian. His greatest works are his *Confessions*, an autobiography that describes his conversion, and *The City of God*. The latter was a response to Rome's sack by the Goths in 410. Augustine separated the fate of Christianity from that of the Roman Empire. He contrasted the secular world—the city of Man—with the spiritual—the City of God. The former was selfish and evil, the latter unselfish and good. All states, even a Christian Rome, were part of the City of Man and, therefore, corrupt and destined to pass away. Only the City of God was eternal and unaffected by earthly calamities.

•••—Read the **Document**
St. Augustine of Hippo, *Theory of the "Just War"* at **myhistorylab.com**

SUMMARY

 WHO WERE the early peoples of Italy?

Italy before Rome. Early and influential invaders of the Italian peninsula included the Etruscans, Greeks, and Celts. Starting around 800 B.C.E., the Etruscans established themselves as a military ruling class in northern Italy. *page 144*

WHAT PATTERNS of Roman governance were set in the royal period?

Royal Rome. Rome began as a small settlement in Latium in central Italy ruled by Etruscan kings. These kings, like later rulers of Rome, had the power of *imperium*. The importance of family, clientage, and the division of society into two broad classes were other enduring patterns that were set in this period. *page 144*

WHAT CULTURES most influenced Roman culture, and why?

The Republic. Rome became a republic in 509 B.C.E. The Roman constitution divided power between elected magistrates, the chief of whom were two consuls; an appointed Senate, whose members served for life; and popular assemblies. During the third century B.C.E., the aristocratic patricians were forced to share power with the common people, the plebeians. The institution of clientage by which clients pledged their loyalty to powerful patrons in return for legal and political protection was an important part of Roman political life. Rome expanded and engaged in the first of many conflicts with Carthage. In the third century B.C.E. Rome turned to the east and defeated the Hellenistic monarchies that had succeeded Alexander's empire. Macedon and Greece fell under Roman rule. This led to the adoption of Greek culture by the Roman aristocracy and the rapid Hellenization of Roman culture. *page 146*

 WHY DID a growing gap between the wealthy and everyone else contribute to political instability?

Roman Imperialism. By the early fourth century, Rome had expanded to control all of Italy through a policy of conquest, alliances, colonies of Roman veterans, and generosity to foes who submitted. Between 264 and 146 B.C.E., Rome fought three wars with Carthage for control of the western Mediterranean. These Punic Wars ended with the destruction of Carthage but led to social and political disorder in Italy. Many small farmers lost their land, and efforts by the Gracchi brothers to resolve the problems ended in their murders. *page 152*

 WHAT WERE the central features of Octavian rule?

The Fall of the Republic and the Augustan Principate. The Roman Republic was destroyed by social unrest and rivalry among ambitious generals and politicians, the most successful of whom was Julius Caesar. After a civil war that followed Caesar's assassination in 44 B.C.E., his nephew Octavian emerged as the most powerful man in Rome. Under the title of Augustus, he set up a system that preserved the façade of republican institutions but was in fact a monarchy. *page 156*

 WHAT ROLE did cities play in the Roman Empire?

Peace and Prosperity: Imperial Rome. The Roman Empire stretched from Scotland to Iraq. Rome fostered the growth of cities, developed the rule of law, built a vast network of roads and other public works, and established peace and stability between 14 and 180 C.E. *page 158*

 HOW DID Paul resolve the central dilemma of the relationship between Judaism and early Christianity?

The Rise of Christianity. Christianity arose in the Roman province of Judaea in the first century C.E. Paul believed that Christianity was a universal religion that should be known beyond the Jewish community. Christianity spread throughout the empire despite occasional persecutions by the Roman state, which itself became Christian in the late fourth century. *page 162*

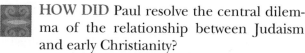 **WHY DID** the capital of the empire move from Rome to Constantinople, and what was the significance of this shift?

The Third and Fourth Centuries: Crisis and Late Empire. In the third century C.E., the Roman peace collapsed under the pressure of invasions by barbarians in the West and the Sasanids in the East. Rival generals murdered emperors and usurped the throne. The economy declined. The state exacted more and more taxes and resources from its citizens. The emperors Diocletian

and Constantine managed to halt the decline, but in the fifth century C.E. Roman authority in the West collapsed. In the East, however, a Christian Roman Empire based in the city of Constantinople survived and evolved into the Byzantine Empire that did much to preserve the Greek and Roman heritage for another thousand years. *page 164*

KEY TERMS

agape (ah-gah-PAY) (p. 163)
Arianism (p. 169)
Augustus (p. 157)
Catholic (p. 163)
censor (p. 148)
equestrians (p. 153)
Eucharist (p. 163)
heretics (p. 163)
humanitas (p. 151)
imperator (p. 157)
imperium (p. 144)
latifundia (lah-tee-foon-dee-ah) (p. 153)

"**mystery religions**" (p. 162)
Nicene Creed (p. 169)
orthodox (p. 163)
patrician (p. 146)
Pharisees (p. 162)
plebeian (p. 146)
populares (p. 153)
Punic Wars (p. 149)
syncretism (p. 167)
tetrarchy (p. 165)
tribunes (p. 148)

REVIEW QUESTIONS

1. How did the institutions of family and clientage and the establishment of patrician and plebeian classes contribute to the stability of the early Roman Republic? How important was education to the success of the republic?

2. Discuss Rome's expansion to 265 B.C.E. How was Rome able to conquer and control Italy? In their relations with Greece and Asia Minor in the second century B.C.E., were the Romans looking for security? Wealth? Power? Fame?

3. Explain the clash between the Romans and the Carthaginians in the First and Second Punic Wars. Could the wars have been avoided? How did Rome benefit from its victory over Carthage? What problems were created by this victory?

4. How did Greek culture influence Roman beliefs and practices?

5. What were the problems that plagued the Roman Republic in its final century? What caused these problems and how did the Romans try to solve them? To what extent was the republic destroyed by ambitious generals who loved power more than Rome itself?

6. Discuss the Augustan constitution and government. What solutions did Augustus provide for the problems that had plagued the Roman Republic? Why was the Roman population willing to accept Augustus as head of the state?

7. Despite unpromising beginnings, Christianity was enormously popular by the fourth century C.E. Why were Christians persecuted by Roman authorities? What were the more important reasons for Christianity's success?

8. Consider three theories that scholars have advanced to explain the decline and fall of the Roman Empire. What are the difficulties involved in explaining the fall? What explanation would you give?

Note: To learn more about the topics in this chapter, please turn to the Suggested Readings at the end of the book. For additional sources related to this chapter please see www.myhistorylab.com

PEARSON myhistorylab Connections

Reinforce what you learned in this chapter by studying the many documents, images, maps, review tools, and videos available at **www.myhistorylab.com**

Research and Explore

◉ Watch the Video   *Defining Imperialism*

◉ Watch the Video   *Roman Roads*

((●● Hear the **Audio**

Hear the audio file for Chapter 6
at **www.myhistorylab.com**

7

China's First Empire, 221 B.C.E.–589 C.E.

((•—[Hear the **Audio** for **Chapter 7** at www.myhistorylab.com

Han Dynasty aristocrat out driving in his horse cart. Bronze relic excavated from a tomb in Kansu in northwestern China in 1969. Grave goods were a part of Chinese tradition for centuries.

What might this relic suggest about the social status of the individual buried in the tomb where this was found?

ne hallmark of Chinese history is its striking continuity of culture, language, and geography. The Shang and Zhou dynasties were centered in north China along the Yellow River or its tributary, the Wei. The capitals of China's first empire were in exactly the same areas, and north China would remain China's political center up to the present. If Western civilization had experienced similar continuity, it would have progressed from Thebes in the valley of the Nile to Athens on the Nile; Rome on the Nile; then, in time, to Paris, London, and Berlin on the Nile; and each of these centers of civilization would have spoken Egyptian and written in Egyptian hieroglyphics.

These continuities do not mean that China was unchanging. One key turning point came in the third century B.C.E., when the old, quasi-feudal, multistate Zhou system gave way to a centralized bureaucratic government. The new centralized state built an empire stretching from the steppe in the north to Vietnam in the south.

The history of the first empire is composed of three segments: the Qin Dynasty, the Former Han Dynasty, and the Later Han Dynasty. The English word China is derived from the name of the first dynasty. The Qin overthrew the previous Zhou Dynasty in 256 B.C.E. and went on to unify China in 221 B.C.E. In reshaping China, the Qin developed such momentum that it became overextended and collapsed a single generation after the unification. The succeeding Han dynasties each lasted about 200 years, the Early Han from 206 B.C.E. to 8 C.E., the Later Han (founded by a descendant of the Former Han rulers) from 25 to 220 C.E. Historians usually treat each of the Han dynasties as a separate period of rule, although they were nearly continuous and shared many institutions and cultural traits. So deep was the impression left by these two dynasties on the Chinese that even today they call themselves the "Han people"—in contrast to Mongols, Manchus, Tibetans, and other minorities—and they call their ideographs "Han writing." ■

QIN UNIFICATION OF CHINA

Among the territorial states of the Late Zhou era, none was more innovative and ruthless than Qin (pronounced "chin"). Its location on the Wei River in northwest China—the same area from which the Zhou had launched their expansion a millennium

HOW DID the Qin
unify China?

GLOBAL PERSPECTIVE

CHINA'S FIRST EMPIRE

Were there world-historical forces that produced great empires in China, India, and the Mediterranean at roughly the same time? Certainly these empires had similar features. All three came after revolutions in thought. The Han built on Zhou thought (it would be hard to imagine the Han bureaucratic state without Legalism and Confucianism), just as Rome used Greek thought, and the Mauryan Empire, Buddhist thought. In each case, the conception of universal political authority sustaining the empire derived from earlier philosophies. All three were Iron Age empires, joining their respective technologies with new organizational techniques to create superb military forces. All three had to weld together diverse regions into a single polity. All three created legacies that continued long after the empire had disappeared.

The differences between the empires are also instructive. Consider China and Rome. In China the pervasive culture—the

only higher culture in the area—was Chinese, even before the first empire arose. This culture had been slowly spreading for centuries and in places outran the polity. Even the Ch'u people south of the Yangzi, while viewed as "semibarbarian" by northern Chinese, had a variation of the same common culture. Thus cultural unity had paved the way for political unity. In contrast, the polyglot empire of Rome encompassed quite different peoples, including older civilizations. The genius of Rome, in fact, was to fashion a government and a set of laws that could contain and reconcile its diverse cultures.

Geographically, however, Rome had an easier time of it, for the Mediterranean offered direct access to most parts of the empire and was a thoroughfare for commerce. In contrast, China was largely landlocked. It was composed of several regional economic units, each of which, located in a segment of a river basin separated from the others by natural barriers, looked inward. It

earlier—gave it strategic advantages: It controlled the passes leading out onto the Yellow River plain, so it was easy to defend and was a secure base from which to attack other states. From the late fourth century B.C.E., the Qin conquered a part of Sichuan and thus controlled two of the most fertile regions of ancient China. It welcomed Legalist administrators, who developed policies for enriching the country and strengthening its military. Despite its harsh laws, farmers moved to Qin from other areas, attracted by the order and stability of its society. Its armies had been forged by centuries of warfare against the nomadic raiders whose lands half encircled it. To counter these raiders, its armies adopted nomadic skills, developing cavalry in the fourth century. Other states regarded the Qin as tough, crude, and brutal but recognized its formidable strengths.

In 246 B.C.E. the man who would unify China succeeded to the Qin throne at the age of 13. He grew to be vigorous, ambitious, intelligent, and decisive. He is famous as a Legalist autocrat, but he was well liked by his ministers, whose advice he usually followed. (See Chapter 2 for a description of Legalism.) In 232 B.C.E., he began the campaigns that destroyed the six remaining territorial states. On completing his conquests in 221 B.C.E., to raise himself above the kings of the former territorial states, he adopted the glorious title that we translate as "emperor"—a combination of ideographs hitherto used only for gods or mythic heroes. Then, aided by talented officials, this First Qin Emperor set about applying to all of China the reforms that had been effective in his own realm. His accomplishments in the eleven years before his death, in 210 B.C.E., were stupendous.

Having conquered the civilized world of north China and the Yangzi River basin, the First Emperor sent his armies to conquer new lands. They reached the northern edge of the Red River basin in what is now Vietnam. They occupied China's southeastern coast and the area encompassing the present-day city of Guangzhou (see Map 7–1). In the north and the northwest, the emperor's armies fought against the Xiongnu, Altaic-speaking Hunnish nomads. During the previous age, northern border states had built long walls to protect settled lands from incursions by horse-riding raiders. The

View the Image
The Great Wall of China
at **myhistorylab.com**

was the genius of Chinese administration to overcome physical and spatial barriers and integrate the country politically.

A second difference was that government in Han China was more orderly, more complex, and more competent than that of Rome. For example, civil officials controlled the Chinese military almost until the end, whereas in later Roman times, emperor after emperor was set on the throne by the army or the Praetorian Guard. The Roman Empire was not a Chinese-type, single-family dynasty.

A third difference was in the military dynamics of the two empires. Roman power was built over centuries. Its history is the story of one state growing in power by steady increments, imposing its will on others, and gradually piecing together an empire. Not until the early centuries C.E. was the whole empire in place. China, in contrast, remained a multistate system right up to 232 B.C.E. and then, in a sudden surge, was unified by one state in eleven years. The greater dynamism of China during the first

empire can be explained, perhaps, by the greater military challenge it faced across its northern border: an immense Xiongnu nomadic empire. Because the threat was more serious than that any European barbarian enemy posed to Rome, the Chinese response was correspondingly massive. (Some historians say that Chinese expansion to the north and northwest drove the Xiongnu—the Huns—westward, displacing Germanic tribes that flooded into Europe and pressed against Roman frontiers.)

Focus Questions

◆ What challenges did the Roman, Han, and Mauryan empires face in conquering and integrating new territories? How did they meet these challenges?

◆ Compare and contrast the Roman and Han empires. What qualities did they have in common? How did they differ?

Qin emperor had them joined into a single Great Wall that extended 1,400 miles from the Pacific Ocean into Central Asia. Construction of the Great Wall cost the lives of vast numbers of conscripted laborers—by some accounts, 100,000; by others, as many as 1 million.

The most significant reform, carried out by the Legalist minister Li Si, extended the Qin system of bureaucratic government to the entire empire. Li Si divided China into forty prefectures, which were further subdivided into counties. The county heads were responsible to prefects, who, in turn, were responsible to the central government. Officials were chosen by ability. Bureaucratic administration was impersonal, based on laws to which all were subject. No one, for example, escaped taxation. This kind of bureaucratic centralism broke sharply with the old Zhou pattern of establishing dependent principalities for members of a ruler's family.

Furthermore, to ensure the smooth functioning of local government offices, former aristocrats of the territorial states were removed from their lands and resettled in the capital, near present-day Xian. They were housed in mansions on one side of the river, from which they could gaze across at the enormous palace of the First Emperor.

Other reforms further unified the First Emperor's vast domain. Roads were built radiating out from the capital city. The emperor decreed a system of uniform weights and measures. He unified the Chinese writing system, establishing standard ideographs. He established uniform axle lengths for carts. Even ideas did not escape the drive toward uniformity. Following the precepts of Legalism, the emperor and his advisers launched a campaign for which they have subsequently been

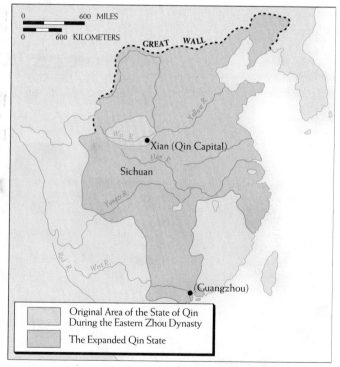

MAP 7–1. The Unification of China by the Qin State.
Between 232 and 221 B.C.E. the Qin state expanded and unified China.

Why did Qin expansion fail to move westward?

Read the Document
Li Si and the Legalist Policies of Qin Shihuang (280–208 B.C.E.)
at **myhistorylab.com**

✓●—Study and Review
at **myhistorylab.com**

QUICK REVIEW

Qin Reforms

◆ Extension of Qin bureaucracy to entire empire

◆ Building of roads

◆ Creation of a unified writing system

◆ Creation of unified system of weights and measures

⚙●—View the Image
Qin Shihuang's Terra-Cotta Soldiers
at **myhistorylab.com**

WHAT IS the dynastic cycle?

dynastic cycle
The term used to describe the rise, decline, and fall of China's imperial dynasties.

denounced: They collected and burned the books of Confucianism and other schools, and were said to have buried alive scholars opposed to the Legalist philosophy. Only useful books on agriculture, medicine, or Legalist teachings were spared.

But the Qin had changed too much, too quickly. To pay for the roads, canals, and the Great Wall, burdensome taxes were levied on the people. Commoners hated conscription and labor service, and nobles resented their loss of status. Merchants were exploited; scholars, except for Legalists, were oppressed. After the First Emperor died, in 210 B.C.E., intrigues broke out at court, and rebellions arose in the land. At the end, the short-lived dynasty was destroyed by the domino effect of its own legal codes. When the generals sent to quell a rebellion were defeated, they joined the rebellion rather than returning to the capital and incurring the severe punishment decreed for failure. The Qin collapsed in 206 B.C.E.

In 1974 a farmer near Xian discovered the army of 8,000 life-size terra-cotta horses and soldiers that guarded the tomb of the First Emperor. The historical record tells us that in the tomb itself, under a mountain of earth, are a replica of his capital; a relief model of the Chinese world with quicksilver rivers; other warriors with chariots of bronze; and the remains of horses, noblemen, and criminals sacrificed to accompany in death the emperor whose dynasty was to have lasted for 10,000 generations.

FORMER HAN DYNASTY (206 B.C.E.–8 C.E.)

THE DYNASTIC CYCLE

Confucian historians have seen a pattern in every dynasty of long duration. They call it the **dynastic cycle**. The stages of the cycle are interpreted in terms of the "Mandate of Heaven." The cycle begins with internal wars that eventually lead to the military unification of China. Unification is proof that heaven has given the unifier the mandate to rule. The first ruler, strong and vigorous, restores peace and order to China. Economic growth follows, almost automatically. The peak of the cycle is marked by public works, energetic reforms, and aggressive military expansion. During this phase, China appears invincible. But then the cycle turns downward. The costs of expansion, coupled with increasing opulence at the court, place a heavy burden on tax revenues just as they are beginning to decline. The vigor of the monarchs wanes. Intrigues develop at court. Central controls loosen, and provincial governors and military commanders gain autonomy. Finally, public works fall into disrepair, floods and pestilence occur, rebellions break out, and the dynasty collapses. For Confucian historians, the last emperors in a cycle are not only politically weak but also morally culpable.

The Great Wall of China. It was originally built during the Qin Dynasty (256–206 B.C.E.), but what we see today is the wall as it was completely rebuilt during the Ming Dynasty (1368–1644 C.E.).

Paolo Koch/Photo Researchers, Inc.

What purpose was the original Great Wall built to serve?

EARLY YEARS OF THE FORMER HAN DYNASTY

The first sixty years of the Han were the early phase of its dynastic cycle. After the collapse of the Qin, one rebel general gained control of the Wei basin and went on to unify China. He became the first emperor of the Han Dynasty and is known by his posthumous title of Gaozu (r. 206–195 B.C.E.). He rose from plebeian origins to

A Closer Look

The Terra-Cotta Army of the First Qin Emperor

In 1974 a Xian farmer, drilling for water, discovered the tomb of the First Qin Emperor (256–210 B.C.E.). To date, 8,000 warriors, copper horses, and war chariots have been found. The emperor's 76-meter-high burial chamber, which according to the records of history has a starry firmament and rivers of mercury, has not yet been excavated.

Government workshops molded arms, legs, torsos, and heads, which were then assembled. Some warriors wore tunics, some breastplates, and others fish-scale armor. There were eight basic face masks, and after the molding, details, such as mustaches, were added with clay. No two faces are alike. The completed warrior was painted with lacquer, though most color has disappeared during the 2,300 years since the "army" was drawn up in formation.

The workers who buried the emperor were sealed in the tomb to keep its location a secret. But in vain. Early grave robbers stole the valuable weapons that the warriors held (note the cupped hands) but ignored the worthless clay statues. After that, its location was unknown for two millennia.

Questions

1. How did the legalism of the Qin state affect its armies?

2. Why did the emperor have this ghostly army fabricated? Did he plan to lead it in an afterlife?

myhistorylab To examine this image in an interactive fashion, please go to **www.myhistorylab.com**

become emperor, which would happen only once again in Chinese history. Gaozu built his capital at Chang'an, not far from the capitals of the previous dynasties. It took the emperor and his immediate successors many years to consolidate their power because they consciously avoided actions that would remind the populace of the hated Qin despotism. They made punishments less severe and reduced taxes. Good government prevailed, the economy rebounded, granaries were filled, and the government accumulated vast cash reserves. Later historians often singled out the early Han rulers as model sage-emperors.

HAN WUDI

The second phase of the dynastic cycle began with the rule of Wudi (the "martial emperor"), who came to the throne in 141 B.C.E. at the age of 16 and ruled for fifty-four years (141–87 B.C.E.). Wudi was daring, vigorous, and intelligent but also superstitious, suspicious, and vengeful. He wielded tremendous personal authority.

Building on the prosperity achieved by his predecessors, Wudi initiated new economic policies. He had a canal built from the Yellow River to the capital in northwest China, linking the two major economic regions of north China. He established "ever-level granaries" throughout the country so that the surplus from bumper crops could be bought and then resold in time of scarcity. To increase revenues, he levied taxes on merchants, debased the currency, and sold some offices. Wudi also moved against merchants who had built fortunes in untaxed commodities by reestablishing government monopolies—a practice of the Qin—on copper coins, salt, iron, and liquor. For fear of Wudi, no one spoke out against the monopolies, but a few years after his death, a famous debate was held at the court.

The "Salt and Iron Debate" was frequently cited thereafter in China, and in Japan and Korea as well. On one side, quasi-Legalist officials argued that the state should enjoy the profits from the sale of salt and iron. On the other side, Confucians argued that these resources should be left in private hands, for the moral purity of officials would be sullied by dealings with merchants. The Confucian scholars who compiled the historical account of the debate presented themselves as the winners, but state monopolies became a regular part of Chinese government finance.

Wudi also aggressively expanded Chinese borders—a policy that would characterize every strong dynasty. His armies swept south into what is today northern Vietnam and northeast across Manchuria to establish a military outpost in northern Korea that would last until 313 C.E.

THE XIONGNU

Xiongnu

A tribal confederation of nomadic pastoralists who controlled vast territories northwest of the Han Empire; to Europeans, they were the Huns.

The principal threat to the Han was from the **Xiongnu**, a nomadic pastoral people who lived to the north. Their mounted archers could raid China and flee before an army could be sent against them. To combat them, Wudi employed the entire repertoire of policies that would become standard thereafter. When possible he made allies of border nomads, who would fight against more distant tribes. Allies were permitted to trade with Chinese merchants; they were awarded titles and honors; and their kings were sent Chinese princesses as brides. (See Document, "Chinese Women among the Nomads" on page 182.) When trade and titles did not work, he used force. Between 129 and 119 B.C.E. he sent several armies of more than 100,000 troops into the steppe, destroying Xiongnu power south of the Gobi Desert. To establish a strategic line of defense aimed at the heart of the Xiongnu Empire further to the west, Wudi then sent 700,000 Chinese colonists to the arid Kansu panhandle and extended the Great Wall

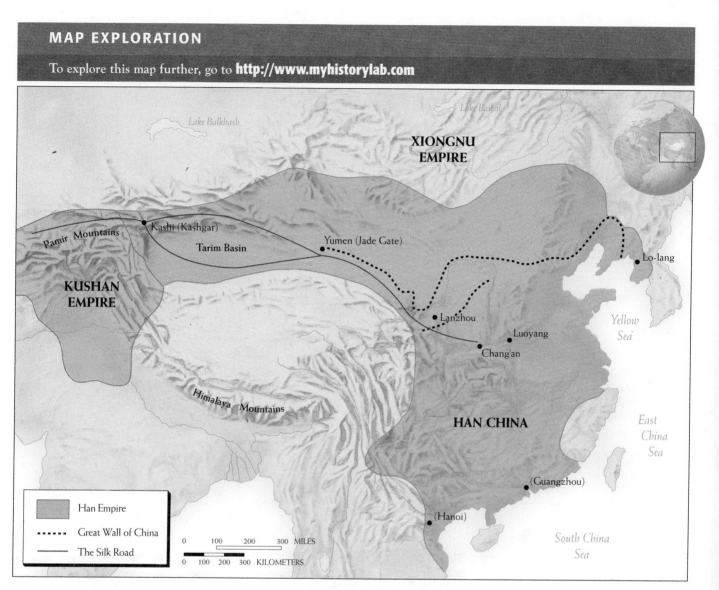

MAP EXPLORATION

To explore this map further, go to **http://www.myhistorylab.com**

MAP 7–2.   The Han Empire 206 B.C.E.–220 C.E.

At the peak of Han expansion, Han armies advanced far out into the steppe north of the Great Wall and west into Central Asia. The Silk Road to Rome passed through the Tarim Basin to the Kushan Empire, and on to western Asia and the Middle East.

Why did the Han seek to expand their empire to the west and south?

to the Yumen (Jade Gate) outpost at the eastern end of the Tarim basin. From this out-post, Chinese influence was extended over the rim oases of Central Asia, establishing the **Silk Road** that linked Chang'an with Rome (see Map 7–2).

GOVERNMENT DURING THE FORMER HAN

To demonstrate how different they were from the Qin, early Han emperors set up some Zhou-like principalities, small, semiautonomous states with independent lords. But this was a token gesture. The principalities were closely superintended and then curtailed after several generations. Despite repudiating the Qin, the Han basically

Silk Road
Trade route from China to the West that stretched across Central Asia.

DOCUMENT

Chinese Women among the Nomads

The first of these selections is the lament of Xijun, a Chinese lady sent by Wudi in about 105 B.C.E. to be the wife of a nomad king of the Wusun people of Central Asia. Once there, she found her husband to be old and decrepit. He saw her only once or twice a year, when they drank a cup of wine together. They could not converse, as they had no language in common. The second selection, written centuries later, is by the Tang poet Du Fu, who visited the village of another woman sent to be the wife of a nomad king.

- **WHAT** does the fate of the women in these poems suggest about the foreign policy of the rulers of ancient China?

1.

My people have married me
In a far corner of Earth;
Sent me away to a strange land,
To the king of the Wu-sun.
A tent is my house,
Of felt are my walls;
Raw flesh my food

With mare's milk to drink.
Always thinking of my own country,
My heart sad within.
Would I were a yellow stork
And could fly to my old home!

2.

Ten thousand ranges and valleys approach the Ching Gate
And the village in which the Lady of Light was born and bred. She went out from the purple palace into the desert-land; She has now become a green grave in the yellow dusk. Her face!—Can you picture a wind of the spring? Her spirit by moonlight returns with a tinkling Telling her eternal sorrow.

[1] *Source:* From *Chinese Poems* by Arthur Waley. Copyright © 1946 by George Allen and Unwin Ltd., an imprint of HarperCollins Publishers Ltd. Reprinted by permission of the Arthur Waley Estate.

[2] *Source:* From *The Jade Mountain* translated by Witter Bynner, Copyright 1929 and renewed 1957 by Alfred A. Knopf, a division of Random House, Inc. Used by permission of Alfred A. Knopf, a division of Random House, Inc.

---

continued the Qin form of centralized bureaucratic administration. Officials were organized by grades and were paid salaries in grain, plus cash or silk. They were recruited by sponsorship or recommendation: Provincial officials had the duty of recommending promising candidates. A school established at Chang'an was said to have 30,000 students by the Later Han. Bureaucracy grew until, by the first century B.C.E., there were more than 130,000 officials—perhaps not too many for a population that had reached 60 million.

During the Han Dynasty, this "Legalist" structure of government became partially Confucianized. It did not happen overnight. The first Han emperor despised Confucians as bookish pedants—he once urinated in the hat of a scholar. But Confucian ideas proved useful. The Mandate of Heaven provided an ethical justification for dynastic rule. A respect for old records and the written word fit in well with the vast bookkeeping the empire entailed. Gradually the Confucian classics were accepted as the standard for education. Confucianism was seen as shaping moral men who would be upright officials, even in the absence of external constraints. Increasingly, laws were interpreted and applied by men with a Confucian education.

The court during the Han Dynasty exhibited features that would appear in later dynasties as well. All authority centered on the emperor, the all-powerful "son of heaven." When the emperor was weak, however, or ascended to the throne when still a child, others competed to rule in his name. Four contenders for this surrogate role appeared and reappeared through Chinese history: court officials, the empress dowager, court eunuchs, and military commanders.

Court officials were selected for their ability to govern: They staffed the apparatus of government and advised the emperor directly. Apart from the emperor himself, they were usually the most powerful men in China, yet their position was often precarious. Few officials escaped being removed from office or banished once or twice during their careers. Of the seven prime ministers who served Wudi, five were executed.

Of the emperor's many wives, the empress dowager was the one whose child had been named as the heir to the throne. Her influence sometimes continued even after her child became an adult emperor. But she was most powerful as a regent for a child emperor. On Gaozu's death in 195 B.C.E., for example, the Empress Lu became the regent for her child, the new emperor. Aided by her relatives, she seized control of the court and murdered a rival, and when her son was about to come of age, she had him killed and a younger son made the heir, thus continuing her rule as regent. When she died in 180 B.C.E., loyal adherents of the imperial family who had opposed her rule massacred her relatives.

Court eunuchs came mostly from families of low social status. They were brought to the court as boys, castrated, and assigned to work as servants in the emperor's harem. They were thus in contact with the future emperor from the day he was born, became his childhood confidants, and often continued to advise him after he had gained the throne. Emperors found eunuchs useful as counterweights to officials. But to the scholars who wrote China's history, the eunuchs were greedy half-men, given to evil intrigues.

Military leaders, whether generals or rebels, were the usual founders of dynasties. In the later phase of most dynasties, regional military commanders often became semi-independent rulers. A few even usurped the throne. Yet they were less powerful at the Chinese court than they were, for example, in imperial Rome, partly because the military constituted a separate category, lower in prestige than the better-educated civil officials. It was also partly because the court took great pains to prevent its generals from establishing a base of personal power. Appointments to command a Han army were given only for specific campaigns, and commanders were appointed in pairs so that each would check the other.

Another characteristic of government during the Han and subsequent dynasties was that its functions were limited. It collected taxes, maintained military forces, administered laws, supported the imperial household, and carried out public works that were beyond the powers of local jurisdictions. But government in a district that remained orderly and paid its taxes was left largely in the hands of local notables and large landowners. This pattern was not, to be sure, unique to China. Most premodern governments, even those that were bureaucratic, floated on top of their local societies and only rarely reached down and interfered in the everyday lives of their subjects.

THE SILK ROAD

Roman ladies loved diaphanous gowns of Chinese silk. Wealthy Chinese coveted Roman glass and gold. There was not a single camel train that traveled from Chang'an all the way to Rome. Instead, precious cargoes, moving more easily than persons, were passed across empires, like batons in relay races, from one network of merchants to another.

Funerary Figure. This kneeling figure is from the Han Dynasty.

Does this statue seem to represent a particular person? Why or why not?

During the Han and later dynasties, the route began with a network of Chinese or Central Asian traders that stretched from the Chinese capital to Lanzhou in northeastern China, through the Gansu corridor to Yumen or later Dunhuang. It then crossed the inhospitable Tarim basin, intermittently under Chinese military control, from oasis to oasis, to Kashi (Kashgar). From Kashi, the route continued in a northerly sweep to Tashkent, Samarkand, and Bukhara or in a southerly sweep to Teheran, Baghdad, and Damascus, and finally on to the Mediterranean ports of Tyre, Antioch, and Byzantium (Constantinople), which traded with Rome. (See Map 7–2.) Of the goods that departed Chang'an, only a minute portion reached Rome, which was not a destination as much as the center of the westernmost trade network. Only the thinnest trickle of Roman goods reached China.

The Silk Road, and the alternate oceanic route, point up China's isolation from other high centers of civilization. Goods were in transit more than half a year; the distance was measured in thousands of miles; camel caravans at times traveled as little as 15 miles a day. The route was hazardous, the climate extreme. Crossing deserts and mountain passes, travelers experienced cold, hunger, sandstorms, and bandits.

Most Chinese foreign trade was with their immediate steppe neighbors. The Chinese exported silk, lacquer, metal work, and later jewels, musk, and rhubarb (a digestive aid). They imported horses for their army, cattle, sheep, donkeys, and jade from Khotan and also woolens, medicines, indigo, and the occasional exotic animal. Only the most precious goods made their way to distant empires. Silk—light, compact, and valuable—was ideal. The Romans and Chinese had only the vaguest idea of where the other was located and knew nothing of the other's civilization. Romans thought silk came from a plant.

Exotic goods hawked in distant bazaars lend an aura of romance to the "Silk Road," but its true significance was as a transmission belt. In an early age China may have borrowed the chariot, compound bow, wheat, domesticated horses, and the stirrup from western Asia. Even the idea of mold-casting bronze may have come from beyond China's frontiers. Chinese technologies of paper making, iron casting, water-powered mills, and shoulder collars for draft animals, and later the compass and gunpowder, spread slowly from China to the West. Seeds of plants went in both directions, as did germs. During the Later Han, the Roman Empire lost a quarter of its population to an epidemic that, some say, appeared in China forty years later with equally dire results. During the fourteenth century, bubonic plague may have spread through the Mongol Empire from southwestern China to Central Asia to the Middle East, and then on to Europe as the Black Death. Missionary religions traveled east on the Silk Road: Buddhism toward the end of the Han Dynasty and Islam centuries later.

DECLINE AND USURPATION

During the last decade of Wudi's rule in the early first century B.C.E., military expenses ran ahead of revenues. His successor cut back on military costs, eased economic controls, and reduced taxes. But over the next several generations, large landowners began to use their growing influence in provincial politics to avoid paying taxes. State revenues declined. The tax burden on smaller landowners and free peasants grew heavier. In 22 B.C.E., rebellions broke out in several parts of the empire. At court, too, decline set in. There was a succession of weak emperors. Intrigues, nepotism, and factional struggles grew apace. Even officials began to sense that the dynasty no longer had the approval of heaven. The dynastic cycle approached its end.

Watch the Video
The Silk Road: 5,000 miles and 1,500 Years of Cultural Interchange
at **myhistorylab.com**

QUICK REVIEW

Decline of the Han

- Scheming, dissension, and violence in court
- Large landowners gained power
- Free farmers fled south
- Popular rebellions suppressed by generals, who then seized power

Many at the court urged Wang Mang, the regent for the infant emperor and the nephew of an empress, to become the emperor and begin a new dynasty. Wang Mang refused several times—to demonstrate his lack of eagerness—and then accepted in 8 C.E. He drew up a program of sweeping reforms based on ancient texts. He was a Confucian yet relied on new institutional arrangements rather than moral reform to improve society. He revived ancient titles, expanded state monopolies, abolished private slavery (about 1 percent of the population), made loans to poor peasants, and then moved to confiscate large private estates.

These reforms alienated many. Merchants disliked the monopolies. Large landowners resisted the expropriation of their lands. Nature also conspired to bring down Wang Mang: The Yellow River overflowed its banks and changed its course, destroying the northern Chinese irrigation system. Several years of poor harvests produced famines. The Xiongnu overran China's northern borders. In 18 C.E., a secret peasant society rose in rebellion. In 23 C.E., rebels attacked Chang'an, and Wang Mang was killed and eaten by rebel troops. He had tried to found a new dynasty from within a decrepit court without an independent military base. The attempt was futile. Internal wars continued in China for two more years until a large landowner, who had become the leader of a rebel army, emerged triumphant in 25 C.E. Because he was from a branch of the imperial family, his new dynasty was viewed as a restoration of the Han.

Chinese Galloping Horse. China traded with steppe merchants to obtain the horses needed to equip its armies against steppe warriors. Especially desired by the Chinese court were the fabled "blood-sweating" horses of far-off Ferghana (present-day Tajikistan). **How were horses used by the Chinese and by their neighbors?**

See the **Map**

China from the Later Zhou Era to the Han Era at **myhistorylab.com**

CHRONOLOGY

THE DYNASTIC HISTORY OF CHINA'S FIRST EMPIRE

256–206 B.C.E.	Qin Dynasty
206 B.C.E.–**8** C.E.	Former Han Dynasty
25–220 C.E.	Later Han Dynasty

LATER HAN (25–220 C.E.) AND ITS AFTERMATH

FIRST CENTURY

WHY DID the Han Dynasty collapse?

The founder of the Later Han moved his capital east to Luoyang. Under the first emperor and his two successors, there was a return to strong central government and a laissez-faire economy. Agriculture and population recovered. By the end of the first century C.E., China was as prosperous as it had been during the good years of the Former Han. The shift from pacification and recuperation to military expansion came earlier than it had during the previous dynasty. During the reign of the first emperor, south China and Vietnam were retaken. Dissension among the Xiongnu enabled the Chinese to secure an alliance with some of the southern tribes in 50 C.E., and in 89 C.E. Chinese armies crossed the Gobi Desert and defeated the northern Xiongnu. This defeat sparked the migrations, some historians say, that brought those nomadic warriors to the southern Russian steppes and then, in the fifth century C.E., to Europe, where they were known as the Huns of Attila. In 97 C.E. a Chinese general led an army to the shores of the Caspian Sea. The Chinese expansion in inner Asia, coupled with more lenient government policies toward merchants, facilitated the camel caravans that carried Chinese silk across the Tarim basin and, ultimately, to merchants in Iran, Palestine, and Rome.

186   **PART 2**   EMPIRES AND CULTURES OF THE ANCIENT WORLD, 1000 B.C.E. TO 500 C.E.

DECLINE DURING THE SECOND CENTURY

After 88 C.E. the emperors of the Later Han were ineffectual and short-lived. Empresses plotted to advance the fortunes of their families. Emperors turned for help to palace eunuchs. In 159 C.E. a conspiracy of eunuchs in the service of an emperor slaughtered the family of a scheming empress dowager and ruled at the court. When officials and students protested against the eunuch dictatorship, over a hundred were killed and over a thousand were tortured or imprisoned. In another incident in 190 C.E., a general deposed one emperor, installed another, killed the empress dowager, and massacred most of the eunuchs at the court.

In the countryside, large landowners grew more powerful. They harbored private armies. Farmers on the estates of the mighty were reduced to serfs. The landowners used their influence to avoid taxes. Great numbers of free farmers fled south for the same purpose. The remaining freeholders paid ever-heavier taxes and labor services. Many peasants turned to neo-Daoist religious movements that provided the ideology and organization to channel their discontent into action. In 184 C.E. rebellions organized by members of the religious movements broke out against the government. Han generals suppressed the rebellions but stayed on to rule in the provinces they had pacified. In 220 C.E. they deposed the last Han emperor.

A Green Glazed Pottery Model of a Later Han Dynasty Watchtower (87.6 x 35.6 x 38.1 cm). Note the resemblance to later Chinese Buddhist pagodas.

How might watchtowers have been used during the Later Han dynasty?

AFTERMATH OF EMPIRE

For more than three and a half centuries after the fall of the Han, China was disunited. For several generations it was divided into three kingdoms, whose heroic warriors and scheming statesmen were made famous by wandering storytellers. These figures later peopled the *Tale of the Three Kingdoms*, a great romantic epic of Chinese literature.

Chinese history during the post-Han centuries had two characteristics. The first was the dominant role played by the great aristocratic landowning families. With vast estates, huge numbers of serfs, fortified manor houses, and private armies, they were beyond the control of most governments. Because they took over many of the functions of local government, some historians describe post-Han China as having reverted to the quasi-feudalism of the Zhou. The second characteristic of these centuries was that northern and southern China developed in different ways.

In the south, a succession of six, ever-weaker states had their capital at Nanjing. Although these six southern states were called dynasties—and the entire period of Chinese history from 220 B.C.E. to 589 C.E. is called the Six Dynasties era after them—they were in fact short-lived kingdoms plagued by intrigues, usurpations, and coups d'état; frequently at war with northern states; and in constant fear of their own generals. The main developments in the south were (1) continuing economic growth and the emergence of Nanjing as a thriving center of commerce; (2) the ongoing absorption of tribal peoples into Chinese society and culture; (3) large-scale immigrations of Chinese fleeing the north; and (4) the spread of Buddhism and its penetration to the heart of Chinese culture.

In the north, state formation depended on the interaction of nomads and Chinese. During the Han Dynasty, Chinese invasions of the steppe had led to the incorporation of semi-Sinicized Xiongnu as the northernmost tier of the Chinese defense system—just as Germanic tribes had acted as the teeth and claws of the late Roman Empire. But as the Chinese state weakened, the highly mobile nomads broke loose, joined with other tribes, and began to invade China. The short-lived states that they formed are usually referred to as the "Sixteen Kingdoms." One kingdom was founded by invaders of Tibetan stock. Most spoke Altaic languages: the Xianbi (proto-Mongols), the Tuoba (proto-Turks), and the Ruan Ruan (who would later appear in eastern Europe as the Avars). But differences of language and ancestry were less important than these tribes' similarities:

1. All began as steppe nomads with a way of life different from that of agricultural China.

2. After forming states, all became at least partially Sinicized. Chinese from great families, which had preserved Han traditions, served as their tutors and administrators.

3. All were involved in wars—among themselves, against southern dynasties, or against conservative steppe tribes that resisted Sinicization.

4. Buddhism was as powerful in the north as in the south. As a universal religion, it acted as a bridge between "barbarians" and Chinese—just as Christianity was a unifying force in post-Roman Europe. The barbarian rulers of the north were especially attracted to its magical side. Usually Buddhism was made the state religion. Of the northern states, the most durable was the Northern Wei (386–534 C.E.), famed for its Buddhist sculpture.

HAN THOUGHT AND RELIGION

WHAT WAS the extent of Buddhist influence under the Han?

Poems describe the splendor of Chang'an and Luoyang: broad boulevards, tiled gateways, open courtyards, watchtowers, and imposing walls. Most splendid of all were the palaces of emperors, with their audience halls, vast chambers, harem quarters, and parks containing artificial lakes and rare animals and birds. But today little remains of the grandeur of the Han. Whereas Roman ruins abound in Italy and circle the Mediterranean, in China nothing remains above ground. Only the items buried in tombs—pottery, bronzes, musical instruments, gold and silver jewelry, lacquerware, and clay figurines—give a glimpse of the rich material culture of the Han period. Only the paintings on the walls of tombs tell us of its art. But a wealth of written records conveys the sophistication and depth of Han culture. Perhaps the two most important areas were philosophy and history.

HAN CONFUCIANISM

A major accomplishment of the early Han was the recovery of texts that had been lost during the Qin persecution of scholars. Some were retrieved from the walls of houses where they had been hidden; others were reproduced from memory by scholars. Debate arose regarding the relative authenticity of the old and new texts—a controversy that has continued until modern times. In 51 B.C.E. and again in 79 C.E. councils were held to determine the true meaning of the Confucian classics. In 175 C.E. an approved, official version of the texts was inscribed on stone tablets.

The first dictionary was compiled in about 100 C.E. Containing about 9,000 characters, it helped promote a uniform system of writing. In Han times, as today, Chinese from the north could not converse with Chinese from the southeastern coast, but a common written language bridged differences of pronunciation, contributing to Chinese unity. Scholars began writing commentaries on the classics, a major scholarly activity throughout Chinese history. Scholars learned the classics by heart and used classical allusions in their writing.

Han philosophers also extended Zhou Confucianism by adding to it the teachings of cosmological naturalism. Zhou Confucianists had assumed that the moral force of a virtuous emperor would not only order society but also harmonize nature. Han Confucianists explained why. Dong Zhongshu (ca. 179–104 B.C.E.), for example, held that all nature was a single, interrelated system. Just as summer always follows spring, so does one color, one virtue, one planet, one element, one number, and one officer of the court always take precedence over another. All reflect the systematic workings of yang and yin and the five elements. And just as one dresses appropriately to the season, so was it important for the emperor to choose policies appropriate to the sequences inherent in nature. If he was moral, if he acted in accord with Heaven's natural system, then all would go well. But if he acted inappropriately, then Heaven would send a portent as a warning—a blue dog, a rat holding its tail in its mouth, an eclipse, or a comet. If the portent was not heeded, wonders and then misfortunes would follow. It was the Confucian scholars, of course, who claimed to understand nature's messages and advised the emperor.

It is easy to criticize Han philosophy as a pseudoscientific or mechanistic view of nature, but it represented a new effort by the Chinese to encompass and comprehend the interrelationships of the natural world. This effort led to inventions like the seismograph and to advances in astronomy, music, and medicine. It was also during the Han that the Chinese invented paper, the wheelbarrow, the stern-post rudder, and the compass (known as the "south-pointing chariot").

HISTORY

The Chinese were the greatest historians of the premodern world. They wrote more history than anyone else, and what they wrote was usually more accurate. Apart from the *Spring and Autumn Annals* and the scholarship of Confucius himself, history writing in China began during the Han Dynasty. Why the Chinese were so history-minded has been variously explained: because the Chinese tradition is this-worldly; because Confucianists were scholarly and their veneration for the classics carried over to the written word; because history was seen as a lesson book (the Chinese called it a mirror) for statesmen, and thus a necessity for the literate men who operated the centralized Chinese state.

The practice of using actual documents and firsthand accounts of events began with Sima Qian (d. 85 B.C.E.), who set out to write a history of the known world from the most ancient times down to the age of the emperor Wudi. His *Historical Records* consisted of 130 substantial chapters (with a total of over 700,000 characters) divided into "Basic Annals"; "Chronological Tables"; "Treatises" on rites, music, astronomy, the calendar, and so on; "Hereditary Houses"; and seventy chapters of "Biographies," including descriptions of foreign peoples. A second great work, *The Book of the Han*, was written by Ban Gu (d. 92 C.E.). It applied the analytical schema of Sima Qian to a single dynasty, the Former Han, and established the pattern by which each dynasty wrote the history of its predecessor.

QUICK REVIEW

Chinese Historians

- Greatest historians of premodern world
- History seen as a lesson book for statesmen
- Practice of using actual documents and firsthand accounts began with Sima Qian (d. 85 B.C.E.)

●•●-[Read the **Document**
Sima Qian, The Life of Meng Tian, Builder of the Great Wall
at **myhistorylab.com**

NEO-DAOISM

As the Han Dynasty waned, it became increasingly difficult to implement the Confucian ethic in the sociopolitical order. Some scholars abandoned Confucianism altogether in favor of **Neo-Daoism**, or "mysterious learning." A few wrote commentaries on the classical Daoist texts that had been handed down from the Zhou. The *Zhuangzi* was especially popular. Other scholars, defining the natural as the pleasurable, withdrew from society to engage in witty "pure conversations." They discussed poetry and philosophy, played the lute, and drank wine. The most famous were the Seven Sages of the Bamboo Grove of the third century C.E. One sage was always accompanied by a servant carrying a jug of wine and a spade—the one for his pleasure, the other to dig his grave should he die. Another wore no clothes at home. When criticized, he replied that the cosmos was his home, and his house his clothes. "Why are you in my pants?" he asked a discomfited visitor. Still another took a boat to visit a friend on a snowy night, but on arriving at his friend's door, turned around and went home. When pressed for an explanation, he said that it had been his pleasure to go, and that when the impulse died, it was his pleasure to return. This story reveals a scorn for convention coupled with an admiration for an inner spontaneity, however eccentric.

Another concern of what is called Neo-Daoism was immortality. Some sought it in dietary restrictions and yoga-like meditation, some in sexual abstinence or orgies. Others, seeking elixirs to prolong life, dabbled in alchemy, and although no magical elixir was ever found, the schools of alchemy to which the search gave rise are credited with the discovery of medicines, dyes, glazes, and gunpowder.

Meanwhile, popular religious cults arose among the common people. Since they included the Daoist classics among their sacred texts, these popular cults are also called Neo-Daoist. Like most folk religions, they contained an amalgam of beliefs, practices, and superstitions. They had a pantheon of gods and immortals and taught that the good or evil done in this life would be rewarded or punished in the innumerable heavens or hells of an afterlife. These cults had priests, shamans who practiced faith healing, seers, and sorceresses. For a time, they also had hierarchical church organizations, but these were smashed at the end of the second century C.E. Local Daoist temples and monasteries, however, continued until modern times. With many Buddhist accretions, they furnished the religious beliefs of the bulk of the Chinese population. Even in recent decades, these sects flourished in Taiwan and Chinese communities in Southeast Asia. They were suppressed in China in the Maoist era but were revived during the 1990s.

BUDDHISM

Central Asian missionaries, following the trade routes east, brought Buddhism to China in the first century C.E. It was at first viewed as a new Daoist sect, which is not surprising because early translators used Daoist terms to render Buddhist concepts. **Nirvana**, for example, was translated as "not doing" (*wuwei*). In the second century C.E., confusion about the two

Neo-Daoism
A revival of Daoist "mysterious learning" that flourished as a reaction against Confucianism during the Han Dynasty.

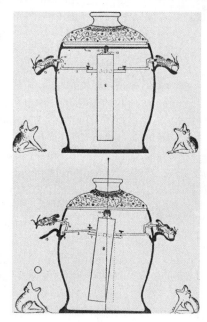

A Chinese Seismograph. The suspended weight swings in the direction of the earthquake. This moves a lever, and a dragon drops a ball into the mouth of one of the four waiting ceramic frogs.

How did the "mysterious learning" of Neo-Daoism contribute to science, technology, and medicine?

Nirvana In Buddhism the attainment of release from the wheel of *karma*.

religions led to the very Chinese view that Laozi had gone to India, where the Buddha had become his disciple, and that Buddhism was the Indian form of Daoism.

As the Han sociopolitical order collapsed in the third century C.E., Buddhism spread rapidly. (There are parallels to the spread of Christianity at the end of the Roman Empire.) Although an alien religion in China, Buddhism had some advantages over Daoism:

1. It was a doctrine of personal salvation, offering several routes to that goal.

2. It upheld high standards of personal ethics.

3. It had systematic philosophies, and during its early centuries in China, it continued to receive inspiration from India.

4. It drew on the Indian tradition of meditative practices and psychologies, which were the most sophisticated in the world.

●◆●⎰Read the **Document**
Faxien, Record of Buddhist Countries,
Chapter Sixteen at **myhistorylab.com**

By the fifth century C.E. Buddhism had spread over all of China (see Map 7–3). Occasionally it was persecuted by Daoist emperors, but most courts supported Buddhism. The "Bodhisattva Emperor" Wu of the southern Liang Dynasty three times gave himself to a monastery and had to be ransomed back by his disgusted courtiers. Temples and monasteries abounded in both the north and the south. There were communities of women as well as of men. Chinese artists produced Buddhist painting and sculpture of surpassing beauty, and thousands of monk-scholars labored to translate sutras and philosophical treatises. Chinese monks went on pilgrimages to India. The record left by Fa Xian, who traveled to India overland and back by sea between 399 and 413 C.E., became a prime source of Indian history.

The Tang monk Xuanzang went to India from 629 until 645. Several centuries later, his pilgrimage was novelized as *Journey to the West.* The novel joins faith, magic, and adventure.

A comparison of Indian and Chinese Buddhism highlights some distinctive features of its spread. Buddhism in India had begun as a reform movement. Forget speculative philosophies and elaborate metaphysics, taught the Buddha, and concentrate on simple truths: Life is suffering, the cause of suffering is desire, death does not stop the endless cycle of birth and rebirth; only the attainment of *nirvana* releases one from the "wheel of *karma.*" Thus, in this most otherworldly of the world's religions, all of the cosmic drama of salvation was compressed into the single figure of the Buddha meditating under the Bodhi tree. Over the centuries, however, Indian Buddhism developed contending philosophies and conflicting sects and, having become virtually indistinguishable from Hinduism, was largely reabsorbed after 1000 C.E.

A mendicant friar of the Tang Dynasty. He is accompanied by a tiger, indicating the extent to which he has become one with nature and with his own true nature.

In what ways did the Chinese adapt Buddhism to fit their culture?

In China, there were a number of sects with different doctrinal positions, but the Chinese genius was more syncretic. It took in the sutras and meditative practices of early Buddhism. It took in the Mahayana philosophies that depicted a succession of Buddhas, cosmic and historical, past and future, all embodying a single ultimate reality. It also took in the sutras and practices of Buddhist devotional sects. Finally, in the Tiantai sect, the Chinese joined together these various elements as different levels of a single truth. Thus the monastic routine of a Tiantai monk would include reading sutras, sitting in meditation, and also practicing devotional exercises.

Socially, too, Buddhism adapted to China. Ancestor worship demanded heirs to perform the sacrifices. Without progeny, ancestors might become "hungry ghosts." Hence, the first son was expected to marry and have children, whereas the second son, if he were

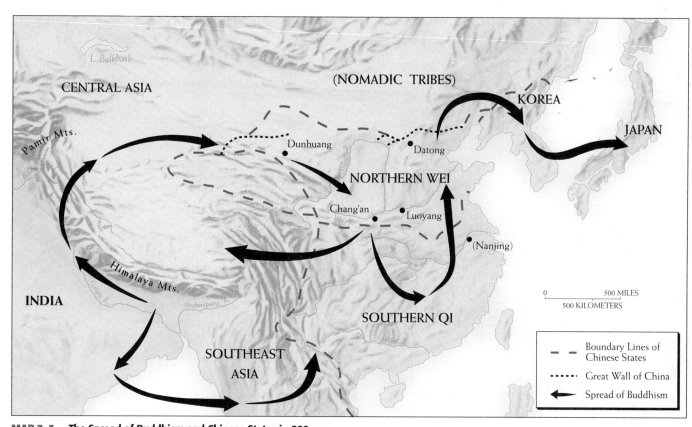

MAP 7–3.   The Spread of Buddhism and Chinese States in 500 C.E.
Buddhism originated in a Himalayan state in northwest India. It spread in one wave south to India and on to Southeast Asia as far as Java. But it also spread into northwest India, Afghanistan, Central Asia, and then to China, Korea, and Japan.

What is the relationship between the spread of Buddhism and trade?

so inclined, might become a monk. The practice also arose of holding Buddhist masses for dead ancestors. Still another difference between China and India was the more extensive regulation of Buddhism by the state in China. Just as Buddhism was not to threaten the integrity of the family, so Buddhism was not to reduce the taxes paid on land. As a result, limits were placed on the number of monasteries, nunneries, and monastic lands, and the state had to give its permission before men or women abandoned the world to enter a religious establishment—though these regulations were not always enforced.

SUMMARY

HOW DID the Qin unify China?

Qin Unification of China. The state of Qin unified China in 221 B.C.E. through military conquest. To the north it built the Great Wall to prevent incursions by the nomadic Xiongnu peoples. It ruled through a centralized bureaucracy in line with its Legalist philosophy. But the pace of its reform was so frenetic and its legal punishments were so harsh that it alienated its people. The Qin collapsed after the death of the First Emperor. *page 175*

WHAT IS the dynastic cycle?

Former Han Dynasty. China's pattern of dynastic cycles—military unification, consolidation, growth, reform, followed by decay and disintegration—began. The Former Han and Later Han, back-to-back dynasties, ruled China for more than four centuries (206 B.C.E.–220 C.E.). A pattern of centralized rule by officials educated in the Confucian classics was established. Ever since this period, the core Chinese population has referred to itself as the "Han people." *page 178*

WHY DID the Han Dynasty collapse?

Later Han and Its Aftermath. The Later Han established a new capital, but in most respects continued Former Han policies. Late in the first century C.E., the first in a line of weak emperors came to power, beginning the process of decline. After the fall of the Han, large landowners gained power and China was fragmented for several centuries. Northern and southern China developed differently. *page 185*

WHAT WAS the extent of Buddhist influence under the Han?

Han Thought and Religion. During long periods of peace and good government, literature, art, and history-writing flourished. Neo-Daoism partially eclipsed Confucianism. Buddhism entered China in the first century and spread rapidly in the third century, as the Han collapsed. *page 187*

KEY TERMS

dynastic cycle (p. 178) **Silk Road** (p. 181)
Neo-Daoism (p. 189) **Xiongnu** (p. 180)
Nirvana (p. 189)

REVIEW QUESTIONS

1. How did Legalism help the Qin unify China? What other factors played a part? What were the main features of Qin administration? Why did the Qin collapse?

2. What was the "dynastic cycle"? In what sense was it a Confucian moral rationalization? Was a cycle of administrative and military decline especially true of Chinese government, or can we see the same pattern elsewhere?

3. Who were the Xiongnu? How did Wudi respond to them?

4. How did the Silk Road work? What items were traded and on what route? What impact did this trade have on Chinese culture?

5. What challenges did the Han face in conquering and integrating new territories into the empire? How did they meet those challenges?

6. Compare and contrast the Roman and Han empires. What qualities did they have in common? How did they differ?

7. Who were the players who sought power at the Han court? Did the means they used reflect the differences in their positions?

8. What roles did Neo-Daoism have on elite Chinese culture and politics? What was its role among the larger populace?

9. Did Buddhism "triumph" in China in the same sense in which Christianity triumphed in the Roman world? Compare China to the Roman Empire. What problems did both empires face, and how did they try to resolve them?

Note: To learn more about the topics in this chapter, please turn to the Suggested Readings at the end of the book. For additional sources related to this chapter please see www.myhistorylab.com

PEARSON
myhistorylab Connections

Reinforce what you learned in this chapter by studying the many documents, images, maps, review tools, and videos available at **www.myhistorylab.com**

Read and Review

✓● Study and Review Chapter 7

●●● Read the Document *Li Si and the Legalist Policies of Qin Shihuang (280–208 B.C.E.), p. 177*
Sima Qian, The Life of Meng Tian, Builder of the Great Wall, p. 188
Faxien, Record of Buddhist Countries, Chapter Sixteen, p. 190

◉ See the Map *China from the Later Zhou Era to the Han Era, p. 185*

◉ Watch the Video *The Silk Road: 5,000 miles and 1,500 Years of Cultural Interchange, p. 184*

◉ View the Image *The Great Wall of China, p. 176*
Qin Shihuang's Terra Cotta Soldiers, p. 178

Research and Explore

◉ Watch the Video *Symbiosis in Central Asia*
Buddhism on the Silk Road
Central and Periphery
Kushan Empire
Silk Road

◉ See the Map *Ancient China*

((●● Hear the Audio

Hear the audio file for Chapter 7
at **www.myhistorylab.com**

8

Imperial China,
589–1368

((•─[Hear the Audio for Chapter 8 at www.myhistorylab.com

"Lady Wenji's Return to China: Wenji Arriving Home." Southern Song Dynasty. Circa 1150 C.E. Lady Wenji, who lived in the second century C.E., was the daughter of a high-ranking official who was abducted by the no-madic Xiongnu. She eventually married and bore two sons. After twelve years in captivity she was ransomed and returned to China, leaving her children behind. Wenji's ordeal became the subject of numerous poems and paintings, such as the one shown here.

Museum of Fine Arts, Boston.

What were some of the roles played by women in China in this period?

T*he Tang (618–907) is everyone's favorite dynasty: open, cosmopolitan, expansionist, exuberant, and creative. It was the example of Tang China that decisively influenced the formation of states and high cultures in Japan, Korea, and Vietnam. Poetry during the Tang attained a peak that has not been equaled since. The Song (960–1279) rivaled the Tang in the arts; it was China's great age of painting and the most significant period for Chinese philosophy since its origins in the Zhou. Although not militarily strong, the Song Dynasty also witnessed an important commercial revolution. The Yuan (1279–1368) was a short-lived dynasty of rule by Mongols during which China became the most important unit in the largest empire the world has yet seen.* ■

REESTABLISHMENT OF EMPIRE: SUI (589–618) AND TANG (618–907) DYNASTIES

In the period corresponding to the European Early Middle Ages, the most notable feature of Chinese history was the reunification of China, the re-creation of a centralized bureaucratic empire consciously modeled on the earlier Han Dynasty (206 B.C.E.–220 C.E.). Reunification, as usual, began in the north. The Northern Wei (386–534), the most enduring of the northern Sino-Turkic states, took the first steps. It moved its court south to Luoyang, made Chinese the language of the court, and adopted Chinese dress and surnames. It also used the leverage of its nomadic cavalry to impose a new land tax, mobilizing resources for state use. The Northern Wei was followed by several short-lived kingdoms. Because the emperors, officials, and military commanders of these kingdoms came from the same aristocratic stratum, the social distance between them was small, and the throne was often usurped.

THE SUI DYNASTY

Sui Wendi (d. 605), a talented general of mixed Chinese-Turkic ancestry, came to power in 581 and began the Sui Dynasty (589–618). He unified the north, restored the tax base, reestablished a centralized bureaucratic government, and went on to conquer

GLOBAL PERSPECTIVE

IMPERIAL CHINA

Rough parallels between China and Europe persisted until the sixth century C.E. Both saw the rise and fall of great empires. At first glance, the three and a half centuries that followed the Han Dynasty appear remarkably similar to the comparable period after the collapse of the Roman Empire: Central authority broke down, private armies arose, and aristocratic estates were established. Barbarian tribes once allied to the empires invaded and pillaged large areas. Otherworldly religions entered to challenge earlier official worldviews. In China, Neo-Daoism and then Buddhism challenged Confucianism, just as Christianity challenged Roman conceptions of the sociopolitical order.

But from the late sixth century C.E., a fundamental divergence occurred. Europe tailed off into centuries of feudal disunity and backwardness. A ghost of empire lingered in the European memory. But the reality, even after centuries had passed, was that tiny areas like France (one seventeenth the size of China), Italy (one thirty-second), or Germany (one twenty-seventh) found it difficult to establish an internal unity, much less re-create a pan-European or pan-Mediterranean empire. In contrast, China, which is about the size of Europe and geographically no

more natural a political unit, put a unified empire back together again, attaining new wealth, power, culture, and unified rule that has continued until the present. What explains the difference?

One reason China re-created its empire was that in China the victory of Buddhism was less complete than that of Christianity in Europe. Confucianism, and its conception of a unified empire, survived within the aristocratic families and at the courts of the Six Dynasties. It is difficult even to think of Confucianism apart from the idea of a universal ruler, aided by men of virtue and ability, ruling "all under Heaven" according to Heaven's Mandate. In contrast, the Roman concept of political order was not maintained as an independent doctrine. Moreover, empire was not a vital concept in Christian thought—except perhaps in Byzantium, where the empire lasted longer than it did in western Europe. The notion of a "Christian king" did appear in the West, but basically, the kingdom sought by Jesus was not of this world.

A second consideration was China's greater cultural homogeneity. It had a common written language that was fairly close to all varieties of spoken Chinese. Minority peoples and even barbarian conquerors—apart from the Mongols—were rapidly

---

QUICK REVIEW

Sui Wendi (d. 605)
- Founder of the Sui Dynasty (589–618)
- Talented ruler who unified China
- Grand Canal constructed and Great Wall rebuilt during his reign

⊙ See the Map
China during the Sui and Tang Dynasties
at **myhistorylab.com**

Chang'an
City in northern China, near present-day X'ian, that served as capital during the Sui and Tang dynasties.

Censorate The branch of the imperial Chinese government that acted as a watchdog, reporting instances of misgovernment directly to the emperor and remonstrating when it considered the emperor's behavior improper.

southern China and unify the country. During his reign, huge palaces arose in his Wei valley capital. The Great Wall was rebuilt. The Grand Canal was constructed, linking the Yellow and Yangzi rivers. This canal enabled the northern conquerors to tap the wealth of central and southern China. Peace was maintained with the Turkic tribes along China's northern borders. Eastern Turkic khans (chiefs) were sent Chinese princesses as brides.

The early years of the second Sui emperor were also constructive, but then Chinese attempts to meddle in steppe politics led to hostilities and wars. Hardships and casualties in campaigns against Korea and along China's northern border produced rising discontent. Natural disasters occurred. The court became bankrupt and demoralized. Rebellions broke out, and once again, there was a free-for-all among the armies of aristocratic military commanders. The winner, and the founder of the Tang Dynasty, was a relative of the Sui empress and a Sino-Turkic aristocrat of the same social background as those who had ruled before him.

Chinese historians often compare the short-lived Sui Dynasty with that of the Qin (256–206 B.C.E.). Each brought all of China under a single government after centuries of disunity. Each did too much, fell, and was replaced by a long-lasting dynasty. The Tang built on the foundations that had been laid by the Sui, just as the Han had built on those of the Qin.

THE TANG DYNASTY

The first Tang emperor took over the Sui capital, renamed it **Chang'an**, and made it his own. Within about a decade the new dynasty had extended its authority over all of China; tax revenues were adequate for government needs; and Chinese armies had begun the campaigns that would push Chinese borders out farther than ever

Sinicized. In contrast, after Rome the Mediterranean fell apart into its component cultures. Latin became the universal language of the Western church, but for most Christians it was a foreign language, a part of the mystery of the Mass, and even in Italy it became an artificial language, separate from the living tongue. European languages and cultures were divisive forces.

✓ • Study and Review
China's Struggle for Cultural and Political Unity, 400 B.C.E.–A.D. 400 at **myhistorylab.com**

A third and perhaps critical factor was China's population density, which was at least fifteen times greater than that of France, Europe's most populous state. Population density explains why the Chinese could absorb barbarian conquerors so much more quickly than could Europe. More cultivators provided a larger agricultural surplus to the northern kingdoms than that enjoyed by comparable kingdoms in Europe. Greater numbers of people also meant better communications and a better base for commerce. To be sure, the centuries that followed the Han saw a decline in commerce and cities. In some areas barter or the use of silk as currency replaced money, but the economic level remained higher than in early medieval Europe. Several of the factors that explain the Sui–Tang regeneration of a unified empire apply equally well or better to the Song and subsequent dynasties. Comparisons across continents are difficult, but it seems likely that Tang and Song China had longer stretches of good government than any other part of the contemporary world. Not until the nineteenth century did comparable bureaucracies of talent and virtue appear in the West.

Focus Questions

◆ In what ways did China and Europe parallel each other in their development until the sixth century C.E.? How did they diverge after that?

◆ Why did China witness the reunification of empire after the fall of the Han Dynasty, whereas after the fall of Rome, Europe was never again united in a single empire?

◆ Why did Tang and Song China enjoy longer stretches of good government than anywhere else in the contemporary world during the same period?

(see Map 8–1 on page 198). Confucian scholars were employed at the court, Buddhist temples and monasteries flourished, and peace and order prevailed, especially from 624 to 755.

The first Tang emperor and his successors worked to reconcile conflicting interests. The emperor wanted a bureaucratic government in which authority was centralized in his own person, but at the same time he had to make concessions to the aristocrats—the dominant elements in Chinese society in the Late Han—who staffed his government and continued to dominate early Tang society.

The degree to which political authority was centralized was apparent in the formal organization of the bureaucracy. At the highest level were three organs: Military Affairs, the Censorate, and the Council of State (see Figure 8–1). Military Affairs supervised the Tang armies with the emperor, in effect, the commander in chief. The **Censorate** had watchdog functions: It reported instances of misgovernment directly to the emperor and could also remonstrate with the emperor when it considered his behavior improper. The Council of State was the most important body. It met daily with the emperor and was made up of the heads of the Secretariat, which drafted policies; the Chancellery, which reviewed them; and State Affairs, which carried them out.

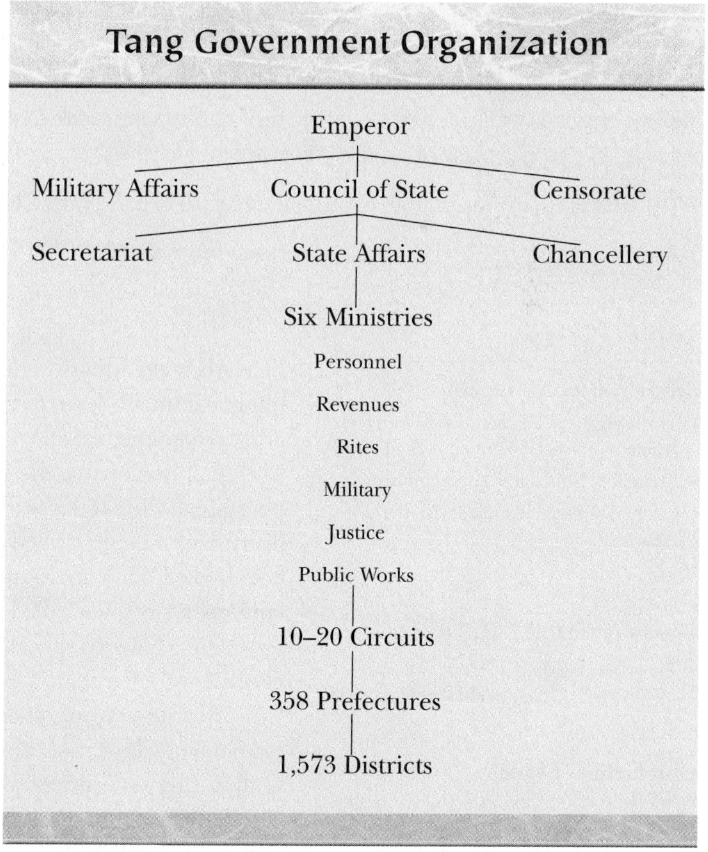

Tang Government Organization

Emperor

Military Affairs — Council of State — Censorate

Secretariat — State Affairs — Chancellery

Six Ministries

Personnel

Revenues

Rites

Military

Justice

Public Works

10–20 Circuits

358 Prefectures

1,573 Districts

FIGURE 8–1. Tang Government Organization.

MAP EXPLORATION

To explore this map further, go to **http://www.myhistorylab.com**

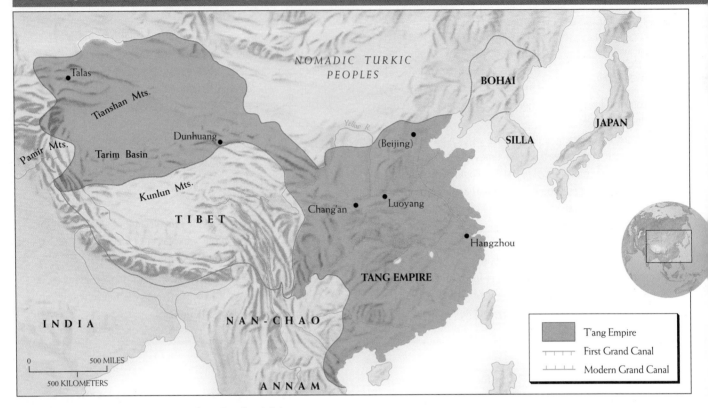

MAP 8–1.   The Tang Empire at Its Peak During the Eighth Century.

The Tang expansion into Central Asia reopened trade routes to the Middle East and Europe. Students from Bohai, Silla (Korea), and Japan studied in the Tang capital of Chang'an and then returned, carrying with them Tang books and technology.

Why did the Chinese Empire continually seek to expand into Central Asia?

QUICK REVIEW

Centralization of Authority

♦ Three organs of bureaucracy: Military Affairs, Censorate, Council of State

♦ Council of State most important body

♦ Council of State met daily with the emperor

•❖•⌐[**Read** the **Document**
Tang Daizong on the Art of Government
at **myhistorylab.com**

examination system
A method of selecting scholar-bureaucrats based on the results of a highly structured, and extremely competitive, series of tests.

Beneath State Affairs were the Six Ministries, which continued as the core of the central government down to the twentieth century; beneath them were the several levels of local administration.

Concessions to the interests of the aristocratic families were embodied in the tax system. All land was declared to be the property of the emperor and was then redistributed to able-bodied cultivators, who paid taxes in labor and grain. Because all able-bodied adult males received an equal allotment of land (women got less), the land-tax system was called the "equal field system." But the system was not egalitarian. Aristocrats enjoyed special exemptions and grants of "rank" and "office" lands that, in effect, confirmed their estate holdings.

Recruitment of officials also favored aristocrats, since most officials either were recommended for posts or received posts because their fathers had been high officials. Only a tiny percentage was recruited through the **examination system**. Those who passed the examinations had the highest prestige and were more likely to have brilliant careers. But only well-to-do families could afford the years of study needed to pass the rigorous examinations, so even the examination bureaucrats were usually aristocrats.

Women of the inner court continued to play a role in government. For example, Wu Zhao (626–ca. 706), a young concubine of the strong second emperor, married his weak heir. When the emperor suffered a stroke in 660, she dominated the court. After his death in 683 she ruled as regent and then, deposing her son, became emperor herself, the only woman in Chinese history to hold the title. She moved the court to Luoyang and proclaimed a new dynasty. A fervent Buddhist with an interest in magic, she saw herself as the incarnation of the messianic Buddha Maitreya and built temples throughout the land. Her sexual appetites were said to have been prodigious. She ruled China until she was 80; she was deposed in 705.

Surprisingly, Empress Wu's machinations may have strengthened the central government. In her struggle for power against the old northwestern Chinese aristocrats, she turned not to members of her family but to the products of the examination system and to a group known as the Scholars of the North Gate. This policy broadened the base of government by bringing in aristocrats from other regions of China. Her rule coincided with the maximal geographical expansion of Tang military power.

After a few years of tawdry intrigues, Xuan Zong came to the throne. In reaction to Empress Wu, he appointed government commissions headed by distinguished aristocrats to reform government finances. Examination bureaucrats lost power. The Grand Canal was repaired and extended. A new census extended the tax rolls. Wealth and prosperity returned to the court. His reign (713–756) was also culturally brilliant.

Chang'an was an imperial city, an administrative center that lived on taxes (see Map 8–2). It was designed to exhibit the power of the emperor and the majesty of his court. The city was laid out on a grid. At the far north of the city, the palace faced south, in keeping with Confucian tradition. In front of the palace was a complex of government offices from which an imposing 500-foot-wide avenue led to the main southern gate. Enclosed by great walls, the city covered 30 square miles. Its population was over 1 million: half within the walls, the other half in suburbs. It was the largest city in the world. (The population of China in the year 750 was about 50 million—about 4 percent of the country's present-day population.) Chang'an was also a trade center from which caravans set out across Central Asia. Merchants from India, Persia, Syria, and Arabia hawked the wares of the Near East and all of Asia in its two government-controlled markets.

THE TANG EMPIRE

A Chinese dynasty is like an accordion, first expanding into the territories of its neighbors and then contracting back to its densely populated core area. The principal threats to the Tang state were from Tibetans in the west, Turks in the northwest and north, and Khitan Mongols in Manchuria.

To protect its border, the Tang employed a four-tier policy. When nothing else would work, the Tang sent armies. But armies were expensive, and military solutions impermanent. For example, in 630 Tang armies defeated the eastern Turks; in 648 they took the Tarim basin, open-

•⁙•⌐Read the Document
An Essay Question from the Chinese Imperial Examination System at **myhistorylab.com**

QUICK REVIEW

Chang'an

- Chang'an was an administrative center that lived on taxes
- Designed to show power and majesty of emperor and his court
- City was laid out on a grid

✓•⌐Study and Review
Comparative Case Study: Women in the Imperial Courts of China and Japan at **myhistorylab.com**

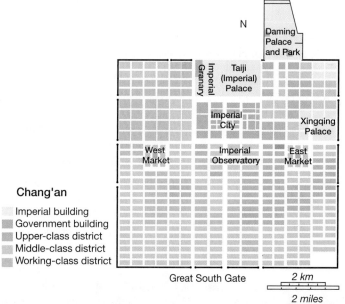

Chang'an
- Imperial building
- Government building
- Upper-class district
- Middle-class district
- Working-class district

MAP 8–2. Chang'an. The great city of Chang'an had been a Chinese capital since the Han period. By the eighth century there were around a half-million people within the city walls, with the same number close by outside, making it the largest city in the world at the time. The rigorous grid structure accommodated a variety of districts, each with its own administration.

HOW DOES the layout of Chang'an exhibit the power of the emperor?

Relief of Tang Emperor's Horse. A bearded "barbarian" groom tends the charger of the second Tang emperor (r. 626–649). This stone relief was found on the emperor's tomb. Note the stirrup, a Chinese invention of the fourth century C.E.

A Relief of Emperor T'ai T'sung's Horse, "Autumn Dew." University of Pennsylvania Museum, Philadelphia (NEG.# S8-62840).

How might stirrups help horsemen? What kinds of activities would be easier with stirrups than without?

Uighur Turk

A pastoralist, Altaic-speaking group based in the plains northwest of China, south of Lake Baikal.

⏵⏵⏵ Read the **Document**
Chinese description of the Tibetans
at **myhistorylab.com**

CHRONOLOGY

IMPERIAL CHINA

589–618	Sui Dynasty
618–907	Tang Dynasty
960–1279	Song Dynasty
1279–1368	Yuan (Mongol) Dynasty

ing trade routes to western Asia for almost a century; and in 657 they defeated the western Turks and extended Chinese influence to petty states near Samarkand. By 698, however, the Turks were invading northeastern China again, and between 711 and 736 they were in control of the steppe from the Oxus River to China's northern frontier. Chinese efforts against Tibet were much the same. From 670 Tibet expanded and threatened China. In 679 it was defeated. In 714 it rose again, wars were fought from 727 to 729, and a settlement was reached in 730. But wars broke out anew. In 752 Tibet entered an alliance with the state of Nan Chao in Yunnan. In 763 Tibetan forces captured and looted Chang'an. They were driven out, but the point remains that no military victory was final.

The second tier of Chinese defenses was to use nomads against other nomads. The critical development for the Tang was the rise to power of the **Uighur Turks**. From 744 to 840, the Uighurs controlled Central Asia and were staunch allies of the Tang. Without their support, the Tang Dynasty would have ended sooner.

A third tier was the defense along China's borders, including the Great Wall. At mid-dynasty, whole frontier provinces in the north and the northwest were put under military commanders, who in time came to control the provinces' civil governments as well. The bulk of the Tang military was in such frontier commands. At times their autonomy posed as much of a threat to the Tang court as to the nomadic enemy.

The fourth line of defense was to bring the potential enemy into the empire as a tributary. The Tang definition of "tributary" included principalities truly dependent on China; Central Asian states conquered by China; enemy states, such as Tibet or the Thai state of Nan Chao in Yunnan, when they were not actually at war with China; the Korean state of Silla, which had unified the peninsula with Tang aid but had then fought Tang armies to a stalemate when they attempted to impose Chinese hegemony; and wholly independent states, such as Japan. All sent embassies bearing gifts to the Tang court, which housed and fed them and sent back costly gifts in return.

For some countries these embassies had a special significance. As the only "developed nation" in eastern Asia, China was a model for countries still emerging as states. An embassy gained access to the entire range of Tang culture and technology. In 640 there were 8,000 Koreans, mostly students, in Chang'an. China was able to exert great influence on its neighbors during their formative stages.

Within China, signs of decline began to appear around the mid-eighth century. China's frontiers started to contract. Tribes in Manchuria became unruly. Tibetans threatened China's western border.

In 751, an overextended Tang army was defeated by Arabs near Samarkand, closing China's caravan trade with the West for more than five centuries. Meanwhile, in 755 a Sogdian general, An Lushan, who commanded three Chinese provinces on the northeastern frontier, led his 160,000 troops in a rebellion that swept across northern China, capturing Luoyang and then Chang'an. The emperor fled to Sichuan—apparently all for love, which was soon lost: Ten years earlier the emperor Xuan Zong had taken a young woman, Yang Guifei, from the harem of his son. So infatuated was he that he neglected to govern. This was fine for a while, because his chief minister governed instead. When the minister died, though, Xuan Zong appointed his concubine's second cousin to the post, initiating a chain of events that

OVERVIEW Chinese Policy toward Barbarians

For much of the history of the Chinese Empire, nomadic peoples from the west and north, whom the Chinese considered to be barbarians, posed a recurrent threat. The imperial Chinese government adopted a variety of strategies for dealing with this threat.

Armies	When nothing else worked, the Chinese went on the offensive and sent armies against the nomads. But armies were expensive, and victories over nomads were transitory. Within a few years the tribes would regroup and menace China anew.
Nomads against nomads	A second strategy was to obtain allies from the nomads along China's borders and use them against more distant nomads. To win over neighboring tribes, a variety of bribes was employed.
Border defense	In the north, an inner line of defense was the Great Wall. Also, late in dynasties, northern provinces were often placed under military governors.
Diplomacy	China sought to neutralize its neighbors by loosely attaching them to its empire. Nomadic tribes, Central Asian states, and Korea became "tributaries" of the emperor. Their rulers sent embassies bearing gifts ("tribute") to the imperial court, which fed and housed them, and sent them home with even costlier gifts and reports of China's power, wealth, splendor, and cultural achievements.

resulted in rebellion. En route to Sichuan, Xuan Zong's soldiers, blaming Yang Guifei for their plight, strangled her.

After a decade of wars and much devastation, a new emperor restored the dynasty with the help of the Uighur Turks, who looted Chang'an as part of their reward. The century of relative peace and prosperity that followed illustrates the resilience of Tang institutions. China was smaller, but military governors maintained the diminished frontiers. Provincial governors were more autonomous, but taxes were still sent to the capital. Occasional rebellions were suppressed. Most of the emperors were weak, but three strong emperors carried out reforms. The most important reform was that of the land system. The official census, on which land allotments and taxes were based, showed a drop in population from 53 million before the An Lushan rebellion to 17 million afterward. The government replaced the equal field system with a tax collected twice a year. The new system, begun in 780, lasted until the sixteenth century. Under it, a fixed quota of taxes was levied on each province. After the rebellion, government revenues from salt and iron surpassed those from land.

During the second half of the ninth century the government weakened further. Most provinces were autonomous, often under military commanders, and resisted central control. Wars, bandits, droughts, and peasant uprisings took their toll. By the 880s warlords had carved all of China into independent kingdoms, and in 907 the Tang Dynasty fell. But within half a century a new dynasty arose. The fall of the Tang did not lead to the centuries of division that had followed the Han. Something had changed within China.

TANG CULTURE

The creativity of the Tang period arose from the juxtaposition and interaction of cosmopolitan, medieval Buddhist, and secular elements. The rise of each of these cultural spheres was rooted in the wealth and the social order of the re-created empire.

Tang culture was cosmopolitan both because of its broad contacts with other cultures and peoples and because of its openness to them. Pilgrims, art, and philosophy flowed between India and China, so the voluptuousness of Indian painting and

View the **Image**
Court Lady Yang Guifei Mounting a Horse
at **myhistorylab.com**

Read the **Document**
Ibn Wahab, an Arab merchant, visits Tang China at **myhistorylab.com**.

sculpture influenced the Tang representation of the *bodhisattva*. Commercial contacts were widespread; foreign goods were sold in Chang'an marketplaces, and Arab and Persian quarters grew up in the seaports of southeastern China. Merchants brought their religions with them. Nestorian Christianity, Zoroastrianism, Manichaeism, Judaism, and Islam entered China at this time. (Most were swept away in the persecutions of the ninth century.)

Central Asian music and musical instruments became so popular they almost displaced the native tradition. Tang ladies adopted foreign hairstyles. Dramas and acrobatic performances by western Asians could be seen in the streets of the capital. In Tang poetry, too, what was foreign was judged on its own merits.

The Tang Dynasty was the golden age of Buddhism in China. Patronized by emperors and aristocrats, the Buddhist establishment acquired vast landholdings and wealth. Temples and monasteries were constructed throughout China. Little of the beauty and sophistication of temple art and architecture has survived in China, except in the Caves of the Thousand Buddhas in China's far northwest, which were sealed during the eleventh century and not rediscovered until the twentieth century. Only during the Tang did China have a "church" establishment that was at all comparable to that of medieval Europe, and even then it was subservient to the state. Buddhist wealth and learning brought with them secular functions: Temples served as schools, inns, or even bathhouses; they lent money; priests performed funerals and dispensed medicines. Occasionally the state moved to recapture the revenues monopolized by temples. The severest persecution, which marked a turn in the fortunes of Buddhism in China, occurred from 841 to 845, when an ardent Daoist emperor confiscated millions of acres of tax-exempt lands, put 260,000 monks and nuns back on the tax registers, and destroyed 4,600 monasteries and 40,000 shrines.

During the early Tang, the principal Buddhist sect was the Tiantai, but after the mid-ninth-century suppression, other sects came to the fore:

1. One devotional sect focused on Maitreya, a Buddha of the future, who will appear and create a paradise on earth. Maitreya was a cosmic messiah, not a human figure. The sect's teachings often furnished the ideology for popular uprisings and rebellions like the White Lotus, which claimed that it was renewing the world in anticipation of Maitreya's coming.

2. Another devotional sect worshiped the **Amitabha Buddha**, the Lord of the Western Paradise or Pure Land. This sect taught that in the early centuries after the death of the historical Buddha, people could obtain enlightenment by their own efforts, but later the Buddha's teachings had become so distorted that humans could obtain salvation only by reliance on Amitabha. All who called on Amitabha with a pure heart and perfect faith would be saved. Amitabha Buddhism developed a congregational form of worship, became the largest sect in China, and deeply influenced Chinese popular religion.

3. A third sect, most influential among the Chinese elites, began in China, where it was known as Chan. In the West, it is better known by its Japanese name, **Zen**. Zen taught that the historical Buddha was only a man and exhorted each person to attain enlightenment by his or her own efforts. Although its monks were well-

Tang Figurine. During the Tang Dynasty (618–907), well-to-do families placed glazed pottery figurines in the tombs of their dead. Perhaps they were intended to accompany and amuse the dead in the afterlife. Note the fancy chignon hairstyle of this female flutist, one figure in a musical ensemble. Today these figurines are sought by collectors around the world.

What are some characteristics of Tang culture?

Amitabha Buddha
The Buddhist Lord of the Western Paradise, or Pure Land.

Zen
A form of Buddhism, which taught that Buddha was only a man and exhorted each person to attain enlightenment by his or her own efforts.

learned, Zen was anti-intellectual in its emphasis on direct intuition into one's own Buddha-nature. Enlightenment was to be obtained by a regimen of physical labor and meditation. To jolt the monk into enlightenment, some Zen sects posed riddles: "If all things return to the One, what does the One return to?" "From the top of a hundred-foot pole, how do you step forward?" The psychological state of the adept attempting to deal with these problems is compared to that of "a mosquito biting an iron ball." The discipline of meditation, combined with a Zen view of nature, profoundly influenced the arts in China and subsequently in Korea and Japan as well.

A third characteristic of Tang culture was the reappearance of secular scholarship and letters. A scholarly bureaucratic complex emerged. Most men of letters were also officials, and most high-ranking officials painted or wrote poems. This secular stream of Tang culture did not oppose Buddhism. Officials were often privately sympathetic to Buddhism, but as men involved in the affairs of government, their values were this-worldly. Court historians revived the Han practice of writing an official history of the previous dynasty. Scholars compiled dictionaries and wrote commentaries on the Confucian classics. More paintings were Buddhist than secular, but Chinese landscape painting had its origins during the Tang. Nowhere, however, was the growth of a secular culture more evident than in poetry, the greatest achievement of Tang letters. An anthology of Tang poetry compiled during the Ming period (1368–1644) contained 48,900 poems by almost 2,300 authors.

The poet Li Bo (701–762) was neither wholly secular nor Buddhist; he might better be called Daoist. He was exceptional among Tang poets in never having sat for the civil service examinations. Large and muscular, he was a swordsman and a carouser. Of the 20,000 poems he is said to have composed, 1,800 have survived, and a fair number have titles like "Bring on the Wine" or "Drinking Alone in the Moonlight." According to legend, he drowned while drunkenly attempting to embrace the reflection of the moon in a lake. His poetry is clear, powerful, passionate, and always sensitive to beauty. It also contains a sense of fantasy, as when he climbed a mountain and saw a star-goddess, "stepping in emptiness, pacing pure ether, her rainbow robes trailed broad sashes." According to Li Bo, life is brief and the universe is large, but this view did not lead him to renounce the world. Rather, he exulted, identifying with the primal flux of yin and yang:

I'll wrap this Mighty Mudball of a world all up in a bag
And be wild and free like Chaos itself![1]

Du Fu (712–770), an equally famous Tang poet, was from a literary family. He failed the metropolitan examination at the age of 23 and spent years wandering, impoverished. He eventually got a government job but fell into rebel hands during the An Lushan rebellion. His poetry is less lyrical and more allusive than Li Bo's. It also reflects more compassion for human suffering: for the mother whose sons have been

Caravaneer on a Camel. The animal's shaggy mane indicates that it is a Bactrian camel from Central Asia.

How did trade influence culture during the Tang and Song dynasties?

●●●–Read the **Document**
T'ang Dynasty Poetry (8th century) Li Po at **myhistorylab.com**

●●●–Read the **Document**
Lu You, excerpt from Diary of a Journey to Sichuan at **myhistorylab.com**

---

[1]S. Owen, *The Great Age of Chinese Poetry: The High T'ang.* © 1980 (New Haven, CT: Yale University Press), p. 125. Reprinted by permission.

A Closer Look

A Tang Painting of the Goddess of Mercy

At the beginning of the twentieth century a sealed cave filled with the arts and objects of Tang China was discovered at Dunhuang in northwestern China, a jumping-off city to the Central Asian Silk Road.

Guanyin, the bodhisattva of compassion and mercy. A bodhisattva is an enlightened being who has postponed entering nirvana until all sentient beings are saved.

"Guanyin" means "hearing sounds," that is to say, hearing the pleas of all supplicants. In India, this bodhisattva was known as Avalokiteshvara and was male. In China, it became a female deity, Guanyin. In Japan it was known as Kannon and was female. Women prayed to it for a safe childbirth.

The donor of the painting was well-to-do and of official rank. His family, in formal dress and poses of piety, is shown as they might have stood in the family ancestral hall, men on the right and women on the left. Younger sons, their wives, and children are in the lower tier.

Questions

1. What, do you imagine, was the purpose of this painting?   2. What social values does the painting depict?

myhist**o**ry**lab**   To examine this image in an interactive fashion, please go to **www.myhistorylab.com**

conscripted and sent to war; for brothers scattered by war; for his own family, to whom he returned after having been given up for dead. Like Li Bo, he felt that humans are short-lived and that nature endures. Visiting the ruins of the palace of the second Tang emperor, he saw "Grey rats scuttling over ancient tiles." "Its lovely ladies are the brown soil" and only "tomb horses of stone remain." Unlike Li Bo, his response to this sad scene was to

> *Sing wildly, let the tears cover your open hands.*
> *Then go ever onward and on the road of your travels,*
> *Meet none who prolong their fated years.*[2]

TRANSITION TO LATE IMPERIAL CHINA: THE SONG DYNASTY (960–1279)

WHAT WAS the agricultural revolution that occurred during the Song Dynasty?

See the **Map**
China under Tang and Song Dynasties
at **myhistorylab.com**

The Song fits the dynastic cycle model of Chinese history. It reunified China in 960, establishing its capital at Kaifeng on the Yellow River (see Map 8–3). Mobilizing its resources effectively, it ruled for 170 years; this period is called the Northern Song. Then it weakened, losing the north in 1127 but continuing to rule the south from a new capital at Hangzhou for another 150 years. The Southern Song fell to the Mongols in 1279.

But there is more to Chinese history than the inner logic of the dynastic cycle. Important longer-term changes cut across dynasties. One such set of changes began during the late Tang and continued into the Song period. Its effects on the economy, society, state, and culture help to explain why China after the Tang did not relapse into centuries of disunity as it had after the Han—and why China never again experienced more than brief intervals of disunity.

AGRICULTURAL REVOLUTION OF THE SONG: FROM SERFS TO FREE FARMERS

Landed aristocrats had dominated local society in China during the Sui and Tang periods. The tillers of their lands were little more than serfs. The aristocracy weakened, however, during and after the Tang. Estates shrank as they were divided among a man's sons after his death. As the aristocrats' landholdings diminished, they were attracted to the capital where they became a metropolitan elite. After the fall of the Tang, the estates were often seized by warlords.

The fading power of the aristocracy and changes in the land and tax systems worked in favor of those who tilled the soil. The end of the equal field system freed farmers to buy and sell land, and ownership of land as private property gave cultivators greater independence. Taxes paid in grain gave way during the Song to taxes in money. The commutation of the labor tax to a money tax gave farmers more control over their time. Conscription, the cruelest and heaviest labor tax of all, disappeared as the conscript armies of the early and middle Tang were replaced by professional soldiers. Changes in technology also benefited the cultivator. New strains of an early-ripening rice permitted double cropping, and new commercial crops were developed.

Hear the **Audio**
at **myhistorylab.com**

QUICK REVIEW

Song Agricultural Revolution
◆ Aristocracy declined
◆ Money taxes replaced labor tax and conscription
◆ New crops and technologies increased productivity

---

[2]Owen, *The Great Age of Chinese Poetry*, pp. 223–224.

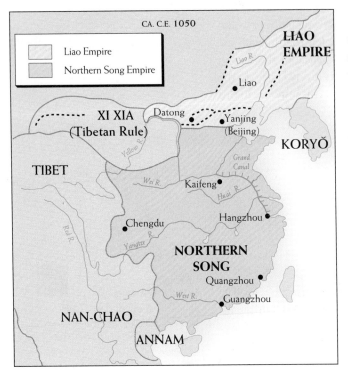

MAP 8–3.   The Northern Song and Liao Empires (Top) and the Southern Song and Jin Empires (Bottom).   During the Northern Song, the Mongol Liao Dynasty ruled only the extreme northern edge of China. During the Southern Song, in contrast, the Manchurian Jin Dynasty ruled half of China.

Why did the authority of the Song Dynasty not extend beyond southern China after 1279?

The disappearance of the aristocrats also increased the authority of the district magistrate, the sole local representative of imperial authority. But there were too many villages in his district for him to be involved regularly in their internal governance. As long as taxes were paid and order was maintained, affairs were left in the hands of the village elites.

One other development that began during the Song—and became vastly more important later—was the appearance of a scholar-gentry class. The typical gentry family contained at least one member who had passed the provincial civil service examination and lived in a district seat or market town. Socially and culturally, these gentry were closer to magistrates than to villagers, but since they usually owned land in the villages, they shared some interests with local landholders. At times they functioned as a buffer between the village and the magistrate's office.

COMMERCIAL REVOLUTION OF THE SONG

Demographic shifts, innovative technologies, the growth of cities, the spread of money, and rising trade all contributed to changes in the countryside. These developments varied by region, but overall the economy reached new prosperity as it underwent a **Song commercial revolution**.

Until late in the Tang, the north had been China's most populous and productive region. But starting in the late ninth century the center of gravity of China's population, agricultural production, and culture shifted to the lower and eastern Yangzi region. Between 800 and 1100 the population of the region tripled, as China's total population increased to about 100 million. Its rice paddies yielded more per acre than the wheat or millet fields of the north, making rice the tax base of the empire. Its wealth led to the establishment of so many schools that the government set regional quotas for the examination system.

Technological advances during the Song included the abacus, the use of gunpowder in grenades and projectiles, and improvements in textiles and porcelains. In north China, the world's most advanced coal and iron-smelting industry developed. Using coke and bellows to heat furnaces to the temperatures required for carbonized steel, it provided superior tools and weapons. Printing began in China with the use of carved seals. The earliest woodblock texts, mostly on Buddhist subjects, appeared in the seventh century. By the tenth century a complete edition of the classics had been published, and by the mid-Song books printed with movable type were fairly common.

Exchange during the Tang had been based largely on silk. During the Northern Song large amounts of copper cash were coined, but the demand rose more rapidly than the supply. Beginning in the Southern Song, silver was minted to complement copper cash.

Cities with more than 100,000 households almost quadrupled in number. The Northern Song capital at Kaifeng is recorded as having had 260,000 households—probably more than 1 million inhabitants—and the Southern Song capital at Hangzhou had 391,000 households. Compare these capitals to those of backward Europe: London during the Northern Song had a population of about 18,000; Rome during the Southern Song had 35,000; and Paris even a century later had fewer than 60,000. These Song capitals were open within and spread beyond their outer walls. Restaurants, theaters, wine shops, and brothels abounded.

Trade between regions during the Song was limited mainly to luxury goods such as silk, lacquerware, medicinal herbs, and porcelains. Only where transport was cheap—along rivers, canals, or the coast—was interregional trade in bulk commodities economical, and even then it was usually carried on only to make up for specific shortages.

Foreign trade reached new heights during the Song. In the north, Chinese traders bought horses from Tibetan, Turkic, and Mongol border states and sold silks and tea. Along the coast, Chinese merchants took over the port trade that during the Tang had been in the hands of Korean, Arab, and Persian merchants. The new hegemony of Chinese merchants was based on improved ships using both sail and oars and equipped with watertight compartments and better rudders. Chinese captains, navigating with the aid of the compass, came to dominate the sea routes from Japan in the north to Sumatra in the south. The content of the overseas trade reflected China's advanced economy: It imported raw materials and exported finished goods. Porcelains were sent to Southeast Asia and then were carried by Arab ships to medieval trading centers on the Persian Gulf and down the coast of East Africa as far south as Zanzibar.

GOVERNMENT: FROM ARISTOCRACY TO AUTOCRACY

The millennium of late imperial China after the Tang is often spoken of as the age of **imperial autocracy** or as China's age of absolute monarchy. Earlier emperors were often personally powerful, but changes during the Song made it easier for emperors to be autocrats.

Song emperors had direct personal control over more offices than their Tang predecessors. The central government was also better funded. Revenues in 1100 were three times the peak revenues of the Tang, partly because of the growth of population and agricultural wealth, and partly because of the establishment of government monopolies on salt, wine, and tea and various duties, fees, and taxes levied on trade. During the Northern Song, these commercial revenues rivaled the land tax; during the Southern Song, they surpassed it.

The disappearance of the aristocracy strengthened the emperors. During the Tang, the emperor had come from the same Sino-Turkic aristocracy as most of his principal ministers, and he ruled on behalf of this aristocracy. During the Song, in contrast, government officials were commoners, mostly products of the examination system. They were separated from the emperor by an enormous social gulf.

Irrigation Methods on a Farm in the Yangzi Valley. A farmer and his wife use their legs and feet to work the square-pallet chain pump, a boy drives a water buffalo to turn a water-pumping device, and another boy fishes.

© Photograph by Wan-go Weng/Collection of H. C. Weng.

What does this image suggest about the productivity of Chinese farms during the Song Dynasty?

Song commercial revolution
The growth in trade, population, technology, money supply, and other factors that reinforced one another to create cycles of commerce-driven economic growth during the Song Dynasty.

QUICK REVIEW

Song Commercial Revolution
- Yangzi basin gains population and power
- Steel, printing, and other technologies improve
- Cash and credit permeate the economy
- More cities have large populations
- Trade increases

Imperial autocracy
The governing style practiced by the Song emperors, in which the ruler exercises unlimited, personal authority.

The Song examination system was larger than that of the Tang, though smaller than it would be under later dynasties. Whereas only 10 percent of officials had been recruited by examination during the Tang, the Song figure rose to over 50 percent and included the most important officials. To pass the examinations, the candidate had to memorize the Confucian classics, interpret selected passages, write in the literary style, compose poems on themes given by the examiners, and propose solutions to contemporary problems in terms of Confucian philosophy. The quality of the officials produced by the Song system was impressive. The Chinese examination system that flourished during the Song continued, with some interruptions, into the twentieth century. The continuity of Chinese government rested on the examination elite with its common culture and values.

The social base for this examination meritocracy was triangular, consisting of land, education, and office. Landed wealth paid the costs of education. Without passing the examinations, an official position was out of reach. And without office, family wealth could not be preserved, since property was divided each time it was inherited. Merchants had wealth but were despised by scholar-officials as grubby profit-seekers and were barred from taking the examinations. Some merchants bought land, and their sons or grandsons became eligible to take the exams. Similarly, a small peasant might build up his holdings, become a landlord, and educate a son or grandson. The system was steeply hierarchical, but it was not closed nor did it produce a new, self-perpetuating aristocracy.

SONG CULTURE

Song culture retained some of the energy of the Tang while becoming more intensely and perhaps more narrowly Chinese. The preconditions for the rich Song culture were a rising economy, an increase in the number of schools and higher literacy, and the spread of printing. Song culture was closely associated with the officials and the scholar-gentry, who were both its practitioners and its patrons. The secular culture of Tang officials became dominant during the Song.

Chinese consider the Song Dynasty the peak of their traditional culture. It was, for example, China's greatest age of pottery and porcelains. High-firing techniques were developed, and kilns were established in every area. Song pottery, with its beautiful glazes and restrained, harmonious shapes, was unlike anything produced in the world before, and it made ceramics a major art form in East Asia. The Song was also an age of great historians. Sima Guang (1019–1086) wrote *A Comprehensive Mirror for Aid in Government*, which treated all Chinese history rather than a particular dynasty. His sophisticated work included a discussion of documentary sources and an explanation of why he chose to rely on one source rather than another.

The greatest achievements of the Song, however, were in philosophy, poetry, and painting. The Song was second only to the Zhou as a creative age in philosophy. A series of original thinkers culminated in the towering figure of Zhu Xi (1130–1200). Zhu Xi studied Daoism and Buddhism in his youth, along with Confucianism. During his thirties he focused on Confucianism, deepening and making more systematic its social and political ethics by joining Buddhist and native metaphysical elements to it. This new Confucianism became a viable alternative to Buddhism for Chinese intellectuals. Comparable figures in other traditions include Saint Thomas Aquinas (1224–1274) of medieval Europe or the Islamic theologian al-Ghazali (1058–1111), each of whom produced a new synthesis or worldview that lasted for centuries (see Chapters 15 and 12, respectively).

An Elegant Song Dynasty Wine Pot with green celadon glaze (24.8 cm high).

Ewer with carved flower sprays. Porcelain with molded and carved low-relief decoration in grayish-green glaze. Northern Song Dynasty (960–1000 © Gift of The Asian Art Museum Foundation).

In what ways is this wine pot "elegant"? Do you think it is an accurate representation of Song culture?

DOCUMENT

Su Dungpo Imagined on a Wet Day, Wearing a Rain Hat and Clogs

After Su's death, a disciple wrote these lines.

A

- **WHAT** does this poem suggest about the social and political roles played by scholars?

When with tall hat and firm baton he stood in council,
The crowds were awed at the dignity of the statesman in him.
But when in cloth cap he strolled with cane and sandals,
He greeted little children with gentle smiles.

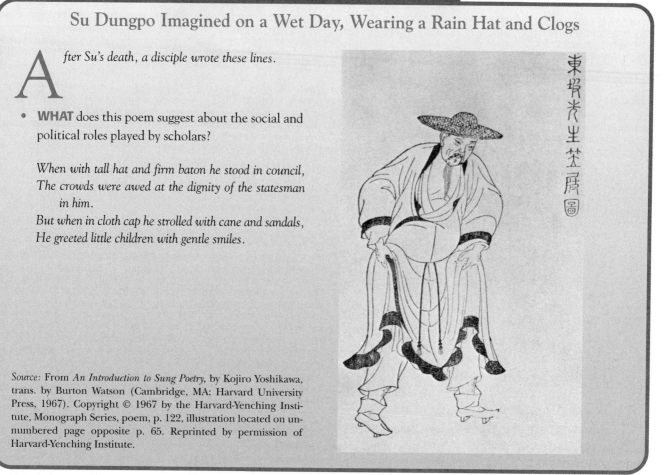

Source: From *An Introduction to Sung Poetry,* by Kojiro Yoshikawa, trans. by Burton Watson (Cambridge, MA: Harvard University Press, 1967). Copyright © 1967 by the Harvard-Yenching Institute, Monograph Series, poem, p. 122, illustration located on unnumbered page opposite p. 65. Reprinted by permission of Harvard-Yenching Institute.

Zhu Xi's teachings became a new orthodoxy, maintained by the civil service examinations. Like the examination system, the imperial institution, the scholar-gentry class, and the land system, his interpretation of Confucianism contributed to continuity and impeded change.

The most famous poet of the Northern Song was Su Dungpo (1037–1101), a man who participated in the full range of the culture of his age: He was a painter and a calligrapher; he practiced Zen and wrote commentaries on the Confucian classics; he superintended engineering projects; and he was a connoisseur of cooking and wine.

Su, a conservative, rose through a succession of posts to become the governor of a province. Eight years later, when the reformers came to power, Su was arrested and spent 100 days in prison, awaiting execution on a charge of slandering the emperor. Instead, he was released and exiled. He wrote, "Out the gate, I do a dance, wind blows in my face; our galloping horses race along as magpies cheer."[3] In exile, he farmed a plot of land at the "eastern slope" from which he took his literary name, Dungpo. After 1086 Su resumed his official career. In 1094 another shift occurred, and Su was exiled to the distant southern island of Hainan. After yet another shift, Su was on his way back to the capital when he died, in 1101. (See Document, "Su Dungpo Imagined on a Wet Day, Wearing a Rain Hat and Clogs.")

---

[3]Yoshikawa, *An Introduction to Sung Poetry,* p. 117.

An ink on silk handscroll, Southern Song Dynasty. The vast expanse of nature is hardly affected by the human presence.

Xia Gui, Chinese (active 1180–after 1224), "Twelve Views of Landscape." Southern Song Dynasty, (1127–1279). Handscroll; ink on silk. 11" x 90 3/4" (28.0 x 230.5 cm) overall. The Nelson-Atkins Museum of Art, Kansas City, Missouri. Purchase: Nelson Trust, 32-159/2. Photograph by John Lamberton.

What evidence of humans is there in this image?

In China, calligraphy and painting were seen as related. The same qualities of line, balance, and strength needed for calligraphy carried over to painting. Chinese calligraphy is immensely pleasing even to the untutored Western eye, and it is not difficult to distinguish between the elegant strokes of Huineng, the last emperor of the Northern Song, and the powerful brushwork of the Zen monk Zhang Jizhi. Song painting was varied, but its crowning achievement was landscapes. Song paintings are different from those of the West. Each stroke of the brush was final; mistakes could not be covered up. Each element in a scene was presented in its most pleasing aspect; the painting was not constrained by single-point perspective. Paintings had no single source of illumination, but contained an overall diffusion of light. Space was an integral part of the painting. If the painting contained human figures at all, they were small in a natural universe that was very large. Chinese painting thus reflected the same worldview as Chinese philosophy or poetry. The painter sought to grasp the inner reality of the scene, and not be bound up in surface details. In paintings by monks or masters of the Zen school, the presentation of an intuitive vision of an inner reality was even more pronounced.

CHINA IN THE MONGOL WORLD EMPIRE: THE YUAN DYNASTY (1279–1368)

WHY WERE the Mongols able to establish such a vast empire?

The Mongols created the greatest empire in the history of the world. It extended from the Caspian Sea to the Pacific Ocean; from Russia, Siberia, and Korea in the north to Persia and Burma in the south. Invasion fleets were even sent to Java and Japan, though without success. Mongol rule in China is one chapter of this larger story.

RISE OF THE MONGOL EMPIRE

The Mongols, a nomadic people, roamed the grasslands north of China where they raised horses and herded sheep. They lived in felt tents, or yurts. Women performed much of the work and were freer than women in China. Families belonged to clans, and related clans made up tribes. Tribes would gather during the annual migration from the summer plains to winter pasturage. Chiefs were elected, chosen for their courage, military prowess, judgment, and leadership. Like Manchu or Turkic, the Mongol tongue was Altaic. The Mongols worshiped nature deities and a supreme sky god. They communicated with their gods through religious specialists called *shamans*. Politically divided, they traded and warred among themselves and with settled peoples on the borders of their vast grassland domains.

The founder of the Mongol Empire, Temujin, was born in 1167. His father, a tribal chief, was poisoned while Temujin was still a child. Temujin fled; years later, he returned to the tribe, avenged his father, and in time became chief himself. Through his shrewd policy of alliances and remarkable survival qualities, he had united all Mongol tribes and had been elected their great khan, or ruler, by the time he was 40. It is by the title *Genghis* (also spelled *Jenghiz* or *Chinggis*) *Khan* that he is known to history. Genghis possessed an extraordinary charisma, and his sons and grandsons also became wise and talented leaders. Why the Mongol tribes should have produced such leaders at this point in history is difficult to explain.

A second conundrum is how the Mongols, who numbered only about 1.5 million, created the army that conquered vastly denser populations. Part of the answer is institutional. Genghis organized his armies into "myriads" of 10,000 troops, with decimal subdivisions of 1,000, 100, and 10. Elaborate signals were devised so that in battle even large units could be manipulated like the fingers of a hand. Mongol tactics were superb: Units would retreat, turn, flank, and destroy their enemies. The historical record makes clear that Genghis's nomadic cavalry had a paralytic effect on the peoples they encountered. The Mongols were peerless horsemen, and their most dreaded weapon was the compound bow, short enough to be used from the saddle yet more powerful than the English longbow.

They were astonishingly mobile. Each man carried his own supplies and covered vast distances quickly. In 1241, for example, a Mongol army had reached Hungary, Poland, and the shore of the Adriatic and was poised for a further advance into western Europe. But when word arrived of the death of the great khan, the army turned and galloped back to Mongolia to help choose his successor.

The Mongol army learned the use of siege weapons from enemies it conquered. Chinese engineers were used in campaigns in Persia. The Mongols also used terror; inhabitants of cities that refused to surrender in the Near East and China were put to the sword. Descriptions of the Mongols by those whom they conquered dwell on their physical toughness and pitiless cruelty.

But the Mongols had strengths that went beyond the strictly military. Genghis opened his armies to recruits from the Uighur Turks, the Manchus, and other nomadic peoples. In 1206 Genghis promulgated laws designed to prevent warring between tribes that would undermine his empire. Genghis also obtained thousands of pledges of personal loyalty from his followers, and he appointed these "vassals" to command his armies and staff his government. This policy gave his forces an inner coherence that countered the divisive effect of tribal loyalties. Unabashedly frank words attributed to Genghis may reveal what lay behind the Mongol drive to conquest: "Man's highest joy is in victory: to conquer one's enemies, to pursue them, to deprive them of their possessions, to make their beloved weep, to ride on their horses, and to embrace their wives and daughters."[4]

Read the Document
Giovanni Di Piano Carpini on the Mongols at **myhistorylab.com**

QUICK REVIEW

Genghis Khan

- Named Temujin at birth, in 1167
- "Khan" means great ruler
- Exceptionally charismatic
- Structured army for easy control, cohesiveness
- Divided empire among four sons

See the Map
The Mongol Empire of Chinggis Khan, ca. 1227, at **myhistorylab.com**

---

[4]J. K. Fairbank, E. O. Reischauer, and A. M. Craig, *East Asia, Tradition and Transformation* (Boston: Houghton Mifflin, 1973), p. 164.

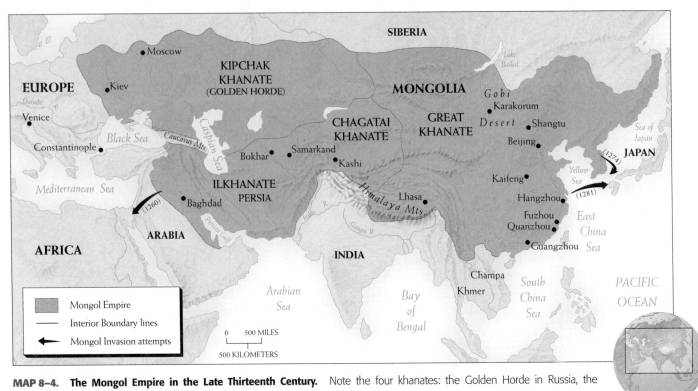

MAP 8–4. The Mongol Empire in the Late Thirteenth Century. Note the four khanates: the Golden Horde in Russia, the Ilkhanate in Persia, Chagatai in Central Asia, and the Great Khanate extending from Mongolia to southern China.

How did the Mongol Empire facilitate trade and communication?

Genghis divided his far-flung empire among his four sons. Over several generations, each of the four khanates became independent. The khanate of Chagatai was in Central Asia and remained purely nomadic. A second khanate of the Golden Horde ruled Russia from the lower Volga. The third was in Persia, and the fourth, led by those who succeeded Genghis as great khans, centered first in Mongolia and then in China (see Map 8–4).

MONGOL RULE IN CHINA

The standard theory used to organize Chinese history is the dynastic cycle, but a second theory explains Chinese history in terms of the interaction between the settled peoples of China and the nomads of the steppe. When strong states emerged in China, their wealth and population enabled them to expand militarily onto the steppe. But when China was weak, the steppe peoples overran China. To review briefly:

1. During the Han Dynasty (206 B.C.E.–220 C.E.), the most pressing problem in foreign relations was the Xiongnu Empire to the north.

2. During the centuries that followed the Han, various nomadic peoples invaded and ruled northern China.

3. The energy and institutions of these Sino-Turkic rulers of the northern dynasties shaped China's reunification during the Sui (589–618) and Tang (618–907) dynasties. The Uighur Turks also played a major role in Tang defense policy.

4. Northern border states became even more important during the Song. The Northern Song (960–1126) bought peace with payments of gold and silver to the Liao. The Southern Song (1126–1279), for all its cultural brilliance, was little more than a tributary state of the Jin Dynasty, which had expanded into northern China.

From the start of the Mongol pursuit of world hegemony, the riches of China were a target. Genghis proceeded cautiously, determined to leave no enemy at his back. He first disposed of the Tibetan state to the northwest of China and then the Manchu state of Jin that ruled north China. Mongol forces took Beijing in 1227, the year Genghis died. They went on to take Luoyang and the southern reaches of the Yellow River in 1234, and all of north China by 1241. During this time, the Mongols were interested mainly in loot. Only later did Chinese advisers persuade them that more wealth could be obtained by taxation.

Kublai, a grandson of Genghis, was chosen as the great khan in 1260. In 1264 he moved his capital from Karakorum in Mongolia to Beijing. It was only in 1271 that he adopted a Chinese dynastic name, the Yuan, and, as a Chinese ruler, went to war with the Southern Song. Once the decision was made, the Mongols swept across southern China. The last Song stronghold fell in 1279.

Kublai Khan's rule in Beijing reflected the mixture of cultural elements in Mongol China. Kublai rebuilt Beijing as a walled city in the Chinese style. But Beijing was far to the north of any previous Chinese capital, away from centers of wealth and population; to provision it, the Grand Canal had to be extended. From Beijing, Kublai could look out onto Manchuria and Mongolia and maintain ties with the other khanates. The city proper was for the Mongols. Chinese were segregated in an adjoining walled city. The palace of the khan was designed by an Arab architect; its rooms were Central Asian in style. Kublai also maintained a summer palace at Shangdu ("Xanadu") in Inner Mongolia, where he could hawk and ride and hunt in Mongol style.

Early Mongol rule in northern China was rapacious and exploitative, but it later shifted toward Chinese forms of government and taxation, especially in the south and at the local level. Because it was a foreign military occupation, civil administration was highly centralized. Under the emperor was a Central Secretariat, and beneath it were ten "Moving Secretariats," which became the provinces of later dynasties. These highly centralized institutions and the arbitrary style of Mongol decision making accelerated the trend toward absolutism that had started during the previous dynasty.

About 400,000 Mongols lived in China during the Yuan period. For such a tiny minority to control the Chinese majority, it had to stay separate. One measure was to make military service a monopoly of Mongols and their nomadic allies. Garrisons were established throughout China with a strategic reserve on the steppe. Military officers were always regarded as more important than civil officials. A second measure was to use ethnic classifications in appointing civil officials. Mongols held the top civil and military posts. Persians, Turks, and other non-Chinese were given high civil posts. Northern Chinese, including Manchus and other border

Kublai Khan. Wearing ermine coat, the Mongol emperor sits on a horse among Mongol warriors at the hunt. At his side is his consort, Chabi.

National Palace Museum, Taiwan, Republic of China.

How did the reign of Kublai Khan combine Mongol and Chinese elements?

⊙─See the **Map**
The Mongol Empire, 1206–1405
at **myhistorylab.com**

peoples, ranked above southern Chinese. Even when the examination system was sporadically revived after 1315, the Mongols and their allies took an easier examination; their quota was as large as that for Chinese, and they were appointed to higher offices.

The result was an uneasy symbiosis. Chinese officials directly governed the Chinese populace, collecting taxes, settling disputes, and maintaining the local order. Few of these officials ever learned to speak Mongolian, and Mongols usually did not bother to learn Chinese: Communication was through interpreters. Yet without the active cooperation of Chinese officials, Mongol rule in China would have been impossible.

FOREIGN CONTACTS AND CHINESE CULTURE

Diplomacy and trade within the greater Mongol Empire brought China into contact with other higher civilizations for the first time since the Tang period. Persia and the Arab world were especially important. Merchants, missionaries, and diplomats voyaged from the Persian Gulf and across the Indian Ocean to seaports in southeastern China; Arab communities in port cities grew. Camel caravans carrying silks and ceramics left Beijing for Baghdad. Chinese communities became established in Tabriz, the center of trading in western Asia, and in Moscow and Novgorod. Knowledge of printing, gunpowder, and Chinese medicine spread to western Asia. Chinese ceramics influenced those of Persia, while Chinese painting influenced Persian miniatures.

•◆•─Read the **Document**
Marco Polo at the Court of Kublai Khan,
ca. 1300 at **myhistorylab.com**

In Europe, knowledge of China was transmitted by the Venetian trader Marco Polo, who claimed to have served Kublai as an official between 1275 and 1292. His book, *A Description of the World*, was translated into most European languages. Many readers doubted that a land of such wealth and culture could exist so far from Europe, but the book excited an interest in geography. When Christopher Columbus set sail in 1492, his goal was to reach Polo's Zipangu (Japan).

The Moroccan Muslim scholar and explorer Ibn Battuta (1304–c. 1370) traveled throughout much of the Mongol world in the fourteenth century. In his account of his journeys, he described the Chinese as wealthy, but disinclined to flaunt their riches.

•◆•─Read the **Document**
The Mongols: An excerpt from the
Novgorod Chronicle, 1315
at **myhistorylab.com**

Mongol toleration encouraged contact across religions. Nestorian Christianity, spreading from Persia to Central Asia, reentered China; Kublai Khan's mother was a Nestorian Christian. Several papal missions were sent from Rome to the Mongol court, and an archbishopric was established in Beijing. Kublai sent a letter to the pope asking him to send a hundred educated men to his court. Tibetan Buddhism was the religion most favored by the Mongols, but Chinese Buddhism also flourished. Priests and monks of all religions were given tax exemptions. Half a million Chinese became Buddhist monks during the Mongol century. Islam made great gains, becoming permanently established in Central Asia and western China. Even Confucianism was regarded as a religion by the Mongols, and its teachers were exempted from taxes.

Despite these wide contacts with other peoples and religions, the high culture of China appears to have been influenced little—partly because China had little to learn from other areas, and partly because the centers of Chinese culture were in the south, the area least affected by Mongol rule. Overall, in reaction to the Mongol conquest, Chinese culture became conservative and turned in on itself.

The major contribution to Chinese arts during the Yuan was by dramatists, who combined poetic arias with vaudeville theater to produce a new operatic drama. Performed by traveling troupes, the operas relied on makeup, costumes, pantomime, and stylized gestures. The women's roles were usually played by men. Except for the

The Journey of Marco Polo. Marco Polo and companions en route to China on the Silk Road.
What role did travelers play in encouraging cross-cultural understanding or curiosity during the Yuan Dynasty?

arias—the highlights of the performance—the dramas used vernacular Chinese, appealing to a popular audience. Justice always triumphed, and the dramas usually ended happily. Yuan drama continued almost unchanged in later dynasties, and during the nineteenth century it merged with a form of southern Chinese theater to become today's Beijing Opera.

LAST YEARS OF THE YUAN

The Yuan was the shortest of China's major dynasties. Little more than a century elapsed between Kublai's move to Beijing in 1264 and the dynasty's collapse in 1368. After the rule of Kublai and his successor, a decline set in. By then, the Mongol Empire as a whole no longer lent strength to its parts. The khanates became separated by religion and culture as well as by distance. Tribesmen in Mongolia thought the great khans in Beijing had become too Chinese, while the court at Beijing never really gained legitimacy among the Chinese. When succession disputes, bureaucratic factionalism, and pitched battles between Mongol generals broke out, the Chinese showed little inclination to rally in support of the dynasty.

Problems arose in the countryside, too. Taxes were heavy, and some local officials were corrupt. The government issued excessive paper money and then refused to accept it in payment for taxes. The Yellow River changed its course, flooding the canals that carried grain to the capital. Further natural disasters during the 1350s led to popular uprisings. The White Lotus sect preached the coming of Maitreya. Regional military commanders, suppressing the rebellions, became warlords. Important economic regions were devastated and partially depopulated. At the end, a rebel army threatened Beijing, and the last Mongol emperor and his court fled on horses to Shangdu. When that city fell, they fled deeper into Mongolia.

SUMMARY

HOW DID the Sui and Tang dynasties re-create China's empire?

Reestablishment of Empire: Sui (589–618) and Tang (618–907) Dynasties. The Sui and Tang dynasties (589–907) reunited China's empire through strong leadership and military conquest. Under the Tang, China expanded into Central Asia. Chang'an, the Tang capital, became the largest city in the world. Tang culture was rich and cosmopolitan, much influenced by its contacts with other cultures and immensely influential on the cultures of Japan, Korea, and Vietnam. The Tang Dynasty was also the golden age of Buddhism in China, and a variety of Buddhist sects flourished. *page 195*

WHAT WAS the agricultural revolution that occurred during the Song Dynasty?

Transition to Late Imperial China: The Song Dynasty (960–1279). Under the Song Dynasty (960–1279), China experienced an agricultural revolution in which large aristocratic estates worked by serfs gave way to small landholdings owned by free farmers. New crops, water control, and fertilizers increased agricultural productivity. Advances in technology led to the invention of printing and the development of a coal and iron-smelting industry. The growth of a money economy encouraged the expansion of trade, both within China and with foreign countries. Song culture was particularly rich in philosophy, poetry, and painting. *page 205*

WHY WERE the Mongols able to establish such a vast empire?

China in the Mongol World Empire: The Yuan Dynasty (1279–1368). After their unification by Genghis Khan (1167–1227), the Mongols created the greatest empire in history. The highly mobile Mongol cavalry overwhelmed Chinese armies. By 1279 the Mongols ruled all of China. But Mongol rule in China was short-lived and enjoyed only shallow Chinese support. Mongol rule in China ended in 1368. *page 210*

KEY TERMS

Amitabha Buddha (p. 202)
censorate (p. 197)
Chang'an (p. 196)
examination system (p. 198)
imperial autocracy (p. 207)
Song commercial revolution (p. 206)
Uighur Turks (p. 200)
Zen (p. 202)

REVIEW QUESTIONS

1. In what ways did China and Europe parallel each other in their development until the sixth century C.E.? How did they diverge after that?

2. Are there similarities between the Qin–Han transition and that of the Sui–Tang? Between Han and Tang expansion and contraction?

3. How did the Chinese economy change from the Tang to the Northern Song to the Southern Song? How did the polity change? How did China's relationships to surrounding states change?

4. What do Chinese poetry and art tell us about Chinese society? What position did poets occupy in Chinese society?

5. Briefly describe the "dynastic cycle" and the "settled Chinese/steppe nomads" theories of Chinese history. What are the strengths and weaknesses of each theory? Is one more useful than the other?

6. Summarize significant developments in Chinese Buddhism during this period. What was the relationship between Buddhism and the state at various times? Between Buddhism and the elite?

7. What drove the Mongols to conquer most of the known world? How could their military accomplish the task? Once they conquered China, how did they rule it? What was the Chinese response to Mongol rule?

Note: To learn more about the topics in this chapter, please turn to the Suggested Readings at the end of the book. For additional sources related to this chapter please see www.myhistorylab.com

PEARSON myhistorylab Connections

Reinforce what you learned in this chapter by studying the many documents, images, maps, review tools, and videos available at **www.myhistorylab.com**

Read and Review

✓• Study and Review Chapter 8

Comparative Case Study: Women in the Imperial Courts of China and Japan, p. 199

•••• Read the Document   *Tang Daizong on the Art of Government, p. 198*

An Essay Question from the Chinese Imperial Examination System, p. 199

Chinese description of the Tibetans, p. 200

Ibn Wahab, an Arab merchant, visits Tang China, p. 201

T'ang Dynasty Poetry (8th century) Li Po, p. 203

Lu You, excerpt from Diary of a Journey to Sichuan, p. 203

Giovanni Di Piano Carpini on the Mongols, p. 211

Marco Polo at the Court of Kublai Khan, c. 1300, p. 214

The Mongols: An excerpt from the Novgorod Chronicle, 1315, p. 215

👁•See the Map   *China during the Sui and Tang Dynasties, p. 196*

China under Tang and Song Dynasties, p. 205

The Mongol Empire, 1206–1405, p. 214

👁•View the Image   *Court Lady Yang Guifei Mounting a Horse, p. 201*

Research and Explore

👁•Watch the Video   *Transit*

👁•See the Map   *The Mongol Empire of Chinggis Khan, ca. 1227, p. 211*

((•• Hear the Audio

Hear the audio file for Chapter 8
at **www.myhistorylab.com**

9
Early Japanese History

A twelfth-century Japanese fan. Superimposed on a painting of a gorgeously clad nobleman and his lady in a palace setting are verses in Chinese from a Buddhist sutra. The aesthetic pairing of sacred and secular was a feature of life at the Heian court. The fan could well have been used by a figure in Sei Shōnagon's *Pillow Book*.

What does the mix of cultural influences displayed here suggest about medieval Japan?

WHAT REVOLUTIONARY changes accompanied the Yayoi?

HOW DID Chinese culture influence Japan?

WHY CAN this period in Japan be described as feudal, and in what sense is this description misleading?

apanese history has three main turning points. Each was marked by a major influx of an outside culture, and each led to a massive restructuring of Japanese institutions. The first came during the third century B.C.E., when Old Stone Age Japan became an agricultural, metalworking society, similar to those on the Korean peninsula or in northeast Asia. The second came during the seventh and eighth centuries, when whole complexes of Chinese culture entered Japan directly. Absorbing these, archaic Japan made the leap to a higher historical civilization associated with the Chinese writing system, Chinese technologies and philosophies, and Chinese forms of Buddhism. Japan remained an independent part of this civilization for more than a millennium. The third turning point occurred in the nineteenth century, when Japan encountered the West. ∎

JAPANESE ORIGINS

THE JŌMON, JAPAN'S OLD STONE AGE

Japanese hotly debate their origins. New archaeological finds are front-page news. During the ice ages, Japan was connected by land bridges to Asia. Woolly mammoths entered the northern island of Hokkaido, and other continental fauna entered the lower islands. Did humans come, too? Because Japan's acidic volcanic soil eats up bones, there are no early skeletal remains. The earliest evidence of human habitation is finely shaped stone tools dating from about 30,000 B.C.E.

Then, from within this hunting and gathering society, in about 10,000 B.C.E., pottery developed. This is the oldest pottery in the world. Archaeologists are baffled by the appearance of pottery in an Old Stone Age hunting, gathering, and fishing society, when in all other early societies it developed along with agriculture as an aspect of New Stone Age culture. Japan's "Jōmon" society is named after the rope-like, cord-pattern (*jōmon*) designs on the pottery. Jōmon people lived in pit-dwellings with thatched roofs; population is extremely difficult to estimate, but there were probably about 200,000 of them.

THE YAYOI REVOLUTION

A second northeast Asian people began migrations down the Korean peninsula and across the Tsushima Straits to Japan from about 300 B.C.E. Their movement may have been caused by Chinese military activities. These people, called the Yayoi, were differ-

GLOBAL PERSPECTIVE

EAST ASIA

Heartland civilizations, as noted in Chapter 2, were few in number. Most of the world became "civilized" as the writing systems, philosophies, and technologies of the heartlands spread to adjacent areas. In East Asia, Chinese civilization spread to Japan, Korea, and Vietnam, just as in the West, the heartland civilization of the Middle East and Greece spread to Rome and Constantinople, and then to the rest of Europe. The transmission was faster in East Asia than in Europe because the early empire had been re-created by the Sui and Tang during the sixth century and was brilliantly vital, whereas the old Western Roman Empire lay in ruins.

When we speak of "East Asia," we refer as much to culture as to geography, to what Japan, Korea, and Vietnam had in common with China. They adopted Confucian and Buddhist teachings and with them conceptions of the universe, state, and human relations. They took in Chinese arts and technologies: painting, music, ceramics, criminal and civil law, medicine, and architecture. To the untutored Western eye, the paintings of China, Japan, and Korea often look much the same. They learned to write using Chinese characters. Since the languages of Japan, Korea, and Vietnam belonged to non-Chinese language families, it was initially as difficult for them to write in Chinese as It would be for us to write in Egyptian hieroglyphics.

We note, too, that Japan in the seventh and eighth centuries was not a blank slate onto which Chinese culture could be simply inscribed. Japan already had in place (and this is true for Korea and Vietnam as well) an agricultural economy, metalworking skills, settled village communities, and an archaic government. The appeal of Chinese civilization was irresistible, but specific needs and conditions shaped its adoption. For example, the archaic Yamato court found Chinese political institutions and tax systems useful in extending its control over outlying regions.

Mongolia, Central Asia, and Tibet stand in stark contrast to Japan, Korea, and Vietnam. Their climates were harsher, their agriculture more rudimentary, and their life-styles largely nomadic and pastoral. Despite their proximity to China and their frequent

Jōmon pottery figure. Did this bow-legged and somehow modern-looking statuette adorn an emperor's tomb in the period before 300 B.C.E.?

What is known about the Jōmon people?

ent from the Jōmon in language, appearance, and level of technology. There is no greater break in the entire Japanese record than that between the Jōmon and the Yayoi, for at the beginning of the third century B.C.E., the bronze, iron, and agricultural revolutions—which in the Near East, India, and China had been separated by thousands of years and each of which on its own had wrought profound transformations—entered Japan simultaneously.

It is uncertain whether the Yayoi came as a trickle and were absorbed—the predominant view in Japan—or whether they came in sufficient numbers to push back the indigenous Jōmon people. DNA studies suggest that modern Japanese and Koreans are closer to the Yayoi than to the Jōmon. In any case, Yayoi culture rapidly replaced that of the Jōmon as far east as the present-day city of Nagoya and diffused more slowly into eastern Japan, where conditions were less favorable for agriculture. Early Yayoi "frontier settlements" were located next to their fields. Their agriculture was primitive. By the first century C.E., the expanding Yayoi population led to wars for the best land. Villages were relocated to defensible positions on low hills away from the fields. A more peaceful order of regional tribal confederations and a ruling class of aristocratic warriors emerged. Late Yayoi excavations once again reveal villages alongside fields and far fewer stone axes.

During the third century C.E. a queen named Pimiko achieved a temporary hegemony over a number of regional tribal confederations. A Chinese chronicle describes Pimiko as a shaman, mature but unmarried. After Pimiko, references to Japan disappeared from the Chinese dynastic histories for a century and a half.

TOMB CULTURE, THE YAMATO STATE, AND KOREA

Emerging directly from Yayoi culture was an era (300–600 C.E.) characterized by giant tomb mounds. (They still dot the landscape near present-day Osaka.) The tombs, patterned on those in Korea, were circular mounds of earth built atop megalithic burial chambers. Like the Yayoi graves that preceded them, early tombs contained mirrors, jewels, and other ceremonial objects. Starting in the fifth century C.E., these objects were replaced by armor, swords, and military trappings,

contacts with it, they were unable or unwilling to adopt its advanced civilization. In effect, on the steppe to the north and west, the Chinese seed fell upon stony places and was scorched or withered away. But in the agricultural lands of Japan, Korea, and Vietnam, it fell on good ground and brought forth fruit.

The difference had consequences. It seems paradoxical that Japan, Korea, and Vietnam, which took in Chinese civilization, became independent nations in recent times, whereas Tibet, Central Asia, and part of Mongolia, which refused Chinese civilization, eventually became a part of China. This is largely because they were at a lower level of development and unable to resist Chinese aggression. But also important is the fact that those countries that took in Chinese political culture used it to develop their own political identities. The self-awareness they developed as a people contributed to their emergence as independent nations. Their feelings toward China were also ambivalent—like those of Westernizing Third World countries toward the West.

Of the countries that took in Chinese civilization, Korea and Vietnam (which will be treated in Chapter 18) were closer to China for longer periods of time and had, as a result, a stronger Chinese imprint. Japan was the most distant, and also the largest and the most populous; consequently it became the most distinctive variant within East Asia. Its literature and arts were brilliant and diverse. Its history was a continuous progression, quite unlike the sequence of dynasties in China.

Focus Questions

- How does Japanese history illustrate the relationship between a "heartland civilization" and adjacent areas?

- Why did Korea, Vietnam, and Japan become independent nations in recent times? What other nations on the periphery of China did not?

reflecting a new wave of continental influences. The flow of people and culture from the Korean peninsula into Japan that began with Yayoi was continuous into historical times.

Japan reappeared in the Chinese chronicles in the fifth century C.E. This period was also covered in the earliest Japanese accounts of their own history, compiled in 712 and 720. These records describe regional aristocracies under the loose hegemony of the "great kings," whose courts were located on the fertile Yamato plain. Regional rulers held parallel political authority over their populations, as can be seen in the spread of tomb mounds for aristocrats throughout Japan. The court was the scene of incessant power struggles. Rebellions were frequent during the fifth and sixth centuries, and there were constant wars with "barbarian tribes" in southern Kyushu and eastern Honshu on the frontiers of "civilized" Japan.

The basic social unit of Yamato aristocratic society was the extended family (*uji*). Groups of specialist workers called *be* were attached to aristocratic families. There was a small class of slaves, but many peasants were neither slaves nor members of aristocratic clans or specialized workers' groups.

Relations with Korea were critical to the Yamato Court. During the fifth and sixth centuries, a three-cornered military balance developed on the Korean peninsula between the state of Paekche in the southwest, Silla in the east, and Koguryo in the north (see Map 9-1 on page 222). Japan was an ally of Paekche and maintained extensive trade and military relations with a weak southern federation known as the Kaya States. Imported iron weapons and tools gave the Yamato military strength. Korean immigrant artisans increased the court's wealth and influence. The first elements of Chinese culture entered Japan through Paekche: Chinese writing was adopted for the transcription of Japanese names during the fifth or sixth century; Confucianism entered in 513, when Paekche sent a "scholar of the Five Classics"; Buddhism arrived in 538 when a Paekche king sent a Buddha image, sutras, and possibly a priest.

C H R O N O L O G Y

EARLY JAPANESE HISTORY

8000–300 B.C.E.	Jōmon culture
Early Continental Influences	
300 B.C.E.–300 C.E.	Yayoi culture
300–680 C.E.	Tomb culture and the Yamato state
680–850 C.E.	Chinese Tang pattern in Nara and Early Heian Japan

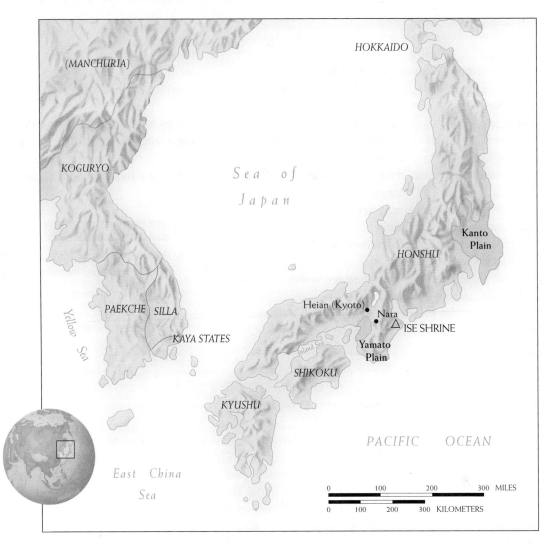

MAP 9–1. Yamato Japan and Korea (ca. 500 C.E.) Paekche was Japan's ally on the Korean peninsula. Silla, Japan's enemy, was the state that would eventually unify Korea. (*Note:* Nara was founded in 710; Heian in 794.)

How did Japan's proximity to Korea and China influence its cultural development?

Eventually the political balance on the Korean peninsula shifted. In 532 Paekche turned against Japan. In 660 Silla, always hostile to Japan, unified the peninsula. But by this time Japan had established direct relations with China.

RELIGION IN EARLY JAPAN

The indigenous religion of the Yamato Japanese was an animistic worship of the forces of nature, later given the name of **Shintō**, or "the way of the gods," to distinguish it from Buddhism. Shintō probably entered Japan as part of Yayoi culture. The underlying forces of nature might be embodied in a waterfall, a twisted tree, a strangely shaped boulder, or a great leader who would be worshiped as a deity after his death. The more potent forces of nature became personified as deities. The sensitivity to nature and natural beauty that pervades Japanese art and poetry owes much to Shintō. Most villages had shamans, female or male religious specialists who, by entering a trance, could directly contact the inner forces of nature and gain the power to foretell the future or heal sickness.

Shintō

"The way of the gods." The animistic worship of the forces of nature that is the indigenous religion of Japan.

The Itsukashima Shrine. On the little island of Miyajima not far from Hiroshima is the lovely Itsukashima shrine dedicated to the daughters of the Shintō god of the moon and oceans. Its outer gate (*torii*) is constructed of camphor logs to resist the salt water. Originally built in the late sixth century, it was rebuilt in the sixteenth.

What does the location of this shrine suggest about how the shrine is meant to be used?

Early Shintō was connected with the state. Each clan had its own nature deity (*kami*) that it claimed as its original ancestor. When Japan was unified by the Yamato court, the myths of several clans were joined into a composite national myth. The deity of the Yamato great kings was the sun goddess, so she became the chief deity. The earliest Japanese histories, the earliest telling of the creation of Japan, switch mid-volume from stories of the gods, interspersed with the genealogies of noble families, to stories of early emperors and events in early Japan. The Japanese emperors, today the oldest royal family in the world, were viewed as the lineal descendants of the sun goddess and as "living gods." Other gods assumed lesser positions appropriate to the status of their clan. The Great Shrine of the sun goddess at Ise has always been the most important in Japan. (See Document, "Darkness and the Cave of High Heaven," on page 224.)

NARA AND HEIAN JAPAN

The second major turning point in Japanese history was the inflow of Chinese civilization between the seventh and twelfth centuries. Roughly speaking, until almost the end of the seventh century the Japanese studied China; during the eighth they implanted Chinese institutions; after that, they modified the institutions to meet Japanese needs. By the eleventh century the creative reworking of Chinese elements had led to distinctive Japanese forms, unlike those of China but equally unlike those of the earlier Yamato court.

HOW DID Chinese culture influence Japan?

COURT GOVERNMENT

The regular embassies to the Tang court that began in 607 C.E. included traders, students, and Buddhist monks as well as representatives of the Yamato great kings. Like Third World students who study abroad today, Japanese who studied in China played key roles in their own government when they returned home. They brought back with them a quickening flow of technology, art, Buddhism, and knowledge of Tang legal and governmental systems. But for Yamato Japanese, the difficulties of mastering Chinese and China's philosophical culture were enormous. Prince Shōtoku (574–622) adopted the Chinese calendar and promulgated Chinese and Buddhist ideas. Fujiwara Kamatari (614–669) at mid-seventh century attempted more extensive reforms, though only a few were realized. Large-scale institutional changes using the Tang model began only in the 680s with the Emperor Temmu and his successor, the Empress Jitō (r. 686–697).

Temmu's life illustrates the interplay between Japanese power politics and the adoption of Chinese institutions. He usurped the throne from his nephew and then used

DOCUMENT

Darkness and the Cave of High Heaven

The younger brother of the sun goddess was a mischief-maker. Eventually the gods drove him out of heaven. On one occasion, he knocked a hole in the roof of a weaving hall and dropped in a dappled pony that he had skinned alive. One weaving maiden was so startled that she struck her genitals with the shuttle she was using and died.

- **Entering** a cave and then reemerging signifies death and rebirth in the religions of many peoples. What does this myth suggest regarding the social relations of the Shintō gods?

The Sun Goddess, terrified at the sight, opened the door of the heavenly rock cave, and hid herself inside. Then the Plain of High Heaven was shrouded in darkness, as was the Central Land of the Reed Plains [Japan]. An endless night prevailed. The cries of the myriad gods were like the buzzing of summer flies, and myriad calamities arose.

The eight hundred myriad gods assembled in the bed of the Quiet River of Heaven. They asked one god to think of a plan. They assembled the long-singing birds of eternal night and made them sing. They took hard rocks from the bed of the river and iron from the Heavenly Metal Mountain and called in a smith to make a mirror. They asked the Jewel Ancestor God to make a string of 500 curved jewels eight feet long. They asked other gods to remove the shoulder blade of a male deer, to obtain cherry wood from Mount Kagu, and to perform a divination. They uprooted a sacred tree, attached the string of curved jewels to its upper branches, hung the large mirror from its middle branches, and suspended offerings of white and blue cloth from its lower branches.

One god held these objects as grand offerings and another intoned sacred words. The Heavenly Hand-Strong-Male God stood hidden beside the door. A goddess bound up her sleeves with clubmoss from Mount Kagu, made a herb band from the spindle-tree, and bound together leaves of bamboograss to hold in her hands. Then she placed a wooden box face down before the rock cave, stamped on it until it resounded, and, as if possessed, she exposed her breasts and pushed her skirt-band down to her genitals. The Plain of High Heaven shook as the myriad gods broke into laughter.

The Sun Goddess, thinking this strange, opened slightly the rock-cave door and said from within: "Since I have hidden myself, I thought that the Plain of Heaven and the Central Land of the Reed Plains would all be in darkness. Why is it that the goddess makes merry and the myriad gods all laugh?"

The goddess replied: "We rejoice and are glad because there is here a god greater than you." While she spoke two other gods brought out the mirror and held it up before the Sun Goddess.

The Sun Goddess, thinking this stranger and stranger, came out the door and peered into the mirror. Then the heavenly Hand-Strong-Male God seized her hand and pulled her out. Another god drew a rope behind her and said: "You may not go back further than this."

So when the Sun Goddess had come forth, the Plain of High Heaven and the Central Land of the Reed Plains once again naturally shone in brightness.

Source: From the *Records of Ancient Matters (Kojiki)*, trans. by Albert Craig, with appreciation to Basil Hall Chamberlain and Donald L. Phillippi.

Tennō

"Heavenly emperor." The official title of the emperor of Japan.

Chinese systems to consolidate his power. He promulgated a Chinese-type law code that greatly augmented the powers of the ruler. He styled himself as the "heavenly emperor," or *tennō*, replacing the title of "great king."

Until the eighth century the capital was usually moved each time an emperor died. Then in 710 a new capital, laid out on a grid like the Chinese capital, Chang'an, was established at Nara. The capital was moved again in 784, and yet again in 794 to Heian (later Kyoto). This site remained the capital until the move to Tokyo in 1869. The superimposition of a Chinese-type capital on a still backward Japan produced a stark contrast. In the villages, peasants—who worshiped the forces in mountains and trees—lived in pit dwellings and either planted in

crude paddy fields or used slash-and-burn techniques of dry-land farming. In the capital, pillared palaces housed the emperor and nobles, descended from the gods on high. They drank wine, wore silk, and enjoyed the paintings, perfumes, and pottery of the Tang. Clustered about the capital were Buddhist temples with soaring pagodas and sweeping tile roofs.

Governments at the Nara and Heian courts were headed by emperors, who were simultaneously Confucian rulers with the majesty accorded by Chinese law and Shintō rulers descended from the sun goddess. Protected by an aura of the sacred, their lineage retained power throughout the rest of Japanese history, though several emperors were killed and replaced by other family members.

Beneath the emperor, the same modified Chinese pattern prevailed. At the top was a Council of State, a powerful office from which leading clans sometimes manipulated authority. Beneath the council were eight ministries—two more than in China. (The extras were a Secretariat and the Imperial Household Ministry.) Local government was handled by sixty-odd provinces, which were further subdivided into districts and villages. In other respects, Japanese court government was unlike that of China. There were no eunuchs and little tension between the emperor and the bureaucracy—the main struggles were between clans. The Tang movement from aristocracy toward meritocracy was also absent in Japan. Family counted for more than grades. A feeble attempt to establish a Chinese-style examination elite failed.

Even during the Nara period the elaborate apparatus of Chinese government was too much. China had a population of 60 million; Nara Japan had 4 or 5 million. With fewer people to govern in Japan and no external enemies, court government focused on care of the imperial house. In the early Heian period, three new departments outside the Chinese system handled most of the functions of government: an office of auditors handled taxation, a bureau of archivists exercised executive power through the drafting of decrees, and police commissioners enforced laws and maintained order in the capital. Power shifted during the Heian period but always revolved around the emperor. Until the mid-ninth century, some emperors ruled directly. In 856, the northern branch of the Fujiwara clan began to establish a stranglehold on power that was not broken until the last half of the eleventh century. In 1072, the Emperor Shirakawa regained control of the government and strengthened the imperial family, but by then the capital was increasingly isolated, and threatening developments were taking place in the countryside.

PEOPLE, LAND, AND TAXES

The life of the common people of Japan remained harsh during the Nara and Heian periods. Estimates of the early Nara population suggest slightly more than 5 million persons; by the end of the Heian period, almost half a millennium later, the number had increased, scholars estimate, to only about 6 million. Why had population not grown more during these fairly peaceful centuries? One factor is that agricultural technology improved only slowly. Metals were still scarce, and wooden plow blades were still in use. Another factor was the frequency of droughts and famines. A third was the effect of continental germs—introduced by embassies or later commercial relations—on a previously isolated Japanese population that had not yet developed immunities. Periodic epidemics swept the court and village communities alike.

Taxes weighed heavily on village populations. In Nara and early Heian Japan, the economy was agricultural. The problem for peasants was to obtain land. The problem for the government, imperial family, nobles, and temples was to find labor to work their extensive landholdings. Japan attempted a solution, using China's so-called equal field system to distribute land to all able-bodied persons and collect from them three

Prince Shōtoku (574–622). A commanding figure at the pre-Nara Yamato court, Prince Shōtoku (shown here with two of his sons) promoted Buddhism and began regular embassies to China. "This world is a lie," he wrote, reflecting the Buddhist belief in an ultimate reality beyond.

How did embassies to China contribute to Japanese culture?

((•—Hear the Audio
at **myhistorylab.com**

In the Heiji War of 1159–1160, regional samurai bands became involved in Kyoto court politics. This is a scroll painting of the burning of the Sanjō Palace.

Handscroll; ink and colors on paper. "Scroll w/depictions of the Night Attack on the Sanjō Palace" from Heiji monogatari emaki, 2nd half of the 13th century.Unknown. Japanese,Kamakura Period.Handscroll; ink & colors on paper.41.3 x 699.7 cm. Fenollosa-Weld C. Photograph © 2007 Courtesy Museum of Fine Arts, Boston.

Did the existence of samurai make Japan "feudal"?

samurai
Professional Japanese warriors.

Read the Document
Murasaki Shikibu, selections from the *Tale of Genji* at **myhistorylab.com**

taxes: a light tax of grain, a light tax of cloth or other local products, and a heavy tax of labor service. But this necessitated elaborate population and land registers. Even in China, with its sophisticated bureaucracy, the system broke down.

The Heian discarded the complex equal field system, and court officials simply gave each governor a quota of taxes to collect from his province. Each governor, in turn, gave quotas to the district magistrates. Governors and magistrates, when they could, collected more than their quotas and pocketed the difference. This surplus collection funded a new local ruling class.

Court nobles and powerful temples used their influence at court to obtain exemptions from taxation for their lands. About half the land in late Heian Japan was converted from tax-paying lands to tax-free estates. Even small landholders often commended their land to nobles, figuring they would be better off as serfs on tax-free estates than as free farmers subject to taxation. The pattern of commendations was random, resulting in estates composed of scattered parcels of land. Noble estate owners appointed stewards from among local notables to manage the land in exchange for a small slice of the cultivators' surplus. Stewards and district magistrates shared an interest in upholding the local order.

RISE OF THE SAMURAI

Nara Japan experimented with a Chinese military system based on conscription, but it proved inefficient. In 792, the court ended conscription and established a system of mounted warriors whose taxes were remitted in exchange for military service. They were stationed in the capital and in the provinces. The Japanese verb "to serve" is *samurau,* so those who served became known as **samurai.** Nonofficial private bands of local warriors replaced the official appointees in the mid-Heian period, and they constituted Japan's military until the fifteenth and sixteenth centuries, when foot soldiers became the core of the military.

Being a samurai was expensive. Horses, armor, and weapons were costly, and their use required long training. The primary weapon was the bow and arrow, used from the saddle. Most samurai were from well-to-do local families. Their initial function was to preserve local order and, possibly, to help with tax collection. But they contributed at times to disorder. From the second half of the ninth century there are accounts of district magistrates leading local forces against provincial governors, doubtless in connection with tax disputes.

Regional military coalitions or confederations first broke into history from 935 to 940, when a regional military leader, a descendant of an emperor, became involved in a tax dispute. He captured several provinces and called himself the new emperor. The Kyoto court responded by recruiting another military band to quell the rebellion. Other regional wars followed, and by the middle of the twelfth century there were regional military bands in every part of Japan. A power struggle at court in 1156 enabled a band led by Taira Kiyomori to seize control of Kyoto and the emperor. But, like the earlier Fujiwara family, he did not change the system. He only imposed a new stratum atop the many power centers already established at court.

ARISTOCRATIC CULTURE AND BUDDHISM

Shintō religious practices and village folkways, an extension of the culture of the late Yamato period, were among the most significant elements of the culture of Nara and early Heian Japan. The tiny aristocracy, about one-tenth of 1 percent of Japan's population, was encapsulated in the routines of court life, most of which had only recently

been imported from China. This cultural gap helps explain why aristocrats found commoners incomprehensible and hardly human. The writings of courtiers reflect little sympathy for the suffering and hardships of the people.

Heian high culture, like a hothouse plant, was protected by the political influence of the court. It was nourished by tax revenues and income from estates. Aristocrats created canons of elegance and taste that are striking even today. The speed with which Tang culture was assimilated and reworked was amazing.

CHINESE TRADITION IN JAPAN

Education at the Nara and Heian courts was largely a matter of reading Chinese books and acquiring the skills needed to compose poetry and prose in Chinese. These were daunting tasks, both because there was no tradition of scholarship in Japan and because the two languages were so dissimilar. But the challenge was met. From the Nara period until the nineteenth century, most philosophical and legal writings, as well as most of the histories, essays, and religious texts in Japan, were written in Chinese. Original Chinese works became part of the Japanese cultural tradition. Chinese history became the mirror in which Japan saw itself, despite the differences between the two societies. Buddhist stories and the books of Confucianism also became Japanese classics. A Western parallel might be the role that "foreign books," such as the Bible and works of Plato and Aristotle, played in medieval and Renaissance England.

BIRTH OF JAPANESE LITERATURE

The first major anthology of poems written in Japanese was the *Collection of Ten Thousand Leaves (Man'yōshū)*, compiled in about 760. It contained 4,516 poems. They reveal a deep sensitivity to nature and strong human relationships between husband and wife, parents and children. They also display a love for the land of Japan and links to a Shintō past.

An early obstacle to the development of Japanese poetry was the difficulty of transcribing Japanese sounds. In the *Ten Thousand Leaves*, Chinese characters were used as phonetic symbols, but there was no standardization. A new syllabic script, *kana*, was developed during the ninth century, which led to the brilliant literature of the Heian period. The greatest works were by Sei Shōnagon and Murasaki Shikibu, daughters of provincial officials serving at the Heian court. The *Pillow Book* of Sei Shōnagon contains sharp, satirical, amusing essays and literary jottings that reveal the demanding aristocratic taste of the early-eleventh-century Heian court.

The Tale of Genji, written by Murasaki Shikibu in about 1010, was the world's first novel. *Genji* is a work of originality and acute psychological delineation of character, for which there was no Chinese model. It tells of the life, loves, and sorrows of Prince Genji, the son of an imperial concubine, and, after his death, of his son Kaoru. The novel spans three quarters of a century and is quasi-historical in nature.

NARA AND HEIAN BUDDHISM

Buddhism came to Japan from China. The Six Sects of the Nara period each represented a separate doctrinal position within Mahayana Buddhism. As in China, monasteries and temples were tied closely to the state. Tax revenues supported them, and monks prayed for the health of the emperor and for rain in time of drought.

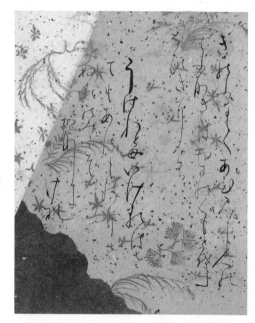

An Album Leaf from the Ishiyama-gire. A part of a collection from the works of thirty-six poets compiled in the early twelfth century. The poem is by Ki no Tsurayuki (868?–945?), who in the preface to another anthology wrote: "The poetry of Japan has its roots in the human heart and flourishes in the countless leaves of words. . . . Hearing the warbler sing among the blossoms and the frog in his fresh waters—is there any living being not given to song? It is poetry which, without exertion, moves heaven and earth, stirs the feelings of gods and spirits invisible to the eye, softens the relations between men and women, calms the hearts of fierce warriors." The calligraphy is by Fujiwara no Sadanobu (1088–1154). The poem is written on layered rice paper with gold and silver and foliage designs. Even to the untutored eye, the effect is elegant.

Calligraphy attributed to Fujiwara no Sadanobu. Album leaf from the "Ishiyama-gire." Heian, period, early 12th century. Ink with gold and silver on decorated and collaged paper, 8 x 6 3/8 in. (20.3 x 16.1 cm). Courtesy of The Freer Gallery of Art, Smithsonian Institution, Washington, DC.

Who wrote Japanese poetry in this period? Who read it?

OVERVIEW   Development of Japanese Writing

No two languages could be more different than Chinese and Japanese. Chinese is monosyllabic, uninflected, and tonal. Japanese is polysyllabic, highly inflected, and atonal. To adopt Chinese writing for use in Japanese was thus no easy task. What the Japanese did at first—when they were not simply learning to write in Chinese—was to use certain Chinese ideographs as a phonetic script. For example, in the *Man'yōshū*, the eighth-century poetic anthology, *shira-nami* (white wave) was written with 之 for shi, for 良 ra, for 奈 na, and for 美 mi. Over several centuries, these phonetic ideographs evolved into a unique Japanese phonetic script:

Original Chinese Ideograph	Simplified Ideograph	Phonetic Script (Kana)
之		し
良		ら
奈		な
美		み

(((•→ Hear the Audio at **myhistorylab.com**

The above examples show how the original ideograph was first simplified according to the rules of calligraphy and was then further simplified into a phonetic script known as *kana*. In modern Japanese, Chinese ideographs are used for nouns, verb stems, and adjectives, and the phonetic script is used for inflections and particles.

学生 は 図書館 へ 行きました Student/as for/library/to/went. (The student went to the library.)

In the above sentence, the Chinese ideographs are the forms with many strokes, and the phonetic script is shown in the simpler, cursive form.

•◦•→ Read the Document
Buddhism in Japan: The Taika Reform Edicts at **myhistorylab.com**

The Hōryūji Temple. Built by Prince Shōtoku in 607, it contains the oldest wooden buildings in the world. They are the best surviving examples of contemporary Chinese Buddhist architecture.

How did Buddhism evolve as it was assimilated into Japanese culture?

The Japanese came to Buddhism from the magic and mystery of Shintō, so Buddhism's appeal lay in its colorful and elaborate rituals, the beauty of its art, and the gods, demons, and angels of the Mahayana pantheon. The mastery of the philosophy took longer. But since Buddhism was no more foreign to Japan than Confucianism and the rest of the Chinese culture that had helped reshape the Japanese identity, there was no bias against it. Consequently, Buddhism entered deeply into Japanese culture and retained its vitality longer than in China.

The great Buddhist sects of the Heian era were Tendai and Shingon. The monk Saichō (767–822) went to China in 804 and returned the following year with the teachings of the Tendai sect (*Tiantai* in Chinese). He preached that salvation was for all who led lives of contemplation and moral purity. He instituted strict rules and a twelve-year training curriculum for novice monks at his mountain monastery. Over the next few centuries the sect grew until thousands of temples had been built on Mount Hiei, which remained a center of Japanese Buddhism until it was destroyed in the wars of the sixteenth century. Many later Japanese sects emerged from within the Tendai fold, stressing one or another doctrine of its syncretic teachings.

The Shingon sect was begun by Kûkai (774–835), an extraordinary figure: a poet, artist, and one of three great calligraphers of the period, who is sometimes credited with inventing the *kana* syllabary and with introducing tea into Japan. Kûkai went to China with Saichō in 804 and returned two years later bearing the Shingon doctrines. Shingon doctrines center on an eternal and cosmic Buddha, of whom all other Buddhas are manifestations. *Shingon* means "true word" or "mantra," a verbal formula

with mystical powers. It is sometimes called esoteric Buddhism because it had secret teachings that were passed from master to disciple. In China, Shingon was persecuted and died out, but it was tremendously successful in Japan.

During the later Heian period, Buddhism began to be assimilated. Folk Shintō took in Buddhist elements, while in elite culture, Shintō was almost entirely absorbed by Buddhism. Shintō deities came to be seen as the local manifestations of universal Buddhas. Often great Buddhist temples had smaller Shintō shrines on their grounds. The Buddha watched over Japan and the cosmos; the shrine deity guarded the temple itself. Not until the mid-nineteenth century was Shintō disentangled from Buddhism, and then it occurred for political ends.

JAPAN'S EARLY FEUDAL AGE

The late twelfth century marked the shift from centuries of rule by a civil aristocracy to centuries of rule by military nobles. It saw the formation of the *bakufu* ("tent government"), a completely non-Chinese type of government. During this time the **shōgun** emerged as the de facto ruler of Japan, although in theory he was a military official of the emperor. New cultural forms emerged, along with changes in family and social organization.

THE KAMAKURA ERA

After Taira Kiyomori seized Kyoto in 1160, other bands still flourished elsewhere in Japan. The Taira, assuming their tutelage over the court would endure, embraced Kyoto's elegant lifestyle, but the Minamoto were rebuilding their strength in eastern Japan. In 1180 Minamoto Yoritomo (1147–1199) seized control of eastern Japan and began the war that ended in 1185 with the downfall of the Taira.

Yoritomo's victory was national. Warriors from every area vied to become his vassals. Yoritomo set up his headquarters at Kamakura, 30 miles south of present-day Tokyo, at the edge of his base of power in eastern Japan (see Map 9–2 on page 230). He called his government the *bakufu* in contrast to the civil government in Kyoto. The offices he established were few and practical and staffed by his vassals. The decisions of these offices were codified in 1232 as the Jōei Code. Yoritomo also appointed military governors in each province and military stewards on the former estates of the Taira and others who had fought against him. These appointments carried the right to some income from the land. The remainder of the income, as earlier, went to Kyoto as taxes or as revenues to the owners of the estates.

When Yoritomo died in 1199, his widow and her Hōjō kinsmen moved to usurp the power of the Minamoto house. The widow, having taken holy orders after her husband's death, was known as the Nun Shōgun. One of her sons was pushed aside. The other became shōgun but was murdered in 1219. After that, the Hōjō ruled as regents for a puppet shōgun, just as the Fujiwara had been regents for figurehead emperors. The Kyoto court led an armed uprising against Kamakura in 1221, but it was quickly suppressed. The Kamakura vassals had become loyal to the *bakufu*, which guaranteed their income from land; their personal loyalty to the Minamoto had ended with the death of Yoritomo.

THE MONGOLS

In 1266 Kublai Khan (see Chapter 8) sent envoys demanding that Japan submit to his rule. The Hōjō at Kamakura refused. The first Mongol invasion fleet arrived in 1274 with 30,000 troops but withdrew after initial victories. The Mongols again sent envoys; this time, they were beheaded. A second invasion of 140,000 troops, an amphibious

WHY CAN this period in Japan be described as feudal, and in what ways is this description misleading?

bakufu
"Tent government." The military regime that governed Japan under the shōguns.

shōgun
A military official who was the actual ruler of Japan in the emperor's name from the late 1100s until the mid-nineteenth century.

Minamoto Yoritomo. Founder of the Kamakura Shogunate. He is depicted here in court robes as a statesman and official though he was, above all, a warrior-general.

Why might Minamoto Yoritomo have wanted to present himself in civilian official dress?

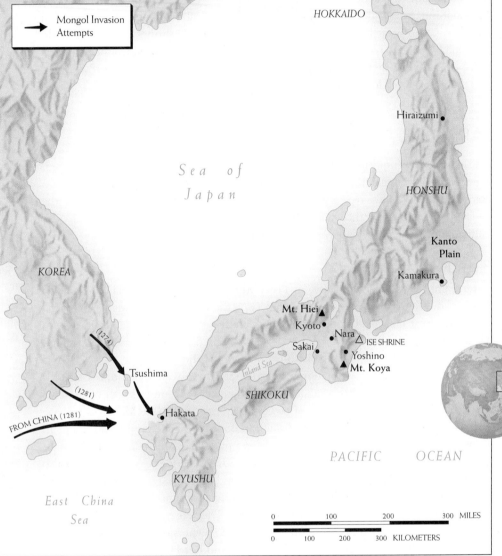

MAP EXPLORATION

To explore this map further, go to **http://www.myhistorylab.com**

MAP 9–2. Medieval Japan and the Mongol Invasions. The *bakufu* at Kamakura and the court at Kyoto were the two centers of power during the Kamakura period, 1185–1333. After 1336 the Ashika-ga *bakufu* was established in Kyoto, absorbing the powers of the court.

What geographic features do Kyoto and Kamakura share? From a geographic point of view, how do these locations differ?

See the Map

Medieval Japan and the Mongol Invasions at **myhistorylab.com**

kamikaze
"Divine winds" that sank a portion of the invading Mongol fleet in Japan in 1281.

force on a scale unprecedented in world history, arrived in 1281, two years after Kublai had completed his conquest of southern China. With gunpowder bombs and phalanx-es of archers protected by a forward wall of soldiers carrying overlapping shields, the Mongol forces overmatched the Japanese tactics of fierce individual combat. But a wall of stone had been erected along the curved shoreline of Hakata Bay in northwestern Kyushu, and the Mongols were held off for two months until **kamikaze**, or "divine

winds," sank a portion of their fleet and forced the rest to withdraw. Preparations for a third expedition ended with Kublai's death in 1294. The burden of repelling the Mongols fell on Kamakura's vassals in Kyushu. But as no land was taken, there were few rewards for those who had fought, and dissatisfaction was rife.

THE QUESTION OF FEUDALISM

Scholars often contend that Yoritomo's rule marks the start of feudalism in Japan. Feudalism may be defined in terms of three criteria: lord–vassal relationships, fiefs given in return for military service, and a warrior ethic. Can Kamakura Japan be described in these terms?

Certainly, the mounted warriors who made up the armies of Yoritomo were predominantly his vassals, not his kin. As for fiefs, the answer is ambiguous. Kamakura vassals received rights to income from land in exchange for military service, but the income was usually a slice of the surplus from the estates of Kyoto nonmilitary aristocrats. Fiefs, as such, did not appear until the late fifteenth century.

There is no ambiguity, however, regarding the warrior ethic, which had been developing among regional military bands for several centuries before 1185. The samurai prized martial qualities such as bravery, cunning, physical strength, and endurance. They gave their swords names. Their sports were hunting, hawking, and archery. Warriors thought of themselves as a military aristocracy that practiced the "way of the bow and arrow."

But warrior bands were only part of society. Kamakura Japan still had two political centers: The *bakufu* had military authority, while the Kyoto court continued the late Heian pattern of civil rule. Yoritomo's vassal band was small, numbering perhaps 2,000 before 1221 and 3,000 thereafter, mostly concentrated in eastern Japan. The local social order of the late Heian era continued, and Kamakura vassals depended on the cooperation of existing power holders. In short, while the Kamakura vassals themselves could be called feudal, they were only a thin skin on the surface of a society constructed according to older principles.

THE ASHIKAGA ERA

At times, formal political institutions seem rocklike in their stability, and history unfolds within the framework they provide. Then, almost as if a kaleidoscope had been shaken, the old institutions collapse and are swept away. In their place appear new institutions and new patterns of personal relations that, often enough, had begun to take shape within the confines of the old. It is not easy to explain the timing of such upheavals, but they are easy to recognize. One occurred in Japan between 1331 and 1336.

By 1331, various tensions had developed within Kamakura society. Because the patrimony of a warrior was divided among his children, vassals became poorer over time. Kamakura vassals were dissatisfied with the Hōjō monopolization of key *bakufu* posts. While the ties of vassals to Kamakura weakened, the ties to other warriors within their region grew stronger until new regional bands were ready to emerge. The precipitating event was a revolt in 1331 by an emperor who thought emperors should actually rule. Kamakura sent Ashikaga Takauji (1305–1358), the head of a branch family of the Minamoto line, to put down the revolt; instead he joined it. Other regional lords then rose up and destroyed the Hōjō *bakufu* in Kamakura.

What emerged from the confusion of the period from 1331 to 1336 was a new *bakufu* in Kyoto and semiautonomous regional states in the rest of Japan.

CHRONOLOGY

GOVERNMENT BY MILITARY HOUSES

1160–1180	Taira rule in Kyoto
1185–1333 KAMAKURA *BAKUFU*	
1185	Founded by Minamoto Yoritomo
1219	Usurped by Hōjō
1221	Armed uprising by Kyoto court
1232	Formation of Jōei Code
1274 and 1281	Invasions by Mongols
1336–1467 ASHIKAGA *BAKUFU*	
1336-1392	Southern Court
1467	Start of Warring States period

QUICK REVIEW

Mongol Invasion

◆ 1266: Kublai Khan demands Japan submit to his rule

◆ 1274: Invasion fleet withdraws after initial victories

◆ 1281: Huge invasion force destroyed by *kamikaze*, or "divine winds"

Japanese Sword.
From medieval times, Japanese artisans have made the world's finest swords. They became a staple export to China. Worn only by samurai, they were also an emblem of class status, distinguishing the warriors from commoners.

Who were the samurai, and what roles did they play in Japanese history?

A Closer Look

The East Meets the East

Mongols invaded Japan in 1274 and 1281. Battles were fought. The invaders were eventually routed by typhoons known as kamikaze or "divine winds."

Takezaki Suenaga, one hand on the reins and one on his bow, fights bravely against the Mongol invaders. He wears armor of braided plates and helmet, and presses on despite the wounds suffered by his horse. (He later commissioned the scroll, as a record of his exploits, to be passed down to his descendants.)

Mongol warriors, bearing composite bows and spears, continue their attack, despite the shower of Japanese arrows. One Mongol, struck by an arrow, turns away.

"A bomb bursting in air." Gunpowder was invented in Song China in about 1000 C.E. and quickly gave rise to a variety of weapons. Song Chinese used these weapons when the Mongols invaded China, and the Mongols used them when they invaded Japan.

Questions

1. Why did the Mongols invade Japan?
2. How did the Japanese respond?
3. What does this picture reveal?

myhistorylab To examine this image in an interactive fashion, please go to **www.myhistorylab.com**

---

daimyo
Lords who owned vast estates and held regional power.

Each regional state was governed by a lord, now called a **daimyo**, and a small warrior band. The *bakufu* offices established by Ashikaga Takauji were simple and functional: a samurai office for police and military matters; an administrative office for financial matters; a documents office for land records; and a judicial board to settle disputes. They were staffed by Takauji's vassals. The *bakufu* also appointed vassals to watch over its interests in the far north, in eastern Japan, and in Kyushu.

The pattern of rule in the outlying regions was diverse. All regional lords or daimyo were the vassals of the shōgun, but the relationship was often nominal. The relationship between the *bakufu* and regional lords fluctuated from 1336 to 1467. The third shōgun, for example, tightened his grip on the Kyoto court, improved relations with the great Buddhist temples and Shintō shrines, and established ties with Ming China. His military campaigns dented the autonomy of regional lords. But even the third shōgun had to rely on his daimyo and their armies. To strengthen them for campaigns, he gave them new authority, which created problems for his successors. As ties of personal loyalty wore thin, new local warrior bands began to form.

WOMEN IN WARRIOR SOCIETY

The Nun Shōgun was one of a long line of important women in Japan. In Japanese mythology, the sun goddess ruled the Plain of High Heaven, while the late Yayoi shaman-ruler Pimiko was probably not an exceptional figure. Empresses ruled in Yamato and Nara courts, and they were followed by great women writers in the Heian period. Under the Kamakura *bakufu*, there was only one Nun Shōgun, but daughters as well as sons of warrior families often trained in archery and other military arts. As long as society was stable, women fared relatively well. But as fighting became more common in the fourteenth century, their position began to decline, and as warfare be-came endemic in the fifteenth, their status plummeted. The warrior's fief—his reward for serving his lord in battle and the lord's surety for his continuing service—became all important. To protect it, multigeniture, in which daughters as well as sons inherit-ed property, gave way to unigeniture, inheritance by the most able son.

View the Image
Japanese Court Ladies
at **myhistorylab.com**

Study and Review
Women in the Imperial Courts of China
and Japan at **myhistorylab.com**

AGRICULTURE, COMMERCE, AND MEDIEVAL GUILDS

Population figures for medieval Japan are rough estimates at best, but recent scholar-ship suggests 6 million for the year 1200 and 15 million for 1600. Much of the increase occurred during the late Kamakura and Ashikaga periods, when the country was fairly peaceful. The increase was brought about by land reclamation and improvements in agricultural technology. Iron-edged tools became available to all. New strains of rice were developed. Irrigation and diking improved. Double cropping began with vegeta-bles planted during the fall and winter in dry fields, which were flooded and planted with rice during the spring and summer.

In the Nara and early Heian periods, the economy was almost exclusively agricultural. Japan had no money, no commerce, and no cities—apart from Nara, which developed into a temple town living on assigned revenues, and Kyoto, where taxes were consumed. Follow-ing the example of China, the government had established a mint, but little money actually circulated. Taxes were paid in labor or grain. Commerce consisted of barter transactions, with silk or grain as the medium of exchange. Artisans produced for the noble households or temples to which they were attached. Peasants were economically self-sufficient.

From the late Heian period, partly as a side effect of fixed tax quotas, more of the growing agricultural surplus stayed in local hands, though not in the hands of the cul-tivators. This trend accelerated during the Kamakura and Ashikaga periods, as warriors took increasingly larger slices of the income of estates. As the income of civil nobles decreased, artisans detached themselves from noble households and began to produce for a wider market. Military equipment was an early staple of commerce, but gradually *sake*, lumber, paper, vegetable oils, salt, and products of the sea also became commer-cialized. A demand for copper coins appeared, and since they were no longer minted in Japan, huge quantities were imported from China.

During the Kamakura period, independent merchants appeared to handle the products of artisans. Some trade networks spread over all Japan. More often, artisan and merchant guilds, not unlike those of medieval Europe, paid a fee to obtain monop-oly rights in a given area. Kyoto guilds paid fees to powerful nobles or temples, and later to the Ashikaga *bakufu*. In outlying areas guild privileges were obtained from the regional lords. From the Kamakura period onward, markets were held periodically in many parts of Japan, by a river or at a crossroads. Some place-names in Japan today re-veal such an origin. Yokkaichi, today an industrial city, means "fourth-day market." It began as a place where markets were held on the fourth, fourteenth, and twenty-fourth days of each month. From the fifteenth century such markets were held with increasing frequency until, eventually, permanent towns were established.

BUDDHISM AND MEDIEVAL CULTURE

The Nara and Heian periods are often referred to as Japan's classical age. The period that followed—say, from 1200 to 1600—is often called medieval. It was medieval in the root sense of the word in that it lay between the other two major spans of premodern Japanese history. It also shared some characteristics that we label medieval in Europe and China. However, there is one salient difference. Medieval Japanese culture was a direct outgrowth of the classical age; one can even say that during the early Kamakura there was an overlap. In contrast, Europe was torn by barbarian invasions, and a millennium separated the classical culture of Rome from high medieval culture. In China, too, the era of political disunity and barbarian invasions lasted 400 years, and it was during these years that its medieval Buddhist culture blossomed.

The results of the historical continuity in Japan are visible in every branch of its culture. The earlier poetic tradition continued with great vigor. The flat *Yamato-e* style of painting continued, as did artisanal production, using the same techniques. Just as Heian estates, and the authority of the court, continued into the Kamakura era, so did Heian culture extend into medieval Japan.

Nonetheless, medieval Japanese culture had some distinctly new characteristics. First, as the leadership of society shifted from court aristocrats to military aristocrats, new forms of literature appeared. The medieval military tales were as different from *The Tale of Genji* as the armor of the mounted warrior was from the no less colorful silken robes of the court nobility. Second, a new wave of culture entered from China. If the Nara and Heian had been shaped by Tang culture, medieval Japan—though not its institutions—was shaped by Song culture. The link is immediately apparent in the ink paintings of medieval Japan. Third, and most important, the medieval centuries were Japan's age of Buddhist faith. A religious revolution occurred during the Kamakura period and deepened during the Ashikaga.

JAPANESE PIETISM: PURE LAND AND NICHIREN BUDDHISM

Among the doctrines of the Heian Tendai sect was the belief that the true teachings of the historical Buddha had been lost and that salvation could be had only by calling on the name of Amida, the Buddha who ruled over the Western Paradise, or **Pure Land**. The doctrine that the world had fallen on evil times and that only faith would suffice was given credence by earthquakes, epidemics, fires, and banditry in the capital, as well as wars throughout the land. During the tenth and eleventh centuries, itinerant preachers began to spread Pure Land doctrines and practices beyond the narrow circles of Kyoto.

Two early Kamakura figures stand out as religious geniuses who experienced the truth of Pure Land Buddhism within themselves. Hōnen (1133–1212) was perhaps the first to say that the invocation of the name of Amida alone was enough for salvation; faith, not works or rituals, was what counted. These claims brought Hōnen into conflict with the older Buddhist establishment and marked the emergence of Pure Land as a separate sect. Later, Shinran (1173–1262) taught that even a single invocation in praise of Amida, if done with perfect faith, was sufficient for salvation. But perfect faith was a gift from Amida and could not be obtained by human effort. Shinran taught that pride was an obstacle to purity of heart. One of his most famous sayings is "If even a good man can be reborn in the Pure Land, how much more so a wicked man"[1]—the wicked man is less inclined to assume that he is the source of his own salvation and therefore more apt to place his complete trust in Amida. Shinran broke with many of the practices of earlier Buddhism: He ate meat, married a nun, and taught that all occupations were equally "heavenly" if performed with a pure heart. Exiled from Kyoto, he traveled

Pure Land

In Buddhism, the celestial realm of the bodhisattva, Amida.

---

[1] R. Tsunoda, W. deBary, and D. Keene, *Sources of Japanese Tradition* (New York: Columbia University Press, 1958), p. 217.

about Japan establishing "True Pure Land" congregations. (When the Jesuits arrived in Japan in the sixteenth century, they called this sect "the devil's Christianity.")

Pure Land Buddhism became the dominant form of Buddhism in Japan and remains so today. It was also the only sect in medieval Japan—apart from the Tendai sect on Mount Hiei—to develop political and military power. As a religion of faith, it developed a strong church as protection for the saved while they were still in this world. As peasants became militarized during the fifteenth century, some Pure Land village congregations created self-defense forces. At times they rebelled against feudal lords. In one instance, Pure Land armies ruled the province of Kaga for over a century. These congregations were smashed during the late sixteenth century, and the sect depoliticized.

A second devotional sect was founded by Nichiren (1222–1282), who believed that the Lotus Sutra perfectly embodied the teachings of the Buddha. He instructed his adherents to chant, over and over, "Praise to the Lotus Sutra of the Wondrous Law," usually to the accompaniment of rapid drumbeats. Like the repetition of "Praise to the Amida Buddha" in the Pure Land sect or comparable verbal formulas in other religions around the world, the chanting optimally induced a state of religious rapture. The goal of an internal spiritual transformation was common to both the devotional and the meditative sects of Buddhism. Nichiren was remarkable for a Buddhist in being both intolerant and nationalistic. He blamed the ills of his age on rival sects and asserted that only his sect could protect Japan. He predicted the Mongol invasions, and his sect claimed credit for the "divine winds" that sank the Mongol fleets. Even his adopted Buddhist name, the Sun Lotus, combined the character for the rising sun of Japan with that of the flower that had become the symbol of Buddhism.

ZEN BUDDHISM

Meditation had long been a part of Japanese monastic practice. Zen teachings and meditation techniques were introduced by monks returning from study in Song China. Eisai (1141–1215) brought back the teachings of the Rinzai sect in 1191, and Dōgen (1200–1253) the Sōtō teachings in 1227. Eisai's sect was patronized by the Hōjō rulers in Kamakura and the Ashikaga in Kyoto. Dōgen established his sect on Japan's western coast, far from centers of political power.

Zen was a religion of paradox. Its monks were learned, yet it stressed a return to the uncluttered "original mind." Zen was punctiliously traditional, yet Zen was also iconoclastic. Its sages were depicted in paintings as tearing up sutras to make the point that it is religious experience and not words that count. Buddhism stressed compassion for all sentient beings, yet in Japan the Zen sect included many samurai whose duty it was to kill their lord's enemies.

Zen influenced the arts of medieval Japan. The most beautiful gardens were in Zen temples. The most famous, at Ryōanji, consists of fifteen rocks set in white sand. Zen monks, such as Josetsu, Shūbun (ca. 1415) and Sesshū (1420–1506), number among the masters of ink painting. Because the artist's creativity itself was seen as grounded in his experience of meditation, a painting of a waterfall was viewed as no less religious than a painting of the mythic Zen founder Bodhidharma.

NŌ PLAYS

Another vital product of Ashikaga culture is the Nō play, a unique mystery drama that is the world's oldest living dramatic tradition. The play is performed on a simple wooden stage by male actors wearing robes of great beauty and carved, painted masks of enigmatic expressions. The text is chanted to the accompaniment of flute and drums. The language is poetic. The action is slow and highly stylized: Circling about the stage can represent a journey, and a vertical motion of the hand, the reading of a letter. At a

Kûya Invoking Buddha. The mid-Heian monk Kûya (903–972) preached Pure Land doctrines in Kyoto and throughout Japan. Little Buddhas emerge from his mouth.

Why does it make sense to depict a Pure Land monk with little Buddhas coming out of his mouth?

critical juncture in most plays, the protagonist is possessed by the spirit of another and performs a dance. Nō plays reveal a medley of themes present in medieval culture. Some pivot on incidents in the struggle between the Taira and the Minamoto. Buddhist ideas of impermanence, of this world as a place of suffering, and of the need to relinquish worldly attachments are found in many plays. Some plays are close to fairy tales, whereas some are based on stories from China.

SUMMARY

 WHAT REVOLUTIONARY changes accompanied the Yayoi?

Japanese Origins. Old Stone Age Japan became an agricultural, metalworking society when new technologies came to Japan from Korea in the third century B.C.E. By the fifth century C.E., the Yamato court ruled most of Japan. It was heavily influenced by Korea. Shintō nature worship was practiced in villages and associated with the government. *page 219*

 **HOW DID** Chinese culture influence Japan?

Nara and Heian Japan. In the seventh century, the second main turning point of their history, the Japanese began to adopt and adapt many features of Chinese culture, including Buddhism and Chinese writing, literature, and political institutions. Japan was ruled by a civil aristocracy under the emperor. An enormous gulf existed between aristocrats and commoners. Japanese government was heavily influenced by the Chinese imperial system. Japanese culture, however, was increasingly self-confident and was aristocratic in its tastes and forms of expression. Noblewomen wrote many of the great works of Japanese literature during this age. Buddhism became increasingly assimilated. *page 223*

 WHY CAN this period in Japan be described as feudal, and in what ways is this description misleading?

Japan's Early Feudal Age. In the eighth century mounted warriors called samurai began to dominate local society. By the late 1100s, power passed from the civil bureaucracy to military aristocrats. The shōguns' power was based on their ability to command the loyalty of military vassals. Minamoto Yoritomo's seizure of power in 1185 marked the beginning of Japan's feudal age. He established the *bakufu*, or "tent government," in Kamakura. In 1274 and 1281, Mongol invaders sent by Kublai Khan

retreated from Japan. In 1336, Ashitaga Takauji moved his *bakufu* to Kyoto. Women's status declined, while Buddhist sects reflected Japanese concerns. *page 229*

KEY TERMS

bakufu (bah-koo-foo) (p. 229)
daimyo (dye-myoh) (p. 232)
kamikaze (p. 230)
Pure Land (p. 234)

samurai (p. 226)
Shintō (p. 222)
shōgun (p. 229)
Tennō (ten-noh) (p. 224)

REVIEW QUESTIONS

1. In what sense was Japanese society during the Yayoi period defined by its eastern frontier? What changes in its early frontier society led to the building of tombs and the emergence of the Yamato great kings?

2. Discuss Japan's cultural ties with China during the Nara and Heian periods. How did Chinese culture affect Japanese government and religion? How did the Japanese change what they borrowed? Was the relation of Japanese culture to China like that of American culture to England?

3. Trace the rise in Japan of a society dominated by military lords and their vassals. Do the late Heian, Kamakura, and Ashikaga represent successive stages in the development of Japanese "feudalism"?

4. Compare and contrast Heian court culture with the "feudal" culture of the Kamakura and Ashikaga eras.

5. Trace the development of Japanese Buddhism. What sects emerged, and why?

6. What was the overall trajectory of the status of women in Japan, from the Yayoi period to the Ashikaga era? What caused changes in women's status?

Note: To learn more about the topics in this chapter, please turn to the Suggested Readings at the end of the book. For additional sources related to this chapter please see www.myhistorylab.com

myhistorylab Connections

Reinforce what you learned in this chapter by studying the many documents, images, maps, review tools, and videos available at **www.myhistorylab.com**

Read and Review

✓•─[**Study** and **Review**   Chapter 9

•ᐧ•─[**Read** the **Document**   *Murasaki Shikibu, selections from The Tale of Genji, p. 226*
Buddhism in Japan: The Taika Reform Edicts, p. 228

•─[**View** the **Image**   *Japanese Court Ladies, p. 233*

✓•─[**Study** and **Review**   *Women in the Imperial Courts of China and Japan, p. 233*

Research and Explore

◉─[**See** the **Map**   *Medieval Japan and the Mongol Invasions, p. 230*

───((•─[**Hear** the **Audio** ───

Hear the audio file for Chapter 9
at **www.myhistorylab.com**

RELIGIONS OF THE WORLD

BUDDHISM

Hinduism, Buddhism, and Jainism all arose out of the spiritual ferment of Vedic India after 700 B.C.E. Buddhism shares a kinship with the other two religions much as Judaism, Christianity, and Islam have a relationship.

The founder of Buddhism, Siddhartha Gautama, was born about 563 B.C.E., a prince in a petty kingdom near what is now the border of India and Nepal. He was reared amid luxury and comforts, married at 16, and had a child. According to legend, at age 29 he saw a decrepit old man, sick and suffering, and a corpse. He suddenly realized that all humans would suffer the same fate. Gautama renounced his wealth and family and entered the life of a wandering ascetic. He visited famous teachers, for almost six years practiced extremes of ascetic self-deprivation, and finally discovered the Middle Path between self-indulgence and self-mortification. He attained *nirvana* at the age of 35, becoming the *Buddha*, or Enlightened One. The rest of his eighty years the Buddha spent teaching others the truths he had learned.

Basic to the Buddha's understanding of the human condition were the "Four Noble Truths": (1) All life is suffering—an endless chain of births and rebirths (*karma*); (2) the cause of the suffering is desire—it is desire that binds humans to the wheel of *karma*; (3) escape from suffering and endless rebirths can come only by the cessation of desire and the attainment of *nirvana*; (4) the path to *nirvana* is eightfold, requiring right views, thought, speech, actions, living, efforts, mindfulness, and meditation. Buddhists say that *nirvana* cannot be described: It is the ground of all existence, ineffable, and beyond time and space—an ultimate reality that may be experienced but not grasped intellectually.

The Buddha was a religious teacher, not a social reformer, yet his religious understanding led to ethical conclusions. He condemned the caste system that flourished in the India of his day. He denounced war, slavery, and the taking of life. He opposed appeals to miracles. He did not demand a blind faith in his doctrines: He told his followers to accept his teachings only after they had tested them against their own experience. He taught that poverty was a cause of immorality and that it was futile to attempt to suppress crime with punishments. He identified with all humanity, saying, "He who attends on the sick attends on me."

Because the goal of Buddhism is for all humans to become buddhas, some have called Buddhism the most contemplative and otherworldly of the great world religions. For the spiritually unprepared, and even for the historical Buddha, the way was not easy, and one lifetime was not enough.

Teenage Buddist monks walk past the ornate facade and towering stupa of Shwedagon Pagoda in Yangon, Myanmar (Burma).

William Waterfall/PacificStock.com

What is the role of monks in a Buddhist society?

Monks and nuns might practice the Eightfold Path, meditate for months and years, and experience an inner spiritual awakening, but only a few would gain enlightenment, the release from karmic causation. Most could only hope for a rebirth in a higher spiritual state—to begin again closer to the goal.

For laypeople the emphasis of Buddhism was on ethical living in human society as a preparation for a more dedicated religious quest in a future life.

Buddhism spread rapidly along the Ganges River and through northern India. In the time of King Ashoka (272–232 B.C.E.) of the Mauryas, it spread to southern India, Ceylon, and beyond. This was its great missionary age. As it spread throughout India its influence on religious practice at the village level was enormous, and its meditative techniques helped reshape Hindu yogic exercises. Eventually, however, Buddhism in India was re-Hinduized. It developed competing schools of metaphysics, a pantheon of gods and cosmic Buddhas, and devotional sects focusing on one or another of these cosmic figures. Its original character as a reform movement of Hinduism was lost, and between 500 and 1500 C.E. it was largely reabsorbed into Hinduism.

Beyond India, two major currents of Buddhism spread over Asia. One, known as the "Way of the Elders" (*Theravada*), swept

Two Seated Buddhas. This fifth- to sixth-century C.E. painting adorns a wall of a cave in Ajanta, India.

Borromeo/Art Resource, New York.

Why does Buddhist art sometimes show more than one Buddha?

Tibetan Buddhist nuns. The nuns belong to a Tibetan sect of the Mahayana (Greater Vehicle) Buddhism that swept north to Central Asia and Tibet, and then east to China, Korea, and Japan. Behind them, prayer flags blow in the wind.

What is the difference between Mahayana and Theravada Buddhism?

through continental Southeast Asia and the islands that are today Indonesia. The Theravada teaching was close to early Indian Buddhism and, as it spread, it carried with it other strands of Indian culture as well. Buddhism remains the predominant religion of Burma, Thailand, Cambodia, and Laos, although it must contend with more recent secular ideologies. In Thailand it remains the state religion: Thai kings rule as Buddhist monarchs; Thai boys spend short periods as Buddhist monks; and Thai temples (*wats*) continue as one center of village life. Before the spread of Islam, Buddhism also once flourished in Malaya, Sumatra, and Java.

The second major current, known as the "Greater Vehicle" (*Mahayana*), spread through northwest India to Afghanistan and Central Asia, and then to China, Tibet and Mongolia, Vietnam, Korea, and Japan. In each region the pattern that unfolded was different. In what is today Pakistan, Afghanistan, and Central Asia, Buddhism was overtaken and replaced by Islam. Mahayana doctrines entered Tibet during the sixth century C.E. and became firmly established several centuries later.

Today Tibetan Buddhism is the predominant religion of Tibet, Nepal, Sikkim, Bhutan, and Mongolia (although in Mongolia it is severely curtailed by Chinese authorities). In China, and then spreading from China to Korea, Vietnam, and Japan, Mahayana

Buddhism saw its fullest development. One key doctrine in this current was the ideal of the *bodhisattva*, a being who had gone all the way to *nirvana*, but held back in order to help others attain salvation.

Another Mahayana doctrine, that of the Chan (in China) or Zen (in Japan) sect, stressed meditation and perhaps was closer to the teachings of the historical Buddha.

In China, the Tang Dynasty (618–907) was the great Buddhist age, a time of unparalleled creativity in religious art, sculpture, and music. After that, although Buddhism continued to flourish at the village level, the governing scholar-gentry class shifted to the more worldly doctrines of Neo-Confucianism. In Vietnam, Korea, and Japan, the overall process replicated that of China, but the shift occurred later and with many local variations.

During modern times Buddhism—like all structures of faith—has struggled, with the secular doctrines of the scientific, and industrial, and communist revolutions exerting a powerful influence in the nineteenth and twentieth centuries. The future is unclear, but undoubtedly Buddhism will be powerfully affected by the ongoing transformations of Asian societies.

◆ Is Buddhism's relation to Hinduism parallel to Christianity's relation to Judaism?

◆ How do the teachings of the Buddha compare with Christian doctrine?

10

The Formation of Islamic Civilization, 622–1000

((•●[Hear the Audio for Chapter 10 at www.myhistorylab.com

Islamic Astronomy. Initially Muslim astronomers believed that the earth rested motionless at the center of a series of eight spheres, the last of which was studded with fixed stars revolving daily from east to west and at times from west to east. Muslim astronomers were influenced by and improved on Sanskrit, Sasanian, Syriac, and Greek texts on astronomy. *Rami*, the Sagittarius in this illustration from an eighteenth-century copy of a book by 'Abd al-Rahman ibn 'Ubmar al-Sufi (d. 986), has a set of twenty-nine gold spots that represent a stellar constellation.

How did Islam preserve Classical learning?

T he diverse, but identifiable civilization that we call "Islamic" is the last great civilization to appear to date. The basic elements of the Islamic worldview derived from a single, prophetic-revelatory event, the Prophet Muhammad's proclamation of the Qur'an.[1] This event galvanized diverse, polytheistic Arabs into a new unity—the monotheistic, egalitarian community (umma) of "submitters" (muslims) to God.

This community expanded far beyond Arabia; Persians, Indians, and others made it a great universalist tradition. Arab military prowess and cultural pride joined with a new religious orientation to initiate one of the most lasting revolutions in history, but peoples of the older Eurasian heartlands converted this revolution into a new civilization. Their acceptance of the Islamic vision of society (and reality) as more compelling than any older one— Jewish, Roman, Greek, Persian, Christian, or Buddhist—gave rise to a multifaceted Islamic civilization.

((●—[Hear the Audio
at **myhistorylab.com**

---
[1]Qur'an is a more accurate English transliteration of the Arabic word than *Koran*; similarly, *Muhammad* is preferable to *Mohammed*, *Muslim* to *Moslem*, *emir* to *amir*, and *ulama* to *ulema*.

THE EARLY ISLAMIC WORLDS OF ARAB AND PERSIAN CULTURES

The rise of Arabic, Persian, and Turkish Islamic cultures as core religious and cultural worlds of Islamic civilization is a pivotal moment in world history. In its first three centuries, the Islamic polity was arguably the most dynamic, multiethnic, multilingual imperial realm of its time. In the same age, Tang Chinese emperors renewed and restored the old Han imperium; Charlemagne and the Carolingians carved out a much smaller, more homogeneous empire in relatively underdeveloped western Europe; Byzantium fought to survive against Arab and Turkish arms and turned inward to conserve its traditions; and the regional kingdoms of post-Gupta India remained vulnerable to new forces (including Islamic ones) moving into northwestern India.

Only China compared favorably with the Islamic world during this period in political and military strength, cultural unity, creativity, and self-consciousness. The Tang and the Abbasids wielded commensurate power in their heydays, although the Chinese endured as a centralized state much longer than the Arab Islamic Empire. Certainly these were the era's greatest political

and cultural units. Each had one cultural language: Variations of Chinese were spoken by a large percentage of Chinese subjects, while Arabic became the administrative and religious *lingua franca* of the Islamic Empire, from Morocco to India, as the result of its status as the language of Qur'anic revelation and hence of learning. The two civilizations shared the use of pastoral cavalry as well as the adaptive ability to incorporate new peoples into their larger cultures—although Islamic civilization proved finally more flexible in this regard. Indeed, the great adaptability of Islamic religious traditions and their attendant social orders belie today's widespread misconception of Islamic traditions as inherently inflexible.

Islamic states were spread over vastly more culturally heterogeneous and widely dispersed geographical areas than was the Chinese Empire. Conquest initially fueled the economy of the new Islamic imperial state, but in the long run, trade, artisanal crafts, seafaring technology, and urban commercial centers became the backbone of the Islamic lands' prosperity, as well as the

ORIGINS AND EARLY DEVELOPMENT

WHAT WAS the Qur'anic message as expressed to Muhammad?

THE SETTING

By 600 C.E., the dominant Eurasian political powers, Christian Byzantium and Zoroastrian Sasanid Persia, had battled for West Asian political and cultural ascendancy for over four centuries. Then, in the wake of one final, mutually exhausting conflict (608–627), a new Arab power broke in from the south to weaken the first and destroy the second.

Pre-Islamic Arabia was not just a land of deserts, camels, and pastoralists. Byzantium and Persia had kept the nomads of the Syrian and northern Arabian steppe at bay by enlisting small Arab client kingdoms on the edge of the desert as buffer states. One of the biggest of these kingdoms was Christian in faith. Arab kingdoms had long flourished in the agriculturally rich highlands of southern Arabia, which had direct access to the international oceanic trade along its coasts (see Chapters 4, 5). Some of these kingdoms, including a Jewish one in the sixth century, were independent; others were under Persian or Abyssinian control. In the western Arabian highland of the Hijaz, astride its major trade route, the town of Mecca was a center of the caravan trade and a pilgrimage site because of its famous sanctuary, the **Ka'ba** (or Kaaba), where pagan Arab tribes enshrined gods. The settled Meccan Arabs ran a merchant republic in which tribal values were breaking down under the strains of urban commercial life. Still, these settled Arabs were not cut off from their nomadic relatives who lived on herding and by raiding settlements and caravans.

The Arabic language, a Semitic tongue, defined and linked the Arab peoples, however divided they were by livelihood, religion, blood feuds, and tribal conflict. From the Yemen north to Syria-Palestine and Mesopotamia, Arabs shared a highly developed poetic idiom. Every tribe had a poet to exhort its warriors and insult its enemies before battle. Poetry contests were also held, often in conjunction with annual trade fairs that brought tribes together under a general truce.

Ka'ba

A black meteorite in the city of Mecca that became Islam's holiest shrine.

QUICK REVIEW

Mecca

- Center of caravan trade
- Pilgrimage center because of presence of Ka'ba
- A merchant republic

See the Map
Expansion of Islam at
myhistorylab.com

prime means of disseminating Islamic concepts and traditions to new areas, as regional states replaced the centralized imperial state of the early caliphate.

This Islamic achievement was unique in that the peoples who built it did so by developing new religious, social, and political traditions rather than simply reviving old ones. In later centuries the early Arab impress on Islamic culture and religion was transformed by vast numbers of Persian- and Turkish-speaking Muslims and many regional cultural groups, from Swahili speakers in East Africa to multiple peoples of South and Southeast Asia. Yet in the midst of Islam's diversity, Arabic went abroad with the holy Qur'an as the sacred medium of God's revelation. Since Islam's earliest spread, individual Muslims worldwide have cultivated to some degree Arabic and the Arabic scripture and thus kept in touch with Islam's Arab origins.

This achievement was novel, at least in its global scale. Although the Muslim faith can be seen as a reformation of Jewish and Christian monotheism, it was directed not merely at reforming but subsuming the older Jewish and Christian traditions in a more comprehensive vision of God's plan on earth. And even as Islam can be seen as a reform of Semitic monotheism, Muslims also built on previous Persian, Turkish, and other traditions; they adopted and adapted elements of neighboring African, European, and Asian cultures. As a diverse, international civilization and religious tradition, Islam developed its own distinctive forms that persisted wherever Muslims extended the *umma*.

Focus Questions

◆ Why did only China compare favorably with the Islamic world during the first centuries after the birth of Islam? How were the two civilizations similar, and how were they different?

◆ What is unique about the Islamic achievement? In what ways was it built on the traditions of earlier religions?

Islam is not a "religion of the desert." It began in a commercial urban center and first flourished in an agricultural oasis and small merchant towns of the Hijaz. Its first converts were Meccan townsfolk and date farmers in Yathrib. Before becoming Muslims, most Arabs were animists; fewer were Jews or Christians. North–south caravans passed from Damascus through Mecca to Aden and the Indian Ocean, and no merchant involved in this traffic, as Muhammad himself was, could have been unfamiliar with the diverse cultures along the trade routes. Early Muslim leaders used Arab tribes as warriors and looked to Arab culture for their traditional roots long after the locus of Islamic power had left Arabia. But the empire and civilization they ultimately spawned were centered in the heartlands of Mediterranean and West Asian urban and rural cultures and based more on settled communal existence than on rural or desert tribal societies and economies.

MUHAMMAD AND THE QUR'AN

Muhammad (ca. 570–632) was raised an orphan in a commercial family of the old Meccan tribe of Quraysh. Later, in the midst of a successful business career made possible by his marriage to Khadija (d. ca. 619), an older, wealthy Meccan widow and entrepreneur, he became troubled by the idolatry, worldliness, and lack of social conscience around him. Such failings were equally offensive to sensitive Jewish or Christian morality, with which he was familiar, but these traditions had not displaced Arabian pagan traditions, despite the presence of some Jewish and Christian Arab tribes.

When he was about 40, Muhammad felt himself called by the one God, the God of Abraham, Moses, and Jesus, to "rise and warn" his fellow Arabs about their frivolous disregard for morality and worship of the Creator.

On repeated occasions revelation came to Muhammad through a messenger identified as God's angel, Gabriel. It took the form of a "reciting" (**qur'an**) of God's

Read the Document
Al-Tabari: Muhammad's Call to Prophecy
at **myhistorylab.com**

Qur'an
Meaning "a reciting." The Islamic bible, which Muslims believe God revealed to the Prophet Muhammad.

The Ka'ba in Mecca. In Muslim tradition, the Ka'ba (Arabic "cube") is the site of the first "house of God," founded by Adam, then rebuilt by Abraham and his son Ishmael at God's command. It is held to have fallen later into idolatrous use until Muhammad's victory over the Meccans and his cleansing of the holy house. The Ka'ba is the geographical point toward which all Muslims face when performing ritual prayer. It and the plain of Arafat outside Mecca are the two foci of the pilgrimage of Hajj that each Muslim aspires to make at least once in a lifetime.

The Five Pillars of Islam include the Hajj; what are the other four?

Islam

Meaning "submission." The religion founded by the Prophet Muhammad.

View the Image
The Qur'an at **myhistorylab.com**

Word—now rendered in "clear Arabic" for the Arabs, just as it had been given to previous prophets in Hebrew or other languages for their peoples.

The message of the Qur'an was clear: The Prophet is to warn his people against worshipping false gods and against all immorality, especially injustice to the poor, orphans, widows, and indeed all women. At the end of time, on Judgment Day, every person will be bodily resurrected to face what they have earned: eternal punishment in hellfire or eternal joy in paradise. The way to paradise lies in gratitude to God for His bounties, His revelatory guidance, and His readiness to forgive the penitent. It lies in social justice and obedient worship of God, and in recognition of God's transcendence. The proper human response to God is "submission" (*islam*) to His will, becoming *muslim* ("submissive") in one's worship and morality. All of creation naturally praises and serves God except humans, who can choose to obey or to reject him.

In this Qur'anic message, the ethical monotheism of Judaic and Christian tradition (probably reinforced by Zoroastrian and Manichaean influences) reaches fulfillment in a radically theocentric vision demanding absolute obedience to the Lord of the Universe. The Qur'anic revelations state that Muhammad is only the last in a series of prophets chosen to bring God's word: Noah, Abraham, Moses, Jesus, and nonbiblical Arabian figures like Salih had similar missions previously. The Qur'an is filled with stories of earlier biblical figures, especially Abraham and Moses. Most frequently mentioned from the Christian New Testament is Mary, mother of Jesus. Because the followers of earlier prophets neglected or altered their scriptures' teachings, Muhammad has been given one final reiteration of God's message. Jews, Christians, and pagans are summoned to heed this Qur'anic message.

The Prophet's preaching fell largely on deaf ears in the first years after his calling (traditionally dated to the year 610). A few followed the lead of his wife, Khadija, in recognizing him as a divinely chosen reformer. Some prominent Meccans joined him, but the merchant aristocracy as a whole resisted. His preaching against their gods and goddesses threatened their ancestral ways as well as the Ka'ba pilgrimage shrine and the lucrative trade it attracted. The Meccans began to persecute Muhammad's followers. After the deaths of Khadija and Muhammad's uncle and protector, Abu Talib, the situation worsened; the Prophet even had to send a small band of Muslims to Abyssinia for temporary refuge. Then, because of his growing reputation as a moral leader, Muhammad was called to Yathrib (an important agricultural oasis 240 miles north of Mecca) to arbitrate among its five quarreling tribes, three of which were Jewish. Having sent his Meccan followers ahead, Muhammad fled Mecca in July 622 for Yathrib, afterward known as Medina (*al-Madina*, "the City [of the Prophet]"). Some dozen years later, this "emigration," or **hegira** (in Arabic, *Hajj*), became the starting point for the Islamic calendar, the event marking the creation of a distinctive Islamic community, or **umma.**[2]

Muhammad quickly cemented ties between the Meccan emigrants and the Medinans, many of whom became converts. Raids on his Meccan enemies' caravans established his leadership. They reflect the economic dimension of the Medinan-Meccan struggle. The Arab Jews of Medina largely rejected his religious message and authority. They even made contact with his Meccan enemies, moving Muhammad to turn on them, kill or enslave some, banish others, and take their lands. Many of the Qur'anic revelations from this period pertain to communal order or chastise Jews and Christians who rejected Islam.

Muslim norms took shape in Medina: allegiance to the *umma*; honesty in all one's affairs; modesty in personal habits; abstention from alcohol and pork; fair division of inheritances; improved treatment of women, especially as to property and other rights in marriage; careful regulation of marriage and divorce; ritual ablution before any act of worship, be it reciting the Qur'an or prayer; three (later five) daily rites of worship facing the Meccan shrine of the Ka'ba; payment of a tithe to support less fortunate Muslims; annual daytime fasting for the month of Ramadan and, eventually, pilgrimage to Mecca at least once in a lifetime, if one is able. Five of these essential elements of Islamic became known as The Pillars: (1) *Shahada*, or the Muslim Creed ("There is no God but God and Muhammad is God's prophet"); (2) *Salat*, or prayer; (3) *Sawm*, fasting during Ramadan; (4) *Zakat*, or alms; and (5) **Hajj**, the pilgrimage.

Acceptance of Islamic political authority brought tolerance. A Jewish oasis yielded to Muhammad's authority and was allowed, unlike the resistant Medinan Jews, to keep its lands, practice its faith, and receive protection in return for paying a head tax. This practice was followed ever after for Jews, Christians, and other "people of Scripture" who accepted Islamic rule. After long conflict, the Meccans surrendered to Muhammad, and his acceptance of them into the *umma* set the pattern for the later Islamic conquests. Following age-old practice, Muhammad cemented many of his alliances with marriage (although while Khadija lived, he took no second wife). In the last years of the Prophet's life, the once tiny band of Muslims became the heart of a pan-Arabian tribal confederation, bound together by personal allegiance to Muhammad, submission (*islam*) to God, and membership in the *umma*.

hegira
The flight of Muhammad and his followers from Mecca to Medina in 622 C.E. It marks the beginning of the Islamic calendar.

umma
The Islamic community.

Hajj The pilgrimage to Mecca that all Muslims are enjoined to perform at least once in their lifetime.

---

[2]The twelve-month Muslim lunar year is shorter than the Christian solar year by about eleven days, a difference of about three years per century. Muslim dates are reckoned from the month in 622 in which Muhammad began his hegira (Arabic: *Hijra*). Thus Muslims celebrated the start of their lunar year 1401 in November 1980 (1979–1980 C.E. = A.H. [Anno Hegirae] 1400), whereas it was only 1,358 solar years from 622 to 1980.

WOMEN IN EARLY ISLAMIC SOCIETY

The *umma* is a central concern in Islam, and the family is the core of the *umma*. Consequently, family law played a central role in the development of Islamic law. It is Islamic family law that stipulates the rights of women and men.

The Qur'an introduced into Arabian society radical new ideas that dramatically improved the status of women. For example, it prohibited the common practice of female infanticide, stating that all children should have the opportunity to live. The Qur'an recognizes a woman's right to contract her own marriage and stipulates that she, and not her male relatives, receives the dowry from her husband. Legally, a woman entering marriage was not an object to be bought and sold but rather a party to a negotiated contract. A woman was also guaranteed the right to inherit, own, and manage property.

Women are therefore afforded many rights in the Qur'an. Yet the Qur'an does not assume the full gender equality advocated in some modern societies in the twenty-first century. Islamic law stipulates that the father or senior male controls and guides the family unit. A male receives a larger share in inheritance and has fewer restrictions in initiating a divorce; also, a man's eyewitness testimony carries more weight in court than a woman's. Even though the Qur'an introduced many positive changes for women, it also presupposed and legitimated a patriarchal society and did not outlaw all customs that practically and symbolically kept women from full equality.

Polygamy is a practice often identified with Islam. The Qur'an tolerates this (preexisting) practice but seeks to control and regulate it. It states that a man can have up to four wives provided he can treat them all equally and fairly (Q. 4:3). Some Muslims interpret this verse as effectively prohibiting polygamy because it is manifestly impossible to treat and love two or more women "equally." And in fact, monogamy is globally the predominant Muslim marital practice.

Another practice commonly associated with Islam is female veiling, *hijab*, which is understood by Muslims as a practice of modesty. The veil is a generic term that applies to various types of body or facial covering, such as *chador* and *burqa*. Veiling of women was customary in a number of pre-Islamic societies, notably among upper-class women in the Byzantine and Sasanid empires. It was, and still is, common in parts of the Mediterranean. Islam did not invent the veil, nor does the Qur'an specifically stipulate veiling, let alone repression of women. Rather, it emphasizes that both men and women are responsible for their actions and should dress and act modestly. It does stipulate that women should guard their modesty and "draw their veils over their bosom and display their beauty only to their husbands and their fathers" (Q. 24:31).

As with many religious dictums, whatever their spirit, implementation has proven problematic. Though the original intention of veiling was to protect women and their honor, the veil and the derivative idea of seclusion often largely barred women from public life until the twentieth century. These and other Qur'anic verses have been used literally to justify patriarchy and keep women from exercising the full rights that the Qur'an affords them. With more modern education, many Muslim women have turned to the Qur'an to interpret these verses anew to stipulate practices that are both Islamic and compatible with modern ideas of equality. And of course different Islamic cultures, from Indonesia to North Africa to Europe and America, differ greatly in how literally or liberally they apply traditional practices and customs.

QUICK REVIEW

Women's Rights in the Qur'an

- Infanticide—commonly practiced on females—prohibited
- Women contract their own marriages, receive dowries
- Women can inherit, own, and manage property
- Society assumed to be patriarchal

Veiling. There are many different forms of veiling. These photos illustrate three. The left-hand photo shows a young woman dressed in contemporary clothing with just her head covered. The middle photo shows a Yemeni woman with all but her eyes covered. The right-hand photo shows an Afghani woman who is fully covered.

Why is there so much variation in veiling practices?

In early Islamic history, many women—such as the wives of Muhammad (Khadija and A'isha)—played influential roles. They were instrumental in defining certain aspects of Islamic law and even commanded troops in warfare. In medieval times, however, women were not, with a few notable exceptions, prominent in the public sphere. As in many other places around the world, women were largely cut off from public political, social, and educational activities. These negative effects are still visible today in many Middle Eastern, African, and Asian regions even as women generally are increasingly negotiating their way into the public sphere.

EARLY ISLAMIC CONQUESTS

In 632 Muhammad died, leaving neither a son nor a designated successor. The new *umma* faced its first major crisis. A political struggle between Meccan and Medinan factions ended in a pledge of allegiance to Abu Bakr, the most senior of the early Meccan converts. Following old Arabian patterns, many tribes renounced allegiance to the Prophet after his death. Nevertheless, Abu Bakr's rule (632–634) as Muhammad's successor, or "caliph" (*khalifa*), reestablished Medinan hegemony and at least nominal religious conformity for much of Arabia. The Arabs were forced to recognize in the *umma* a new kind of supratribal community that demanded more than allegiance to a particular leader.

WHY WAS Islam able to expand rapidly?

COURSE OF CONQUEST

Under the next two caliphs, Umar (634–644) and Uthman (644–656), Arab armies moved beyond the peninsula, intent on more than traditional bedouin booty raids. In one of history's most astonishing expansions, by 643 they had conquered the Byzantine and Sasanid territories of the Fertile Crescent, Egypt, and most of Iran. For the first time in centuries the lands from Egypt to Iran came under one rule. Finally, Arab armies swept west over the Byzantine-controlled Libyan coast and, in the east, pushed to the Oxus, defeating the last Sasanid ruler by 651.

An interlude of civil war followed during the contested caliphate of Muhammad's cousin and son-in-law Ali (656–661). Then the fifth caliph, Mu'awiya (661–680), directed further expansion and initiated the new Umayyad Dynasty, which survived despite a second civil war (680–692) until 750. In the Mediterranean, an Islamic fleet conquered Cyprus, plundered Sicily and Rhodes, and crippled Byzantine sea power. By 680 control of greater Persia was solidified by permanent Arab garrisoning of Khorasan, much of Anatolia was raided, Constantinople was besieged (but not taken), and Armenia was under Islamic rule.

Succeeding decades saw the eastern Berbers of Libyan North Africa defeated and converted to Islam in substantial numbers. With their help, "the West" (al-Maghrib, modern Morocco and Algeria) fell quickly. In 711 raids into Spain began (memory of the Berber Muslim leader of the first invaders, Tariq, lives on in the name of *Gibraltar*, from *Jabal Tariq*, "Mount Tariq"). By 716 the disunited Spanish Visigoth kingdoms had fallen, and much of Iberia was under Islamic control. Pushing north into France, the Arabs were finally checked by Charles Martel with a defeat at Tours (732). At the opposite end of the empire, buoyed by large-scale Arab immigration, Islamic forces consolidated their holdings as far as the Oxus River (Amu Darya) basin of Khorasan, and in 710 these forces reached the Indus region. Islamic power was supreme from the Atlantic to Central Asia (see Map 10–1).

FACTORS OF SUCCESS

This rapid expansion was possible because of the weakened military and economic condition of the Byzantines and Sasanids, the result of their chronic warfare with one another. The new Islamic vision of society and life also united the Arabs and attracted others. Its corollary was the commitment among the Islamic leadership to extend "the abode of submission" (Dar al-Islam) abroad. However, too much has been made of Muslim zeal for martyrdom. Assurance of paradise for those engaged in **jihad**, "just struggle (in the path of God)," is less likely to have motivated the average Arab tribesman—who, at least at the beginning, was usually only nominally Muslim—than did promise of booty. Life in the Peninsula was hard, so the hope of greater prosperity must have been compelling.

Still, religious zeal was important, especially as time went on. The early policy of sending Qur'an reciters among the Arab armies to teach essentials of Muslim faith and practice had its effects. Another factor was the leadership of the first caliphs and field generals, which, combined with Byzantine and Iranian weakness, gave Arab armies a distinct advantage. Some populations even welcomed Islamic rule as a relief from Byzantine or Persian oppression. Crucial here was Muslim willingness to allow Christian, Jewish, and even Zoroastrian groups to continue as minorities (with their own legal systems and no military obligations) under protection of Islamic rule. In return, they had to recognize Islamic political authority, pay a non-Muslim head tax (jizya), and not proselytize or interfere with Muslim religious practice. (Ironically, with time, the head tax and other strictures on non-Muslims encouraged many Christians and Jews to convert.)

Finally, the astute policies of the early leaders helped give the conquests overall permanence: relatively little bloodshed, destruction, or disruption in conquest; adoption of existing administrative systems (and personnel) with minimal changes; adjustment of unequal taxation; appointment of capable governors; and strategic siting of new garrison towns like Basra, Kufa, and Fustat (later Cairo).

jihad

"Struggle in the path of God." Although not necessarily implying violence, it is often interpreted to mean holy war in the name of Islam.

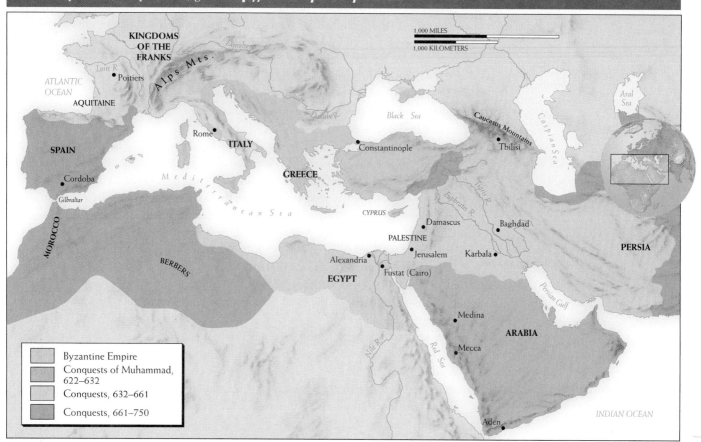

Byzantine Empire
Conquests of Muhammad, 622–632
Conquests, 632–661
Conquests, 661–750

MAP 10–1. Muslim Conquests and Domination of the Mediterranean to about 750 C.E. The rapid spread of the Islamic religious and political-military presence is shown here. Within 125 years of Muhammad's preaching, Muslim hegemony extended from Spain to Central Asia.

Why did so many subject peoples welcome Islamic rule?

THE NEW ISLAMIC WORLD ORDER

Although they were quick to adopt and adapt existing traditions in the lands they conquered, the Muslims brought with them a new worldview that demanded a new political, social, and cultural order, however long it might take to implement. Beyond military and administrative problems loomed the more important question of the nature of Islamic society. Under the Prophet the new community of the *umma* had replaced, at least in theory, the tribal, blood-based sociopolitical order in Arabia. Yet once the Arabs (most of whom became Muslims) had to rule non-Arabs and non-Muslims, new problems tested the ideal of an Islamic polity. Chief among these were leadership and membership qualifications, social order, and religious and cultural identity.

WHAT ROLES did the caliphate and the *ulama* play in Islamic states?

THE CALIPHATE

Allegiance to Muhammad had rested on his authority as divine spokesperson and gifted leader. His first successors were chosen much as were Arab *shaykhs* ("sheiks"), or tribal chieftains: by agreement of the leading elders, of the new religious "tribe" of

caliphate
The true line of succession to Muhammad.

imam
Islamic prayer leader.

emir
An Islamic military commander.

•♦•⌐Read the Document
Al-Tabari and Ibn Hisham, from
"The Founding of the Caliphate"
at **myhistorylab.com**

Muslims on the basis of superior personal qualities and the precedence in faith conferred by piety and association with the Prophet. The true line of succession to Muhammad was known as the **caliphate**, and the successors' titles were "successor" (*khalifa*, or caliph), "leader" (*imam*—literally, the one who stands in front to lead ritual worship), and "commander (*emir*) of the faithful." These names underscored religious and political authority, which most Muslims recognized in the caliphs Abu Bakr and Umar, and potentially in Uthman and Ali. Unfortunately, by the time of Uthman and Ali, dissension led to civil war. Yet the first four caliphs had all been close to Muhammad, and this gave their reigns a nostalgic aura of purity, especially as the later caliphal institution was based largely on sheer power legitimized by hereditary succession. (See Document, "Al-Mawardi and al-Hilli.")

The nature of Islamic leadership became an issue with the first civil war (656–661) and the recognition of Mu'awiya, a kinsman of Uthman, as caliph. He founded the first dynastic caliphate, that of his Meccan clan of Umayya (661–750). Umayyad descendants held power until they were ousted in 750 by the Abbasid clan, which based its legitimacy on descent from Abbas, an uncle of the Prophet. The Umayyads had the prestige of the office held by the first four, "rightly guided" caliphs. But many also deemed them to be worldly kings compared to the first four, "true" successors to Muhammad.

The Abbasids took the caliphate by open rebellion in 750, having exploited pious dissatisfaction with Umayyad worldliness, non-Arab Muslim resentment of Arab preference (primarily in Iran), and dissension among Arab tribal factions in the garrison towns. For all their stress on the Muslim character of their caliphate, the Abbasids were scarcely less worldly and continued the hereditary rule begun by the Umayyads. This they did well enough to retain control of most of the far-flung Islamic territories until 945, when the Shi'ite Buyid Dynasty took control in Baghdad and relegated the caliph to largely symbolic status. Thereafter, although their line continued until 1258, the caliphate was primarily a titular office representing an Islamic unity that existed largely in name only.

THE *ULAMA*

Although the caliph could exert his power to influence religious matters, he was never "emperor and pope combined," as European writers have claimed. Religious leadership in the *umma* devolved instead on another group. The functional successors of the Prophet in society at large were those Muslims recognized for piety and learning and as informal or even formal (as with state-appointed judges) authorities. Initially, they were the "Companions" (male and female) of Muhammad with greatest stature in the old Medinan *umma*—including the first four caliphs. This generation was replaced by those younger followers most concerned with preserving, interpreting, and applying the Qur'an and with maintaining the norms of the Prophet's original *umma*. Because the Qur'an contained few legal prescriptions, they had to draw on precedents from Meccan and Medinan practice, as well as oral traditions from and about the Prophet and Companions. They also had to standardize grammatical rules for a common Arabic language based on the Qur'an and pre-Islamic poetry. Furthermore, they had to improve the phonetic, cursive Arabic script, a task done so well that the script was gradually applied as the standard alphabetic script for other languages wherever Islamic culture became dominant: among Iranians, Turks, Indians, Indonesians, Malays, East Africans, and others. Along with these and other religious, intellectual, and cultural achievements, Muslim scholars developed an enduring pattern of education based on study under those persons highest in the unbroken cross-generational chain of trustworthy Muslims linking the current age with that of the earliest *umma*.

DOCUMENT

Al-Mawardi and al-Hilli

At his death, the Prophet left his followers without explicit instructions on leadership and governance of the umma. The question of political authority became hotly contested, which resulted ultimately in the major division between Sunni and Shi'i Muslims that has prevailed to this day. Below are two important later interpretations of political legitimacy by an influential Sunni official, al-Mawardi (974–1058), and a leading Shi'a theologian, al-Hilli (1250–1326).

- **WHAT** are the essential characteristics of a ruler according to both thinkers? What do these thinkers have in common, and what are their differences?

AL-MAWARDI

The *Imamate*: God, whose power be glorified, has instituted a chief of the Community as a successor to Prophethood and to protect the Community and assume the guidance of its affairs. Thus the *Imamate* is a principle on which stands the bases of the religious Community and by which its general welfare is regulated, so that the common good is assured by it. . . .

Thus the obligatory nature of the *Imamate* is established, and it is an obligation performed for all by a few, like fighting in a holy war, or the study of the religious sciences. . . .

As for those persons fitted for the *Imamate*, the conditions related to them are seven: . . . Justice in all its characteristics. . . . Knowledge requisite for independent judgment (*ijtihad*) about revealed and legal matters. . . . Soundness of the senses in hearing, sight, and speech, in a degree to accord with their normal functioning. . . . Soundness of the members from any defect that would prevent freedom of movement and agility. . . . Judgment conducive to the governing of subjects and administering matters of general welfare. . . . Courage and bravery to protect Muslim territory and wage the *jihad* against the enemy. . . . Pedigree: he must be of the tribe of Quraysh, since there has come down an explicit statement on this, and the consensus has agreed . . . .

He must maintain the Religion according to the principles established and agreed upon by the earliest . . . .

Al-Hilli

He who is worthy of the *Imamate* is a person appointed and specified by God and His Prophet, not any chance person; it is not possible that there be more than one person at any one period who is worthy . . . . Hence the *Imamate* is *lutf* [God's kindness to humans in guiding them]. . . .

It is necessary that the *Imâm* be immune to sin; otherwise he would need a Imâm, or spiritual guide, and that is impossible. And also if he committed sin, he would lose his place in men's hearts, and the value of his appointment would be nullified. And because he is the guardian of the law . . . he must be immune to sin . . . which no one perceives but God the most high. Hence . . . the *Imâm* must be appointed by God, not by the people.

Agreement has been reached that in appointing the *Imâm* the specification can be made by God and His Prophet, or by a previous *Imâm* . . . . [There is disagreement over] whether or not his appointment can be in a way that is other than specification (by God and the Prophet). He who knows the unseen make[s] it known. And that comes about in two ways: (1) by making it known to someone immune to sin, such as the Prophet, and then he tells us of the *Imâm*'s immunity to sin and of this appointment; (2) by the appearance of miracles wrought by his hand to prove his veracity in claiming the *Imamate*. Sunnis say that whenever the people [*umma*] acknowledge any person as chief, and are convinced of his ability and his power increases, he becomes the *Imâm*.

The *Imâm* [must] be absolutely the best of the people of his age, because he takes precedence over all. . . .

Source: From *The Middle East and Islamic World Reader* by Marvin Gettlemen and Stuart Schar © 2003 by Marvin Gettlemen and Stuart Schar. Reprinted by permission of Grove Press.

A Closer Look

The Dome of the Rock, Jerusalem (Interior)

The Dome of the Rock (completed in 691) is the earliest monumental structure of Islamic architecture. Apparently the earliest architectural and artistic project of the Ummayad Dynasty, it was constructed on the "Temple Mount" sacred site created in Herodian times. The best interpretation today is that it was built to signal prominently the success of Islam as the completion of Jewish and Christian monotheistic religion. Its magnificent mosaic tile ornamentation has been renewed on its exterior in Ottoman times (see exterior photograph on p. 253), but inside, as in this photograph, we see much of the original decoration in all its magnificence, along with the later marble covering sheathing walls, piers, and spandrels. The octagonal shape follows that of the Byzantine *martyria* and the wooden dome, stone and brick masonry, and careful symmetry of design derive from Byzantine church architecture.

The decorative mosaics display vegetal designs that are mixed with jewels, crowns, and breastplates, many from Sasanid and Byzantine insignia. The latter may well be regalia of kings defeated by the Muslims, while the trees depicted may recall Solomon's palace in Jerusalem, which is often referred to in early medieval traditions. Barely visible here are also bird wings, palmettes, and floral composites of Persian design that run around the interior.

The long gold mosaic written inscription running completely around the building below the ceiling of the dome contains carefully chosen Qur'anic passages about Christ, none of which contradict Christian doctrine. This may be the earliest medieval use of writing in building decoration.

The rock over which the entire dome is built became in Muslim tradition the spot from which Muhammad's night ascension to the heavens (treated in the sources sometimes as visionary, sometimes as physical) began, although an older Muslim tradition marks it as the spot from which God returned to heaven after creating the earth.

Questions

1. Is the Dome of the Rock a late-antique Byzantine building (perhaps designed and built in part by Christian artisans), or a signal Muslim structure that uses pre-Islamic themes and motifs but combines them in novel ways to signal/symbolize Islam's reform of monotheism and the new Islamic imperium? Or could it be both? Discuss.

The Dome of the Rock in Jerusalem.
An early example of Islamic architecture, it dates from 685 and the first wave of Arab expansion. It is built over the rock from which Muslims believe Muhammad had a heavenly ascension experience and on which Jews believe Abraham prepared to sacrifice Isaac. The Dome of the Rock has symbolic significance for Muslims because the site is associated with the life of the Prophet. For a few years of Muhammad's time in Medina, Muslims even faced Jerusalem when they prayed, before a new Qur'anic revelation changed the direction to Mecca.

What are other examples of sites that are important, for different reasons, to two or more faiths?

These scholars came to be known as **ulama** ("persons of right knowledge"). Their personal legal opinions and collective discussions of issues, from theological doctrine to criminal punishments, established a basis for religious and social order. By the ninth century they had largely defined the understanding of the divine law, or *Shari'a*, that Muslims ever after have held to be definitive for legal, social, commercial, political, ritual, and moral concerns. This understanding and the methods by which it was derived form the Muslim science of jurisprudence (*fiqh*), the core discipline of Islamic learning.

The centers of *ulama* activity were Medina, Mecca, and especially Iraq (Basra and Kufa, later Baghdad), then Khorasan, Syria, North Africa, Spain, and Egypt. In Umayyad times, the *ulama* criticized caliphal rule when it strayed too far from Muslim norms. Gradually the *ulama* became a new elite identified with the upper class of each regional society under Islamic rule. Caliphs and their governors regularly sought their advice, but often only for moral or legal (the two are, in Muslim view, the same) sanction of a contemplated (or accomplished) action. Some *ulama* gave dubious sanctions and compromised themselves. Yet incorruptible *ulama* were seldom persecuted for their opinions (unless they supported sectarian rebellions), mostly because of their status and influence among rank-and-file Muslims.

Thus, without building a formal clergy, Muslims developed a workable moral-legal system based on a formally trained, if informally organized, scholarly elite and a

ulama

"Persons with correct knowledge." The Islamic scholarly elite who served a social function similar to the Christian clergy.

QUICK REVIEW

Religious Authority of the *Ulama*

- Opinions of *ulama* became the basis for religious and social order
- *Ulama* became a social and political elite
- *Ulama* were rarely prosecuted for their opinions

Ritual Worship. These illustrations show the sequence of movement prescribed for the ritual worship of *Salat* that each Muslim should perform five times a day. Various words of praise, prayer, and Qur'an recitation accompany each position and movement. The ritual symbolizes complete obedience to God as the one, eternal, omnipotent Lord of the universe.

How do the rituals depicted here convey an impression of submission?

tradition of concern with religious ideals in matters of public affairs and social order. If the caliphs and their deputies were seldom paragons of piety and were often ruthless, they had at least to act with circumspection and support pious standards publicly. Thus the *ulama* shared leadership in Muslim societies with the rulers, even if unequally—an enduring pattern in Islamic states.

THE *UMMA*

A strength of the Qur'anic message was its universality. By the time of the first conquests, the new state was already so rooted in Islamic ideals that non-Arab converts had to be accepted, even if it meant loss of tax revenue. The social and political status of new converts was, however, clearly second to that of Arabs. Umar had organized the army register, or **diwan**, according to tribal precedence in conversion to, or (for Christian Arab tribes) fighting for, Islam. The *diwan* served as the basis for distributing and taxing the new wealth, which perpetuated Arab precedence. The new garrisons, which rapidly became urban centers of Islamic culture, kept the Arabs enough apart that they were not simply absorbed into the cultural patterns or traditions of the new lands. The dominance of the Arabic language was ensured by the centrality of the Qur'an in Muslim life and the notion of its perfect Arabic form, together with the increasing administrative use of Arabic to replace Aramaic, Greek, Middle Persian, or Coptic.

Non-Arab converts routinely attached themselves to Arab tribes as "clients," which assured protection and a place in the *diwan*. Still, this meant accepting a permanent second-class citizenship. Although many non-Arabs, especially Persians, mastered Arabic and prospered, dissatisfaction among client Muslims led to uprisings against caliphal authority. Persian-Arab tensions were especially strong in Umayyad and early Abbasid times. Nevertheless, a Persian cultural renaissance eventually raised the Islamicized, or modern Persian language to high status in Islamic culture. Consequently, it profoundly affected Islamic religion, art, and literature.

Caliphal administration joined with the evolution of legal theory and practice and the consolidation of religious norms to give stability to the emerging Islamic society. So powerful was the Muslim vision of society that, upon the demise of a caliph, or even a dynasty such as the Umayyads, the *umma* and the caliphal office continued. There were, however, conflicting notions of that vision. In the first three Islamic centuries, two major interpretations crystallized that reflected idealistic interpretations of the *umma*, its leadership, and membership. When neither proved practical, they became minority visions that continued to fire the imaginations of some but failed to win broad-based support. A third, "centrist," vision found favor with the majority because it spoke to a wide spectrum and accommodated inevitable compromises in the cause of Islamic unity.

The most radical idealists traced their origin to the first civil war (656–661). They were the Kharijites, or "seceders" from Ali's camp, because, in their view, he compromised with his enemies. The Kharijites' demanded that the Muslim polity be based on strict Qur'anic principles. They espoused total equality of the faithful and held that the leader of the *umma* should be the best Muslim, whoever that might be. They took a rigorist view of membership in the *umma*: Anyone who committed a major sin was no longer a Muslim. Extreme Kharijites called on true Muslims to rebel against the morally compromised reigning caliph. The extremist groups were constant rallying points for opposition to the Umayyads and the Abbasids. More moderate Kharijites tolerated less-than-ideal Muslims and caliphs, yet they retained a strong sense of the moral imperatives of Muslim duty. Their ideals influenced wider Muslim pietism and even today moderate Kharijite groups survive in Oman and North Africa.

diwan
High governmental body in many Islamic states.

Ashura. As Shi'ites, Iranians stage elaborate passion plays, or *Taziyehs*, during the Ashura commemorations of the martyrdom of Imam Hussein b. 'Ali. These plays are performed annually during the first ten days of the Muslim lunar month of Muharram. Here is the culminating scene from a *Taziyeh* in Tehran on December 27, 2009, with one of the warriors of the Umayyad caliph Yazid standing over the body of the martyred Hussein, son of 'Ali and grandson of the Prophet Muhammad, who was slain at Kerbala on 10 Muharram, 680.

What are the basic beliefs of Shi'ites?

A second position was defined largely in terms of leadership of the *umma*. Muhammad had no surviving sons. Ali, who was both Muhammad's son-in-law and his cousin, claimed the caliphate in 656. Ali's blood tie with Muhammad was augmented, for many, by belief in the Prophet's designation of him as the next true Muslim leader, or *imam*. Ali's claim was contested by Mu'awiya in the first Islamic civil war. When Mu'awiya took over after a Kharijite murdered Ali in 661, many of Ali's followers felt that Islamic affairs had gone awry. The roots of the "partisans of Ali" (*Shi'at Ali*, or simply the **Shi'a**, or *Shi'ites*) go back to Ali's murder and especially to that of his son Husayn at Karbala, in Iraq, at the hands of Umayyad troops in 680.

Numerous rebellions in Umayyad times rallied around a person who claimed to be a true successor. The Abbasids based their right to the caliphate on membership in Muhammad's clan of Hashim. The major Shi'ite pretenders who emerged in the ninth and tenth centuries based their claims on both the Prophet's designation and their descent from Ali and Fatima, Muhammad's daughter. They also stressed the idea of a divinely inspired knowledge passed on by Muhammad to his designated heirs. Thus the true Muslim was the faithful follower of the *imams*, who carried Muhammad's blood and spiritual authority.

Shi'ites saw Ali's assassination and the massacre of Husayn and his family as proofs of the evil nature of this world's rulers, and as rallying points for true Muslims. Their martyrdom was extended to a line of Alid *imams* that varied among different groups of Shi'ites. True Muslims, like their *imams*, must suffer. But they would be vindicated by a *mahdi*, or "guided one," who would usher in a messianic age and judgment day that would see the faithful rewarded. (In the Sunni tradition, which we discuss next, similar "mahdist" movements arose occasionally as well.)

In later history Shi'ites did rule Islamic states, but only after 1500, in Iran, did Shi'ism prevail as the majority faith in a major state. The Shi'ite vision of the true *umma* has not been able to dominate the larger Islamic world.

Most Muslims ultimately accepted a third, less sharply defined position on leadership and membership in the *umma*. In part a compromise, it proved acceptable both to lukewarm Muslims or pragmatists and to persons of intense piety. To emphasize the correctness of their views, they eventually called themselves *Sunnis*—followers of the tradition (**sunna**) established by the Prophet and the Qur'an. Sunnis encompass a wide range of reconcilable ideas and groups. They have made up the broad middle spectrum of Muslims who tend to put communal solidarity and maintenance of the Islamic polity above purist adherence to particular tenets. They have been inclusivist rather than exclusivist, a trait that has typified the Islamic (unlike the Jewish or Christian) community through most of its history.

This centrist position provided the most workable basis for the new Islamic state. Its basic ideas were threefold: (1) The *umma* is theocratic, a state under divine authority, which translates into a nomocracy under the authority the Shari'a. The sources of guidance are, first, the Qur'an; second, Muhammad's precedent; and, third and fourth, the interpretive efforts and consensus of the Muslims (in practice, of the *ulama*). (2) The caliph is the absolute temporal ruler, charged with administering and defending the Abode of Islam and protecting

Shi'a
The minority of Muslims who trace their beliefs from the caliph Ali who was assassinated in 661 C.E.

sunna
Meaning "tradition." The dominant Islamic group whose followers are called Sunnis.

CHRONOLOGY

ORIGINS AND EARLY DEVELOPMENT OF ISLAM

ca. 570	Birth of Muhammad
622	The Hegira (*Hijra*, "emigration") of Muslims to Yathrib (henceforward *al-Madina*, "The City [of the Prophet]"); beginning of Muslim calendar
632	Death of Muhammad; Abu Bakr becomes first "successor" (*Khalifa*, caliph) to leadership, reigns 632–634
634–644	Caliphate of Umar; rapid conquests in Egypt and Iran
644–656	Caliphate of Uthman (member of Umayyad clan); more conquests; Qur'an text established; growth of sea power
656–661	Contested caliphate of Ali; first civil war
661–680	Caliphate of Mu'awiya; founding of Umayyad Dynasty (661–750); capital moved to Damascus; more expansion

Muslim norms; he possesses no greater authority than other Muslims in matters of faith. (3) A person who professes to be Muslim by witnessing that "There is no god but God, and Muhammad is his Messenger" should be considered a Muslim (because "only God knows what is in the heart"), and not even a mortal sin excludes such a person automatically from the *umma*.

Under increasingly influential *ulama* leadership, these and other basic premises of Muslim community became the theological underpinnings internationally of both the caliphal state and the majority Islamic social order.

THE HIGH CALIPHATE

WHY DID the caliphal empire decline?

The consolidation of the caliphal institution began with the victory of the Umayyad caliph Abd al-Malik in 692 in a second civil war. The ensuing century and a half mark the era of the "high caliphate," the politically strong, culturally vibrant, wealthy, and centralized institution that flourished first under the Umayyads in Damascus and then in the Abbasid capital of Baghdad.[3] The "golden age" of caliphal power and splendor came in the first century of Abbasid rule, during the caliphates of the fabled Harun al-Rashid (786–809) and his son, al-Ma'mun (813–833).

●◆●[Read the Document
Baghdad: City of Wonders
at **myhistorylab.com**

THE ABBASID STATE

The Abbasids' revolution effectively ended Arab dominance as well as Umayyad ascendancy (except in Spain). The shift of the imperial capital from Damascus to the new "city of peace" built at Baghdad on the Tigris (762–766) symbolized the geographic shift in cultural and political orientation under the new regime. In line with this, more Persians entered the bureaucracy. The Abbasids' disavowal of Shi'ite hopes for a divinely inspired imamate reflected their determination to gain the support of a broad spectrum of Muslims, even if they still stressed their descent from al-Abbas (ca. 565–653), uncle of both Muhammad and Ali.

mamluk Slave soldiers who converted to Islam, the *mamluks* eventually became a powerful military caste and even governed Egypt from 1250 to 1517.

Whereas the Umayyads had relied on Syrian Arab forces, the Abbasids used Arabs and Persians as well as provincial mercenaries for their main troops. Beginning in the ninth century, they enlisted slave soldiers (**mamluks**), mostly Turks from the northern steppes, as their personal troops. The officers of these troops, themselves *mamluks*, soon seized positions of power in the central and provincial bureaucracies and the army. Eventually the caliphs were dominated by their *mamluk* officers. This domination led to increasing alienation of the Muslim populace from their own rulers. This was evident in Iraq itself, where unrest with his overbearing Turkish guard led the Abbasid caliph to remove the government from Baghdad to the new city of Samarra 60 miles up the Tigris, where it remained from 836 to 892 (see Map 10–2).

The Great Mosque of Samarra. Built in the mid-ninth century by the Abbasid caliph al-Mutawakkil, this Friday, or congregational, mosque has a prayer space larger than nine football fields, making it the largest such enclosed space in the Islamic world. The style of the minaret recalls the ziggurats of ancient Babylon.

Why was early Abbasid rule attractive to large numbers of people?

SOCIETY

The deep division between rulers and populace—the functionally secular state and its subjects—became typical of Islamic societies. However, even while provincial rulers' independence reduced Abbasid central power after the mid-ninth century, such rulers nominally recognized caliphal authority. This gave them legitimacy as guardians of the Islamic socioreligious order, which meanwhile found its real cohesiveness in the Muslim ideals being standardized and propagated by the *ulama*.

---

[3]This periodization of early Islamic government follows that of M. G. S. Hodgson, *The Venture of Islam*, Vol. 1 (Chicago: University of Chicago Press, 1984), pp. 217–236.

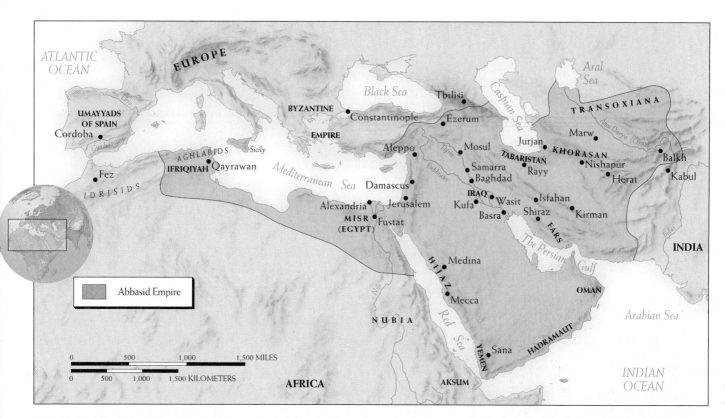

MAP 10–2. The Abbasid Empire, ca. 900 C.E. A great diversity of peoples and nations were united by the Abbasids. Their capital at Baghdad became the center of a trading network that linked India, Africa, and China.

Which Muslim regions were not part of the Abbasid Empire and why?

Full conversion of the populace of the Islamic Empire lagged behind centralization of political power and development of Islamic socioreligious institutions. Iraq and Iran saw the fullest Islamization of local elites before the mid-twelfth century, followed by Spain, North Africa, and Syria. Conversion and fuller Islamization increased Muslim self-confidence and diminished the need for centralized caliphal power.[4]

DECLINE

The eclipse of the caliphal empire was foreshadowed at the outset of Abbasid rule when one of the last Umayyads fled west to Spain, where he founded a Spanish Islamic state (756–1030) that produced the spectacular Moorish culture of Spain. The Spanish Umayyads grew so strong that they claimed the title of caliph in 929. In all the Abbasid provinces, regional governments were always potential independent states. In North Africa in 801 Harun al-Rashid's governor set up his own state in modern Tunisia. In Egypt, the Fatimids set up Shi'ite rule in 969 and claimed to be the only true caliphate.

In the East, Iranian lands grew harder for Baghdad to control. Beginning in 821 in Khorasan, Abbasid governors or rebels started independent dynasties repeatedly for the next two centuries, and the caliph usually had to recognize them. Among the longest-lived of these Iranian dynasties were the Samanids, who ruled at Bukhara as nominal Abbasid vassals from 875 until 999. They gave northeastern Iran a long period of economic and political security from Turkish steppe invaders. Under their

QUICK REVIEW

Abbasid State

- Ruled from Baghdad
- Arab dominance replaced by Eastern, especially Persian, influence
- Leaders of slave soldiers (*mamluks*) gained power
- Splendid court left rich cultural legacy

---

[4]Richard W. Bulliet, *Conversion to Islam in the Medieval Period* (Cambridge, MA: Harvard University Press, 1979), especially pp. 7–15, 128–138.

sultans Rulers who have almost complete sovereignty over a certain domain without claiming the title of caliph.

aegis, Persian poetry and Arabic scientific studies began a Persian Islamic cultural renaissance and an influential scientific tradition.

Of greatest consequence for the Abbasid caliphate was the rise in the mountains south of the Caspian of a Shi'ite clan, the Buyids, who took over Abbasid rule in 945. Henceforth the caliph and his descendants were largely puppets in the hands of a Buyid "commander" (*emir*). In 1055 the Buyids were replaced by the more famous, Turkish-speaking Seljuk **sultans**. By this time the caliphal office had long been under the control of the ruler in Baghdad, and this was to remain the case until the Mongols destroyed even nominal Abbasid caliphal authority in 1258 (see Chapter 12).

ISLAMIC CULTURE IN THE CLASSICAL ERA

WHAT WERE the main achievements of "classical" Islamic culture?

The pomp and splendor of the Abbasid court became the stuff of legends, such as those preserved much later in *A Thousand and One Nights*. Their rich cultural legacy was made possible by a strong army and central government and vigorous internal and external trade, probably stimulated by the prosperous Tang Chinese Empire with which Islamic lands had overland and maritime contact. Material factors, such as the introduction of paper manufacture from China through Samarkand about 750, or the flight of Byzantine scholars east to new Abbasid centers of learning, contributed to the intellectual vibrancy of the early Abbasid era.

INTELLECTUAL TRADITIONS

The Abbasid heyday was marked by sophisticated tastes and insatiable thirst for all knowledge. An Arab historian called Baghdad "the market to which the wares of the sciences and arts were brought, where wisdom was sought as a man seeks after his stray camels, and whose judgment of values was accepted by the whole world." Contacts (primarily among intellectuals) between Muslims and Christian, Jewish, Zoroastrian, and other "protected" communities contributed to the cosmopolitanism of the age. Some older intellectual traditions experienced a revival. Philosophy, astronomy, mathematics, medicine, and other natural sciences enjoyed strong interest and patronage. In Islamic usage, philosophy and the sciences were subsumed under *falsafa* (from Greek *philosophia*). Islamic culture took over the tradition of rational inquiry from the Hellenic world and preserved and developed it when Europe was a cultural backwater.

An Illustration from *The Maqamat* of al Hariri (d. 1122), a masterpiece of Arabic literature of the later Middle Ages. Its entertaining stories, written in rhymed prose, have passed into popular lore in the Islamic world.

What are some characteristics of Arabic literature?

CHRONOLOGY	
"CLASSICAL" PERIOD OF THE HIGH CALIPHATE	
786–809	Caliphate of Harun al-Rashid; apogee of caliphal power
813–833	Caliphate of al-Ma'mun; patronage of translations of Greek, Sanskrit, and other works into Arabic; first heavy reliance on slave soldiers (*mamluks*)
875	Rise of Samanid power at Bukhara; patronage of Persian poetry paves way for Persian literary renaissance
909	Rise of Shi'ite Fatimid Dynasty in North Africa
945–1055	Buyid emirs rule the eastern empire at Baghdad; Abbasid caliphs become largely figureheads
1055	Buyids replaced by Seljuk sultans as effective rulers at Baghdad and custodians of the caliphate

Arabic translations of Greek and Sanskrit works stimulated progress in astronomy and medicine. Translation reached its peak in al-Ma'mun's new academy headed by a Nestorian Christian, Hunayn ibn Ishaq (d. 873), noted for his medical and Greek learning. There were Arabic translations of everything from the Greek works of Galen, Ptolemy, Euclid, Aristotle, Plato, and the Neo-Platonists to Indian Sanskrit fables earlier translated into Middle Persian under the Sasanids. Such translations stimulated not only Arabic learning, but later also that of the less advanced European world.

LANGUAGE AND LITERATURE

Arabic language and literature developed greatly in the new empire. A significant genre of Arabic writing emerged. Known as *adab*, or "manners" literature, it included essays and didactic literature influenced by Persian letters. Poetry also flourished by building on the tradition of the Arabic ode, or **qasida**. Grammar was central to the interpretation of the Qur'an that occupied the *ulama* and undergirded an emerging religious-learning curriculum. Historical, geographical, and biographical writing became major Arabic genres. They owed much to the ancient accounts of "the battle days of the Arabs" but sought to record the lives of the Prophet and Companions, and then those of subsequent generations. Such records of persons were crucial to judging the reliability of the "chains" of transmitters accompanying each traditional report, or **hadith**. A *hadith* reports words or actions ascribed to Muhammad and the Companions; it became the chief source of Muslim legal and religious norms alongside the Qur'an, as well as the basic unit of most prose genres. The work of al-Shafi'i (d. 820) on legal reasoning was the shining exemplar of the many collections of the *hadith* that were mined by preachers and interpreters of the law.

ART AND ARCHITECTURE

In art and architecture the Abbasid era saw the crystallization of a "classical" Islamic style by about 1000 C.E. Except for ceramics and calligraphy, most Islamic art and architecture had clear antecedents in Greco-Roman, Byzantine, or Persian art. But older forms and motifs were now used in new ways and combinations, and they spread to new locales—generally from east (especially the Fertile Crescent) to west (Syria, Egypt, North Africa, and Spain). Sasanid stucco decoration techniques and designs turned up, for example, in Egypt and North Africa. Chronologically, urban Iraq developed an Islamic art first, then made its influence felt east and west, whether in Bukhara or in Syria and North Africa. Also new were the combination and elaboration of discrete forms, as in the case of the colonnade (or hypostyle) mosque or complex arabesque designs.

Muslims had reason to be self-confident about their faith and culture. Most monuments of the age express the distinctiveness they felt. Particular formal items, such as calligraphic motifs and inscriptions on buildings, came to characterize Islamic architecture and define its functions. Most striking was the avoidance of pictures or icons in

qasida
Some of the most elaborate poems in the world, they generally run 50–100 lines, have a single, unifying theme, regular rhyme and meter, and speak in praise of a ruler or an idea.

hadith
A saying or action ascribed to Muhammad.

The Congregational Mosque. Two examples of the finest congregational mosques of the classical Islamic world. The large courtyards and pillared halls of these buildings were intended not only for worship, but also for mass community gatherings for official communications or mustering troops in time of war. Their splendor announced the presence and power of Islamic rule. The top photo shows the Great Mosque at Qayrawan in modern Tunisia, built during the eighth and ninth centuries. The bottom photo shows the Spanish Umayyad mosque in Córdoba, built in the eighth to tenth centuries in a series of roofed extensions—unlike the mosque of Qayrawan, which has only one great hall and covered colonnades around its central courtyard.

(A) Werner Forman Archive, Art Resource, New York; (B) Adam Lubroth, Art Resource, New York.

How does the layout of these mosques comment on the role of the community in early Islam?

The Qur'an. Gold-embellished page from an eighth- or ninth-century Qur'an in Kufic script (23.8 × 35.5 cm). The earliest Qur'ans were oriented horizontally and lettered in angular Kufic script (named for the city of Kufa in Iraq).

Arabic Manuscript: 30.60 Page from a Koran, 8th–9th century. Kufic script. H: 23.8 x W: 35.5 cm. Courtesy of the Freer Gallery of Art, Smithsonian Institution, Washington, DC: Purchase, F1930.60r.

Why would a Qur'an be written in an artful script, in a manuscript incorporating gold?

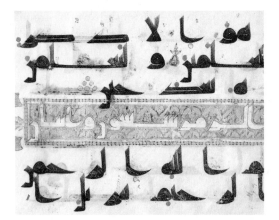

public art. This was, of course, in line with the Muslim aversion both to any hint of idolatry and to the strongly iconic Byzantine Christian art. Although this iconoclasm later diminished, it was a telling expression of the general thrust of Muslim faith and the culture it animated. Overall, the Muslims' artistic achievements before the year 1000 impress us with a quality that is distinctively and "classically" Islamic, whatever the details of particular examples.[5]

SUMMARY

WHAT WAS the Qur'anic message as expressed to Muhammad?

Origins and Early Development. The Prophet Muhammad (ca. 570–632) was the founder of Islam. Born in the Arabian commercial city of Mecca, he was influenced by contact with Arab Christians and with Jews. At about age 40, he had a religious experience during which, Muslims believe, God's messenger angel Gabriel repeatedly performed recitation (*qur'an*) of God's word to him. The message of the Qur'an was (1) social justice and worship of the one true God are required of every person; (2) at the end of time, people will be resurrected and judged by God, who will reward or punish them according to how they have lived; and (3) the proper response to God is submission (*islam*) to his will by becoming a *muslim* ("one who submits"). *page 242*

HOW DID the status of women improve under Islam?

Women in Early Islamic Society. Islamic law emphasizes community, and family is the foundation of community. The Qur'an recognizes many more rights for women than traditional Arabian custom permitted, but the social vision expressed in the Qur'an is still fundamentally patriarchal. *page 246*

WHY WAS Islam able to expand rapidly?

Early Islamic Conquests. By the time of Muhammad's death, his followers had conquered all of Arabia. Under his successors, the caliphs, Muslim Arab armies conquered most of the Near East, North Africa, Spain, Sasanid Iran, and northwest India. Many of the peoples of these territories welcomed Islamic rule as liberation from Persian or Byzantine domination and eventually converted to Islam and became part of the *umma*, the community of Islamic believers. *page 247*

WHAT ROLES did the caliphate and *ulama* play in Islamic states?

The New Islamic World Order. Disputes over the succession to the Prophet divided Muslims. The *ulama*, Islamic religious and legal scholars, played a prominent part in Islamic society as interpreters of Islamic tradition and law. Islamic unity and preservation of the community (*umma*) withstood the idealistic challenges of the Kharijites and the Shi'ites, largely thanks to the broad appeal of centrist Sunni interpretations of the faith. *page 249*

WHY DID the caliphal empire decline?

The High Caliphate. Under the Abbasid caliphs who ruled from the city of Baghdad, the Islamic Empire began to splinter. Large parts of the empire—Spain, North Africa, Iran—seceded. Military commanders (*emirs*) in Baghdad reduced the caliphs to mere figureheads by the tenth century. *page 256*

[5]Grabar, *Formation of Islamic Art*, (New Haven: Yale University Press, 1973), pp. 1–103, 206–213.

WHAT WERE the main achievements of "classical" Islamic culture?

Islamic Culture in the Classical Era. Islamic culture enjoyed its "classical" phase under the Abbasids. Arabic translations of Greek and Sanskrit works stimulated progress in astronomy and medicine. Arabic literature and poetry flourished. As the sacred medium of God's final revelation, the Arabic language spread throughout the Islamic world. Arabic artists and architects built on Greco-Roman, Byzantine, and Persian traditions to develop a distinctive Islamic style in decoration, painting, and architecture. *page 258*

KEY TERMS

caliphate (KAY-liff-AYT) (p. 250)

diwan (dih-WAHN) (p. 254)

emir (ee-MEER) (p. 250)

hadith (ha-DEETH) (p. 259)

Hajj (HADJ) (p. 245)

hegira (hih-JEYE-rah) (p. 245)

imam (ih-MAHM) (p. 250)

islam (p. 244)

jihad (jih-HAHD) (p. 248)

Ka'ba (KAAH-ba) (p. 242)

mamluk (MAM-look) (p. 256)

qasida (kuh-SEE-duh) (p. 259)

qur'an (koh-RAN) (p. 244)

Shi'a (SHEE-ah) (p. 255)

sultans (p. 258)

sunna (SOO-nah) (p. 255)

ulama (OO-luh-MAAH) (p. 253)

umma (UHM-uh) (p. 245)

REVIEW QUESTIONS

1. Describe Arabian society before Islam. What were the prime targets of the Qur'anic message in that society?

2. What are the main features of the Islamic worldview? How do Islamic ideas about history, salvation, law, social justice, and other key issues compare to those of Christianity and Judaism?

3. What rights for women did the Qur'an support that were not widely accepted in Arab society? In what areas can the Qur'an be seen as limiting women's rights?

4. What were the primary kinds of leadership in the early Islamic polities? To what extent was political and religious leadership separated in different offices and functions?

5. Discuss the conversion of subject populations in the early centuries of Islamic empire. What were the incentives and obstacles to conversion?

6. As time passed after Muhammad's death and Muslim territory expanded, were Muslims successful in preserving the community envisioned in the Qur'an? Discuss why or why not.

7. Why were the initial Arab armies so successful?

8. Why was the imperial caliphal state eclipsed? What were some of the lasting accomplishments of the Umayyad and Abbasid empires?

9. What are the doctrinal differences between Kharijites, Shi'ites, and Sunnis? In what sense are Sunnis "centrist"?

10. Discuss the "classical" culture of the golden age of the caliphate. What role did foreign traditions play in it? What were some of its prominent achievements?

Note: To learn more about the topics in this chapter, please turn to the Suggested Readings at the end of the book. For additional sources related to this chapter please see www.myhistorylab.com

myhistorylab Connections

Reinforce what you learned in this chapter by studying the many documents, images, maps, review tools, and videos available at **www.myhistorylab.com**

Read and Review

✓ **Study** and **Review** Chapter 10

Read the Document *Al-Tabari: Muhammad's Call to Prophecy, p. 243*

Al-Tabari and Ibn Hisham, from "The Founding of the Caliphate," p. 250

Baghdad: City of Wonders, p. 256

View the Image *The Qur'an, p. 244*

Research and Explore

See the Map *Expansion of Islam, p. 243*

Hear the Audio

Hear the audio file for Chapter 10 at **www.myhistorylab.com**

11

The Byzantine Empire and Western Europe to 1000

((•─Hear the **Audio** for Chapter 11 at www.myhistorylab.com

Hagia Sophia. One of the greatest achievements of Byzantine civilization, Hagia Sophia (the Church of Holy Wisdom) was completed in 537 C.E. by Anthemius of Tralles and Isidore of Miletus. Circled with numerous windows, the great dome floods the hall with light and, together with the church's many other windows, mosaics, and open spaces, gives the interior a remarkable airiness and luminosity. After the Turkish conquest of Constantinople in 1453, Hagia Sophia was transformed into a mosque.

What impression do you get from looking at this space? Do you think the architects wished to convey this feeling?

*T*he early Middle Ages (or early medieval period) marks the birth of Europe. Greco-Roman culture combined with Germanic culture and an evolving Christianity to create distinctive political and cultural forms. In government, religion, and language, what had been the northern and western provinces of the Roman Empire grew apart from the eastern Byzantine world and a Mediterranean-based Islamic Arabia.

German tribes had been settling peacefully around the Roman Empire since the first century B.C.E., but in the fourth century C.E. they began to migrate directly into it from the north and east. During the fifth century they turned fiercely against their hosts, largely because the Romans treated them so cruelly. To the south, Arab dominance transformed the Mediterranean and challenged Western trade with the East. Western Europe became insular. Forced to manage by themselves, western Europeans learned to develop their native resources. The reign of Charlemagne saw a modest renaissance of antiquity, aided by Byzantium and Arabia. The peculiar social and political forms that emerged during this period—manorialism and feudalism—successfully coped with unprecedented chaos on local levels, while nourishing the growth of distinctively Western institutions. ■

THE END OF THE WESTERN ROMAN EMPIRE

In the early fifth century, Italy and Rome suffered a series of devastating blows. In 410 the Visigoths sacked Rome. In 452 the Huns, led by Attila—known to contemporaries as the "scourge of God"—invaded Italy. And in 455 Rome was overrun by the Vandals.

By the mid-fifth century, power in western Europe had passed to barbarian chieftains. In 476, the traditional date given for the fall of the Roman Empire, the barbarian

HOW DID the Byzantine Empire continue the legacy of the Roman Empire?

263

THE EARLY MIDDLE AGES

In western Europe, the centuries between 400 and 1000 witnessed both the decline of Classical civilization and the birth of a new European civilization. Beginning with the fifth century, a series of barbarian invasions separated western Europe culturally from its Classical age. This prolonged separation was unique to western Europe. Along with the invasions themselves and the new cultural traits they brought into Europe, it was pivotal to the development of European civilization. Although some important works and concepts survived from antiquity due largely to the Christian church, Western civilization labored for centuries to recover its rich classical past in "renaissances" stretching into the sixteenth century. Out of this mixture of barbarian and surviving (or recovered) classical culture, Western civilization was born. With the aid of a Christian church eager to restore order and centralized rule, the Carolingians created a new, albeit fragile, imperial tradition. But Western society remained highly fragmented politically and economically during the Early Middle Ages. Meanwhile, many of the world's other great civilizations of the first millennium C.E. were peaking.

In China, particularly in the seventh and eighth centuries, Tang Dynasty rulers also sought ways to secure their borders against foreign expansion, mainly pastoral nomads. China at this time was far more cosmopolitan and politically unified than western Europe, and also centuries ahead in technology. By the tenth century, the Chinese were printing with movable type, an invention the West did not achieve until the fifteenth century, and then very likely borrowed in prototype from China. The effective authority of Chinese rulers extended far beyond their immediate centers of government. The Tang Dynasty held sway over their empire in a way Carolingian rulers could only imagine.

In Japan, the Yamato court (300–680), much like the court of the Merovingians and Carolingians, struggled to unify and control the countryside. Shintō, a religion friendly to royalty, aided the Yamato. As in the West, a Japanese identity evolved through struggle and accommodation with outside cultures, especially with the Chinese, the dominant influence on Japan between the seventh and twelfth centuries. But foreign cultural influence, again as in the West, never managed to eradicate the

Odovacer (ca. 434–493) deposed the last Western Roman emperor. The Eastern emperor Zeno (r. 474–491) recognized Odovacer's authority in the West, and Odovacer acknowledged Zeno as sole emperor, contenting himself to serve as Zeno's Western viceroy. By the end of the fifth century the Ostrogoths had settled in Italy, the Franks in northern Gaul, the Burgundians in Provence, the Visigoths in southern Gaul and Spain, the Vandals in Africa and the western Mediterranean, and the Angles and Saxons in England (see Map 11–1 on page 266).

The barbarians admired Roman culture and had no desire to destroy it. Except in Britain and northern Gaul, Roman law, government, and language (Latin) coexisted with the new Germanic institutions. Only the Vandals and the Anglo-Saxons refused to profess titular obedience to the emperor in Constantinople.

The Visigoths, the Ostrogoths, and the Vandals were Christians, which helped them accommodate to Roman culture, but they followed the Arian creed, which was considered heretical in the West. Around 500, the Franks converted to the Orthodox, or "Catholic," form of Christianity supported by the bishops of Rome. As we will see, the Franks ultimately dominated most of western Europe, helping convert the Goths and other barbarians to Roman Christianity.

A gradual interpenetration of two strong cultures—a creative tension—marked the period of the Germanic migrations. Despite the Western military defeat, the Goths and the Franks became far more romanized than the Romans were germanized. Latin language, Nicene Christianity, and eventually Roman law and government were to triumph in the West during the Middle Ages.

THE BYZANTINE EMPIRE

Imperial power shifted to the eastern part of the Roman Empire, whose center was the city of Byzantium (modern-day Istanbul). Between 324 and 330, Emperor Constantine the Great rebuilt and renamed the city after himself. Constantinople

indigenous culture. By the ninth century a distinctive Sino-Japanese culture existed. Like western Europe, Japan remained a fragmented land during these centuries, despite a certain allegiance and willingness to pay taxes to an imperial court. Throughout Japan, as in western Europe, the basic unit of political control consisted of highly self-conscious and specially devoted armed retainers. A system of lordship and vassalage evolved around bands of local mounted warriors known as samurai. Through this system, local order was maintained in Japan until the fifteenth century. Like the Merovingian and Carolingian courts, the Japanese court had to tolerate strong and independent regional rulers.

While western Europe struggled for political and social order in the fourth and fifth centuries, Indian civilization basked in a golden age under the reign of the Guptas (320–467). In this era of peace and stability, when a vocationally and socially limiting caste system neatly imposed order on Indian society from Brahmans to outcasts, culture, religion, and politics flourished.

In the seventh century, Islamic armies emerged from the Arabian Peninsula, conquered territory from India to Spain by 710, and gave birth to a powerful new international civilization. Cosmopolitan and culturally vibrant, this civilization flourished despite the breakdown of Islamic political unity beginning in the ninth and tenth centuries. Islamic cultural strides in this era overshadowed the modest cultural renaissance in the West under Charlemagne.

Focus Questions

◆ What caused the prolonged separation of western European civilization from its Classical past? What were the consequences of this separation for western Europe?

◆ Which other society most resembled that of western Europe during this period? Why?

◆ While western Europe struggled to regain order, unity, and contact with its Classical past, what was happening in the other great civilizations of the world?

remained the capital of both the old Roman and the new Byzantine Empires until the eighth century, when Charlemagne reclaimed the Western Roman Empire's imperial title. The term *Byzantine* refers to the Greek, Hellenistic, Roman, and Judaic monotheistic elements that distinguish the culture of the East from the Latin West.

The history of the Byzantine Empire has three distinct periods:

1. From the rebuilding of Byzantium as Constantinople in 324, through an early period of expansion and splendor, to the beginning of the Arab expansion and the spread of Islam in 632.

2. A time of sustained contraction and splintering, from 632 to the conquest of Asia Minor by the Saljuq Turks in 1071 or, as some prefer, to the fall of Constantinople to the Western Crusaders in 1204.

3. From either 1071 or 1204 to the catastrophic fall of Constantinople to the Ottoman Turks in 1453, the end of the empire in the East.

THE REIGN OF JUSTINIAN

The first period of Byzantine history (324–632) was by far its greatest, and its pinnacle was the reign of the emperor Justinian (r. 527–565). He ruled with the assistance of his remarkable wife, Theodora. The daughter of a circus bear trainer, Theodora had allegedly been an entertainer and a prostitute

Justinian as Conqueror. A classical ivory carving of Justinian celebrating his conquests in Italy, North Africa, and West Asia, ca. 500 C.E.

What were some of Justinian's nonmilitary achievements?

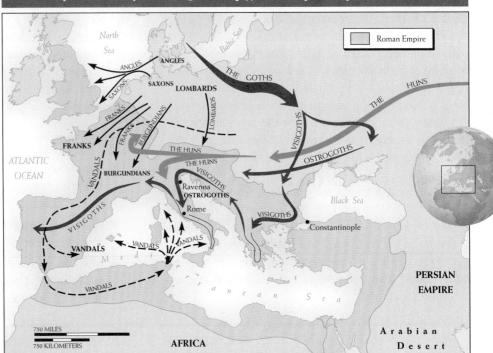

MAP EXPLORATION

To explore this map further, go to **http://www.myhistorylab.com**

MAP 11–1.   Barbarian Migrations into the West in the Fourth and Fifth Centuries.

The forceful intrusion of Germanic and non-Germanic tribes into the empire from the last quarter of the fourth century through the fifth century made for a constantly changing pattern of movement and relations. The map shows the major routes taken by the usually unwelcome newcomers and the areas most deeply affected by the main groups.

Which part of the Roman Empire was least affected by barbarian migrations?

View the Image
Emperor Justinian at **myhistorylab.com**

Read the Document
Reign Justinian: Secret History, Procopius
at **myhistorylab.com**

Read the Document
Prologue, Corpus Civilis, ca. 530
at **myhistorylab.com**

QUICK REVIEW

Justinian Government

♦ *Corpus Juris Civilis* collated and revised Roman law

♦ Close ties between rulers and church

♦ Empire had many large cities and was the crossroads of Asian and European civilizations

in her youth. She equaled her husband in intelligence and exceeded him in toughness. In 532, when a riot threatened to overthrow their administration, he planned to flee. She convinced him to stay and put down the rebellion by ordering the slaughter of tens of thousands of protesters.

Under Justinian, the empire's strength lay in its more than 1,500 cities. Constantinople was the largest, with perhaps 350,000 inhabitants, and it was the crossroads of Asian and European cultures. Larger provincial cities had populations of approximately 50,000. These towns were administered at first by councils of wealthy local landowners, the *Decurions*. Being heavily taxed, these landowners were prone to rebellion. Consequently, by the sixth century the emperor had replaced them with governors chosen for their personal loyalty. Tighter central control was justified by the need to resist barbarian pressures from the north and east.

Justinian's policy—"one God, one empire, one religion"—was to centralize government by imposing legal and doctrinal conformity throughout his domain. To this end he ordered a codification of existing law. The result was the *Corpus Juris Civilis*, or "Body of Civil Law," organized in four parts. The *Code* revised imperial edicts issued by emperors since the reign of Hadrian (r. 117–138). The *Novellae*, or "New Things," dealt with decrees issued by emperors since 534, including Justinian.

OVERVIEW   Barbarian Invasions of the Western Roman Empire

The Germanic tribes—the barbarians—who overran the Western Roman Empire had coexisted with the Romans for centuries in a relationship marked more by the commingling of cultures and trade than by warfare. The arrival of the Huns from the east in the late fourth century, however, caused many of the tribes, beginning with the Visigoths in 376, to flee westward and seek refuge within the empire. They found the western half of the empire weakened by famine, disease, high taxation, and an enfeebled military. The Romans lost control of their frontiers, and in the fifth century, the tribes overran the West and set up their own domains. The following is a list of the most important tribes and the areas they controlled by the year 500.

TRIBES	AREA OF CONTROL
Anglo-Saxons	Most of England
Franks	Northeast France
Burgundians	Eastern-central France
Alemanni	Switzerland
Visigoths	Most of Spain and southern France
Suevi	Northwest Spain
Vandals	North Africa
Ostrogoths	Italy, Austria, Croatia, Slovenia

The *Digest* organized opinions penned by famous jurists, and the *Institutes* was a kind of textbook for scholars. Because Roman law emphasized the authority of a single sovereign, later European rulers found Justinian's collection useful when they struggled to centralize power. Between the Renaissance and the nineteenth century, his code helped shape many governments.

Empress Theodora and her Attendants ca. 547 c.e. A mosaic from the Basilica of S. Vitale in Ravenna, Italy.

Was Theodora typical of powerful women in this era? Explain.

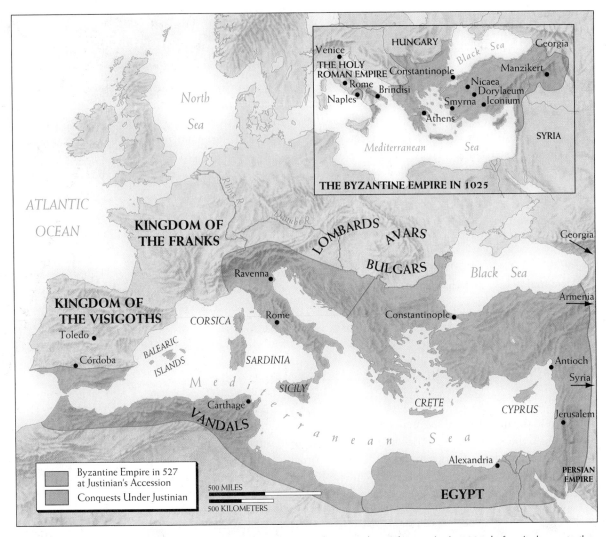

MAP 11–2.   The Byzantine Empire at the Death of Justinian.   The inset shows the empire in 1025, before its losses to the Seljuk Turks.

How did Justinian attempt to re-create the Roman Empire?

Justinian attempted to regain control of the Western Roman Empire, but his success was partial and temporary. He reoccupied Italy, North Africa, and parts of Spain but at a cost that his beleaguered empire could ill afford (see Map 11–2).

Nomadic Avars, Slavs, and Bulgars invaded the lands north and west of Constantinople in the sixth and seventh centuries. The Slavs were converted to Eastern Orthodoxy (Byzantine Christianity) by two learned missionaries sent from Constantinople: the future Saints Cyril and Methodius. They created a Greek-based alphabet adapted to writing the Slavic language. When the Bulgars conquered and absorbed the Slavs, this script was revised; it is now known as Cyrillic or Old Church Slavonic. It facilitated the spread of Byzantine Christianity and culture in eastern Europe and Russia.

During the reign of Emperor Heraclius (r. 610–641), the empire turned east. Heraclius spoke only Greek, not Latin. He spent his entire reign resisting Persian and Islamic invasions, the former successfully, the latter in vain. In 628 he defeated the Persian king Chosroes. After 632, Islamic armies progressively overran the empire. Not until the reign of Leo III of the Isaurian Dynasty (r. 717–740) did the Byzantines repel Arab armies and regain at least most of Asia Minor, but the larger Mediterranean empire was lost forever. The downsized empire was restructured by creating provincial strongholds under the direct authority of imperially appointed generals, allowing a more disciplined and flexible use of military power in time of crisis.

THE IMPORTANCE OF CONSTANTINOPLE

As the capital of the Eastern Roman Empire and an immense commercial network, Constantinople was vital to the Empire and featured prominently in the psyche of its neighbors and enemies. The Byzantines claimed that two-thirds of the world's wealth was concentrated in their capital.[1] Since all the city's economic activity was strictly regulated, a large bureaucratic corpus arose that featured its own aristocracy.[2] This class was soon influential at court and stood counter to the landed nobility, ensuring that the empire never became a feudal order.

Constantinople's riches attracted merchants from all over Europe and the Muslim world. By 1143, Constantinople contained Genoan, Pisan, French, Venetian, Jewish, and Muslim "quarters," or areas reserved for the homes and businesses of outsiders. The existence of such collectives meant that their sponsor nations developed an active interest in the economic affairs of the city, while native Byzantines felt betrayed by their government. This tension affected the political landscape of the entire region. For allowing the masses to exact bloody retribution on the merchant quarters, Andronicus I rose to power and eventually usurped the throne.[3] Constantinople's fame was far-reaching. The Varangian Guard, a fearsome force that served as palace bodyguards, was composed entirely of Scandinavian and English soldiers, young men who had left their homelands to seek their fortune in the "Empress of Cities." The city suffered numerous sieges in its history, with each failed attempt only adding to the perceived glory of success. Constantinople was such an object of fascination to Arab empires that mystical traditions proclaimed the Muslim conquest of Constantinople as one of the six portents of *ashrat al sa'a*, the end of the world.[4]

THE HEIGHT OF BYZANTINE IMPERIAL POWER IN THE TENTH CENTURY

The military reforms of the seventh and eighth centuries allowed the Byzantine Empire to deal more successfully with its enemies, leading to a period of stability and peace in the middle of the tenth century. Under rulers of the Macedonian Dynasty, founded by Basil I (867-886), the eastern Mediterranean was again under Byzantine control. Bulgarian advances into Byzantine territory were brought to a halt by the fiercest military emperor of the dynasty, Basil II (r. 976-1025), known as the "Bulgar-slayer."

The tenth century became a period of strong imperial rule. Macedonian rule brought forth a flourishing age of art, culture, and literature personified in the period's philosopher-king, Emperor Constantine VII *Porphyrogenitus* (i.e. "born in the 'imperial

Ruins of Constantinople. The walls of the city of Constantinople were built in the fifth century and were expanded and improved until the fifteenth century.

What were some of the symbolic roles played by Constantinople?

👁 See the **Map**
The Byzantine Empire under Justinian at **myhistorylab.com**

---

[1] Robert de Claris, "La conquête de Constantinople," in *Three Old French Chronicles of the Crusades*, ed. Edward N. Stone (Seattle, WA, 1939), Chapter 81.

[2] George Ostrogorsky, *History of the Byzantine State* (New Brunswick, NJ: Rutgers University Press, 1999), p. 253.

[3] Charles M. Brand, *Byzantium Confronts the West 1180–1204* (Cambridge, MA: Harvard University Press, 1968), p. 41.

[4] Nadia Maria El-Cheikh, *Byzantium Viewed by the Arabs* (London, England: Harvard University Press, 2004), p. 67.

purple' "), sole ruler from 945 to 959. The University of Constantinople and the intellectuals who attended this institution in the eleventh century were products of the Macedonian revival. They included, most famously, Michael Psellus, the author of *The Chronography*, an account of the reigns of fourteen Byzantine emperors and empresses. Economically speaking, the Macedonian rule was a period of "state-controlled" growth, when imperial legislation restrained the growth of large landowners in order to protect small landowners and peasants.

The military peace that made this revival possible began to dissolve with the loss of the last stronghold of the Byzantine Empire in the West: Bari, a town in southern Italy which fell to the Norman kings of France in 1071. In the same year, Muslim Saljuq Turks destroyed the imperial army at the battle of Manzikert in 1071 and overran Anatolia, the heartland from which Constantinople recruited its soldiers. Thereafter, the Byzantine Empire was forced to fight against enemies on two fronts, while it continued to serve as a bastion of the religious and cultural heritage of the West.

After two decades of steady Turkish advances, the Eastern emperor Alexius I Comnenus (r. 1081–1118) called for Western aid in 1092. Three years later, the West launched the first Crusade. A century later (1204), the Fourth Crusade stopped in Constantinople en route to Jerusalem, but not to rescue the Eastern capital; Latin Crusaders inflicted more damage on Eastern Christendom's holy city than all previous non-Christian invaders had done. (See Chapter 15.)

See the Map
Byzantium 1000–1100
at **myhistorylab.com**

THE RELIGIOUS DIVERSITY OF CHRISTENDOM

Religious belief alternately served and undermined imperial political unity. In 391, Christianity became the official faith of the Eastern Empire, while all other religions and sects were deemed "demented and insane." The patriarch of Constantinople crowned Byzantine emperors. Patriarchs in other cities received generous endowments of land and gold from rich donors, empowering the church to act as the state's welfare agency. Great wealth and prestige bound the clergy tightly to state service.

Christianity was the dominant faith, but large numbers of Jews lived within the Byzantine Empire. Roman law had protected them, so long as they did not proselytize Christians, but some Byzantine emperors tried to induce or to compel their conversion to Christianity. Neither approach was successful.

Although the state religion was Orthodox Christianity, some Christian heresies attracted large followings and occasionally received imperial support. Justinian, for instance, was passionately orthodox, but Theodora was a Monophysite, a variant of the faith that was popular in the East. Monophysites taught that Christ had a single, immortal nature and was not a union of eternal God and mortal man. Byzantine art portrays Christ, a self-same person with God, as impassive and transcendent, not as a suffering mortal man. The modern Coptic, Syrian, and Armenian churches endorse this belief. It was condemned as a heresy in the West in 451.

Eastern and Western theologians also disagreed on whether the Holy Spirit proceeded from both the Son and the Father. This dispute dates back to the first Ecumenical Council in Nicaea (modern Iznik, a city in western Turkey) convened in 325. There the council established 'The Orthodox Creed' also known as 'The Nicene Creed.' It was adopted with certain changes by the ecumenical council of Constantinople (381) and by subsequent ecumenical councils of the Eastern Orthodox Church. According to the Nicene-Constantinopolitan Creed, the Holy Spirit proceeded from the Father alone, unlike the post-sixth century versions accepted by the

Virgin and Child with Saints and Angels. A sixth-century icon of the Virgin and Child surrounded by warrior saints (Theodore on the left; George on the right) and wary angels. A rare survivor of eighth-century iconoclasm.

What is iconoclasm?

DOCUMENT

The Nicene Creed

The Nicene-Constantinopolitan Creed is the first official pronouncement of the Christian belief system and the first official definition of the Christian "orthodox" faith. As such, the creed distinguished orthodox belief or "correct" belief, from heretical versions.

- **THE NICENE** Creed emphasizes the two natures of Christ. Which "unorthodox" beliefs does this document aim to uproot? Historically, how did the controversy surrounding the term *filioque* arise? Please discuss the significance of the term starting from the Nicene Creed.

"We believe in one God, the Father Almighty, maker of all things visible and invisible; and in one Lord Jesus Christ, the Son of God, the only begotten of his Father, of the substance of the Father, God of God, Light of Light, very God of very God, begotten, not made, being of one substance with the Father. By whom all things were made, both which [are] in heaven and in earth. Who for us men and for our salvation came down [from heaven] and was incarnate and was made man. He suffered and the third day he rose again, and ascended into heaven. And he shall come again to judge both the quick and the dead. And [we believe] in the Holy Ghost. And whosoever shall say that there was a time when the Son of God was not, or that before he was begotten he was not, or that he was made of things that were not, or that he is of a different substance or essence [from the Father] or that he is a creature, or subject to change or [convert] - all that say so the Catholic and Apostolic Church anathematizes them.

Source: Philip Schaff and Henry Wace, eds., *The Seven Ecumenical Councils, vol. 14, A Select Library of Nicene and Post-Nicene Fathers of the Christian Church* (Grand Rapids, MI, 1957).

Western Church, which included the phrase "from the Son" (*filioque*). (See Document, "The Nicene Creed.")

Some scholars perceive here a hidden political concern: By protecting the unity and majesty of the Father, Eastern theology was safeguarding the unity and majesty of the emperor himself, from whom all power on earth was believed properly to flow. The Eastern emperors claimed absolute sovereignty, both secular and religious. They practiced Caesaropapism, or the emperor acting as if he held authority over the church as well as over his kingdom. By comparison, the West nurtured a separation of church and state that began to flower in the eleventh century.

A dispute over the use of sacred images (icons) in worship, which erupted in the eighth century, further divided the East and West. In 726, Emperor Leo III (r. 717–741) forbade the use of images and icons by all Christians. His intention may have been to weaken the monastic owners of popular icons and to court populations influenced by Muslim and Jewish contempt for image worshipers. At any rate, his attack on traditional practices shocked the West and helped drive the Roman popes into an alliance with Europe's strongest emerging rulers, the Frankish kings. Constantinople underwent a spate of iconoclasm (destruction of icons) but reversed itself in the mid-ninth century and restored respect for sacred images.

The Eastern church rejected several requirements of Roman Christianity. It denied the existence of Purgatory; permitted lay divorce and remarriage; allowed priests, but not bishops, to marry; and embraced vernacular liturgies in place of Greek and Latin. In these matters Eastern Christians gained opportunities and rights Christians in the West would not enjoy until at least the Protestant Reformation in the sixteenth century.

Having accumulated for centuries, differences between the Eastern and Roman churches finally resulted in a schism in 1054. The pope's envoy, Cardinal

●●●─[Read the **Document**
Epitome Iconoclastic Seventh Synod, 754 at **myhistorylab.com**

Humbertus, who was sent to Constantinople to try to resolve some of the points in contention, excommunicated his Eastern colleagues, and they in turn condemned the West. The result was a breach that remained until 1965, when a Roman pope and the patriarch of Constantinople met to revoke the mutual condemnations of 1054.

THE IMPACT OF ISLAM ON EAST AND WEST

HOW DID the Islamic world influence medieval Western civilization?

A new drama began to unfold in the sixth century with the rise of Islam (see Chapter 10). Emperors in Constantinople struggled with invading Arab armies. Unlike Germanic invaders, who absorbed and adapted Roman culture and religion, the Arabs ultimately imposed their own culture and religion on the lands they conquered.

An Arab-Berber army under Tariq ibn Ziyad (Gibraltar, "mountain of Tariq," is named after him) conquered Visigothic Spain in 711, beginning a 700-year reign in what is today Andalusia. By the middle of the eighth century Arabs were masters of the southern and eastern Mediterranean coastline, territories today held, for the most part, by Islamic states. Muslim armies also pushed north and east through Mesopotamia and Persia and beyond. The Muslim conquerors generally tolerated Christians and Jews, provided they paid taxes and made no efforts to proselytize Muslim communities. The Arabs forbade mixed marriages and any conscious cultural interchange. Special taxes on conquered peoples encouraged them to convert to Islam.

Assaulted from East and West, Christian Europe developed a lasting fear and suspicion of the Muslims. Eventually, Byzantine Emperor Leo III (r. 717–740) stopped Arab armies at Constantinople after a year's siege (717–718). In subsequent centuries the Byzantines further secured their borders and for a time expanded militarily and commercially into Muslim lands. In the West, the Franks under Charles Martel defeated a raiding party of Arabs on the western frontier of the Frankish kingdom near Tours (today in central France) in 732, ending the possibility of Arab expansion into the heart of Europe. The Mediterranean remained something of a "Muslim lake" during the High Middle Ages, and the center of the evolving western European civilization shifted north. Yet positive contact and influence continued between Muslims and Christians. Western trade with the East continued to be of great importance to the Carolingians.

BYZANTIUM'S CONTRIBUTION TO ISLAMIC CIVILIZATION

The Islamic Empire found itself face to face with Byzantium: An astonishingly vital, young phenomenon confronted what then seemed to be an exhausted, ancient empire. A sequence of Islamic invasions and sieges did not, however, destroy the Byzantines, and eventually borders between the two empires were more or less established.

With the slowdown of Muslim expansion, commerce and exchange with Byzantium intensified. The caliphates of Islam regarded Byzantium as a model. The splendor of court culture and ceremony was adopted from the Byzantines with the intent to intimidate and impress; Byzantine architecture and craftsmanship were much admired; and Byzantine art and iconography formed a foundation for later Arab illuminations and artwork.[5]

Arab empire-builders were curious about earlier peoples and wished to associate themselves with an older tradition of authority. In the Byzantines, they saw the greatest challenge to the legitimacy of the Islamic Empire. The Muslims also wanted to understand their faith in intellectual terms. From these diverse motives there developed considerable interest in Ancient Greek learning, particularly in works on logic, philosophy, and medicine. A great deal of translation was underway by the ninth century, facilitated by such learned figures as the Caliph Ma'mun.[6] Texts were acquired from Byzantium; commentaries by Arab scholars noted that Christianity had suppressed the study of these same works for religious reasons.

THE WESTERN DEBT TO ISLAM

Arab invasions and presence in the Mediterranean area during the Early Middle Ages contributed both directly and indirectly to the formation of western Europe. They did so indirectly by driving west Europeans back onto their native tribal and inherited Judeo-Christian, Greco-Roman, and Byzantine resources, from which they created a Western culture of their own. Also, by diverting the attention and energies of the Byzantine Empire during the formative centuries, the Arabs prevented it from expanding into western Europe. That allowed two Germanic peoples to gain ascendancy: first the Franks and then the Lombards, who invaded Italy in the sixth century and settled in the Po valley.

Despite hostilities between the Christian West and the Muslim world, there was creative interchange between them, with the West having the most to gain. Arab civilizations were enjoying their golden age. Between the eighth and tenth centuries, Moorish Córdoba was a model multicultural city embracing Arabs, Berbers, Spanish Christian converts to Islam, and native Jews. The Arabs taught Western farmers how to irrigate fields and Western artisans how to tan leather and refine silk. The West also gained from its contacts with Arabic scholars. Ancient Greek works on astronomy, mathematics, and medicine became available in Latin translation, thanks to the Arabs. Down to the sixteenth century, the basic gynecological and child-care manuals guiding the work of Western midwives and physicians were compilations made by the Baghdad physician Al-Razi (Rhazes), the philosopher and physician Ibn-Sina (Avicenna) (980–1037), and Ibn Rushd (Averröes) (1126–1198), who was also Islam's greatest authority on Aristotle. Jewish scholars made important contributions; the great Moses Maimonides (1135–1204) wrote in both Arabic and Hebrew. The Arabs, exceptional poets, gave the West its most popular book, the folk tales of *The Arabian Nights*.

THE DEVELOPING ROMAN CHURCH

WHAT WAS the doctrine of papal primacy?

Throughout the period of imperial decline, Germanic invasions, and Islamic expansion, one Western institution remained firmly entrenched and gained in strength: the Christian church. The church sought to organize itself according to the centralized, hierarchical administrative structure of the empire, with strategically placed "viceroys" (bishops) in European cities who looked for spiritual direction to their leader, the bishop of Rome (later pope). As the Western Empire crumbled, local bishops and cathedral chapters (ruling bodies of clergy) filled the vacuum of authority. The local cathedral became the center of urban life and the local bishop the highest authority for those who remained in the cities. In Rome, on a larger and more fateful scale, the pope took control of the city as the Western emperors gradually departed and died out. Western Europe soon discovered that the Christian church was its best repository of Roman administrative skills and classical culture.

The Christian church had been graced with special privileges, great lands, and wealth by Emperor Constantine, whose Edict of Milan in 313 gave Christians a favored status within the empire. In 380 Emperors Theodosius I (r. ca. 379–395) and Gratian I

---

[5]El-Cheikh, *Byzantium Viewed by the Arabs*, pp. 154, 60, 194.

[6]Irfan Shahid, "Byzantium and the Islamic World," in *Byzantium, a World Civilization*, ed. Angeliki E. Laiou and Henry Maguire (Washington, DC: Dumbarton Oaks Research Library and Collection, © 1992), 51.

Religious Diversity. A Muslim and a Christian play the *ud* or lute together, from a thirteenth-century *Book of Chants* in the Escorial Monastery of Madrid. Medieval Europe was deeply influenced by Arab-Islamic culture, transmitted particularly through Spain. Some of the many works in Arabic on musical theory were translated into Latin and Hebrew, but the main influence on music came from the arts of singing and playing spread by minstrels.

A Moor and a Christian playing the lute, miniature in a book of music from the "Cantigas" of Alfonso X "the Wise" (1221–1284). Thirteenth century (manuscript). Monastero de El Escorial, El Escorial, Spain/index/bridgeman Art Library.

What kinds of exchanges took place between Muslims and western Europeans during the Middle Ages?

QUICK REVIEW

Monasticism

♦ First monks, like Anthony of Egypt, were hermits

♦ Basil the Great encouraged service

♦ Benedict of Nursia developed hierarchical, self-sufficient monasteries

♦ Monks were disciplined, respected by public

◆◆◆ Read the Document

St. Benedict's Rules for Monks
at **myhistorylab.com**

---

apostolic primacy

The doctrine that the popes are the direct successors to the Apostle Peter and, as such, heads of the church.

(r. 367–383) raised Christianity to the official religion of the empire. Both Theodosius and his predecessors acted as much for political effect as out of religious conviction; in 313 Christians composed about one-fifth of the population of the empire, making Christianity the strongest among the empire's competing religions. Mithraism, a religion popular among army officers and restricted to males, was its main rival.

The church could act as a potent civilizing and unifying force. It had a religious message of providential purpose and individual worth that could give solace and meaning to life at its worst. It had a ritual of baptism and a creedal confession that united people beyond the traditional barriers of social class, education, and gender. And alone in the West, the church retained an effective hierarchical administration, staffed by the best educated minds in Europe and centered in emperorless Rome.

MONASTIC CULTURE

Monastic culture proved again and again to be the peculiar strength of the church during the Middle Ages. The first monks were hermits, such as Anthony of Egypt (ca. 251–356), who felt compelled to withdraw from society and give up all worldly attachments to pursue a purely spiritual life. So many people were attracted to the hermits' movement that communal organizations had to be devised to serve them. The monastic life, which was guided by the biblical "counsels of perfection" (chastity, poverty, and obedience), came to be regarded as the purest form of religious practice. Basil the Great (329–379), whose rule (regulations to govern a monastery) spread widely throughout the East, urged monks to leave their protected enclaves and serve the needs of others by caring for orphans, widows, and the infirm.

The great organizer of Western monasticism was Benedict of Nursia (ca. 480–547). In 529 he established a monastery at Monte Cassino, in Italy, founding the form of monasticism—Benedictine—that quickly came to dominate in the West. Benedict wrote a sophisticated *Rule for Monasteries*, a comprehensive plan that both regimented and enriched monastic life. Benedictine monasteries were hierarchically organized and directed by an abbot. Periods of study and religious devotion (about four hours each day of prayers and liturgical activities) alternated with manual labor (up to eight hours, including copying manuscripts)—a program that carefully promoted the religious, intellectual, and physical well-being of the monks. During the Early Middle Ages Benedictine missionaries Christianized both England and Germany. Their disciplined organization and devotion to hard work made the Benedictines an economic and political power as well as a spiritual force wherever they settled.

THE DOCTRINE OF PAPAL PRIMACY

Constantine and the Eastern emperors looked on the church as little more than a department of the state. The bishops of Rome, however, opposed royal intervention. Taking advantage of imperial weakness and distraction, they developed the doctrine of "papal primacy," which raised the bishop of Rome to an unassailable supremacy within the church. As the "pope," he was both head of the Roman Catholic Church and Christ's vicar on earth, continuing the line of Christ's apostles from St. Peter. The new title put him in a position to claim power within the secular world, giving rise to repeated conflicts between church and state throughout the Middle Ages.

Pope Damasus I (366–384) laid the foundation for papal claims to absolute authority by asserting Rome's **apostolic primacy**. He pointed to Jesus' words to Peter in the Gospel of Matthew (16:18): "Thou art Peter, and upon this rock I will build my church." Because tradition maintained that Peter was the first bishop of Rome and that he died there, Damasus insisted that Rome's popes, Peter's successors, were heirs to the role Jesus had decreed for Peter. Pope Leo I (440–461) assumed the title *pontifex maximus*—"supreme priest"—and laid claim to a **"plenitude of power,"** supremacy over all other bishops in the church. Pope Gelasius I (492–496) stated that the authority of the clergy was "more weighty" than the power of kings, for priests were given charge over divine affairs.

DIVISION OF CHRISTENDOM

The division of Christendom into Eastern (Byzantine) and Western (Roman Catholic) churches has its roots in the Early Middle Ages and was due in part to linguistic and cultural differences. In East and West, church organization closely followed that of the secular state. A novel combination of Greek, Roman, and Asian elements shaped Byzantine culture, giving Eastern Christianity a stronger mystical dimension than Western Christianity. This difference in outlook may have predisposed Eastern patriarchs to submit more passively than Western popes ever could to royal intervention in their affairs.

Differences in doctrine and practice were exacerbated when the Eastern and Western churches both claimed jurisdiction over newly converted areas in the northern Balkans. Beyond these issues, three major factors lay behind the religious break between East and West. The first revolved around questions of doctrinal authority. The Eastern church put more stress on the authority of the Bible and the ecumenical councils of the church in the definition of Christian doctrine than on the counsel and decrees of the bishop of Rome. The claims of Roman popes to a special primacy of authority were unacceptable to the East, where regional churches were independent and autonomous. This basic issue of authority lay behind the mutual excommunication of Pope Nicholas I and Patriarch Photius in the ninth century, and that of Pope Leo IX (through his ambassador to Constantinople, Cardinal Humbert) and Patriarch Michael Cerularius in 1054.

A second major issue in the separation of the two churches was the Western addition of the *filioque* clause to the Nicene-Constantinopolitan Creed. According to this anti-Arian clause, the Holy Spirit proceeds "also from the Son" (*filioque*) as well as from the Father, making clear the Western belief that Christ was fully of one essence with God the Father and not a lesser being.

The third factor was the iconoclastic controversy of the first half of the eighth century. As noted earlier, after 725 the Byzantine emperor Leo III (r. 717–741) attempted to force Western popes to abolish the use of images in their churches. This stand met fierce official and popular resistance. To punish the West, Leo confiscated valuable papal lands. This direct challenge to the papacy coincided with a threat to Rome and the Western church from the Lombards of northern Italy. Assailed on two fronts, the Roman papacy seemed doomed. But the papacy has been one of the most resilient and enterprising institutions in Western history. In 754 Pope Stephen II (r. 752–757) formed an alliance with the Franks' ruler, Pepin III, to defend the church against the Lombards and to serve as a Western counterweight

plenitude of power
The teaching that the popes have power over all other bishops of the church.

●●●-⎰Read the **Document**
Pope Leo I on Bishop Hilary of Arles
at **myhistorylab.com**

CHRONOLOGY

MAJOR POLITICAL AND RELIGIOUS DEVELOPMENTS OF THE EARLY MIDDLE AGES

313	Emperor Constantine issues the Edict of Milan
325	Council of Nicaea defines Christian doctrine
410	Rome invaded by Visigoths under Alaric
413–426	Saint Augustine writes *The City of God*
451–453	Europe invaded by the Huns under Attila
476	Barbarian Odovacer deposes Western emperor and rules as king of the Romans
529	Saint Benedict founds monastery at Monte Cassino
533	Justinian codifies Roman law
732	Charles Martel defeats Arabs at Tours
754	Pope Stephen II and Pepin III ally

to the Eastern emperor. This marriage of religion and politics created a new Western church and empire and determined much of the course of Western history thereafter.

THE KINGDOM OF THE FRANKS

WHY DID
Charlemagne's empire break up after his death?

MEROVINGIANS AND CAROLINGIANS: FROM CLOVIS TO CHARLEMAGNE

Clovis and his successors gave the Franks a major role in the recovery of western Europe. The territory under their control included modern France, Belgium, the Netherlands, and western Germany. In attempting to govern this extensive kingdom, the Merovingians encountered the most persistent problem of medieval political history—the competing claims of the "one" and the "many," the struggle of a lone king to impose centralized government on local magnates.

The Merovingian kings addressed this problem by making pacts with the landed nobility and by creating the royal office of count. The counts were men without possessions to whom the king gave great lands in the expectation that they would be loyal officers. But once established in office, the Merovingian counts became territorial rulers in their own right. The Frankish kingdom progressively fragmented into independent regions and tiny principalities. The Frankish custom of dividing the kingdom equally among the king's legitimate male heirs only made matters worse. By the seventh century, the Frankish king lacked effective executive power. Real power was concentrated in the office of the Mayor of the Palace, who was the spokesman at the king's court for the great landowners. Through this office, the Carolingian dynasty rose to power.

The Carolingians took their name from the dynasty's greatest ruler, Carolus (later to be known as Charlemagne). They controlled the office of the Mayor of the Palace for over one hundred years, starting with Pepin I, who died in 639. Pepin II (d. 714) ruled in fact, if not in title, over the Frankish kingdom. His illegitimate son, Charles Martel ("the Hammer," d. 741), created a great cavalry by bestowing lands known as *benefices* or **fiefs** on powerful nobles, who, in return, agreed to be ready to serve as the king's army. It was such an army that checked the Arabs at Tours in 732. Then, with the enterprising connivance of the pope, the Carolingians simply expropriated the Frankish crown in 751.

The fiefs so generously bestowed by Charles Martel to create his army came in large part from landed property that he usurped from the church. His alliance with the landed aristocracy permitted the Carolingians to have some measure of political success where the Merovingians had failed. The Carolingians created counts almost entirely out of the landed nobility from which the Carolingians themselves had risen. The Merovingians, in contrast, had tried to compete directly with these great aristocrats by raising the landless to power. By playing to strength rather than challenging it, the Carolingians strengthened themselves, at least for the short term. The church, by this time dependent on the protection of the Franks against the Eastern emperor and the Lombards, had no choice but to tolerate the seizure of its lands. Later, the Franks partially compensated the church for the lands.

The church played a large and enterprising role in the Frankish government. By Carolingian times, monasteries were a dominant force. Their intellectual achievements made them respected repositories of culture. Their religious teaching and example imposed order on surrounding populations. Their relics and rituals made them magical shrines to which pilgrims came in great numbers. Thanks to their donated

QUICK REVIEW

Merovingians
- Frankish dynasty founded by Clovis
- Created royal office of count
- Fragmentation of kingdom
- Mayor of the Palace gained power

fief
Land granted to a vassal in exchange for services, usually military.

lands and serf labor, many had become very profitable farms and landed estates. By Merovingian times, the higher clergy were already employed in tandem with counts as royal agents. It was the policy of the Carolingians to use the church to pacify conquered neighboring tribes—Frisians, Thuringians, Bavarians, and especially the Franks' archenemies, the Saxons.

Conversion to Nicene Christianity became an integral part of the successful annexation of conquered lands and people; the cavalry broke bodies, while the clergy won hearts and minds. The Anglo-Saxon missionary Saint Boniface (b. Wynfrith, ca. 680–754) was the most important of the German clergy who served Carolingian kings in this way. Christian bishops in missionary districts and elsewhere became lords, appointed by and subject to the king—an ominous integration of secular and religious policy in which lay the seeds of the later Investiture Controversy of the eleventh and twelfth centuries (see Chapter 15).

The church helped the Carolingians with more than territorial expansion. Pope Zacharias (r. 741–752) sanctioned Pepin the Short's termination of the vestigial Merovingian Dynasty and the Carolingian accession to kingship of the Franks. According to legend, Saint Boniface annointed Pepin, thereby investing Frankish rule with a sacral character from the start.

Zacharias's successor, Pope Stephen II (r. 752–757), appealed directly to Pepin when he was driven from Rome in 753 by the Lombards. In 754 the Franks and the church formed an alliance against the Lombards and the Eastern emperor, whose power was greater than the Franks' power in central Italy at the time. Carolingian kings became the protectors of the Catholic Church and thereby "kings by the grace of God." Pepin gained the title *patricius Romanorum*, "father-protector of the Romans," a title heretofore borne only by the representative of the Eastern emperor. In 755 the Franks defeated the Lombards and gave the pope the lands surrounding Rome, creating what came to be known as the **Papal States**. During this time the papacy began to circulate a fraudulent document, *Donation of Constantine*, which was intended to prove to the Franks that the church was the heir to the legacy of Rome's empire. It was exposed as a forgery in the fifteenth century.

The papacy had looked to the Franks for an ally strong enough to protect it from the Eastern emperors. It is an irony of history that the church found in the Carolingian Dynasty a Western imperial government that drew almost as slight a boundary between state and church as did Eastern emperors. Although preferable to Eastern domination, Carolingian patronage of the church proved to be no less constraining.

REIGN OF CHARLEMAGNE (768–814)

Charlemagne, the son of Pepin the Short, continued the role of his father as papal protector in Italy and his policy of territorial conquest in the north. After defeating the Lombards of northern Italy in 774, Charlemagne took the title "King of the Lombards." He subjugated surrounding pagan tribes, foremost among them the Saxons, and brought the Danubian plains into the Frankish orbit by the virtual annihilation of the Avars, a tribe related to the Huns. The Arabs were chased beyond the Pyrenees. By the time of his death on January 28, 814, Charlemagne's kingdom embraced modern France, Belgium, Holland, Switzerland, almost the whole of Germany, much of Italy, a portion of Spain, and the island of Corsica (see Map 11–3, on page 278).

Encouraged by ambitious advisers, Charlemagne reached to be a universal emperor. His sacred palace city, Aachen (in French, Aix-la-Chapelle), was constructed in conscious imitation of the courts of the ancient Roman and the contemporary Eastern emperors. Although he permitted the church its independence, he looked after it paternalistically. He used the church above all to promote social stability and hierarchical

Papal States

Territory in central Italy ruled by the pope until 1870.

QUICK REVIEW

Church and State

◆ Church played a large role in the Frankish government

◆ Christian bishops became lords in service of the king

◆ Papacy looked to Franks for protection from the Eastern emperors

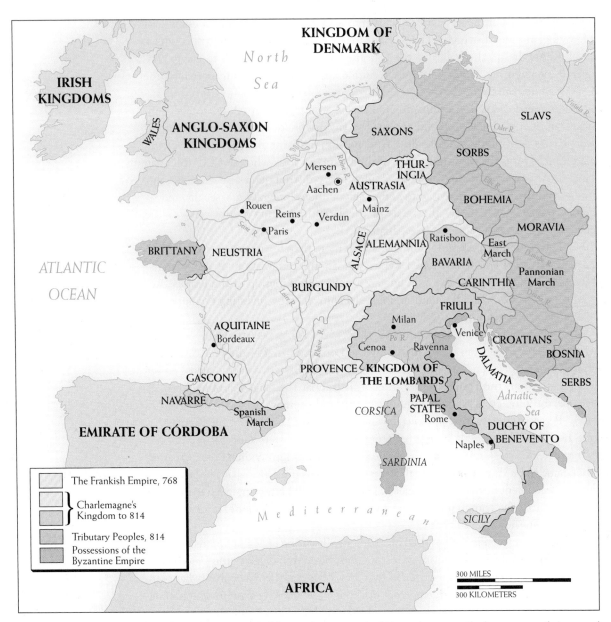

MAP 11–3.   The Empire of Charlemagne to 814.   Building on the successes of his predecessors, Charlemagne greatly increased the Frankish domains. Such traditional enemies as the Saxons and the Lombards fell under his sway.

How does the extent of Charlemagne's empire compare with that of the ancient western Roman Empire?

⊙ See the Map

Charlemagne's Empire, 814
at **myhistorylab.com**

order throughout the kingdom. Frankish Christians were ceremoniously baptized, professed the Nicene Creed (with the *filioque* clause), and learned in church to revere Charlemagne.

Charlemagne realized his imperial pretensions on Christmas Day 800, when Pope Leo III (795–816) crowned him emperor. This event created what would later be called the Holy Roman Empire, a revival, based after 870 in Germany, of the old Roman Empire in the West. The coronation benefited both the church and Charlemagne. Before his coronation, he had been a minor Western potentate in the eyes of Eastern emperors; afterward, Eastern emperors recognized his imperial dignity.

Charlemagne stood six feet, three and one half inches tall—a fact confirmed when his tomb was opened and exact measurements of his remains were taken in 1861. He was restless, ever ready for a hunt. Informal and gregarious, he insisted on the presence of friends even when he bathed and was widely known for his practical jokes, lusty good humor, and warm hospitality. People and gifts came to Aachen from all over the world; in 802, Charlemagne received a white elephant from the caliph of Baghdad, Harun-al-Rashid.

Charlemagne had five official wives in succession, and many mistresses and concubines, and he sired numerous children. This created problems. His oldest son by his first marriage, Pepin, was jealous of the attention Charlemagne showed to the sons of his second wife. Fearing the loss of paternal favor, Pepin joined a conspiracy against his father. He spent the rest of his life in confinement in a monastery after the plot was exposed.

Charlemagne governed his kingdom through counts, of whom there were perhaps as many as 250. Each count had three main duties: to maintain a local army loyal to the king, to collect tribute and dues, and to administer justice throughout his district. This last responsibility was undertaken through a district law court known as the *mallus*, which heard testimony from the parties involved in a dispute or crime, passed judgment, and assessed a monetary compensation to be paid to the injured party. In cases where guilt or innocence was unclear, recourse was often taken to judicial duels or "divine" tests and ordeals. Among these was the length of time a defendant's hand took to heal after immersion in boiling water.

As in Merovingian times, many counts used their official position and new judicial powers to their own advantage. As they grew stronger and more independent, they came to regard the land grants with which they were paid as hereditary positions rather than generous royal donations. This development signaled the impending fragmentation of Charlemagne's kingdom.

Charlemagne never solved the loyalty problem. Ecclesiastical agents proved no better than secular ones; except for their attendance to the liturgy and to church prayers, landowning bishops were largely indistinguishable from the lay nobility. Charlemagne sensed—rightly, as the Gregorian reform of the eleventh century would prove—that the emergence of a distinctive and reform-minded class of ecclesiastical landowners would be a danger to royal government. Charlemagne purposefully treated his bishops as he treated his counts, that is, as vassals who served at the king's pleasure.

Charlemagne used his wealth to attract Europe's best scholars to Aachen. Theodulf of Orleans (d. 821), Angilbert (d. 814), and Charlemagne's biographer Einhard (ca. 770–840) developed court culture and education. The renowned Anglo-Saxon master Alcuin of York (735–804), who became director of the king's palace school in 782, brought classical and Christian learning to Aachen and was handsomely rewarded for his efforts with several wealthy monastic estates. Although Charlemagne appreciated learning for its own sake, he also intended to upgrade the administrative skills of the royal bureaucracy. By preparing the sons of nobles to run the religious and secular offices of the realm, court scholarship served kingdom building. With its special concentration on grammar, logic, rhetoric, and basic mathematics, the school provided training in the basic tools of bureaucracy. Charlemagne's scholars created a new, clear style of handwriting—Carolingian minuscule—and fostered the use of accurate Latin in official documents, developments that helped increase lay literacy. Charlemagne's sister Gisela oversaw the copying of classical manuscripts, thereby preserving the treasures of antiquity. Through personal correspondence and visitations, Alcuin created a community of scholars and clerics at court and infused administration with a sense of comradeship and common purpose. A modest renaissance, or rebirth, of antiquity occurred in the palace school as scholars collected and preserved ancient manuscripts. Alcuin worked on a correct text of the Bible and made editions of the monastic *Rule* of Saint Benedict. These scholarly activities served official efforts to bring uniformity to church law and liturgy, educate the clergy, and improve moral life within the monasteries.

Charlemagne. An equestrian figure of Charlemagne (or possibly one of his sons) from the early ninth century.

Bronze equestrian statuette of Charlemagne, 3/4 view, from Metz Cathedral, ninth–tenth century. Louvre, Paris, France. Copyright Bridgeman-Giraudon/Art Resource, New York.

Would you consider Charlemagne a successful leader? Why or why not?

Read the Document

Life of Charlemagne (early ninth century) Einhard, at **myhistorylab.com**

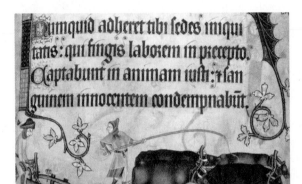

Plowing the Fields. The invention of the moldboard plow greatly improved farming. The heavy plow cut deeply into the ground and furrowed it. This illustration from the Luttrell Psalter (ca. 1340) also shows that the traction harness, which lessened the strangulation effect of the yoke on the animals, had not yet been adopted. Indeed, one of the oxen seems to be on the verge of choking.

What other improvements in farming practice occurred during this period?

manors

Village farms owned by a lord.

demesne

The part of a manor that was cultivated directly for the lord of the manor.

serfs

Peasants tied to the land they tilled.

QUICK REVIEW

Serfs

- Status varied: free and unfree
- All owed dues in kind to the lord of the manor
- Much discontent, many escaped

three-field system

A medieval innovation that increased the amount of land under cultivation by leaving only one-third fallow in a given year.

The agrarian economy of the Middle Ages was organized and controlled through village farms known as **manors**. Peasants labored as farmers in subordination to a lord, a more powerful landowner who gave them land and a dwelling in exchange for their services and a portion of their crops. That part of the land farmed by the peasants for the lord was the **demesne**, which on average made up about one-quarter to one-third of the arable land. All crops grown there were harvested for the lord.

Peasants were treated according to their social status and the size of their landholdings. A freeman—that is, a peasant with hereditary property (property free from the claims of an overlord)—became a **serf** by surrendering his property to a greater landowner (a lord) in exchange for protection and assistance. The free serf received his land back from the lord with a clear definition of his economic and legal rights. Although the land was no longer his property, he had full possession and use of it, and the number of services and amount of goods he was to supply to the lord were carefully spelled out. Peasants who entered the service of a lord with little real property to bargain with (perhaps only a few farm implements and animals) ended up as unfree serfs and were much more vulnerable to the lord's demands, spending up to three days a week working the lord's fields. Truly impoverished peasants who lived and worked on the manor as serfs had the lowest status and were the least protected.

Serfs were subject to so-called dues in kind: firewood for cutting the lord's wood, sheep for grazing their sheep on the lord's land, and the like. Thus the lord, who for his part furnished shacks and small plots of land from his vast domain, had at his disposal an army of servants who provided him with everything from eggs to boots. That many serfs were discontented is reflected in the high number of recorded escapes. An astrological calendar from the period marks the days most favorable for escaping. Fugitive serfs roamed the land as beggars and vagabonds, searching for new and better masters.

By the time of Charlemagne, the moldboard plow, which was especially needed in northern Europe where the soil was heavy, and the three-field system of land cultivation were coming into use. These developments greatly improved agricultural productivity. Unlike the older "scratch" plow, which crisscrossed the field with only slight penetration, the moldboard cut deep into the soil and turned it to form a ridge, providing a natural drainage system for the field as well as permitting the deep planting of seeds. Unlike the earlier two-field system of crop rotation, which simply alternated fallow with planted fields each year, the **three-field system** increased the amount of cultivated land by leaving only one-third fallow in a given year.

As owners of the churches on their lands, the lords had the right to raise chosen serfs to the post of parish priest, placing them in charge of the churches on the lords' estates. Church law directed the lord to set a serf free before he entered the clergy, but lords preferred a "serf priest," one who not only said the Mass on Sundays and holidays but also continued to serve his lord during the week. Like Charlemagne with his bishops, Frankish lords cultivated a docile parish clergy.

Ordinary people baptized themselves and their children, confessed the Creed Mass, tried to learn the Lord's Prayer, and received last rites from the priest when death approached. Local priests were no better educated than their congregations, and instruction in the meaning of Christian doctrine and practice remained minimal. People became particularly attached to the more tangible veneration of relics and saints. Charlemagne shared many of the religious beliefs of his ordinary subjects: He collected and venerated relics, made pilgrimages to Rome, frequented the church of Saint Mary in Aachen several times a day, and directed in his last will and testament that much of his great treasure be spent to endow Masses and prayers for his departed soul.

BREAKUP OF THE CAROLINGIAN KINGDOM

Late in life, an ailing Charlemagne knew that his empire was ungovernable. The seeds of dissolution lay in regionalism. In medieval society, a direct relationship existed between physical proximity to authority and loyalty to authority. Local people obeyed local lords more readily than they obeyed a glorious but distant king. Charlemagne had been forced to recognize and even to enhance the power of regional magnates in order to win needed financial and military support.

The Carolingian kings did not give up easily, however. Charlemagne's only surviving son and successor, Louis the Pious (r. 814–840), had three sons by his first wife. Louis acted early in his reign to break the tradition of dividing his kingdom equally among his sons. Instead, Louis made his eldest son, Lothar (d. 855), co-regent and sole imperial heir in 817. He gave Lothar's brothers important but much lesser assigned hereditary lands: Pepin (d. 838) became king of Aquitaine and Louis "the German" (d. 876) became king of Bavaria.

In 823 Louis's second wife, Judith of Bavaria, bore him a fourth son, Charles (d. 877). Determined that her son should receive more than just a nominal inheritance, the queen incited the brothers Pepin and Louis to war against Lothar and persuaded their father to divide the kingdom equally. As the bestower of crowns upon emperors, the pope had an important stake in the preservation of the revived Western Empire and the imperial title, so the pope condemned Louis and restored Lothar to his original magnificent inheritance. But this stirred the resentments of Lothar's brothers, including his half-brother, Charles, who joined in renewed war against him.

In 843, with the Treaty of Verdun, peace finally came to Louis's surviving heirs (Pepin had died in 838). The great Carolingian Empire was partitioned into three equal parts. Lothar received a middle section, which came to be known as Lotharingia and embraced roughly modern Holland, Belgium, Switzerland, Alsace-Lorraine, and Italy. Charles the Bald received the western part of the kingdom, or roughly modern France, and Louis the German came into the eastern part, or roughly modern Germany. Although Lothar retained the imperial title, the universal empire ceased to exist. Not until the sixteenth century, with the election in 1519 of Charles I of Spain as the Holy Roman Emperor Charles V, would the Western world again see a kingdom as vast as Charlemagne's.

Carolingian fragmentation continued. When Lothar died in 855, his kingdom was divided equally among his three surviving sons, leaving it much smaller and weaker than the kingdoms of Louis the German and Charles the Bald. Henceforth, western Europe would be divided into an eastern and a western Frankish kingdom—roughly Germany and France—at war over the fractionalized middle kingdom, a contest that has continued into modern times.

The political breakdown of the Carolingian Empire coincided with new external threats. In the late ninth and tenth centuries, successive waves of Normans (North men), better known as Vikings, swept into Europe from Scandinavia. *Vikings* was a catchall term for Scandinavian peoples who visited Europe alternately as gregarious traders and savage raiders, and their exploits have been preserved in sagas that reveal a cultural world filled with mythical gods and spirits. Taking to sea in oceangoing longboats of rugged, doubled-hulled construction, they terrified their neighbors to the south, invading and occupying English and European coastal and

QUICK REVIEW

Charlemagne's Successors

- Louis the Pious (r. 814–840) made his son Lothar sole imperial heir

- Civil war broke out between Lothar and Louis's other sons

- The Treaty of Verdun (843) divided the empire into three equal parts

A Closer Look

A Multicultural Book Cover

Carolingian education, art, and architecture served royal efforts to unify the kingdom by fusing inherit-ed Celtic-Germanic and Greco-Roman-Byzantine cultures. Charlemagne, his son, and grandsons deco-rated their churches with a variety of art forms, among them illuminated manuscripts, such as the bejeweled metalwork that became the binding of the *Lindau Gospels* (ca. 870).

The Christ seen here reflects early Christian art and Byzantine theology, which did not endow divinity with human suffering. So impassive is this Christ that he seems almost to smile on the cross.

However, the surrounding panels show the angels in heaven and Christ's followers on earth writhing with grief.

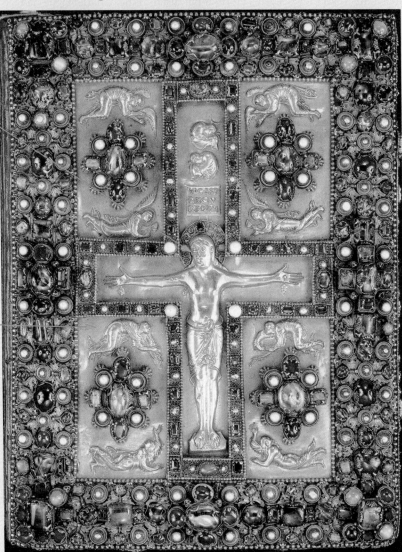

Questions

1. Does the inclusiveness of this book cover suggest a shared heritage among the Celts, Germans, Greeks, Romans, and Byzantines?

2. How does this composite of cultures on the book cover compare with their actual historical relations in the ninth century?

3. Since the nonsuffering Christ on the book cover pres-ents a distinctive Byzantine icon, does this suggest agreement among the parties over the portrayal of the Savior's crucifixion?

4. Do the agonizing figures on the book cover (both an-gels and humans) represent other religious traditions that prefer a suffering Christ upon the cross?

myhistorylab   To examine this image in an interactive fashion, please go to **www.myhistorylab.com**

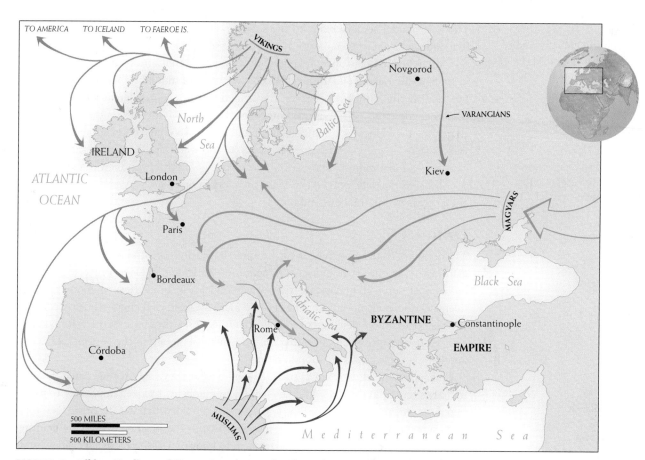

MAP 11–4. Viking, Muslim, and Magyar Invasions to the Eleventh Century. Western Europe was sorely beset by new waves of outsiders from the ninth to the eleventh century. From north, east, and south, a stream of invading Vikings, Magyars, and Muslims brought the West at times to near collapse and of course gravely affected institutions within Europe.

How did early medieval Europe respond to invasions?

river towns. In the ninth century, the Danes briefly besieged Paris, while other Vikings turned York into a major trading post for their woolens, jewelry, and ornamental wares. Erik the Red made it to Greenland, and his son Leif Erikson wintered in Newfoundland 500 years before Columbus. In the eleventh century Christian conversions and English defeat of the Norwegians effectively restricted Vikings to their Scandinavian homelands.

Magyars, or Hungarians, who were great horsemen, also swept into western Europe from the eastern plains, while Muslims made incursions across the Mediterranean from North Africa (see Map 11–4). The Franks built fortified towns and castles in strategic locations as refuges. When they could, they bought off the invaders with grants of land and payments of silver. In the resulting turmoil, local populations became more dependent than ever on local strongmen for life and livelihood, creating the essential precondition for the maturation of feudal society.

FEUDAL SOCIETY

The Middle Ages were characterized by a chronic absence of effective central government and the constant threat of famine, disease, and foreign invasion. In this state of affairs the weaker sought the protection of the stronger, and the true lords and masters became those who could guarantee immediate protection from rapine and starvation.

See the **Map**
Viking Muslim and Magyar Invasions 1000
at **myhistorylab.com**

Magyars
The majority ethnic group in Hungary.

WHAT IS a feudal society?

feudal society

The social, political, military, and economic system that prevailed in the Middle Ages and beyond in some parts of Europe.

vassal

A person granted an estate or cash payments in return for accepting the obligation to render services to a lord.

●●●Read the Document
Feudalism, 1083, Archbishop of Cologne
at **myhistorylab.com**

fealty

An oath of loyalty by a vassal to a lord, promising to perform specified services.

The term **feudal society** refers to the social, political, military, and economic system that emerged from these conditions.

In a feudal society, people require firm assurance that others can be depended on in time of dire need. Feudalism is above all a system of mutual rights and responsibilities. During the Early Middle Ages, the landed nobility became great lords who ruled over their domains as miniature kingdoms. They maintained their own armies and courts, regulated local tolls, and even minted their own coins. Large groups of warrior **vassals** were created by extensive bestowals of land, and these developed into a prominent professional military class with its own code of knightly conduct. In feudal society, most serfs docilely worked the land, the clergy prayed and gave counsel, and lords and knights maintained law and order.

ORIGINS

The origins of feudal government can be found in the divisions and conflicts of Merovingian society. In the sixth and seventh centuries, individual freemen began to solve the problem of survival by placing themselves under the protection of more powerful freemen, who built up armies and became local magnates. Freemen who so entrusted themselves to others were described collectively as *vassi* ("those who serve"), from which evolved the term *vassalage*, meaning the placement of oneself in the personal service of another who promises protection in return.

Landed nobles, like kings, tried to acquire as many vassals as they could, because military strength in the Early Middle Ages lay in numbers. It proved impossible to maintain these growing armies within the lord's own household, which was the original custom, or to support them by special monetary payments, so the practice evolved of granting them land as a "tenement." Such land came to be known as a *benefice*, or a *fief*, and vassals were expected to dwell on it and maintain their horses and other accouterments of war in good order. Originally vassals, therefore, were little more than gangs-in-waiting.

VASSALAGE AND THE FIEF

Vassalage involved **fealty** to the lord. To swear fealty was to promise to refrain from any action that might threaten the lord's well-being and to perform personal services for him on his request. Chief among the expected services was military duty as a mounted knight. This could involve a variety of activities: a military expedition, escort duty, standing castle guard, or the placement of one's own fortress at the lord's disposal, if the vassal was of such stature as to have one. Continuous bargaining and bickering occurred over the terms of service.

Limitations were placed on the number of days a lord could require services from a vassal. In France in the eleventh century, about forty days of service per year were considered sufficient. It also became possible for vassals to buy their way out of military service by a monetary payment known as *scutage*. The lord, in turn, applied this payment to the hiring of mercenaries, who often proved more efficient than contract-conscious vassals. Beyond his military duty, the vassal was also expected to give the lord advice when he requested it and to sit as a member of his court when it was in session.

CHRONOLOGY	
CAROLINGIAN DYNASTY (751–987)	
750–800	Fraudulent Donation of Constantine created in an effort to counter Frankish domination of church
751	Pepin III "the Short" becomes king of the Franks
755	Franks drive Lombards out of central Italy; creation of Papal States
768–814	Charlemagne rules as king of the Franks
774	Charlemagne defeats Lombards in northern Italy
800	Pope Leo III crowns Charlemagne
814–840	Louis the Pious succeeds Charlemagne as "emperor"
843	Treaty of Verdun partitions the Carolingian Empire
870	Treaty of Mersen further divides Carolingian Empire
875–950	Invasions by Vikings, Muslims, and Magyars
962	Ottonian Dynasty succeeds Carolingian in Germany
987	Capetian Dynasty succeeds Carolingian in France

The lord's obligations to his vassals were very specific. He was, first of all, obligated to protect the vassal from physical harm and to stand as his advocate in public court. After fealty was sworn and homage paid, the lord provided for the vassal's physical maintenance by the bestowal of a benefice, or fief. The fief was simply the physical or material wherewithal to meet the vassal's military and other obligations. It could take the form of liquid wealth as well as the more common grant of real property. There were so-called money fiefs, which empowered a vassal to receive regular payments from the lord's treasury. Such fiefs created potential conflicts because they made it possible for one country to acquire vassals among the nobility of another. Normally, the fief consisted of a landed estate of anywhere from a few to several thousand acres, but it could also take the form of a castle.

In Carolingian times, a benefice, or fief, varied in size from one or more small villas to several *mansi*, which were agricultural holdings of 25 to 48 acres. The king's vassals received benefices of at least 30 and as many as 200 such mansi. Royal vassalage with a benefice understandably came to be widely sought by the highest classes of Carolingian society. As a royal policy, however, it proved deadly to the king. Although Carolingian kings jealously guarded their rights over property granted in benefice to vassals, resident vassals were still free to dispose of their benefices as they pleased. Vassals of the king, strengthened by his donations, in turn created their own vassals. These vassals, in turn, created still further vassals of their own—vassals of vassals of vassals—in a reverse pyramiding effect that fragmented land and authority from the highest to the lowest levels by the late ninth century.

Beginning with the reign of Louis the Pious (r. 814–840), bishops and abbots swore fealty and received their offices from the king as a benefice. The king formally invested these clerics in their offices during a special ceremony in which he presented them with a ring and a staff, the symbols of high spiritual office. This presumptuous practice of lay investiture, like the Carolingian confiscation of church land mentioned earlier, was a sore point for the church. In the eleventh and twelfth centuries it would provoke a great confrontation between church and state as reform-minded clergy rebelled against what they believed to be involuntary clerical vassalage.

FRAGMENTATION AND DIVIDED LOYALTY

In addition to the fragmentation brought about by the multiplication of vassalage, effective occupation of the land led gradually to claims of hereditary possession. Hereditary possession became a legally recognized principle in the ninth century and laid the basis for claims to real ownership. Further, vassal engagements came to be multiplied in still another way as enterprising freemen sought to accumulate as much land as possible. One man could become a vassal to several different lords. This development led in the ninth century to the concept of a "liege lord"—one master whom the vassal must obey even to the harm of the others, should a direct conflict among them arise.

The problem of loyalty was reflected not only in the literature of the period, with its praise of the virtues of honor and fidelity, but also in the development of the ceremonial acts by which a freeman became a vassal. In the mid-eighth century, an "oath of fealty" highlighted the ceremony. A vassal reinforced his promise of fidelity to the lord by swearing a special oath with his hand on a sacred relic or the Bible. In the tenth and eleventh centuries, paying homage to the lord involved not only the swearing of such an oath but also the placement of the vassal's hands between the lord's and the sealing of the ceremony with a kiss.

Despite their problems, feudal arrangements provided stability throughout the Early Middle Ages and aided the difficult process of political centralization during

Lord and Vassal. A seventh-century portrayal of a vassal, who kneels before his lord and inserts his hands between those of his lord in a gesture of mutual loyalty: the vassal promising to obey and serve his lord, the lord promising to support and protect his vassal.

Spanish School (seventh century). Lord and vassal, decorated page (vellum). Archivo de la Corona de Aragon, Barcelona, Spain/Index/Bridgeman Art Library.

What caused fragmentation in the feudal system?

the High Middle Ages. The genius of feudal government lay in its adaptability. Contracts of different kinds could be made with almost anybody, as circumstances required. The process embraced a wide spectrum of people, from the king at the top to the lowliest vassal in the remotest part of the kingdom. The foundations of the modern nation-state would emerge in France and England from the fine-tuning of essentially feudal arrangements as kings sought to adapt their goal of centralized government to the reality of local power and control.

SUMMARY

HOW DID the Byzantine Empire continue the legacy of the Roman Empire?

The End of the Western Roman Empire. In the fifth century, Roman authority in the West collapsed under the impact of Germanic invasions. Imperial power shifted to the eastern part of the Roman Empire—known as the Byzantine Empire—with its capital at Constantinople. The Byzantine Empire would endure until the Ottoman Turks captured Constantinople in 1453. The peak of Byzantine power occurred during the reign of Justinian (527–565), whose achievements included the *Corpus Juris Civilis*, a codification of Roman law on which most European law was based until the nineteenth century. The Byzantine Empire helped protect medieval western Europe from Muslim invaders and preserved much of classical learning. *page 263*

HOW DID the Islamic world influence medieval Western civilization?

The Impact of Islam on East and West. Islamic Arab armies conquered most of the Mediterranean rim. Christian Europe developed a lasting fear and suspicion of Muslims. Franks under Charles Martel defeated an Arab raiding party in central France in 732. Christian-Muslim trade continued, and the Islamic world acted as a conduit for classical learning to the West. Córdoba was a thriving multicultural city. *page 272*

WHAT WAS the doctrine of papal primacy?

The Developing Roman Church. The church was the strongest and most prestigious institution in early medieval Europe, where it filled the vacuum created by the collapse of Roman authority. Monastic culture was especially strong. The greatest organizer of Western monasticism was Saint Benedict of Nursia (480–547). Benedictine monasteries were an economic, political, and spiritual force throughout the West. With the collapse of imperial authority in the West, the bishops of Rome—the popes—developed the doctrine of papal primacy by which they claimed supreme authority over church doctrine and the clergy. These claims were unacceptable in the East, where a

separate Greek Orthodox Church developed under the control of the Byzantine emperors. *page 273*

WHY DID Charlemagne's empire break up after his death?

The Kingdom of the Franks. The Frankish ruler Charlemagne (r. 768–814) sought to re-create a universal Western empire and was crowned emperor by the pope in 800. Charlemagne's realm embraced modern France, Belgium, Holland, and Switzerland, most of Germany, and parts of Italy and Spain. He formed a close alliance with the church and relied on churchmen as royal agents and administrators. His palace school at Aachen was the center of a modest renaissance of classical learning under scholars such as Alcuin of York (735–804). But Charlemagne's empire proved to be ungovernable. Charlemagne had increased the power of local lords whose support he needed to rule, but their power and wealth became so great that they were able to put their self-interest above royal authority. After Charlemagne's death, his empire dissolved amid quarrels among his heirs, the revolts of powerful nobles, and invasions by Vikings, Magyars, and Muslims. *page 276*

WHAT IS a feudal society?

Feudal Society. The Middle Ages were characterized by a chronic absence of central government and the constant threat of famine, disease, and invasion. Lords were those who could guarantee protection under these conditions. In feudal society, a local lord offered security in return for allegiance from his dependents or vassals. It was a system of mutual rights and responsibilities. Medieval vassals pledged fealty to their lord in return for a fief, or grant of land. They promised to support their "liege lord" with troops or money when he called on them for aid.

The feudal economy was organized and controlled through agrarian villages known as manors, worked by free peasants who had their own modest property and economic and legal rights, or by serfs, impoverished peasants who were bound to the land and obliged to provide their lords with an array of services, dues in kind, and products. *page 283*

KEY TERMS

apostolic primacy (p. 274)
demesne (dih-MEEN) (p. 280)
fealty (p. 284)
feudal society (p. 284)
fiefs (p. 276)
Magyars (p. 283)

manors (p. 280)
Papal States (p. 277)
plenitude of power (p. 275)
serf (p. 280)
three-field system (p. 280)
vassals (p. 284)

REVIEW QUESTIONS

1. Trace the history of Christianity to the reign of the emperor Charlemagne. How did the church become a political power in the Western Roman Empire?

2. How did the Franks become the dominant force in western Europe? What were the characteristics of Charlemagne's rule? Why did his empire break apart?

3. How did the Merovingians attempt to solve the problem of "the one versus the many"? To what extent did they succeed? How did the Carolingian approach differ? Was it more successful?

4. How and why was the history of the eastern or Byzantine half of the Roman Empire so different from the western half? What were the major political and religious differences? How would you compare Justinian to Charlemagne?

5. Compare and contrast the teachings of Islam, Roman Catholicism, and Byzantine or Orthodox Christianity. Are they irreconcilable?

6. Discuss the role of Islam in the cultural development of western Europe. What impacts, direct or indirect, of Islam would you characterize as positive, and why? What about negative impacts?

7. What were the defining features of feudalism? Is a feudal society a "backward" society?

8. Why were trust and loyalty such important issues in western Europe's feudal period? Can you think of a social structure in which trust and loyalty are more important than they are in feudal society? Can you think of one where trust and loyalty are less important?

Note: To learn more about the topics in this chapter, please turn to the Suggested Readings at the end of the book. For additional sources related to this chapter please see www.myhistorylab.com

PEARSON myhistorylab Connections

Reinforce what you learned in this chapter by studying the many documents, images, maps, review tools, and videos available at **www.myhistorylab.com**

Read and Review

✓ ⎡Study and Review Chapter 11

⦁⦁⦁⎡Read the Document Reign Justinian: Secret History, Procopius, p. 266

Prologue, Corpus Civilis, ca. 530, p. 266

Epitome Iconoclastic Seventh Synod 754, p. 271

St. Benedict's Rules for Monks, p. 274

Pope Leo I on Bishop Hilary of Arles, p. 275

Life of Charlemagne (early ninth century) Einhard, p. 279

Feudalism, 1083, Archbishop of Cologne, p. 284

◉⎡See the Map Charlemagne's Empire, 814, p. 278

Viking Muslim and Magyar Invasions, 1000, p. 283

◉⎡View the Image Emperor Justinian, p. 266

Research and Explore

◉⎡See the Map The Byzantine Empire under Justinian, p. 269

◉⎡See the Map Byzantium, 1000–1100, p. 270

((•⦁⎡**Hear** the **Audio**

Hear the audio file for Chapter 11
at **www.myhistorylab.com**

12

The Islamic World, 1000–1500

((•─Hear the Audio for Chapter 12 at www.myhistorylab.com

Islamic World Map. The geographical treatise and collection of wondrous tales, *The Wonders of Creation*, was popular in medieval and early modern Islamic society. The map shown here portrays several creatures supporting the world in the firmament. North is oriented at the bottom. Africa is the large triangular landmass jutting upward.

How does the perspective of this world map comment on the worldview of Islam in this period?

THE ISLAMIC HEARTLANDS

ISLAMIC INDIA AND SOUTHEAST ASIA

Centralized caliphal power in the Islamic world had broken down by the mid-tenth century. Regional Islamic states with distinctive political and cultural identities dominated—a pattern that would endure to modern times (see Map 12–1 on page 292). Yet the diverse Islamic lands remained part of a larger civilization. Muslims from Córdoba in Spain could (and did) travel to Bukhara in Transoxiana or Zanzibar or Malaysia and feel at home. Regionalism and cosmopolitanism, diversity and unity, have characterized Islamic civilization ever since.

The next 500 years saw the growth of a truly international Islamic community, united by shared norms of communal order represented and maintained by Muslim religious scholars

GLOBAL PERSPECTIVE

THE EXPANSION OF ISLAMIC CIVILIZATION, 1000–1500

In Islamic and other Asian territories, the period from about 1000 to around 1500 is difficult to characterize simply. The spread of Islam to new peoples or their ruling elites is an obvious theme. However, the history of Islam in India, for example, is hardly the history of India as a whole. The vast conquests and movements of Mongols and Central Asian Turks out of inner Asia were among the most striking developments in this period. Their effects on the societies they conquered were often cataclysmic, whether in China, South Asia, West Asia, or eastern Europe. These conquests and migrations wiped out much of the existing orders and forced countless refugees to flee to new areas. After the initial conquests, however, the empires created by these pastoral warriors, or *ghazis,* of Central Asia helped facilitate the movement across the Eurasian continent of people, merchandise, ideas, and, in the fourteenth century, the Bubonic pandemic. They also contributed, even if unintentionally, new, often significant human resources to older civilizations, such as those of China, the Islamic heartlands, and South Asia.

In this era, Islam became a truly cosmopolitan tradition of religious, cultural, political, and social values and institutions.

This achievement was possible because Islamic culture was highly adaptable and open to "indigenization," or a syncretistic blending of cultural traits, even in seemingly hostile contexts of polytheistic Hindu, South Asian, and African societies. The ability to adapt while maintaining the core tenets of the Muslim faith enabled Islamic religion and culture to take root in many different regions of the globe. Also in this period, distinct traditions of art, language, and literature, for all their regional diversity, became part of a larger Muslim whole. Islamic civilization had none of the territorial contiguity or linguistic and cultural homogeneity of either Chinese or Japanese civilization. Nevertheless, the Islamic world did become a recognizable international reality, a true *Dar al-Islam*, or "House of Islam," in which a Muslim could travel among and exchange ideas and goods with Muslims of radically different backgrounds from Morocco to China and encounter them as brothers/sisters of the *umma*. Ibn Battuta (1304–c. 1370), a Moroccan jurist, traveled for thirty years through Egypt to India and then to parts of Southeast Asia and China before returning to dictate his *Travels in Asia and Africa, 1325–1354.* As an Islamic judge and Arabic speaker, he was able to journey the length

(ulama). Sufism, the strand of Islam that stressed spirituality and allegiance to a spiritual master, gained popularity, especially after 1200. The growth of Sufi affiliations or brotherhoods influenced Muslim life everywhere, often countering the more legalistic aspects of ulama conformity. Shi'ite ideas offered another alternative vision. Movements loyal to Ali and his heirs challenged but failed to reverse centrist Sunni predominance among the majority of Muslims, even though Shi'ite dynasties ruled much of the Islamic heartlands in the tenth and eleventh centuries.

A cultural renaissance fueled the spread of modern Persian as the major language of Islam alongside Arabic. The Persian-dominated Iranian and Indian Islamic world became more distinct from the western Islamic lands where Arabic prevailed.

Two Asian steppe peoples, the Mongols and the Turks, controlled much of the Islamic world in these centuries, but with different results. Turkish rulers—the Saljuq sultans in Iran and Anatolia, and the "slave-kings" of both the Mamluk sultanate in Egypt and the Delhi sultanate in north India—infused Islamic cultures with Turkish influence. The Mongols conquered much of the Islamic heartlands in the thirteenth century, but their culture and religion did not become dominant. Instead, in this age Islam became the major new influence in Central, South, and Southeast Asia, as well as sub-Saharan Africa. ■

THE ISLAMIC HEARTLANDS

RELIGION AND SOCIETY

HOW DID the Sunni, Shi'ite, and Sufi traditions develop between the years 1000 and 1500?

In this period Islamic society was shaped by the consolidation and institutionalization of Sunni legal and religious norms, Sufi traditions and personal piety, and Shi'ite legal and religious norms.

and breadth of the global Islamic world and feel himself still within the bounds of one civilization.

Indian traditional culture was not bound up with a missionary religious tradition like that of Islam, and the developing caste system closely associated with Hindu traditions was less adaptable and much more tied to its homeland. Yet in this age Hindu kingdoms flourished in Indonesia, although these kingdoms mostly rejected the caste system and thus accommodated Hinduism and Indian culture to local conditions. Buddhism, another highly adaptable religion, was expanding across much of Central and Eastern Asia, thereby solidifying its place as an international missionary tradition.

Christianity, by contrast, was not rapidly expanding in Africa, Asia, or Europe. The somewhat disastrous experience of the Crusades (see Chapter 15) brought Europeans into closer contact with the Islamic world than ever before but did not attract converts to Christianity or increase European power in the Mediterranean. In the year 1000 Europe was almost a cultural and political backwater compared to major Islamic or Hindu states, let alone China. By 1500, however, European Christianity was poised for internal revolution and international expansion. European civilization was riding the crest of a commercial and cultural renaissance, enjoying economic and political growth, and starting global exploration for gold and silver to trade with more prosperous and cultured Asian lands. The impact on the Indian Ocean and Chinese-Japanese trade and shipping entrepôts was not immediate; it was only after the mid–eighteenth century that European exploration and trade initiatives became full-scale imperial expansion and rule that changed the rest of the globe profoundly.

See the Map
The Spread of Islam
at **myhistorylab.com**

Focus Questions

◆ What impact did the Mongols and Central Asian Turks have on the Islamic world?

◆ Why were Muslims and Buddhists more successful than Hindus and Christians in spreading their faiths in this era? What does this suggest about the characteristics of a successful world religion?

CONSOLIDATION OF A SUNNI ORTHOPRAXY

The *ulama* (both Sunni and Shi'ite) gradually became entrenched religious, social, and political elites throughout the Islamic world, especially after the breakdown of centralized power in the tenth century. Their integration into local merchant, landowning, and bureaucratic classes led to stronger identification of these groups with Islam.

From the eleventh century, the *ulama*'s power and fixity as a class were expressed in the institution of the **madrasa**, or college of higher learning. On the one hand, the *madrasa* had grown up naturally as individual experts frequented a given mosque or private house and attracted students seeking to learn the Qur'an, the *hadith* ("Tradition"), jurisprudence, Arabic grammar, and the like. On the other hand, rulers endowed the *madrasas* with buildings, scholarships, and salaried chairs, so that they could control the *ulama* by appointing teachers and influencing the curriculum. In theory, such control might combat unwelcome sectarianism. Unlike the university, with its corporate organization and institutional degrees, the *madrasa* was a support institution for individual teachers, who personally certified students' mastery of particular subjects. It gave an institutional base to Islam's long-developed system of students seeking out the best teachers and studying texts with them until they received the teachers' formal certification, or "permission" to transmit and teach those same texts themselves.

Largely outside *ulama* control, popular "unofficial" piety flourished in local pilgrimages to saints' tombs, in folk celebrations of Muhammad's birthday and veneration of him in poetry, and in ecstatic chant and dance among Sufi groups. But the shared traditions of family and civil law, daily worship rituals, fasting in **Ramadan**, and the Hegira united almost all Muslims, even most Kharijites or Shi'ites. In the Christian world, theological dogmas determined sectarian identity. Muslims, however, tended to define Islam in terms of what Muslims do—by practice rather than by beliefs. The chief

madrasa
An Islamic college of higher learning.

Ramadan
The month each year when Muslims must fast during daylight hours.

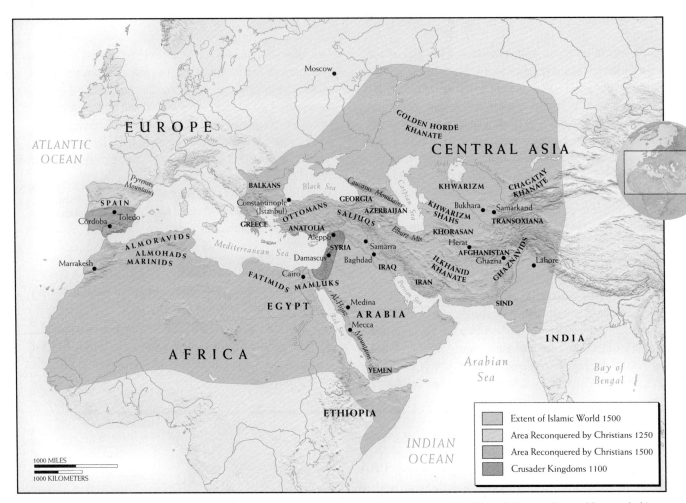

MAP 12–1.   The Islamic World, 1000–ca. 1500. Compare this map with Map 10–1 on page 249. Although the Muslim world expanded into Africa, India, and Central Asia, it also lost Spain to Christian reconquest.

Given the many Muslim states shown on this map, to what extent is it correct to speak of a single Islamic civilization?

arbiters of "normative" Sunni and Shi'ite Islam among the *ulama* were the *faqihs*, or legal scholars, not the theologians.

Sunni orthopraxy, or "correct religious practice," discouraged religious or social innovations. It was well established by the year 1000 as the dominant tradition, even though Shi'ite aspirations often made themselves felt either politically or theologically. The emergence of a conservative theological orientation tied to one of the four main Sunni legal schools, the Hanbalites (after Ibn Hanbal, d. 969) narrowed the scope for creative doctrinal change. The Hanbalites relied on a literalist reading of the Qur'an and the *hadith*. The *ulama* also became more socially conservative as they were integrated into social aristocracies. *Ulama* were often as committed to the status quo as rulers.

SUFI PIETY AND ORGANIZATION

Sufi piety stresses the spiritual and mystical dimensions of Islam. The term **Sufi** apparently came from the Arabic *suf* ("wool"), based on the old ascetic practice of wearing only a coarse woolen garment. Sufi simplicity and humility had roots with the Prophet and Companions but developed as a distinctive tendency when, after about 700 C.E., male and female pietists emphasized a godly life over and above mere observance of Muslim duties. Some stressed ascetic avoidance of temptations, others loving devotion to God. Sufi piety bridged the abyss between human and Divine that Muslim

‣‣‣─[Read the Document
Al-Ghazali, excerpt from Confessions, at **myhistorylab.com**

Sufi
Sufism is a mystic tradition within Islam that encompasses a diverse range of beliefs and practices dedicated to Divine love and the cultivation of the elements of the Divine within the individual human being. The chief aim of all Sufis is to let go of all notions of duality, including a conception of an individual self, and to realize the Divine unity.

insistence on an omniscient, omnipotent God implies. Socially, Sufi piety merged with folk piety in such popular practices as saint veneration, shrine pilgrimage, ecstatic worship, and seasonal festivals. Sufi writers collected stories of saints, wrote treatises on the Sufi path, and composed some of the world's finest mystical poetry.

Some Sufis were revered as spiritual masters and saints. Their disciples formed brotherhoods with their own distinctive mystical teaching, Qur'an interpretation, and devotional practice. These fraternal orders became the chief instruments of the spread of Muslim faith, as well as a locus of popular piety in almost all Islamic societies. Organized Sufism has always attracted members from the populace at large (in this, it differs from monasticism), as well as those dedicated to poverty or other radical disciplines. Indeed, Sufi orders became in this age one of the typical social institutions of everyday Islamic life. Whether Sunni or Shi'ite, many Muslims have ever since identified in some degree with a Sufi order.

CONSOLIDATION OF SHI'ITE TRADITIONS

Shi'ite traditions crystallized between the tenth and twelfth centuries. Many states now came under Shi'ite rulers, but only the Fatimids in Egypt established an important empire. A substantial Shi'ite populace developed only in Iran, Iraq, and the lower Indus (Sind).

Two Shi'ite groups emerged as the most influential. The first were the "Seveners," or "Isma'ilis," who recognized Isma'il (d. ca. 760), first son of the sixth Alid *imam*, as the seventh *imam*. Their thought drew on Gnostic and Neo-Platonic philosophy, knowledge of which they reserved for a spiritual elite. Isma'ili groups were often revolutionary.

By the eleventh century, however, the majority of Shi'ites accepted a line of twelve *imams*, the last of whom is said to have disappeared in Samarra (Iraq) in 873 into a cosmic concealment from which he will eventually emerge as the Mahdi, or "Guided One," to usher in the messianic age and final judgment. These "Twelvers" still focus on the martyrdom of the twelve *imams* and look for their intercession on the Day of Judgment. They have flourished best in Iran, home of most Shi'ite thought. The Buyids who took control of the Abbasid caliphate in 945 were Twelvers. The Safavids made Twelver doctrine the Iranian "state religion" in the sixteenth century (see Chapter 20).

REGIONAL DEVELOPMENTS

After the tenth century the western (or Mediterranean) half of the Islamic world had two regional foci: (1) Spain (**Al-Andalus**), Moroccan North Africa, and, to a lesser extent, West Africa; and (2) Egypt, Syria-Palestine, Anatolia, Arabia, and Libyan North Africa. The history of the eastern half of the Islamic world in the period between 1000 and 1500 was marked by the violent Mongol incursions of the thirteenth century.

SPAIN, NORTH AFRICA, AND THE WESTERN MEDITERRANEAN ISLAMIC WORLD

The grandeur of Spanish or Andalusian Islamic culture is visible still in Córdoba's Great Mosque and the remnants of the Alhambra Palace. In European tradition, the *Chanson de Roland* recalls Charlemagne's retreat through the Pyrenees after failing to check the first Spanish Umayyad's growing power. That ruler, Abd al-Rahman I (r. 756–788), was the founder of the cosmopolitan tradition of Spanish Umayyad culture at Córdoba, the cultural center of the Western world for the next two centuries. Renowned for medicine, science, literature, intellectual life, commercial activity, public baths and gardens, and courtly elegance, Córdoba reached its zenith under Abd al-Rahman III (r. 912–961),

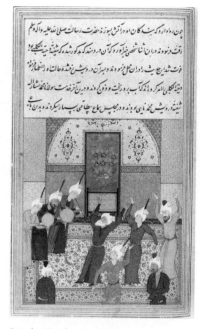

Dancing Dervishes. This image from a 1552 Persian manuscript depicts a Sufi master dancing with his disciples. Sufis often use music and bodily movement to induce ecstatic experiences, which they feel bring them closer to God.

What role did Sufis play in the spread of Islam during this period?

QUICK REVIEW

Islamic Higher Education

♦ *Madrasa:* college of higher learning

♦ *Madrasas* were support institutions for individual teachers

♦ Operated within Islamic tradition of students seeking best teachers

WHO WERE the Mamluks, and why were they able to withstand the Mongols?

Al-Andalus
The Arabic name given to those parts of the Iberian Peninsula governed by Muslims, or Moors, at various times between 711 and 1492.

The Alhambra. Built in the fourteenth century, the Alhambra's serene, almost severe aspect belies its spectacular interior ornamentation. Considered one of the greatest examples of Islamic architecture and one of the most beautiful of all surviving medieval buildings, the Alhambra rises within its curtain walls above Granada, the last of the great Andalusian Moorish cities.

What were some highlights of Moorish culture?

•○•─Read the Document
Ibn Rushd Averroes 12th century
at **myhistorylab.com**

Decorated Ceramic Bowl. A glazed ceramic bowl with a gazelle or antelope, symbolic of beauty and grace. From North Africa, Tunisian area, Fatimid (tenth–twelfth centuries).

Who were the Fatimids?

Reconquista
The Christian reconquest of Spain from the Muslims from 1000 to 1492.

who took the title of caliph in 929. His absolutist, but benevolent, rule saw a largely unified, peaceful Islamic Spain. The mosque-university of Córdoba that he founded attracted students from Europe as well as the Islamic world.

A sad irony of this cosmopolitan world was recurring religious exclusivism, as well as conflict among Muslims and Christians alike. Abroad, Abd al-Rahman III checked both Fatimid power in North Africa and northern Spain's Christian kingdoms, making possible a golden era of Moorish power and culture. After his death, fragmentation into warring Muslim principalities allowed a resurgence of Spain's Christian states from about 1000 until 1085, when the city of Toledo fell permanently into Christian hands.

Brief Islamic revivals in Spain and North Africa came under African reform movements of the Almoravids and Almohads. The Almoravids originated as a religious-warrior brotherhood among Berber nomads in West Africa. Having subdued northwestern Africa, in 1086 they carried their zealotry from their new capital of Marrakesh into Spain, reuniting its Islamic kingdoms. They persecuted arabized Christians (Mozarabs) as well as some Moorish Jews. Ensuing wars began the final major phase of the Spanish "Reconquest" (**Reconquista**), in which Christian rulers regained and Christianized Iberia. These conflicts are best known in the West for the exploits of El Cid (d. 1099), the mercenary adventurer who became the Spanish national hero.

The Almohads ended Almoravid rule in Morocco in 1147 and then conquered much of southern Spain. Before their demise (1225 in Spain; 1275 in Africa), they stimulated a brilliant revival of Moorish culture. During this era, paper manufacture reached Spain and then the rest of western Europe from the Islamic world. The westward odyssey of Indian fable literature through Iran and the Arab world ended in Spanish and Latin translations in thirteenth-century Spain. The greatest lights of this Spanish Islamic intellectual world were the major philosopher and physician Ibn Rushd (Averroës, d. 1189); the great Muslim mystical thinker Ibn al-Arabi (d. 1240); and the famous Jewish Arab philosopher Ibn Maymun (Maimonides, d. 1204).

EGYPT AND THE EASTERN MEDITERRANEAN ISLAMIC WORLD: THE FATIMIDS AND THE MAMLUKS

The major Islamic presence in the Mediterranean from the tenth to the twelfth centuries was that of the Shi'ite Fatimids, who claimed descent from Muhammad's daughter, Fatima. They began as a Tunisian dynasty, then conquered Morocco, Sicily, and Egypt (969), where they built their new capital, Cairo (*al-Qahira*, "the Victorious"). Their rule as Isma'ili Shi'ite caliphs (see Chapter 10) meant that for a time there were three "caliphates": in Baghdad, Córdoba, and Cairo. Content to rule a Sunni majority in Egypt, they sought recognition as true imams by other Isma'ili groups and were able briefly to take western Arabia and most of Syria from the Buyid "guardians" of the Abbasid caliphate (see Chapter 10).

Fatimid rule spawned two splinter groups that have played visible, if minor, roles in history. The Druze of modern Lebanon and Syria originated around 1020 with members of the Fatimid court who professed the divinity of one of the Fatimid caliphs. The tradition they founded is too far from Islam to be considered a Muslim sect. The Isma'ili Assassins, on the other hand, were a radical Muslim movement founded by a Fatimid defector in the Elburz Mountains of Iran around 1100. The name "Assassins" derives not from their infamous political assassinations, but from a European corruption of Arabic *Hashishiyyin* ("users of hashish"). This likely stemmed from the report that they used drugs to manipulate followers into undertaking usually suicidal assassination missions. Their movement was eradicated by the Mongols in the thirteenth century.

The Fatimids built the al-Azhar Mosque in Cairo as a center of learning, a role it maintains today, albeit for Sunni, not (as then) Shi'ite, scholarship. Fatimid rulers treated Egypt's Coptic Christians generally as well as they did their Sunni majority, and many Copts held high offices. Jews also generally fared well under Fatimid rule.

After 1100 the Fatimids weakened, falling in 1171 to Salah al-Din (Saladin, 1137–1193), a general and administrator under the Turkish ruler of Syria, Nur al-Din (1118–1174). Saladin, a Sunni Kurd, is well known in the West for his battles with the Crusaders, especially the retaking of Jerusalem (1187). After Nur al-Din's death, Saladin added Syria-Palestine and Mesopotamia to his Egyptian dominions and founded the Ayyubid Dynasty that, under his successors, controlled all three areas until Egypt fell to the Mamluks in 1250 and most of Syria and Mesopotamia to the Mongols by 1260.

Like Nur al-Din, and on the model of the Saljuks (see Chapter 10), Saladin founded *madrasas* to teach Sunni law. His and his Ayyubid successors' reigns in Egypt saw the entrenchment of a self-conscious Sunnism under a program of mutual recognition and teaching of all four Sunni schools of law. Henceforward Shi'ite Islam disappeared from Egypt.

The heirs of the Fatimids and Saladin in the eastern Mediterranean were the redoubtable Mamluk **sultans** ("[those with] authority"). The Mamluks were chiefly Circassians from the Caucasus, captured in childhood and trained as slave-soldiers. The first Mamluk sultan, Aybak (r. 1250–1257), and his successors were elite Turkish and Mongol slave-officers originally from the bodyguard of Saladin's dynasty. Seizing power in Egypt from the Ayyubids, they became the only Islamic dynasty to withstand the Mongols. Their victory at Ain Jalut in Palestine (1260) ended the Mongols' westward movement. The Mamluk state was based on a military fief system and total control by the slave-officer elite. Whereas the early Mamluks were often succeeded by sons or brothers, succession after 1400 was typically a survival of the fittest; no sultan reigned more than a few years.

The Mamluk sultan Baybars (r. 1260–1277), conqueror of the last Crusader fortresses, figures prominently in Arab legend. To legitimize his rule, he revived the Abbasid caliphate at least in name after Baghdad's devastation by the Mongols (1258) by installing an uncle of Baghdad's last Abbasid as caliph in Cairo. He made treaties with Byzantine and European sovereigns, and with the newly converted Muslim ruler, or *khan*, of the Golden Horde—the Mongol Tatars of southern Russia. His public works in Cairo were numerous, and he extended Mamluk rule south to Nubia and west among the Berbers.

As trade relations with Mongol domains improved after 1300, the Mamluks prospered, commanding a large empire. However, the Black Death epidemic of

CHRONOLOGY

WESTERN ISLAMIC LANDS

756–1021	Spanish Umayyad Dynasty
912–961	Rule of Abd al-Rahman III; height of Umayyad power and civilization
969–1171	Fatimid Shi'ite Dynasty in Egypt
ca. 1020	Origin of Druze community (Egypt/Syria)
1056–1275	Almoravid and Almohad dynasties in North and West Africa, Spain
1096–1291	Major European Christian crusades into Islamic lands; some European presence in Syria-Palestine
1171	Fatimids fall to Saladin, Ayyubid lieutenant of the ruler of Syria
1189	Death of Ibn Rushd (Averroës), philosopher
1204	Death of Musa ibn Maymun (Maimonides), philosopher, Jewish savant
1240	Death of Ibn al-Arabi, theosophical mystic
1250–1517	Mamluk sultanate in Egypt and (from late 1200s) Syria; claimed the Abbasid caliphate
1258	Hulagu Khan's Mongols sack Baghdad, ending Abbasid era
1260	Mamluk victory at Ain Jalut halts Mongol advance into Syria
ca. 1300	Ottoman state founded in western Anatolia
1406	Death of Ibn Khaldun, historian, social philosopher
1453	Byzantine empire ends with conquest of Constantinople by Ottoman forces under Sultan Mehmet I (1451–1481)

sultans
Rulers who have almost complete sovereignty over a certain domain without claiming the title of caliph.

QUICK REVIEW

The Mamluks

◆ Only Islamic dynasty to withstand Mongols

◆ Based in eastern Mediterranean, Cairo

◆ Patronized scholars and artists

Mamluk Bottle. This elegant glass bottle was made in Mamluk workshops in Syria in the mid-fourteenth century for the Yemenite ruler.

John Tsantes/Courtesy of the Freer Gallery of Art, Smithsonian Institution, Washington, DC.

◆◆ Read the Document
al-Tha'Alibi, Recollections of Bukhara, at **myhistorylab.com**

QUICK REVIEW

Ghaznavid Culture

- ◆ Mahmud of Ghazna supported Persian arts, scholarship
- ◆ Mathematician/scientist al-Biruni
- ◆ Poet Firdawsi helped establish "New Persian" language

Mamluk Trade. Trade in spices and other precious commodities between the Mamluks and western Europe was significant. In this painting from about 1500, we see Venetian ambassadors received by the governor of Damascus, who sits on a low platform wearing a distinctive, horn-shaped turban.

What kinds of goods were traded between Christian Europe and the Muslim Mediterranean?

1347–1348 in the Arab Middle East hurt the Mamluk and other regional states badly. Still, the Mamluks survived even the Ottoman conquest of Egypt in 1517 to continue there as Ottoman governors into the nineteenth century.

Architecture, much of which still graces Cairo, remains the major Mamluk bequest to posterity. In addition, mosaics, calligraphy, and metalwork were among the arts and crafts of special note. The Mamluks were great patrons of scholars who excelled in history, biography, astronomy, mathematics, and medicine. The most important of these was Ibn Khaldun (d. 1406). Born of a Spanish Muslim family in Tunis, he settled in Cairo as an adult. He is still recognized as the greatest Muslim social historian and philosopher of history.

THE ISLAMIC EAST: ASIA BEFORE THE MONGOL CONQUESTS

The Persian dynasties of the Samanids at Bukhara (875–999) and the Buyids at Baghdad (945–1055) were the major successors to eastern Abbasid dominion. Their successes epitomized the rise of regional states that undermined the caliphate from the ninth century onward. Similarly, their demise reflected another emerging pattern: the ascendancy of Turkish slave-rulers (like the Mamluks in the west) and Oghuz Turkish peoples, known as Turkomans. With the Saljuqs, what began with the use of Turkish slave troops in ninth-century Baghdad ended in the permanent presence of Turkish ruling dynasties in Islamic lands. As late converts, they became typically the most zealous of Sunni Muslims.

The rule of the Samanids in Transoxiana was ended by a Turkoman group in 999, but they had already lost eastern Iran south of the Oxus in 994 to one of their own slave governors, Subuktigin (r. 976–997). He set up his own state at Ghazna in modern Afghanistan, whence he and his son and successor, Mahmud of Ghazna (r. 998–1030), launched successful campaigns against his former masters. The Ghaznavids are notable for their patronage of Persian literature and culture and their conquests in northwestern India, which began a lasting Muslim presence in India. Mahmud was their greatest ruler. He is still remembered for his booty raids and destruction of temples in western India. At its peak, his empire stretched from western Iran to the Oxus and Indus.

Mahmud attracted to Ghazna numerous Khurasani Persian scholars and artists, notably the great scientist and mathematician al-Biruni (d. 1048), and the poet Firdawsi (d. ca. 1020). Firdawsi's *Shahnama* ("The Book of Kings") is the masterpiece of Persian literature, an epic of 60,000 verses that helped fix the "New Persian" language already developed especially by the earlier, prolific Khurasani poet, the Isma'ili Shi'ite Rudaki (d. ca. 941). It also helped revive pre-Islamic cultural traditions of the greater Iranian world, which became a hallmark of later Persian literature. After Mahmud the empire declined, although Ghaznavids ruled at Lahore until 1186.

The Saljuqs were the first major Turkish dynasty of Islam. They were a steppe clan who settled in Transoxiana, became avid Sunnis, and extended their sway over Khorasan in the 1030s. In 1055 they took Baghdad. As the new guardian of the caliphate and master of an Islamic empire, the Saljuq leader Tughril Beg (r. 1037–1063) took the title of *sultan* to signify his temporal authority. He and his early successors made various Iranian cities their capitals instead of Baghdad.

As new Turkish tribes joined their ranks, the Saljuqs brought Islamic rule for the first time into the central Anatolian plateau at Byzantine expense, even capturing the Byzantine emperor in their victory at

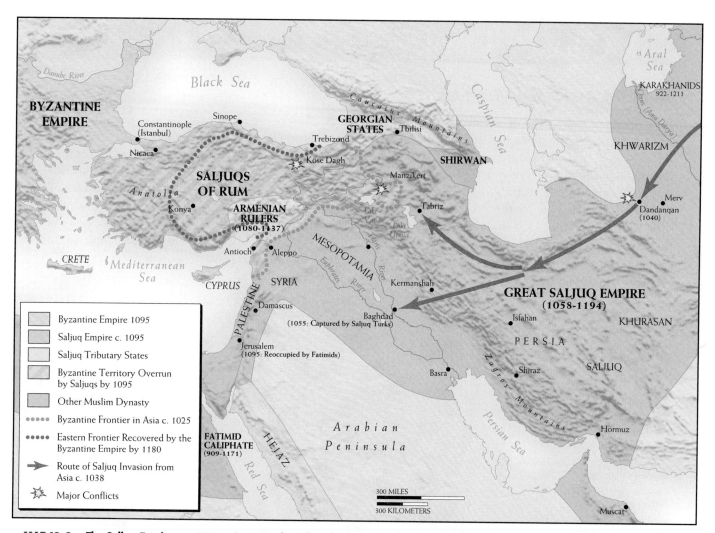

MAP 12–2.   The Saljuq Empire, ca. 1095. By 1200, the Saljuqs had conquered Persia, Mesopotamia, and Syria and defeated Byzantine armies at Manzikert in 1071, altering the balance of power in the eastern Mediterranean and Near East.

How do the Saljuq conquests reveal the power of steppe peoples to overturn settled societies?

Manzikert, in Armenia, in 1071 (see Map 12–2). They also conquered much of Syria and wrested Mecca and Medina from the Shi'ite Fatimids. Turkish rule in Anatolia dates from 1077, when the Saljuq governor there formed a separate sultanate. Known as the Saljuqs of Rum ("Rome," i.e., Byzantium), these rulers were only displaced after 1300 by the Ottomans, another Turkish dynasty, who eventually conquered not only Anatolia but southeastern Europe (see Chapter 20).

The most notable Saljuq was the vizier Nizam al-Mulk, the real power behind two sultans from 1063 to 1092. In his time new roads and caravanserais (inns) for trade and pilgrimage were built, canals were dug, mosques and other public buildings were founded (including the first great Sunni *madrasas*), and science and culture were patronized. He also founded in 1067 what some contend was the first Muslim "university," the legal-theological *madrasa* of the Nizamiyyah in Baghdad. He subsequently established similar *madrasas* in Mesopotamia and Persia. He supported an accurate calendar reform and authored a major work on the art of governing, the *Siyasatnameh*. Before his murder by an Isma'ili assassin in 1092, he appointed as professor in the

QUICK REVIEW

Saljuq Culture

- Vizier Nizam al-Mulk established numerous *madrasas*
- Muhammad al-Ghazali, Muslim religious thinker
- Umar Khayyam, astronomer, mathematician, poet

A Closer Look

Al-Hariri, *Assemblies* (*Maqamat*)

The *maqama* was a type of rhymed Arabic prose narrative that began most prominently with the tenth-century writer Badi' al-Zaman al-Hamadhani and reached its apogee with Muhammad al-Hariri of Basra (1054–1122). Hariri's *Assemblies* is comprised of 50 rhetorically extravagant stories usually centered on the exploits of a picaresque trickster, Abu Zayd, who exposes the foibles of the powerful and prideful and is generally a confidence man who makes his way by his wits. The best illustrations of Hariri's *Assemblies* were done by the Iraqi miniature painter Yahya al-Wasiti in 1237. Here, one of al-Wasiti's illustrations for the 43rd *maqama* shows in realistic detail the arrival in a village of the narrator al-Harith and Abu Zayd on camels. Note that although Muslims have often avoided visual depiction of human beings as infringing on God's creativity, magnificent miniatures such as this were created in many different ages and places in the traditional Islamic world.

The village mosque's minaret is shown clearly here, with the rest of the village depicted as a line of houses along a street with glimpses of inhabitants engaged in everyday activities (spinning, talking, etc.) in the interior of the houses. The stylized layout and motifs (e.g., the plants) of the painting are nonetheless quite dynamic, with many people and animals engaged in different acts and activities.

Within the tightly composed picture there are various animals (goats, poultry, water buffalo) depicted, just as there are villagers, all subordinated to, and on a different plane from, the two arriving figures and the receiving villager in the foreground.

Questions

1. What kinds of activity and people can you pick out in the village? What sources of livelihood can you identify? What kinds of animals? How does the artist communicate so much activity and dynamism in such a small space?

2. Other than the minaret, what distinguishes the mosque from the rest of the village? What formal mechanisms does al-Wasiti use to make the scene dynamic despite the portrayal of characters in a stylized manner and layout?

Annotations by Susan Douglass.

Nizamiyyah Muhammad al-Ghazali (d. 1111), probably the greatest Muslim religious thinker. He also patronized the mathematician and astronomer Umar Khayyam (d. 1123), whose Western fame rests on the poetry of his "Quatrains," or *Ruba'iyat*.

Iranian Saljuq rule crumbled and by 1194 was wholly wiped away by another Turkish slave dynasty from Khwarizm in the lower Oxus basin. By 1200 these Khwarizm-Shahs had built a large, if shaky, empire and sphere of influence covering Iran and Transoxiana. In the same era the Abbasid caliph at Baghdad, al-Nasir (r. 1180–1225), established an independent caliphal state in Iraq. Neither his heirs nor the Khwarizm-Shahs were long to survive.

ISLAMIC ASIA IN THE MONGOL AGE

The building of a vast Mongol Empire spanning Asia from China to Poland in the thirteenth century proved momentous not only for eastern Europe and China (see Chapter 8), but also for Islamic Eurasia and India. A Khwarizm-Shah massacre of Mongol ambassadors brought down the full wrath of the Great Khan, Genghis (ca. 1162–1227), on the Islamic east. He razed entire cities from Transoxiana and Khorasan to the Indus (1219–1222). After his death, his empire's division into four khanates under his four sons gave the Islamic world respite. But in 1255 Hulagu Khan (r. 1256–1265), a grandson of Genghis, led a massive army again across the Oxus. Adding Turkish troops to his forces (Mongol armies typically included many Turks), he went from victory to victory, destroying every Iranian state. In 1258, when the Abbasid caliph refused to surrender, Hulagu's troops plundered Baghdad, killing at least 80,000 inhabitants, including the caliph and his sons.

Hulagu's wife, with Nestorian Christians and Buddhists in his inner circle, persuaded him to spare the Christians of Baghdad. He followed this policy in later conquests, including the sack of Aleppo—which, like Baghdad, resisted. Thus, when Damascus surrendered Western Christians had hopes of seeing Mamluk Cairo and Islamic power collapse, but Hulagu's drive west was delayed by rivalry with his kinsman Berke. A Muslim convert, Berke ruled the khanate of the Golden Horde, the southern-Russian Mongol state north of the Caucasus. He was in contact with the Mamluks, and some of his Mongols even helped them defeat Hulagu in Palestine (1260), stopping a Mongol advance into Egypt. A treaty in 1261 between the Mamluk sultan and Berke established an alliance confirming the breakup of Mongol unity and autonomy for the four khanates: in China (the Yuan Dynasty), Iran (the Ilkhans), Russia (the Golden Horde), and Transoxiana (the Chagatays).

Hulagu and his heirs ruled the old Persian Empire from Azerbaijan for seventy-five years as viceroys (Il-Khans) of the Great Khan of China's viceroys (*Il-Khans*). As elsewhere, the Mongols did not eradicate the society they inherited. Their native paganism and Buddhist and Christian leanings yielded to Muslim faith, although they practiced religious tolerance. After 1335 the Ilkhanid Empire broke up into provinces, and for fifty years Iran was again fragmented.

This situation prepared the way for a new Turko-Mongol conquest from Transoxiana, under Timur-i Lang ("Timur the Lame," or "Tamerlane," 1336–1405). Even Genghis Khan could not match Timur in the savagery of military campaigns. Timur's raiding between 1379 and 1405 was not aimed at empire-building, but sheer conquest. In successive campaigns he swept everything before him in a flood of devastation: eastern Iran (1379–1385); western Iran, Armenia, the Caucasus, and upper Mesopotamia (1385–1387); southwestern Iran, Mesopotamia, and Syria (1391–1393); Central Asia from Transoxiana to the Volga and as far as Moscow (1391–1395); North India (1398); and northern Syria and Anatolia (1400–1402). Timur's sole positive contributions seem to have been the buildings he sponsored at Samarkand, his capital. He left behind him ruins, death, disease, and political chaos across the entire eastern Islamic world, which did not soon recover. His was, however, the last great steppe invasion, for firearms soon destroyed the steppe horsemen's advantage.

Timur's sons ruled after him in Transoxiana and Iran (1405–1494). The most successful Timurid was Shahrukh (r. 1405–1447), who for a time controlled a united Iran. His capital, Herat, became an important center of Persian Islamic culture and Sunni piety. He patronized the famous Herat school of miniature painting as well as Persian literature and philosophy. The Timurids had to share Iran with Turkoman dynasties in western Iran, once even losing Herat to one of them. They and the Turkomans were the last Sunnis to rule Iran. Both were eclipsed at the end of the fifteenth century by the militant Shi'ite dynasty of the Safavids, who ushered in a new, Shi'ite era in the Iranian world (see Chapter 20).

THE SPREAD OF ISLAM BEYOND THE HEARTLANDS

WHAT WERE the main ways Islam spread beyond Eurasia?

The period from roughly 1000 to 1500 saw Islamic civilization spread to become a lasting religious, cultural, social, and political force in new regions (see Map 12–1). Expanding not only from Mesopotamia, Persia, and the Black Sea north to Moscow under the Golden Horde, but also west to the Balkans and the Danube basin under the Ottoman Turks, Islamic rule covered the greater part of Eurasia in this era (see Chapter 20). Meanwhile, India, Malaysia, Indonesia, inland West Africa, and coastal East Africa became major spheres of Islamic political, social, cultural, and commercial presence. In all these regions Sufi orders were most responsible for converting people and spreading Islamic cultural influences, though merchants, too, were major agents of cultural Islamization.

Conquest was a third (but demographically less important) means of Islamization (and either Arabization or Persianization) in these regions. Sometimes only ruling elites, sometimes wider circles, became Muslims, but in India, Southeast Asia, and sub-Saharan Africa much of the populace retained their languages, heritage, and religious traditions, while their elites learned Arabic and/or Persian as second or third languages. Nonetheless, in the most important of these regions, India, the coming of Islam brought epochal changes.

ISLAMIC INDIA AND SOUTHEAST ASIA

Indian Islamic civilization (like earlier Indian civilization) was formed by creative interaction between invading foreigners and indigenous peoples. The early Arab and Turkish invaders were a foreign Muslim minority; their heirs were truly "Indian" as well as Islamic, adding a new dimension to both Indian and Islamic civilization. From then on, Indian civilization would both include and enrich Islamic traditions.

THE SPREAD OF ISLAM TO SOUTH ASIA

HOW DID trade and Sufi orders spread Islam?

Well before the Ghaznavids came to the Punjab, Muslims were to be found even outside the original Arab conquest areas in Sind (see Map 12–3). Muslim merchants had settled in the port cities of Gujarat and southern India as diaspora communities to profit from internal Indian trade as well as from trade with the Indies and China. Wherever Muslim traders went, converts to Islam were attracted by business advantages as well as by the

MAP EXPLORATION

To explore this map further, go to **http://www.myhistorylab.com**

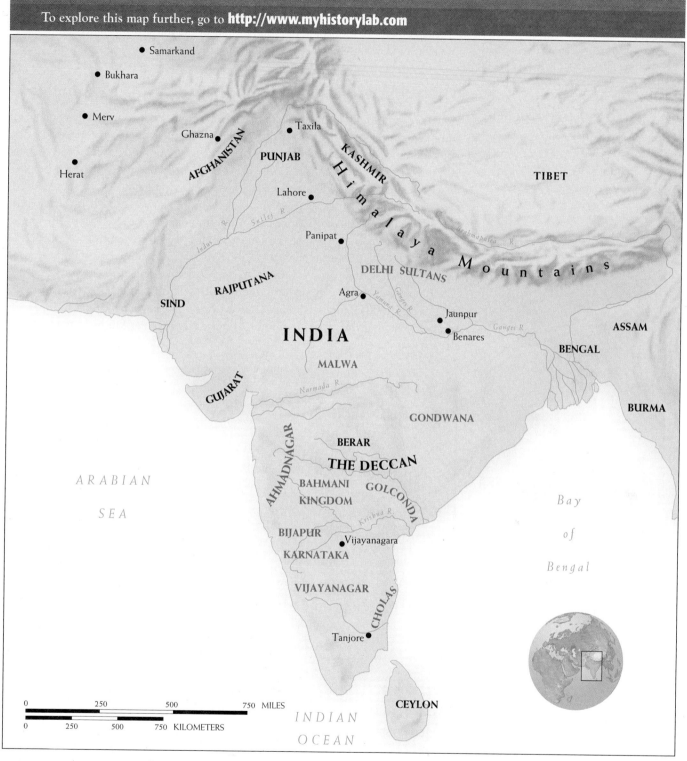

MAP 12–3.   The Indian Subcontinent, 1000–1500.

Shown are major kingdoms and regions.

Where in India were the principal Islamic states located during this period?

View the Image
The Indian Ocean Dhow Sailing Vessel, at **myhistorylab.com**

Deccan
Large plateau with varying terrain that constitutes most of southern India.

WHAT ALLOWED Muslim rulers eventually to dominate India?

The Qutb Minar (Victory Tower) in Delhi is an example of classic Indo-Muslim architecture. Constructed in the twelfth century, this soaring tower of red sandstone commemorated Islamic military victory.

What features of this tower reflect Indian cultural traditions?

straightforward ideology and practice of Islam and its officially egalitarian, "classless" ethic. Sufi orders had gained a foothold in the central **Deccan** and in the south, giving today's south Indian Muslims old roots. Sufi piety also drew converts in the north, especially when the Mongol devastation of Iran in the thirteenth century sent refugees into North India. Muslim refugees strengthened Muslim life in the subcontinent.

MUSLIM-HINDU ENCOUNTER

From the outset Muslim leaders had to rule a land dominated by utterly different cultural and religious traditions. Much as early Muslim rulers in Iranian territories had given Zoroastrians legal status as "people of Scripture" (like Christians and Jews; see Chapter 10), the first Arab conquerors in Sind (711) had treated Hindus as "protected peoples" under Muslim sovereignty. These precedents gave Indian Muslim rulers a legal basis for coexistence with their Hindu subjects but did not remove Hindu resistance to Islamic rule.

The chief obstacle to Islamic expansion in India was the strength of the Hindu warrior class that emerged after the Hun and other Asian invasions of the fifth and sixth centuries. Apparently descended from invaders and the native Hindu warrior (Kshatriya) class, they were known from about the mid-seventh century as *Rajputs*. The Rajputs were a large group of northern Indian clans sharing a fierce warrior ethic and strong Hindu cultural and religious traditionalism. They fought the Muslims with great tenacity, but their inability to unite brought them under Muslim domination in the sixteenth century (see Chapter 20).

C H R O N O L O G Y

EASTERN ISLAMIC LANDS

875–999	Persian Samanid Dynasty, centered at Bukhara
ca. 941	Death of Rudaki, first Persian epic poet, father of "New Persian"
945–1055	Persian Buyid Shi'ite Dynasty in Baghdad controls caliphs
994–1186	Ghaznavid Dynasty in Ghazna (modern Afghanistan) and Lahore (modern Pakistan), founded by Subuktigin (r. 976–997) and his son, Mahmud of Ghazna (r. 998–1030)
ca. 1020	Death of Firdawsi, compiler of the Persian national epic, the *Shahnama*
ca. 1050	Death of al-Biruni, scientist, mathematician, and polyglot
1055–1194	Saljuq rule in Baghdad
1063–1092	Viziership of Nizam al-Mulk
1067	Nizam al-Mulk founds Nizamiyya Madrasa in Baghdad
1111	Death of al-Ghazali, theologian and scholar
1219–1222	Genghis Khan plunders eastern Iran to Indus region
1258	Hulagu Khan conquers Baghdad
1260–1335	Hulagu and his Il-Khanid successors rule Iran
1261	Mamluk-Mongol treaty halts westward Mongol movement
1379–1405	Campaigns of Timur-i Lang (Tamerlane) devastate entire Islamic East
1405–1447	Shahrukh, Timurid ruler at Herat, great patron of arts and philosophy
1405–1494	Timurids, successors of Tamerlane, rule in Transoxiana and Iran

ISLAMIC STATES AND DYNASTIES

A series of Turkish-Afghan rulers known as the "Slave Sultans of Delhi" extended and maintained Islamic power over North India for nearly a century (1206–1290). Such slave-soldiers, or **mamluks**, figured prominently in the leading elites of the new regime, much as they did in the Mamluk Dynasty in Egypt. Five descendants of Iltutmish ruled after him until 1266. The most vigorous of these was his daughter Raziyya, who ruled as sultana from 1237 to 1241.

Four later Muslim dynasties—the Khaljis, Tughluqs, Sayyids, and Lodis—continued the Delhi sultanate until nearly 1500. This run of Muslim dynasties was interrupted by Timur's Mongol-Turkish invasion and sack of Delhi in 1398, from which the city took decades to recover. However, even before this devastation—roughly from the mid-1300s—the sultanate's central authority waned. In the two centuries before the advent of the Mughals in the mid-sixteenth century, many regions became partially or wholly independent, smaller sultanates, Rajput kingdoms, or tiny Hindu or Muslim principalities. The sultanate was often only the most prominent among various kingdoms. Regional rule predominated across the subcontinent.

The most important independent Islamic state was that of the Bahmanids in the Deccan (1347–1527). These rulers were famous for architecture and the intellectual life of their court, as well as for containing the powerful South Indian Hindu state of Vijayanagar (1336–1565). (The first documented use of firearms in the subcontinent was in a Bahmani battle with the raja of Vijayanagar in 1366.) Most regional capitals fostered a rich cultural life. Jaunpur, to the north of Benares (Varanasi), for example, became an asylum for artists and intellectuals after Timur's sack of Delhi and boasted an impressive tradition of Islamic architecture. Kashmir, an independent sultanate from 1346 to 1589, was a literary center where many Indian texts were translated into Persian.

SOUTHEAST ASIA

Islam spread into Southeast Asia as a result of a natural extension of long-distance Islamic (Arab and Persian) and Indian trade across the Indian Ocean, land and sea migrations of scholars and merchants, and socialization of Indian peoples of South Asia. This extension of much older trade contacts eastward beyond the Indian subcontinent had unique characteristics of its own. Because of their geographic location, the islands in Southeast Asia readily connected India and China and thus became an important trade route by the fifteenth century. The spread of Islam in this region was not a steady, progressive development. Rather, the proliferation of Islam was idiosyncratic, and a number of distinct Islamic traditions emerged, centered largely around five areas: Java, Sumatra, Melaka, Acheh, and Moluccas (see Map 12–4 on page 304).

In some areas, such as the Moluccas, traditional Muslim beliefs coexisted with ancestor-worship, sorcery, or magic. Various central Islamic rites such as the pilgrimage (*Hajj*) were perceived to be an Arab custom and thus optional for "true" Muslims. Eventually, many political leaders adopted a more stringent Islamic practice, largely because this aided in greater centralization and consolidation of power.

One of the greatest sources of tension and conflict in this area was only tangentially related to distinct religious views: It was the struggle between the center and the periphery. Before the arrival of the Dutch in the early seventeenth century, the various urban rulers, typically located in port cities, benefited from the new global economy. They sought to subsume under their control the hereditary chiefs, who had also converted to Islam, by invoking Islam and their vision of a perfect society. The local

HOW DID local traditional beliefs shape Muslim practice in Southeast Asia?

mamluks
Slave-soldiers who converted to Islam, the mamluks eventually became a powerful military caste and even governed Egypt from 1250 to 1517.

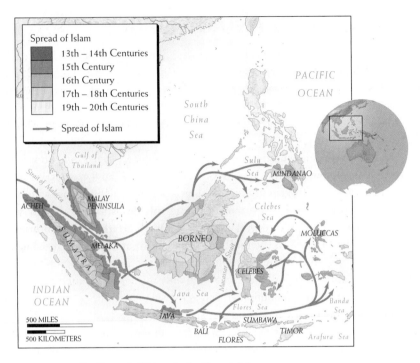

MAP 12–4.   The Spread of Islam in Southeast Asia.

What were the main reasons for the spread of Islam in Southeast Asia?

traditions proved to be durable, especially in the rural areas. Muslims in Southeast Asia therefore adapted Islam to their needs and customs rather than simply replacing the indigenous practices with the new universal and foreign religion.

RELIGIOUS AND CULTURAL ACCOMMODATION

HOW DID Islam become an enduring part of Indian civilization?

Despite the division of the subcontinent into multiple political units, the five centuries after Mahmud of Ghazna saw Islam become an enduring, influential element of Indian culture—especially in the north and the Deccan. The Delhi sultans were able, except for Timur's invasion, to fend off the Mongols, as had the Mamluks in Egypt. They thereby provided a political and social framework within which Islam could take root. Although a Muslim minority of Persianized Turks and Afghans continued to rule a Hindu majority, conversion went on at various levels of society. **Ghazis** ("warriors") carried Islam by conquest to pagan groups in eastern Bengal and Assam. Some Hindu converts came from the ruling classes serving Muslim overlords. Sufi orders converted many Hindus among the lower classes. The Muslim aristocracy, initially mostly foreigners, was usually treated in Indian society as a separate caste group. Lower class Hindu converts were assimilated into lower "Muslim castes," often identified by occupation. (See Document, "How the Hindus Differ from the Muslims" on page 306.)

ghazis
Warriors who carried Islam by force of arms to pagan groups.

Sanskrit had long been the common Indian scholarly language, but in this period regional languages, such as Tamil in the south, achieved literary and administrative status, and Persian became the intellectual and cultural language of the North Indian ruling elites. However, the infusion of substantial numbers of Muslims into the subcontinent produced a new language, **Urdu-Hindi**, with both Perso-Arabic and Indic ele-

Urdu-Hindi
A language that combines Persian-Arabic and native Indian elements. Urdu is the Muslim version of the language. Hindi is the Hindu version.

OVERVIEW Major Islamic Dynasties, 1000s–1500s

DYNASTY	LOCATION	DYNASTY	LOCATION
(Spanish) Umayyads	Spain (756–1031)	"Great" Saljuqs Saljuqs (of Rum)	Iraq, Iran (1038–1194); Anatolia (1077–1307)
Almoravids	North Africa, Spain (1056–1147)	Abbasids	Based in Iraq (749–1258)
Almohads	North Africa, Spain (1130–1269)	Ghaznavids	Transoxiana, NW India (977–1186)
Fatimids	North Africa, then Egypt, Syria (909–1171)	Khwarizm-Shahs	Central Asia, Iran (c. 1077–1231)
Ayyubids	Egypt, Syria, Yemen (1169–late 1400s)	Ilkhanids	Iran (1256–1353)
Mamluks	Egypt, Syria (1250–1517)	Timurids	Transoxiana, Iran (1370–1506)
Samanids	Khurasan, Transoxiana (819–1005)	Delhi Sultans	Northern India (1206–1555)
Buyids	Iran, Iraq (932–1062)	Bahmanids and successors	Deccan/Central India (1347–1527)

ments. It began to take shape soon after the eleventh-century Muslim influx and developed in response to the increasing need of Hindus and Muslims for a shared language. It became the spoken idiom of the Delhi region and a literary language of North Indian and Deccan Muslims in the seventeenth and eighteenth centuries. Indo-European in grammar, it used Perso-Arabic vocabulary and script and was at first called *Hindi* ("Indian") or *Dakani* ("southern"), then in British times *Hindustani*. Eventually *Urdu* became the name for its Islamic version, based on its Perso-Arabic, Turkish heritage, and *Hindi* for the version associated with Hindu culture and its Sanskrit heritage. Ultimately, Urdu became the official national language of modern Pakistan, and Hindi, of modern India.

Indian Muslims, both immigrants and converts, were susceptible to Hindu influence (in language, marriage customs, and caste consciousness), much like Muslims in Africa and Asia. Unlike earlier immigrant elites, they were never utterly absorbed into Hindu culture but remained in some measure a group apart, proud to be distinct. The Muslim ruling classes saw themselves as protectors and propagators of Islam in India, and most of the Delhi sultans sought formal recognition for their rule from the nominal Abbasid caliphs in Baghdad or, in Mamluk times, in Cairo.

Nevertheless, the reciprocal influence of Muslims and Hindus was inevitable, especially in popular piety and among the masses as opposed to the ruling elites. Sufi devotion had an appeal similar to that of Hindu devotional, or **bhakti** movements (see Chapter 4), and each influenced the other. Some of India's most revered Sufi and *bhakti* saints date from the fourteenth and fifteenth centuries. During this period, various theistic mystics strove to transcend Hindu-Muslim antagonism and exclusivism. They typically preached devotion to a God who saves his worshipers without regard to either Hindu caste obligations or legalistic Muslim observance. The poet-saints Ramananda (d. after 1400) and Kabir (d. ca. 1518) were the two most famous such reformers.

bhakti
Hindu devotional movements.

DOCUMENT

How the Hindus Differ from the Muslims

*A*l-Biruni (d. ca. 1050), the greatest scholar-scientist of medieval Islam, was born in north-eastern Iran. He spent much of his life at the court of Mahmud of Ghazna, whom he accompanied on expeditions into northwestern India. Alongside his scientific work, he learned Sanskrit, studied the Hindus, and wrote a History of India. The following selections from this work illustrate the reach and sophistication of his mind.

- **HOW DOES** the emphasis on purity and the impurity of foreigners that Biruni imputes to the Hindus compare with the attitudes of Islam? Other religions? Does this passage suggest why the Hindu tradition has remained largely an Indian one while Islam became international? To what might Biruni be referring in his comments on the relative absence of religious controversy among Hindus?

. . . The barriers which separate Muslims and Hindus rest on different causes.

First, they differ from us in everything which other nations have in common. And here we first mention the language, although the difference of language also exists between other nations. If you want to conquer this difficulty (i.e., to learn Sanskrit), you will not find it easy, because the language is of an enormous range, both in words and inflections, something like the Arabic, calling one and the same thing by various names, both original and derived, and using one and the same word for a variety of subjects, which, in order to be properly understood, must be distinguished from each other by various qualifying epithets. . . .

Secondly, they totally differ from us in religion, as we believe in nothing in which they believe, and vice versa.

On the whole, there is very little disputing about theological topics among themselves; at the utmost, they fight with words, but they will never stake their soul or body or their property on religious controversy. On the contrary, all their fanaticism is directed against those who do not belong to them—against all foreigners. They call them *mleecha*, i.e., impure, and forbid having any connection with them, be it by intermarriage or any other kind of relationship, or by sitting, eating, and drinking with them, because thereby, they think, they would be polluted. They consider as impure anything which touches the fire and the water of a foreigner; and no household can exist without these two elements. Besides, they never desire that a thing which once has been polluted should be purified and thus recovered, as, under ordinary circumstances, if anybody or anything has become unclean, he or it would strive to regain the state of purity. They are not allowed to receive anybody who does not belong to them, even if he wished it, or was inclined to their religion. This, too, renders any connection with them quite impossible, and constitutes the widest gulf between us and them.

In the third place, in all manners and usages they differ from us to such a degree as to frighten their children with us, with our dress, and our ways and customs, and as to declare us to be devil's breed, and our doings as the very opposite of all that is good and proper. By the by, we must confess, in order to be just, that a similar depreciation of foreigners not only prevails among us and the Hindus, but is common to all nations towards each other.

Source: From Edward C. Sachau, *Alberuni's India*, Vol. 1 (London: Kegan Paul, Trench, Truebner, 1910), pp. 17, 19, 20.

HINDU AND OTHER INDIAN TRADITIONS

WHAT WERE some characteristics of Hindu culture in this period?

The history of India from 1000 to 1500 was also important for the religious and cultural communities of India that as a whole vastly outnumbered the Muslims. The Jain tradition flourished, notably in Gujarat, Rajputana, and Karnataka. In the north Muslim conquests effectively ended Indian Buddhism—which had already been waning—by the eleventh century.

Hindu religion and culture flourished even under Muslim rule, as the continuing social and religious importance of the Brahmans and the popularity of *bhakti* movements throughout India attest. This was an age of Brahmanic scholasticism that produced many commentaries and manuals but few seminal works. *Bhakti* creativity was much greater. The great Hindu Vaishnava Brahman Ramanuja (d. 1137) reconciled *bhakti* ideas with the classical Upanishadic Hindu worldview in the Vedantin tradition. *Bhakti* piety permeates the masterpiece of Hindu mystical love poetry, Jayadeva's *Gita Govinda* (twelfth century), which is devoted to Krishna, the most important of Vishnu's incarnations.

The south continued to be the center of Hindu cultural, political, and religious activity. The major dynastic state in the south in this age was that of the Cholas, who flourished from about 900 to 1300 and patronized a famous school of bronze sculpture at their capital, Tanjore. Their mightiest successor, the kingdom of Vijayanagar (1336–1565), subjugated the entire south in the fourteenth century and resisted its Muslim foes longer than any other kingdom. Vijayanagar itself was one of India's most lavish cities and a center of the cult of Shiva before its destruction by the Deccan Bahmanid sultan.

Krishna Dancing on the Head of the Serpent Kaliya. This fifteenth-century bronze figure from Vijayanagar is based on the legend of how Kaliya infested the Jumna River's waters until Krishna leaped in and emerged dancing on the vanquished snake.
Asian Art Museum of San Francisco. The Avery Brundage Collection B65B72.
How were Islam and Hinduism altered by their contact with each other?

SUMMARY

 HOW DID the Sunni, Shi'ite, and Sufi traditions develop between the years 1000 and 1500?

Religion and Society. Between 1000 and 1500, the most important developments for the shape of Islamic society were of Sunni and Shi'ite legal and religious norms and of Sufi traditions and personal piety. Sunnism was the dominant tradition across the Islamic world. In both main branches of Islam, the *ulama* became the religious, social, and political elites and discouraged religious innovation. Shi'ism flourished in Iran under the Savafid rulers. Sufi piety stresses the spiritual and mystical dimensions of Islam. Sufi fraternal orders, whether Sunni or Shi'ite, became the chief instruments for spreading the Muslim faith in most Islamic societies. *page 290*

 WHO WERE the Mamluks, and why were they able to withstand the Mongols?

Regional Developments. Despite general religious tolerance and high cultural achievements, the Muslims were gradually pushed out of Spain by the Spanish Christian states between 1000 and 1492. In Egypt, the Shi'ite Fatamids established a separate caliphate from 969 to 1171.

●●●─Read the Document
A Contemporary Describes Timur
at **myhistorylab.com**

The Mamluks, elite Turkish and Mongol slave-officers, were the only Muslim dynasty to withstand the Mongol invasions, thanks to military might and strong government. The Saljuqs, based in Anatolia and Iraq, were the first major Turkish dynasty of Islam. Other notable Islamic dynasties were the Ghaznavids in Transoxiana and the Khwarizm-Shahs in Persia. In 1255 the Mongols invaded the Muslim world and swept all before them, conquering Transoxiana, Persia, and Iraq, where they captured Baghdad and killed the last Abbasid caliph in 1258, before being defeated by the Mamluks in Syria in 1260. Thereafter, the Mongols established the Ilkhanid Dynasty in Persia and converted to Islam. Another wave of Turko-Mongol conquest under Timur-i Lang further devastated much of the Near East between 1379 and 1405. *page 293*

WHAT WERE the main ways Islam spread beyond Eurasia?

The Spread of Islam beyond the Heartlands. Islamic rulers controlled most of Eurasia in the 1000–1500 period. Islam also gained influence in India, Malaysia,

Indonesia, and parts of West and East Africa. Trade and commerce, Sufi orders, and conquest were among the means by which Islam spread. *page 300*

HOW DID trade and Sufi orders spread Islam?

The Spread of Islam to South Asia. Muslim traders, as well as Sufi brotherhoods, spread Islam in India, where it appealed to local needs and, for traders, seemed to offer business advantages. *page 300*

WHAT ALLOWED Muslim rulers eventually to dominate India?

Muslim–Hindu Encounter. Hindus enjoyed protected status under Muslim rule in India, but they still resisted. Over time, lack of Hindu unity allowed Muslim rulers to increase their power. *page 302*

HOW DID local traditional beliefs shape Muslim practice in Southeast Asia?

Islamic States and Dynasties. The Delhi sultanate, in which mamluks were prominent, maintained power in Northern India for much of this period. A variety of smaller, independent states emerged starting in the mid-1300s, including the Islamic Bahmanids in the Deccan. In Southeast Asia, Islam was spread by Muslim merchants and traders, as well as by Sufi brotherhoods, and wherever it took root, it blended with local customs. *page 303*

HOW DID Islam become an enduring part of Indian civilization?

Religious and Cultural Accommodation. A new language, Urdu-Hindi, combined Persian-Arabic and indigenous Indian elements. There was reciprocal influence between Muslims and Hindus. *page 304*

WHAT WERE some characteristics of Hindu culture in this period?

Hindu and Other Indian Traditions. Buddhism all but disappeared from India during these years, but Hindu religion and culture flourished, even under Muslim control. Hindu devotional, or *bhakti*, movements were especially creative. *page 306*

KEY TERMS

Al-Andalus (p. 293)
bhakti (p. 305)
Deccan (p. 302)
ghazis (p. 305)
madrasa (p. 291)
mamluk (p. 303)

Ramadan (p. 291)
Reconquista (p. 294)
Sufi (soo-FEE) (p. 292)
sultans (p. 295)
Urdu-Hindi (p. 305)

REVIEW QUESTIONS

1. In the 1000–1500 period, why did no Muslim leader build a unified large-scale Islamic empire of the extent of the early Abbasids?

2. How were the *ulama* educated? What was their relationship to political leadership? What social roles did they play? What was the role of the *madrasas* in Islamic culture and civilization?

3. What was the impact of the institutionalization of Sufi piety and thought? What were the social and political roles of Sufism?

4. Discuss cultural developments in Spain before 1500. Why was Córdoba such a model of civilized culture? What were some of the distinguishing features of al-Andalus?

5. Why did Islam survive the successive invasions by steppe peoples (Turks and Mongols) from 945 on? What were the lasting results of these "invasions" for the Islamic world?

6. What were the primary obstacles to stable rule for India's Muslim invaders and immigrants? How did they deal with these obstacles?

7. What are some examples of reciprocal influence between Muslim and Hindu traditions in India?

8. What were noteworthy characteristics of the spread of Islam in Southeast Asia?

Note: To learn more about the topics in this chapter, please turn to the Suggested Readings at the end of the book. For additional sources related to this chapter please see www.myhistorylab.com

myhistorylab Connections
PEARSON

Reinforce what you learned in this chapter by studying the many documents, images, maps, review tools, and videos available at **www.myhistorylab.com**

Read and Review

✓●─ **Study** and **Review** Chapter 12

●●●─ **Read** the Document *Al-Ghazali, excerpt from Confessions, p. 292*
Ibn Rushd Averroes 12th century, p. 294
al-Tha'Alibi, Recollection of Bukhara, p. 296
A Contemporary Describes Timur, p. 307

●●─ **View** the Image *The Indian Ocean Dhow Sailing Vessel, p. 302*

Research and Explore

◉─ See the Map *The Spread of Islam, p. 291*

◉─ See the Map *Delhi Sultanate, 1236 C.E.*

((●─ **Hear** the **Audio**

Hear the audio file for Chapter 12
at **www.myhistorylab.com**

13

Ancient Civilizations of the Americas

((•▶[Hear the Audio for Chapter 13 at www.myhistorylab.com

A Mixtec View of Creation. In this manuscript, which predates the Spanish conquest, the Mixtec Indians of Oaxaca, Mexico, illustrate how their gods created the world. The complex narrative depicted here relates the creation of the Mother and Father of the gods by Lord and Lady One-Deer.

What is the connection between religious authority and political power in Native American civilizations, and how does this compare with other civilizations in the premodern period?

umans first settled the American continents between 12,000 and 30,000 years ago. At that time glaciers locked up much of the world's water, lowering the sea level and opening a land bridge between Siberia and Alaska. The earliest undisputed archaeological evidence of humans in Tierra del Fuego, at the southern tip of South America, dates to 11,000 years ago, indicating that by then the immigrants' descendants had spread over all of both North and South America. When the glaciers receded the oceans rose, severing Asia from America. The inhabitants of the Americas were isolated from the inhabitants of Africa and Eurasia and would remain so until 1492.

Although isolated from one another, the peoples of the Americas, Africa, and Eurasia experienced similar cultural changes at the end of the Paleolithic. Some people shifted from

GLOBAL PERSPECTIVE

ANCIENT CIVILIZATIONS OF THE AMERICAS

Civilization in the Americas before 1492 developed independently of civilization in the Old World. As the pharaohs of Egypt were erecting their pyramid tombs, the people of the desert Pacific coast of Peru were erecting temple platforms. While King Solomon ruled in Jerusalem, the Olmec were creating their monumental stone heads. As Rome reached its apogee and then declined, so did the great city of Teotihuacán in the Valley of Mexico. As Islam spread from its heartland, the rulers of Tikal brought their city to its greatest splendor before its abrupt collapse. Maya mathematics and astronomy rivaled those of any other peoples of the ancient world. And as the aggressive nation-states of Europe were emerging from their feudal past, the Aztecs and Incas were consolidating their great empires. The agriculture, engineering, and public works of these states—as exemplified by the famous Aztec drainage systems, the floating gardens or *chiampas* of Lake Texcoco, and the Inca system of roads and their terraced agriculture—exquisitely demonstrate an ability to master the most challenging environments.

The encounter between Old World and New commencing at the close of the fifteenth century, however, proved devastating for American civilizations. The same naval and military technology that allowed Europeans to embark on the voyages of discovery and fight destructive wars among themselves caught the great native empires unprepared. More important, however, was what historian Alfred Crosby has called the "Columbian Exchange." The peoples of the New World exchanged trade goods, ideas, technology, and microbes among themselves, along north–south trade routes that linked the American Southeast and Southwest to Mesoamerica, and the peoples of the northern Andes to those of the central and southern regions, as well as east–west routes linking eastern North America with the Great Lakes region and beyond. The coming of the Spanish profoundly disturbed both the patterns of trade and the ecological balance. Most significant, the Spanish introduced new epidemic diseases against which the peoples of the New World did not possess immunity. During the first century after the encounter

hunting and gathering to an agricultural way of life. Scholars of the early Americas call this the Paleoindian period.

Between approximately 8000 B.C.E. and 2000 B.C.E., in what is termed the Archaic period, climatic changes occurred in Central America. Large animals, including mammoth, became extinct, altering humans' food supply. The diet of maize (corn), beans, and squash came to predominate. The domestication of new crops led to a much more sedentary life. New kinds of weapons and tools were developed to secure and process new foods.

After about 2000 B.C.E., during what is called the Formative period, remarkable civilizations emerged as societies grew increasingly stratified, villages coalesced into urban centers, monumental architecture was erected, and artistic traditions developed. The two most prominent centers of pre-Columbian American civilization—and the focus of this chapter—were Mesoamerica, in what is today Mexico and Central America, and the Andean region of South America. At the time of the European conquest of the Americas in the sixteenth century, two relatively recent, expansionist empires—the Aztecs, or Mexica, in Mesoamerica, and the Inca in the Andes—dominated their respective environments. Spanish conquerors obliterated both of these empires and nearly succeeded in obliterating native culture. But in both regions, Native American traditions have endured, overlaid and combined in complex ways with Spanish culture, to provide clues to the pre-conquest past. ■

RECONSTRUCTING THE HISTORY OF NATIVE AMERICAN CIVILIZATION

WHAT PROBLEMS do scholars face in reconstructing the history of Native American civilizations?

Andean civilizations in South America never developed writing, and in Mesoamerica much of the written record was destroyed by time and conquest. Archaeologists have been able to create a picture of the economic and social organization of ancient American civilizations, but archaeology alone cannot produce the kind of narrative history that thousands of years of written records have made possible for Eurasian civilizations.

...es, killing vast numbers of people and affording the ... ...chological edge, played a key role in the con... ...es of the New World.

...rtant in understanding the ability of small num... ...ans to conquer these advanced civilizations, how... ...e nature of the civilizations themselves. Neither the ... ...nor their cultures were static or immobile; they were ... ...y not, in one historian's words, "a people without history," ...f much of that history is lost to us because of the absence or ...struction of written records. The European invaders succeeded ...ost rapidly in toppling the most organized of the societies in the New World, the Aztecs and the Inca, precisely because these societies were organized, centralized, and hierarchical.

It is important to remember that the history of New World civilizations in the face of the encounter was tightly linked to internal developments before the arrival of Europeans. The Aztecs and Incas, in particular, ruled over different peoples, many of whom resented their subjugation and saw in the arrival of the Europeans an opportunity to assert their autonomy. Thus the Spanish in Mexico and, to a lesser extent, in Peru, found allies among the local peoples willing to do much of the fighting for them. When Hernán Cortés faced the Aztecs in the decisive battle for their capital city, Tenochtitlán, he did so with at least 30,000 indigenous warriors by his side. Consequently, the Spanish intruded into a political situation that was itself already in flux and prepared to respond to the introduction of new military and cultural forces.

Focus Questions

◆ Why is it important to bear in mind that the civilizations of the New World had long and rich histories before the arrival of Europeans? Why is it so difficult to discover the details of the history of the peoples of the Americas? What are our major sources of information?

◆ What role did the environment play in the formation of American civilizations?

However, from the ancient civilization of the Maya in Mesoamerica specimens of writing survive, and scholars have deciphered their script and attached names, dates, and events to silent ruins.

We also have accounts of the history and culture of the Aztecs and Inca produced by Spanish missionaries and officials. Although these accounts are invaluable sources of information, they are also obviously biased. Scholars seeking to understand Native American civilization have had to rely on the language and categories of European thought to investigate peoples and cultures that had nothing to do with Europe. Columbus and other early explorers (see Chapter 17), believing they had reached the East Indies, called the people they met in the Caribbean "Indians." This misnomer stuck and extended to all Native American peoples who, of course, had other names for themselves. The name *America* itself is European, taken from Amerigo Vespucci (1451–1512), a Florentine who explored the coast of Brazil in 1501 and 1502.

●[View the Image

Mayan Ruins, at **myhistorylab.com**

MESOAMERICA: THE FORMATIVE PERIOD AND THE EMERGENCE OF MESOAMERICAN CIVILIZATION

Mesoamerica (meaning "middle America") extends from Central Mexico into Central America (see Map 13–1 on page 314). This is a region of great physical diversity, ranging from lowland tropical rain forests to temperate highlands with fertile basins and valleys. Lowland regions include the Yucatán Peninsula and the Gulf and Pacific coasts. Highland regions include Mexico's central plateau and the mountainous areas of Guatemala. Most of Mesoamerica's mineral resources are found in the highlands. The lowlands were the source of many important trading goods, including hardwoods, plant dyes, and the prized feathers of exotic birds.

WHAT GROUP dominated Olmec society?

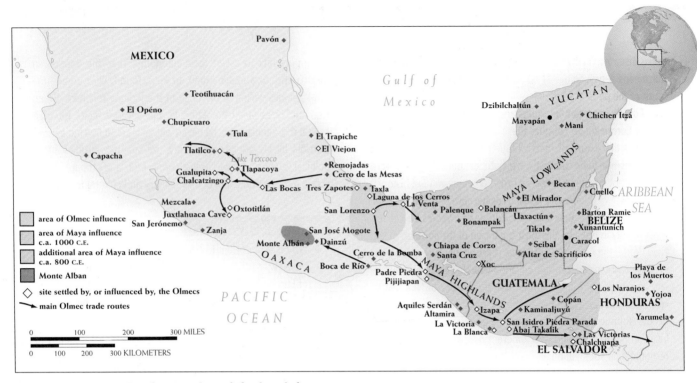

MAP 13–1. **Mesoamerica: The Formative and Classic Periods.**

What Role did trade play in the formation of Mesoamerican civilizations?

✓•—Study and Review
at **myhistorylab.com**

obsidian
A hard volcanic glass that was widely used in Mesoamerica.

Aztec Calendar Stone. When the Aztec "calendar" was unearthed in Mexico in 1790, it confirmed the greatness and complexity of the Americas' pre-Columbian civilizations.

What system was the basis for the Aztec calendar?

Mesoamerica also designates a distinctive cultural tradition that emerged in this region between 1000 and 2000 B.C.E., manifested itself in a succession of impressive states until the coming of European conquerors in the sixteenth century, and continues to express itself in the lives of indigenous peoples. Mesoamerica is not culturally homogeneous: The peoples of Mesoamerica were and are ethnically and linguistically diverse. There was no single Mesoamerican civilization, nor was there a single linear development of civilization in the region. Nonetheless, Mesoamerican civilizations shared many traits, including writing, a sophisticated calendrical system, many gods and religious ideas, a ritual ball game, and urban centers with religious and administrative buildings symmetrically arranged around large plazas.

Long-distance trade linked the peoples of Mesoamerica. Metallurgy came late to Mesoamerica, and it was used primarily for ceremonial objects rather than for weapons and tools. Mesoamericans made weapons and other tools from **obsidian**, a volcanic glass capable of holding a razor-sharp edge, and for that reason a valued trade commodity.

Mesoamerican history before the Spanish conquest is conventionally divided into four major periods: Archaic, Formative, Classic, and Post-classic. The term *Classic*, with its connotations of "best" or "highest," derives from European historical frameworks. It reflects the view of many early Mesoamericanists that the Classic period, which corresponds more or less to the time during which the Maya civilizations of the southern Yucatán erected dated stone monuments called stelae, was the high point of Mesoamerican civilization. Despite various controversies, this chronology continues to provide a useful framework.

The transition from hunting and gathering to settled village life occurred gradually in Mesoamerica during the Archaic period. The cornerstone of the process was the domestication of maize (corn) and other staple crops, including beans and squash. Other plants native to the Americas that were domesticated in this period include tomatoes, chili peppers, and avocado. Maize and beans were particularly important

Figure 13.1 Number of Domesticated Species Compared[*]

	Continent			
	Eurasia	**Sub-Saharan Africa**	**The Americas**	**Australia**
Domesticated Species	13	0	1	0

[*]A species is defined as a wild mammal weighing on the average over 100 pounds. Thirteen species were domesticated in Eurasia in antiquity: sheep, goats, cows, pigs, horses, Arabian camels, Bactrian camels, donkeys, reindeer, water buffalo, yak, Bali cattle, and mithan. Only one species was domesticated in the Americas: llamas (alpacas), which are found in the Andes.

Adapted from Jared Diamond, *Guns, Germs, and Steel* (New York: W. W. Norton, 1997).

because together they provide a richer source of protein than the grains that were the basis of the Neolithic revolution in the ancient Near East and China. Mesoamerica was poor in sources of animal protein, having only a few small domesticated animals—among them dogs and turkeys—and no large herd animals like the cattle, sheep, and goats of the Old World (see Figure 13–1).

The domestication of maize, beans, and other plants secured the people of Mesoamerica an adequate and dependable diet. Over time they devised myriad ways to prepare and store these staples. Since the conquest, maize has also been one of Mesoamerica's major contributions to the world.

Probably because they had no large draft animals, the people of the Americas never developed the wheel. (They did make wheeled toys, however.) In Mesoamerica, humans did all the carrying. And because there were neither horses nor chariots, wars in Mesoamerica—and in Andean South America—were fought by foot soldiers.

Between 5000 and 2500 B.C.E. villages began to appear in both highland and lowland regions of Mesoamerica. By about 2000 B.C.E. settled agricultural life had taken hold in much of the region. As in the Old World, people began to make fired clay vessels, and ceramic technology appeared. Nomadic hunter-gatherers have little need of storage, but farmers do, and clay vessels filled that need. Pottery is also a medium for artistic expression, and it played a role in religion and ritual observance.

MESOAMERICAN BALLGAMES

Peoples throughout ancient Mesoamerica played a complicated ball game that originated before 1700 B.C.E. Ruins of approximately 1,500 ball courts from different eras have been unearthed from the Southwest of the United States to the Amazon, as well as on Cuba. Early Spanish explorers and missionaries witnessed the game among the Aztecs and were fascinated.

The game involved multiple players—team sizes differed from area to area—contesting a hard rubber ball, apparently without using their hands. Courts were shaped in the form of an "I" and were usually at least as long as a modern football field. The goal was to move the ball to the opponents' end court. At some point in the Classic period, the game came to involve shooting the ball through a stone hoop.

The Mesoamerican ball game was very dangerous and often violent. The rubber balls were hard, so players wore elaborate protective headgear and padding for both arms and legs, as portrayed in ancient sculpture and paintings. Some sculptures

QUICK REVIEW

Transition to Settled Village Life

- Occurred during Archaic period
- Cornerstone of process was domestication of maize
- Mesoamerica had few domesticated animals

Ball Court at Monte Alban. Like most ball-game courts that have survived throughout Mesoamerica, the ball court at the Monte Alban Temple Complex in Oaxaca has an "I" shape with a long, narrow alley flanked on both sides by stone walls.

What purposes did Mesoamerican ball games serve?

◆●◆─[Read the Document
Victory over the Underworld,
at **myhistorylab.com**

portray women in sports gear, though it is unclear whether women actually competed. The players, like modern sports figures, occupied prestigious positions in their societies.

Games often carried elaborate political and ritualistic overtones. Some accounts tell of political disputes being settled by playing a ball game instead of warfare. For some peoples, the game served to reenact major events recorded in mythology. (See p. 320 regarding the Maya ball games.) On other occasions the games were rigged to reenact past warfare, with the team of the side that had lost the war losing the game. In some cases, losers were sacrificed.

THE OLMEC

((◉●─[Hear the Audio
Early Americas
at **myhistorylab.com**

By about 1500 B.C.E. Mesoamerica's agricultural villages were beginning to coalesce into more complicated societies with towns, monumental architecture, class divisions, long-distance trade, and sophisticated artistic traditions (see Map 13–1). The most prominent Early Formative period culture is the Olmec, centered on the lowlands of Mexico's Gulf coast. Most knowledge about the Olmecs comes from the archaeological sites of San Lorenzo and La Venta. San Lorenzo, first occupied in about 1500 B.C.E., had developed into a prominent center by about 1200 B.C.E. It included public buildings, a drainage system linked to artificial ponds, and a ball court. The center flourished until about 900 B.C.E., and was abandoned by about 400 B.C.E. As San Lorenzo declined, La Venta rose to prominence, flourishing from about 900 to 400 B.C.E. La Venta's most conspicuous feature is the 110-foot Great Pyramid, which stands at one end of a group of platforms and plazas aligned along a north–south axis. Many artifacts were buried along the center line of this axis.

The population of San Lorenzo and La Venta was never great, probably less than 1,000 people. The monumental architecture and sculpture at these sites—including massive stone heads, thought to be portraits of rulers, carved from basalt from quarries as much as 65 miles away—suggest that Olmec society was dominated by an elite class of ruler-priests able to command the labor of farmers who lived in outlying villages.

Among the most pervasive images in Olmec art is that of the were-jaguar, a half-human, half-feline creature. The were-jaguar may have been a divine ancestor figure, perhaps providing the elite with the justification for their authority. Similarities between the were-jaguar iconography and that of later Mesoamerican deities suggest some of the underlying continuities linking Mesoamerican societies over time.

The raw material for many Olmec artifacts, such as jade and obsidian, comes from other regions of Mesoamerica. Control of trade in such high-status materials by the Olmec elite contributed to their prestige and authority.

CHRONOLOGY

**MAJOR PERIODS IN ANCIENT
MESOAMERICAN CIVILIZATION**

8000–2000 B.C.E.	Archaic
2000 B.C.E.–150 C.E.	Formative (or Pre-Classic)
150–900 C.E.	Classic
900–1521 C.E.	Post-Classic

Olmec Monument. A large carved monument from the Olmec site of La Venta with a naturalistically rendered human figure.

What does the size of Olmec carvings suggest about Olmec political power?

THE VALLEY OF OAXACA AND THE RISE OF MONTE ALBAN

Olmec civilization had disappeared by about 200 B.C.E. Some of the most significant settlements in the Late Formative period were in the Valley of Oaxaca. Around 500 B.C.E., Monte Albán was built on a hill where three branches of the valley meet. Its population grew to about 5,000, and it emerged as the capital of a state that dominated the Oaxaca region. Carved images of bound prisoners imply that warfare played a role in establishing its authority. These images also suggest an early origin for the ritual human sacrifice that characterized most Mesoamerican cultures. Monte Albán maintained its independence against the growing power of the greatest city of the Classic period, Teotihuacán.

THE EMERGENCE OF WRITING AND THE MESOAMERICAN CALENDAR

The earliest evidence of writing and the Mesoamerican calendar has been found in the Valley of Oaxaca. The Mesoamerican calendar is based on two interlocking cycles, each with its own day and month names. One cycle, tied to the solar year, was of 365 days; the other was of 260 days. Combining the two cycles produced a "century" of 52 years, the amount of time required before a particular combination of days in each cycle would repeat itself. The hieroglyphs found in Oaxaca relate to the 260-day cycle. At the time of the Spanish conquest, all the peoples of Mesoamerica used the 52-year calendrical system.

THE CLASSIC PERIOD IN MESOAMERICA

The Classic period was a time of cultural florescence. In central Mexico, it saw the rise of Teotihuacán, a great city that rivaled the largest cities of the world at the time. The Maya, who built densely populated cities in the seemingly inhospitable rain forests of the southern Yucatán, developed a sophisticated system of mathematics and Mesoamerica's most advanced hieroglyphic writing. Indeed, urban life in Classic Mesoamerica was richer and grander than that of contemporaneous Europe north of the Alps.

Scholars have recently made enormous strides in understanding Classic civilization. Progress in deciphering Maya hieroglyphics has opened a window on politics and statecraft. Archaeological studies have broadened our understanding of Teotihuacán and Maya cities, providing clues to the lives of the people who lived in them.

Classic cities, with their many temples, plazas, and administrative buildings, were religious and administrative centers whose rulers combined secular and religious authority. Warfare was common, and Classic rulers did not hesitate to use force to expand their authority. Ritual sacrifice of captive enemies was widespread.

TEOTIHUACÁN

In the Late Formative period two centers competed for dominance over the rapidly growing population of the Valley of Mexico. Cuicuilco was located at the southern end of the valley, whereas Teotihuacán was located about 30 miles northeast of Mexico City. When a volcano destroyed Cuicuilco in the first century C.E., Teotihuacán grew into a great city, perhaps Mesoamerica's first city-state, dominating central Mexico for centuries and strongly influencing the rest of Mesoamerica.

Natural advantages contributed to Teotihuacán's rise. A network of caves recently discovered under its most prominent monument, the Pyramid of the Sun (the name by which the Aztecs knew it), may have been considered an entrance to the underworld. Stone quarried from the caves was used to construct the city, creating a symbolic link between the city's buildings and its sacred origins. Teotihuacán is also near a source of obsidian, and it straddled a trade route to the Gulf Coast and southern Mesoamerica. It was surrounded by fertile farmland.

At its height around 500 C.E., Teotihuacán extended over almost 9 square miles and had a population of more than 150,000, making it one of the largest cities in the world at the time. Its size and organization suggest that it was ruled by a powerful, centralized authority. It was laid out on a rigid grid plan dominated by a broad, 3-mile-long thoroughfare known as the Avenue of the Dead. Religious and administrative structures and a market occupy the center of the city. At one end of the Avenue of the Dead is the so-called Pyramid of the Moon, and near it, to one side, is the 210-foot-high

QUICK REVIEW

The Mesoamerican Calendar

♦ Calendar based on two interlocking cycles

♦ First cycle, tied to solar year, was 365 days; the second was 260 days

♦ Two cycles produced a "century" of 52 years

WHAT WERE some of the main achievements of the Classic period civilizations in Mesoamerica?

Watch the **Video**
Teotihuacán Ruins in Mexico
at **myhistorylab.com**

A Closer Look

The Pyramid of the Sun in Teotihuacán

Teotihuacán, located outside Mexico City, remains one of the most important and most mysterious of all the great pre-Columbian archaeological sites. It was a vast city with a population in the hundreds of thousands, flourishing at its height in about 500 C.E. and becoming abandoned about 800 C.E., hundreds of years before the rise of the Aztec Empire. Extremely little is actually known about this city, including the name it inhabitants gave it. The name "Teotihuacán," meaning Where the Gods Were Born, is the name that the Aztecs gave to it long after it had been abandoned. They also gave names to many of the surviving structures and streets in the city.

The Pyramid of the Sun is the second largest pyramid on the American continents and the third in the world, being just over 200 feet high. It was constructed during the first two centuries C.E. The religious rituals for which it was intended are unclear, though human sacrifice appears to have occurred on it. The great structure, which was probably topped by a small frame temple, is located over a system of subterranean caves linked to the pyramid. This and other monuments in Teotihuacán were admired by the later peoples who lived in central Mexico who associated the site with their own myths. At the time Cortés arrived, the Aztec emperor Moctezuma visited the site, apparently hoping to receive guidance or wisdom from the ancients who had once inhabited it.

This somewhat romanticized painting by Jorge Pérez de Lara in 1878 indicates how the Pyramid of the Sun and the area surrounding it looked in the decades before formal archaeological excavations began in 1905 and the pyramid was restored in 1910 as part of the centennial of Mexican independence.

This photo illustrates how tourists encounter the site today, with the great pyramid having been reconstructed now for over a century. In ancient times, the pyramid was apparently covered by plaster and painted red. Much archaeological work remains to be carried out on the Pyramid of the Sun and Teotihuacán as a whole.

Picture Desk, Inc./Kobal Collection.

Questions

1. How might you imagine the reactions of successive generations of visitors to the ruins of the Pyramid of the Sun? For example, what were the reactions of the pre-Aztec peoples who encountered it as an abandoned site, the Aztecs who considered it a sacred place, the early Spanish who were amazed at the size of the edifice, later archaeologists, and still later tourists? How do differing expectations determine what people experience when visiting ancient sites? Why is it so difficult to imagine ancient urban sites, now abandoned with only monuments remaining, as places once inhabited by tens of thousands of people?

2. How does archaeological evidence, in the Americas or elsewhere in the world, differ from written records or the artistic record?

3. How could the restoration of the Pyramid of the Sun in 1910 be used to link modern and ancient Mexico? Do you know of other restorations of ancient sites carried out by modern governments?

myhistorylab   To examine this image in an interactive fashion, please go to **www.myhistorylab.com**

Pyramid of the Sun. More than 2,000 residential structures surround the city center. The lavish homes of the city's elite lie nearest the center. Most of the city's residents lived in walled apartment compounds that were also centers of craft manufacture with neighborhoods devoted to pottery, obsidian work, and other specialties. Parts of the city were reserved for foreign traders. Murals adorned the interiors of many residences, of common people as well as the elite. The humble dwellings of poor farmers—who were apparently forced to abandon their villages and move to Teotihuacán—occupied the city's periphery.

Teotihuacán's influence extended throughout Mesoamerica. In the central highlands, dispersed settlements were consolidated into larger centers laid out similarly to Teotihuacán, suggesting conquest and direct control—a Teotihuacán empire. The city's influence in more distant regions may have reflected close trading ties. The city's obsidian and pottery were exchanged widely for items like the green feathers of the quetzal bird and jaguar skins, valued for ritual garments.

Among the deities of Teotihuacán are a storm god and his goddess counterpart, who may be linked to the Aztec's rain god. The people of Teotihuacán also worshiped a feathered serpent, recognizably antecedent to the god the Aztecs worshiped as Quetzalcoatl and the Maya as Kukulcan. Murals also suggest that the Teotihuacán elite, like the Maya and later Mesoamerican peoples, drew their own blood as a form of sacrifice to the gods. They also practiced human sacrifice.

After 500 C.E. Teotihuacán's influence began to wane, and in the eighth century its authority collapsed. A fire swept through the city, destroying the ritual center and the residences of the elite and hinting at an internal revolt. Although a substantial population remained, the city never regained its former status. It retained a hold on the imagination of succeeding generations of Mesoamericans, however, much as the ruins of ancient Greece and Rome influenced later Europeans. The name by which we know it, Teotihuacán, was given by the Aztecs and means "City of the Gods." It was still a revered pilgrimage site at the time of the Spanish conquest.

THE MAYA

Maya civilization arose in southern Mesoamerica. The earliest distinctively Maya urban sites date to around 800 B.C.E.. The most important of these is Nakbé. The pyramid structures so popularly identified with Mayan culture were fully developed between 300 B.C.E. and 300 C.E. During the later Classic period, Maya civilization experienced a remarkable florescence in the lowland jungles of the southern Yucatán. It is this last era about which scholars now possess the most knowledge, because of inscriptions on stone monuments. More scholarship and archaeological exploration have been devoted to the Mayan peoples than any other culture of Mesoamerica, and our understanding of Classic Maya civilization has changed radically in recent decades. The Maya have also entered the modern popular imagination.

All the pre-Spanish societies of Mesoamerica were literate, recording historical and religious information on scrolled or screenfold books made with deerhide or bark paper. Only a handful of these books, four of them Mayan, have survived. (Spanish priests, who viewed native religious texts as idolatrous, burned almost all of them.) The Maya of the Classic period, who developed Mesoamerica's most advanced writing system, were unique in the extent to which they inscribed writing and calendrical symbols in stone, pottery, and other imperishable materials.

Teotihuacán. Temple façade showing Quetzalcoatl, the feathered serpent, as well as the god Tlalc, with round eyes.

What were important features of religious belief in Teotihuacán?

QUICK REVIEW

Teotihuacán
- Population of more than 150,000 at its height
- Dominated by Avenue of the Dead
- Influence of city extended throughout Mesoamerica

View the Image
A Mayan Town, at **myhistorylab.com**

Tikal, the largest city, probably had a population of between 50,000 and 70,000 at its height. Terracing, irrigation systems, and other agricultural technologies increased yields enough to support dense populations. Powerful ruling families and their elite retainers dominated cities, supported by a far larger class of farmer-commoners. Maya inscriptions mostly recount important events in the lives of rulers. Warfare between cities was chronic. As murals and sculptures show, captured prisoners were sacrificed to appease the gods and glorify the victorious ruler.

The Maya believed that the world had gone through several cycles of creation before the present one. They recognized no clear distinction between a natural and a supernatural world or between religious and political authority. Rulers claimed association with the gods to justify their authority. They wore special regalia and performed rituals—including bloodletting ceremonies, the sacrifice of captives, and ball games—to sustain the gods and the cosmic order.

The Classic Maya developed a sophisticated mathematics and were among the first peoples in the world to invent the concept of zero. In addition to the 52-year calendar they shared with other Mesoamerican societies, the Maya developed an absolute calendar, known as the **Long Count**. The Long Count calendar—like the Jewish, Christian, or Muslim calendars—was anchored to a fixed starting point in the past. The calendar had great religious as well as practical significance for the Maya. They viewed the movements of the celestial bodies to which the calendar was tied—including the sun, moon, and Venus—as deities. The complexity and accuracy of their calendar reflect Maya skills in astronomical observation. They adjusted their lunar calendar for the actual length of the lunar cycle (29.53 days) and may have had provisions like our leap years for the actual length of the solar year. The calendar's association with divine forces and the esoteric knowledge required to master it must have been important sources of prestige and power for its elite guardians.

Long Count
A Mayan calendar that dated from a fixed point in the past.

During the Classic period many independent units, each composed of a capital city and smaller subject towns and villages, alternately vied and cooperated with each other, rising and falling in relative prominence. Tikal, at its height the largest Classic Maya city, is also one of the most thoroughly studied. The residential center covers more than 14 square miles and has more than 3,000 structures. The city follows the uneven terrain of the rain forest and is not laid out on a grid. Monumental causeways link the major structures of the site. Tikal benefited from its strategic position. It is located near a source of flint, valued as a raw material for stone tools, and swamps that with modification might have been agriculturally productive. It has access to river systems that lead both to the Gulf and the Caribbean coasts, giving it control of the trade between those regions.

A single dynasty of thirty-nine rulers reigned in Tikal from the Early Classic period until the eighth century. Early rulers in this Jaguar Paw line were buried in a structure known as the North Acropolis, and the inscriptions associated with their tombs provide details, including in many cases their names, the dates of their rule, and the dates of major military victories. Late in the fourth century links developed between Tikal and Teotihuacán. One ruler, Curl Nose, who ascended to the throne in 379, may have married into the ruling family from the Teotihuacán-dominated city of Kaminaljuyu in the southern highlands.

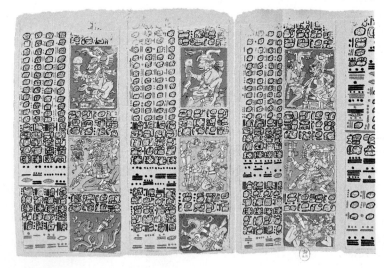

Maya Calendar. This copy of a page from the Dresden codex shows detailed calendrical observations and astronomical predictions. The original calendar was inscribed on stone tablets.

How did the Mayan calendar relate to Mayan religious beliefs?

For about a hundred years beginning in the mid-sixth century, Tikal and most other lowland Maya sites lost much of their influence and may have suffered a serious defeat at the hands of the city of Caracol. Then in 682 the ruler Ah Cacau (r. 682–723?) ascended the throne and initiated a new period of vigor and prosperity for Tikal, again expanding its influence through conquest and strategic marriage alliances. Ah Cacau and his two immediate successors, Yax Kin (r. 734–?) and Chitam (r. 769–?), began an ambitious building program, creating most of Tikal's surviving monumental structures. Chitam was the last ruler in the Jaguar Paw Dynasty. After he died Tikal again declined, and, like other sites in the southern lowlands, it never recovered.

Similar dynastic histories have emerged from research at other Classic Maya sites. Inscriptions in the shrine above the tomb of Lord Pacal (r. 615–683), the greatest ruler of the city of Palenque, record the city's entire dynastic history back to mythic ancestors. Two of the rulers in this genealogy were women, including Pacal's mother, Lady Zac Kuk (r. 612–640).

Mayan Mural. This reproduction of one of the remarkable murals found at the Maya site of Bonampak shows the presentation of captives to the city's ruler, Chan Muan.

What roles did captives play in Mayan society?

Between 800 and 900 C.E. Classic civilization collapsed in the southern lowlands. The ruling dynasties all came to an end, the construction of monumental architecture and sculpture with Long Count dates ceased, and the great cities were virtually abandoned. The cause of the collapse is still unknown. Factors that may have contributed to it include intensifying warfare, population growth, and attempts to increase agricultural production that ultimately backfired.

The focus of Maya civilization shifted to the northern Yucatán. There the site of Chichén Itzá, located next to a sacred well, flourished from the ninth to the thirteenth centuries. Stylistic resemblances between Chichén Itzá and Tula, the capital of the Post-Classic Toltec Empire in central Mexico (discussed next), suggest ties between the two cities. After Chichén Itzá's fall, Mayapan became the main Maya center. By the time of the Spanish conquest it too had lost sway, and the Maya had divided into small, competing centers.

THE POST-CLASSIC PERIOD

WHAT ROLE did human sacrifice play in the Aztec Empire?

After Teotihuacán collapsed in the eighth century, warfare increased, and several smaller militaristic states emerged, centered around fortified hilltop cities. Interregional trade and market systems became increasingly important, and secular and religious authority began to diverge.

THE TOLTECS

About 900 C.E. a people known as the Toltecs rose to prominence. Their capital, Tula, is located near the northern periphery of Mesoamerica. Like Teotihuacán, it lay close to an important source of obsidian. The Toltecs themselves were apparently descendants of one of many "barbarian" northern peoples (like the later Aztecs) who began migrating into Mesoamerica during the Late Classic period.

Later Aztec mythology glorified the Toltecs as the fount of civilization, attributing to them a vast and powerful empire to which the Aztecs were the legitimate heirs. Other Mesoamerican peoples at the time of the conquest also assigned legendary status to the

Tula Statuary. Tula, now Hidalgo, Mexico, was the capital of the Toltec civilization. These enormous statues, known as the Atlantes, stand atop the remains of the ancient Toltec pyramid raised in ancient Tula.

Why did the Aztecs claim links with the Toltecs?

Mexica
The Aztecs' name for themselves.

Toltecs. The archaeological evidence for a Toltec empire, however, is ambiguous. Tula, with 35,000 to 60,000 people, was never as large or as organized as Teotihuacán. Toltec influence reached many regions of Mesoamerica, and the city established extensive trade routes, especially for luxury goods. Archaeologists are uncertain whether that influence translated into political control. Toltec iconography, which stresses human sacrifice, death, blood, and military action, supports their warlike reputation. Their deities are clearly antecedent to those worshiped by the Aztecs, including the feathered serpent Quetzalcoatl and the warlike trickster Tezcatlipoca.

Whatever the reality of Toltec power, it was short-lived. By about 1100 Tula was in decline and its influence gone.

THE AZTECS

The people commonly known as the Aztecs referred to themselves as the **Mexica**, a name that lives on as *Mexico*. When the Spanish arrived in 1519, the Aztecs dominated much of Mesoamerica. Their capital city, Tenochtitlán, was the most populous yet seen in Mesoamerica. Built on islands and landfill in the southern part of Lake Texcoco in the Valley of Mexico, it was home to at least 200,000 people. It had great temples and palaces. Bearing tribute to its rulers and goods to its great markets, canoes crowded the city's canals, and pedestrians thronged its streets and the great causeways linking it to the mainland. The city's traders brought precious goods from distant regions; vast wealth flowed in constantly from subject territories. Yet the Aztecs were relative newcomers, the foundation of their power being less than 200 years old.

We have more information about the Aztecs than any other preconquest Mesoamerican people. Many of the Spanish conquistadors recorded their experiences, and postconquest administrators and missionaries collected valuable information. Although filtered through the bitterness of defeat for the Aztecs and the biases of the conquerors, these records nevertheless provide detailed information about Aztec society and Aztec history.

According to their own legends, the Aztecs were originally a nomadic people inhabiting the shores of a mythical Lake Aztlán northwest of the Valley of Mexico. At the urging of their patron god Huitzilopochtli, they began to migrate, arriving in the Valley of Mexico early in the thirteenth century. Scorned by the people of the cities and states already there, but prized and feared as mercenaries, they ended up in the marshy land on the shores of Lake Texcoco. They finally settled on the island that became Tenochtitlán in 1325 after seeing an eagle perched there on a prickly pear cactus, an omen Huitzilopochtli had said would identify the end of their wandering.

The Aztecs initially accepted a position as tributaries and mercenaries for Azcazpotzalco, then the most powerful state in the valley, but soon became trusted allies with their own tribute-paying territories and claims through marriage to descent from the Toltecs. In 1428, under their fourth ruler, Itzcoatl (r. 1427–1440), the Aztecs formed a triple alliance with Texcoco and Tlacopan, turned against Azcazpotzalco, and became the dominant power in the Valley of Mexico. Less than 100 years before the arrival of Cortés, the Aztecs began the aggressive expansion that brought them their vast tribute-paying empire (see Map 13–2).

Itzcoatl also laid the foundation of Aztec imperial ideology. He ordered the burning of all the ancient books in the valley, expunging any history that conflicted with Aztec pretensions, and restructured Aztec religion and ritual to support and justify Aztec preeminence. The Aztecs now presented themselves as the divinely ordained suc-

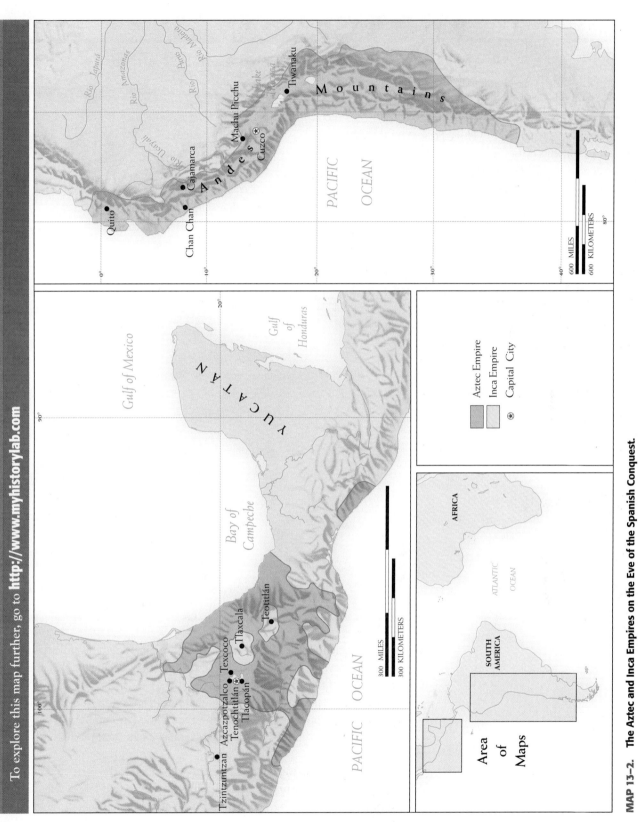

MAP EXPLORATION

To explore this map further, go to **http://www.myhistorylab.com**

MAP 13–2.   The Aztec and Inca Empires on the Eve of the Spanish Conquest.
What were the chief differences between the Aztec and Inca empires?

DOCUMENT

Nezahualcoyotl of Texcoco Sings of the Giver of Life

Nezahualcoyotl, ruler of Texcoco, lived from 1402 to 1472 and was admired as a philosopher-king. In this poem he sings of the presence of the Giver of Life who invents himself and of the ability of human beings to invoke this divinity, but at the same time he emphasizes the impossibility of achieving any close relationship with the divinity.

- In what ways does this song remind you of the thought and religious traditions of the early civilizations of China, India, Egypt, and Greece? What are the characteristics of "He Who invents Himself"? What kind of relationship can human beings achieve with this being? Why does the singer compare seeking the Giver of Life with seeking someone among flowers?

In no place can be the house of He Who invents Himself.
But in all places He is invoked,
in all places He is venerated,
His glory, His fame are sought on the earth.
It is He Who invents everything
He is Who invents Himself: God.
In all places He is invoked,
in all places He is venerated,
His glory, His fame are sought on the earth.
No one here is able,
no one is able to be intimate
with the Giver of Life;
only He is invoked, at His side,

near to Him,
one can live on the earth.
He who finds Him,
knows only one thing; He is invoked,
at His side, near to Him,
one can live on the earth.
In truth no one is intimate with You,
O Giver of Life!
Only as among the flowers,
we might seek someone,
thus we seek You,
we who live on the earth,
while we are at Your side.
Our hearts will be troubled,
only for a short time,
we will be near You and at Your side.
The Giver of Life enrages us,
He intoxicates us here.
No one can be perhaps at His side,
be famous, rule on the earth.
Only You change things
as our hearts know it:
No one can be perhaps at His side,
be famous, rule on the earth.

Source: Excerpt (pp. 86–88) from *Fifteen Poets of the Aztec World,* by Miguel Leon-Portilla. Copyright © 1992 by Miguel Leon-Portilla. Reprinted by permission of University of Oklahoma Press.

cessors to the ancient Toltecs, and with each new conquest and the growing splendor of Tenochtitlán, they seemed to ratify that claim. (See Document, "Nezahualcoyotl of Texcoco Sings of the Giver of Life.")

Aztec conquests ultimately included almost all of central Mexico. To the west, however, they were unable to conquer the rival Tarascan Empire with its capital of Tzintzuntzan. And within the Aztec realm several pockets, most prominently Tlaxcala, remained unsubdued.

The Aztec Empire was extractive. After a conquest, the Aztecs usually left the local elite in power but demanded heavy tribute in goods and labor. Tribute included goods of all kinds, including agricultural products, fine craft goods, gold and jade, textiles, and precious feathers. This wealth underwrote the grandeur of Tenochtitlán, making it "a beautiful parasite, feeding on the lives and labour of other peoples and casting its shadow over all their arrangements."[1]

---

[1]Inga Clendinnen, *Aztecs: An Interpretation* (Cambridge: Cambridge University Press, 1991), p. 8.

Human sacrifice on a prodigious scale was central to Aztec ideology. The Aztecs believed that Huitzilopochtli, as sun god, required human blood to sustain him as he battled the moon and stars each night to rise again each day. The prime candidates for sacrifice were war captives, and the Aztecs often engaged in "flowery wars" with traditional enemies just to obtain captives. On major festivals, thousands of victims might perish. Led up the steps of the temple of Huitzilopochtli, a victim was thrown backward over a stone, his arms and legs pinned, while a priest cut out his heart. He would then be rolled down the steps of the temple, his head placed on a skull rack, and his limbs butchered and distributed to be eaten. Small children were sacrificed to the rain god Tlaloc, who was believed to be pleased by their tears.

Victims were also selected as stand-ins for particular gods, to be sacrificed after a series of rituals. For example, each year a beautiful male youth was chosen to represent the powerful god Tezcatlipoca. All year, the chosen one wandered through the city dressed as the god and playing the flute. A month before the end of his reign he was given four young women as wives. Twenty days before his death he was dressed as a warrior, and for a few days he virtually ruled the city. Then he was sacrificed.

No other Mesoamerican people practiced human sacrifice on the scale of the Aztecs. It must have intimidated subject peoples. It may also have reduced the population of fighting-age men from conquered provinces, and with it the possibility of rebellion. Together with the heavy burden of tribute, human sacrifice fed resentment and fear, which may help explain why so many subject peoples were willing to throw in their lot with Cortés when he challenged the Aztecs.

Three great causeways linked Tenochtitlán to the mainland. These met at the ceremonial core of the city, dominated by a double temple dedicated to Huitzilopochtli and Tlaloc. The palaces of the ruler and high nobles lay just outside the central precinct. The ruler's palace was the empire's administrative center, with government officials, artisans and laborers, gardens, and a zoo of exotic animals. The rest of the city was divided into four quarters, which were further divided into numerous wards (*calpulli*). Some *calpulli* were specialized, reserved for merchants (*pochteca*) or artisans. The city was laid out on a grid formed of streets and canals. Agricultural plots of great fertility known as *chinampas* bordered the canal and the lake shores. Aqueducts carried fresh water from springs on the lake shore into the city. A massive dike kept the briny water of the northern part of Lake Texcoco from contaminating the waters around Tenochtitlán.

Aztec society was hierarchical, authoritarian, and militaristic. It was divided into two broad classes, noble and commoner, with merchants and certain artisans forming an intermediate category. The nobility enjoyed great wealth and luxury. Laws and regulations relating to dress reinforced social divisions.

The Aztecs were morally austere. They valued obedience, respectfulness, discipline, and moderation. Laws were strict and punishment was severe. Standards for the nobility were higher than for commoners, and punishments for sexual and social offenses were more strictly enforced the higher one stood in the hierarchy. Drunkenness was frowned upon and harshly punished among the elite. Parents would even execute their own children for breaking moral laws and customs.

The Founding of Tenochtitlán. According to legend, the tribal god Huitzilopochtli led the Aztecs/Mexica to a spot where an eagle sat atop a prickly pear cactus (*tenochtli*) growing out of a rock and told them to build their capital there. This symbol now graces the Mexican flag. This image first appeared in the *Codex Mendoza*, a pictorial history of the Aztecs, presumably prepared for the first viceroy of New Spain, Antonio Mendoza, around 1541.

How did the Aztecs build their empire?

calpulli
The wards into which the Aztec capital, Tenochtitlán, was divided.

View the Image
Aztec Warriors at **myhistorylab.com**

Human Sacrifice. Illustration from a colonial-era manuscript volume, known as the Codex Magliabecchiano, presenting Aztec ritual sacrifice on a temple altar.

What role did human sacrifice play in Aztec society?

See the **Map**
Pre-Columbian Civilization in Mesoamerica, at **myhistorylab.com**

The highest rank in the nobility was that of *tlatoani* (plural *tlatoque*), or ruler of a major political unit. The highest were the rulers of the three cities of the Triple Alliance; of them, the highest was the *tlatoani* of Tenochtitlán. Below them were the *tetcutin*, lords of subordinate units. And below them were the *pipiltin*, who filled the bureaucracy and the priesthood.

The bulk of the population was made up of commoners who farmed the *chinampas*, harvested fish from the lake, and provided labor for public projects. All commoners belonged to a *calpulli*, each of which had its own temple. Girls and boys alike received training in ritual and ideology in the song houses attached to these temples. Some criminal offenses were punished with enslavement, and serfs worked the estates of noblemen.

Professional traders and merchants— *pochteca*—were important figures in Aztec society. Their activities, backed by the threat of Aztec armies, were a key factor in spreading Aztec influence. Artisans of luxury goods—including lapidaries, feather workers, and goldsmiths—also had their own *calpulli* and enjoyed a special status.

Markets were central to Aztec economic life. The great market at Tlatelolco, adjacent to Tenochtitlán, impressed the Spaniards with its great size, orderliness, and variety of goods. More than 60,000 people went there daily. Market administrators, both women and men, regulated transactions. Cacao beans and cotton cloaks served as mediums of exchange.

Above all else, Aztec society was organized for war. Although there was no standing army as such, all young men received military training. Combat was a matter of individual contests, not the confrontation of massed infantry. A warrior's goal was to subdue and capture prisoners for sacrifice. Prowess in battle, as measured by the number of prisoners a warrior captured, was key to social advancement, and failure brought social disgrace.

Women could inherit and own property. They traded in the marketplace, and their craftwork could provide income. Women had access to priestly roles, although they were barred from high religious positions. In general, the Aztec emphasis on warfare left women excluded from positions of high authority. A woman's primary role was to bear children, and childbirth was compared to battle. Death in childbirth, like death in battle, guaranteed rewards in the afterlife.

ANDEAN SOUTH AMERICA: THE PRECERAMIC AND INITIAL PERIODS

HOW DID Andean peoples modify their environments?

The Andean region of South America—primarily modern Peru and Bolivia—also had a long history of indigenous civilization. This is a region of dramatic contrasts. South of the equator, a narrow strip of desert lines the Pacific coast. Beyond this strip the Andes Mountains rise abruptly. Small river valleys descend the western face of the mountains, cutting the desert plain to create a series of oases. The cold waters of the Humboldt Current sweep north along the coast from the Antarctic, carrying rich nutrients that support abundant sea life. Within the Andes are regions of high peaks and steep terrain, regions of grassland (*puna*), and deep, warm, fertile intermontane valleys. The eastern slopes of the mountains, covered with dense vegetation, descend into the great tropical rain forest of the Amazon basin (see Figure 13–2).

From ancient times, the people of the coast lived by exploiting the marine resources of the Pacific and by cultivating maize, beans, squash, and cotton. They also engaged in long-distance trade by sea along the Pacific coast.

The people of the highlands domesticated several plants native to the Andean region, including the potato, other tubers, and a grain called quinoa, which they cultivated on the high slopes of the Andes. In the intermontane valleys they cultivated maize. And in the *puna* grasslands they kept herds of llamas and alpacas for their fur and meat and as beasts of burden. Since ancient times, highland communities maintained access to the different resources available in different altitude zones. They share this adaptation, which anthropologists sometimes call *verticality*, with people in other mountainous regions, such as the Alps and the Himalayas.[2]

Andean civilization is conventionally divided into seven periods: Preceramic, Initial, Early Horizon, Early Intermediate, Middle Horizon, Late Intermediate, and Late Horizon. The Early, Middle, and Late Horizons are periods in which a homogeneous art style spread over a wide area. The Intermediate periods are characterized by regional stylistic diversity. Although there have been archaeological excavations of spectacular Andean sites, such as Machu Pichu, Andean archaeology has been less developed than that of other regions of pre-Columbian America, in large measure because of the difficulty of reaching the sites.

The earliest monumental architecture in Peru dates to the early third millennium B.C.E., roughly contemporary with the Great Pyramids of Egypt. Mostly near the shore, these earliest centers of Norte Chico civilization consist of ceremonial mounds and plazas and predate the introduction of pottery to Peru.

Coastal people at this time subsisted primarily on the bounties of the sea, supplemented with squash, beans, and chili peppers cultivated in the floodplains of the coastal rivers. They also cultivated gourds—for use as containers and utensils—and cotton. The cotton fishing nets and other textiles of this period represent the beginning of the sophisticated Andean textile tradition. The Norte Chico civilization appears to have been in decline by about 1800 B.C.E.

The earliest public buildings in the highlands date to before 2500 B.C.E. These are typically stone-walled structures enclosing a sunken fire pit used to burn ritual offerings. The distribution of these structures, first identified at the site of Kotosh, suggests that highland people shared a set of religious beliefs that archaeologists have called the *Kotosh religious tradition*. Highland people during the late preceramic period cultivated maize as well as potatoes and other highland tubers. Llamas and alpacas were fully domesticated by about 2500 B.C.E. There is little evidence of social stratification for

Grassy plain 13,000 ft. above sea level
Uplands: 10,500–12,500 ft. above sea level
Frost-free valleys 7,500–10,000 ft. above sea level
Lower slopes of mountains: 2,400–7,000 ft. above sea level
Dry coastal region: 2,400 ft. above sea level

FIGURE 13–2. **The Andean environment packs tremendous ecological diversity into a small space.**

CHRONOLOGY

PERIODS OF ANDEAN CIVILIZATION

ca. 3000–ca. 2000 B.C.E.	Preceramic
ca. 2000–ca. 800 B.C.E.	Initial
ca. 800–ca. 200 B.C.E.	Early Horizon
ca. 200 B.C.E.–ca. 600 C.E.	Early Intermediate
ca. 600–ca. 800/1000 C.E.	Middle Horizon
ca. 800/1000–ca. 1475	Late Intermediate
ca. 1475–1532	Late Horizon (Inca Empire)

---

[2]Michael Mosley, *The Incas and Their Ancestors* (New York: Thames and Hudson, 1992), p. 42.

the late preceramic period. The public structures of both the coast and the highlands appear to have been centers of community ritual for relatively egalitarian societies.

The introduction of pottery to Peru around 2000 B.C.E. corresponds to a major shift in settlement and subsistence patterns on the coast, marking the beginning of the Initial period. People became increasingly dependent on agriculture as well as on maritime resources. They moved their settlements inland, built irrigation systems, and began cultivating maize. They built large and impressive ceremonial centers, with forms that varied by region. Population grew and society became gradually but increasingly stratified. Incised carvings of bodies with severed heads at Cerro Sechín and Sechín Alto in the Casma suggest growing conflict. Centers apparently remained independent of one another.

CHAVÍN DE HUANTAR AND THE EARLY HORIZON

 WHY DID Chavín influence spread?

The large coastal centers of the Initial period declined early in the first millennium B.C.E. At about the same time, beginning around 900 B.C.E., a site in the highlands, Chavín de Huantar, was growing in influence (see Map 13–3). Located on a trade route between the coast and the lowland tropical rain forest, Chavín was the center of a powerful religious cult with a population of perhaps 3,000 at its height. The architecture of its central temple complex reflects coastal influence. Its artistic iconography draws on many tropical forest animals, including monkeys, serpents, and jaguars. The structure known as the Old Temple is honeycombed with passageways and drains; archaeologists think water was channeled through these drains to produce a roaring sound. At the end of the central passageway is an imposing stela carved in the image of a fanged deity that combines human and feline features. A small hole in the ceiling above suggests that it may have been an oracle whose "voice" was that of a priest in the gallery above.

MAP 13–3. Pre-Inca sites discussed in this chapter.

What were the differences between highland and coastal cultures in early South American history?

Between about 400 and 200 B.C.E. Chavín influence spread widely throughout Peru, probably because of the prestige of its cult. The florescence of Chavín was marked by important technological innovations in ceramics, weaving, and metallurgy. Excavations at Chavín and other Early Horizon sites point to increasing social stratification. Examination of skeletal remains, for example, suggests that people who lived closer to the ceremonial center ate better than people living on the margins of the site.

THE EARLY INTERMEDIATE, MIDDLE HORIZON, AND LATE INTERMEDIATE PERIODS

HOW DO Tiwanaku and Huari foreshadow the achievements of the Inca?

Signs of increasing warfare accompany the collapse of the Chavín culture and the ideological unity it had brought to the Andes. During the Early Intermediate period, increasing regional diversity combined with increasing political centralization as the first territorial states emerged in the Andes. Among the best-known of these cultures are the Nazca on the south coast of Peru and the Moche on the north coast.

NAZCA

The Nazca culture, which flourished from about 100 B.C.E. to about 700 C.E., was centered in the Ica and Nazca valleys. The people of the Nazca valley built underground aqueducts to tap groundwater and divert it into irrigation canals. Cahuachi, the largest Nazca site, was empty most of the year, filling periodically with pilgrims during religious festivals. It may have been the capital of a Nazca confederation, with each of its many temple platforms representing a member unit.

The earlier Paracas culture on the south coast produced some of the world's finest, most intricate textiles. The Nazca, too, are renowned for their textiles and their polychrome pottery, elaborately decorated with images of Andean plants and animals. They may be most famous, however, for their colossal earthworks, or geoglyphs, the so-called Nazca lines. These were created by brushing away the dark gravel of the desert to reveal a lighter-colored surface. Some geoglyphs depict figures like hummingbirds, spiders, and killer whales that appear on Nazca pottery. These are usually located on hillsides visible to passersby. Others, usually consisting of radiating lines and geometric forms, are drawn on Nazca's pampa flats and are only visible from the air.

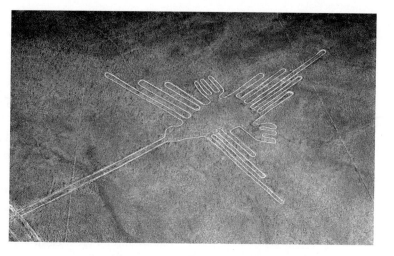

The Nazca Geoglyph located in the Peruvian desert depicts a vast hummingbird. The lines were constructed by the Nazca people probably sometime between 250 C.E. and 600 C.E. They appear to have been sacred paths walked by Nazca people perhaps somewhat as medieval Europeans walked a labyrinth. At the summer solstice the final parallel line points to the sun. The features of this and other geoglyphs can only be discerned from the air, and their exact purpose remains a matter of speculation.

How do these geoglyphs illustrate the connection between culture and the environment?

MOCHE

The Moche culture flourished from about 200 to 700 C.E. on the north coast of Peru. At its height it dominated all the coastal river valleys for 370 miles. The culture takes its name from the Moche valley, the site of two huge structures, the Pyramid of the Sun and the Pyramid of the Moon. The cross-shaped Pyramid of the Sun, the largest adobe structure in the Americas, was some 1,200 feet long by 500 feet wide and rose in steps to a height of 60 feet. It was made with more than 143 million adobe bricks, each of which had a mark that probably identified the group that made it. Archaeologists think the marks enabled Moche lords to be sure that subject groups fulfilled their tribute obligations. The Moche area may have been divided into northern and southern realms, with each valley ruled from its own center, Pampa Grande or Cerro Blanco.

The Moche were skilled potters, producing molded and painted vessels that reveal much about Moche life, religion, and warfare. Realistic portrait vessels may depict actual people. Other vessels provide evidence about the appearance of Moche architecture and the kind of regalia worn by the elite. The discovery in the late 1980s of the undisturbed tombs of Moche rulers suggests that a central theme in Moche iconography—the sacrifice ceremony—was an actual ritual. Depictions of the sacrifice ceremony show elaborately dressed figures drinking the blood of sacrificed prisoners. The Moche were also the most sophisticated metalsmiths in the Andes. They developed innovative alloys, cast weapons and agricultural tools, and used the lost-wax process to create small, intricate works. As with so many of the pre-Columbian peoples, the reason for the decline of the Moche is uncertain.

Moche Earspool. This magnificent earspool of gold, turquoise, quartz, and shell was found in the tomb of the Warrior Priest in the Moche site of Sipan, Peru, 300 C.E.

Courtesy of UCLA Fowler Museum of Cultural History/Susan Einstein/Christopher B. Donnan.

What processes did the Moche use in their metalwork?

TIWANAKU AND HUARI

In the fifth century C.E., as Teotihuacán was reaching its height in Mesoamerica, the first expansionist empires were emerging in the Andean highlands. One of these was centered at Tiwanaku in the Bolivian altiplano near the south shore of Lake Titicaca;

quipu
Knotted string used by Andean peoples for record keeping.

the other was at Huari, in the south-central highlands of Peru. Although they differ in many ways, both are associated with productive new agricultural technologies, and both show evidence of a form of statecraft that reflects Andean verticality and foreshadows the administrative practices of the later Inca Empire. The artistic symbolism of both also shares many features, suggesting a shared religious ideology. Archaeologists still do not have a firm grip on the chronology of Tiwanaku and Huari or the relationship between them.

Tiwanaku lies at more than 12,600 feet above sea level, making it the highest capital in the ancient world. Construction apparently began at the site in about 200 C.E. It began its expansionist phase from about 500 to 600 C.E. and collapsed 500 years later, in the eleventh century. The city occupied 1 to 2 two square miles and may have had a population of 20,000 to 40,000 people at its height. Laid out on a grid, it is dominated by several large and impressive public structures and ceremonial gateways. The enormous effort expended in transporting the stone for these monuments indicates the power of the Tiwanaku rulers over the labor of their subjects.

A system of raised-field agriculture on the shores of Lake Titicaca provided Tiwanaku with its economic base. This system involved farming on artificial platforms capped with rich topsoil and separated by basins of water. Experimental reconstructions have shown it to be extremely productive.

Tiwanaku dominated the Titicaca basin and neighboring regions. It probably exerted its influence through its religious prestige and by establishing colonies and religious-administrative structures in distant territories. As with other cultures in the region, human sacrifice played a part in Tiwanaku rituals.

The Huari Empire flourished from about 600 to 800 C.E., dominating the highlands from near Cuzco in the south to Cajamarca in the north. For a brief period it also extended a fortified colony into Tiwanaku territory. The capital, Huari, covers about 1.5 square miles. It consists of a sprawl of large, high-walled stone enclosures, and it had a population of 20,000–30,000.

Huari is located in an intermontane valley and its rise is associated with the development of techniques for terracing and irrigating the slopes of the valley to increase their productivity. The spread of this beneficial technology may have facilitated the expansion of the Huari Empire, explaining its acceptance without signs of military domination. Huari administrative centers were undefended and built in accessible places. Many archaeologists think they may have functioned like later Inca administrative centers, housing a small Huari elite that organized local labor for state projects. Again like the Inca, Huari administrators used **quipu** record-keeping devices made of string. Inca *quipu*, however, used knots, whereas Huari *quipu* used different colored string.

THE CHIMU EMPIRE

Although there is evidence of Huari influence on the Peruvian north coast, it is unlikely to have taken the form of direct political control. After the demise of Moche authority, two new states emerged on the north coast. One, named for the site of Sican, was centered in the Lambayeque valley. The central figure in Sican iconography, the Sican Lord, may have been a representation of a mythical founder figure named Nyamlap, mentioned in post-conquest Spanish chronicles. Like their Moche predecessors in the Lambayeque valley, the Sican people were skilled smiths who produced sumptuous gold objects.

The other new north coast state, known as Chimu, was centered in the Moche valley. In two waves of expansion the Chimu built an empire that incorporated the Lambayeque valley and stretched for 800 miles along the coast, from the border of Ecuador in the north to the Chillon valley in the south. The administrative capital of this empire, Chan Chan, was a vast city in the Moche valley. Its walls enclosed 8 square miles, and its central core covered over 2 square miles. Serving as the focus of the city were some ten immense adobe-walled enclosures known as *ciudadelas*. With their large open plazas, their administrative and storage facilities, and their large burial mounds, these probably housed the empire's ruling elite. Surrounding them were smaller compounds that probably housed the lesser nobility. And surrounding these were the homes and workshops of the artisans and workers who served the elite. Two areas were apparently transport centers, where llama caravans brought raw materials to the capital from the empire's territories. The total population of the city was between 30,000 and 40,000. Human sacrifice probably marked some Chimu ceremonies.

About 1470, only sixty years before the arrival of the Spaniards, the Chimu Empire was swept away by a powerful new state from the southern highlands of Peru, the Inca Empire.

Machu Picchu. The Inca city of Machu Picchu perches on a saddle between two peaks on the eastern slopes of the Andes.

Why would the Inca have situated Machu Picchu in such a remote location?

THE INCA EMPIRE

In 1532, when Francisco Pizarro encountered it, the Inca Empire was one of the largest states in the world. Its domains encompassed the area between the Pacific coast and the Amazon basin for some 2,600 miles, from southern Colombia to northern Chile (see Map 13–2). Its ethnically and linguistically diverse population numbered in the millions, with settlements linked by excellent roads. The Incas inhabited the lowland river valleys along the coast and the highlands, but did not settle in the Amazon rain forest.

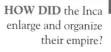

HOW DID the Inca enlarge and organize their empire?

The Inca themselves called their domain *Tawantinsuyu*, the Land of the Four Quarters. Their capital, Cuzco, lay at the intersection of these divisions. Home to the ruler (Inca) and the ruling elite, it was a city of great splendor and magnificence. Its principal temples, dedicated to the sun and moon, gleamed with gold and silver. Its outer boundaries had been drawn to resemble the shape of a vast puma.

The origins of the Inca are obscure. According to Inca traditions, expansion began in the fifteenth century in the wake of a revolt of the Chanca people that nearly destroyed Cuzco. Inca Yupanqui, son of the city's aging ruler, led a heroic resistance and crushed the revolt. Assuming the name Pachacuti, he laid the foundations of Inca statecraft; he and his successors expanded their domains to bring the blessings of civilization to the rest of the Andean world. There is clearly an element of imperial propaganda in this legend. The Inca did expand dramatically in the fifteenth century, but archaeological evidence suggests that they had been expanding their influence for decades and perhaps centuries before the Chanca revolt.

The Inca enlarged their empire through a combination of alliance and intimidation as well as conquest. They organized their realm into a hierarchical administrative structure and imposed a version of their language, **Quechua**, as the administrative language of the empire. (Quechua is still widely spoken in the Peruvian Andes.) The Inca emperorship was not conveyed by direct inheritance. A dispute over the royal succession was occurring at the time of the Spanish arrival and was exploited by the Spanish.

The Inca and the peoples they ruled were extremely devout in their religion. The Inca saw themselves in a profound relationship to their dead forebears; they

Mummified remains. A mummy, exhumed at the cemetery at Puruchuco-Huaquerones, with a feathered headdress, thought to signify high status.

What kinds of bodies were most likely to be mummified in Inca culture?

Quechua
The Inca language.

mita
The Inca system of forced labor in return for gifts and ritual entertainments.

Mitimaqs
Communities whom the Incas forced to settle in designated regions for strategic purposes.

mamakuna
Inca women who lived privileged but celibate lives and had important economic and cultural roles.

chicha
A maize beer brewed by the *mamakuna* for the Inca elite.

The Inca *Quipumayoc*. The grand treasurer shown holding a *quipu*, a device made of knotted strings, used to record administrative matters and sacred histories. Information was encoded in the colors of the strings and the style of the knots.

How did the Inca organize their empire?

deeply honored their ancestors. Mummified bodies of ancestors were preserved, especially among the elite. Property of the dead was owned communally. Consequently, the property of a deceased Inca emperor was not inherited by his successor but by his descendants, a group known as a Panaca. When a new Inca emperor came to power, he had to undertake military expansion to provide property for his own descendants.

The official Inca religion was organized in a strongly hierarchical fashion, as were the gods being worshiped. Incas sacrificed animals to their gods and, on occasions of great communal difficulty, also sacrificed human beings, often children. Beyond the major population centers, religion was essentially folk worship of spirits rather than formal gods.

Unlike the Aztecs, who extracted primarily economic tribute from their subject peoples, the Inca relied on various forms of labor taxation. They divided agricultural lands into several categories, allowing local populations to retain some for their own support and reserving others for the state and the gods. In a system known as the **mita**, local people worked for the state on a regular basis, receiving in return gifts and lavish state-sponsored ritual entertainments. Men also served in the army and labored on the construction of vast public works projects, building cities and roads, and terracing hillsides. In a policy that reflects the Andean practice of colonizing ecologically varied regions, the Inca also designated entire communities as **Mitimaqs**, moving them about to best exploit the resources of their empire. They sometimes settled loyal people in hostile regions and moved hostile people to loyal regions.

The Inca employed several groups of people in what amounted to full-time state service. One of these, the **mamakuna**, consisted of women who lived privileged but celibate and carefully regulated lives in cities and towns throughout the empire. *Mamakuna* might also be given in marriage by Inca rulers to cement alliances. These so-called Virgins of the Sun played an important economic as well as religious role, weaving textiles and brewing the maize beer known as **chicha** for the Inca elite. Textiles were highly prized in Andean society. Cloth and clothing were not only a principal source of wealth and prestige in Inca society, they were also a means of communication. Complex textile patterns served as insignia of social status, indicating a person's rank and ethnic affiliation. *Chicha* had great ritual importance and was consumed at state religious festivals. Another group of full-time state workers, the *yanakuna*, were men whose duties included tending the royal llama herds.

The Incas made their presence felt in their empire through regional administrative centers and warehouses linked by a remarkable system of roads. The centers served to organize, house, and feed people engaged in *mita* labor service and to impress upon them the power and beneficence of the state with feasting and ritual. The wealth of the empire, collected in storehouses, sustained the *mita* laborers, fed and clothed the army, and enriched the Inca elite. Although the Inca lacked writing, they kept detailed administrative records on their string *quipu*.

To move their armies, administer their domains, and distribute the wealth of their empire efficiently, the Inca built more than 14,000 miles of road. These ranged from narrow paths to wide thoroughfares. Rope suspension bridges crossed gorges and rivers, and stairways eased the ascent of steep slopes. A system of relay runners sped messages to Cuzco from the far reaches of the empire. This road system later facilitated Spanish conquest of the empire.

Over their long history the people of the Andes adapted to their challenging environment in ways that allowed them to prosper, bringing more land under cultivation than is the case today. Building on ancient Andean traditions, the Inca engineered a productive economy that brought its people a measure of well-being that would not survive the destruction of the empire by Spanish invaders. When those invaders arrived in the 1530s, they found the Inca Empire in political strife as two brothers contested the title of Inca. The Spanish also confronted an Inca population that had been significantly lessened by a small pox epidemic during the previous decade. That disease, introduced to Mexico in 1520, had spread rapidly in the Americas and reached the Andes before the Europeans themselves. The Spanish conquest meant that the most extensive and administratively sophisticated empire of pre-Columbian America had endured less than a century.

SUMMARY

 WHAT PROBLEMS do scholars face in reconstructing the history of Native American civilizations?

Reconstructing History. Some Maya written accounts survive, but much of the history of Native Americans is reconstructed through archaeological evidence. Accounts written after the Spanish conquest can provide valuable information, but they must be interpreted carefully. *page 312*

 WHAT GROUP dominated Olmec society?

Mesoamerica. Mesoamerica means "middle America." It extends from central Mexico to Central America. Although there was no single Mesoamerican civilization, the civilizations of the Olmecs, the peoples of Monte Albán and Teotihuácan, the Maya, the Toltecs, and the Aztecs shared many features: urban centers with monumental buildings arranged on large plazas, writing, a sophisticated calendrical system, religious ideas that included human sacrifice, and the cultivation of certain crops, especially maize and beans. The cities of Mesoamerica were also linked by trade. Elite ruler-priests dominated Olmec society, and probably other Mesoamerican societies. *page 313*

 WHAT WERE some of the main achievements of the Classic period civilizations in Mesoamerica?

The Classic Period. The great city of Teotihuacán influenced much of Mesoamerica. Maya civilization featured writing, sophisticated mathematics and astronomy, and religious ritual. *page 317*

WHAT ROLE did human sacrifice play in the Aztec Empire?

The Post-Classic Period. Warfare increased, and secular and religious authority began to separate as the Classic period's political structures disintegrated. The brief era of

Toltec power was followed by the Aztecs, who established the largest Mesoamerican state before the coming of the Spanish in the sixteenth century. The Aztec Empire depended on tribute from conquered peoples. Aztec society was organized for war and was divided into nobles and commoners, with merchants and certain artisans forming intermediate categories. The Aztecs practiced wide-scale human sacrifice to provide blood to the sun god. Most of the victims were captured warriors, so the Aztecs went to war frequently. Women could own property and participate in trade but were subordinate to men and excluded from positions of high authority. *page 321*

 HOW DID Andean peoples modify their environments?

Andean South America. Monumental architecture and public buildings in Peru date from the third millennium B.C.E. When pottery first appeared in Peru, around 2000 B.C.E., a process of increasing reliance on agriculture began. This process was reinforced by expanding ceremonial centers and population growth. *page 326*

WHY DID Chavín influence spread?

Chavín de Huantar. Chavín de Huantar was a trade center. It was also the home of a powerful religious cult that gained regional influence because of its prestige. *page 328*

 HOW DO Tiwanaku and Huari foreshadow the achievements of the Inca?

Early Intermediate, Middle Horizon, and Late Intermediate Periods. Territorial states including the Nazca and the Moche were followed by the expansionist Tiwanaku and Huari empires. Tiwanaku and Huari rulers, like the Incas later on, were able to mobilize large numbers of laborers for immense state projects. The Chimu Empire was swept away by the Incas. *page 328*

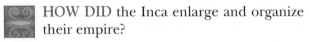

HOW DID the Inca enlarge and organize their empire?

The Inca Empire. The Incas built the most extensive Andean empire. It extended for 2,600 miles from Ecuador to Chile between the Pacific coast and the Amazon basin. Inca rule relied on conquest, intimidation, and alliances with other peoples. The Inca exacted taxation in terms of forced labor and constructed over 14,000 miles of roads and numerous rope bridges. Although the Inca lacked writing, they kept detailed accounts using knotted strings. *page 331*

KEY TERMS

calpulli (p. 325)
chicha (p. 332)
Long Count (p. 320)
Mexica **(meh-HEE-kah)**
    (p. 322)
mamakuna (p. 332)
mita (p. 332)

Mitimaqs (p. 332)
obsidian (p. 314)
Quechua **(KEHTCH-oo-ah)**
    (p. 331)
quipu **(KEE-poo)** (p. 330)

REVIEW QUESTIONS

1. What tools have historians used to study the early history of peoples in the Americas? How has understanding of Native American civilizations changed over time?

2. Describe the rise of civilization in Mesoamerica and Andean South America. What does it have in common with the rise of civilization elsewhere? In what ways was it unique?

3. What role did the environment play in the formation of American civilizations?

4. The appearance of monumental architecture in the ancient world was often associated with hierarchical agricultural societies. Was this the case for the Peruvian coast?

5. What were some of the accomplishments of the Classic civilizations of Mesoamerica? How do they compare with contemporary civilizations elsewhere in the world?

6. How was the Aztec Empire organized? How does it compare to the early empires of the ancient world in the Near East, Europe, and Asia?

7. How was the Inca Empire organized? How does it compare to the early empires of the ancient world in the Near East, Europe, and Asia?

8. Both the Aztec and Inca empires fell in the early sixteenth century when confronted with Spanish forces of a few hundred men. What factors might have contributed to their defeat?

Note: To learn more about the topics in this chapter, please turn to the Suggested Readings at the end of the book. For additional sources related to this chapter please see www.myhistorylab.com

PEARSON
myhistorylab Connections

Reinforce what you learned in this chapter by studying the many documents, images, maps, review tools, and videos available at **www.myhistorylab.com**

Read and Review

✔●─[**Study** and **Review**   Chapter 13

●●●●─[**Read** the **Document**   *Victory over the Underworld,*
p. 316

●●●─[**View** the **Image**   *Mayan Ruins, p. 313*
A Mayan Town, p. 319
Aztec Warriors, p. 325

●●●─[**Watch** the **Video**   *Teotihuacán Ruins in Mexico, p. 317*

((●●─[**Hear** the **Audio**   *Early Americas, p. 316*

Research and Explore

◉─[**See** the **Map**   *Pre-Columbian Civilization in Mesoamerica, p. 326*

◉─[**See** the **Map**   *Civilizations in North America*

((●●─[**Hear** the **Audio** ─

Hear the audio file for Chapter 13
at **www.myhistorylab.com**

14

Africa ca. 1000–1700

((•─ Hear the Audio for Chapter 14 at www.myhistorylab.com

The Great Mosque at Kilwa, ca. 1100 C.E. The Swahili city of Kilwa, on the coast of present-day Tanzania, was likely founded by Muslim traders with strong links to the Indian Ocean world. The insides of its domes were lined with Chinese porcelain. Now in ruins, this large congregational mosque was probably in its day the largest fully enclosed structure in sub-Saharan Africa.

What characterizes Swahili culture?

Different parts of the African continent had very different histories early in the second millennium C.E. Many regions had substantial interactions with the Islamic and European worlds; others engaged in trade and cultural exchanges within the continent.

The Atlantic slave trade affected almost all of Africa between the fifteenth and nineteenth centuries. This subject is treated in detail in Chapter 17, but here, we cannot overlook its importance in disrupting and reconfiguring African economies, social organization, and politics.

We begin with Africa above the equator, where Islam's influence increased and substantial kingdoms and empires flourished. Then we discuss West, East, central, and southern Africa and the effects of Arab-Islamic and European influence. ■

GLOBAL PERSPECTIVE

AFRICA, 1000–1700

Long-distance trade—the supply-and-demand-driven movement of goods, people, and cultural attitudes and practices—typically stimulates historical change. This was as true in Africa in the early second millennium as in the Americas, Europe, Asia, or anywhere in the world. Different regions in Africa were oriented differently in relation to trade routes and trading partners, and these regions developed in markedly different ways between 1000 and 1700.

The North African coast and the Sahel lay amidst trading networks linking the Mediterranean world, the growing *Dar al-Islam* ("House of Submission"—the Islamic realm), and the rich kingdoms of West Africa. The East African coast was integrated into the trading and cultural networks of the Indian Ocean basin and was firmly engaged with the Muslim world there. The rest of sub-Saharan Africa was culturally diverse; people here engaged primarily in intra-African trade with cultures that occupied other ecological niches. It is important to remember that Africa is a

See the Map
Trade Routes in Africa
at **myhistorylab.com**

continent that is home to many societies with different histories, languages, religions, and cultures. In this way it is

similar to Europe, but Africa is also much larger than Europe and more ethnically and culturally diverse.

Along the Mediterranean, the key new factor in African history at this time was the Ottomans' imperial expansion into Egypt and the **Maghreb**. The long Ottoman hegemony altered the political configuration of the Mediterranean world. Merchants and missionaries carried Islam and Arabian cultural influences across the Sahara from North Africa and the Middle East to the western, central, and Nilotic Sudan, where Muslim conversion played a growing social and political role, especially among the ruling elites who profited most from brokering trade between their lands and the Islamic north. Islam provided a shared arena of expression for at least some classes and groups in societies over a vast area from Egypt to Senegambia. In Africa as elsewhere, new converts modified Islam through a process of syncretism. Distinctively African

See the Map
Discovery: The Maghrib
and West Africa,
Fourteenth Century
at **myhistorylab.com**

forms of Islam emerged, faithful to the central tenets of the religion, but differing in observances and customs from those of the Arabian cultural

NORTH AFRICA AND EGYPT

HOW DID the Ottomans govern North Africa and Egypt?

Dar al-Islam
In Arabic, the "House of Submission," or Islamic world. This term has many shades of meaning, ranging from a place where the government is under Muslim control to a place where individuals are free to practice Islamic beliefs.

Maghreb
Literally, in Arabic, "place of sunset," or the west; refers to the northwest of Africa, and specifically what is now Morocco.

Sharifs
A term for leaders who are direct descendants of the Prophet Muhammad through his first grandson, Hasan ibn Ali.

Watch the Video
Piracy at **myhistorylab.com**

As we saw in Chapter 12, Egypt and other North African societies played a central role in Islamic and Mediterranean history after 1000 C.E. From Tunisia to Egypt, Sunni religious and political leaders and their Shi'ite, especially Isma'ili, counterparts struggled for the minds of the masses. By the thirteenth century, the Shi'ites had become a small minority among Muslims in Mediterranean Africa. In general, a feisty regionalism characterized states, city-states, and tribal groups north of the Sahara and along the lower Nile. No single power controlled them for long. Regionalism persisted even after 1500, when most of North Africa came under the influence—and often, direct control—of the Ottoman Empire centered in Istanbul.

By 1800 the nominally Ottoman domains from Egypt to Algeria were effectively independent. In Egypt the Ottomans had established direct rule after their defeat of the Mamluks in 1517, but by the seventeenth century power had passed to Egyptian governors descended from the Mamluks. The Mediterranean coastlands between Egypt and Morocco were officially Ottoman provinces, or regencies, but by the eighteenth century, Algiers, Tripoli (in modern Libya), and Tunisia had institutionalized their own political structures.

Morocco, ruled by a succession of *Sharifs* (leaders claiming descent from the family of the Prophet Muhammad), was the only North African sultanate to remain fully independent after 1700. The most important *Sharifian* Dynasty was that of the Sa'dis (1554–1659). One major reason for Morocco's independence was that its Arab and Berber populations united after 1500 to oppose the Portuguese and the Spaniards.

sphere, especially in attitudes toward women and relationships between the sexes.

South of the Sahara, dynamic processes of state-building and trade were the main forces for cultural change. In central and South Africa, except along the eastern coast, and in the West African forests, older African traditions held sway, and there was little or no evidence of Islam beyond individual Muslims involved in trade. On the eastern coast, however, Islam influenced the development of the Swahili culture and language, a unique blend of African, Indian, and Arabian traditions, and Islamic traders linked the region to India, China, and the Indies. In sub-Saharan Africa, the spread of Islam took place almost entirely through peaceful means.

Along the Atlantic and Indian Ocean coasts of Africa, the key development of the fifteenth century was the arrival of ships carrying traders and missionaries from Christian Europe. The strength of African societies and the biological dangers to Europeans venturing into the interior meant that most of the trade between the African interior and Europeans on both coasts remained under the control of Africans for generations. Even before Europeans themselves reached the interior, however, the trade in slaves, weapons, and gold that they fostered greatly altered African political and social structures not only along the coasts but also in regions untouched by the outsiders. The European voyages of discovery of the fifteenth and sixteenth centuries presaged the African continent's involvement in a new, expanding, and, by the eighteenth century, European-dominated global trading system. This system generally exploited rather than bolstered African development, as the infamous Atlantic slave trade (see Chapter 17) and the South African experience illustrate.

((••⎯Hear the Audio
Influences in Africa 2
at **myhistorylab.com**

Focus Questions

◆ Where in Africa was Islamic influence concentrated? How did Islam spread? What does this reveal about the relationship between commerce and cultural diffusion?

◆ Why did different regions in Africa develop in different ways between 1000 and 1700?

THE SPREAD OF ISLAM SOUTH OF THE SAHARA

HOW DID Islam spread south of the Sahara?

Islamic influence in sub-Saharan Africa began as early as the eighth century. By 1800 it affected most of the Sudanic belt and the coast of East Africa. The process was generally peaceful, gradual, and partial. Conversion to Islam was rare beyond the ruling or commercial classes, and Islamic faith tended to coexist or blend with indigenous beliefs. Agents of Islam brought commercial and political changes as well as the Qur'an, new religious practices, and literate culture.

In East Africa, Muslim traders moving down the coastline with the ancient monsoon trade routes had begun to "Islamize" ports and coastal regions even before 800 C.E. From the thirteenth century on, Islamic trading communities and city-states developed along the coast from Mogadishu to Kilwa.

⊙⎯See the Map
East African Coast to 1600
at **myhistorylab.com**

In the western and central parts of the continent, Islam was introduced primarily by traders from North Africa and the Nile valley. Berbers who plied the desert routes (see Chapter 5) to trading towns such as Awdaghast on the edge of the Sahel as early as the eighth century were Islam's chief agents. From there Islam spread south to centers such as Kumbi Saleh and beyond, southeast across the Niger, and west into Senegambia. Migrating Arab tribal groups that settled in the central sub-Saharan Sahel also helped spread Islam.

The year 985 marks the first time a West African royal court—that of the kingdom of Gao, east of the Niger bend—officially became Muslim (see Chapter 5), though Gao rulers did not try to convert their subjects.

By contrast, the rulers of the later kingdom of Ghana long maintained their indigenous traditions even though they traded with Muslims and had Muslim advisers.

Starting in the 1030s zealous militants known as Almoravids (see Chapter 12) began a conversion campaign that eventually swept into Ghana's territory, taking first Awdaghast and later, in 1076, Kumbi Saleh. Thereafter, the forcibly converted Soninke ruling group of Ghana spread Islam among their own populace and farther south in the savannah. They converted Mande-speaking traders, who brought Islam south into the forests.

Farther west, the Fulbe rulers of Takrur became Muslim in the 1030s and propagated their new faith among their subjects. The Fulbe, or Fulani, remained important carriers of Islam over the next eight centuries as they migrated gradually into new regions as far east as Lake Chad, where some rulers were Muslim as early as 1100.

Major groups in West Africa strongly resisted Islamization, especially the Mossi kingdoms founded in the Volta region at Wagadugu around 1050 and Yatenga about 1170.

SAHELIAN EMPIRES OF THE WESTERN AND CENTRAL SUDAN

WHAT WERE the four most important states in the Sahel between 1000 and 1600?

As we noted in Chapter 5, substantial states had risen in the first millennium c.e. in the Sahel just south of the Sahara.[1] From about 1000 to 1600, four of these developed into relatively long-lived empires: Ghana, Mali, and Songhai in the western Sudan, and Kanem-Bornu in the central Sudan.

GHANA

Ghana established the model for later Sahelian empires in the western Sudan. Well north of modern Ghana (and unrelated to it except by name), it lay between the inland Niger Delta and the upper Senegal. A Ghanaian kingdom existed as early as 400–600 c.e., but Ghana emerged as a regional power only near the end of the first millennium to flourish for about two centuries. Its capital, Kumbi (or Kumbi Saleh), on the desert's edge, was well sited for the Saharan and Sahelian trade networks. Ghana's major population group was the Soninke; *Ghana* is the Soninke term for "ruler."

Ghanaian rulers were descended matrilineally (through the previous king's sister) and ruled through a council of ministers. Contemporaneous reports, especially from the eleventh-century Muslim writer al-Bakri, indicate that the king was supreme judge and held court regularly to hear grievances. The royal ceremonies held in Kumbi Saleh were embellished with the wealth and power befitting a king held to be divinely blessed, and perhaps semidivine.

Slaves were at the bottom of Ghana's hierarchical society; farmers and draftsmen above them; merchants above them; and the king, his court, and the nobility on top. Ghana's power rested on a solid economic base. Tribute from the empire's many chieftaincies and taxes on royal lands and crops supplemented duties levied on all incoming and outgoing trade. This trade—north–south between the Sahara and the savannah, and especially east–west through the Sahel between Senegambia and more easterly trading towns like Gao on the Niger Bend—involved a variety of goods. Imported salt, cloth, and metal goods such as copper from the north were probably exchanged for gold

---

[1]S. K. and R. J. McIntosh, *Prehistoric Investigations in the Region of Jenne, Mali* (Oxford: Oxford University Press 1980), pp. 41–59, 434–461; R. Oliver, *The African Experience* (New York: HarperCollins, 1991), pp. 90–101.

and kola nuts from the south. The regime apparently also controlled the gold (and, presumably, the slave) trade that originated in the savanna to the south and west.

Although the Ghanaian king and court did not convert to Islam, they made elaborate arrangements to accommodate Muslim traders and government servants in a separate settlement a few miles from Khumbi's royal preserve. Muslim traders were prominent at court, literate Muslims administered the government, and Muslim legists advised the ruler.

A huge, well-trained army secured royal control, enabling the kings to extend their sway in the late tenth century to the Atlantic shore and to the south (see Map 14–1 on page 342). In 992, Ghanaian troops wrested Awdaghast from the Berbers. The empire was, however, vulnerable to attack from the desert, as Almoravid Berber forces proved in 1054 when they took Awdaghast in a single raid.

Ghana's empire was probably destroyed in the late twelfth century by the anti-Muslim Soso people from the mountains southeast of Kumbi Saleh; they were a Malinke clan who had long been part of the Ghanaian Empire. Their brief ascendancy between 1180 and 1230 ended the once great transregional power centered at Kumbi Saleh.[2]

MALI

With Ghana's collapse and the Almoravids' focus on North Africa, the western Sudan broke up into smaller kingdoms. In the early twelfth century Takrur's control of the Senegal valley and the gold-producing region of Galam made it the strongest state in the western Sudan. Like Ghana, however, it was soon eclipsed, first by the brief Soso ascendancy and then by the rise of Mali.

In the mid-thirteenth century, the Keita ruling clan of Mali forged a new and lasting empire, built on monopolization of the lucrative north–south gold trade. The Keita kings dominated enough of the Sahel to control the flow of West African gold from the Senegal regions and the forestlands south of the Niger to the trans-Saharan trade routes and the influx of copper and salt in exchange. Based south of their Ghanaian predecessors, in the fertile land along the Niger, they controlled all trade on the upper Niger, as well as the Gambia and Senegal trade to the west. They used captives for plantation labor in the Niger inland delta to produce surplus food for trade.

Agriculture and cattle farming were the primary occupations of Mali's population. Rice was grown in the river valleys and millet in the drier parts of the Sahel. Together with beans, yams, and other agricultural products, this made for a plentiful food supply. Fishing flourished along the Niger and elsewhere. Cattle, sheep, and goats were plentiful. The chief craft specialties were metalworking (iron and gold) and weaving of cotton grown within the empire.

The Malinke, a southern Mande-speaking people of the upper Niger region, formed the core population of the new state. They apparently lived in walled urban settlements typical of the western savanna region. Each walled town held 1,000 to 15,000 people and was linked to neighboring cities by trade and intermarriage.

The Keita Dynasty had converted to Islam around 1100 C.E. Keita's rulers even claimed descent from Muhammad's famous *muezzin* Bilal ibn Ribah, a former black slave from Abyssinia whose son was said to have settled in the Mande-speaking region. During Mali's heyday in the thirteenth and fourteenth centuries, its kings often

[2]D. Conrad and H. Fisher, "The Conquest That Never Was: Ghana and the Almoravids, 1076," *History in Africa* 9 (1982): 1–59; 10 (1983): 53–78.

QUICK REVIEW

Mali

- Keita clan forged Mali in mid-thirteenth century
- Keita kings controlled the flow of West African gold
- Agriculture and cattle farming were primary occupations of Mali's people

The Great Mosque at Jenne. Jenne was one of the important commercial centers controlled by the empire of Mali in the thirteenth and fourteenth centuries. The thriving market in front of the mosque reflects the enduring vitality of trade and commerce in the region.

How widely was Islam adopted in western Sudan?

muezzin
The leader of a mosque's call to prayers.

MAP EXPLORATION

To explore this map further, go to **http://www.myhistorylab.com**

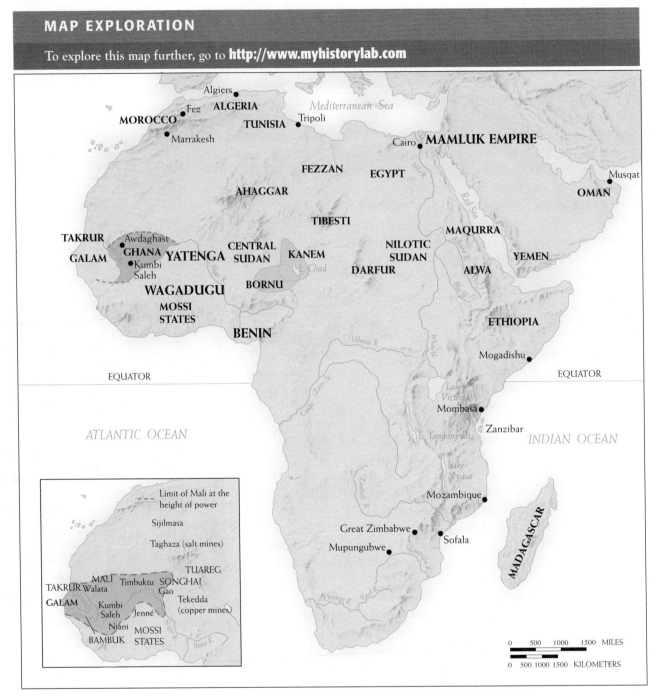

MAP 14–1.   Africa ca. 900–1500. Shown are major cities and states referred to in the text. The main map shows the region of West Africa occupied by the empire of Ghana from ca. 990 to ca. 1180. The inset shows the region occupied by Mali between 1230 and 1450.

Why was Ghana's location important for its prosperity?

●●●● Read the Document

Excerpts from Sundiata: An Epic of Old Mali, 1235 at **myhistorylab.com**

made the pilgrimage to Mecca, bringing back with them military aids, such as Barbary war horses, and new ideas about political and military organization. Through Muslim traders' networks, Mali was connected to other areas of Africa, especially to the east.

Mali's imperial power was built largely by the Keita King Sundiata (or Sunjaata, r. 1230–1255). Sundiata and his successors exploited their agricultural resources, significant population growth, and Malinke commercial skills to build an empire even more powerful than that of Ghana. Sundiata extended his control west to the Atlantic coast and east beyond Timbuktu. By controlling the commercial entrepôts of Gao, Walata, and Jenne, he dominated the Saharan as well as the Niger trade. He built his capital, Niani, into a major city. Niani was located on a tributary of the Niger in the savannah at the edge of the forest in a gold- and iron-rich region. It had access to the forest trade products of gold, kola nuts, and palm oil; it was easily defended by virtue of its surrounding hills; and it was readily reached by river.

The empire that Sundiata and his successors built ultimately encompassed three major regions and language groups of Sudanic West Africa: (1) the Senegal region (including Takrur), populated by speakers of the West Atlantic Niger-Kongo language group; (2) the central Mande states between Senegal and Niger, occupied by the Niger-Kongo-speaking Soninke and Mandinke; and (3) the peoples of the Niger in the Gao region who spoke Songhai, the only Nilo-Saharan language west of the Lake Chad basin. Mali was less a centralized bureaucratic state than the center of a vast sphere of influence that included provinces and tribute-paying kingdoms. Many individual chieftaincies were independent but recognized the sovereignty of the supreme, sacred *mansa*, or "emperor," of the Malian realms.

The greatest Keita king was Mansa Musa (r. 1312–1337), famous for his pilgrimage through Mamluk Cairo to Mecca in 1324. He spent or gave away so much gold in Cairo alone that he started massive inflation lasting over a decade. He brought many Muslim scholars, artists, scientists, and architects back to Mali, where he consolidated his power and secured peace throughout his vast dominions. The devout ruler fostered the spread of Islam. Under Musa's rule, Timbuktu became famous for its *madrasas* and libraries, making it the leading intellectual center of sub-Saharan Islam and a major trading city of the Sahel—roles it retained long after Mali's empire declined.[3]

After Musa, rivalries for the throne diminished Mali's dominance. The empire slowly withered until a new Songhai power supplanted it after about 1450.

SONGHAI

There was a Songhai kingdom around Gao, on the eastern arc of the great bend of the Niger, as early as the eleventh or twelfth century. In 1325 Mansa Musa gained control of the Gao region. Mali's domination ended with the rise of a dynasty in Gao known as the Sunni or Sonni around 1375. The kingdom became an imperial power under the greatest Sunni ruler, Sonni Ali (r. 1464–1492). For more than a century the Songhai Empire was arguably the most powerful state in Africa (see Map 14–2 on page 344). With a strong military built around a riverboat flotilla and cavalry, Sonni Ali took Jenne and Timbuktu. He pushed the Tuareg Berbers back into the northern Sahel and Sahara and stifled threats from the southern forestland.

QUICK REVIEW

King Sundiata (r. 1230–1255)

♦ Built Mali's imperial power

♦ Mali's empire was more powerful than its Ghanaian predecessor

♦ Empire encompassed three major regions: Senegal, the central Mande states, and the peoples of Niger in the Gao region

●●●—Read the **Document**
The Travels of Ibn Battuta "Ibn Battuta in Mali" at **myhistorylab.com**

●●●—Read the **Document**
Al-Umari describes Mansa Musa of Mali at **myhistorylab.com**

mansa
Malian emperor, from Mandinka word meaning "king of kings."

Mansa Musa, King of Mali. The fourteenth-century Catalan Atlas shows King Mansa Musa of Mali, seated on a throne holding a nugget of gold. A camel rider approaches him.

Why would a fourteenth-century European atlas show Mansa Musa?

[3]For more on Mali, especially its wealth and Timbuktu's role as a center of scholarship, see E. Gilbert and J. T. Reynolds, *Africa in World History: From Prehistory to the Present* (Upper Saddle River, NJ: Prentice Hall, 2008), pp. 106-109.

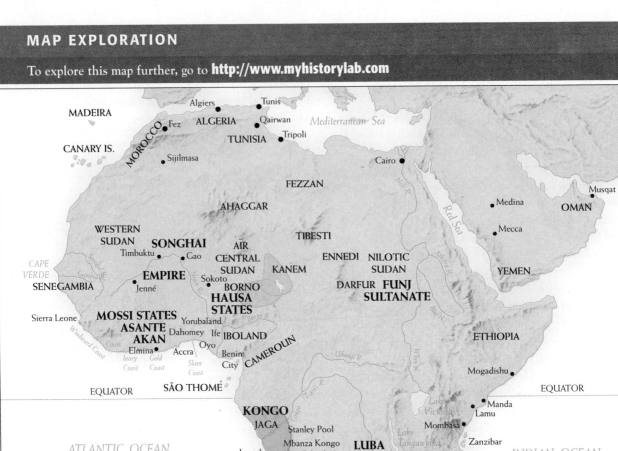

MAP EXPLORATION

To explore this map further, go to **http://www.myhistorylab.com**

MAP 14–2. **Africa ca. 1500–1700.** Important towns, regions, peoples, and states. The inset shows the empire of Songhai at its greatest extent in the early sixteenth century.

What was Songhai's major source of wealth?

His successor Askia Muhammad al-Turi (r. 1493–1528) continued Sonni Ali's expansionist policies. Between them, these two rulers built an empire that stretched west nearly to the Atlantic, northwest into the Sahara, and east into the central Sudan. Like their Ghanaian predecessors, they took advantage of their control of access to gold and other West African commodities to cultivate and expand the caravan trade to the North African coast. This provided their major source of wealth.

Unlike Sonni Ali, who maintained his people's traditional faith, Askia Muhammad and his Askia successors were emphatically Muslim. At-Turi modeled the Songhai state on the Islamic empire of Mali. (See Document, "Muslim Reform in Songhai.") In his reign, many Muslim scholars came to Gao, Timbuktu, and Jenne. He appointed Muslim judges (*qadis*) throughout the empire and made Timbuktu a major intellectual and legal training center. He replaced native Songhais with Arab Muslim immigrants as government officials. Like Mansa Musa before him, Muhammad made a triumphal pilgrimage to Mecca, where he was hailed as "Caliph of the western Sahara." From his vast royal treasury he supported the poor and Sufi leaders, or **marabouts**, and built mosques throughout the realm. Nevertheless, he failed to Islamize the empire or to ensure a strong central state for his successors.

The last powerful Askia leader was Askia Dawud (r. 1549–1583), under whom Songhai prosperity and intellectual life reached its apogee. Both trans-Saharan trade and royal patronage of the arts rose to new levels. Still, difficulties mounted. The last Askias battled the Mossi to the south and Berbers from the north. Civil war broke out over the royal succession in 1586, dividing the empire. In 1591 an assay sent by the Sa'dis of Morocco used superior gunpowder weapons, coupled with the aid of disaffected Songhai princes, to defeat the last Askia of Gao, and the Gao Empire collapsed.

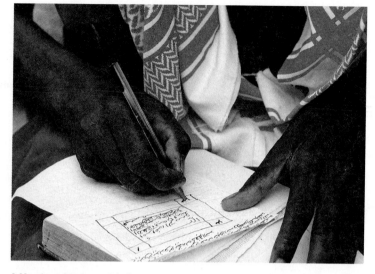

A Marabout Creates a *Grigri*. A verse from the Qur'an is copied onto a piece of paper, which will be folded and put in a leather pouch. The pouch is worn as an amulet, to protect the wearer from sickness, harm, or evil.

Are you aware of the use of amulets in non-Muslim religious traditions?

marabout

In Sunni Islam as practiced in West Africa, a *marabout* is a spiritual leader, versed in the Koran, who often guides the personal lives of his followers.

See the Map

African Empires in the Western Sudan at **myhistorylab.com**

KANEM AND KANEM-BORNU

A fourth sizable Sahelian Empire—this one in the central Sudan—arose after 1100. Called Kanem, it began as a southern Saharan confederation of the nomadic tribes known as Zaghawah. By the twelfth century a Zaghawah group, the Kanuri, had settled in Kanem. From there they began a campaign of military expansion during the thirteenth century. Their leader, Mai Dunama Dibbalemi (r. ca. 1221–1259), was a contemporary of Sundiata in Mali. Dibbalemi was a Muslim, and he used a synthesis of Islam and African traditions of sacred kingship to sanction his rule. Islam provided a rationale for expansion through *jihad*, or holy "struggle" against polytheists.

Dibbalemi and his successors extended Kanuri power north into the desert and northeast along the Sahelian-Saharan fringe. In both directions they controlled important trade routes—north to Libya and east to the Nile. The next two centuries saw the mixing of Kanuri and local Kanembu peoples. There was a corresponding transformation of the

CHRONOLOGY

SAHELIAN EMPIRES OF THE WESTERN SUDAN

ca. 990–ca. 1180?	Empire of Ghana
1076	Ghana loses Awdaghast to Almoravids
1180–1230	Soso clan controls old Ghanaian territories
ca. 1230–1450	Empire of Mali, founded by Sundiata
1230–1255	Reign of Sundiata
1312–1337	Reign of Mansa Musa
1340–1370s	Independent Songhai state emerges in Gao after throwing off Malian rule
ca. 1450–1591	Songhai Empire at Gao
1462–1492	Reign of Sonni Ali
1493–1591	Askia Dynasty rules Songhai Empire
1493–1528	Reign of Askia Muhammad al-Turi
1549–1583	Reign of Askia Dawud

DOCUMENT

Muslim Reform in Songhai

Around 1500 Askia Muhammad al-Turi, the first Muslim Songhai ruler, wrote to the North African Muslim theologian Muhammad al-Maghili (d. 1504) about proper Muslim practices. In these excerpts from al-Turi's seventh question, we glimpse the new convert's zeal for conformity to traditional religious norms, as well as the king's desire for bettering social order and his concern for justice. The answers from al-Maghili reflect the puritanical "official line" of the conservative ulama who did not want to allow syncretism to emerge among newly converted groups.

- **WHAT** are the problems and corresponding solutions described in the letters? Which problem did al-Maghili find most serious? Why? Which do you think would have been most serious? Why?

FROM ASKIA MUHAMMAD AL-TURI'S SEVENTH QUESTION

Among the people [of the Songhay Empire], there are some who claim knowledge of the supernatural through sand divining and the like, or through the disposition of the stars . . . [while] some assert that they can write (talismans) to bring good fortune . . . or to ward off bad fortune. . . . Some defraud in weights and measures. . . .

One of their evil practices is the free mixing of men and women in the markets and streets and the failure of women to veil themselves . . . [while] among the people of Djenné [Jenne] it is an established custom for a girl not to cover any part of her body as long as she remains a virgin . . . and all the most beautiful girls walk about naked . . . .

So give us legal ruling concerning these people and their ilk, and may God Most High reward you!

FROM MUHAMMAD AL-MAGHILI'S ANSWER

The answer—and God it is who directs to the right course—is that everything you have mentioned concerning people's behavior in some parts of this country is gross error. It is the bounden duty of the commander of the Muslims and all other believers who have the power to change every one of these evil practices.

As for any who claims knowledge of the supernatural in the ways you have mentioned . . . he is a liar and an unbeliever. . . . Such people must be forced to renounce it by the sword. Then whoever renounces such deeds should be left in peace, but whoever persists should be killed with the sword as an unbeliever; his body should not be washed or shrouded, and he should not be buried in a Muslim graveyard. . . .

As for defrauding in weights and measures it is forbidden (*haram*) according to the Qur'an, the Sunna and the consensus of opinion of the learned men of the Muslim community. It is the bounden duty of the commander of the Muslims to appoint a trustworthy man in charge of the markets, and to safeguard people's means of subsistence. He should standardize all the scales in each province. . . . Similarly, all measures both large and small must be rectified so that they conform to a uniform standard. . . .

Now, what you mentioned about the free mixing of men and women and leaving the pudenda uncovered is one of the greatest abominations. The commander of the Muslims must exert himself to prevent all these things. . . . He should appoint trustworthy men to watch over this by day and night, in secret and in the open. This is not to be considered as spying on the Muslims; it is only a way of caring for them and curbing evildoers, especially when corruption becomes widespread in the land as it has done in Timbuktu and Djenné . . . .

Source: From *The African Past*, trans. by J. O. Hunwick, reprinted in Basil Davidson (Grosset and Dunlap, The Universal Library), pp. 86–88. Reprinted by permission of Curtis Brown Ltd. Copyright © 1964 by Basil Davidson.

---

shaykh
Arabic word for a tribal elder or Islamic scholar; can also be rendered as sheikh, sheik, or cheikh.

Kanuri leader from nomadic **shaykh** to Sudanic king and of Kanem from a nomadic to a largely sedentary, quasi-feudal kingdom. Like Mali to the west, Kanem's dominion was of two kinds: direct rule over and taxation of core territories, and indirect control over and collection of tribute from a wider region of vassal chieftaincies. Islamic acculturation progressed most rapidly in the core territories.

Civil strife, largely over royal succession, weakened the Kanuri state. After 1400 the locus of power shifted from Kanem to Bornu, southwest of Lake Chad. Here, in the 1490s, a new Kanuri Empire arose almost simultaneously with the collapse of the Askia Dynasty of the Songhai Empire at Gao. Firearms and Turkish military instructors acquired after a pilgrimage to Mecca enabled the Kanuri leader Idris Alawma (r. ca. 1575–1610) to unify Kanem and Bornu. He set up an avowedly Islamic state and extended his rule as far as Hausaland, between Bornu and the Niger. The center of trading activity as well as political power now shifted from the Niger Bend east to Kanuri-controlled territory.

Deriving its prosperity from the trans-Saharan trade, Idris Alawma's regional empire survived for nearly a century. It was broken up by a long famine, Tuareg attacks, weak leadership, and loss of control over trade to smaller, better-organized Hausa states to the west. The ruling dynasty held out until 1846, but by 1700 its power had been sharply reduced.

CHRONOLOGY

CENTRAL SUDANIC EMPIRES

ca. 1100–1500	Kanuri Empire of Kanem
ca. 1220s–1400	Height of empire of Kanem
ca. 1221–1259	Reign of Mai Dunama Dibbalemi
ca. 1575–1610	Reign of Idris Alawma, major architect of the Kanem-Bornu state
ca. 1575–late 1600s (1846)	Kanuri Empire of Kanem-Bornu

THE EASTERN SUDAN

The Christian states of Maqurra and Alwa in the Nilotic Sudan, or Nubia, lasted for more than 600 years, beginning in the early seventh century. They maintained political, religious, and commercial contact with Egypt, the Red Sea world, and much of the Sudan.

After 1000 C.E. Maqurra and Alwa continued treaty relations with their more powerful northern Egyptian neighbors. However, the Mamluks intervened repeatedly in Nubian affairs, and Arab nomads constantly threatened the Nubian states. Both Maqurra and Alwa were subject to immigrating Muslim Arab tribesmen and to traders and growing Muslim minorities. Long-term intermingling of Arabic and Nubian cultures created a new Nilotic Sudanese people and culture.

A significant factor in the gradual disappearance of Christianity in Nubia was its elite character there and its association with the Egyptian world of Coptic Christianity. Maqurra became officially Muslim at the beginning of the fourteenth century, although Christianity persisted briefly. The Islamization of Alwa came later, under the long-lived Funj sultanate that replaced the Alwa state.

The Funj state flourished between the Blue and White Niles and to the north along the main Nile from just after 1500 until 1762. The Funj were originally cattle nomads who apparently adopted Islam soon after setting up their kingdom. During the late sixteenth and seventeenth centuries, the Funj developed an Islamic society whose Arabized character was unique in sub-Saharan Africa. A much reduced Funj state survived until an Ottoman Egyptian invasion in 1821.

WHY DID Christianity gradually disappear in Nubia?

THE FORESTLANDS—COASTAL WEST AND CENTRAL AFRICA

WEST AFRICAN FOREST KINGDOMS: THE EXAMPLE OF BENIN

Many states with distinct political, religious, and cultural traditions had developed in the southern and coastal regions of West Africa. The forest kingdom of Benin reflects the sophistication of West African culture before 1500; its art, in particular, is renowned for its enduring beauty.

HOW DID the arrival of Europeans affect the peoples of West and central Africa?

oba

Title of the king of Benin.

uzama

An order of hereditary chiefs in Benin.

((•●⏻Hear the Audio

Influences in Africa 2

at **myhistorylab.com**

The Edo speakers of Benin have occupied the southern Nigerian region between Yorubaland and the Ibo peoples east of the lower Niger for millennia. Traditional Edo society is organized according to a patrilineal system emphasizing primogeniture. The village is the fundamental political unit, and authority is built around the organization of males into age-grade units.[4]

Traditional Edo culture was closely linked to that of Ife, one of the most prominent Yoruba states northwest of Benin. A distinct kingdom of Benin existed as early as the twelfth century, and traditional accounts of both Ife and Edo agree that an Ife prince was sent to rule in Benin around 1300. The power of the *oba*, or king, was sharply limited by the Edo leaders who invited the foreign ruler. These leaders were known as the *uzama*, an order of hereditary chiefs. According to tradition, the fourth *oba* managed to wrest more control from these chiefs and expanded his ceremonial authority. In the fifteenth century, with King Ewuare, Benin became a royal autocracy and a large state of regional importance.

Ewuare rebuilt the capital—known today as Benin City—and named it and his kingdom Edo. He exercised his sweeping authority in light of the deliberations of a royal council. Ewuare formed this council not only from the palace *uzama* but also from the townspeople. He gave each chief specific administrative responsibilities and rank in the government hierarchy. Ewuare and his successors developed a tradition of military kingship and engaged in major wars of expansion, into Yorubaland to the west and Ibo country to the east, across the Niger River. They claimed for the office of *oba* an increasing ritual authority that presaged more radical developments in the king's role.

In the seventeenth century the *oba* was transformed from a military leader into a religious figure with supernatural powers. Human sacrifice, specifically of slaves, seems to have accompanied the cult of deceased kings and became even more frequent later in the nineteenth century. Succession by primogeniture was discontinued, and the *uzama* chose *obas* from any branch of the royal family.

Benin's court art—the splendid terra-cotta, ivory, and especially the famous brass sculpture of Ife-Benin—is among the glories of human creativity. Some scholars trace the artistic and technical lineage of these magnificent works to the sculptures of the Nok culture of ancient West Africa (see Chapter 5). Cast bronze plaques depicting legendary and historical scenes were mounted in the royal palace in Benin City before the sixteenth century. There are also brass heads, apparently of royalty, that resemble the many life-size terra-cotta and brass heads found at Ife. Similar sculptures have been found both to the north and in the Niger Delta.

EUROPEAN ARRIVALS ON THE COASTLANDS: SENEGAMBIA AND THE GOLD COAST

Along the coasts of West and central Africa, between 1500 and 1800, the changes wrought by the burgeoning Atlantic slave trade are notorious (see Chapter 17). But there were other significant developments. The introduction of food crops from the Americas—maize, peanuts, squash, sweet potatoes, cocoa, and cassava (manioc)—had far-reaching impacts. Africa's gradual involvement in the emerging global economic system paved the way for European colonial domination. The European names for segments of the coastline—the Grain (or Pepper) Coast, the Ivory Coast, the Gold Coast, and the Slave Coast—identify the main exports that could be extracted by ship.

CHRONOLOGY		
BENIN		
ca. 1100–1897	Benin state	
ca. 1300	First Ife king of Benin state	
1440–1475	Reign of Ewuare	

---

[4]A. F. C. Ryder, *Benin and the Europeans, 1485–1897* (New York: Longman, 1969), p. 1. Ryder's work is a basic reference for the following brief summary about Benin.

A Closer Look

Benin Bronze Plaque with Chief and Two Attendants

BENIN ARTISTS AND ARTISANS produced spectacular sculptures from the late thirteenth century until the coming of the British in 1897. Their figures typically have the head-to-body proportions of this example, about one to four—perhaps emphasizing the head's importance as a marker of identity and behavior and a symbol of life. The details of the clothing might have been "readable" as to the wearer's rank and family. The stylized faces are typical of Benin bronzes (often actually of brass); dating the piece is hard, but given the two small European figures depicted in the upper field and the sophisticated detail, it is most likely sixteenth or seventeenth century.

The royal figure here has an elaborate headdress with two feathers on top and pendant plumes behind; two bead necklaces, one with leopard teeth mixed in; armlets and anklets; a loincloth; a leopard skin with fringe; a quadrangular bell on a double necklace; a spear with leaf-shaped blade; and an ornamented shield.

Two European figures, possibly Portuguese, are shown from the waist up; both have long moustaches, clublike weapons, plumed helmets, neck ruffs, and armor.

The two royal attendants are carrying round fans, wearing helmets, and adorned like the king with bracelets.

Benin Plaque. Brass. Lost wax. W. Africa 16th–17th century C.E. Hillel Burger/Peabody Museum, Harvard University © President and Fellows of Harvard College. All rights reserved.

Questions

1. The sophisticated Benin bronze artistry allowed for highly detailed sculpture that, for all its stylization, captured its subjects vividly and in great detail. What do you make of the differences between the depictions of the Benin Africans and the two European figures?

2. It has been speculated that this was a piece of court art and the depiction of the royal figure and attendants was intended to exalt royal power and prestige. Do you see evidence of this? If so, what is the evidence?

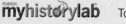

To examine this image in an interactive fashion, please go to **www.myhistorylab.com**

Ife figure, ca. twelfth – fifteenth centuries C.E. The serene classicism of Ife art is equaled only by that of ancient Greece.

What other artistic traditions seem to be linked to Ife?

In West Africa, Senegambia—which takes its name from the Senegal and Gambia rivers—was one of the earliest regions affected by European trade. Senegambia's maritime trade with European powers, like the older overland trade from the interior, was primarily in gold and products such as salt, cotton goods, hides, and copper. For roughly a century Senegambian states also provided slaves for European purchase; perhaps a third of all African slaves exported during the sixteenth century came from Senegambia. Thereafter, however, the focus of the slave trade shifted south and east along the coast (see Chapter 17). Over time, Portuguese-Africans and the British came to control the Gambia River trade, while the French won the Senegal River markets.

The Gold Coast was another West African coastal district heavily affected by the arrival of international maritime trade. As the name suggests, after 1500 the region served as the outlet for the gold fields in the forestland of Akan. Beginning with the Portuguese at Elmina in 1481, but primarily after 1600, European states and companies built coastal forts to protect their trade and to serve as depots for inland goods. The trade in gold, kola nuts, and other commodities seems to have encouraged the growth of larger states, perhaps because they could better handle and control the overland commerce.

The intensive contact of the Gold Coast with Europeans also led to the importation and spread of American crops, notably maize and cassava. The success of these crops in West and central Africa likely contributed to substantial population growth in the sixteenth and seventeenth centuries. The Gold Coast was an importer of slaves until long after 1500. Slaves became major exports in the late seventeenth century, especially in the Accra region. The economy was so disrupted by the slave trade that gold mining declined sharply. Eventually more gold came into the Gold Coast from the sale of slaves than went out from its mines (see Chapter 17).

CENTRAL AFRICA: THE KONGO KINGDOM AND ANGOLA

Before 1500 natural barriers—including swamps in the north, coastal rain forests to the west, highlands to the east, and deserts in the south— impeded international contact and trade with the vast center of the continent. In tropical central Africa, there had long been regional interactions in movements of peoples and in trade and culture (see Chapter 5). Political, economic, and social units varied in size; peoples such as the Lunda and the Luba, on the southern savannah below the rain forest, carved out sizable kingdoms by the fifteenth century and expanded their control over neighboring areas into the eighteenth century.

The Portuguese came to the western coastal regions looking for gold and silver but found none. Ultimately, their main export was slaves. At first, slaves were taken for gang labor to the Portuguese sugar plantations on Sao Tomé island in the Gulf of Guinea and then, in vast numbers, to perform similar plantation labor in Brazil. In the 1640s the Dutch briefly succeeded the Portuguese as the major suppliers of African slaves to English and French plantations in the Caribbean.

The Kongo Kingdom was located on a fertile, well-watered plateau south of the lower Zaïre River valley. Astride the border between forest and grassland, the Kongo kings had built a central government based on a pyramid structure of tax or tribute collection, dating from the fourteenth century. The king's authority was tied to his role as a spiritual spokesman for the

CHRONOLOGY

CENTRAL AFRICA

1300s	Kongo Kingdom founded
1483	Portuguese come to central African coast
ca. 1506–1543	Reign of Affonso I as king of Kongo
1571	Angola becomes Portuguese proprietary colony

gods or ancestors. By 1600 Kongo was half the size of England and boasted a high state of specialization in weaving and pottery, salt production, fishing, and metalworking.

When the Portuguese came to central Africa in 1483, Kongo was the major state with which they dealt. The Portuguese brought Mediterranean goods, preeminently luxury textiles from North Africa, to trade; slaves became the primary export. Although imported luxuries augmented the prestige and wealth of the ruler and his elites, they did nothing to replace the labor pool lost to slavery. At first the Portuguese put time and effort into education and Christian proselytizing, but the desire for more slaves eventually outweighed these concerns. As demand grew, local rulers increasingly attacked neighbors to garner slaves for Portuguese traders (see Chapter 17).

The Kongo ruler Affonso I (r. ca. 1506–1543) was a Christian convert who initially welcomed Jesuit missionaries and supported conversion. But in time he broke with the Jesuits. Affonso had constant difficulty curbing the more exploitative slaving practices and independent-minded provincial governors, who undermined royal authority by dealing directly with the Portuguese. Affonso's successor finally restricted Portuguese activity to Mpinda harbor and the Kongo capital of Mbanza Kongo (São Salvador). A few years later, Portuguese attempts to name the Kongo royal successor caused a bloody uprising against them that led in turn to a Portuguese boycott on trade with the kingdom.

Thereafter, disastrous internal wars shattered the Kongo state. Slavery contributed to provincial unrest. Independent Portuguese traders and adventurers soon did their business outside government channels and tried to manipulate the Kongo kings.

Kongo, however, enjoyed renewed vigor in the seventeenth century. The Kongo kings ruled as divine-right monarchs at the apex of a complex sociopolitical pyramid. Royal power came to depend on hired soldiers armed with muskets. The financial base of the kingdom rested on tribute from officials and taxes and tolls on commerce. Christianity, the state religion, was accommodated to traditional beliefs. Sculpture, iron and copper technology, dance, and music flourished.

To the south, in Portuguese Angola, the experience was even worse than in Kongo. The Ndongo Kingdom flourished among the Mbundu people during the sixteenth century, though the Portuguese controlled parts of Angola as a proprietary colony (the first white colonial enterprise in black Africa). By the end of the 1500s Angola was exporting thousands of slaves yearly through the port of Luanda. In less than a century the hinterland had been depopulated. New internal trade in salt and the spread of American food crops such as maize and cassava (which became part of the staple diet of the populace) produced some positive changes in the interior, but in the coastal region the Portuguese brought catastrophe.

Queen Nzinga of Ndongo, who ruled from 1615 to 1660. This contemporary engraving shows her negotiating a treaty with the Portuguese. She is seated on the back of a slave.

Who seems to have the most power in this scene?

•◆–[Read the **Document**
Voyage from Lisbon
at **myhistorylab.com**

◉–[View the Image
Loango, the Capital of the Kingdom of the Congo at **myhistorylab.com**

EAST AFRICA

SWAHILI CULTURE AND COMMERCE

HOW DID Swahili language and culture develop?

The participation of East African port towns in the lucrative South Seas trade was ancient. Arabs, Indonesians, and even some Indians had been absorbed into what had become, during the first millennium C.E., a predominantly Bantu-speaking population from Somalia south. From the eighth century onward Islam traveled with Arab and Persian sailors and merchants to these southerly trading centers of what the Arabs called the land of the *Zanj*, or "Blacks" (hence "Zanzibar"). Conversion to Islam, however, occurred only along the coast. In the thirteenth century Muslim traders

•◦•─[Read the Document
Descriptions of the cities of Zanj
at **myhistorylab.com**

Swahili
A language and culture that developed from the interaction of Africans and Arabs along the East African coast.

QUICK REVIEW

East African Port Towns
- Part of trade with Middle East, Asia, and India
- Tied together by common language, Swahili
- Swahili civilization reached its peak in the fourteenth and fifteenth centuries

The Malindi Mosque on Zanzibar Island is an example of Islamic influence in Swahili culture.

What are some other examples of Islamic influence on Swahili culture?

Moors
The Spanish and Portuguese term for Muslims.

from Arabia and Iran began to dominate coastal cities from Mogadishu to Kilwa. By 1331 the traveler Ibn Battuta wrote of Islamic rulers, inhabitants, and mosques all along the coast.[5]

A shared language called **Swahili**, or Kiswahili (from the Arabic plural *sawahil*, "coastlands"), developed along the coast. Its structure is Bantu; its vocabulary is largely Bantu but incorporates many words with Arabic roots; it is written in Arabic script. Like the language, Swahili culture is basically African with a large contribution by Arab, Persian, and other extra-African elements. This admixture created a new consciousness and identity. Today, many coastal peoples who share the Swahili language join African to Persian, Indian, Arab, and other ancestries.

Like the Swahili language and culture, the spread of Islam was largely limited to the coastal civilization, with the possible exception of the Zambezi valley, where Muslim traders penetrated upriver. This contrasts with the Horn of Africa, where Islamic kingdoms developed both in the Somali hinterland and on the coast.

Swahili civilization reached its apogee in the fourteenth and fifteenth centuries. The harbor trading towns were the administrative centers of the local Swahili states, and most of them were sited on coastal islands or easily defended peninsulas. Merchants came from abroad and from the African hinterlands. These towns were impressive, with stone mosques, fortress-palaces, harbor fortifications, fancy residences, and commercial buildings combining African and Arabo-Persian elements.

The Swahili states' ruling dynasties were probably African in origin, though elite families often included Arab or Persian members. Swahili coastal centers boasted an advanced, cosmopolitan culture; by comparison, most of the populace in the small villages lived in mud or sometimes stone houses and earned their living farming or fishing. Society seems to have consisted of three principal groups: the local nobility, the commoners, and resident foreigners engaged in commerce. Slaves constituted a fourth class, although their local extent (as opposed to their sale) is disputed.

The flourishing trade of the coastal centers was based on ivory taken from inland elephants. Other exports included gold, slaves, turtle shells, ambergris, leopard skins, pearls, fish, sandalwood, ebony, and cotton cloth. The chief imports were cloth, porcelain, glassware, glass beads, and glazed pottery. Cowrie shells were a common currency in the inland trade, but coins minted at Mogadishu and Kilwa from the fourteenth century on were increasingly used in the trading centers.

THE PORTUGUESE AND THE OMANIS OF ZANZIBAR

The original Swahili civilization declined in the sixteenth century. Trade waned with the arrival of the Portuguese, who destroyed both the Islamic commercial monopoly on the oceanic trade and the main Islamic city-states along the coast. Decreases in rainfall or invasions of Zimba peoples from inland regions may also have contributed to the decline.

The Portuguese undoubtedly intended to gain control of the South Seas trade (see Chapter 17). In Africa, as everywhere, they saw the **Moors** (the Spanish and Portuguese term for Muslims) as their implacable enemies; they viewed the struggle to wrest the commerce and the ports of Africa and Asia from Islamic control as a Christian crusade.

---

[5]*Travels in Asia and Africa, 1325–1354*, trans. and selected by H. A. R. Gibb (New York: Robert M. McBride, 1929), pp. 110–113.

After the initial Portuguese victories along the African coast, there was no concerted effort to spread Christianity beyond fortified coastal settlements. Thus the long-term cultural and religious consequences of the Portuguese presence were slight. The Portuguese did, however, cause widespread economic decline. Inland Africans refused to cooperate with them, and Muslim coastal shipping from India and Arabia was reduced sharply. Ottoman efforts in the late sixteenth century failed to defeat the Portuguese, but after 1660 the strong eastern Arabian state of Oman raided the African coast with impunity. In 1698 the Omanis took Mombasa and ejected the Portuguese everywhere north of Mozambique.

Under the Omanis, Zanzibar became a new and major power center in East Africa. Control of the coastal ivory and slave trade fueled prosperity by the later eighteenth century. Zanzibar itself benefited from the introduction of clove cultivation in the 1830s; cloves became its staple export. (The clove plantations also became the chief market for a new internal slave trade.) Omani African sultans dominated the east coast until 1856, when Zanzibar and its coastal holdings became independent under a branch of the same family that ruled in Oman. Zanzibar passed eventually to the British in the late 1880s. Still, the Islamic imprint on the coast survives today.

CHRONOLOGY

EAST AND SOUTHEAST AFRICA

900–1500	"Great Zimbabwe" civilization
ca. 1200–1400	Development of Bantu Kiswahili language
ca. 1300–1600	Height of Swahili culture
1698	Omani forces take Mombasa, oust Portuguese from East Africa north of the port of Mozambique
1741–1856	United sultanate of Oman and Zanzibar

SOUTHERN AFRICA

SOUTHEASTERN AFRICA: "GREAT ZIMBABWE"

About the same time that the east coast trading centers were beginning to flourish, a different kind of civilization was thriving farther south, in the rocky, savannah-woodland watershed between the Limpopo and Zambezi rivers (now southern Zimbabwe). This civilization was sited far enough inland never to have felt the impact of Islam. It was founded in the tenth or eleventh century by Bantu-speaking Shona people, and it became a large and prosperous state between the late thirteenth and late fifteenth centuries. We know it only through the archaeological remains of approximately 150 settlements.

The most impressive of these ruins is the apparent capital known today as "Great Zimbabwe," a huge site encompassing two major building complexes. One, called the acropolis, is a series of stone enclosures on a high hill. It overlooks a larger enclosure that contains many ruins and a circular tower, all surrounded by a massive wall some 32 feet high and up to 17 feet thick. The acropolis complex may have contained a shrine, whereas the larger enclosure was apparently the royal palace and fort. The stonework reflects a

HOW DID slavery affect race relations in Cape Colony?

See the Map
African Climate Zones and Bantu Migration Routes, ca. 3000 B.C.E.
at **myhistorylab.com**

Great Zimbabwe. Ruins of the Conical Tower inside the Great Enclosure at Great Zimbabwe.

What were some probable sources of Great Zimbabwe's power?

prazeros

Portuguese and mixed-race owners of large estates in the Zambezi valley.

Carving from Great Zimbabwe. This soapstone carving of a bird comprises the top portion of a monolith from Great Zimbabwe, c. 1200 – 1400 C.E. [H: Bird—14 1/2″ (36.8 cm); H: Monolith—5′ 4 1/2″ (1.64 m).] Stone-carved birds are national emblems in Zimbabwe and were commonly found on walls and monoliths dating back to Great Zimbabwe in the eleventh century.

What is known about the culture at Great Zimbabwe?

wealthy and sophisticated society. Artifacts from the site include gold and copper ornaments, soapstone carvings, and imported beads, as well as glass and porcelain of Chinese, Syrian, and Persian origins.

The state seems to have partially controlled the gold trade between inland areas and the east coast port of Sofala. Its territory lay east and south of substantial gold-mining enterprises. This large settlement was probably home to the ruling elite of a prosperous empire. Its wider domain was made up mostly of smaller settlements whose inhabitants lived by subsistence agriculture and cattle raising.

Earlier Iron Age sites farther south suggest that other large state entities may have preceded Great Zimbabwe. The specific impetus for Great Zimbabwe may have been a significant immigration around 1000 C.E. of Late Iron Age Shona speakers who brought with them mining techniques and farming innovations, along with their ancestor cults. Improved farming and animal husbandry could have led to substantial population growth. The expanding gold trade linked the flourishing of Zimbabwe to that of the East African coast from about the thirteenth century.

We may never know why this impressive civilization declined after dominating its region for nearly 200 years. It appears that the northern and southern sectors of the state split up, and people moved away from Great Zimbabwe, probably because the farming and grazing land there was exhausted. The southern successor kingdom, Changamire, was powerful from the late 1600s until about 1830. The northern successor state, which stretched along the Zambezi, was known to the first Portuguese sources as the kingdom ruled by the Mwene Mutapa, or "Master Pillager," the title of its sixteenth-century ruler, Mutota, and his successors.

THE PORTUGUESE IN SOUTHEASTERN AFRICA

Portuguese attempts to obtain gold from the Zambezi region of the interior by controlling trade on the Swahili coast were failures. The Portuguese then established fortified posts up the Zambezi and meddled in Shona politics. In the 1690s the Changamire Shona Dynasty conquered the northern Shona territory and pushed the Portuguese out of gold country.

All along the Zambezi, a lasting consequence of Portuguese intrusion was the creation of quasi-tribal chiefdoms. These were led by **prazeros**, interracial descendants of the area's first Portuguese estate holders, Africans, and Indian immigrants. By the end of the eighteenth century, they formed a few clanlike groups that controlled vast landholdings and commanded armies, often made up largely of slaves. They functioned as warlords, too strong for either the Portuguese or the regional African rulers to control.

SOUTH AFRICA: THE CAPE COLONY

In South Africa the Dutch planted European colonials almost inadvertently, yet the consequences were far-reaching. The first Cape settlement was built in 1652 by the Dutch East India Company as a resupply point for Dutch vessels traveling between the Netherlands and the East Indies. The support station grew gradually, becoming by century's end a large settler community (the population of the colony in 1662, including slaves, was 392; by 1714 it had reached 3,878).[6] These settlers were the forebears of the Afrikaners of modern South Africa.

Local Khoikhoi people were gradually incorporated into the colonial economy. The Khoikhoi (see Chapter 5) were mostly pastoralists; they had neither traditions of strong political organization nor an economic base beyond their herds. At first they freely bartered livestock for iron, copper, and tobacco. However, when settlers began to

---

[6]R. Elphick and H. Giliomee, *The Shaping of South African Society, 1652–1820* (Cape Town: Longman, 1979), p. 4.

displace the Khoikhoi in the southwestern Cape, conflicts ensued. The results were the consolidation of European landholdings and a breakdown of Khoikhoi society. Dutch military success led to even greater control over the Khoikhoi by the 1670s. Treated as free persons, they became the chief source of colonial wage labor—labor that was in ever greater demand as the colony grew.

The colony also imported slaves from all along the South Seas trade routes, including India, East Africa, and Madagascar. Slavery set the tone for relations between the emergent, and ostensibly "white," Afrikaner population and the "coloreds" of other races. Free or not, the latter were eventually all too easily identified with slave peoples.

After the first settlers spread out around the company station, nomadic white livestock farmers, or *Trekboers*, moved more widely afield, leaving the richer but limited farming lands of the coast for the drier interior tableland. There they contested wider groups of Khoikhoi cattle herders for the best grazing lands. The Trekboers developed military techniques—notably the "commando," a collective civilian raid—to secure their way of life by force. Again the Khoikhoi were the losers. By 1700 they were stripped almost completely of their own pasturages, and their way of life was destroyed. Increasing numbers of Khoikhoi took up employment in the colonial economy. Others moved north to join with other refugees from Cape society (slaves, mixed bloods, and some freedmen) to form raiding bands operating along the frontiers of Trekboer territory close to the Orange River. The disintegration of Khoikhoi society continued in the eighteenth century, accelerated sharply by smallpox—a European import against which this previously isolated group had no immunity.

Cape society in this period was diverse. The Dutch East India Company officials (including Dutch Reformed ministers), the emerging Afrikaners (both settled colonists and Trekboers), the Khoikhoi, and the slaves played differing roles. Intermarriage and cohabitation of masters and slaves added to the social complexity, despite laws designed to check such mixing. Accommodation of nonwhite minority groups within Cape society proceeded; the emergence of *Afrikaans*, a new vernacular language of the colonials, shows that the Dutch immigrants themselves were subject to acculturation. By the time of English domination after 1795, the sociopolitical foundations of modern South Africa—and the bases of *apartheid*—were firmly laid.

Early European View of Khoikhoi. This seventeenth-century illustration of Khoikhoi reflects a European view of daily life near the Cape of Good Hope.

What economic role did the Khoikhoi play in the Cape Colony?

Trekboers
White livestock farmers in Cape Colony.

Afrikaans
The new language, derived from Dutch, that evolved in the seventeenth- and eighteenth-century Cape Colony.

apartheid
"Apartness," the term referring to racist policies enforced by the white-dominated regime that existed in South Africa from 1948 to 1992.

SUMMARY

HOW DID the Ottomans govern North Africa and Egypt?

North Africa and Egypt. Developments in African history from 1000 to 1700 varied from region to region. In North Africa, the key new factor was the imperial expansion of the Ottoman Empire as far west as Morocco. But the development of independent regional rulers soon rendered Ottoman authority in North Africa purely nominal. *page 338*

HOW DID Islam spread south of the Sahara?

The Spread of Islam South of the Sahara. Islam was introduced between the eighth century and 1800. In most cases, the process was slow, peaceful, and partial; ruling elites and traders were more likely to practice Islam, whereas most commoners followed traditional practices. *page 339*

WHAT WERE the four most important states in the Sahel between 1000 and 1600?

Sahelian Empires of the Western and Central Sudan. Several substantial states arose south of the Sahara: Ghana, Mali, Songhai, and Kanem. The ruling elites of these states converted to or were heavily influenced by Islam, although most of their populations practiced local religions or engaged in syncretism. Much of the wealth of these states was tied to their control of the trans-Saharan trade routes. *page 340*

WHY DID Christianity gradually disappear in Nubia?

The Eastern Sudan. The Nubian Christian states of Maqurra and Alwa were gradually Islamized. *page 347*

HOW DID the arrival of Europeans affect the peoples of West and central Africa?

The Forestlands: Coastal West and Central Africa. In the coastal forestlands of West Africa, a substantial kingdom arose in Benin, famous for its brass sculptures. Senegambia and the Gold Coast were influenced by contact with European traders and the introduction of food crops from the Americas. Social, political, and economic structures in Kongo and Angola were disrupted by Portuguese slave trading. *page 347*

HOW DID Swahili language and culture develop?

East Africa. On the east coast, Islam influenced the development of the distinctive Swahili culture and language, and Islamic traders linked the region to India and East Asia. Omanis gained control of Zanzibar. *page 351*

HOW DID slavery affect race relations in Cape Colony?

Southern Africa. The ruins at Great Zimbabwe leave many questions unanswered. The Portuguese followed the Zambezi to the gold fields that fed the trade at the Swahili coast, but they were unable to profit much. In southernmost Africa, Trekboers displaced Khoikhoi. The Trekboers imported slaves from India and other parts of Africa, and soon the master–slave relationship became their model for all interactions with nonwhites. *page 353*

KEY TERMS

Afrikaans (AF-rih-KAHNS) (p. 355)
apartheid (a-PART-HAYT) (p. 355)
Dar al-Islam (DAR-ahl-his-LAHM) (p. 338)
Maghreb (MUHG-ruhb) (p. 338)
mansa (MAHN-sah) (p. 343)
marabouts (MAYR-uh-booz) (p. 345)
Moors (p. 352)

muezzin (myoo-EHZ-ihn) (p. 341)
oba (OH-bah) (p. 348)
prazeros (p. 354)
Sharifs (shuh-REEFS) (p. 338)
shaykh (SHAYK) (p. 346)
Swahili (swah-HEE-lee) (p. 352)
Trekboers (TREHK-borz) (p. 355)
uzama (p. 348)

REVIEW QUESTIONS

1. Why did Islam succeed in the Sudanic belt and East Africa? What role did warfare play in its success? What role did trade have in it?

2. What is the importance of the empires of Ghana, Mali, and Songhai to world history? Why was the control of the trans-Saharan trade so important to these kingdoms? What was the importance of Islamic culture to them? Why did each of these empires break up?

3. What was the impact of the introduction of food crops from the Americas on various regions of Africa during this period?

4. How did Swahili culture form? Describe its defining characteristics. Why has its impact on the East African coast endured?

5. What was the impact of the Portuguese on East Africa and central Africa? How did European coastal activities affect the African interior?

6. Why did Ottoman influence decline in northern Africa in the eighteenth century?

7. How did the Portuguese and Dutch differ from or resemble the Arabs and other Muslims who came as outsiders to sub-Saharan Africa?

8. What is known about Great Zimbabwe? What questions remain? How might the remaining questions be answered?

9. Discuss the diversity of Cape society in South Africa before 1700. Who were the Trekboers, and what was their conflict with the Khoikhoi? How was the basis for apartheid formed in this period?

Note: To learn more about the topics in this chapter, please turn to the Suggested Readings at the end of the book. For additional sources related to this chapter please see www.myhistorylab.com

PEARSON
myhistörylab Connections

Reinforce what you learned in this chapter by studying the many documents, images, maps, review tools, and videos available at **www.myhistorylab.com**

Read and Review

✓•—⎡Study and **Review** Chapter 14

•⎡Read the Document Excerpts from Sundiata: An Epic of
Old Mali, 1235, p. 342
The Travels of Ibn Battuta "Ibn Battuta in Mali," p. 343
Al-Umari describes Mansa Musa of Mali, p. 343
Voyage from Lisbon, p. 351
Descriptions of the cities of Zanj, p. 352

⊙—⎡See the Map Trade Routes in Africa, p. 338
Discovery: The Maghrib and West Africa, Fourteenth
  Century, p. 338
East African Coast to 1600, p. 339
African Empires in the Western Sudan, p. 345
African Climate Zones and Bantu Migration Routes,
  ca. 3000 B.C.E., p. 353

•⎡View the Image Loango, the Capital of the Kingdom of
the Congo, p. 351

((•—⎡Hear the Audio Influences in Africa 2, p. 339
Influences in Africa 2, p. 348

Research and Explore

⊙⎡Watch the Video Piracy, p. 338

⊙⎡Watch the Video West African States

——— ((•—⎡**Hear** the **Audio** ———

Hear the audio file for Chapter 14
at **www.myhistorylab.com**

15

Europe to the Early 1500s: Revival, Decline, and Renaissance

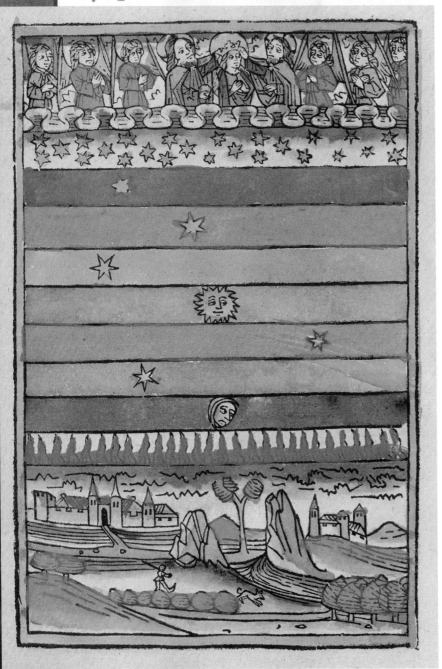

((•—Hear the Audio for Chapter 15 at www.myhistorylab.com

The Medieval Universe. In medieval Europe, the traditional geocentric or earth-centered universe was usually depicted by concentric circles. In this popular German work on natural history, medicine, and science, Konrad von Megenberg (1309–1374) depicted the universe in a most unusual but effective manner. The seven known planets are contained within straight horizontal bands that separate the earth below from heaven, populated by the saints, above.

Which realm seems more important to the artist, heaven or earth?

The High Middle Ages (the eleventh through the thirteenth centuries in Europe) were a period of political expansion and consolidation and of intellectual flowering and synthesis. The Latin, or Western, church established itself as a spiritual authority independent of secular monarchies, which became more powerful and self-aggrandizing. The parliaments and popular assemblies that accompanied the rise of these monarchies laid the foundations of modern representative institutions.

An agricultural revolution increased food supplies and populations. Trade and commerce revived, towns expanded, banking and credit developed, and a "new rich" merchant class rose to power in Europe's cities. Universities were established. Contact with the Arab world gave access to the writings of the ancient Greek philosophers, which stimulated the great expansion of Western culture during the late Middle Ages and the Renaissance.

The late Middle Ages and the Renaissance, roughly from 1300 to 1500, were a time of both unprecedented calamity and bold new beginnings in Europe. France and England grappled with each other in a bitter conflict known as the Hundred Years' War (1337–1453). Bubonic plague (the "Black Death") killed as much as one third of the population in many regions between 1348 and 1350. A schism divided the church (1378–1417). And in 1453

THE HIGH MIDDLE AGES IN WESTERN EUROPE

With its borders finally secured, Western Europe during the High Middle Ages was able to concentrate on its political institutions and cultural development, which had been ignored during the early Middle Ages. For Western Europe, the High Middle Ages were a period of clearer self-definition during which individual lands gained much of the geographic shape we recognize today. Europe also began to escape its relative isolation from the rest of the world, which had prevailed since the early Middle Ages. Two factors contributed to this increased engagement: the Crusades and renewed trade along the Silk Road linking China and Europe, made possible by the Mongol conquests in Asia.

Under the Song Dynasty (960–1279), before Mongol rule, China continued its technological advance. In addition to the printing press, the Chinese invented the abacus and gunpowder. They also enjoyed a money economy unknown in the West. But culturally, these centuries between 1000 and 1300 were closed and narrow by comparison with those of the Tang Dynasty. Politically, the Song were far more autocratic. This was also an era of expansion for Chinese trade, and one of the few in Chinese history in which merchants as a group were able to advance in wealth and status. Although the imperial reach of the Song was limited, Chinese culture in this period was more open to outside influences than in any previous era.

In the late twelfth century Japan shifted from civilian to military rule; the Kamakura *bakufu* governed by mounted warriors who were paid with rights to income from land in exchange for their military services. This rise of a military aristocracy marked the beginning of Japan's "medieval," as distinct from its "classical," period. Three Mongol invasions in the thirteenth century also fostered a strong military to resist them. With a civilian court also in existence, Japan actually had a dual government (that is, two emperors and two courts) until the fourteenth century. However, this situation differed greatly from the deep and permanent national divisions developing at this time among the emerging states and autonomous principalities of Western Europe.

the Turks captured Constantinople. But at the same time, the late Middle Ages witnessed a rebirth that would continue into the seventeenth century. Scholars began criticizing medieval assumptions about the nature of God, humankind, and society. Printing was invented, and local languages—Europe's vernaculars—gained recognition. Patriotism and incipient nationalism became major forces in the independent nation-states of Europe. ◼

REVIVAL OF EMPIRE, CHURCH, AND TOWNS

WHAT IMPACT did the Crusades have on medieval European society?

OTTO I AND THE REVIVAL OF THE EMPIRE

The fortunes of both the old empire and the papacy began to revive when the Saxon Henry I ("the Fowler"; d. 936) became the first non-Frankish king of Germany in 918. Henry rebuilt royal power. His son Otto I (r. 936–973) maneuvered his relatives into power in Bavaria, Swabia, and Franconia and then invaded Italy and proclaimed himself its king in 951. In 955 he defeated the Hungarians at Lechfeld, securing German borders against new barbarian attacks and earning the title "the Great."

Otto enlisted the help of the church in rebuilding his realm. He appointed bishops and abbots to administer his land, since these men possessed a sense of universal empire but they could not marry and found families to compete with his own. In 961, Otto responded to a call for help from Pope John XII (955–964), and in 962, Otto received in return an imperial coronation. The church was brought ever more under royal control, but it was increasingly determined to assert its independence.

THE REVIVING CATHOLIC CHURCH: THE CLUNY REFORM MOVEMENT AND THE INVESTITURE STRUGGLE

Otto's successors became so preoccupied with Italy that they allowed their German base to disintegrate. As the German Empire began to crumble in the eleventh century, the church, unhappy under imperial domination, declared its independence by embracing the Cluny reform.

The great monastery at Cluny had been founded in 910 in east-central France. The Cluny reformers maintained that clergy should not be subservient to kings; clergy should

Within the many developing autonomous Islamic lands at this time, the teachings of Muhammad created an international culture. Religious identity enabled Muslims to transcend their new and often very deep regional divisions. Similarly, Christianity allowed Englishmen, Frenchmen, Germans, and Italians to think of themselves as one people and to unite in crusades to the Holy Land. As these Crusades got under way in the late eleventh century, Islam too was on the march, penetrating Anatolia and Afghanistan and impinging upon India, where it met a new challenge in Hinduism.

The legacy of the Crusades was mixed. They accomplished few of the goals that originally motivated the European Crusaders; the Holy Land remained under Islamic control, the Crusader kingdoms there collapsed within a few generations of their founding, and the animosity toward Christians fostered by the Crusades resonates even today in the Middle East. Still, the Crusades brought Europeans into more direct and frequent contact with the non-European world than they had known since the heyday of the Roman Empire. Crusaders sampled and sent home products from the Middle East, Asia, and North Africa, creating new tastes in food, art, and even fashion. The resulting growth in demand for these products impelled rising numbers of European merchants to seek these products beyond Europe. Eventually Europeans sought to bypass the Islamic world entirely and secure supplies of Eastern products, especially spices, by going directly to the sources in India and East Asia. By such development European isolation was ended.

Focus Questions

- ◆ How did the High Middle Ages in Europe differ from the early Middle Ages?

- ◆ What was the legacy of the Crusades for Europe? In what ways did they signal the start of new relationships between Europe and the wider world?

serve under the direct authority of the pope. They denounced "secular" parish clergy, who lived with concubines in marriage-like relationships. Distinctive features of Western religion—separation of church and state, and the celibacy of the Catholic clergy—had their origins in the Cluny reform movement. From Cluny, reformers were dispatched throughout France and Italy, and in the late eleventh century the papacy embraced their proposals.

Pope Gregory VII (r. 1073–1085) advocated other reforms, too. In 1075, he condemned under penalty of excommunication the well-established custom of a king appointing bishops to administer his estates, "investing" them with the ring and staff that symbolized their ecclesiastical office. Emperor Henry IV of Germany saw this as a direct challenge to his authority. In contrast, Germany's territorial princes supported the pope, for they believed that anything that weakened the emperor strengthened them.

The lines of battle were quickly drawn. Henry assembled his loyal German bishops at Worms in January 1076 and had them proclaim their independence from Gregory. Gregory promptly excommunicated Henry and absolved all Henry's subjects from loyalty to him. The German princes were delighted, and Henry faced a general revolt. He had no choice but to come to terms with Gregory. In a famous scene, he prostrated himself outside the pope's castle in northern Italy in January 1077, reportedly standing barefoot in the snow off and on for three days before the pope gave him absolution. Papal power seemed to triumph, but the struggle was not yet over.

The Investiture Controversy was finally settled in 1122 with the Concordat of Worms in which the new Emperor Henry V (r. 1106–1125) agreed not to invest bishops with the ring and staff, and Pope Calixtus II (r. 1119–1124) recognized the emperor's right to grant bishops their secular fiefs. The emperor effectively retained the right to nominate or veto a candidate. The settlement created separate spheres of ecclesiastical and secular authority; it also set the stage for future conflicts between church and state.

THE CRUSADES

What the Cluny reform was to the clergy, the **Crusades** to the Holy Land were to the laity: an outlet for the heightened religiosity of the late eleventh and twelfth centuries.

QUICK REVIEW

Church and State

- ◆ Investiture crisis centered on authority to appoint and control clergy

- ◆ Pope Gregory excommunicated Henry IV when Henry proclaimed his independence from the papacy

- ◆ Crisis settled in 1122 with Concordat of Worms

Crusades
Religious wars directed by the church against "infidels" and "heretics."

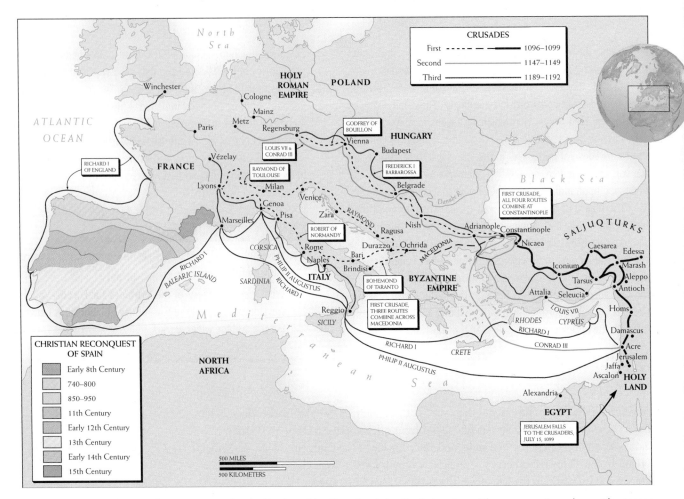

MAP 15–1. The Early Crusades. Routes and several leaders of the Crusades during the first century of the movement are shown. The names on this map do not exhaust the list of great nobles who went on the First Crusade. The even showier array of monarchs of the Second and Third Crusades still left the Crusades, on balance, ineffective in achieving their goals.

What obstacles did the Crusaders encounter?

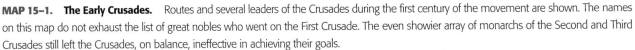

Late in the eleventh century, the Byzantine Empire was under severe pressure from the Seljuk Turks. The Eastern emperor, Alexius I Comnenus, appealed for Western aid. At the Council of Clermont in 1095, Pope Urban II responded by launching the First Crusade. Scholars debate the motives of the Crusaders. Genuine religious piety played a major part. The papacy promised Crusaders forgiveness for all their sins should they die in battle, and a crusade to the Holy Land was the ultimate religious pilgrimage. The pope and others may also have hoped to stabilize the West by sending large numbers of restless, feuding young nobles off to foreign lands. (About 100,000 took part in the First Crusade.) Younger sons of noblemen, for whom there were no estates at home, may have hoped that a crusade would make their fortunes. Urban also saw the Crusades as an opportunity to reconcile Eastern and Western Christianity.

Drawn by the dream of liberating the holy city of Jerusalem, which the Seljuk Turks had held since the seventh century, three great armies gathered in France, Germany, and Italy. As the Crusaders marched by different overland routes toward Constantinople, they seized the opportunity to rid Europe of Jews as well as Muslims. Jewish communities, especially in the Rhineland, suffered bloody pogroms (see Map 15–1).

The Eastern emperor was suspicious of the uncouth, spirited soldiers who gathered at his capital, and his subjects, whose villages the Westerners plundered, were openly hostile. Nevertheless, the Crusaders succeeded in doing what Byzantine armies had failed to do. They routed the Seljuks, and on July 15, 1099, they took the city of Jerusalem. They owed their success to their superior military discipline and weaponry and to the fact that the Muslims failed to unite to oppose them.

The victorious Crusaders set up a "kingdom of Jerusalem" composed of a number of tiny feudal states. These were tenuously held islands in a sea of Muslims intent on their destruction. As the Crusaders built castles for the defense of their new territories, their focus shifted from conquest to economic development. Some, like the military-religious order of the Knights Templar, acquired vast fortunes.

After about forty years, the Crusader states began to fall. The Second Crusade, preached by the Cistercian monk Bernard of Clairvaux (1091–1153), attempted a rescue but met with dismal failure. In October 1187, Saladin (r. 1138–1193), king of Egypt and Syria, reconquered Jerusalem, a victory so brilliant and unexpected that Pope Urban III was said to have dropped dead upon hearing about it. Save for a brief interlude in the thirteenth century, the holiest of cities remained in Islamic hands until the twentieth century.

The Third Crusade in the twelfth century (1189–1192) attempted to reclaim Jerusalem, under three of Europe's greatest rulers: Richard the Lion-Hearted of England, Frederick Barbarossa of the Holy Roman Empire, and Philip Augustus of France. Barbarossa died in an accident en route to the front, and Philip Augustus returned to France to prey on Richard's lands. Left alone, Richard could do little. On his way home, Richard was captured by Emperor Henry VI. England paid a huge ransom to win his release. Popular resentment at the failed, costly venture contributed to the events that produced the Magna Carta in 1215, an effort to curb the power of England's kings.

Politically and religiously the first three Crusades were a failure. But they stimulated Western trade with the East, as Venetian, Pisan, and Genoan merchants followed the Crusaders across Byzantium to lucrative new markets.

Venetian commercial ambitions shaped the Fourth Crusade. Thirty thousand Crusaders gathered in Venice in 1202, intending to sail to Egypt. When they could not raise the money to pay for their transport, they negotiated: In exchange for passage, they agreed to take the rival Christian port of Zara for Venice. Europe was stunned, but worse was to come. The Crusaders were next diverted to Constantinople, which fell to their assault in 1204. A Latin ascended the Byzantine throne, and Venice became the dominant commercial power in the eastern Mediterranean.

Pope Innocent III was chagrined by the misdirection of a Crusade he had authorized, but once Constantinople was in Latin hands, he changed his mind. The opportunity to bring Greek Christians under the control of the Latin church was too tempting. The Greeks, however, could not be reconciled to Latin rule, and in 1261 the man they recognized as their legitimate emperor, Michael Paleologus, recaptured the city. He had help from Venice's rival, Genoa. The Fourth Crusade did nothing to heal the political and religious divisions that separated East and West.

TOWNS AND TOWNSPEOPLE

In the eleventh and twelfth centuries, most towns were small. Only about 5 percent of western Europe's population were urban dwellers, but they were some of the most creative members of medieval society.

•••—Read the **Document**
Arab-Syrian Gentleman Discusses Franks
at **myhistorylab.com**

👁—See the **Map**
The Major Crusades
at **myhistorylab.com**

•••—Read the **Document**
The Magna Carta 1215
at **myhistorylab.com**

((•—Hear the **Audio**
at **myhistorylab.com**

CHRONOLOGY

THE CRUSADES

1095	Pope Urban II launches the First Crusade
1099	The Crusaders take Jerusalem
1147–1149	The Second Crusade
1187	Jerusalem retaken by the Muslims under Saladin
1189–1192	Third Crusade
1202–1204	Fourth Crusade

Foundry in Florence. Skilled workers were an integral component of the commerce of medieval towns. This scene shows the manufacture of cannons in a foundry in Florence.

What parts of this image are most detailed? Why?

A Closer Look

European Embrace of a Black Saint

St. Maurice, patron saint of Magdeburg, Germany, was a third-century Egyptian Christian, who commanded the Egyptian legion of the Roman army in Gaul. In 286 C.E. he and his soldiers were executed for impiety after refusing to worship the Roman gods. Maurice's cult began in 515, and he became a favorite saint of Charlemagne and other pious, warring German kings.

Portrayed as a white man for centuries, St. Maurice first appeared as a black man in the mid-thirteenth century. In the era of the Crusades, rulers had their eyes on new possessions in the Orient, and an Eastern-looking patron saint (Maurice) seemed the perfect talisman as Western merchants and armies ventured forth to trade and conquer. At this time, artists also began to paint as a black man one of the three Magi who visited baby Jesus on his birthday. The name Maurice was close to the German word for black dye ("Mauro") and later Moors ("Mohren"). Progressively, the third-century saint was transformed into a black African. By the fifteenth and sixteenth centuries, his head adorned the coats-of-arms of leading Nuremberg families who traded in the Near East, among them the Tuchers, Nuremberg's great cloth merchants, and Albrecht Dürer, Germany's most famous Renaissance artist.

Questions

1. Did Charlemagne and other German kings embrace Maurice as their favorite saint for mercenary, religious, or military motives?

2. Was racism behind the portrayal of Maurice as a white man for eleven centuries, before painters presented him as the black saint he had always been?

3. Why would some of Nuremberg's wealthy, leading families adorn their coats-of-arms with the head of an African saint?

Towns were dominated at first by the feudal lords whose charters guaranteed the towns' safety. The purpose of towns was originally to concentrate skilled laborers who could manufacture the finished goods desired by lords and bishops. As towns grew, they attracted serfs who used their skills and industriousness to raise themselves into higher social ranks. Lords in the countryside had to offer serfs better terms of tenure to keep them on the land, so the growth of towns improved conditions for all serfs.

The first merchants may have been enterprising serfs. Long-distance traders were often people who had nothing to lose and everything to gain from the enormous risks of foreign trade. They traveled together in armed caravans and convoys, buying goods and products as cheaply as possible at the source and selling them for all they could get in Western ports (see Map 15–2 on page 366). Merchants were outside the traditional social groups of nobility, clergy, and peasantry, but as they gained wealth, they gained respect and imitators. They also challenged traditional authority.

Townspeople needed simple, uniform laws and a government sympathetic to new forms of business activity. Commerce was incompatible with the fortress mentality of the lords of the countryside. Merchants especially wanted to end the arbitrary tolls and tariffs imposed by regional magnates. Small shopkeepers and artisans identified far more with merchants than with aloof lords and bishops. The lesser nobility (small knights) outside the towns also supported the new mercantile economy. During the eleventh and twelfth centuries, the burgher upper classes successfully challenged the old noble urban lords. Towns allied with kings against the nobility in the countryside, rearranging the centers of power and dissolving classic feudal government. Many towns in the High and Late Middle Ages formed their own independent communes.

With urban autonomy came new models of self-government. Around 1100 the old urban nobility and the new burgher upper class merged into an urban patriciate. From this new ruling class was born the aristocratic town council. Enriching and complicating the situation was the fact that small artisans and craftspeople slowly developed their own protective associations or **guilds** and began to gain a voice in government. The towns' opportunities for the "little person" had created the slogan "Town air brings freedom." Townspeople thought of themselves as citizens with basic rights, not subjects at the mercy of their masters' whim.

Towns became a major force in the transition from feudal societies to national governments. They were a ready source of educated bureaucrats and lawyers who knew Roman law, the tool for running the state. Money earned by townspeople enabled kings to hire their own armies, freeing them from dependence on the nobility. Towns, in turn, won royal political recognition and had their constitutions guaranteed. In France, towns became integrated early into royal government. In Germany, they fell under ever tighter control by the princes. In Italy, uniquely, towns became genuine city-states during the Renaissance.

Towns attracted Jews, who plied trades in small businesses. Many became wealthy as moneylenders to kings, popes, and businesspeople. Jewish intellectual and religious culture both dazzled and threatened Christians. Suspicion and distrust among Christians led to an unprecedented surge in anti-Jewish sentiment in the late twelfth and early thirteenth centuries.

In the twelfth century, translations and commentaries by Byzantine and Spanish Islamic scholars introduced western Europeans to the works of Aristotle, Euclid, and Ptolemy, the texts of Greek physicians and Arab mathematicians, and the corpus of Roman law. The resulting intellectual ferment gave rise to modern Western universities such as Bologna (established 1158) and the University of Paris.

In the High Middle Ages, people assumed that truth was already known and only needed to be properly organized, elucidated, and defended. Under this model of learning, known as **Scholasticism**, students summarized and compared the traditional authorities,

QUICK REVIEW

Town Charters

- Towns originally dominated by feudal lords
- Town charters granted townspeople safety and independence
- Growth of towns improved conditions for serfs generally

The University of Bologna in central Italy was distinguished as the center for the revival of Roman law. This carving on the tomb of a Bolognese professor of law shows students attending one of his lectures.

Why were universities important in medieval history?

guild

An association of merchants or craftsmen that offered protection to its members and set rules for their work and products.

Scholasticism

Method of study based on logic and dialectic that dominated the medieval schools. It assumed that truth already existed; students had only to organize, elucidate, and defend knowledge learned from authoritative texts, especially those of Aristotle and the Church Fathers.

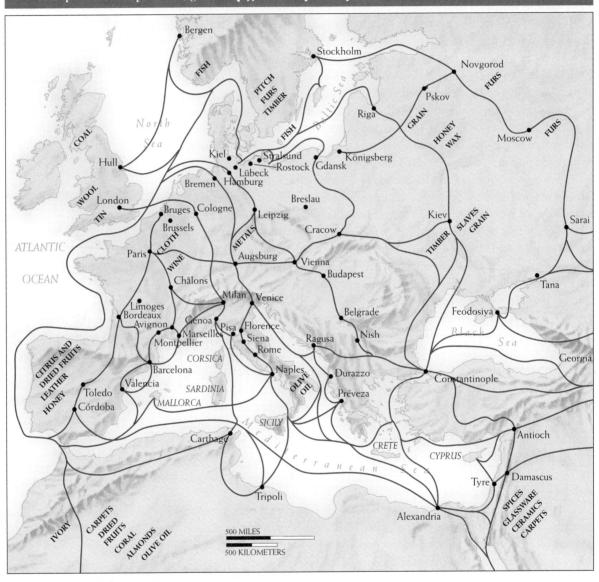

MAP 15–2.   Medieval Trade Routes and Regional Products.   Trade in Europe varied in intensity and geographical extent in different periods during the Middle Ages. The map shows some of the channels that came to be used in interregional commerce. Labels tell part of what was carried in that commerce.

How strong were the connections among Europe, the Middle East, and Africa at this time?

elaborated their arguments pro and con, and drew the logical conclusions. After Aristotle's works were popularized in the West, logic and dialectic became the new tools for disciplining thought and knowledge. Dialectic was the art of discovering a truth by pondering the arguments against it. Together with aspiring philosophers, theologians, and lawyers, even medical students learned their vocation by debating the authoritative texts in their field, not by clinical medical practice.

Peter Abelard (1079–1142) was the boldest advocate for the new Aristotelian learning. The leading philosopher and theologian of his day, he became Master of Students at Notre Dame. His thinking was unique in its appreciation of subjectivity. He claimed, for instance, that a person's motives determined whether the person's actions were good or evil, not the acts themselves. He also said that an individual's feeling of repentance was a more important factor in receiving God's forgiveness than the church's sacrament of penance.

His audacious logical critique of religious doctrine earned him powerful enemies. Abelard, as he laments in his autobiography, played into their hands by seducing Heloise, a young woman he was hired to tutor. She was the niece of a powerful church leader. After she became pregnant, Abelard wed her—but kept the marriage secret, for university teachers, like clergy, were required to be celibate. Her uncle hired men to castrate Abelard. Thereafter he became a monk, and she entered a convent. They exchanged letters in which he denigrated his love for her as wretched desire. Repentance failed to ingratiate him with the church authorities. In 1121, his works were burned, and in 1140, nineteen propositions that he had taught were condemned as heresies. Heloise outlived him by twenty years and won renown for her efforts to improve conditions for cloistered women.

•◦◈—Read the Document
Abelard Defends Himself
at **myhistorylab.com**

regular clergy
Monks and nuns who belong to religious orders.

secular clergy
Parish clergy who did not belong to a religious order.

MEDIEVAL SOCIETY

THE ORDER OF LIFE

In the art and literature of the Middle Ages, three basic social groups were represented: the landed nobility; the clergy; the peasantry and village artisans. After the eleventh century, long-distance traders and merchants emerged as a fourth social group.

No medieval social group was absolutely uniform. Noblemen formed a broad spectrum. Dignity and status within the nobility were directly related to the exercise of authority over others. By the Late Middle Ages, separate classes of higher and lower nobility had evolved in both town and country. The higher were the great landowners and territorial magnates, long the dominant powers in their regions; the lower were petty landlords, the descendants of minor knights, newly rich merchants, or wealthy farmers.

Waging war was the nobleman's sole profession. In the eighth century, the adoption of stirrups made mounted warriors Europe's most valued military assets. The chief virtues of these knights were physical strength, courage, and belligerency.

By the Late Middle Ages, several factors forced the landed nobility into a steep economic and political decline from which it never recovered. Climatic changes and agricultural failures created large famines, while the great plague (discussed later) brought about unprecedented population losses. Changing military tactics (the use of infantry and heavy artillery during the Hundred Years' War) made the noble cavalry nearly obsolete. And the alliance of wealthy towns with the king weakened the nobility. After the fourteenth century, land and wealth counted for far more than lineage as qualification for entrance into the highest social class.

Unlike the nobility or peasantry, one was not born into the clerical estate. It was acquired by religious training and ordination and was, in theory, open to anyone. There were two fundamental categories of clergy. The **regular clergy** were the monks who lived according to a special ascetic rule (*regula*) in cloisters apart from the world. In the thirteenth century, two new orders were sanctioned, the Franciscans and the Dominicans, whose members went out into the world to preach the church's mission and to combat heresy. The **secular clergy**, who lived and worked directly among the laity in the world (*saeculum*), formed a vast hierarchy. At the top were the wealthy cardinals, archbishops, and bishops. Below them were the urban priests, the cathedral canons, and the court clerks. Finally, there was the great mass of poor parish priests, who were neither financially nor intellectually much above the common people they served.

During most of the Middle Ages, the clergy were honored as the first estate, and theology was the queen of the sciences. There was great reverence for the clergy's function as mediators between God and humanity. The priest brought the Son of God down to

WHAT NEW group was added to the three traditional groups in medieval society?

Dominicans (top) and Franciscans (bottom). Unlike the other religious orders, the Dominicans and Franciscans did not live in cloisters but wandered about preaching and combating heresy. They depended for support on their own labor and the kindness of the laity.

Cliche Bibliothèque Nationale de France, Paris.

Why are books so prominent in both these images?

earth when he celebrated the sacrament of the Eucharist, and his absolution released penitents from punishment for sin. Mere laypeople did not presume to judge priests.

The largest and lowest social group in medieval society was one on whose labor the welfare of all others depended: the agrarian peasantry. Many peasants lived and worked on the manors of the nobility. The lord of the manor required a certain amount of produce (grain, eggs, and the like) and services from the peasant families, and he held judicial and police authority over them. The lord owned and operated the machines that processed crops into food and drink, and he had the right to subject his tenants to exactions known as *banalities*. He could, for example, force them to breed their cows with his bull, and pay for the privilege, or make their wine in his wine press. The lord also collected as an inheritance tax a serf's best animal. Without the lord's permission, a serf could neither travel nor marry outside the manor in which he served. Serfs were not chattel slaves, however. It was to a lord's advantage to keep his serfs healthy and happy; his welfare, like theirs, depended on a successful harvest. Serfs had their own dwellings and modest strips of land, and they lived off the produce of their own labor. They could sell any surpluses, and serfs could pass their property on to their children.

Two basic changes transformed the peasantry during the Middle Ages. The first was the increasing importance of single-family holdings: As families retained property from generation to generation, family farms replaced manorial units. The second was the conversion of the serf's dues into money payments, a change made possible by the revival of trade and the return of a monetary economy. By the thirteenth century, many peasants held their land as rent-paying tenants and no longer had servile status.

In the mid-fourteenth century, when the great plague and the Hundred Years' War created a labor shortage, nobles in England and France tried to turn back the clock by increasing taxes on the peasantry and restricting their migration to the cities. Their efforts triggered rebellions, which were brutally crushed. As growing national sentiment would break European society's political unity, and heretical movements end its nominal religious unity, the peasantry's revolts revealed the absence of medieval social unity.

MEDIEVAL WOMEN

The image of women in the Middle Ages was quite different than the reality of women's lives. The image was sketched by celibate male clergy who viewed virginity as morally superior to marriage and claimed that women were physically, mentally, and morally inferior to men. They defined only two respectable roles for women: subjugated housewife or confined nun. Many medieval women were neither.

The clerical view of women was contradicted both within the church itself and in secular society. During the twelfth and thirteenth centuries, the burgeoning popularity of the cult of the Virgin Mary, of chivalric romances, and of courtly love literature celebrated women as natural moral superiors of men. Peter Lombard (1100–1169), an influential theologian, taught that God created Eve from Adam's rib because God intended woman neither to rule nor to be ruled but to be at man's side as his partner in a mutual relationship.

Germanic law treated women better than Roman law had done, recognizing basic rights. German women could inherit, administer, and dispose of property, and they could take men to court and sue for bodily injury and rape. German women married husbands of similar age, and a German bride was entitled to a gift of property from her husband that she retained in case of his death.

The nunnery was an option for single women who could afford it: Entrance required a dowry. Within a nunnery a woman could rise to a position of leadership and exercise authority, but even cloistered women had to submit to supervision by male clergy. The number of women in cloisters was never very large; in late medieval England no more than 3,500 women entered the cloister.

QUICK REVIEW

Peasant Life

◆ Peasants were the largest and lowest social group

◆ Many peasants worked on manors

◆ Serfs were not chattel slaves

Medieval Marketplace. A fifteenth-century rendering of an eleventh- or twelfth-century marketplace. Medieval women were active in all trades, but especially in the food and clothing industries.

© Scala/Art Resource, New York.

How did the realities of women's lives compare to the image cultivated by Christian clergy?

In the ninth century, the Carolingian monarchs obeyed the church and began to enforce monogamy. This was both a gain and a loss for women. Wives were accorded greater dignity and legal security, but their burdens as household managers and bearers of children multiplied. The life span of Frankish women decreased in the ninth century.

The vast majority of medieval women worked for income. Between the ages of 10 and 15, girls and boys were apprenticed to learn productive trades. Married women often operated their own shops or became partners in the shops of their husbands. Women appeared in virtually every "blue-collar" trade, from butcher to goldsmith, but mostly worked in the food and clothing industries. Women belonged to guilds, just like men, and they could become craftmasters, but they were paid less than men who did the same jobs. In the late Middle Ages, townswomen had some opportunities for schooling and to acquire **vernacular** literacy, but they were excluded from the learned professions of scholarship, medicine, and law.

vernacular
The everyday language spoken by the people, as opposed to Latin.

GROWTH OF NATIONAL MONARCHIES

ENGLAND: HASTINGS (1066) TO MAGNA CARTA (1215)

Medieval England's political destiny was determined by the response to the death of the childless Anglo-Saxon ruler Edward the Confessor (r. 1042–1066). Through a connection with Edward's mother, a Norman princess, Duke William of Normandy (d. 1087) laid claim to the English throne. The Anglo-Saxon assembly preferred a native nobleman, Harold Godwinsson (ca. 1022–1066). William invaded England, defeating Harold's army at Hastings on October 14, 1066. William I "the Conqueror" was crowned king of England in Westminster Abbey.

William established a strong monarchy but kept the Anglo-Saxon tax system, the practice of court writs (legal warnings) as a flexible form of central control over localities, and the Anglo-Saxon quasi-democratic tradition of frequent *parleying*—that is, the holding of conferences between the king and lesser powers who had vested interests in royal decisions. The result was a balancing of monarchical and parliamentary elements that continues to characterize English government today.

William's grandson, Henry II (r. 1154–1189), had large French holdings through inheritance and his marriage to Eleanor of Aquitaine (1122–1204). Henry II's increasing autocracy was met with strong political resistance from both the nobility and the clergy. Under Henry's successors, the brothers Richard the Lion-Hearted (r. 1189–1199) and John (r. 1199–1216), burdensome taxation turned resistance into rebellion. With the full support of the clergy and the townspeople, the barons forced King John to recognize the **Magna Carta** ("Great Charter") in 1215, a document that reaffirmed traditional rights and personal liberties. This famous cornerstone of modern English law put limits on royal power and secured the right of representation in government to the privileged.

HOW DID England and France develop strong royal governments by the thirteenth century?

▪●◆ Read the **Document**
The Battle of Hastings 1066
at **myhistorylab.com**

◉ See the **Map**
England and France ca. 1180
at **myhistorylab.com**

Magna Carta
The "Great Charter" limiting royal power that the English nobility forced King John to sign in 1215.

Battle of Hastings. William the Conqueror on horseback urging his troops into combat with the English at the Battle of Hastings (October 14, 1066).

Detail from the Bayeux Tapestry, scene 51, c. 1073–1083. Musee de la Tapisserie, Bayeaux, France. Photo copyright Bridgeman-Giraudon/Art Resource, New York.

How did changes in military tactics influence relationships between monarchs and nobles in the Middle Ages?

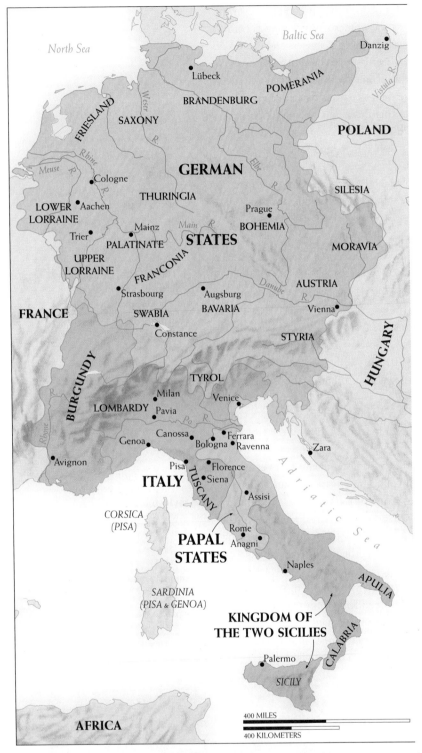

FRANCE: BOUVINES (1214) TO THE REIGN OF LOUIS IX

Powerful feudal princes dominated France from the beginning of the Capetian Dynasty (987) until the reign of Philip II Augustus (1180–1223). During this period, the Capetian kings wisely concentrated their limited resources on securing the territory surrounding Paris, by then the center of French government and culture.

The Duke of Normandy, who after 1066 was master of England, was also a vassal of the French king. Philip Augustus acted decisively to maintain control over his Norman vassal: His armies occupied all the English territories on the French coast except for Aquitaine. At Bouvines on July 27, 1214, the French won handily over the English and their German allies. The victory unified France around the monarchy and thereby laid the foundation for French ascendancy in the Late Middle Ages.

Louis IX (r. 1226–1270), the grandson of Philip Augustus, embodied the medieval view of the perfect ruler. He inherited a unified and secure kingdom. Under him, the efficient French bureaucracy became an instrument of order and fair play in local government. He sent royal commissioners to monitor the local officials and act as champions of the people. Louis abolished private wars and serfdom within his own royal domain, gave his subjects the right of appeal from local to higher courts, and made the tax system more equitable. The French people came to associate their king with justice, and a unifying national identity grew strong.

During Louis's reign, French society and culture became an example to all of Europe, a pattern that continued into the modern period. Northern France became the showcase of monastic reform, chivalry, and Gothic art and architecture. It was the golden age of Scholasticism, and Europe's greatest thinkers converged on Paris.

THE HOHENSTAUFEN EMPIRE (1152–1272)

While stable governments developed in both England and France during the Middle Ages, the Holy Roman Empire fragmented (see Map 15–3). Frederick I Barbarossa (1152–1190), the first of the Hohenstaufens, reestablished

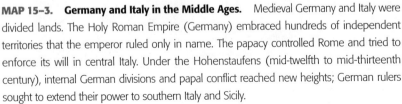

MAP 15–3. Germany and Italy in the Middle Ages. Medieval Germany and Italy were divided lands. The Holy Roman Empire (Germany) embraced hundreds of independent territories that the emperor ruled only in name. The papacy controlled Rome and tried to enforce its will in central Italy. Under the Hohenstaufens (mid-twelfth to mid-thirteenth century), internal German divisions and papal conflict reached new heights; German rulers sought to extend their power to southern Italy and Sicily.

Why were emperors unable to unite Germany and Italy in the Middle Ages?

imperial authority but also initiated a new phase in the contest between popes and emperors. In 1186 his son—the future Henry VI (r. 1190–1197)—married Constance, heiress to the kingdom of Sicily. The Papal States were now encircled, antagonizing the popes. When Henry VI died in 1197, Germany was thrown into civil war. Henry VI's four-year-old son, Frederick, had for his own safety been made a ward of Pope Innocent III (r. 1198–1215). Innocent had both the motive and the means to challenge the Hohenstaufens.

In December 1212, the pope supported his ward's coronation as Emperor Frederick II. But Frederick soon disappointed his papal sponsor by giving the German princes what they wanted—undisputed authority over their territories. Germany was fragmenting into petty kingdoms. The papacy punished Frederick by excommunicating him (four times) and leading German princes in revolt against him. This transformation of the papacy into a formidable political and military power made the church highly vulnerable to criticism from religious reformers and royal apologists.

When Frederick died in 1250, the German monarchy died with him. The princes established an electoral college in 1257 to pick the emperor, and the "king of the Romans" became their puppet.

POLITICAL AND SOCIAL BREAKDOWN

HUNDRED YEARS' WAR

The Hundred Years' War (1337–1453) started when the English king Edward III (r. 1327–1377), grandson of Philip the Fair of France (r. 1285–1314), claimed the French throne. But the war was more than a dynastic quarrel. England and France were territorial and economic rivals with a long history of animosity, making the Hundred Years' War a struggle for national identity.

France had three times the population of England, was far wealthier, and fought on its own soil. But most major battles were stunning English victories. Unlike England, France was still struggling to make the transition from a fragmented feudal society to a centralized modern state. France's defeats also resulted from incompetent leadership and English military superiority. The English infantry was more disciplined than the French, and English archers could fire six arrows a minute with enough force to pierce the armor of a knight at 200 yards. Eventually, thanks in part to the inspiring leadership of Joan of Arc (1412–1431) and a sense of national identity and self-confidence, the French were able to expel the English. By 1453, all that remained to the English was their coastal enclave of Calais.

The Hundred Years' War had lasting political and social consequences. It devastated France, but it also awakened French nationalism and hastened the country's transition from a feudal monarchy to a centralized state. In both France and England the burden of the war fell most heavily on the peasantry, who were forced to support it with taxes and services.

THE BLACK DEATH

Agricultural improvements spurred population growth in the Late Middle Ages. Europe's population roughly doubled between the years 1000 and 1300. There were more people than there was food to feed them or jobs to employ them, and the average European faced the probability of extreme hunger at least once during his or her expected thirty-five-year life span. Between 1315 and 1317, for example, cold weather and crop failures produced a great famine. Decades of overpopulation, economic depression, famine, and bad health made Europeans vulnerable to a virulent plague that struck with full force in 1348.

WHAT WERE the consequences of the Black Death?

See the Map
The Hundred Years' War
at **myhistorylab.com**

See the Map
The 100 Years' War
at **myhistorylab.com**

See the Map
Black Death and Peasant Revolts
at **myhistorylab.com**

Read the Document
Black Death, 1349, Henry Knighton
at **myhistorylab.com**

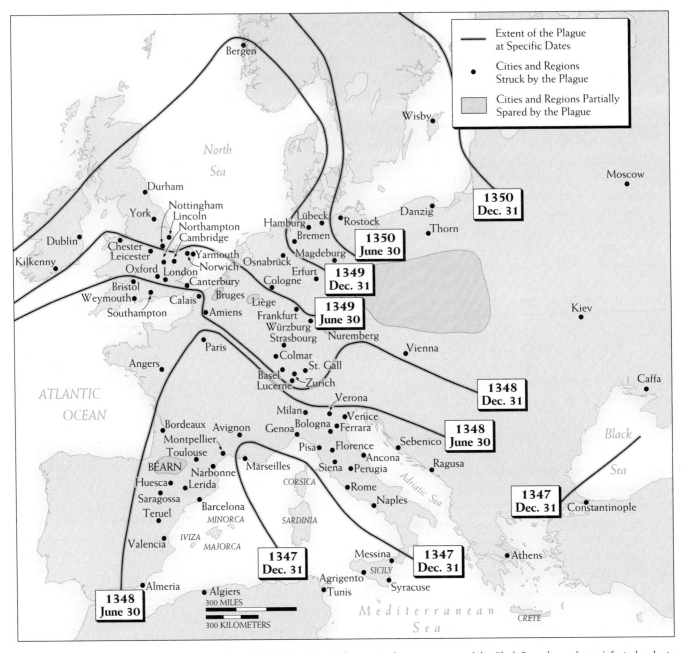

MAP 15–4. Spread of the Black Death. Apparently introduced by sea-borne rats from areas around the Black Sea where plague-infested rodents have long been known, the Black Death had great human, social, and economic consequences. According to one of the lower estimates, it killed 25 million people in Europe. The map charts the spread of the plague in the mid-fourteenth century. Generally following trade routes, it reached Scandinavia by 1350, and some believe it then went on to Iceland and even Greenland. Areas off the main trade routes were largely spared.

What were some social and economic consequences of the plague?

Black Death

The bubonic plague that killed millions of Europeans in the fourteenth century.

The **Black Death**, so-called because it discolored the body, followed the trade routes from Asia into Europe. Appearing in Sicily in late 1347, it entered Europe through the port cities of Venice, Genoa, and Pisa in 1348, and swept rapidly northward. Areas outside the major trade routes, like Bohemia, remained virtually unaffected. Bubonic plague made numerous reappearances in succeeding decades. It is estimated that western Europe had lost as much as two-fifths of its population by the early fifteenth century (see Map 15–4).

The plague was transmitted by fleas and rats, but it also entered the lungs and could be spread by sneezes. Contemporary physicians had little understanding of how diseases worked. Popular wisdom held that bad air caused the disease. Some thought that earthquakes had released poisonous fumes. Psychological reactions varied tremendously. Some hoped that moderation and temperance would save them; some indulged in sexual promiscuity; some fled in panic; some developed a morbid religiosity. Parades of flagellants whipped themselves, hoping to induce God to show mercy and intervene. Jews were baselessly accused of spreading the disease, and pogroms flared. The church tried to maintain order, but across western Europe people developed an obsession with death and a deep pessimism that endured for decades.

Whole villages vanished. The labor supply shrank, so wages increased and those of skilled artisans soared. Many serfs substituted money payments for their labor services and pursued more rewarding jobs in the cities. Agricultural prices fell because of lowered demand, and the price of luxury and manufactured goods—the work of skilled artisans—rose. The noble landholders suffered the greatest decline in power. They were forced to pay more for finished products and for farm labor, while receiving a smaller return on their agricultural produce. Rents declined everywhere.

Some landowners converted arable land to sheep pasture, substituting more profitable wool production for labor-intensive grain crops. The propertied classes also used their political influence to pass repressive legislation that forced peasants to stay on their farms and froze wages at low levels. The result was an eruption of peasant rebellions in France and England.

Although the plague hit urban populations hard, cities recovered relatively quickly. Cities had always protected their interests by regulating competition and immigration from rural areas. After the plague, the reach of such laws was extended to include the lands of nobles and landlords, many of whom were now integrated into urban life. Guilds used their political influence to pass restrictive legislation that protected their markets. Master artisans wanted to keep their numbers low to limit competition, but the journeymen they employed wanted access to the guild so that they could set up shops of their own. To the old conflict between the urban patriciate and the guilds was now added a struggle within the guilds themselves.

There was gain as well as loss for the church, too. Many clergy died—up to one-third in places—as they dutifully ministered to the sick and dying. As a great landholder, the church's income and, therefore, its political influence declined. But it received new revenues from the vastly increased demand for religious services for the dead and the dying and from new gifts and bequests.

Watch the Video
at **myhistorylab.com**

QUICK REVIEW

The Black Death

- Popular name for bubonic plague
- High mortality
- Spread along trade routes
- Many contemporary theories about its causes and cure
- Altered fundamental socioeconomic relationships

Black Death. Men and women carrying plague victims in coffins to the burial ground in Tournai, Belgium, 1349.

How did the high mortality rates of the Black Death alter socioeconomic relationships?

Read the Document
Peasant Revolt in England
at **myhistorylab.com**

ECCLESIASTICAL BREAKDOWN AND REVIVAL: THE LATE MEDIEVAL CHURCH

BONIFACE VIII AND PHILIP THE FAIR

By the fourteenth century popes faced rulers far more powerful than themselves. When Pope Boniface VIII (r. 1294–1303) issued a bull, *Clericis Laicos*, which forbade lay taxation of the clergy without prior papal approval, King Philip the Fair of France (r. 1285–1314) unleashed a ruthless antipapal campaign. Boniface made a last-ditch stand against state control of national churches when he issued the bull *Unam Sanctam* in

WHY DID France's king support the Great Schism?

Read the Document
Unam Sanctam 1302, Pope Boniface VIII
at **myhistorylab.com**

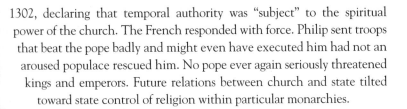

Papal Authority. Pope Boniface VIII (r. 1294–1303), who opposed the taxation of the clergy by the kings of France and England, issued one of the strongest declarations of papal authority, the bull *Unam Sanctam*. This statue is in the Museo Civico, Bologna, Italy.

Scala/Art Resource, New York.

Why did royal power grow relative to papal power in this period?

Curia
The papal government.

Great Schism
The appearance of two, and at times three, rival popes between 1378 and 1415.

Holy Roman Empire
The revival of the old Roman Empire, based mainly in Germany and northern Italy, that endured from 870 to 1806.

1302, declaring that temporal authority was "subject" to the spiritual power of the church. The French responded with force. Philip sent troops that beat the pope badly and might even have executed him had not an aroused populace rescued him. No pope ever again seriously threatened kings and emperors. Future relations between church and state tilted toward state control of religion within particular monarchies.

THE GREAT SCHISM (1378–1417) AND THE CONCILIAR MOVEMENT TO 1449

Boniface VIII's successor, Clement V (r. 1305–1314), moved the papal court to Avignon on the southeastern border with France, where it remained until Pope Gregory XI (r. 1370–1378) reestablished the papacy in Rome in 1377. When Pope Urban VI (r. 1378–1389) proclaimed his intention to reform the papal government in the **Curia**, France's Charles V (r. 1364–1380) feared a loss of influence. Charles V supported the **Great Schism**, which began on September 20, 1378, when thirteen cardinals (twelve of whom were French) elected a cousin of the French king as Pope Clement VII (r. 1378–1397). Clement returned to Avignon. Allegiance to the competing papal courts divided along political lines. England and its allies—the **Holy Roman Empire** (based on the old Roman Empire, mostly Germany and northern Italy), Hungary, Bohemia, and Poland—retained their allegiance to Urban VI. France and its orbit—Naples, Scotland, Castile, and Aragon—supported Clement VII. In 1409 a council at Pisa deposed both the Roman and the Avignon popes and elected yet another pope, recognized by neither Rome nor Avignon. This intolerable situation lasted until November 1417, when a church legal council elected a new pope, Martin V (r. 1417–1431), and reunited the church.

The papacy regained much of its prestige and authority. But the recourse to church councils had planted the conviction that the leader of an institution must be responsive to its members.

THE RENAISSANCE IN ITALY (1375–1527)

WHY WAS the Renaissance a transition from the medieval to the modern world?

Renaissance
The revival of ancient learning and the supplanting of traditional religious beliefs by new secular and scientific values that began in Italy in the fourteenth and fifteenth centuries.

The **Renaissance** is the term used to describe fourteenth- and fifteenth-century efforts to revive ancient learning. It marked a transition from the medieval to the modern world. Medieval Europe, especially before the twelfth century, had been a fragmented feudal society with an agricultural economy, its thought and culture dominated by the church. Renaissance Europe, especially after the fourteenth century, was characterized by growing national consciousness and political centralization, an urban economy based on organized commerce and capitalism, and ever greater secular control of thought and culture.

The distinctive features and achievements of the Renaissance are most striking in Italy from roughly 1375 to 1527, the year of the infamous sack of Rome by imperial soldiers. What was achieved in Italy during these centuries deeply influenced northern Europe.

THE ITALIAN CITY-STATE: SOCIAL CONFLICT AND DESPOTISM

The Renaissance began in the cities of late medieval Italy. Italy was the natural gateway between East and West; Venice, Genoa, and Pisa traded with the Middle East throughout the Middle Ages. During the thirteenth and fourteenth centuries, the trade-rich Italian cities became powerful city-states, dominating the political and economic life of their regions. By the fifteenth century, the great Italian cities had become the bankers for much of Europe. There were five major states in Italy: the duchy of Milan, the republics of Florence and Venice, the Papal States, and the kingdom of Naples.

Social strife and competition for political power were so intense within the cities that most had evolved into despotisms by the fifteenth century. Venice, ruled by a successful merchant oligarchy, was the notable exception. Elsewhere, the new social classes and divisions within society produced by rapid urban growth fueled chronic, near-anarchic conflict. In Florence, true stability was not established until the ascent to power in 1434 of the wealthy Cosimo de' Medici (1389–1464), who controlled the city from behind the scenes. His grandson Lorenzo the Magnificent (1449–1492, r. 1478–1492) ruled Florence in near-totalitarian fashion.

Despotism was less subtle elsewhere in Italy. Dominant groups in many cities cooperated in the hiring of a strongman, known as a *podesta*, to maintain law and order. Political turbulence and warfare also fostered diplomacy. City-states strove to stay abreast of foreign military developments and, if shrewd enough, gained power and advantage without actually going to war.

HUMANISM

Humanism was the scholarly study of the Latin and Greek classics and the ancient Church Fathers, both for their own sake and to promote a rebirth of ancient norms and values. Humanists advocated the ***studia humanitatis***, a liberal arts program that embraced grammar, rhetoric, poetry, history, politics, and moral philosophy. The first humanists were orators and poets. They wrote original literature inspired by the newly discovered works of the ancients, and they taught rhetoric within the universities. They were sought as secretaries, speech writers, and diplomats in princely and papal courts.

Classical and Christian antiquity had been studied before, but the Italian Renaissance of the Late Middle Ages was more secular and lay dominated, had broader interests, recovered more manuscripts, and possessed far superior technical skills compared to earlier rebirths of antiquity. Unlike their Scholastic rivals, humanists drew their own conclusions after reading original sources in Latin or Greek. (See Document, "Pico della Mirandola States the Renaissance Image of Man" on page 376.)

Francesco Petrarch (1304–1374), the father of humanism, celebrated ancient Rome in his writings and tirelessly collected ancient manuscripts. His critical textual studies, elitism, and contempt for the allegedly useless learning of the Scholastics were shared by many later humanists. Dante Alighieri's (1265–1321) *Vita Nuova* and *Divine Comedy*—together with Petrarch's sonnets—form the cornerstones of Italian vernacular literature. Petrarch's student and friend Giovanni Boccaccio (1313–1375) wrote the *Decameron*, 100 bawdy tales told in various voices, and assembled an encyclopedia of Greek and Roman mythology.

The classical ideal of a useful education that produces well-rounded, effective people inspired far-reaching reforms. The most influential Italian Renaissance tract on education, Pietro Paolo Vergerio's (1349–1420) *On the Morals That Befit a Free Man*, was written directly from classical models. Vittorino da Feltre (d. 1446) directed his students to a highly disciplined reading of ancient authors, together with vigorous physical exercise.

Educated and cultured noblewomen had a prominent place at Renaissance courts, among them Christine de Pisan (1365–1434). She was an expert in classical, French, and Italian languages and literature whose most famous work, *The City of Ladies*, describes the accomplishments of history's great women.

humanism
The study of the Latin and Greek classics and of the Church Fathers both for their own sake and to promote a rebirth of ancient norms and values.

studia humanitatis
During the Renaissance, a liberal arts program of study that embraced grammar, rhetoric, poetry, history, philosophy, and politics.

●●●–⊏**Read** the **Document**
Letters to Cicero, 14th c., Petrarch
at **myhistorylab.com**

●●●–⊏**Read** the **Document**
Dante's Divine Comedy, 1321
at **myhistorylab.com**

DOCUMENT

Pico della Mirandola States the Renaissance Image of Man

One of the most eloquent Renaissance descriptions of the abilities of humankind comes from the Italian humanist Pico della Mirandola (1463–1494). In his famed Oration on the Dignity of Man (ca. 1486), Pico described humans as free to become whatever they choose.

- **In what** does the dignity of humankind consist? Does Pico reject the biblical description of Adam and Eve's fall? Does he exaggerate a person's ability to choose freely to be whatever he or she wishes? What inspired such seeming hubris during the Renaissance?

The best of artisans [God] ordained that that creature (man) to whom He [God] had been able to give nothing proper to himself should have joint possession of whatever had been peculiar to each of the different kinds of being. He therefore took man as a creature of indeterminate nature and, assigning him a place in the middle of the world, addressed him thus: "Neither a fixed abode nor a form that is thine alone or any function peculiar to thyself have we given thee, Adam, to the end that according to thy longing and according to thy judgment thou mayest have and possess what abode, what form, and what functions thou thyself shalt desire. The nature of all other beings is limited and constrained within the bounds of laws prescribed by Us. Thou, constrained by no limits, in accordance with thine own free will, in whose hand We have placed thee, shalt ordain for thyself the limits of thy nature. We have set thee at the world's center that thou mayest from thence more easily observe whatever is in the world. We have made thee neither of heaven nor of earth, neither mortal nor immortal, so that with freedom of choice and with honor, as though the maker and molder of thyself, thou mayest fashion thyself in whatever shape thou shalt prefer. Thou shalt have the power to degenerate into the lower forms of life, which are brutish. Thou shalt have the power, out of thy soul's judgment, to be reborn into the higher forms, which are divine." O supreme generosity of God the Father, O highest and most marvelous felicity of man! To him it is granted to have whatever he chooses, to be whatever he wills.

Source: From Giovanni Pico della Mirandola, *Oration on the Dignity of Man*, in *The Renaissance Philosophy of Man*, ed. by E. Cassirer et al., Phoenix Books, 1961, pp. 224–225. Reprinted by permission of The University of Chicago Press.

RENAISSANCE ART IN AND BEYOND ITALY

Throughout Renaissance Europe, the values and interests of the laity were less subordinated to those of the clergy than in previous centuries. In education, culture, and religion, the secular world's purely human pursuits were appreciated as ends in themselves.

This perspective is especially prominent in the painting and sculpture of the High Renaissance (late fifteenth and early sixteenth centuries), when Renaissance art reached its maturity. In imitation of Greek and Roman art, painters and sculptors created well-proportioned and even heroic figures. Whereas Byzantine and Gothic art had been religious and idealized, Renaissance art, especially in the fifteenth century, reproduced nature and human nature realistically in both its physical beauty and grotesqueness.

Italian artists led the way, taking advantage of new technical skills and materials developed during the fifteenth century: oil paints, the technique of shading to enhance realism (**chiaroscuro**), and sizing figures to convey to the viewer a feeling of continuity with a painting (linear perspective). Compared with their flat Byzantine and Gothic counterparts, Renaissance paintings seem filled with energy and life. The great masters of the High Renaissance include Leonardo da Vinci (1452–1519), Raphael (1483–1520), and Michelangelo Buonarroti (1475–1564). A modernizing, experimental style known as **Mannerism** followed, reaching its peak in the late sixteenth and early seventeenth centuries. Tintoretto (d. 1594) and the Spaniard El Greco (d. 1614) were Mannerism's supreme representatives.

⊙ View the Image
Da Vinci, Mona Lisa
at **myhistorylab.com**

⊙ View the Image
Michelangelo's David
at **myhistorylab.com**

chiaroscuro
The use of shading to enhance naturalness in painting and drawing.

Mannerism
A style of art in the mid- to late sixteenth century that permitted artists to express their own "manner" or feelings in contrast to the symmetry and simplicity of the art of the High Renaissance.

⊙ Watch the Video
at **myhistorylab.com**

ITALY'S POLITICAL DECLINE: THE FRENCH INVASIONS (1494–1527)

Italy's autonomous city-states had always cooperated to oppose foreign invaders. In 1494, however, Naples, supported by Florence and the Borgia pope Alexander VI (1492–1503), prepared to attack Milan. The Milanese despot Ludovico il Moro (r. 1476–1499) invited the French to revive their dynastic claim to Naples. Within five months the French king Charles VIII (r. 1483–1498) had crossed the Alps and raced as conqueror through Florence and the Papal States into Naples. Ferdinand of Aragon (r. 1479–1516), who was also king of Sicily, helped create a counteralliance, the League of Venice, which forced Charles to retreat. The French returned to Italy under Louis XII (r. 1498–1515), this time assisted by the Borgia pope Alexander VI (1492–1503). Alexander, probably the most corrupt pope in history, sought to secure a political base in Romagna, officially part of the Papal States, for his son Cesare. Seeing that a French alliance could allow him to reestablish control over the region, Alexander abandoned the League of Venice. Louis successfully invaded Milan in August 1499. In 1500 he and Ferdinand of Aragon divided Naples between themselves, while the pope and Cesare Borgia conquered the Romagna.

In 1503 Cardinal Giuliano della Rovere became Pope Julius II (1503–1513). He suppressed the Borgias and placed their newly conquered lands in Romagna under papal jurisdiction. After securing the Papal States with French aid, Julius changed sides and sought to rid Italy of the French invaders. Julius, Ferdinand of Aragon, and Venice formed a Holy League in October 1511, and soon Emperor Maximilian I (r. 1493–1519) and the Swiss joined them. By 1512 the French were in full retreat.

Jan van Eyck, "Adam and Eve" (1432). In the wings of the Dutch painter Jan van Eyck's earliest work, the Ghent Altarpiece, Adam and Eve appear after their fall. Unlike the Italian Renaissance masters, the Netherlandish master portrays them as true-to-life humans, not heroic, idealized figures. Above their heads their son Cain kills his brother Abel, a commentary on human behavior after the Fall.

Why would church paintings be important during this period?

⊙ See the **Map**
Empire and the Papacy in Italy
at **myhistorylab.com**

Michelangelo's "Creation of Adam." The High Italian Renaissance obsession with the muscular, robust, heroic body finds expression in Michelangelo's rendering of the "The Creation of Adam" in the Sistine Chapel.

What emotional responses does this image seem designed to elicit in viewers?

Niccolò Machiavelli. Santi di Tito's portrait of Machiavelli, perhaps the most famous Italian political theorist, who advised Renaissance princes to practice artful deception and inspire fear in their subjects if they wished to succeed.

Scala/Art Resource, New York.

Is Machiavelli's advice still relevant today?

••••⌐**Read** the **Document**
The Prince, 1519, Machiavelli
at **myhistorylab.com**

WHAT WERE the bases for the rise of the modern sovereign state in the fifteenth century?

The French invaded Italy again under Francis I (r. 1515–1547). French armies massacred Swiss soldiers of the Holy League in 1515. That victory won from the Medici pope Leo X (r. 1513–1521) an agreement known as the Concordat of Bologna (1516), which gave the French king control over the French clergy and the right to collect taxes from them in exchange for French recognition of the pope's superiority over church councils. This helped keep France Catholic after the outbreak of the Protestant Reformation. But the new French entry into Italy also led to the first of four major wars with Spain in the first half of the sixteenth century, the Habsburg–Valois wars, none of which France won.

NICCOLÒ MACHIAVELLI

These invasions made a shambles of Italy. Niccolò Machiavelli (1469–1527) became convinced that Italian political unity and independence were ends that justified any means. Machiavelli admired the heroic acts of ancient Roman rulers, what Renaissance people called their *Virtù*. Juxtaposing the strengths of idealized ancient Romans with the failures of his contemporaries, Machiavelli became famously cynical. Only an unscrupulous strongman, he concluded, could impose order on so divided and selfish a people. Machiavelli hoped to see a strong ruler emerge from the Medici family. But the second Medici pope, Clement VII (r. 1523–1534), watched helplessly as Rome was sacked by the army of Emperor Charles V (r. 1519–1556) in 1527, the year of Machiavelli's death.

REVIVAL OF MONARCHY: NATION BUILDING IN THE FIFTEENTH CENTURY

After 1450, unified national monarchies progressively replaced fragmented and divisive feudal governance. The dynastic and chivalric ideals of feudalism did not disappear: Minor territorial princes survived, and representative assemblies even gained influence in some regions. But by the late fifteenth and early sixteenth centuries, the old problem of the one and the many was being decided in favor of monarchy.

In the feudal monarchy of the High Middle Ages, the basic powers of government were divided between the king and his semi-autonomous vassals. The nobility and the towns acted with varying degrees of success through such evolving representative bodies as the English Parliament, the French Estates General, and the Spanish Cortes to thwart the centralization of royal power. As a result of the Hundred Years' War and the schism in the church, however, the landed nobility and the clergy were in decline in the Late Middle Ages. Towns began to ally with the king, and townspeople staffed the royal offices. This new alliance between king and town slowly broke the bonds of feudal society and facilitated the rise of the modern sovereign state.

In a sovereign state, the powers of taxation, war making, and law enforcement are concentrated in the monarch and exercised by his chosen agents. Monarchies began to create standing national armies in the fifteenth century. As the noble cavalry receded and the infantry and the artillery became the backbone of armies, mercenary soldiers were recruited from Switzerland and Germany to form the mainstay of the "king's army." The growing cost of warfare increased the need to develop new national sources of royal income. The highest classes stubbornly believed they were immune from government taxation, so royal revenue grew at the expense of those least able to resist and least able to pay. Monarchs had several options. As feudal lords they could collect rents from their royal domain. They might also levy national taxes on basic

CHRONOLOGY

MAJOR POLITICAL EVENTS OF THE ITALIAN RENAISSANCE (1375–1527)

1378–1382	Ciompi revolt in Florence
1434	Medici rule in Florence established by Cosimo de' Medici
1454–1455	Treaty of Lodi allies Milan, Naples, and Florence (in effect until 1494)
1494	Charles VIII of France invades Italy
1495	League of Venice unites Venice, Milan, the Papal States, the Holy Roman Empire, and Spain against France
1499	Louis XII invades Milan (the second French invasion of Italy)
1500	The Borgias conquer Romagna
1512–1513	The Holy League (Pope Julius II, Ferdinand of Aragon, Emperor Maximilian I, and Venice) defeat the French
1513	Machiavelli writes *The Prince*
1515	Francis I leads the third French invasion of Italy
1516	Concordat of Bologna between France and the papacy
1527	Sack of Rome by imperial soldiers

food and clothing, such as the *gabelle* or salt tax in France and the *alcabala* or 10 percent sales tax on commercial transactions in Spain. Kings could also levy direct taxes on the peasantry and on commercial transactions in towns under royal protection. The French **taille** was such a tax. Sale of public offices and the issuance of high-interest government bonds were innovative fund-raising devices. Kings turned for loans to rich nobles and to the great bankers of Italy and Germany.

taille
A direct tax imposed by the French monarchy on land owned by non-nobles.

MEDIEVAL RUSSIA

In the late tenth century Prince Vladimir of Kiev (r. 972–1015), then Russia's dominant city, received delegations of Muslims, Roman Catholics, Jews, and Greek Orthodox Christians, each group hoping to win the Russians to its religion. Prince Vladimir chose Greek Orthodoxy, adding a new cultural bond to the long-standing commercial ties between Russia and the Byzantine Empire.

Vladimir's successor, Yaroslav the Wise (r. 1016–1054), developed Kiev into a magnificent political and cultural center, but after his death, rivalry among princes made it just one of several national centers.

Mongol (or Tatar) armies (see Chapters 8 and 12) invaded Russia in 1223, and Kiev fell in 1240. Russian cities became tribute-paying principalities of the segment of the Mongol Empire called the **Golden Horde**, which had its capital on the lower Volga. Mongol rule further separated Russia from the West but left Russian political institutions and religion largely intact. Thanks to their far-flung trade, the Mongolians brought most Russians greater peace and prosperity than they had enjoyed before. The princes of Moscow grew wealthy and expanded the principality. Ivan III, called Ivan the Great (d. 1505), brought all of northern Russia under Moscow's control and ended Mongol rule in 1480. By the last quarter of the fifteenth century, Moscow had replaced Kiev as the political and religious center of Russia. In Russian eyes it was destined to become the "third Rome" after the fall of Constantinople to the Turks in 1453.

•◆•〔Read the **Document**
Vladimir Kiev's Acceptance of Christianity
at **myhistorylab.com**

Golden Horde
Name given to the Mongol rulers of Russia from 1240 to 1480.

FRANCE

There were two cornerstones of French nation building in the fifteenth century: England's retreat from the continent following its loss of the Hundred Years' War, and the defeat of Charles the Bold (r. 1467–1477) and his duchy of Burgundy. The dukes of Burgundy were probably Europe's strongest rulers in the mid-fifteenth century, and they hoped to build a dominant middle kingdom between France and the Holy Roman Empire. Continental powers joined forces to oppose them, and Charles the Bold was killed in battle at Nancy in 1477.

The dissolution of Burgundy left Louis XI (r. 1461–1483) free to secure the monarchy in his expanded kingdom. Louis harnessed the nobility and expanded trade and industry. It was because Louis's successors inherited such a secure and efficient government that France was able to pursue Italian conquests in the 1490s and to fight a long series of losing wars with the Habsburgs in the first half of the sixteenth century. By the mid-sixteenth century France was again a defeated nation, almost as divided as it had been during the Hundred Years' War.

SPAIN

Spain, too, became a strong country in the late fifteenth century. Both Castile and Aragon had been poorly ruled kingdoms until the 1469 marriage of Isabella of Castile (r. 1474–1504) and Ferdinand of Aragon (r. 1479–1516). Castile was by far the richer and more populous of the two. Each retained its own government agencies and cultural traditions. Together, Isabella and Ferdinand were able to subdue their realms, secure their borders, and venture abroad militarily. Townspeople allied themselves with the crown and progressively replaced the nobility within the royal administration. The crown also extended its authority over the wealthy chivalric orders.

Spain had long been remarkable as a place where Islam, Judaism, and Christianity coexisted with a certain degree of toleration. This toleration ended decisively. Ferdinand and Isabella exercised almost total control over the Spanish church as they placed religion in the service of national unity. They appointed the higher clergy and the officers of the Inquisition. Spanish spiritual life became uniform and regimented, which is a major reason Spain became a base for Europe's Counter-Reformation in the sixteenth century.

See the **Map**
Spain 1491
at **myhistorylab.com**

The anti-French marriage alliances Isabella and Ferdinand arranged for their children influenced European history for decades. Their patronage of the Genoese adventurer Christopher Columbus (1451–1506) led to the creation of the Spanish Empire in the New World. Gold and silver from mines in Mexico and Peru helped make Spain Europe's dominant power in the sixteenth century.

ENGLAND

The last half of the fifteenth century was especially difficult for the English. Following the Hundred Years' War, civil war broke out in England between two rival branches of the royal family, the House of York and the House of Lancaster. This conflict, named the Wars of the Roses (York's symbol, according to legend, was a white rose, and Lancaster's a red rose), kept England in turmoil from 1455 to 1485.

The Lancastrian monarchy of Henry VI (r. 1422–1461) was challenged by the Duke of York and his supporters in prosperous southern towns. In 1461 Edward IV (r. 1461–1483), son of the Duke of York, seized power. His brother and successor was Richard III (r. 1483–1485), whose reign saw the growth of support for the exiled Lancastrian Henry Tudor. Henry returned to England to defeat Richard in 1485 and became King Henry VII (r. 1485–1509), founder of a Tudor dynasty that endured until 1603.

To bring the rival royal families together and give his offspring an incontestable hereditary claim to the throne, Henry married Edward IV's daughter, Elizabeth of York. With the aid of a much-feared instrument of royal power, the Court of Star Chamber, he imposed discipline on the English nobility. He shrewdly construed legal precedents to the advantage of the crown and used English law to further his own ends. He confiscated so much noble land and wealth that he was able to govern without depending on Parliament for grants. Henry constructed a powerful monarchy that became one of early modern Europe's most exemplary governments during the reign of his granddaughter, Elizabeth I (r. 1558–1603).

SUMMARY

 WHAT IMPACT did the Crusades have on medieval European society?

Revival of Empire, Church, and Towns. Germany's Otto I breathed new life into both empire and papacy. In the tenth century, the Cluny reform movement increased popular respect for the church and strengthened the clergy. In the Investiture Controversy, the papacy secured the independence of the clergy by enlisting the support of the German princes against the Holy Roman Emperors, thus weakening imperial power in Germany. The Crusades were based on the intense passions of popular piety. The rise of merchants, self-governing towns, and universities helped restructure power. By supporting rulers against the nobility, towns gave kings the resources to build national governments. *page 360*

 WHAT NEW group was added to the three traditional groups in medieval society?

Medieval Society. In theory, medieval society was divided into three main groups: clergy (those who prayed), nobility (those who fought as mounted warriors), and laborers (peasants and artisans). But merchants became a fourth group. Women faced constraints, but their lives were far richer and more varied than Christian imagery suggested. *page 367*

HOW DID England and France develop strong royal governments by the thirteenth century?

Growth of National Monarchies. Much of medieval history involved the struggle by rulers to assert their authority over powerful local lords and the church. In England and France, monarchs and nobles reached accommodation, and national identity was strengthened. The Holy Roman Empire, however, disintegrated. *page 369*

 WHAT WERE the consequences of the Black Death?

Political and Social Breakdown. Both the Hundred Years' War and the Black Death weakened the nobility. Bubonic plague devastated areas surrounding trade routes. Population loss had many consequences, including a shortage of labor and high demand for luxury goods leading to a rise in status for artisans. Cities and kings were, on balance, strengthened. *page 371*

 WHY DID France's king support the Great Schism?

Ecclesiastical Breakdown and Revival: The Late Medieval Church. By the end of the thirteenth century, kings had become more powerful than popes, and the French king, Philip the Fair, was able to defy the papacy. In the fourteenth century, the Great Schism further weakened papal prestige. The papacy never recovered its authority over national rulers. *page 373*

WHY WAS the Renaissance a transition from the medieval to the modern world?

The Renaissance in Italy (1375–1527). The Renaissance, which began in the Italian city-states in the late fourteenth century, marks the transition from the medieval to the modern world. Humanism promoted a rebirth of ancient norms and values and the classical ideal of an educated, well-rounded person. The growth of secular values led to a great burst of artistic activity by artists such as Leonardo da Vinci, Raphael, and Michelangelo. The political weakness of the Italian states invited foreign intervention. The sack of Rome in 1527 marks the end of the Renaissance. *page 374*

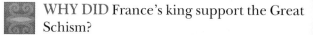

WHAT WERE the bases for the rise of the modern sovereign state in the fifteenth century?

Revival of Monarchy: Nation Building in the Fifteenth Century. By the fifteenth century, England, France, and Spain had developed into strong national monarchies with centralized bureaucracies and professional armies. Although medieval institutions, such as the English Parliament, limited royal power in theory, in practice monarchs in these countries held unchallenged authority. In previous centuries, the Great Schism, the Hundred Years' War, and the Black Death weakened the church and the nobility. Townspeople supported the kings. A similar process was beginning in Russia, where the rulers of Moscow were extending their authority after throwing off Mongol rule. *page 378*

KEY TERMS

Black Death (p. 372)

chiaroscuro (KEY-ahr-uh-SKYOOR-oh) (p. 376)

Crusades (p. 361)

Curia (p. 374)

Golden Horde (p. 379)

Great Schism (p. 374)

guild (p. 365)

Holy Roman Empire (p. 374)

humanism (p. 375)

Magna Carta (p. 369)

Mannerism (p. 376)

regular clergy (p. 367)

Renaissance (p. 374)

Scholasticism (p. 365)

secular clergy (p. 367)

studia humanitatis (p. 375)

taille (p. 379)

vernacular (p. 369)

REVIEW QUESTIONS

1. How do you account for the success of the Cluny reform movement? Can major features of the modern Catholic Church be found in the Cluny reforms?

2. Was the Investiture Controversy a political or religious conflict? Summarize the respective arguments of Gregory VII and Henry IV. Is the conflict a precedent for the modern doctrine of the separation of church and state?

3. Why did Germany remain divided while France and England began to coalesce into reasonably strong states during the High Middle Ages?

4. How did the responsibilities of the nobility differ from those of the clergy and the peasantry during the High Middle Ages? How did each social class contribute to the stability of society?

5. Describe the circumstances that gave rise to towns. How did towns change traditional medieval society?

6. How did the Hundred Years' War, the Black Death, and the Great Schism in the church affect the course of history? Which had the most lasting effects on the institutions it touched?

7. Was the church an aggressor or a victim in the Late Middle Ages and the Renaissance? How successful was it in its confrontations with Europe's emerging dynastic states?

8. What was "reborn" in the Renaissance? Were the humanists the forerunners of modern secular education and culture or eloquent defenders of a still medieval Christian view of the world against the church's secular and pagan critics?

9. Historians find features of modern states developing in Europe during the Late Middle Ages and Renaissance. What modern features can you identify in the governments of the Italian city-states, the northern monarchies, and in Russia?

Note: To learn more about the topics in this chapter, please turn to the Suggested Readings at the end of the book. For additional sources related to this chapter please see www.myhistorylab.com

myhistorylab Connections

Reinforce what you learned in this chapter by studying the many documents, images, maps, review tools, and videos available at **www.myhistorylab.com**

Read and Review

✓ **Study** and **Review** Chapter 15

Read the **Document** *Expulsion, Jews from France 12th Century, p. 362*
Arab-Syrian Gentleman Discusses Franks, p. 363
The Magna Carta 1215, p. 363
Medieval Town Customs: Town, Chester, England, p. 365
Abelard Defends Himself, p. 367
The Battle of Hastings 1066, p. 369
Black Death, 1349, Henry Knighton, p. 371
Peasant Revolt in England, p. 373
Unam Sanctam 1302, Pope Boniface VIII, p. 373
Letters to Cicero, 14th c., Petrarch, p. 375
Dante's Divine Comedy, 1321, p. 375
The Prince, 1519, Machiavelli, p. 378
Vladimir Kiev's Acceptance of Christianity, p. 379

See the **Map** *The Major Crusades, p. 363*
England and France ca. 1180, p. 369
The Hundred Years' War, p. 371
100 Years' War, p. 371
Black Death and Peasant Revolts, p. 371
Empire and the Papacy in Italy, p. 377
Spain 1491, p. 380

View the **Image** *Da Vinci, Mona Lisa, p. 376*
Michelangelo's David, p. 376

Research and Explore

Watch the **Video** *Plague, p. 373*

See the **Map** *Medieval Manor*

(((•—[**Hear** the **Audio**

Hear the audio file for Chapter 15
at **www.myhistorylab.com**

16

Europe 1500–1650: Expansion, Reformation, and Religious Wars

((•──Hear the Audio for Chapter 16 at www.myhistorylab.com

Allegory of the Jesuits and their missions in the four continents from the church of San Pedro, Lima, Peru. Anonymous painter (eighteenth century). St. Ignatius is flanked on his left by Francis Xavier, sporting a chasuble with Asian motifs. In the background, Jesuits living all over the world and occupying a variety of hierarchies within the church, including those wearing Chinese costumes and prelate robes, preside over the conversion of the faithful in India, China, Africa, and the Americas. Like Atlas, the Jesuits carry the globe on their shoulders.

Why do you think the peoples of India, China, Africa, and the Americas are shown smaller than the European missionaries in this painting?

or Europe the late fifteenth and sixteenth centuries were years of unprecedented territorial expansion. Permanent colonies were established in the Americas, and the exploitation of the New World's human and mineral resources began.

Starting early in the sixteenth century, a powerful religious movement spread rapidly throughout northern Europe, altering society and politics as well as the spiritual lives of individuals. Attacking what they believed to be burdensome superstitions and corrupt practices, Protestant reformers led a revolt against the medieval church. Hundreds of thousands of people from all social classes set aside the beliefs of centuries and adopted a simplified religious practice.

The Protestant Reformation challenged aspects of the Renaissance, especially its tendency to follow classical sources in glorifying human nature and its loyalty to traditional religion. Protestants were more impressed by the human potential for evil than by the inclination to do good. But Protestants also embraced many Renaissance values, especially humanist educational reforms and the study of ancient languages, which gave them tools to master Scripture and challenge the papacy. Reform within the church (Counter-Reformation) gave birth to new religious orders and won many Protestant converts back to Catholicism.

As different groups identified their political and social goals with either Protestantism or Catholicism, bloody confrontations spread across Europe. During the Thirty Years' War (1618–1648), international armies of varying religious persuasions clashed in central and northern Europe. ■

386

GLOBAL PERSPECTIVE

EUROPEAN EXPANSION

The European turn to the Atlantic was a consequence of its weakness in the East due to Muslim domination there. However, a recovering Europe was now able to compete for access to valuable goods in Eastern markets by navigating the high seas. In the late fifteenth and the sixteenth centuries, Europeans sailed far from their own shores to Africa, southern and eastern Asia, and the New World of the Americas. From Japan to Peru, they directly confronted civilizations other than their own and that of Islam, with which they already had contact in the form of trade and, more often, by force of arms. A major motivation for the voyages, which began with a reconnaissance of the West African coast, was to circumvent the Muslim monopoly on the movement of spices from the Indian Ocean into Europe, a grip that had only strengthened with the rise of the Ottomans. A wealthier, more self-confident Europe, now recovered from the great plague-induced population decline of the fourteenth century—its taste for Asian spices long-since whetted during the Crusades—was ready to take those spices at their sources.

For much the same reasons (trade and self-aggrandizement) voyages of exploration also set forth from Ming China—especially between 1405 and 1433—reaching India, the Arabian Gulf, and East Africa. Had those voyages been followed up, they might have prevented Europeans from establishing a presence in the Indian Ocean. But the Chinese faced both serious pressures on their northern and western borders, and the problem of administrating a vast, multicultural empire stretching into Central Asia, where non-Chinese rivals had to be kept under control. Moreover, the dominant Neo-Confucian philosophy espoused by the scholar-bureaucrats in the imperial court disdained merchants and commerce, extolling instead a peasant agrarian economy.

These factors led the Chinese to turn inward and abandon overseas trade and exploration precisely at the moment when Europeans were exploring the coast of Africa on their way to the Indian Ocean. It was a fateful choice because it meant that the Asian power best able to resist the establishment of European commercial and colonial empires in the Indian Ocean had

THE DISCOVERY OF A NEW WORLD

WHY DID western Europeans start exploring, trading, and settling around the world in the fifteenth century?

((•—Hear the Audio at **myhistorylab.com**

The discovery of the Americas dramatically expanded the horizons of Europeans, both geographical and intellectual. Knowledge of the New World's inhabitants and exploitation of its mineral and human wealth set new cultural and economic forces in motion. Beginning with the voyages of the Portuguese and Spanish in the fifteenth century, commercial supremacy progressively shifted from the Mediterranean and Baltic seas to the Atlantic seaboard, and western Europe's global expansion began in earnest (see Map 16–1 on page 388).

THE PORTUGUESE CHART THE COURSE

Seventy-seven years before Columbus sailed under Spain's flag, Portugal's Prince Henry the Navigator (1394–1460) began exploration of Africa's Atlantic coast. The Portuguese first sought gold and slaves. During the second half of the fifteenth century, the Portuguese delivered 150,000 slaves to Europe. By the end of that century, they were hoping to find a sea route around Africa to spice markets in Asia.

Overland routes to India and China had long existed, but they were difficult, expensive, and monopolized by Venetians and Turks. The first exploratory voyages were slow and tentative, but they provided experience that taught sailors the skills needed to cross the oceans to the Americas and Asia.

In 1455, the pope gave the Portuguese rights to all the lands, goods, and slaves they might discover from the coast of Guinea to the Indies. The church hoped that conquests would be followed by mass conversions. The explorers also kept an eye out for "Prester John," rumored to be a potential Christian ally against the Muslims. Bartholomew Dias (d. 1500) opened the Portuguese Empire in the East when he rounded the Cape of Good Hope at the tip of Africa in 1487. A decade later, in 1498,

abdicated that role, leaving a vacuum of power for Europeans to fill. Still, Chinese merchants continued to ply ocean trade routes and settle as far from home as the Philippines and, in later centuries, the west coasts of North and South America. Wherever there was commerce in Chinese goods, there were Chinese merchants, albeit now operating without support from their government.

Although parallels may be drawn between the court culture of the Forbidden Palace in Beijing and that of King Louis XIV in seventeenth-century France, the Chinese government, with its philosophy of Confucianism, remained more unified and patriarchal than its counterparts in the West. The Chinese, at first, tolerated other religions, warmly embracing Jesuit missionaries, in part because political power in China was not bound to a particular religion. The Japanese were also admirers of the Jesuits, who arrived in Japan with the Portuguese in 1543. The admiration was mutual, leading to 300,000 Christian converts by 1600. Tolerance of Christianity did not last as long

in Japan as in China. Hideyoshi, in his drive for internal unity, banned Christianity in the late sixteenth century. Nonetheless China and Japan, as well as many Islamic societies, including the Ottomans and the Mughals, demonstrated more tolerance for foreign religions, such as Christianity, than did the West for Islam, or Asian religious traditions.

Focus Questions

◆ Why did Europeans launch voyages of exploration in the fifteenth and sixteenth centuries? What role did the Crusades and the rise of the Ottoman Empire play in this enterprise?

◆ Why did the Chinese voyages of exploration under the Ming come to a halt? What were the consequences for world history?

◆ What was the biological impact of the European discovery of America?

Vasco da Gama (d. 1524) stood on the shores of India. When he returned to Portugal, his cargo was worth sixty times the cost of the voyage. Later, the Portuguese established colonies in Goa and Calcutta and successfully challenged the Arabs and the Venetians for control of the European spice trade.

While the Portuguese concentrated on the Indian Ocean, the Spanish set sail across the Atlantic, hoping to establish a shorter route to the East Indies. Rather than beat the Portuguese at their own game, however, Columbus unwittingly discovered the Americas.

THE SPANISH VOYAGES OF CHRISTOPHER COLUMBUS

On October 12, 1492, after a thirty-three-day voyage from the Canary Islands, Columbus landed in San Salvador (Watlings Island) in the eastern Bahamas. He thought San Salvador was an outer island of Japan, for his knowledge of geography was based on Marco Polo's thirteenth-century account of his years in China and a global map by a Nuremberg mapmaker, which showed only ocean between the west coast of Europe and the east coast of Asia (see Map 16–2 on page 389).

Naked, friendly natives met Columbus and his crew. They were Taino Indians, who spoke a variant of the Arawak language. Believing he had landed in the East Indies, Columbus called these people Indians. The natives' generosity amazed Columbus, as they freely gave his men corn, yams—and many sexual favors. "They never say no," Columbus marveled, observing how easily they could be enslaved.

Soon Amerigo Vespucci (1451–1512), after whom America is named, and Ferdinand Magellan (1480–1521) carefully explored the coastline of South America. Their travels proved that the new lands were part of an entirely unknown continent that opened on the great Pacific Ocean.

Christopher Columbus in old age (d. 1506) by Sebastiano del Piombo.

What did Columbus intend to do when he sailed west across the Atlantic?

●◆●⊣Read the Document

Duarte Barbosas to Africa, India
at **myhistorylab.com**

●◆●⊣Read the Document

Columbus journal and letter
at **myhistorylab.com**

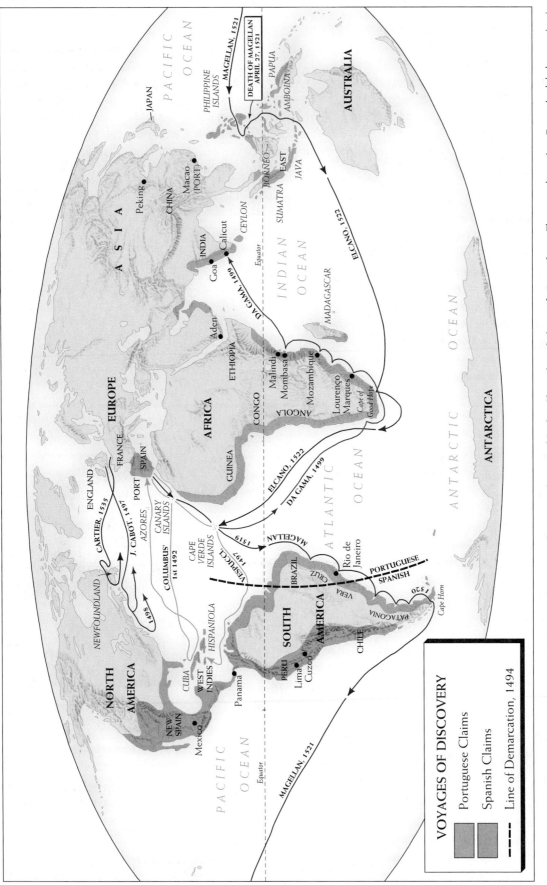

MAP 16–1. European Voyages of Discovery and the Colonial Claims of Spain and Portugal in the Fifteenth and Sixteenth Centuries. The map dramatizes Europe's global expansion in the fifteenth and sixteenth centuries.

Why did western Europeans want to find a sea route to Asia?

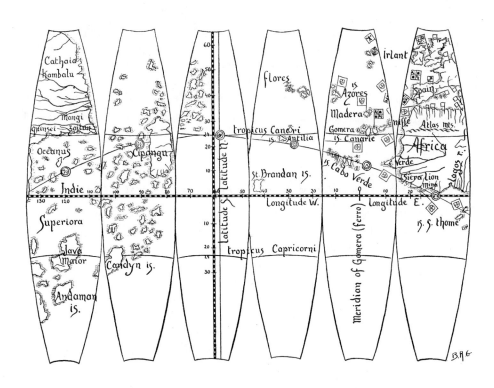

MAP 16–2. Martin Behaim's "Globe Apple." What Columbus knew of the world in 1492 was contained in this map by Nuremberg geographer Martin Behaim (1440–1507), creator of the first spherical globe of the earth. The ocean section of Behaim's globe is reproduced here. Departing the Canary Islands (in the second section from the right), Columbus expected his first major landfall to be Japan, or what he calls Cipangu (in the second section from the left). When he landed at San Salvador, he thought he was on an outer island of Japan; after reaching Cuba, he believed it to be Japan. Only slowly did it dawn on him that these new lands had never before been seen by Europeans.

From Admiral of the Ocean Sea by Samuel Eliot Morison. Copyright 1942 © renewed 1970 by Samuel Eliot Morison. By permission of Little, Brown and Company, Boston, MA.

How did this map influence Columbus's worldview?

QUICK REVIEW

Impact of Columbus's First Voyage on Europe and America

◆ Spurred other European nations to colonial expansion

◆ Financed Spain's role in the age's political and religious conflicts

◆ Brought disease, war, and destruction to native peoples

IMPACT ON EUROPE AND AMERICA

Unbeknownst to those who undertook and financed it, Columbus's first voyage marked the beginning of more than three centuries of Spanish conquest, exploitation, and administration of a vast American empire. The wars Christian Aragon and Castile waged against the Islamic Moors had just ended, and the early Spanish explorers retained their zeal for converting non-Christians.

The voyages to the New World had important consequences for both Europe and America. They created Europe's largest and longest-surviving trading bloc and yielded great wealth for Spain. This wealth fueled European-wide economic expansion and spurred other European countries to undertake their own colonial ventures.

European expansion also had major consequences for ecosystems. Numerous species of fruits, vegetables, and animals were introduced to Europe from America and vice versa. European diseases also devastated America's natives. (See the discussion of the "Columbian Exchange" in Chapter 17.) Spain's imprint on the new territories—Roman Catholicism, economic dependence, and a hierarchical society—is still visible today (see Chapter 33).

THE REFORMATION

The **Reformation** was a sixteenth-century religious movement that sought to reform the church. It led to the establishment of Protestantism and the religious division of Western Christendom.

WHO WERE the early Protestant leaders?

RELIGION AND SOCIETY

The Reformation broke out first in the free imperial cities of Germany and Switzerland. There were sixty-five such cities, each a small kingdom unto itself. Most had Protestant movements. Some turned Protestant and remained so, while others developed mixed confessions that allowed Catholics and Protestants to coexist.

Reformation
The sixteenth-century religious movement that sought to reform the Roman Catholic Church and led to the establishment of Protestantism.

Certain groups favored the Reformation more than others. In many places, trade guilds were in the forefront of the Reformation. Evidence suggests that people who felt bullied by either local or distant authority—a guild by an autocratic local government, a city by a prince or king—saw the Protestant movement as an ally.

Social and political experience thus coalesced with religious issues in both town and countryside. When Martin Luther wrote, preached, and sang about a priesthood of all believers and ridiculed papal laws as arbitrary human inventions, he touched political as well as religious nerves.

POPULAR MOVEMENTS AND CRITICISM OF THE CHURCH

The Protestant Reformation could not have occurred without the monumental crises of the late medieval church and the Renaissance papacy. Laity and clerics alike began to seek a more heartfelt, idealistic piety. The Late Middle Ages saw independent lay and clerical efforts to reform local religious practice.

A variety of factors contributed to lay criticism of the church. The laity in the cities was learning more about the world and those who controlled their lives. They traveled widely—as soldiers, pilgrims, explorers, and traders. New postal systems and the printing press increased the information at their disposal. The new age of books and libraries raised literacy and heightened lay curiosity, confidence, and criticism.

SECULAR CONTROL OVER RELIGIOUS LIFE

On the eve of the Reformation, Rome's international network of church offices began to be pulled apart by a growing sense of regional identity (incipient nationalism) and the increasing competence of local secular administrations. Rare was the late medieval German town that did not have complaints about the maladministration, concubinage, or fiscal misconduct of its clergy.

City governments also sought to restrict clerical privileges and to improve local religious life by bringing the clergy under the local tax code and by endowing new clerical positions for well-trained and conscientious preachers.

THE NORTHERN RENAISSANCE

The scholarly works of northern humanists created a climate favorable to religious and educational reforms. Northern scholars tended to come from more diverse social backgrounds and to be more devoted to religious reforms and new lay freedoms than were their Italian counterparts.

The growth of schools and lay education combined with the invention of cheap paper to create a mass audience for printed books. Johann Gutenberg (d. 1468) invented printing with movable type in the German city of Mainz around 1450. By 1500, printing presses operated in more than 200 cities throughout Europe, providing a new medium for politicians, humanists, and reformers alike.

The most famous northern humanist was Desiderius Erasmus (1466–1536). Idealistic and pacifistic, Erasmus aspired to unite the classical ideals of humanity and civic virtue with the Christian ideals of love and piety. He summarized his own beliefs with the phrase *philosophia Christi*, a simple, ethical piety in imitation of Christ, as opposed to what he saw as the dogmatic, ceremonial, and factious religious practice of his contemporaries. Erasmus edited the works of the Church Fathers and published a Greek edition of the New Testament (1516), which became the basis for a new, more accurate Latin translation (1519). Martin Luther later used both of these works as the basis for his famous German translation.

QUICK REVIEW

Criticism of the Church

- Many people did not see the church as a foundation for religious piety
- Laity and clerics were interested in alternatives and reform
- Laypersons were increasingly willing to take initiative

⊙—View the **Image**
Early Print Shop
at **myhistorylab.com**

QUICK REVIEW

Desiderius Erasmus (1466–1536)

- Most famous northern humanist
- Saw study of Bible and classics as best path to reform
- Edited the works of the Church Fathers and completed a Greek edition of the New Testament

The best known early English humanist was Sir Thomas More (1478–1535), a close friend of Erasmus. More's *Utopia* (1516), a criticism of contemporary society, depicts an imaginary society based on reason and tolerance that requires everyone to work and has rid itself of all social and political injustice. Although More himself remained staunchly Catholic, humanism paved the way for the English Reformation.

In Spain, humanism served the Catholic Church. Francisco Jiménez de Cisneros (1437–1517) was a confessor to Queen Isabella and, after 1508 Grand Inquisitor, a position from which he was able to enforce the strictest religious orthodoxy. Jiménez was a conduit for humanist scholarship and learning. He founded the University of Alcalá near Madrid, printed a Greek edition of the New Testament, and translated many religious tracts that aided clerical reform and control of lay religious life. His greatest achievement, taking fifteen years to complete, was the Complutensian Polyglot Bible, a six-volume work that placed the Hebrew, Greek, and Latin versions of the Bible in parallel columns.

The Gutenberg Bible.   Print and Protestantism would drive the history of the sixteenth century. Well established by the mid-fifteenth century, the printing press made possible the diffusion of both secular and religious learning. In addition to Humanistic scholarship, print also served the educational and propaganda campaigns of princes and religious reformers, increasing literacy in both Latin and vernacular languages. Among the printed works preparing the way none was more stimulating than Gutenberg's Latin Bible. In the mid-1520s Martin Luther made separate German translations of the New and the Old Testaments, henceforth to become the battering rams of the Protestant Reformation.

Why were Bibles printed in the vernacular particularly important to Protestants?

MARTIN LUTHER AND GERMAN REFORMATION TO 1525

Unlike France and England, late medieval Germany lacked the political unity to enforce "national" religious reforms during the Late Middle Ages. As popular resentment of clerical immunities and ecclesiastical abuses spread, opposition to Rome formed. German humanists had long voiced such criticism, and by 1517 it provided a solid foundation for Martin Luther's reform.

Luther (1483–1546) was educated by teachers who had been influenced by the Northern Renaissance. His family hoped he would study law, but instead he entered a monastery and was ordained in 1507. In 1510 he traveled to Rome and witnessed the abuses for which the papacy was being criticized. In 1511, he was transferred to the Augustinian monastery in Wittenberg, where he earned his doctorate in theology and became a leader within the monastery, the new university, and the spiritual life of the city.

Luther was plagued by the disproportion between his own sense of sinfulness and the perfect righteousness that God required for salvation according to medieval theology. Traditional church teaching and the sacraments were no consolation. Between 1513 and 1518 Luther gradually concluded that the righteousness God demands does not come from religious works but is present in full measure in those who believe and trust in the redemptive life and death of Christ. Luther's belief is known as "justification by faith alone."

◉ ┤View the Image
Martin Luther
at **myhistorylab.com**

The Electoral Princes of Saxony, by Lucas Cranach the Elder (ca. 1532). The three princes Luther served: Frederick the Wise, John the Constant, and John Frederick the Magnanimous.

Why did some German princes support Luther?

indulgence
Remission of the temporal penalty of punishment in purgatory that remained after sins had been forgiven.

•❖•⌐Read the Document
Erasmus Julius Excluded Heaven
at **myhistorylab.com**

ninety-five theses
Document posted on the door of Castle Church in Wittenberg, Germany, on October 31, 1517, by Martin Luther protesting, among other things, the selling of indulgences.

•❖•⌐Read the Document
Martin Luther's Ninety-Five Theses
1517 at **myhistorylab.com**

Diet of Worms
The meeting of the representative (diet) of the Holy Roman Empire presided over by the Emperor Charles V at the German city of Worms in 1521 at which Martin Luther was ordered to recant his ninety-five theses.

Luther criticized the church practice of granting **indulgences**. According to medieval theology, God rightly imposed punishments for all sins. When a penitent received absolution from a priest for a mortal sin, God's eternal penalty was transformed into a temporal penalty, a "work of satisfaction" that could be performed in earthly time (for example, through prayers, fasting, almsgiving, and pilgrimages). Penitents who failed to complete their works of satisfaction would suffer in purgatory unless they received an indulgence, a remission of the temporal penalty. Originally, indulgences had been granted for significant self-sacrifice, such as going on a Crusade to the Holy Land.

In 1343, Pope Clement VI (r. 1342–1352) had proclaimed the existence of a "treasury of merit," an infinite reservoir of good works in the church's possession that could be dispensed at the pope's discretion. The church sold "letters of indulgence," which covered the works of satisfaction owed by penitents. By Luther's time, they were regularly dispensed for small cash payments and presented as remitting not only the donor's punishments but also those of their dead relatives presumed to be suffering in purgatory.

In 1517, an indulgence was preached on the borders of Saxony in the territories of Archbishop Albrecht of Mainz, who had large debts. The selling of the indulgence was a joint venture by Albrecht, German bankers, and Pope Leo X (r. 1513–1521), half the proceeds going to the pope and half to Albrecht and his creditors. The famous indulgence preacher John Tetzel (d. 1519) exhorted the crowds: "Don't you hear the voices of your dead parents and other relatives crying out, 'Have mercy on us, for we suffer great punishment and pain. From this you could release us with a few alms.' "[1]

When Luther, according to tradition, posted his **ninety-five theses** for reform on the door of Castle Church in Wittenberg, on October 31, 1517, he protested the impression that indulgences actually remitted sins and released the dead from punishment in purgatory. Luther believed such claims made salvation look like something that could be bought and sold.

Luther's proposals made him famous overnight. They were embraced by humanists, but the church began disciplinary proceedings. Emperor Maximilian I's death in January 1519 diverted official attention to the contest for a new emperor. Charles I of Spain, then 19 years old, succeeded his grandfather and became Emperor Charles V (r. 1519–1556). The electors won political concessions from Charles that prevented him from taking unilateral action against Germans, something for which Luther later had cause to be grateful. (See Map 16–3.)

In a June 1519 debate with Professor John Eck (1486–1543), Luther challenged the infallibility of the pope and the inerrancy of church councils, arguing for the first time that Scripture held sole and sovereign authority over faith. He burned all his bridges to the old church when he defended John Huss, a condemned heretic. In 1520, Luther issued three pamphlets elaborating on his beliefs. In April 1521, Luther defended his religious teaching before the imperial **Diet of Worms**, over which newly elected Emperor Charles V presided. Ordered to recant, Luther declared that he could not act against Scripture, reason, and his own conscience. On May 26, 1521, he was placed under the imperial ban and became an "outlaw." Friends hid him in a secluded castle, where he spent almost a year translating the New Testament into German and attempting by correspondence to oversee the first stages of the Reformation in Wittenberg.

---

[1]*Die Reformation in Augenzeugen Berichten*, ed. by Helmar Judghans (Dusseldorf: Karl Rauch Verlag, 1967), p. 44.

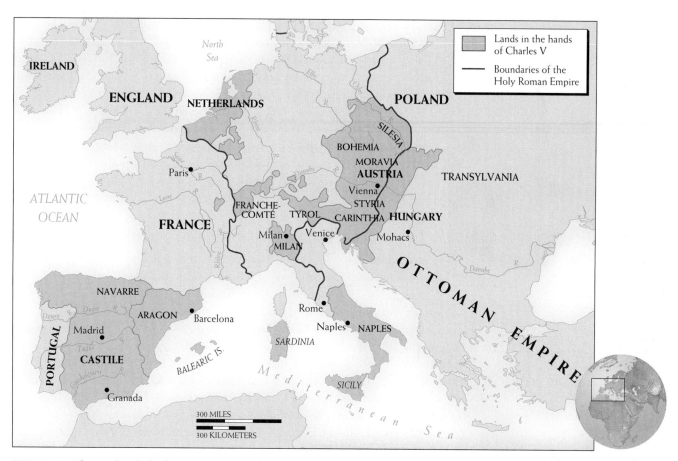

MAP 16–3.   The Empire of Charles V.   Dynastic marriages and good fortune concentrated into Charles's hands rule over the lands shown here, plus Spain's overseas possessions. Crowns and titles rained down on him; election in 1519 as emperor gave him new burdens and responsibilities.

What were the geographical advantages and disadvantages of the empire of Charles V?

The Reformation was greatly helped in these early years by the emperor's wars with France (the Habsburg-Valois Wars) and the advance of the Ottoman Turks into eastern Europe. Against both adversaries Charles V needed German troops, so he promoted friendly relations with the German princes. In 1526, each German territory was given freedom to enforce the Edict of Worms against Luther "so as to be able to answer in good conscience to God and the emperor." German princes effectively gained religious sovereignty. In 1555, the Peace of Augsburg enshrined local control over religion in imperial law.

In the late 1520s and the 1530s, Protestant preachers built sizable congregations in many cities that pressured urban governments to adopt religious reforms. Many magistrates had long pushed for reform and welcomed the preachers as allies. Religious reform became a territorial political movement as well, led by the elector of Saxony and the prince of Hesse. Like the urban magistrates, the princes recognized political and economic opportunities for themselves in the demise of the Roman Catholic Church, and they urged the reform on their neighbors. By the 1530s, there was a powerful Protestant alliance prepared for war with the Catholic emperor.

There were early divisions within the Protestant movement. German peasants, for example, had at first believed Luther to be an ally. They solicited his support of their political and economic rights, including their revolutionary request for release

View the Image
Martin Luther Statue in Hesse Germany
at **myhistorylab.com**

See the Map
Religious Divisions of Europe
at **myhistorylab.com**

Read the Document
Against Murderous Thieving Hordes
Peasants at **myhistorylab.com**

Execution of a Peasant Leader. The punishment of a peasant leader in a village near Heilbronn. After the defeat of rebellious peasants in and around the city of Heilbronn, Jacob Rorbach, a well-to-do peasant leader from a nearby village, was tied to a stake and slowly roasted to death.

Why did Luther not support rebellious peasants?

⊙ See the **Map**
The Swiss Confederation
at **myhistorylab.com**

transubstantiation
The doctrine that the entire substances of the bread and wine are changed in the Eucharist into the body and blood of Christ.

consubstantiation
The doctrine that the substances of both bread and wine, and the body and blood of Christ, are present in the Eucharistic offering.

⊙ View the **Image**
Anabaptist Torture in Muenster
at **myhistorylab.com**

from serfdom. But Lutherans were not social revolutionaries. Luther believed that Christian freedom was an inner release from guilt and anxiety, not the right to an egalitarian society. When the peasants revolted in 1524–1525, Luther condemned them as "unchristian" and urged the princes to crush their revolt without mercy. Tens of thousands of peasants died.

Luther also had a disturbing perspective on Jews. In 1523 he published the pamphlet, "Jesus Christ Was Born a Jew," in which he urged Christians to be kind to Germany's Jews in the hope that they might convert to reformed Christianity. But in the late 1530s and early 1540s, he urged German princes forcibly to remove nonconverting Jews to a land of their own, as France, Spain, and Bohemia had already done. Instead, the Jews found a protector in Emperor Charles V.

ZWINGLI AND THE SWISS REFORMATION

Switzerland was a loose confederacy of thirteen autonomous cantons or states and allied areas. Some became Protestant, some remained Catholic, and a few managed to compromise. The two preconditions of the Swiss Reformation were the growth of national sentiment and a desire for church reform.

Ulrich Zwingli (1484–1531), based in Zurich, was widely known for opposing superstition and the sale of indulgences. Zwingli's reform guideline was simple and effective: Whatever lacked literal support in Scripture was to be neither believed nor practiced. After a public disputation in January 1523, Zurich became effectively a Protestant city and the center of the Swiss Reformation. Its harsh discipline in pursuit of religious ideals made it one of the first examples of a "puritanical" Protestant city.

Landgrave Philip of Hesse (1504–1567) sought to unite Swiss and German Protestants in a mutual defense pact. His efforts were spoiled by theological disagreements between Luther and Zwingli over the nature of Christ's presence in the Eucharist. Zwingli maintained a symbolic interpretation of Christ's words, "This is my body," claiming that Christ was only spiritually present in the bread and wine of the Eucharist. Luther insisted that Christ's human nature shared the properties of his divine nature; where Christ was spiritually present, he could also be bodily present. For Luther, the Eucharistic miracle was not **transubstantiation**, as Rome taught, but "**consubstantiation**": Christ's body and blood being one with, but not of, the bread and wine of the Eucharist. Philip of Hesse brought Luther and Zwingli together in October 1529, but they were unable to work out their differences. The disagreement splintered the Protestant movement theologically and politically.

ANABAPTISTS AND RADICAL PROTESTANTS

Many people wanted a more rapid and thorough implementation of primitive Christianity. The most important of these radical groups were the Anabaptists, the sixteenth-century ancestors of the modern Mennonites and Amish. The Anabaptists rejected infant baptism, insisting that only the baptism of a consenting adult conforms to Scripture. (*Anabaptism* derives from the Greek word meaning "to rebaptize.") Anabaptists withdrew from society to form communities modeled on the example of the first Christians. Political authorities saw their separatism as a threat, and in 1529 rebaptism became a capital offense throughout the Holy Roman Empire.

JOHN CALVIN AND THE GENEVAN REFORMATION

Calvinism was the religious ideology that inspired or accompanied massive political resistance in France, the Netherlands, and Scotland. Believing in both divine predestination and the individual's responsibility to create a godly society, Calvinists were zealous reformers. In a famous and controversial study, *The Protestant Ethic and the Spirit of Capitalism* (1904), the German sociologist Max Weber argued that this peculiar combination of religious confidence and self-disciplined activism produced an ethic congenial to emergent capitalism.

On May 21, 1536, Geneva voted to adopt the Reformation: "to live according to the Gospel and the Word of God . . . without . . . any more masses, statues, idols, or other papal abuses." John Calvin (1509–1564), a reform-minded humanist and lawyer, arrived in Geneva soon thereafter. He wrote articles for the governance of the new church, as well as a catechism to guide and discipline the people. Calvin's measures were too strong for Genevans' tastes, however, and in February 1538 the reformers were exiled from the city.

Calvin then spent two years in Strasbourg, a model Protestant city. He married and wrote a second edition of his masterful *Institutes of the Christian Religion*, which many consider the definitive theological statement of the Protestant faith. Calvin was invited to return to Geneva in 1540.

Calvin and his followers thought the "elect" should live a manifestly God-pleasing life. The consistory, a judicial body composed of clergy and laity, enforced strict moral discipline and was unpopular with many Genevans. But after 1555 the city's magistrates were all devout Calvinists, and more than one-third of Geneva's population was Protestants who had been driven out of France, England, and Scotland, so Calvin had strong support.

Christ Blessing the Children, by Lucas Cranach the Elder (1538). This novel painting was a Lutheran protest against the Anabaptists, who refused to recognize the efficacy of infant baptism. Appealing to the example of Jesus, who had been baptized as an adult, Anabaptists (the name means "rebaptism") disavowed their infant baptism and sought another when they were old enough to grasp what it meant. Here, Jesus joins a throng of new mothers to caress, kiss, and commend their babies to God. After 1529, Anabaptism became a capital offense in the Holy Roman Empire.

Why were there early divisions within the Protestant movement?

•••—Read the **Document**
Calvin Ecclesiastical Ordinances
at **myhistorylab.com**

•••—Read the **Document**
Calvin on Predestination 16th century
at **myhistorylab.com**

CHRONOLOGY

PROGRESS OF PROTESTANT REFORMATION ON THE CONTINENT

1517	Luther posts ninety-five theses against indulgences
1519	Charles I of Spain elected Holy Roman emperor (as Charles V)
1519	Luther challenges infallibility of pope and inerrancy of church councils at Leipzig Debate
1521	Papal bull excommunicates Luther for heresy
1521	Diet of Worms condemns Luther
1521–1522	Luther translates the New Testament into German
1524–1525	Peasants' Revolt in Germany
1529	Marburg Colloquy between Luther and Zwingli
1530	Diet of Augsburg fails to settle religious differences
1531	Formation of Protestant Schmalkaldic League
1536	Calvin arrives in Geneva
1540	Jesuits, founded by Ignatius of Loyola, recognized as order by pope
1545–1563	Council of Trent institutes reforms and responds to the Reformation
1546	Luther dies
1547	Armies of Charles V crush Schmalkaldic League
1555	Peace of Augsburg recognizes rights of Lutherans to worship as they please

POLITICAL CONSOLIDATION OF THE LUTHERAN REFORMATION

In the 1530s German Lutherans formed regional consistories, which oversaw and administered the new Protestant churches. These consistories replaced the old Catholic episcopates. Under the leadership of Philip Melanchthon (1497–1560), educational reforms established compulsory primary education, schools for girls, a humanist revision of the school curriculum, and instruction of the laity in the new religion.

The Reformation also took root elsewhere. In Denmark, Lutheranism became the state religion under Christian III (r. 1536–1559). In Sweden, Gustavus Vasa (r. 1523–1560) confiscated church property and subjected the clergy to royal authority. The absence of a central political authority made Poland a model of religious pluralism and toleration in the second half of the sixteenth century.

Charles V attempted to enforce a compromise agreement between Protestants and Catholics in 1540–1541. Then he turned to a military solution: In 1547 imperial armies crushed the Protestant Schmalkaldic League. The emperor issued the Augsburg Interim, an order that Protestants everywhere must readopt Catholic beliefs and practices. But Protestants resisted fiercely, and the emperor relented. The Peace of Augsburg in September 1555 made the division of Christendom permanent by recognizing what had already been established in practice: *cuius regio, eius religio*, meaning that the ruler of a land would determine the religion of the land. Lutherans were permitted to retain all church lands forcibly seized before 1552. Those discontented with the religion of their region were permitted to migrate. Calvinism, however, was not recognized by the Peace of Augsburg. Calvinists organized to lead national revolutions throughout northern Europe.

THE ENGLISH REFORMATION TO 1553

Late medieval England had a well-earned reputation for defending the rights of the crown against the pope. The marriage of King Henry VIII (r. 1509–1547) finally precipitated England's break with the papacy.

Henry married Catherine of Aragon (d. 1536), a daughter of Ferdinand and Isabella of Spain and the aunt of Emperor Charles V, in 1509. By 1527 the union had produced only a single surviving child, Mary Tudor (d. 1558). Henry came to believe that his marriage was cursed because Catherine had briefly been the wife of his late brother, Arthur.

Henry wanted to marry Anne Boleyn (ca. 1504–1536), one of Catherine's young ladies in waiting. This required papal annulment of the marriage to Catherine, which Henry could not get. Henry's ministers proposed a simple solution: The king could declare his supremacy over English spiritual affairs, as he did over English temporal affairs. Then he could decide the status of his own marriage.

●—[Read the Document
The Act of Supremacy (England), 1534
at **myhistorylab.com**

In 1529 Parliament convened for what would be a seven-year session. In 1533 the "Reformation Parliament" put the clergy under royal jurisdiction, and Henry wed the pregnant Anne Boleyn. Parliament's later Act of Supremacy declared Henry "the only supreme head on earth of the church of England."

Despite his political break with Rome, Henry continued to endorse Catholic doctrine in a country seething with Protestant sentiment. When Edward VI (r. 1547–1553), Henry's son by his third wife, Jane Seymour, became king at age 10, his regents enacted much of the Protestant Reformation. In 1553, when Mary Tudor

●—[View the Image
Thomas Cranmer's Execution
at **myhistorylab.com**

succeeded to the throne, she restored Catholic doctrine and practice with a single-mindedness that rivaled that of her father. It was not until the reign of Anne Boleyn's daughter Elizabeth I (r. 1558–1603) that a lasting religious settlement was worked out in England.

DOCUMENT

Ignatius of Loyola's "Rules for Thinking with the Church"

As leaders of the Counter-Reformation, the Jesuits attempted to live by and instill in others the strictest obedience to church authority. The following are some of the eighteen rules included by Ignatius in his Spiritual Exercises to give Catholics positive direction. These rules also indicate the Catholic reformers' refusal to compromise with Protestants.

- **Would** Protestants find any of Ignatius's "rules" acceptable? Might any of them be controversial among Catholic laity as well as among Protestant laity?

In order to have the proper attitude of mind in the Church Militant we should observe the following rules:

1. Putting aside all private judgment, we should keep our minds prepared and ready to obey promptly and in all things the true spouse of Christ our Lord, our Holy Mother, the hierarchical Church.

2. To praise sacramental confession and the reception of the Most Holy Sacrament once a year, and much better once a month, and better still every week. . . .

3. To praise the frequent hearing of Mass. . . .

4. To praise highly the religious life, virginity, and continence; and also matrimony, but not as highly. . . .

5. To praise the vows of religion, obedience, poverty, chastity, and other works of perfection and supererogation. . . .

6. To praise the relics of the saints . . . [and] the stations, pilgrimages, indulgences, jubilees, Crusade indulgences, and the lighting of candles in the churches.

7. To praise the precepts concerning fasts and abstinences . . . and acts of penance. . . .

8. To praise the adornments and buildings of churches as well as sacred images. . . .

9. To praise all the precepts of the church. . . .

10. To approve and praise the directions and recommendations of our superiors as well as their personal behaviour. . . .

11. To praise both the positive and scholastic theology. . . .

12. We must be on our guard against making comparisons between the living and those who have already gone to their reward, for it is no small error to say, for example: "This man knows more than St. Augustine"; "He is another Saint Francis, or even greater." . . .

13. If we wish to be sure that we are right in all things, we should always be ready to accept this principle: I will believe that the white that I see is black, if the hierarchical Church so defines it. For I believe that between . . . Christ our Lord and . . . His Church, there is but one spirit, which governs and directs us for the salvation of our souls.

Source: From *The Spiritual Exercises of St. Ignatius*, trans. by Anthony Mottola, pp. 139–141. Copyright © 1964 by Doubleday, a division of Bantam, Doubleday, Dell Publishing Group, Inc. Used by permission of Doubleday, a division of Random House, Inc.

CATHOLIC REFORM AND COUNTER-REFORMATION

The medieval church had already faced internal criticisms and efforts at reform before the **Counter-Reformation** was launched in reaction to Protestant successes.

Sixteenth-century popes had resisted efforts to change the laws and institutions of the church. Many new religious orders, however, led a broad revival of piety within the church. The Society of Jesus (the Jesuits) was instrumental in the success of the Counter-Reformation. Organized by Ignatius of Loyola in the 1530s, within a century the society had more than 15,000 members scattered throughout the world, including thriving missions in India, Japan, and the Americas.

Ignatius of Loyola (1491–1556) began his spiritual pilgrimage in 1521 while recuperating from battle wounds. Reading Christian classics, he was so impressed with the heroic self-sacrifice of the church's saints that he underwent a profound

Counter-Reformation

The sixteenth-century reform movement in the Roman Catholic Church in reaction to the Protestant Reformation.

Watch the **Video**
at **myhistorylab.com**

QUICK REVIEW

The Jesuits

- The Society of Jesus founded in 1530s by Ignatius of Loyola
- Achieve spiritual self-mastery through discipline and passion for spirituality

The Miracle of St. Ignatius of Loyola, by Peter Paul Rubens. Here, the founder of the Society of Jesus, surrounded by angels and members of the new Jesuit Order, preaches to an aroused assembly.

What elements of this painting capture the spirit of the Counter-Reformation?

◉⌐View the Image
Ignatius of Loyola,
at **myhistorylab.com**

◆●◆⌐Read the Document
Council of Trent 1545–1563
at **myhistorylab.com**

religious conversion. Ignatius devised a program of religious and moral self-discipline called the *Spiritual Exercises*, which outlined a path to absolute spiritual self-mastery. Ignatius believed that a person could shape his or her own behavior, even create a new religious self, through disciplined study and regular practice. Ignatius's exercises were intended to teach Catholics to submit to higher church authority and spiritual direction. (See Document, "Ignatius of Loyola's 'Rules for Thinking with the Church'" on page 397.) The potent combination of discipline, self-control, and passion for traditional spirituality and mystical experience helped counter the Reformation and won many Protestants back to Catholicism, especially in Austria and Germany.

Pope Paul III (r. 1534–1549) called a general council to reassert church doctrine. Three sessions, spread over eighteen years, met in the imperial city of Trent in northern Italy under firm papal control. The Council of Trent's most important reforms concerned internal church discipline. The selling of church offices was forbidden. The authority of local bishops was strengthened. Parish priests were required to be neatly dressed, educated, strictly celibate, and active among their parishioners. The council did not make a single doctrinal concession to the Protestants, instead reaffirming traditional beliefs and practices. Parish life revived under the guidance of a devout and better-trained clergy.

THE REFORMATION AND DAILY LIFE

HOW DID family life change during the Reformation era?

Although politically conservative, the Reformation brought about far-reaching changes in traditional religious practices and institutions.

RELIGION IN FIFTEENTH-CENTURY LIFE

In the fifteenth century, the church calendar regulated daily life. About one-third of the year was given over to some kind of religious observance or celebration. Clerics made up 6 to 8 percent of the total population of the great cities of central Europe, exercising considerable political as well as spiritual power.

Monasteries and nunneries were influential institutions. Local aristocrats were closely identified with particular churches and chapels. The Mass and liturgy were read entirely in Latin. Images of saints were regularly displayed, and on certain holidays their relics were paraded about and venerated. Pilgrims gathered by the thousands at religious shrines, searching for cures or seeking diversion. Several times during the year, special preachers appeared with letters of indulgence to sell. Many clergy lived openly with concubines and had children in relationships tolerated by the church if penitential fines were paid.

People complained about the clergy's exemption from taxation and, in many instances, also from the civil criminal code. People grumbled about having to support church offices whose occupants actually worked elsewhere, and many felt that the church had too much influence over education and culture.

RELIGION IN SIXTEENTH-CENTURY LIFE

In these same cities after the Reformation had firmly established itself, the same aristocratic families governed; the rich generally got richer and the poor poorer. But overall numbers of clergy fell by two-thirds and religious holidays shrank by one-third. Monasteries and nunneries were nearly absent, many having been transformed into hospices for the sick and poor or into educational institutions. In the churches, which had also been reduced in number by at least a third, worship was conducted almost completely in the vernacular. Local shrines were closed down, and anyone found openly venerating saints, relics, and images was subject to fine and punishment. Copies of Luther's translation of the New Testament, or excerpts from it, were in private homes. The clergy could marry, and most did. They paid taxes and were punished for their crimes in civil courts. Domestic moral life was regulated by committees composed of roughly equal numbers of laity and clergy, over whose decisions secular magistrates had the last word.

Not all Protestant clergy were enthusiastic about this new lay authority in religion, and the laity, too, was ambivalent about some aspects of the Reformation. Over half of the original converts returned to the Catholic fold before the end of the sixteenth century. Half of Europe's population was Protestant in the mid-sixteenth century, but by the mid-seventeenth century only a fifth remained Protestant.[2]

FAMILY LIFE IN EARLY MODERN EUROPE

Changes in the timing and duration of marriage, family size, and infant and child care suggest that social and economic pressures were influencing family life. The Reformation was only one factor in these changes.

Between 1500 and 1800, men and women in western Europe and England married at later ages than they had previously: men in their mid- to late twenties and women in their early to mid-twenties. After the Reformation, both Protestants and Catholics required parental consent and public vows in church before a marriage could be deemed fully licit. Late marriage in the West reflected the difficulty couples had supporting themselves independently. In the sixteenth century, one in five women never married, and an estimated 15 percent were widows. Women who bore children for the first time at advanced ages had higher mortality rates. Delayed marriage increased premarital sex and the number of illegitimate children.

Marriage tended to be "arranged" in the sense that the parents met and discussed the terms of the marriage. But the wealth and social standing of the bride and the bridegroom were not the only things considered. By the fifteenth century, it was usual for the future bride and bridegroom to have known each other, and their feelings were respected by parents.

The western European family was conjugal, or nuclear, consisting of two parents and two to four children who survived into adulthood. Infant mortality and child death were common. The family lived within a larger household, including in-laws, servants, laborers, and boarders.

Artificial birth control has existed since antiquity, but early birth control measures were not very effective, and for both historical and moral reasons the church opposed them. The church and physicians encouraged women to suckle their own newborns rather than hand them off to wet nurses (lactating women who sold their services). Because nursing has a contraceptive effect, some women nursed to space out their pregnancies, while those who wanted many children used wet nurses.

[2]Geoffrey Parker, *Europe in Crisis, 1598–1648* (Ithaca, NY: Cornell University Press, 1979), p. 50.

See the Map
Europe after the Reformation
at **myhistorylab.com**

QUICK REVIEW

Marriage, 1500–1800

- Couples married later in life
- 20 percent of women never married
- Couples had children every two years; many died
- "Wet nursing" was controversial
- Remarriage after death of a spouse was often quick

Portrait of His Wife and Two Elder Children, by Hans Holbein the Younger (1528). German-English painter Hans Holbein's painting of his wife and two of his children.

What was it like to be a child in early modern Europe?

A Closer Look

A Contemporary Commentary of the Sexes

G.1431; R8.MGVK*1   Taming of the Lion   [334 x 477]   1524   Berlin

Taming the Lion

A No man is ever so high or good
That he cannot be managed by a woman
Who does his will
In friendly love and service.

B Although he is tyranical wild,
He is soon calmed by a woman.
She boldly strokes his open mouth,
His anger fades, he does not bite.

C The lion, most lordly of beasts,
Famous for his strength and nobility,
Favors us women with heartfelt gifts
And good humor accompanies his kindness.

D How wonderfully you reflect
Your taming at woman's hand,
Bearing patiently what another
Does to you against your will.

E O powerful king and greatest lord
Your equal is neither near nor far.

Excelling all, both large and small,
Upon your head should lie a crown.

F Lord lion, although you are feared by all,
A woman knows how to saddle you,
Bending you to her will by love.
True love finds a home with a good man.

G How well you have been groomed!
Now how lively and cheerful!
One so spirited
May have the company of women.

H Lord lion, you may have your every wish.
Cover your trail with your tail
And you will not be tracked down.
Those who love in secret know this well.

Lion I let the women amuse themselves by serving me.
What harm can they possibly do me?
If I want, I can suddenly turn fierce again.
He is a fool who lets himself be taught by women.

Questions

1. In the scene above, who controls the relationship between the sexes? Is the lion a truly forbidding patriarch, or is the matriarch the one on top?

2. How does this artistic portrayal of womankind compare with the lives of historical women featured in the chapter?

3. Compare the scene with: "Christ Blessing the Children" (p. 395); Holbein's portrait of his wife and children (p. 399); and Hans Baldung Grien's portrayal of witches (p. 406).

4. What general conclusions can be drawn about the relationship of the sexes?

Family life had features that seem cold and distant to us today. Children between the ages of 8 and 13 were sent from their homes into apprenticeships, school, or employment. Widowers and widows often remarried within a few months of a spouse's death, and marriages with extreme disparity in age between partners also suggest limited affection. In response to such modern-day criticism, it must be remembered that a well-apprenticed child was a self-supporting child, and hence one with a future. Given the primitive living conditions, contemporaries appreciated the utilitarian and humane side of marriage and understood when widowers and widows quickly remarried.

Read the **Document**
Office and Dutie Husband Juan Luis Vives
at **myhistorylab.com**

THE WARS OF RELIGION

After the Council of Trent adjourned in 1563, Catholics began a Jesuit-led counteroffensive against Protestants. At the time of John Calvin's death in 1564, Geneva had become both a refuge for Europe's persecuted Protestants and an international school for Protestant resistance, producing leaders fully equal to the new Catholic challenge. Genevan Calvinism and the reformed Catholicism of the Council of Trent were two equally dogmatic, aggressive, and irreconcilable church systems.

WHY DID religious divisions lead to war?

Calvinism adopted a presbyterian form of church government, in which elders representing individual congregations determined church policy. By contrast, the Counter-Reformation affirmed Catholicism's dedication to a centralized episcopal system, governed by a clerical hierarchy and owing absolute obedience to the pope. Calvinism attracted proponents of political decentralization who opposed totalitarian rulers, whereas Catholicism was congenial to proponents of absolute monarchy who believed that order required "one king, one church, one law."

Wars of religion were both national conflicts and international wars. Catholics and Protestants struggled for control of France, the Netherlands, and England. The Catholic governments of France and Spain fought the Protestant regimes in England and the Netherlands. The Thirty Years' War, which began in 1618, drew in every major European nation before it ended.

FRENCH WARS OF RELIGION (1562–1598)

When Henry II (r. 1547–1559) died in 1559, his sickly 15-year-old son, Francis II (d. 1560), came to the throne under the regency of the queen mother, Catherine de Médicis (1519–1589). With the monarchy weakened, three powerful families competed for control. The Guises were by far the strongest, and they were militant Catholics. The Bourbon and Montmorency-Châtillon families, in contrast, developed strong Huguenot sympathies, largely for political reasons. (French Protestants were called **Huguenots**.)

Huguenots
French Calvinists.

Ambitious aristocrats and discontented townspeople joined Calvinist churches in opposition to the Guise-dominated French monarchy. Many apparently hoped to establish within France a principle of territorial sovereignty akin to that secured within the Holy Roman Empire by the Peace of Augsburg.

After Francis II died, Catherine de Médicis continued as regent for her second son, Charles IX (r. 1560–1574). Wanting a Catholic France but not a Guise-dominated monarchy, Catherine sought allies among the Protestants. Early in 1562 she granted Protestants limited freedoms—though even limited royal toleration ended when the Duke of Guise surprised a Protestant congregation worshiping illegally at Vassy in Champagne and proceeded to massacre several score of them, marking the beginning of the French wars of religion.

In 1572, apparently to cover up her role in an attempt to assassinate a Huguenot leader, Catherine convinced Charles that a Huguenot coup was afoot. On the eve of Saint Bartholomew's Day, August 24, 1572, 3,000 Huguenots were butchered in Paris. Within three days an estimated 20,000 Huguenots were executed throughout France.

The St. Bartholemew's Day Massacre. In this notorious event, here depicted by the contemporary Protestant painter François Dubois, 3,000 Protestants were slaughtered in Paris, and an estimated 20,000 others died throughout France. The massacre transformed the religious struggle in France from a contest for political power into an all-out war between Protestants and Catholics.

Do you think these events would be portrayed differently by a Catholic artist?

Read the Document
Account: Massacre
St. Bartholomew 1572
at **myhistorylab.com**

This event changed the nature of Protestant–Catholic conflict both within France and beyond. In Protestant eyes, it became an international struggle for survival against an adversary whose cruelty justified any means of resistance.

Henry III (r. 1574–1589) sought to steer a middle course, and in this effort he received support from a growing body of neutral Catholics and Huguenots who put the political survival of France above its religious unity. Such *politiques*, as they were called, were prepared to compromise religious creeds to save the nation. Henry III allied with his Protestant cousin and heir, Henry of Navarre, against the Catholic League, supported by the Spanish, which dominated Paris in the mid-1580s. When a fanatical Dominican friar murdered Henry III, the Bourbon Henry of Navarre became Henry IV of France (r. 1589–1610).

Henry IV believed that a royal policy of tolerant Catholicism would be the best way to achieve peace. On July 25, 1593, he publicly abjured the Protestant faith and embraced the traditional religion of his country. "Paris is worth a Mass," he is reported to have said. Henry IV's famous Edict of Nantes (1598) recognized and sanctioned minority religious rights within what was to remain an officially Catholic country. This religious truce granted the Huguenots, who by this time numbered well over a million, freedom of public worship, the right of assembly, admission to public offices and universities, and permission to maintain fortified towns.

Read the Document
The Edict of Nantes 1598
at **myhistorylab.com**

Henry IV was assassinated in 1610. Although he is best remembered for the Edict of Nantes, the political and economic policies he put in place laid the foundations for the transformation of France into the absolutist state it would become in the seventeenth century.

IMPERIAL SPAIN AND THE REIGN OF PHILIP II (1556–1598)

Until the English defeated his mighty Armada in 1588, Philip II of Spain was the late-sixteenth century's greatest ruler. He focused first on Turkish expansion. On October 7, 1571, a Holy League of Spain, Venice, and the pope defeated the

Turks at Lepanto. Before the engagement ended, 30,000 Turks had died and over one-third of the Turkish fleet had been sunk or captured. But Philip failed when he attempted to impose his will within the Netherlands and on England and France.

The Netherlands was the richest area in Europe. Its merchant towns were Europe's most independent, and many were Calvinist strongholds. A stubborn opposition to the Spanish overlords formed when Philip II insisted on enforcing the decrees of the Council of Trent in the Netherlands. William of Nassau, the Prince of Orange (r. 1533–1584), emerged as the leader of a broad movement for the Netherlands' independence from Spain. Like other successful rulers in this period, William of Orange was a *politique* who placed the Netherlands' political autonomy and well-being above religious creeds.

The ten largely Catholic southern provinces (roughly modern Belgium) came together in 1576 with the seven largely Protestant northern provinces (roughly the modern Netherlands) in unified opposition to Spain. This union, known as the Pacification of Ghent, declared internal regional sovereignty in matters of religion. In January 1579 the southern provinces made peace with Spain. The northern provinces continued the struggle. Spain was preoccupied with France and England, and the northern provinces drove out all Spanish soldiers by 1593.

ENGLAND AND SPAIN (1558–1603)

Elizabeth I (r. 1558–1603), the daughter of Henry VIII and Anne Boleyn, may have been the most astute politician of the sixteenth century. She repealed the anti-Protestant legislation of her predecessor Mary Tudor and guided a religious settlement through Parliament that prevented England from being torn asunder by religious differences in the sixteenth century.

Catholic extremists hoped to replace Elizabeth with the Catholic Mary Stuart, Queen of Scots (1542–1587), but Elizabeth acted swiftly against assassination plots and rarely let emotion override her political instincts.

Elizabeth dealt cautiously with the Puritans, Protestants who sought to "purify" the national church. The Puritans had two special grievances: (1) the retention of Catholic ceremony and vestments within the Church of England, and (2) the continuation of the episcopal system of church governance. Sixteenth-century Puritans were not separatists, however. They worked through Parliament to create an alternative national church of semiautonomous congregations governed by representative presbyteries (hence, Presbyterians). More extreme Puritans wanted every congregation to be autonomous. Elizabeth refused to tolerate these Congregationalists, whose views she considered subversive.

Despite religious differences, both Elizabeth and Spain's Philip II hoped to maintain a peaceful coexistence between their nations. Nonetheless, a series of events—culminating in Elizabeth's execution of Mary, Queen of Scots, on February 18, 1587—led inexorably to war between England and Spain. On May 30, 1588, a mighty fleet of 130 Spanish ships bearing 25,000 sailors and soldiers set sail for England. But the day belonged completely to the English. English and Dutch ships, assisted by an "English wind," dispersed the waiting Spanish fleet, over a third of which never returned to Spain.

The Milch Cow. This sixteenth-century satirical painting depicts the Netherlands as a land all the great powers of Europe wish to exploit. Elizabeth of England is feeding her (England had long-standing commercial ties with Flanders); Philip II of Spain is attempting to ride her (Spain was trying to reassert its control over the entire region); William of Orange is trying to milk her (he was the leader of the anti-Spanish rebellion); and the king of France holds her by the tail (France hoped to profit from the rebellion at Spain's expense).

The "Milch Cow." Rijksmuseum, Amsterdam.

Which character shown here could be considered most successful in the way history actually played out?

◉ See the Map
The Netherlands during the Dutch Revolt, ca. 1580
at **myhistorylab.com**

Elizabeth I (1558–1603), Standing on a Map of England in 1592. An astute, if sometimes erratic, politician in foreign and domestic policy, Elizabeth was one of the most successful rulers of the sixteenth century.

National Portrait Gallery, London/SuperStock.

What qualities of kingship are conveyed in this portrait of Elizabeth I?

The Armada's defeat gave heart to Protestant resistance everywhere. Spain never fully recovered. By the time of Philip's death on September 13, 1598, his forces had been rebuffed by the French and the Dutch. His seventeenth-century successors were all inferior leaders. The French soon dominated the Continent, while the Dutch and the English whittled away Spain's overseas empire. Elizabeth died on March 23, 1603, leaving behind her a strong nation poised to expand into a global empire.

THE THIRTY YEARS' WAR (1618–1648)

The Thirty Years' War in the Holy Roman Empire was the last and most destructive of the wars of religion. Religious and political hatreds had become entrenched, and various groups were determined to sacrifice all for their territorial sovereignty and religious beliefs. As the conflicts multiplied, it became the worst European catastrophe since the Black Death of the fourteenth century. When the hostilities ended in 1648, the peace terms shaped much of the map of northern Europe as we know it today.

During the second half of the sixteenth century, Germany was an almost ungovernable land of 360 autonomous political entities. In 1555, the Peace of Augsburg had given each a significant degree of sovereignty within its own borders. Political decentralization and fragmentation characterized Germany as the seventeenth century opened; it was not a unified nation like Spain, England, or even strife-torn France. (See Map 16–4.)

The Holy Roman Empire was about equally divided between Catholics and Protestants, the latter having perhaps a slight numerical edge by 1600. After the Peace of Augsburg, Lutherans had gained political control in many Catholic areas, as had the Catholics in a few previously Lutheran areas. There was also religious strife between liberal and conservative Lutherans and between Lutherans and the growing numbers of Calvinists. Calvinism had not been recognized as a legal religion by the Peace of Augsburg, but it established a strong foothold within the empire when the devoutly Calvinist Elector Frederick III (r. 1559–1576) made it the official religion within the Palatinate in 1559. By 1609 Palatine Calvinists headed a Protestant defensive alliance supported by Spain's sixteenth-century enemies: England, France, and the Netherlands.

Jesuits were also active within the Holy Roman Empire. From staunchly Catholic Bavaria, supported by Spain, Jesuits launched successful missions throughout the empire. In 1609 Maximilian, Duke of Bavaria (1573–1651), organized a Catholic League to counter the Palatine-based Protestant alliance. When the Catholic League fielded a great army, it launched the Thirty Years' War.

In 1648 all hostilities within the Holy Roman Empire were brought to an end by the Treaty of Westphalia. It firmly reasserted the major feature of the Peace of Augsburg: Rulers were again permitted to determine the religion of their lands. The treaty also gave the Calvinists their long-sought legal recognition, while denying it to sectarians. The independence of the Swiss Confederacy and the United Provinces of Holland, long recognized in fact, now became law.

The Treaty of Westphalia perpetuated German division and political weakness into the modern period, although Austria and Brandenburg-Prussia attained international significance during the seventeenth century. In Europe at large, distinctive nation-states, each with its own political, cultural, and religious identity, reached maturity in the seventeenth century and firmly established the competitive nationalism of the modern world.

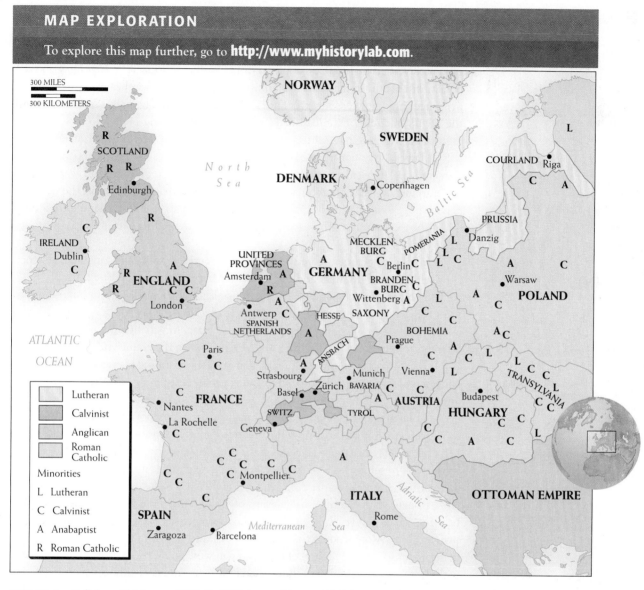

MAP EXPLORATION

To explore this map further, go to **http://www.myhistorylab.com**.

MAP 16–4.   Religious Division ca. 1600. By 1600 few could expect Christians to return to a uniform religious allegiance. In Spain and southern Italy Catholicism remained relatively unchallenged, but note the existence elsewhere of large religious minorities, both Catholic and Protestant.

Why did the wars of religion fail to reestablish religious uniformity in the Holy Roman Empire?

SUPERSTITION AND ENLIGHTENMENT: THE BATTLE WITHIN

Religious reform and warfare moved intellectuals to rethink human nature and society. One side of that reconsideration was dark and cynical, perhaps because the peak years of religious warfare had also been those of the great European witch hunts. Another side was brilliantly skeptical and constructive, reflecting the growing scientific movement of the years between 1500 and 1700.

WHO WERE some of the most significant writers and thinkers between 1500 and 1700?

Two Witches by Hans Baldung Grien (1523). German artist Hans Baldung Grien presents the powers and temptations of two enchanted, monumental witches as they sow the wind.

What types of people were most vulnerable to accusations of witchcraft?

◆◆◆ Read the Document
Malleus Maleficarum 1486
at **myhistorylab.com**

QUICK REVIEW

Witch Hunts

- "Cunning folk" traditionally helped villagers
- Christian clergy monopolized "magic"
- Older, single women were most vulnerable to accusations of witchcraft
- Witch trials could be destabilizing

Watch the Video
at **myhistorylab.com**

WITCH HUNTS AND PANIC

The witch hunts and panics that erupted in almost every Western land reveal the dark side of early modern thought and culture. Between 1400 and 1700, courts sentenced an estimated 70,000 to 100,000 people to death for harmful magic (*maleficium*) and diabolical witchcraft. In addition to harming their neighbors, witches were said to fly to mass meetings known as *sabbats*. They were accused of indulging in sexual orgies with the devil, practicing cannibalism (especially the devouring of small Christian children), and engaging in a variety of rituals that denied or perverted Christian beliefs.

Many factors contributed to the great witch panics of the second half of the sixteenth and the early seventeenth centuries. Religious division and warfare were major influences. The church had traditionally provided defenses against the devil and demons; the Reformation forced people to find alternative ways to handle their anxieties. The growing strength of governments intent on weeding out nonconformists also played a part.

In village societies, feared and respected "cunning folk" had long helped people cope with natural disasters and disabilities by magical means. For local people, these were important services, and possession of magical powers made one an important person in the village. Vulnerable people, such as old, single women, often claimed power. Witch beliefs may also have been a way for villagers to defy urban Christian society's attempts to impose its beliefs, laws, and institutions on the countryside.

The Christian clergy also practiced magic, transforming bread and wine into the body and blood of Christ, and converting eternal punishments for sins into temporal ones. Clergy exorcised demons, too. In the late thirteenth century the church declared its magic the only legitimate magic. Since such power was not human, the theologians reasoned, anyone who practiced magic outside the church did so on behalf of the devil. Attacking accused witches became a way for the church to extend its spiritual hegemony. To accuse, try, and execute witches was a declaration of moral and political authority.

Roughly 80 percent of the victims of witch hunts were women, most single and between 45 and 60 years of age. Older single women were particularly vulnerable for many reasons. More women than men laid claim to supernatural powers, so they were at disproportionate risk. Many of these women were midwives, so they were associated with deaths during childbirth. Both the church and their neighbors were prepared to think and say the worst about them.

Many factors helped end the witch hunts. A more scientific worldview made it difficult to believe in the powers of witches. Witch hunts also tended to get out of hand. Tortured witches sometimes alleged having seen leading townspeople at sabbats, at which point the trials threatened anarchy.

WRITERS AND PHILOSOPHERS

By the end of the sixteenth century, many could no longer embrace either the old Catholic or new Protestant absolutes. Intellectually as well as politically, the seventeenth century would be a period of transition. Some writers and philosophers of the late sixteenth and seventeenth centuries tried to straddle the two ages (Cervantes and Shakespeare), others ignored or opposed new developments that seemed to threaten traditional values (Pascal), and still others embraced emerging ideas and social structures (Spinoza, Hobbes, and Locke).

In Spain, the intertwining of Catholic piety and Spanish political power fostered a literature preoccupied with medieval chivalric virtues, especially honor and loyalty.

Generally acknowledged to be the greatest Spanish writer of all time, Miguel de Cervantes Saavedra (1547–1616) educated himself by insatiable reading in vernacular literature and immersion in the school of life. In 1570 he became a soldier and was decorated for gallantry at Lepanto (1571). He began his most famous work, *Don Quixote*, in prison in 1603, after conviction for theft.

Many believe the intent of *Don Quixote* was to satirize the chivalric romances so popular in Spain, but Cervantes shows deep affection for his characters. Don Quixote, a none-too-stable middle-aged man, is driven mad by reading too many chivalric romances. He comes to believe that he is an aspirant to knighthood and must prove his worthiness. He acquires a rusty suit of armor, mounts an aged horse, and chooses for his inspiration a peasant girl whom he fancies to be a noble lady. Sancho Panza, a wise peasant who serves as Don Quixote's squire, watches with skepticism and sympathy as his lord repeatedly makes a fool of himself. The story ends tragically with Don Quixote's humiliating defeat by a well-meaning friend who forces him to renounce his quest for knighthood. Throughout *Don Quixote*, Cervantes juxtaposed the down-to-earth realism of Sancho Panza with the old-fashioned religious idealism of Don Quixote. Cervantes admired the one as much as the other and demonstrated that to be truly happy, men and women need dreams—even impossible ones—just as much as a sense of reality.

Surprisingly little is known about William Shakespeare (1564–1616), the greatest playwright in the English language. He apparently worked as a schoolteacher, acquiring broad knowledge of Renaissance learning and literature. He took the new commercialism and the bawdy pleasures of the Elizabethan Age in stride and with amusement. References to contemporary political events fill his plays. By modern standards he was a political conservative, accepting the social rankings and the power structure of his day and demonstrating unquestioned patriotism.

Shakespeare was a playwright, actor, and part owner of a theater. His work brought together the best past and current achievements in the dramatic arts. He particularly mastered the psychology of human motivation and passion. Shakespeare wrote histories, comedies, and tragedies. Four of his best tragedies were written within a three-year period: *Hamlet* (1603), *Othello* (1604), *King Lear* (1605), and *Macbeth* (1606). In his lifetime and ever since, Shakespeare has been immensely popular with both audiences and readers. As Ben Jonson (1572–1637), a contemporary classical dramatist who created his own school of poets, put it in 1623: "He was not of an age, but for all time."

Blaise Pascal (1623–1662) was a French mathematician and a physical scientist widely acclaimed by his contemporaries. He was torn between the continuing dogmatism and the new skepticism of the seventeenth century. Pascal believed that reason and science, though attesting to human dignity, remained of no avail in religion. Here only the reasons of the heart and a "leap of faith" could prevail. Pascal saw two essential truths in the Christian religion: A loving God, worthy of human attainment, exists; and human beings, because they are corrupted in nature, are utterly unworthy of God.

Pascal made a famous wager with the skeptics. It is a better bet, he argued, to believe that God exists and to stake everything on his promised mercy than not to do so; if God does exist, everything will be gained by the believer, whereas the loss incurred by having believed in a nonexistent God is minimal. Pascal urged his contemporaries to seek self-understanding by "learned ignorance" and to discover humankind's greatness by recognizing its misery, thereby countering what he saw as the false optimism of the new rationalism and science.

Leviathan. Thomas Hobbes's political treatise, *Leviathan*, portrayed rulers as absolute lords over their lands, incorporating in their persons the individual wills of all their people.

Look closely at this picture: What does it show?

•◆•┤Read the Document
Leviathan at **myhistorylab.com**

The most controversial thinker of the seventeenth century was Baruch Spinoza (1632–1677), the son of a Jewish merchant of Amsterdam. He criticized the dogmatism of Dutch Calvinists and championed freedom of thought. Spinoza's most influential writing, *Ethics*, appeared after his death in 1677. Religious leaders universally condemned it for its apparent espousal of pantheism. According to Spinoza there is only one substance, which is self-caused, free, and infinite, and God is that substance. Everything that exists is in God and cannot even be conceived of apart from him. Such a doctrine is not literally pantheistic, but in Spinoza's view, statements about the natural world are also statements about divine nature. Mind and matter are seen to be extensions of the infinite substance of God; what transpires in the world of humankind and nature is a necessary outpouring of the Divine.

Thomas Hobbes (1588–1679) was the most original political philosopher of the seventeenth century. Although he never broke with the Church of England, he came to share basic Calvinist beliefs, especially the low view of human nature and the ideal of a commonwealth based on a covenant, both of which find eloquent expression in his political philosophy. Hobbes was an enthusiastic supporter of the new scientific movement. During the 1630s he visited Paris, where he came to know Descartes; after the outbreak of the Puritan Revolution (see Chapter 19) in 1640, he lived as an exile in Paris until 1651. Hobbes also spent time with Galileo (see Chapter 21) in Italy and took a special interest in the works of William Harvey, the physiologist famed for the discovery of how blood circulates through the body.

Hobbes was driven to political philosophy by the English Civil War (see Chapter 19). In 1651 his *Leviathan* appeared. Its subject was the political consequences of human passions, and its originality lay in (1) its making natural law, rather than common law (i.e., custom or precedent), the basis of all positive law, and (2) its defense of a representative theory of absolute authority against the theory of the divine right of kings. Hobbes maintained that statute law found its justification only as an expression of the law of nature and that rulers derived their authority from the consent of the people.

The key to Hobbes's political philosophy is a brilliant myth of the original state of humankind. According to this myth, human beings in the natural state are generally inclined to a "perpetual and restless desire of power after power that ceases only in death."[3] Whereas earlier and later philosophers saw the original human state as a paradise from which humankind had fallen, Hobbes saw it as a corruption from which only society had delivered people. According to Hobbes, people escape the impossible state of nature only by entering a social contract that creates a commonwealth tightly ruled by law and order. The social contract obliges every person, for the sake of peace and self-defense, to agree to set aside personal rights. The social contract also establishes the coercive force necessary to compel compliance. Hobbes conceived of the ruler's power as absolute and unlimited. There is no room in Hobbes's political philosophy for political protest in the name of individual conscience or for resistance to legitimate authority by private individuals—features of *Leviathan* criticized by Catholics and Puritans alike.

John Locke (1632–1704) has proved to be the most influential political thinker of the seventeenth century.[4] His political philosophy was embodied in the so-called Glorious Revolution of 1688 to 1689 (Chapter 19). Although he was not as original as Hobbes, his political writings were a major source of the later Enlightenment criticism of absolutism, and they gave inspiration to both the American and French Revolutions.

---

[3]*Leviathan*, Parts I and II, ed. by H. W. Schneider (Indianapolis, IN: Bobbs-Merrill, 1958), p. 86.
[4]Locke's scientific writings are discussed in Chapter 23.

Locke's two most famous works are the *Essay Concerning Human Understanding* (1690) (discussed in Chapter 21) and *Two Treatises of Government* (1690), in which he argued that rulers are not absolute in their power. Rulers remain bound to the law of nature, which is the voice of reason, teaching that "all mankind [are] equal and independent, [and] no one ought to harm another in his life, health, liberty, or possessions,"[5] since all human beings are the images and property of God. People enter social contracts, empowering legislatures and monarchs to arbitrate their disputes, precisely to preserve their natural rights, not to give rulers an absolute power over them. From Locke's point of view, absolute monarchy was "inconsistent" with civil society and could be "no form of civil government at all."[6]

SUMMARY

 WHY DID western Europeans start exploring, trading, and settling around the world in the fifteenth century?

The Discovery of a New World. In the late fifteenth century, Europe began to expand around the globe. Driven by both commercial and religious motives, the Portuguese pioneered a sea route around Africa to India and the Far East, and the Spanish discovered the Americas. The social, political, and biological consequences were immense. *page 386*

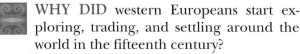 **WHO WERE** the early Protestant leaders?

The Reformation. The Reformation began in Germany with Martin Luther's attack on indulgences in 1517. The Reformation shattered the religious unity of Europe. In Switzerland, Zwingli and Calvin launched their own versions of Protestantism. In England, Henry VIII repudiated papal authority when the pope refused to grant him a divorce. The different Protestant sects were often as hostile to each other as they were to Catholicism. The Roman Catholic Church also acted to reform itself. The Council of Trent tightened church discipline and reaffirmed traditional doctrine. The Jesuits converted many Protestants back to Catholicism. *page 389*

 HOW DID family life change during the Reformation era?

The Reformation and Daily Life. The Reformation led to far-reaching changes in religious beliefs, practices, and institutions. Family life changed in this period, as couples married later in life. *page 398*

 WHY DID religious divisions lead to war?

The Wars of Religion. The religious divisions of Europe led to more than a century of warfare from the 1520s to 1648. The chief battlegrounds were in France, the Netherlands, and Germany. When the Thirty Years' War ended in 1648, Europe was permanently divided into Catholic and Protestant areas. *page 401*

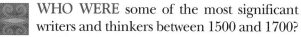 **WHO WERE** some of the most significant writers and thinkers between 1500 and 1700?

Superstition and Enlightenment: The Battle Within. The Reformation led to both dark and constructive views of human nature. Witch crazes erupted across Europe. Thousands of innocent people, mostly women, were persecuted and executed as witches between 1400 and 1700. In literature and philosophy, these years witnessed an outpouring of creative thinking. Among the greatest thinkers of the age were Cervantes, Shakespeare, Pascal, Spinoza, Hobbes, and Locke. *page 405*

KEY TERMS

consubstantiation (p. 394)
Counter-Reformation (p. 397)
Diet of Worms (p. 392)
Huguenots (HYEW-guh-nahts) (p. 401)
indulgence (p. 392)
ninety-five theses (p. 392)
Reformation (p. 389)
transubstantiation (p. 394)

---

[5]*The Second Treatise of Government*, ed. by T. P. Peardon (Indianapolis, IN: Bobbs-Merrill, 1952), chap. 2, sects. 4–6, pp. 4–6.

[6]Ibid.

REVIEW QUESTIONS

1. What impact did expansion have on European economies?

2. What were the main problems of the church that contributed to the Protestant Reformation? Why was the church unable to suppress dissent as it had earlier?

3. How did the theologies of Luther, Zwingli, and Calvin differ? Were their differences only religious, or did they have political consequences for the Reformation as well?

4. Why did the Reformation begin in Germany and not in France, Italy, England, or Spain?

5. What was the Catholic Reformation? Did the Council of Trent alter the character of traditional Catholicism?

6. Why did Henry VIII break with the Catholic Church? Was the "new" religion he established really Protestant?

7. Were the wars of religion really over religion? Explain.

8. Henry of Navarre (later Henry IV of France), Elizabeth I, and William of Orange have been called *politiques*. What does that term mean, and how might it apply to each?

9. Why was England more successful than other lands in resolving its internal political and religious divisions peacefully during the sixteenth and seventeenth centuries?

10. Consider some of the leading intellectuals of this period: Cervantes, Shakespeare, Pascal, Spinoza, Hobbes, and Locke. Whose ideas do you find most challenging, and why? Which one would you most like to meet?

Note: To learn more about the topics in this chapter, please turn to the Suggested Reading s at the end of the book. For additional sources related to this chapter please see www.myhistorylab.com

PEARSON
myhistorylab Connections

Reinforce what you learned in this chapter by studying the many documents, images, maps, review tools, and videos available at **www.myhistorylab.com**

Read and Review

Research and Explore

((•—Hear the Audio

Hear the audio file for Chapter 16
at **www.myhistorylab.com**

CHRISTIANITY

RELIGIONS OF THE WORLD

Christianity is based on the teachings of Jesus of Nazareth, a Jew who lived in Palestine during the Roman occupation. His simple message of faith in God and self-sacrificial love of one's neighbor attracted many people. The Roman authorities, perceiving his large following as a threat, crucified him. After Jesus' crucifixion, his followers proclaimed that he had been resurrected from the dead and that he would return in glory to defeat sin, death, and the devil, and take all true believers with him to heaven—a radical vision of judgment and immortality that has driven Christianity's appeal since its inception. In the teachings of the early church, Jesus became the Christ, the son of God, the long-awaited Messiah of Jewish prophecy. His followers called themselves Christians.

Christianity proclaimed the very incarnation of God in a man, the visible presence of eternity in time. According to early Christian teaching, the power of God's incarnation in Jesus lived on in the preaching and sacraments of the church under the guidance of the Holy Spirit. According to the Christian message, in Jesus, eternity has made itself accessible to every person here and now and forevermore.

The new religion attracted both the poor and powerless and the socially rising and well-to-do. For some, the gospel of Jesus promised a better material life. For others, it imparted a sense of spiritual self-worth regardless of one's place or prospects in society.

In the late second century the Romans began persecuting Christians as "heretics" (because of their rejection of the traditional Roman gods) and as social revolutionaries (for their loyalty to a lord higher than the emperor of Rome). At the same time dissenting Christians, particularly sects claiming direct spiritual knowledge of God apart from Scripture, internally divided the young church. To meet these challenges the church established effective weapons against state terrorism and Christian heresy: an ordained clergy, a hierarchical church organization, orthodox creeds, and a biblical canon (the New Testament). Christianity not only gained legal status within the Roman Empire, but also, by the fourth century, most favored religious status thanks to Emperor Constantine's embrace of it.

Pentecost. This exquisite enamel plaque, from the Mosan school that flourished in France in the eleventh and twelfth centuries, shows the descent of the Holy Spirit upon the apostles, fifty days after the resurrection of Jesus, on the ancient Jewish festival called the "feast of weeks," or Pentecost.

Mosan, The Pentecost, ca. 1150—1175. Champleve enamel on copper gilt; 4 1/16 x 4 1/6 in. (10.3 x 10.3cm). The Metropolitan Museum of Art, The Cloisters Collection, 1965 (65.105). Photograph 1989 The Metropolitan Museum of Art.

How did the church gain power in Europe?

After the fall of the Western Roman Empire in the fifth century C.E., Christianity became one of history's great success stories. Aided by the enterprise of its popes and the example of its monks, the church cultivated an appealing lay piety centered on the Lord's Prayer, the Apostles' Creed, veneration of the Virgin, and the sacrament of the Eucharist. Clergy became both royal teachers and bureaucrats within the kingdom of the Franks. Despite a growing schism between the Eastern (Byzantine) and Western churches, and a final split in 1054, by 1000 the church held real economic and political power. In the eleventh century reform-minded prelates put an end to presumptuous secular interference in its most intimate spiritual affairs by ending the lay investiture of clergy in their spiritual offices. For several centuries thereafter the church remained a formidable international force, able to challenge kings and emperors and inspire Crusades to the Holy Land.

By the fifteenth century the new states of Europe had stripped the church of much of its political power. It was thereafter progressively confined to spiritual and moral authority. Christianity's greatest struggles ever since have been not with kings and emperors over political power, but with materialistic philosophies and worldly ideologies, matters of spiritual and moral hegemony within an increasingly pluralistic and secular

Gay bishop. V. Gene Robinson is applauded after his investiture as the Episcopal Church's bishop of New Hampshire in March 2004. Robinson is the Episcopal Church's first openly gay bishop. The issue of homosexuality has divided Christian churches across the world.

What other controversies have divided Christians?

world. Since the sixteenth century a succession of humanists, skeptics, Deists, Rationalists, Marxists, Freudians, Darwinians, and atheists have attempted to explain away some of traditional Christianity's most basic teachings. In addition, the church has endured major internal upheavals. After the Protestant Reformation (1517–1555) made the Bible widely available to the laity, the possibilities for internal criticism of Christianity multiplied geometrically. Beginning with the split between Lutherans and Zwinglians in the 1520s, Protestant Christianity has fragmented into hundreds of sects, each claiming to have the true interpretation of Scripture. The Roman Catholic Church, by contrast, has maintained its unity and ministry throughout perilous times, although present-day discontent with papal authority threatens the modern Catholic Church almost as seriously as the Protestant Reformation once did.

Christianity has remained remarkably resilient. It possesses a simple, almost magically appealing gospel of faith and love in and through Jesus. In a present-day world whose religious needs and passions still run deep, evangelical Christianity has experienced a remarkable revival. The Roman Catholic Church, still troubled by challenges to papal authority, has become more pluralistic than in earlier periods. The pope has become a world figure, traveling to all continents to represent the church and advance its position on issues of public and private morality. A major ecumenical movement emerging in the 1960s has promoted unprecedented cooperation among evangelical Christian denominations. Everywhere Christians of all stripes are politically active, spreading their divine, moral, and social messages. Meanwhile, old hot-button issues, such as the ordination of women, are being overtaken by new ones, particularly the marriage of gay men and women and the removal of clergy who do not maintain the moral discipline of their holy orders.

- Over the centuries what have been some of the chief factors attracting people to Christianity?

- What forces have led to disunity among Christians in the past? What factors cause tensions among modern Christians?

17

Conquest and Exploitation: The Development of the Transatlantic Economy

((•—Hear the Audio for Chapter 17 at www.myhistorylab.com

Negroes for Sale.

A Cargo of very fine stout Men and Women, in good order and fit for immediate service, just imported from the Windward Coast of Africa, in the Ship Two Brothers.——

Conditions are one half Cash or Produce, the other half payable the first of January next, giving Bond and Security if required.

The Sale to be opened at 10 o'Clock each Day, in Mr. Bourdeaux's Yard, at No, 48, on the Bay.

May 19, 1784.   JOHN MITCHELL.

Thirty Seasoned Negroes

To be Sold for Credit, at Private Sale.

AMONGST which is a Carpenter, none of whom are known to be dishonest.

Also, to be sold for Cash, a regular bred young Negroe Man-Cook, born in this Country, who served several Years under an exceeding good French Cook abroad, and his Wife a middle aged Washer-Woman, (both very honest) and their two Children. Likewise, a young Man a Carpenter.

For Terms apply to the Printer.

Slave Auction Notice. Africans who survived the voyage across the Atlantic were immediately sold into slavery in the Americas. This eighteenth-century advertisement relates to a group of slaves whose ship had stopped at Charleston, South Carolina, and then landed elsewhere in the region to auction its human cargo. Notice the concern to assure potential buyers that the slaves were healthy, as a small-pox epidemic was then raging on the mainland.

Why were Africans treated as commodities during the era of the transatlantic slave trade?

T*he fifteenth-century encounter between the European and American continents changed the entire world. Centuries of European domination and government made the Americas a region where European languages, legal and
political institutions, trade patterns, and religion prevail. African populations,
economies, and political structures were altered by the slave trade into the*
Americas. *Europe gained more influence over other world cultures than it could otherwise
have achieved.*

GLOBAL PERSPECTIVE

THE ATLANTIC WORLD

The exchanges of people, goods, ideas, and plants, animals, and microorganisms between the American, European, and African continents in the fifteenth and sixteenth centuries transformed world history. In the Americas, the native peoples—whose ancestors had migrated from Asia millennia before—had established a wide variety of civilizations. Some of their most remarkable architectural monuments and cities were constructed during the very centuries when European civilizations were reeling from the collapse of Roman power. (See Chapter 13.) While trade and culture had long linked parts of Africa and regions in Eurasia (see Chapter 14) the civilizations of the Americas and the civilizations of Eurasia and Africa had had no significant contact with each other prior to the era of European exploration.

Within half a century of the landing of Columbus, millions of America's native peoples in Florida, the Caribbean islands, Mesoamerica, and South America had experienced the impact of Europeans intent on conquest, exploitation, and religious conversion. The Europeans' rapid conquest was the result of several factors—their advanced weapons and navies; the new diseases they brought with them; and internal divisions among the Native Americans. Thereafter, Spain and Portugal dominated Central and South America (what we now, as a result of this history, call Latin America), and England, France, and Holland set out to settle North America. The Europeans imported their own food crops, such as wheat and apples, while also taking advantage of American plants, such as potatoes, corn, tomatoes, and tobacco.

Throughout the Americas and the Caribbean basin, Europeans established economies of exploitation. In Latin America, they developed various institutions to extract native labor. Plantation owners from the Mid-Atlantic English colonies through the

El Morro, Puerto Rico. This fortress was built by the Spanish in the sixteenth century to protect Spain's valuable trading rights against British, Dutch, and pirate ships.

Why did Spain strive to control sea lanes?

((•—Hear the Audio
at **myhistorylab.com**

Within decades of the European voyages of discovery, Native Americans, Europeans, and Africans began to interact in a manner unprecedented in human history. The Native Americans of North and South America encountered bands of European conquerors and missionaries. Technological and military superiority as well as political divisions among the Native Americans allowed the Europeans to realize their material and religious ambitions. By the middle of the sixteenth century Europeans had begun to import Africans into the American continents as chattel slaves, converting them to Christianity in the process. By the close of the sixteenth century Europe, the Americas, and Africa had become linked in a vast transatlantic economy that extracted material and agricultural wealth from the American continents largely on the basis of the nonfree labor of impressed Native Americans and imported African slaves.

The next century would see English and French colonists settling in North America and the Caribbean, introducing both Protestantism and different political values. As they exploited the North American wilderness, the colonists interacted with Native Americans, sometimes destroying indigenous cultures and whole peoples, sometimes converting Native Americans to Christianity; Native Americans, too, were drawn into the transatlantic economy.

Beginning in the sixteenth century, the importation of African slaves and the use of slave labor were fundamental to the plantation economy that eventually extended from Maryland to Brazil. Slaveholding and economic entanglement in the slave trade also extended into the British colonies north of Maryland. The slave trade intimately connected portions of Africa to the transatlantic economy. The slave trade had a devastating effect on the African people and cultures involved in it, but it also enriched the Americas with African culture and religion. ■

Caribbean and into Brazil preferred slaves forcibly imported from Africa. African slaves were hardier than indigenous laborers, who lacked immunity to European diseases, and they could be better controlled than indentured servants from Europe. With the exception of tobacco, plantation crops derived largely from the Old World; some Africans were already familiar with the cultivation of, for example, rice. The emergent Atlantic world drew the economies and peoples of Europe, Africa, and the Americas into a vast worldwide web of production based on slave labor.

Slavery had its most striking impact on the lives of the millions of humans who over the centuries were torn from their birthplaces, their families, and their cultures. The slave trade corroded the political and social structures of African societies. African slaves suffered from high mortality and sharply reduced birthrates; they were subjected to harsh working conditions and brutally dehumanizing treatment.

Focus Questions

◆ How did the encounter of Europe and Africa with the Americas change the global ecological balance?

◆ Why was the Spanish Empire based on economies of exploitation? How was the labor of non-European peoples drawn into the economy of this empire?

◆ How and why did the plantation economy develop? Why did it rely on African slaves for its labor? What were the consequences of the slave trade for individuals and institutions in each of the three continents constituting the Atlantic world?

◆ Why do we think of the plantation economy as a global, rather than regional, system of production? Why was it the "engine" of Atlantic basin trade?

PERIODS OF EUROPEAN OVERSEAS EXPANSION

Since the late fifteenth century, European contacts with the rest of the world have gone through four distinct stages. The first was the European discovery, exploration, initial conquest, and settlement of the Americas and commercial expansion elsewhere. The second was an era of trade rivalry among Spain, France, and Great Britain. During this period (to 1820), the British colonies of North America and the Spanish colonies of Mexico and Central and South America broke free from European control. The third period spanned the nineteenth century and was characterized by the development of European empires in Africa and Asia. Imperial ideology at this time involved theories of trade, national honor, race, religion, and military strength. The last period of European experience with empire occupied the mid-twentieth century and was a time of decolonization—a retreat from empire.

WHAT WERE the four periods of European contact with the world?

Technological advantages—naval power and gunpowder, not innate cultural superiority—enabled Europeans to exercise global dominance disproportionate to Europe's size and population for four and a half centuries. The legacy of European imperialism continues to influence contemporary events.

MERCANTILIST THEORY OF ECONOMIC EXPLOITATION

The early modern European empires of the sixteenth through the eighteenth centuries were based on commerce. Extensive trade rivalries sprang up around the world, and competitors developed navies to protect their interests. Spain, with the largest empire, constructed elaborate naval, commercial, and political structures to exploit and govern it.

WHAT WAS mercantilism?

Mercantilism. As this painting of the Custom House Quay in London suggests, trade from European empires and the tariffs imposed on it were expected to generate revenue for the home country. But behind many of the goods carried in the great sailing ships in the harbor and landed on these docks lay the labor of African slaves working on the plantations of North and South America.

Samuel Scott, "Old Custom House Quay" Collection. V&A Images, the Victoria and Albert Museum, London.

What kinds of trade goods are visible in this painting?

These empires depended largely on slave labor. The Atlantic slave trade forcibly brought together the lives and cultures of peoples in Africa and the New World. It also enriched many European merchants.

To the extent that any formal economic theory lay behind the conduct of these empires, it was **mercantilism**, a system in which governments heavily regulate trade and commerce to increase national wealth. From beginning to end, the economic well-being of the home country was the primary concern. Mercantilists believed that a nation had to gain more gold and silver bullion than its rivals and that one nation's economy could grow only at the expense of others. Nations grew by establishing colonies overseas to provide markets and natural resources for the home country, which furnished military security and political administration for the colonies. The home country and its colonies were to trade exclusively with each other. The colonies were assumed to be inferior partners in a monopolistic relationship.

By the early eighteenth century, it was clear that mercantilist assumptions did not correspond with reality. Colonial and home markets did not mesh. Spain, for instance, could not produce enough goods for South America, while manufacturing in the British North American colonies challenged production in England and led to British attempts to limit certain colonial industries. Colonists of different countries wished to trade with each other. English colonists could buy sugar more cheaply from the French West Indies than from English suppliers. The eighteenth century became the "golden age of smugglers."[1] Governments could be dragged into war by clashes among their colonies. Problems associated with the mercantile empires led to conflicts around the world.

ESTABLISHMENT OF THE SPANISH EMPIRE IN AMERICA

 WHAT ROLES did the Roman Catholic Church play in Spanish America?

mercantilism
Term used to describe close government control of the economy that sought to maximize exports and accumulate as much precious metal as possible to enable the state to defend its economic and political interests.

●◆●[Read **the Document**
2nd Letter, Hernan Cortez to King Charles V
at **myhistorylab.com**

●◆●[Read **the Document**
del Castillo, History of Conquest
at **myhistorylab.com**

CONQUEST OF THE AZTECS AND THE INCAS

Within twenty years of the arrival of Columbus (1451–1506), Spanish explorers in search of gold had claimed the major islands of the Caribbean and brutally suppressed the native peoples. These actions presaged what was to occur on the continent.

In 1519 Hernán Cortés (1485–1547) landed in Mexico with about 500 men and a few horses. He opened communication with Moctezuma II (1466–1520), the Aztec emperor. Moctezuma may initially have believed Cortés to be the god Quetzalcoatl, who, according to legend, had been driven away centuries earlier but had promised to return. Whatever the reason, Moctezuma hesitated to confront Cortés, attempting at first to appease him with gifts of gold. Cortés forged alliances, most importantly with Tlaxcala, a traditional enemy of the Aztecs. His forces then marched on the Aztec capital of Tenochtitlán (modern Mexico City), where Moctezuma welcomed him. Cortés soon made Moctezuma a prisoner. When Moctezuma died in unexplained circumstances, the Spaniards were driven from Tenochtitlán and nearly wiped out. But they returned, and the Aztecs were defeated in late 1521. Cortés proclaimed the Aztec Empire to be New Spain.

---

[1]Walter Dorn, *Competition for Empire, 1740–1763* (New York: Harper, 1940), p. 266.

In 1532, Francisco Pizarro (ca. 1478–1541) landed on the western coast of South America to take over the Inca Empire. His force included about 200 men armed with guns, swords, and horses. Pizarro lured the Inca ruler, Atahualpa (ca. 1500–1533), into a conference, then seized him and had him garroted in 1533. The Spaniards then captured Cuzco, the Inca capital, ending the Inca Empire. The Spanish faced insurrections, however, and fought among themselves for decades. Effective royal control was not established until the late 1560s.

The conquests of Mexico and Peru are among the most dramatic and brutal events in modern world history. Small military forces armed with advanced weapons and in alliance with indigenous enemies of the rulers subdued two advanced, powerful peoples. European diseases, especially smallpox, aided the conquest, since much of the native population succumbed to diseases against which they had no immunity. But beyond the drama and bloodshed, these conquests marked a turning point. Whole civilizations with long histories and a record of enormous social, architectural, and technological achievement were effectively destroyed. Native American cultures endured, but European culture had the upper hand.

THE ROMAN CATHOLIC CHURCH IN SPANISH AMERICA

The Spanish conquest of the West Indies, Mexico, and South America opened a vast region to the Roman Catholic faith. Religion played a central role; as in the reconquest of the Iberian Peninsula from the Moors, the obligation Christians felt to spread their faith was used to justify military conquest and political control. As a consequence, the Roman Catholic Church in the New World was a conservative force working to protect the power and prestige of the Spanish authorities. Indeed, the papacy turned over much of the control of the church in the New World to the Spanish monarchy. In the sixteenth century, as the papacy and the Habsburg monarchy fought Protestantism, the Roman Catholicism that spread throughout the Spanish domains of America was the zealous faith of the Counter-Reformation.

The Roman Catholic Church, with the aid first of the Franciscans and the Dominicans and later the Jesuits, sought to convert the Native Americans and eradicate Indian religious practices. Converts, however, did not enjoy equality with Europeans. Real tension existed between the early Spanish conquerors and the mendicant friars. Without conquest the church could not convert the Native Americans, but the priests often deplored the harsh conditions imposed on indigenous peoples. By far the most effective and outspoken critic was Bartolomé de Las Casas (1474–1566), a Dominican. He contended that conquest was not necessary for conversion. One result of his campaign was new royal regulations after 1550.

Las Casas's writings inspired the "**Black Legend,**" according to which all Spanish treatment of Native Americans was inhumane. Although substantially true, the Black Legend exaggerated the case against Spain. Certainly the rulers of the native empires had often themselves been cruel to their subject peoples.

By the end of the sixteenth century, the church in Spanish America largely upheld the colonial status quo. Although individual priests defended the communal rights of Native American tribes, the colonial church prospered through its

QUICK REVIEW

Francisco Pizarro (ca. 1478–1541)

◆ Invasion force landed in South America in 1532

◆ Forces included 200 men, horses, guns, and swords

◆ Executed the Inca ruler and captured Cuzco in 1533

Spanish Conquest of Mexico. A sixteenth-century drawing depicts a battle during the Spanish conquest of Mexico. The Aztecs are on the right. Note how the Spaniards bring up the rear, behind their native allies, the Tlaxcalteca.

How does the position of the Tlaxcalteca leading the attack on the Aztecs offer a different perspective on the conquest of the Americas?

•••⌐Read the **Document**
New Laws Indies for Good Treatment 2
at **myhistorylab.com**

Black Legend
The argument that Spanish treatment of Native Americans was uniquely inhumane.

•••⌐Read the **Document**
Account of Devastation of Indies
at **myhistorylab.com**

exploitation of the resources of the New World. By the late eighteenth century, the Roman Catholic Church had become one of the most conservative forces in Latin American society.

ECONOMIES OF EXPLOITATION IN THE SPANISH EMPIRE

HOW DID Spaniards attempt to control labor in the Americas?

Colonial Spanish America had an economy of exploitation in two senses. First, its organization of labor involved dependent servitude or slavery. Second, America's resources were exploited for the economic advantage of Spain.

VARIETIES OF ECONOMIC ACTIVITY

conquistadores
A term meaning "conquerors"; the Spanish conquerors of the New World.

The early **conquistadores** ("conquerors") had been interested primarily in gold, but by the middle of the sixteenth century silver mining provided the chief source of metallic wealth. The great silver mining centers were in northern Mexico and Potosí, in present-day Bolivia. The Spanish crown received one-fifth (the *quinto*) of all mining revenues. Overall, silver was a great source of wealth, and its production for the benefit of Spaniards and the Spanish crown epitomized the extractive economy on which Latin American colonial life was based.

The Silver Mines of Potosí. Worked by conscripted Indian laborers under extremely harsh conditions, these mines provided Spain with a vast treasure in silver.

What does the puny size of the Indians in this painting suggest about their status in the Spanish American society?

This extractive economy required labor, but there were too few Spanish colonists to provide it, and most of the colonists who came to the Americas did not want to work for wages. So, the Spaniards turned first to the native population for workers and then to African slaves. Indian labor dominated on the continent and African labor in the Caribbean.

The Spanish devised a series of institutions to exploit Native American labor. The first was the *encomienda*, a formal grant by the crown of the right to the labor of a specific number of Native Americans for a particular time. But the Spanish monarchy was distressed by reports from clergy that the Native Americans were being mistreated and feared that *encomienda* holders were becoming a powerful noble class in the New World. *Encomienda* as an institution declined by the middle of the sixteenth century.

encomienda
The grant by the Spanish crown to a colonist of the labor of a specific number of Native Americans for a set period of time.

The *encomienda* was followed by another arrangement of labor servitude, the *repartimiento*, which was largely copied from the *mita* labor practices of the Incas. *Repartimiento* required adult male Native Americans to devote a set number of days of labor annually to Spanish economic enterprises. The time limitation on *repartimiento* led some Spanish managers to work teams of men to exhaustion—sometimes to death—before replacing them with the next rotation.

repartimiento
A labor tax in Spanish America that required adult male Native Americans to devote a set number of days a year to Spanish economic enterprises.

Outside the mines, the *hacienda* dominated rural and agricultural life in Spanish colonies on the continent. Royal land grants led to the establishment of large landed estates owned by *peninsulares* (whites born in Spain) or Creoles (whites born in America). The core activity of the haciendas, livestock grazing, required less labor than did the mines. But laborers on the hacienda were usually in formal servitude to the owner and had to buy goods for everyday living on credit from him. They were rarely able to repay their debts and thus could not leave. This system was known as **debt peonage**. The hacienda economy produced foodstuffs for mining areas and urban centers, and haciendas became one of the most important features of Latin American life.

COMMERCIAL REGULATION AND THE FLOTA SYSTEM

Because Queen Isabella of Castile (r. 1474–1504) had commissioned Columbus, the legal link between the New World and Spain was the crown of Castile. Its powers were subject to few limitations. Government of America was assigned to the Council of the Indies, which, in conjunction with the monarch, nominated the viceroys of New Spain and Peru. These viceroys were the chief executives in the New World. Each of the viceroyalties included subordinate judicial councils known as *audiencias*. Local officers included the *corregidores*, who presided over municipal councils. These offices provided the monarchy with a vast array of opportunities for patronage. Political power flowed from the top of this political structure downward; there was little or no local initiative or self-government (see Map 17–1).

hacienda
A large landed estate in Spanish America.

peninsulares
Native-born Spaniards who emigrated from Spain to settle in the Spanish colonies.

debt peonage
A system that forces agricultural laborers (peons) to work and live on large estates (*haciendas*) until they have repaid their debts to the estate's owner.

MAP EXPLORATION

To explore this map further, go to **http://www.myhistorylab.com**

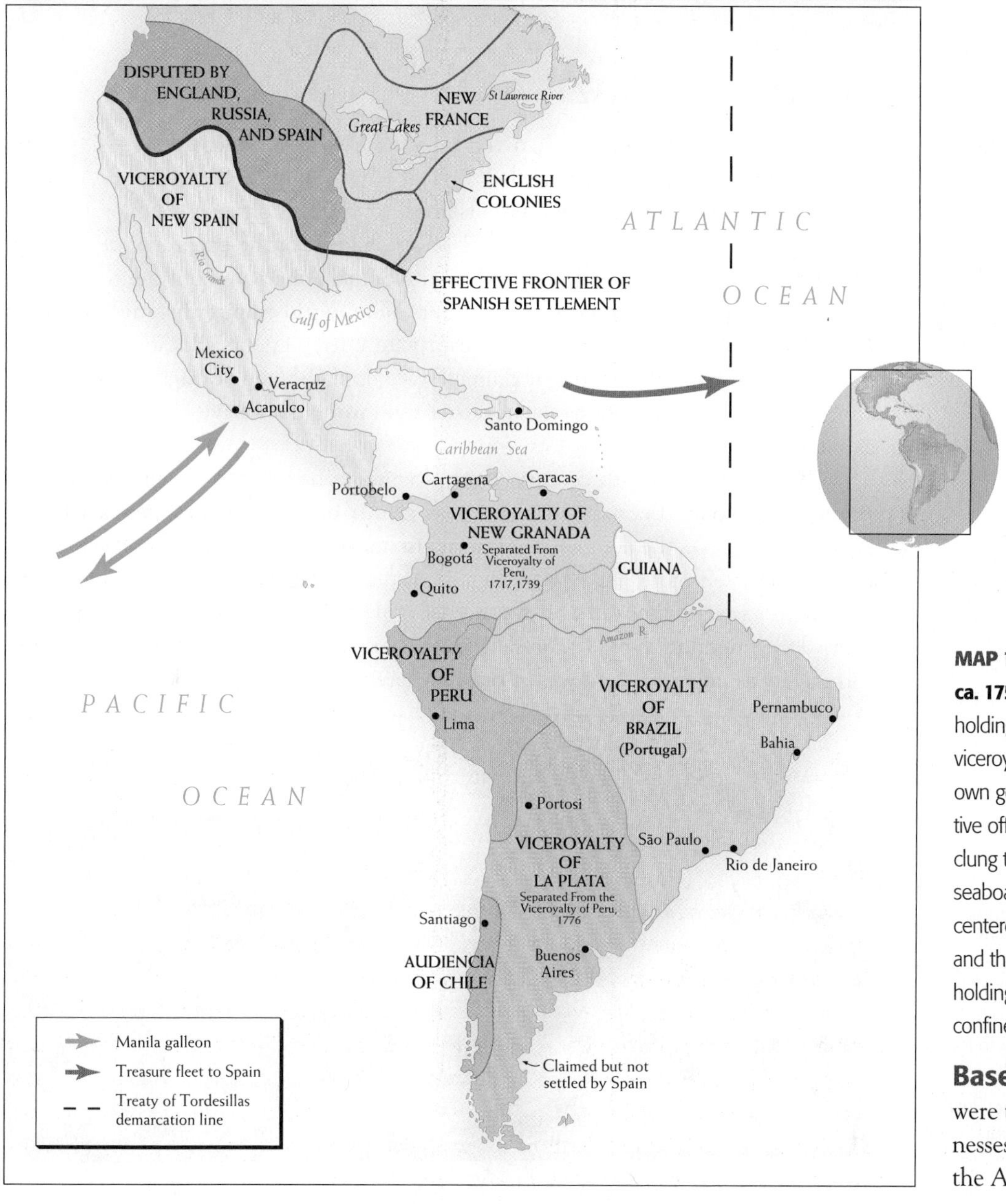

MAP 17–1.   The Americas, ca. 1750. Spain organized its vast holdings in the New World into viceroyalties, each of which had its own governor and other administrative officials. The English colonies clung to the North American seaboard. French possessions centered on the St. Lawrence River and the Great Lakes. Portuguese holdings in Brazil were mostly confined to the coast.

Based on this map, what were the strengths and weaknesses of the Spanish Empire in the Americas?

Colonial political structures supported the commercial goals of Spain. Spanish control of its American empire involved a system of monopolistic trade regulation, although Spain's trade monopoly was often breached. The Casa de Contratación (House of Trade) in Seville regulated all trade with the New World; it was the single most influential institution of the Spanish Empire. Each year a fleet of commercial vessels (the *flota*) controlled by Seville merchants, escorted by warships, carried merchandise from Spain to a few specified ports in America. These included Portobello, Veracruz, and Cartagena; there were no authorized ports on the Pacific coast. Buenos Aires and other areas received goods only after the shipments had been unloaded at an authorized port. After selling their wares, the ships were loaded with silver and gold bullion. They usually wintered in heavily fortified Caribbean ports and then sailed back to Spain. Each year a Spanish ship also crossed the Pacific from Spanish Manila to Acapulco, bringing Chinese silk and porcelain. It returned to Manila laden with Mexican silver. The *flota* system worked imperfectly, but trade outside it was illegal. Spanish colonists were prohibited from trading directly with each other, and foreign merchants were forbidden to breach the Spanish monopoly.

COLONIAL BRAZIL

HOW WERE sugar and slavery entwined in colonial Brazil?

◉ See the **Map**

Spanish and Portuguese Exploration at **myhistorylab.com**

QUICK REVIEW

Brazil's Colonial Economy

◆ Indigenous peoples were nomads, so Portuguese entrepreneurs imported African slaves for labor

◆ Sugar production and gold mining were most significant elements of economy

◆ Portuguese crown was less involved in colonial administration than Spanish crown

Spain and Portugal originally had rival claims to the Americas. In 1494, by the Treaty of Tordesillas, the pope divided the seaborne empires of Spain and Portugal by drawing a line west of the Cape Verde Islands. In 1500 a Portuguese explorer landed on the coast of present-day Brazil, which extended east of the papal line of division, and thus Portugal gained a major hold on the South American continent. Portugal, however, had fewer resources to devote to its New World empire than did Spain. Its rulers left exploitation of the region to private entrepreneurs. Because the native peoples in the lands that Portugal claimed were nomadic, the Portuguese, unlike the Spanish, imported Africans as slaves rather than using the native Indian population as their workforce.

By the mid-sixteenth century, sugar production had gained preeminence in the Brazilian economy. Because sugarcane was grown on large estates (*fazendas*) with African slave labor, the dominance of sugar also meant the dominance of slavery. Slavery became even more important when, in the early eighteenth century, significant gold deposits were discovered in southern Brazil. The expansion of gold mining increased the importation of African slaves. Nowhere, except perhaps in the West Indies, was slavery as important as it was in Brazil, where it persisted until 1888.

Sugar plantations of Brazil and the West Indies were a major source of the demand for slave labor. Slaves are here shown grinding sugarcane and refining sugar, which was then exported to the consumer markets in Europe.

How did the labor requirements for sugar production differ from those for other colonial economic activities?

The taxation and administration associated with gold mining brought new, unexpected wealth to the Portuguese monarchy, allowing it to rule without recourse to the Cortés or traditional parliament for taxation. Through transatlantic trade the new wealth generated from Brazilian gold also filtered into all the major trading nations, which could sell their goods to Portugal as well as profit from the slave trade.

In Brazil, the basic unit of production was the plantation, which did not require a vast colonial administration; agricultural products were much easier to keep track of than the precious metals of Spanish American mines. The Portuguese were willing to allow more local autonomy than was Spain. In Spanish America the use of Native American labor was supervised by the government. Brazil, less dependent on Native American labor, felt no such constraints. Indeed, the Portuguese government condoned policies whereby indigenous tribes were driven into the back country or exterminated. Throughout the eighteenth century the Portuguese government favored the continued importation of slaves.

FRENCH AND BRITISH COLONIES IN NORTH AMERICA

Both England and France had important sugar islands in the Caribbean with plantations worked by African slaves. The trade and commerce of the northern British colonies were closely related to meeting the needs of these islands. The major presence of both nations, however, spread across different parts of the North American continent.

French explorers had pressed down the St. Lawrence River valley in Canada during the seventeenth century. French fur traders and Roman Catholic Jesuit missionaries had followed, with the French government supporting the missionary effort. By the end of the seventeenth century, a significant but sparsely populated French presence existed in Canada (see Map 17–1). The largest settlement was Quebec, founded in 1608. Since trade rather than settlement generally characterized the French effort, there was little conflict between the French and the Native Americans; some Frenchmen married Native American women. It was primarily through the fur trade that French Canada participated in the early transatlantic economy.

From the first successful settlement in Jamestown, Virginia, in 1607, through the establishment of Georgia in 1733, English colonies spread along the eastern seaboard of the future United States. The Dutch, Swedes, and others founded settlements too, but all of them were taken over during the seventeenth century by the English. Settlements were founded for a variety of reasons. Virginia and New Amsterdam (after 1664, New York) aimed for profits through farming and trade. Others, such as the Carolinas, were developed by royal favorites who were given vast land tracts. James Oglethorpe founded Georgia as a refuge for English debtors. The pursuit of religious liberty was the driving force of the Pilgrim and Puritan founders of Massachusetts, the Baptist Roger Williams in Rhode Island, the Quaker William Penn in Pennsylvania, and the Roman Catholic Lord Baltimore in Maryland.

With the exception of Maryland, these colonies were Protestant. The Church of England dominated the southern colonies. In New England, varieties of Protestantism associated with or derived from Calvinism were in the ascendancy. In their religious affiliations, the English-speaking colonies manifested two important traits derived from the English experience. First, much of their religious life was organized around self-governing congregations. Second, their religious outlook derived from those forms of Protestantism that were suspicious of central political authority. In this regard, their

HOW WERE the economies of the French and British North American colonies integrated into the transatlantic economy?

Read the **Document**
Albanel from Jesuit Relation
at **myhistorylab.com**

See the **Map**
European Empires ca. 1600
at **myhistorylab.com**

Fur Trade. A Native American hands a pelt to a European buyer while two spectators—one European, one Indian—nonchalantly observe the transaction. By 1700 the fur trade had decimated the beaver population in southern Canada and New England.

1777 engraving. © The Granger Collection, New York.

How did the relationships between French traders and Native Americans tend to differ from the relationships between English settlers and Native Americans?

((•--[Hear the Audio
at **myhistorylab.com**

QUICK REVIEW

British North America

◆ Jamestown, Virginia: Became first successful British settlement in 1607

◆ Religion shaped the organization of British colonies

◆ English colonies had a complex relationship with Native Americans

Columbian Exchange
Biological exchange of plants, animals, and diseases between the Americas and the rest of the world.

 WHAT WAS the "Columbian Exchange"?

cultural and political outlook differed sharply from that of the Roman Catholics of the Spanish Empire. In a sense, the ideologies of the extreme Reformation and Counter-Reformation confronted each other in the Americas.

The English colonists had complex interactions with the Native American populations. They had only modest interest in missionary enterprise. New diseases imported from Europe took a high death toll among the native population. North America had no large Native American cities; indigenous populations were dispersed, and intertribal animosity was intense. The English often encountered well-organized resistance, as from the Powhatan conspiracy in Virginia and the Pequots in New England. The most powerful of the Native American groups was the Iroquois Nation, organized in the early eighteenth century in New York. The Iroquois battled successfully against other tribes and long negotiated successfully with both the Dutch and the English. The English often used one tribe against another, and the Native Americans also tried to use the English or the French in their own conflicts. Struggles between the English settlers and the Native Americans rarely resulted in full victory for either side. From the late seventeenth century through the American Revolution, Native American alliances became important for the Anglo-French conflict on the Continent, which was intimately related to their rivalry over transatlantic trade (see Chapter 19).

The economies of the English-speaking colonies were primarily agricultural. From New England through the Middle Atlantic, small farms were mostly tilled by free white labor; from Virginia southward a plantation economy dependent on slavery predominated. The principal ports of Boston, Newport, New York, Philadelphia, Baltimore, and Charleston were the chief centers through which goods moved back and forth between the colonies and England and the West Indies. The commercial economies of these cities were all related to the transatlantic slave trade.

Until the 1760s the political values of the Americans resembled those of their English counterparts. The colonials were thoroughly familiar with events in England and sent many of their children there to be educated. They were monarchists but suspicious of monarchical power. Their politics involved vast amounts of patronage and individual favors. Their society was clearly hierarchical, with an elite that functioned like a colonial aristocracy and many ordinary people who were dependent on that aristocracy. Throughout the colonies during the eighteenth century, the Anglican Church grew in influence and membership. The prosperity of the colonies might eventually have led them to separate from England, but in 1750 few people thought that would occur.

THE COLUMBIAN EXCHANGE: DISEASE, ANIMALS, AND AGRICULTURE

The European encounter with the Americas produced remarkable ecological transformations that have shaped the world to the present time (see Map 17–2). Alfred Crosby, the leading historian of the process, has named this cross-continental flow the **Columbian Exchange.**

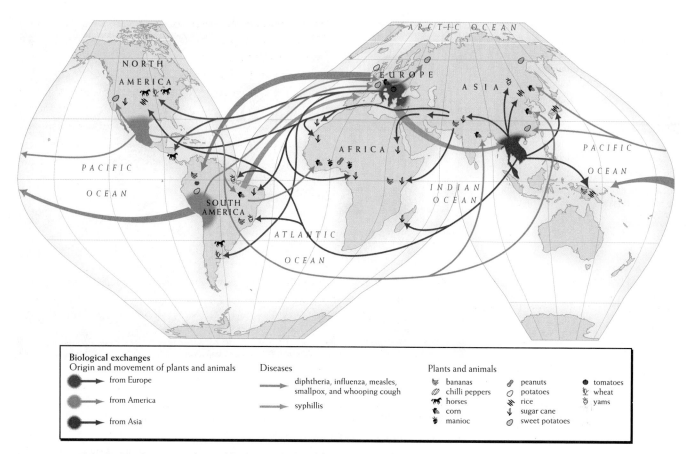

MAP 17–2   Biological Exchanges.   The worldwide movement of plants, animals, and diseases.

How did the Columbian Exchange alter environments around the world?

DISEASES ENTER THE AMERICAS

The American continents had been biologically separated from Europe, Africa, and Asia for tens of thousands of years. The only animal native to the Americas that could serve as a beast of burden was the llama, which could transport only about a hundred pounds. The American continents included vast grassland that lacked grazing animals to transform plants into animal protein. It appears that native peoples had not experienced major epidemics.

By the second voyage of Columbus (1493), that picture began to change in remarkable ways. Columbus brought a number of animals and plants to Hispaniola and other islands of the Caribbean that were previously unknown to the New World. His sailors and the men on subsequent European voyages also carried diseases new to the Americas.

European diseases ultimately played at least as big a role in defeating indigenous Americans as advanced European weaponry did. Much controversy surrounds the question of the actual size of the populations of Native Americans in the Caribbean islands, Mexico, Peru, and the North Atlantic coast. Those populations were significant, with those of Mexico numbering many millions. In the first two centuries after the encounter, wherever Europeans went, extremely large numbers of Native Americans died from diseases they had never before encountered. Smallpox, the most deadly, destroyed millions of people. Bubonic plague, typhoid, typhus, influenza, measles, chicken pox, whooping cough, malaria, and diphtheria produced localized epidemics. An unknown

Smallpox. Introduced by Europeans to the Americas, smallpox had a devastating effect on Native American populations. It swept through the Aztec capital of Tenochtitlán soon after the Spaniards arrived, contributing to the fall of the city. This illustration of the effect of the plague in the Aztec capital is from a postconquest history known as the Florentine Codex compiled for Spanish church authorities by Aztec survivors.

What other diseases did Europeans bring to the Americas?

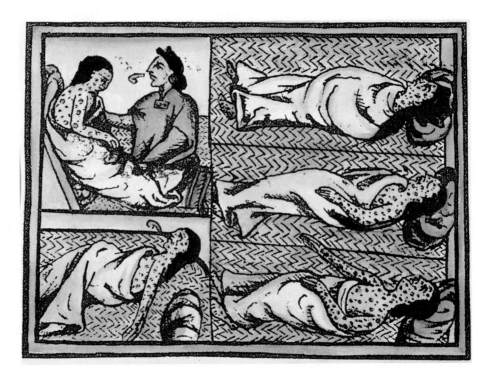

disease, possibly typhus, caused major losses among the Native Americans of New England between approximately 1616 and 1619.

On the reverse side of the equation it seems likely that syphilis originated in the New World. Until the discovery of penicillin in the 1940s, this rampant sexually transmitted disease remained a major public health concern throughout the world.

ANIMALS AND AGRICULTURE

The introduction of European livestock revolutionized American agriculture. The most important new animals were pigs, cattle, horses, goats, and sheep. The horse became first the animal of conquest and then the animal of colonial Latin American culture. Native Americans had no prior experience with such large animals that would obey the will of a human rider; they were initially fearful of the mounted Spanish horsemen. After the conquest, however, the Americas from Mexico southward became the largest horse-breeding region of the world. By the nineteenth century, the possession of horses allowed the Plains Indians of North America to resist European encroachment. Pigs, cattle, and sheep produced enormous quantities of hides and wool. The Americas from the sixteenth century through the present supported a diet more plentiful in animal protein than anywhere else in the world.

Global Foods. A woman in the African country of Uganda offers beans and pineapples for sale, both of which originated in the Americas.

What other American plants were introduced to Africa?

Europeans also brought plants to the New World, including peaches, oranges, grapes, melons, bananas, rice, onions, radishes, and various green vegetables. Sugarcane cultivation created the major demand for slavery. European wheat, over time, allowed the Americas not only to feed themselves but also to export large amounts of grain throughout the world.

The only American animal that came to be raised in Europe was the turkey. The Americas, however, were the source of plants that eventually changed the

OVERVIEW   The Columbian Exchange

To the Americas

Diseases	smallpox, influenza, bubonic plague, typhoid, typhus, measles, chicken pox, malaria, and diphtheria
Animals	pigs, cattle, horses, goats, sheep, chickens
Plants	apples, peaches, pears, apricots, plums, oranges, mangos, lemons, olives, melons, almonds, grapes, bananas, cherries, sugarcane, rice, wheat, oats, barley, onions, radishes, okra, dandelions, cabbages, and other green vegetables

From the Americas

Diseases	syphilis (?)
Animals	turkeys
Plants	maize, tomatoes, sweet peppers, chilis, potatoes, sweet potatoes, squash, pumpkins, manioc (tapioca), beans, cocoa, peanuts, cans, pineapples, guavas, avocados, blueberries, and tobacco

Watch the **Video**
at **myhistorylab.com**

European diet. Maize and potatoes had the greatest impact. Both crops grow rapidly, supplying food quickly and steadily if not attacked by disease. There is good reason to believe the cultivation of the potato was a major cause of the population increase in eighteenth- and nineteenth-century Europe. Africa received many of these same foodstuffs as well. Maize became a staple in Africa. Tobacco also originated in the Americas.

SLAVERY IN THE AMERICAS

Slavery was the final mode of forced or subservient labor in the New World. Unlike the labor exploitation of Native Americans, enslavement of Africans and their descendants extended throughout the Spanish Empire, Portuguese Brazil, and the English-speaking colonies of North America. The heartland of transatlantic slavery lay in the Caribbean islands.

WHY WAS the transatlantic slave trade so economically important?

THE BACKGROUND OF SLAVERY

Virtually every premodern state around the globe depended on slavery to some extent (see Map 17–3 on page 428). Slave institutions in sub-Saharan Africa were ancient. The Islamic states of southwestern Asia and North Africa imported slaves from both the Sudan and Horn of Africa as well as the East African coast, although they took even more slaves from eastern Europe and Central Asia. Both Mediterranean Christian and Islamic peoples were using slaves—mostly Greeks, Bulgarians, Turkish prisoners of war, and Black Sea Tartars, but also Africans—well before the voyages of discovery opened sub-Saharan sources of slaves for the new European colonies overseas.

Read the **Document**
Slavery in Africa late 1700s, Mungo Park
at **myhistorylab.com**

Not all forms of slavery were as dehumanizing as the chattel slavery that came to predominate—with the sanction of Christian authorities—in the Americas. Chattel slaves were outright possessions of their masters, indistinguishable from any material possession; they were not recognized as persons under the law, so they had no legal rights; they could not claim any control over their bodies, their time, their labor, or even their own children.

MAP EXPLORATION

To explore this map further, go to **www.myhistorylab.com**

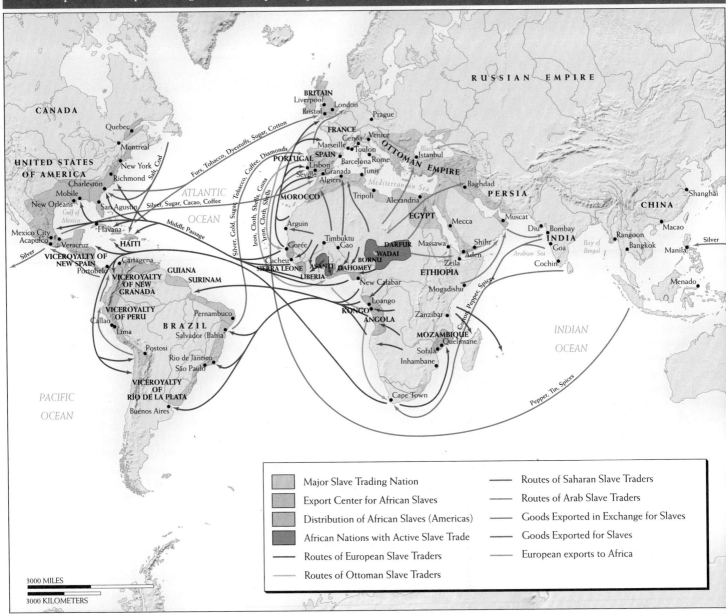

Legend:

- Major Slave Trading Nation
- Export Center for African Slaves
- Distribution of African Slaves (Americas)
- African Nations with Active Slave Trade
- Routes of European Slave Traders
- Routes of Ottoman Slave Traders
- Routes of Saharan Slave Traders
- Routes of Arab Slave Traders
- Goods Exported in Exchange for Slaves
- Goods Exported for Slaves
- European exports to Africa

MAP 17–3.   The Slave Trade, 1400–1860. Slavery is an ancient institution, and complex slave-trading routes were in existence in Africa, the Middle East, and Asia for centuries, but it was the need to supply labor for the plantations of the Americas that led to the greatest movement of peoples across the face of the earth.

How does this map show the global nature of the slave trade?

African societies suffered immense political, economic, and social devastation when they were the chief supplier of slaves to the world. The New World societies that were built to a great extent on the exploitation of African slavery also suffered enduring consequences, including racism.

ESTABLISHMENT OF SLAVERY

As the numbers of Native Americans in South America declined due to disease and exploitation, the Spanish and the Portuguese turned to the labor of imported African slaves. By the late 1500s, in the West Indies and many cities of South America, black slaves surpassed the white population.

On much of the South American continent dominated by Spain, slavery declined during the late seventeenth century, but it continued to thrive in Brazil and in the Caribbean. In British North America, beginning with the importation of slaves to Jamestown in 1619, it quickly became a fundamental institution.

One of the forces that led to the spread of slavery in Brazil and the West Indies was the cultivation of sugar. Sugarcane required a large investment in land and equipment, and only slave labor could provide enough low-cost workers to make the plantations profitable. As the European appetite for sugar grew, so did the slave population. By 1725, black slaves may have constituted almost 90 percent of the population of the West Indies. There and in Brazil and the British colonies in the South, prosperity and slavery went hand in hand. The wealthiest colonies were those that raised consumer staples, such as sugar, rice, tobacco, or cotton, by slave labor.

THE PLANTATION ECONOMY AND TRANSATLANTIC TRADE

The **plantation economy** encompassed plantations that stretched from Maryland through the West Indies and into Brazil. They formed a vast corridor of slave societies in which social and economic subordination was based on both involuntary servitude and race. This kind of society, in its total dependence on slave labor and racial differences, had never existed before. The social and economic influence of plantation slavery persisted through the British effort to outlaw the slave trade during the first half of the nineteenth century, the Latin American wars of independence, the Emancipation Proclamation issued in 1863 in the United States, and the Brazilian emancipation of 1888. Every society in which it existed still contends with its effects.

The slave trade was part of the larger system of transatlantic trade that linked Europe, Africa, and the European colonies in South America, the Caribbean, and North America. The Americas supplied labor-intensive raw materials such as tobacco, sugar, coffee, precious metals, cotton, and indigo. Europe supplied manufactured goods such as textiles, liquor, guns, metal wares, and beads, and cash in various forms. Africa supplied gold, ivory, wood, palm oil, gum, and other products, as well as the slaves whose labor created the American products. By the eighteenth century slaves were Africa's predominant export.

plantation economy
The economic system stretching between the Chesapeake Bay and Brazil that produced crops, especially sugar, cotton, and tobacco, using slave labor on large estates.

SLAVERY ON THE PLANTATIONS

The American plantations to which African slaves arrived were located in rural isolation. The plantation might raise food for its owners and their slaves, but the main production was intended for export. Plantation owners imported virtually all the finished or manufactured goods they used.

The living conditions of plantation slaves varied. Most owners possessed few slaves. Black slaves living in Portuguese areas had the fewest legal protections. In the Spanish colonies the church attempted to provide some protection for black slaves but devoted much more effort to protecting Native Americans. Slave codes were developed in the British and the French colonies during the seventeenth century, but they provided only the most limited protection. Virtually all slave owners feared a slave revolt; slave laws favored the master rather than the slave. Masters were permitted to

See the **Map**
Atlantic Slave Trade
at **myhistorylab.com**

Read the **Document**
Overseer in Cotton Plantation
at **myhistorylab.com**

African American Culture. This eighteenth-century painting depicts a celebration in the slave quarters on a South Carolina plantation. One planter's description of a slave dance seems to fit this scene: the men leading the women in "a slow shuffling gait, edging along by some unseen exertion of the feet, from one side to the other—sometimes curtseying down and remaining in that posture while the edging motion from one side to the other continued." The women, he wrote, "always carried a handkerchief held at arm's length, which was waved in a graceful motion to and fro as she moved."

Abby Aldrich Rockefeller Folk Art Museum, Colonial Williamsburg Foundation, VA.

Why did slave owners suppress traditional African religious practices?

punish slaves by whipping and other harsh corporal punishment, and slaves were often forbidden to gather in groups lest they plan a revolt. Slave marriages generally had no legal standing. The child of an enslaved woman was born a slave, the property of the mother's owner. Owners could separate slave families.

The daily life of most slaves was one of hard agricultural labor, poor diet and clothing, and inadequate housing. The death rate among slaves was high. Their welfare and their lives were sacrificed to make their owners wealthy and to produce the goods demanded by consumers in Europe.

The African slaves who were transported to the Americas were, like the Native Americans, converted to Christianity: in the Spanish domains to Roman Catholicism, and in the English colonies to Protestantism. They were forbidden to practice their traditional faiths: Activities that were not directly related to economic production, or that suggested links to African culture, were suppressed. Some African practices survived in muted forms, however, and slaves managed to mix African religion with Christianity.

European settlers and slave traders were prejudiced against black Africans. Many Europeans thought Africans were savage, and many European languages attached negative connotations to blackness. In virtually all plantation societies, race was an important element in keeping black slaves subservient. Although racial thinking in regard to slavery became more important in the nineteenth century, the fact that slaves were differentiated from the rest of the population by race as well as by their status as chattel property was fundamental to the system.

AFRICA AND THE TRANSATLANTIC SLAVE TRADE

HOW DID the slave trade impact Africa?

The establishment of plantations reliant on slave labor drew Africa and its peoples into the heart of the transatlantic economy. The Portuguese were the principal carriers early in the African slave trade. Their virtual monopoly was broken by the Dutch in the 1640s. The French and the English came into the trade later, yet during the eighteenth century, which saw the greatest number of slaves shipped, they carried almost half the total traffic. Americans, too, were avid slavers who managed to make considerable profits, even after Britain and the United States outlawed the transatlantic slave trade in 1807 and 1808, respectively.

Slaving was an important part of the massive new overseas trade that financed much European and American economic development during the nineteenth century. The success and considerable profits of this trade, bought at the price of immense human suffering, helped propel Europe and some of its colonial offshoots in the Americas into world dominance.

SLAVERY AND SLAVING IN AFRICA

The trade that supplied African slaves to the Mediterranean and Asia long before the fifteenth century has conventionally been termed the "Oriental" slave trade. The Sudan and the Horn of Africa were the main sources of slaves for this trade. The Afro-European trade, conventionally called the **"Occidental" slave trade**, can be traced at

"Occidental" slave trade

The trade in slaves from Africa to the Islamic Mediterranean and Asia that predated the transatlantic slave trade.

least to the thirteenth century, when Europeans established sugarcane plantations on Cyprus. This industry subsequently spread westward to Crete and Sicily and, in the fifteenth century, to the Portuguese Atlantic islands of Madeira and São Tomé. The Portuguese developed the plantation system of slave labor as they began their expansion into the Atlantic. Voyages beginning in the fifteenth century by the Portuguese and other Europeans made the western coasts of Africa as far south as Angola the prime slaving areas. A less important source region for both Occidental and Oriental trades was the eastern coast of Africa below the Horn.

Prior to the full development of the transatlantic slave trade, slavery and slave trading had been no more significant in Africa than anywhere else in the world.[2] Indigenous African slavery resembled that of other premodern societies. Probably about 10,000 slaves per year, most of them female, were taken from sub-Saharan Africa through the Oriental slave trade.

By about 1650 the Occidental slave trade had become as large as the Oriental trade and for the ensuing two centuries far surpassed it. It affected all of Africa, disrupting especially western and central African societies. As a result of the demand for young male slaves on the plantations of the Americas, West Africa experienced a sharp drain on its productive male population. Moreover, as the external trade destroyed the regional male–female population balance, an internal market for female slaves arose. Internal warfare in western and central Africa increased. These developments accelerated during the eighteenth century. Slave prices increased. Owing to population depletion and regional migrations, however, the actual number of slaves sold declined in some areas.

As European and American nations slowly began to outlaw first the slave trade and then slavery itself in the nineteenth century, the Oriental and internal trades increased. Slave exports from East Africa and the Sudan and Horn increased significantly after about 1780, and indigenous African slavery, predominantly of women, also expanded. By about 1850 the internal African trade surpassed the combined Oriental and (outlawed) Occidental trade. This traffic was dominated by the same figures—merchants, warlords, and rulers—who had previously profited from external trade.

African slavery began a real decline only at the end of the nineteenth century, in part because of the dominance of European colonial regimes and in part because of internal changes. The formal end of African indigenous slavery occurred only in 1928 in Sierra Leone. Late in the twentieth century, however, in various locations around the world—mostly places with endemic, severe poverty and weak civil authority, including the Sudan—patterns of involuntary servitude and human trafficking emerged that constitute modern-day slavery.

CHRONOLOGY

CONQUEST OF THE AMERICAS AND THE TRANSATLANTIC SLAVE TRADE

1494	Treaty of Tordesillas divides the seaborne empires of Spain and Portugal
1500	The Portuguese arrive in Brazil
1519–1521	Hernán Cortés conquers the Aztec Empire
1531–1533	Francisco Pizarro conquers the Inca Empire
1607	Jamestown, Virginia, first permanent English settlement in North America
1608	The French found Quebec
1619	First African slaves brought to British North America
1700s	Over 6 million slaves imported from Africa to the Americas
1794	Slavery abolished throughout the French Empire
1807	The importation of slaves abolished in British domains
1808	The importation of slaves abolished in the United States
1817–1820	Spain abolishes the slave trade
1833	Slavery abolished throughout the British Empire
1850	Importation of slaves abolished in Brazil
1874–1928	Indigenous African slavery abolished
1888	Slavery abolished in Brazil

View the Image
West African Slave Market
at **myhistorylab.com**

---

[2]The summary follows closely that of P. Manning, *Slavery and African Life: Occidental, Oriental, and African Slave Trades* (Cambridge: Cambridge University Press, 1990), pp. 127–140.

King Affonso I of the Kongo holds an audience with European ambassadors who kneel before him.

What roles did Africans play in the transatlantic slave trade?

THE AFRICAN SIDE OF THE TRANSATLANTIC TRADE

Africans were actively involved in the transatlantic slave trade. Except for the Portuguese in central Africa, European slave traders generally obtained their human cargoes from Africans at coastal forts or simply at anchorages along the coast. Africans were motivated to control the inland trade, and Europeans were vulnerable to tropical disease. Thus it was largely African middlemen who undertook the actual capture or procurement of slaves and the difficult, dangerous task of marching them to the coast. These middlemen were generally either wealthy merchants who could mount slaving expeditions inland or the agents of African kingdoms who sought to profit from the trade.

The media of exchange for slaves varied. At first they usually involved mixed barter for goods that ranged from gold dust or firearms to beads and alcohol. As time went on they came increasingly to involve monetary payment. This exchange drained productive resources (human beings) from Africa in return for nonproductive wealth.

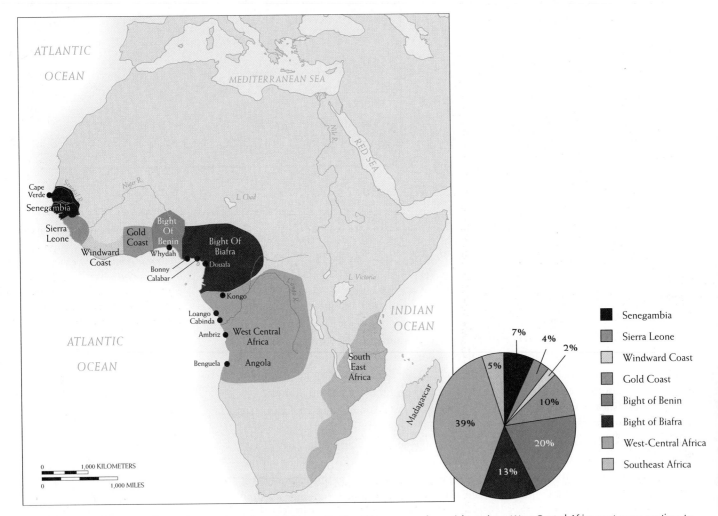

MAP 17–4 Origins of African Slaves Sent to the Americas. Captive Africans came from eight regions. West Central Africa sent more captives to the Americas than any other region.

What factors influenced the origins of enslaved Africans?

The chief western and central African slaving regions provided different numbers of slaves at different times, and the total number of exported slaves varied sharply between periods (see Map 17–4). When one area was unable to produce sufficient numbers to meet demand, the European traders shifted their buying to other points. Between 1526 and 1550 the major sources of slaves for the transatlantic trade were the Kongo-Angola region (34 percent), the Guinea coast of Cape Verde (25.6 percent), and Senegambia (23.5 percent).[3] By contrast, between 1761 and 1810 the French drew some 52 percent of their slaves from Angola and 24 percent from the Bight of Benin, but only 4.8 percent from Senegambia, whereas the British relied most heavily on the Bight of Biafra and central Africa.[4] Traders naturally went where population density and the presence of active African suppliers promised the most slaves and the lowest prices, although prices do not seem to have varied radically in a given period.

THE EXTENT OF THE SLAVE TRADE

The overall number of African slaves exported during the Occidental trade—effectively between 1451 and 1870—is still debated. A major unknown for both the Occidental and the Oriental trades is the number of slaves who died under the brutal conditions to which they were subjected when captured and transported overland and by sea. The **Middle Passage**, the portion of the journey in which Africans were packed onto dangerous and unhealthy boats for the voyage across the Atlantic Ocean, claimed untold numbers; others were lost to other forms of brutality associated with the trade. (See Document, "A Slave Trader Describes the Atlantic Passage" on page 434.)

Historians now estimate that from the sixteenth through the nineteenth century over 35,000 transatlantic slave ship voyages forcibly transported more than 11 million Africans to America. The slave trade varied sharply in extent from period to period (see Figure 17–1). The period of greatest activity, from 1701 to 1810, accounted for over 60 percent of the total. Despite Great Britain's abolition of the slave trade in its colonies in 1807 and the United States' abolition of the slave trade in 1808, the Portuguese still transported more than a million slaves to Brazil between 1811 and 1870. Other nations also continued to trade in slaves in the nineteenth century. In fact, more slaves landed in the Americas in the final years of the trade than during the entire seventeenth century.[5]

Estimates for the older, smaller, and more dispersed Oriental trade are even more problematic, but a figure of million or more is probably realistic. According to one expert's estimate, an additional 15 million people were enslaved within African societies themselves.[6]

Middle Passage

The transatlantic crossing of ships carrying slaves from Africa to the Americas and Caribbean.

[●] View the Image

Diagram: Slave Ship Filled for Middle Passage at **myhistorylab.com**

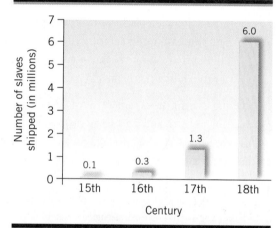

FIGURE 17–1. The Atlantic Slave Trade, 1400–1800. From Caizares-Esguerra, Jorge; Seeman, Eric, The Atlantic in Global History; 1500–2000, © 2007. Electronically reproduced by permission of Pearson Education, Inc., Upper Saddle River, New Jersey.

Why did the slave trade increase so dramatically in the eighteenth century?

---

[3]Scholars have spent decades attempting to assemble trustworthy statistics on the slave trade; the database by Eltis et al., *The Trans-Atlantic Slave Trade: A Database on CD-ROM* (Cambridge and New York: Cambridge University Press, revised 2008), has marshaled a great deal of information in one spot, but new data continue to emerge. Philip Curtin, *The Atlantic Slave Trade: A Census* (Madison: University of Wisconsin Press, 1969), provided the first detailed analysis of the various proposed figures for the slave trade; see especially p. 101.

[4]Curtin, *The Atlantic Slave Trade*, pp. 101, 129; James A. Rawley, *The Trans-Atlantic Slave Trade: A History* (New York: W. W. Norton, 1981), p. 129. Note that precise statistics are subject to revision in light of more recent scholarship; see, for example, Eltis et al., *The Trans-Atlantic Slave Trade: A Database on CD-ROM*.

[5]Rawley, *The Transatlantic Slave Trade*, p. 429; Curtin, *Atlantic Slave Trade*, p. 268.

[6]Manning, *Slavery and African Life*, pp. 37, 170–171.

DOCUMENT

A Slave Trader Describes the Atlantic Passage

During 1693 and 1694, Captain Thomas Phillips carried slaves from Africa to Barbados on the ship Hannibal. The financial backer of the voyage was the Royal African Company of London, which held an English crown monopoly on slave trading. Phillips sailed to the west coast of Africa, where he purchased the Africans who were sold into slavery by an African king. Then he set sail westward.

- **Who** are the various people described in this document who in one way or another were involved in or profited from the slave trade? What dangers did the Africans face on the voyage? What contemporary attitudes could have led this captain to treat and think of his human cargo simply as goods to be transported? What are the grounds of his self-pity for the difficulties he met?

Having bought my complement of 700 slaves, 480 men and 220 women, and finish'd all my business at Whidaw [on the Gold Coast of Africa], I took my leave of the old king and his *cappasheirs* [attendants], and parted, with many affectionate expressions on both sides, being forced to promise him that I would return again the next year, with several things he desired me to bring from England. . . . I set sail the 27th of July in the morning, accompany'd with the East-India Merchant, who had bought 650 slaves, for the Island of St. Thomas. . . . from which we took our departure on August 25th and set sail for Barbadoes.

We spent in our passage from St. Thomas to Barbadoes two months eleven days, from the 25th of August to the 4th of November following: in which time there happened such sickness and mortality among my poor men and Negroes. Of the first we buried 14, and of the last 320, which was a great detriment to our voyage, the Royal African Company losing ten pounds by every slave that died, and the owners of the ship ten pounds ten shillings, being

the freight agreed on to be paid by the charter-party for every Negro delivered alive ashore to the African Company's agents at Barbadoes. . . . The loss in all amounted to near 6500 pounds sterling.

The distemper which my men as well as the blacks mostly died of was the white flux, which was so violent and inveterate that no medicine would in the least check it, so that when any of our men were seized with it, we esteemed him a dead man, as he generally proved. . . .

The Negroes are so incident to [subject to] the small-pox that few ships that carry them escape without it, and sometimes it makes vast havoc and destruction among them. But tho' we had 100 at a time sick of it, and that it went thro' the ship, yet we lost not above a dozen by it. All the assistance we gave the diseased was only as much water as they desir'd to drink, and some palm-oil to annoint their sores, and they would generally recover without any other helps but what kind nature gave them. . . .

But what the smallpox spar'd, the flux swept off, to our great regret, after all our pains and care to give them their messes in due order and season, keeping their lodgings as clean and sweet as possible, and enduring so much misery and stench so long among a parcel of creatures nastier than swine, and after all our expectations to be defeated by their mortality. . . .

No gold-finders can endure so much noisome slavery as they do who carry Negroes; for those have some respite and satisfaction, but we endure twice the misery; and yet by their mortality our voyages are ruin'd, and we pine and fret ourselves to death, and take so much pains to so little purpose.

Source: From Thomas Phillips, "Journal," *A Collection of Voyages and Travels*, Vol. 6, ed. by Awnsham and John Churchill (London, 1746), as quoted in Thomas Howard, ed., *Black Voyage: Eyewitness Accounts of the Atlantic Slave Trade* (Boston: Little, Brown, and Company, 1971), pp. 85–87.

A Closer Look

The Slave Ship *Brookes*

This print, published in 1788 in England by the Plymouth Chapter of the Society for Effecting the Abolition of the Slave Trade, became the single most important and widely circulated abolitionist image of the horrific conditions of the Middle Passage. It records the main decks of the 320-ton slave ship *Brookes*, which measured 25 feet wide and 100 feet long.

The average space for each African destined for slavery in the Americas was 78 inches by 16 inches. The Africans were normally shackled to assure discipline and to prevent their injuring the crew. Iron shackles also prevented Africans from committing suicide on the voyage.

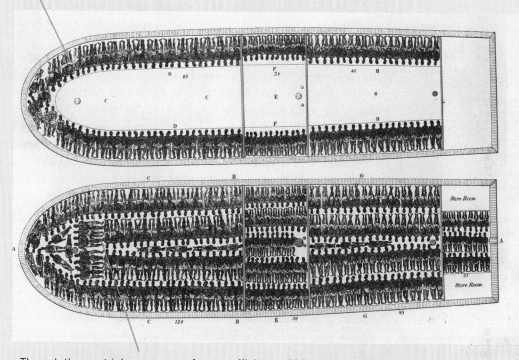

Through the most inhumane use of space efficiency, 609 slaves could be crammed onboard for the nightmarish passage to America. A Parliamentary inquiry in 1788 found that the ship had been designed to carry no more than approximately 450 persons.

(See Document *"A Slave Trader Describes the Atlantic Passage."*)

Questions

1. What response is this image, showing the crowded conditions on the slave ship *Brookes*, expected to arouse in the viewer? How do you think the response of viewers in the early twenty-first century might differ from those in the late-eighteenth and early-nineteenth centuries?

2. In recent years some commentators have criticized this image as indicating passivity on the part of the enslaved Africans and activity only on the part of the abolitionists. Why might this interpretation be directed toward the image?

3. Do you think that British viewers of this image of the *Brookes* would necessarily have associated their own nation with the slave trade? Why or why not?

Job ben Solomon. Captured by Mandingo enemies and sold to a Maryland tobacco planter, Job ben Solomon accomplished the nearly impossible feat of returning to Africa as a freeman. By demonstrating his talents as a Muslim scholar, including his ability to write the entire Qur'an from memory, he astonished his owners and eventually convinced them to let him go home.

"The Fortunate Slave," An Illustration of African Slavery in the early eighteenth century by Douglas Grant (1968). From "Some Memoirs of the Life of Job," by Thomas Bluett 1734. Photo by Robert D. Rubic/Precision Chromes, Inc., Rare Books Division, the New York Public Library, Lenox and Tilden Foundations/Art Resource, New York.

What was a more typical fate for a slave in the Americas?

QUICK REVIEW

Difficulties in Determining Consequences of the Slave Trade

+ Do not know how the slave trade affected specific West African regions

+ Cannot determine number of slaves captured during wars and captured during slave raiding

+ Do not know how slave trading affected commerce in African products

CONSEQUENCES OF THE SLAVE TRADE FOR AFRICA

These statistics hint at the massive impact slave trading had on African life and history. The question of specific effects remains difficult.

We cannot be certain whether the transatlantic trade brought net population loss or gain to specific areas of West Africa. The wide and rapid spread of maize and cassava cultivation after these plants had been imported from the Americas may have fueled African population increases that offset slave-trade losses. We know, however, that slaving took away many of the strongest young men in various areas and, in the Oriental trade zones, most of the young women.

Similarly, we do not know if more slaves were captured as by-products of local wars or from targeted slave raiding. Nor do we know if slaving always inhibited development of trade or perhaps sometimes stimulated it because commerce in a range of African products—from ivory to wood and hides—often accompanied that in slaves. We do know that the exchange of productive human beings for money or goods that were generally not used to build a productive economy was a great loss for African society as a whole.

Finally, because we do not yet have accurate estimates of the total population of Africa at different times over the four centuries of the transatlantic slave trade, we cannot determine with certainty its demographic impact. We can, however, make some educated guesses. If, for example, tropical Africa had possibly 50 million inhabitants in 1600, it would then have had 30 percent of the combined population of the Americas, the Middle East, Europe, and North Africa. If in 1900, after the depredations of the slave trade, it had 70 million inhabitants, its population would have dropped to only slightly more than 10 percent of the combined population of the same world regions. Accordingly, current best estimates indicate that overall African population growth suffered significantly as a result of the devastating numbers of people lost to enslavement or to the increased warfare and decreased birthrate tied to the slave trade. Figures like these also give some idea of slavery's probable impact on Africa's ability to engage with developments that, elsewhere in the world, led to the emergence of the modern industrializing world.[7]

It is important to remember that even in West and central Africa, which bore the brunt of the transatlantic trade, its impact and the response to it were varied. In a few cases, kingdoms such as Dahomey (the present Republic of Benin) seem to have sought and derived immense economic profit by making slaving a state monopoly. Other kingdoms, such as Benin, sought to stay almost completely out of slaving. In instances including the rise of Asante power or the fall of the Yoruba Oyo Empire, it appears that increased slaving was a result as well as a cause of regional instability and change. Increased warfare meant increased prisoners to be enslaved and a surplus to be sold off. Whether slaving was a motive for war is still an unanswered question.

Similarly, the consequences of the major increase in indigenous slavery are unknown, and they varied with the specifics of regional situations. For example, in West Africa relatively more men were taken as slaves than women, whereas in the Sahelian Sudanic regions relatively more women than men were taken. In the west the loss of so many men increased the pressures for polygamy, whereas in the Sahelian Sudanic regions the loss of women may have stimulated polyandry and reduced the birthrate significantly.

---

[7]On all of the preceding points regarding the probable impact of the trade, see Manning, *Slavery and African Life*, pp. 126–148, 168–176. Also consult Eltis et al., *The Trans-Atlantic Slave Trade: A Database on CD-ROM.*

Even though slavery existed previously in Africa, the scale of the transatlantic trade was unprecedented and, hence, had an unprecedented impact on indigenous social, political, and economic realities. The slave trade measurably changed patterns of life and balances of power, whether by stimulating trade or warfare, by disrupting previous market and political structures, by substantially increasing slavery inside Africa, or by disturbing the male–female ratio and, consequently, the workforce balance and birthrate patterns. The overseas slave trade siphoned indigenous energy into ultimately counterproductive or destructive directions. True economic development was inhibited, especially in central and coastal West Africa. The transatlantic slave trade must by any standard be described as one of the most tragic aspects of European involvement in Africa.

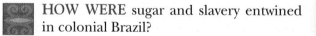 Watch the Video at **myhistorylab.com**

SUMMARY

 WHAT WERE the four periods of European contact with the world?

Periods of European Overseas Expansion. Europe's disproportionate influence on world history has gone through four phases: conquest and commercial exploitation (roughly 1500–1700); trade rivalry, especially among Spain, France, and Great Britain (roughly 1700–1820); European colonization in Africa and Asia (nineteenth century and first half of twentieth century); and decolonization (mid-twentieth century). *page 417*

WHAT WAS mercantilism?

Mercantilist Theory of Economic Exploitation. Early European empires were based on mercantilism, the idea that the nation could be enriched by controlling trade with colonial markets. *page 417*

 WHAT ROLES did the Roman Catholic Church play in Spanish America?

Establishment of the Spanish Empire in America. Within half a century of the landing of Columbus, millions of America's native peoples had encountered Europeans intent on conquest, exploitation, and religious conversion. Because of their advanced weapons, navies, and the new diseases they brought with them, as well as internal divisions among the Native Americans, the Europeans achieved a rapid conquest. The Roman Catholic Church was generally aligned with the conquerers, but some priests became advocates for Native Americans. *page 418*

HOW DID Spaniards attempt to control labor in the Americas?

Economies of Exploitation in the Spanish Empire. In Spanish America, various institutions were developed to extract native labor. The *flota*, controlled by administrators in Seville, sought to monopolize trade. *page 420*

 HOW WERE sugar and slavery entwined in colonial Brazil?

Colonial Brazil. Brazil was Portugal's largest American holding. The Brazilian economy was dominated by sugarcane, which depended on African slave labor. *page 422*

 HOW WERE the economies of the French and British North American colonies integrated into the transatlantic economy?

French and British Colonies in North America. Early French colonists were few in number. They were more interested in commerce (especially transatlantic fur-trading) and Christianity than in settlement, so their relationships with Native Americans were relatively nonconfrontational. English colonists were mostly agriculturalists who had varied and complicated interactions with Native American populations. The economies of North America's port cities were intertwined with the transatlantic slave trade. *page 423*

 WHAT WAS the "Columbian Exchange"?

The Columbian Exchange: Disease, Animals, and Agriculture. Until the European explorations, the civilizations of the Americas, Eurasia, and Africa had had no significant contact with each other. Native Americans had no immunity to several significant European diseases, so many died. Exchanges of plants and animals transformed agriculture in the Americas, Europe, and Africa. *page 424*

WHY WAS the transatlantic slave trade so economically important?

Slavery in the Americas. From the Mid-Atlantic English colonies through the Caribbean and into Brazil, slave-labor plantation systems were established. The economies and peoples of Europe, Africa, and the Americas were thus drawn into a vast worldwide web of production based on slave labor. *page 427*

HOW DID the slave trade impact Africa?

Africa and the Transatlantic Slave Trade. On the African continent, the impact of the slave trade was immense, though difficult to document specifically. The social, economic, and personal effects were enormous, given the extent and duration of the trade. The loss of population and productive resources helped set the stage for European colonization. The Atlantic slave trade's impact continues to be felt at both ends of the original "trade." *page 430*

KEY TERMS

Black Legend (p. 419)
Columbian Exchange (p. 424)
conquistadores (kon-KEES-tuh-DOR-ays) (p. 420)
debt peonage (p. 420)
encomienda **(EN-koh-MYEN-dah)** (p. 420)
hacienda (HAH-see-EN-dah) (p. 420)

mercantilism (MUR-kuhn-tihl-izm) (p. 418)
Middle Passage (p. 433)
"Occidental" slave trade (p. 430)
peninsulares (p. 420)
plantation economy (p. 429)
repartimiento **(ray-PAHR-tih-MYEN-toh)** (p. 420)

REVIEW QUESTIONS

1. How were small groups of Spaniards able to conquer the Aztec and Inca Empires?

2. What was the basis of the mercantilist theory of economics? What was the relationship between the colonial economies and those of the homelands?

3. What was the relationship between conquistadores and missionaries in Spain's American colonies?

4. Describe the economies of Spanish America and Brazil. What were the similarities and differences between them and the British and French colonies in the Caribbean and North America? What role did the various colonies play in the transatlantic economy?

5. Explain the chief factors involved in the Columbian Exchange. Which animals from Europe flourished in the Americas? Why? Which American plants produced broad impact in Europe and elsewhere in the world?

6. Why did forced labor and slavery develop in tropical colonies? How was slavery in the Americas different from slavery in earlier societies?

7. What historical patterns emerged in the slave trade(s) within and out of Africa? Consider the gender and age distribution of slaves, their places of origin, and their destinations.

8. Compare and contrast the Oriental and Occidental slave trades. What was the effect of the transatlantic slave trade on West African societies? On East Africa? What role did Africans themselves play in the slave trade?

Note: To learn more about the topics in this chapter, please turn to the Suggested Readings at the end of the book. For additional sources related to this chapter please see www.myhistorylab.com

PEARSON
myhistorylab Connections

Reinforce what you learned in this chapter by studying the many documents,
images, maps, review tools, and videos available at **www.myhistorylab.com**

Read and Review

✓● Study and Review Chapter 17

●●● Read the Document *2nd Letter, Hernan Cortez to King
Charles V, p. 418*

del Castillo, History of Conquest, p. 418

New Laws Indies for Good Treatment 2, p. 419

Account of Devastation of Indies, p. 419

Albanel from Jesuit Relation, p. 423

*Smallpox epidemic in Mexico 1520 and Smallpox
epidemic in New England, p. 425*

Slavery in Africa late 1700s, Mungo Park, p. 427

Overseer in Cotton Plantation, p. 429

👁 See the Map *Spanish and Portuguese Exploration,
p. 422*

European Empires ca. 1600, p. 423

Atlantic Slave Trade, p. 429

●● View the Image *West African Slave Market, p. 431*

Diagram: Slave Ship Filled for Middle Passage, p. 433

Research and Explore

◉ Watch the Video *Columbian Exchange, p. 427*

◉ Watch the Video *Triangle Trade Routes, p. 437*

((●● Hear the Audio

Hear the audio file for Chapter 17
at **www.myhistorylab.com**

Suggested Readings

Chapter 1

General Prehistory

P. Bogucki, The Origins of Human Society (1999). An excellent summary of recent scholarship on the earliest origins of human societies.

F. Bray, The Rice Economies: Technology and Development in Asian Societies (1986). Still the best authority on the origins of rice cultivation and its effect on the development of ancient Asia.

M. Ehrenberg, Women in Prehistory (1989). An account of the role of women in early times.

C. Freeman, Egypt, Greece and Rome: Civilizations of the Ancient Mediterranean (2004). Good comparative study of Egypt with Greece and Rome.

D.C. Johnson and M.R. Edey, Lucy: The Beginning of Mankind (1981). An account of the African origins of humans.

S.M. Nelson, ed., Ancient Queens: Archaeological Explorations (2003). Reassesses women rulers and female power in the ancient world.

S.M. Nelson and M. Rosen-Ayalon, In Pursuit of Gender: World-wide Archaeological Approaches (2002). Essays on gender and the archaeology of the ancient world.

D.L. Nichols and T.H. Charlton, eds., The Archaeology of City-States: Cross-cultural Approaches (1997). One of a growing body of books and essay collections employing cross-cultural and comparative approaches to world history and archaeology.

M. Oliphant, The Atlas of the Ancient World: Charting the Great Civilizations of the Past (1992). An excellent comprehensive atlas of the ancient world.

P.L. Shinnie, Ancient Nubia (1996). A study of the African state most influenced by Egyptian culture.

Near East

M.E. Auber, The Phoenicians and the West (1996). A new study of an important sea-going people who served as a conduit between East and West.

Ben-Tor, ed., The Archaeology of Ancient Israel (1992). A useful and up-to-date survey.

J. Bottéro, Everyday Life in Ancient Mesopotamia (2001). Interesting vignettes of ancient Mesopotamian life.

H. Crawford, Sumer and the Sumerians (1991). A discussion of the oldest Mesopotamian civilization.

I. Finkelstein and N.A. Silberman, The Bible Unearthed: Archaeology's New Vision of Ancient Israel and the Origin of Its Sacred Texts (2001). An interesting discussion of the insights of recent archaeological finds on the history of the Bible and ancient Israel.

G. Leick, Mesopotamia: The Invention of the City (2002). Good discussion of the urban history of ancient Mesopotamia.

J.N. Postgate, Early Mesopotamia (1992). An excellent study of Mesopotamian economy and society from the earliest times to about 1500 B.C.E., helpfully illustrated with drawings, photos, and translated documents.

D.B. Redford, Akhenaten (1987). A study of the controversial religious reformer.

W.F. Saggs, The Might That Was Assyria (1984). A history of the northern Mesopotamian Empire and a worthy companion to the author's account of the Babylonian Empire in the south.

M. Van de Mieroop, A History of the Ancient Near East, ca. 3000–323 B.C. (2004). An up-to-date comprehensive survey of ancient Near Eastern history.

India

D.P. Agrawal, The Archaeology of India (1982). A fine survey of the problems and data. Detailed, but with excellent summaries and brief discussions of major issues.

C. Chakraborty, Common Life in the Rigveda and Atharvaveda—An Account of the Folklore in the Vedic Period (1977). An interesting attempt to reconstruct everyday life in the Vedic period from the principal Vedic texts.

J.R. Mcintosh, A Peaceful Realm: The Rise and Fall of the Indus Civilization (2002). Discusses what archaeologists have managed to unearth so far regarding Harrapan civilization.

W.D. O'flaherty, The Rig Veda: An Anthology (1981). An excellent selection of Vedic texts in prosaic but very careful translation, with helpful notes on the texts.

J.E. Schwartzberg, ed., A Historical Atlas of South Asia (1978). The definitive reference work for historical geography. Includes chronological tables and substantive essays.

R. Thapar, Early India: From the Origins to A.D. 1300 (2003). A comprehensive introduction to the early history of India.

China

M. Loewe and E. Shaughnessy, eds., The Cambridge History of Ancient China: From the Origins of Civilization to 221 B.C. (1999). A comprehensive and authoritative history of ancient China.

K.C. Chang, The Archeology of Ancient China, 4th ed. (1986). The standard work on the subject.

K.C. Chang, Art, Myth, and Ritual: The Path to Political Authority in Ancient China (1984). A study of the relation between shamans, gods, agricultural production, and political authority during the Shang and Zhou dynasties.

N. Di Cosmo, Ancient China and Its Enemies: The Rise of Nomadic Power in East Asian History (2002). An excellent study of the relationship between China and nomadic peoples that was a powerful force in shaping Chinese and Central Asian history.

C.Y. Hsu, Western Chou Civilization (1988).

D.N. Keightley, The Origins of Chinese Civilization (1983).

M.E. Lewis, Sanctioned Violence in Early China (1990).

X.Q. Li, Eastern Zhou and Qin Civilizations (1986). Includes fresh interpretations based on archaeological finds.

Americas

R.L. Burger, Chavín and the Origins of Andean Civilization (1992). A lucid and detailed account of the rise of civilization in the Andes.

M.D. Coe and R. Koontz, Mexico: From the Olmecs to the Aztecs (2002). Good survey of ancient Mexico.

D. Drew, The Lost Chronicles of the Maya Kings (1999). Fine introduction to the history of Maya civilization.

V.W. Fitzhugh and A. Crowell, Crossroads of Continents: Cultures of Siberia and Alaska (1988). Covers the area where the immigration from Eurasia to the Americas began.

R. Ford, ed., Prehistoric Food Production in North America (1985). Examines the origins of agriculture in the Americas.

P.D. Hunt, Indian Agriculture in America: Prehistory to the Present (1987). Includes a discussion of preconquest agriculture.

A. Knight, Mexico: From the Beginning to the Spanish Conquest (2002). First of a three-volume comprehensive history of Mexico.

C. Morris and A. Von Hagen, The Inka Empire and Its Andean Origins (1993). An overview of Andean civilization with excellent illustrations.

M. Moseley, The Incas and Their Ancestors: The Archaeology of Ancient Peru (1992). An overview of Peruvian archaeology.

J.A. Sabloff, The New Archaeology and the Ancient Maya (1990). A lively account of recent research in Maya archaeology.

I. Silverblatt, Moon, Sun, and Witches: Gender Ideologies and Class in Inca and Colonial Peru (1987). A controversial but thought-provoking discussion of Incan ideas about gender.

Chapter 2

China

R. Bernstein, Ultimate Journey: Retracing the Path of an Ancient Buddhist Monk Who Crossed Asia in Search of Enlightenment (2001). Discusses the diffusion of Buddhism from India to China.

H.G. Creel, What Is Taoism? And Other Studies in Chinese Cultural History (1970).

W.T. de Bary et al., Sources of Chinese Tradition (1960). A reader in China's philosophical and historical literature. It should be consulted for the later periods as well as for the Zhou.

H. Fingarette, Confucius—The Secular as Sacred (1998).

Y.L. Fung, A Short History of Chinese Philosophy, ed. by D. Bodde (1948). A survey of Chinese philosophy from its origins down to recent times.

A. Graham, Disputers of the Tao (1989).

D. Hawkes, Ch'u Tz'u: The Songs of the South (1985).

D.C. Lau, trans., Lao-tzu, Tao Te Ching (1963).

D.C. Lau, trans., Confucius, The Analects (1979).

C. Li, ed., The Sage and the Second Sex: Confucianism, Ethics, and Gender (2000). A good introduction to gender and ethics in Confucian thought.

B.I. Schwartz, The World of Thought in Ancient China (1985).

A. Waley, Three Ways of Thought in Ancient China (1956). An easy yet sound introduction to Confucianism, Daoism, and Legalism.

A. Waley, The Book of Songs (1960).

B. Watson, trans., Basic Writings of Mo Tzu, Hsun Tzu, and Han Fei Tzu (1963).

B. Watson, trans., The Complete Works of Chuang Tzu (1968).

H. Welch, Taoism, The Parting of the Way (1967).

India

A.L. Basham, The Wonder That Was India, rev. ed. (1963). Still unsurpassed by more recent works. Chapter VII, "Religion," is a superb introduction to the Vedic Aryan, Brahmanic, Hindu, Jain, and Buddhist traditions of thought.

W.N. Brown, Man in the Universe: Some Continuities in Indian Thought (1970). A penetrating yet brief reflective summary of major patterns in Indian thinking.

W.T. de Bary et al., Sources of Indian Tradition (1958). 2 vols. Vol. I, From the Beginning to 1800, ed. and rev. by Ainslie T. Embree (1988). Excellent selections from a variety of Indian texts, with good introductions to chapters and individual selections.

P. Harvey, An Introduction to Buddhism (1990). Chapters 1–3 provide an excellent historical introduction.

T.J. Hopkins, The Hindu Religious Tradition (1971). A first-rate, thoughtful introduction to Hindu religious ideas and practice.

K. Klostermaier, Hinduism: A Short History (2000). A relatively compact survey of the history of Hinduism.

J.M. Koller, The Indian Way (1982). A useful, wide-ranging handbook of Indian thought and religion.

R.H. Robinson and W.L. Johnson, The Buddhist Religion, 3rd ed. (1982). An excellent first text on the Buddhist tradition, its thought and development.

R.C. Zaehner, Hinduism (1966). One of the best general introductions to central Indian religious and philosophical ideas.

Israel

A. Bach, ed., Women in the Hebrew Bible: A Reader (1999). Excellent introduction to the ways in which biblical scholars are exploring the role of women in the Bible.

Bright, A History of Israel (1968), 2nd ed. (1972). One of the standard scholarly introductions to biblical history and literature.

W.D. Davies and L. Finkelstein, eds., The Cambridge History of Judaism. Vol. I, Introduction: The Persian Period (1984). Excellent essays on diverse aspects of the exilic period and later.

J. Neusner, The Way of Torah: An Introduction to Judaism (1979). A sensitive introduction to the Judaic tradition and faith.

The Oxford History of the Biblical World, M. D. Coogan, ed. (1998).

Greece

The Cambridge Companion to Greek and Roman Philosophy, D. Sedley ed. (2003).

G.B. Kerferd, The Sophistic Movement (1981). An excellent description and analysis.

J. Lear, Aristotle: The Desire to Understand (1988). A brilliant yet comprehensible introduction to the work of the philosopher.

T.E. Rihil, Greek Science (1999). Good survey of Greek science incorporating recent reseach on the topic.

J.M. Robinson, An Introduction to Early Greek Philosophy (1968). A valuable collection of the main fragments and ancient testimony to the works of the early philosophers, with excellent commentary.

G. Vlastos, The Philosophy of Socrates (1971). A splendid collection of essays illuminating the problems presented by this remarkable man.

G. Vlastos, Platonic Studies, 2nd ed. (1981). A similar collection on the philosophy of Plato.

G. Vlastos, Socrates, Ironist and Moral Philosopher (1991). The results of a lifetime of study by the leading interpreter of Socrates in our time.

Comparative Studies

(Increasingly, world historians are looking at ancient civilizations in relationship to each other rather than as isolated entities to try to understand commonalities and differences in social and cultural development.)

W. Doniger, Splitting the Difference: Gender and Myth in Ancient Greece and India (1999).

G.E.R. Lloyd, The Ambitions of Curiosity: Understanding the World in Ancient Greece and China (2002).

G.E.R. Lloyd, The Way and the Word: Science and Medicine in Early China and Greece (2002).

T. McEvilley, The Shape of Ancient Thought: Comparative Studies of Greek and Indian Philosophies (2002).

Chapter 3

The Rise of Greek Civilization

P. Cartledge, The Spartans (2003). A readable account of this enigmatic people.

J. Chadwick, The Mycenaean World (1976). A readable account by a man who helped decipher Mycenaean writing.

R. Drews, The Coming of the Greeks (1988). A fine discussion of the Greeks' arrival as part of the movements of the Indo-European peoples.

J.V. Fine, The Ancient Greeks (1983). An excellent survey that discusses historical problems and the evidence that gives rise to them.

M.I. Finley, World of Odysseus, rev. ed. (1965). A fascinating attempt to reconstruct Homeric society.

P. Green, Xerxes at Salamis (1970). A lively and stimulating history of the Persian War.

D. Hamel, Trying Neaira (2003). A lively account of the events surrounding a famous jury trial that sheds interesting light on Athenian society in the fourth century B.C.E.

V.D. Hanson, The Western Way of War (1989). A brilliant and lively discussion of the rise and character of the hoplite phalanx and its influence on Greek society.

V.D. Hanson, The Other Greeks (1995). A revolutionary account of the Greek invention of the family farm and its centrality for the shaping of the polis.

D. Kagan, The Great Dialogue: A History of Greek Political Thought from Homer to Polybius (1965). A discussion of the relationship between the Greek historical experience and political theory.

W.K. Lacey, The Family in Ancient Greece (1984).

J.F. Lazenby, The Defense of Greece, 490–479 B.C. (1993). A new and valuable study of the Persian Wars.

J.F. McGlew, Tyranny and Political Culture in Ancient Greece (1993). A recent account of political developments in the Archaic period.

S.G. Miller, Ancient Greek Athletics (2004). The most complete and most useful account of the subject.

O. Murray, Early Greece (1980). A lively and imaginative account of the early history of Greece to the end of the Persian War.

A.M. Snodgrass, The Dark Age of Greece (1972). A good examination of the archaeological evidence.

B.S. Strauss, The Battle of Salamis: The Naval Encounter That Saved Greece and Western Civilization (2004). A lively account of the major naval battle of the Persian Wars and its setting.

A.G. Woodhead, Greeks in the West (1962). An account of the Greek settlements in Italy and Sicily.

W.J. Woodhouse, Solon the Liberator (1965). A discussion of the great Athenian reformer.

Classical and Hellenistic Greece

W. Burkert, Greek Religion (1987). An excellent study by an outstanding student of the subject.

J.R. Lane Fox, Alexander the Great (1973). An imaginative account that does more than the usual justice to the Persian side of the problem.

Y. Garlan, Slavery in Ancient Greece (1988). An up-to-date survey.

P. Green, Alexander to Actium: The Historical Evolution of the Hellenistic Age (1990). A remarkable synthesis of political and cultural history.

C.D. Hamilton, Agesilaus and the Failure of Spartan Hegemony (1991). An excellent biography of the king who was the central figure in Sparta during its domination in the fourth century B.C.E.

N.G.L. Hammond, Philip of Macedon (1994). A new biography of the founder of the Macedonian Empire.

N.G.L. Hammond and G.T. Griffith, A History of Macedonia, Vol. 2, 550–336 B.C. (1979). A thorough account of Macedonian history that focuses on the careers of Philip and Alexander.

R. Just, Women in Athenian Law and Life (1988). An account of women's place in Athenian society.

D. Kagan, The Peloponnesian War (2003). A narrative history of the war.

B.M.W. Knox, The Heroic Temper: Studies in Sophoclean Tragedy (1964). A brilliant analysis of tragic heroism.

D.M. Lewis, Sparta and Persia (1977). A valuable discussion of relations between Sparta and Persia in the fifth and fourth centuries B.C.E.

A.A. Long, Hellenistic Philosophy: Stoics, Epicureans, Sceptics (1974). An account of Greek science in the Hellenistic and Roman periods.

R. Meiggs, The Athenian Empire (1972). A fine study of the rise and fall of the empire, making excellent use of inscriptions.

J.J. Pollitt, Art and Experience in Classical Greece (1972). A scholarly and entertaining study of the relationship between art and history in classical Greece, with excellent illustrations.

J.J. Pollitt, Art in the Hellenistic Age (1986). An extraordinary analysis that places the art in its historical and intellectual context.

E.W. Robinson, Ancient Greek Democracy (2004). A stimulating collection of ancient sources and modern interpretations.

D.M. Schaps, Economic Rights of Women in Ancient Greece (1981).

B.S. Strauss, Athens after the Peloponnesian War (1987). An excellent discussion of Athens' recovery and of the nature of Athenian society and politics in the fourth century B.C.E.

B.S. Strauss, Fathers and Sons in Athens (1993). An unusual synthesis of social, political, and intellectual history.

V. Tcherikover, Hellenistic Civilization and the Jews (1970). A fine study of the impact of Hellenism on the Jews.

G. Vlastos, Socrates, Ironist and Moral Philosopher (1991). The results of a lifetime of study by the leading interpreter of Socrates in our time.

Chapter 4

Iran

M. Boyce, Zoroastrians: Their Religious Beliefs and Practices (1979). A detailed survey by the current authority on Zoroastrian religious history, organized historically and based on extensive research. See Chapters 7–9.

M. Boyce, ed. and trans., Textual Sources for the Study of Zoroastrianism (1984). Well-translated selections from a broad range of ancient Iranian materials and an important introduction that includes Boyce's arguments for a revision of the dates of Zoroaster's life (to between 1400 and 1200 B.C.E.).

J.M. Cook, The Persian Empire (1983). Survey of the Achaemenid period.

J. Curtis, Ancient Persia (1989). Excellent portfolio of photographs of artifacts and sites, with a clear historical survey of the arts and culture of ancient Iran.

W.D. Davies and L. Finklestein, ed., The Cambridge History of Judaism, Vol. 1, Introduction; "The Persian Period." Good articles on Iran and Iranian religion as well as Judaism.

J. Duchesne-Guillemin, trans., The Hymns of Zarathushtra, trans. by M. Henning (1952, 1963). The best short introduction to the original texts of the Zoroastrian hymns.

R.N. Frye, The Heritage of Persia (1963, 1966). A first-rate survey of Iranian history to Islamic times: readable but scholarly. Chapter 6 deals with the Sasanid era.

R. Ghirshman, Iran (1954). Good material on culture, society, and economy as well as politics and history.

R. Ghirshman, Persian Art: The Parthian and Sasanid Dynasties (1962). Superb photographs, and a very helpful glossary of places and names. The text is minimal.

W.W. Malandra, trans. and ed., An Introduction to Ancient Iranian Religion: Readings from the Avesta and Achaemenid Inscriptions (1983). Helpful especially for texts of inscriptions relevant to religion.

Geo Widengran, Mani and Manichaeism (1965). Still the standard introduction to Mani's life and the later spread and development of Manichaeism.

India

A.L. Basham, The Wonder That Was India, rev. ed. (1963). Excellent material on Mauryan religion, society, culture, and history.

A.L. Basham, ed., A Cultural History of India (1975). A fine collection of historical-survey essays by a variety of scholars. See Part I, "The Ancient Heritage" (Chapters 2–16).

N.N. Bhattacharyya, Ancient Indian History and Civilization: Trends and Perspectives (1988). Covers Mauryan and Gupta times as well as earlier periods, with chapters on political systems, cities and villages, ideology and religion, and art.

W.T. de Bary et al., comp., Sources of Indian Tradition, 2nd ed. (1958). Vol. I: From the Beginning to 1800, ed. and rev. by Ainslie T. Embree (1988). Excellent selections from a wide variety of Indian texts, with good introductions to chapters and selections.

S. Dutt, Buddhist Monks and Monasteries of India (1962). The standard work. See especially Chapters 3 ("Bhakti") and 4 ("Monasteries under the Gupta Kings").

D.G. Mandelbaum, Society in India (1972). 2 vols. The first two chapters in Volume I of this study of caste, family, and village relations are a good introduction to the caste system.

B. Rowland, The Art and Architecture of India: Buddhist/ Hindu/Jain, 3rd rev. ed. (1970). The standard work, lucid and easy to read. Note Part Three, "Romano-Indian Art in North-West India and Central Asia." See also the excellent chapters on Sungan, Andhran, and other early Buddhist art (6–8, 14), the Gupta period (15), and the Hindu Renaissance (17–19).

V.A. Smith, ed., The Oxford History of India, 4th rev. ed. by Percival Spear et al. (1981), pp. 71–163. A dry, occasionally dated historical survey. Includes useful reference chronologies. See especially pp. 164–229 (the Gupta period and following era to the Muslim invasions).

R. Thapar, A History of India, Part I (1966), pp. 50–108. Three chapters that provide a basic survey of the period.

R. Thapar, Ashoka and the Decline of the Mauryans (1973). The standard treatment of Ashoka's reign. Three chapters cover the rise of mercantilism, the Gupta "classical pattern," and the southern dynasties to ca. 900 C.E.

S. Wolpert, A New History of India, 2nd ed. (1982). A basic survey history. Chapters 5 and 6 cover the Mauryans, Guptas, and Kushans.

P. Younger, Introduction to Indian Religious Thought (1972). A sensitive attempt to delineate classical concerns of Indian religious thought and culture.

Greek and Asian Dynasties

A.K. Narain, The Indo-Greeks (1957. Reprinted with corrections, 1962). The most comprehensive account of the complex history of the various kings and kingdoms.

F.E. Peters, The Harvest of Hellenism (1970), pp. 222–308. Helpful chapters on Greek rulers of the Eastern world from Seleucus to the last Indo-Greeks.

J.W. Sedlar, India and the Greek World: A Study in the Transmission of Culture (1980). A basic work that provides a good overview.

D. Sinor, ed., The Cambridge History of Early Inner Asia (1990). See especially Chapters 6 and 7.

Chapter 5

R. Bates, V.Y. Mudimbe, and Jean O'Barr, eds., Africa and the Disciplines (1993). Explores how knowledge of Africa has shaped various fields of scholarship. The essay on history by Steven Feierman is particularly relevant to this chapter.

P. Bohannan and P. Curtin, Africa and Africans, rev. ed. (1995). An enjoyable and enlightening discussion of African history and prehistory and of major African institutions (e.g., arts, family life, religion).

R. Bulliet, The Camel and the Wheel (1990). Explains why the camel was chosen over the wheel as a means of transport in the Sahara.

P. Curtin, On the Fringes of History: A Memoir (2005). An engaging autobiography by one of the pioneers in African Studies in the United States; explores what it means to be a historian in the modern world.

P. Curtin, S. Feiermann, L. Thompson, and J. Vansina, African History, rev. ed . (1995). The classic survey history, written by four of the leaders in the field.

T.R.H. Davenport and Christopher Saunders, South Africa: A Modern History, rev. ed. (2000). A comprehensive survey, beginning with coverage of prehistoric southern Africa, the Khoisan peoples, and the Bantu migrations.

B. Davidson, Africa in History, rev. ed. (1995). A sweeping history of the diverse parts of Africa, emphasizing cultural exchange within the continent and beyond.

C.A. Diop, Precolonial Black Africa (1988). A seminal work by the pioneering Afrocentric scholar; his conclusions are controversial, but his writings are always provocative.

P.A. Ebron, Performing Africa (2002). Analyzes the role of performance in the creation and global circulation of African history and identity.

P. Garlake, Early Art and Architecture of Africa (2002). Highlights the diversity and sophistication of early African art and discusses the social context in which it was created.

E. Gilbert and J. Reynolds, Africa in World History, 2nd ed. (2008). The best new survey of African history, placing it in a global context. In conversational prose, the authors attend to environmental factors in African history and emphasize the roles of Western bias in shaping what we now know (and think we know) about Africa.

J. Iliffe, Africans: The History of a Continent (1995). A thematic survey of African history, from the paleontological record to the end of apartheid, with a focus on environment and demography.

E. Isichei, A History of Christianity in Africa: From Antiquity to the Present (1995). An amazing survey of Christianity's role on the African continent, from the time of Christ through European missionaries to the present popularity of Christian faith.

R. Oliver, The African Experience (1991). A masterly, balanced, and engaging sweep through African history.

I. Van Sertima, Black Women in Antiquity, rev. ed. (1988). From Lucy to Hatshepsut and beyond, essays explore the role and status of women in African societies of the past.

L. White et al., eds., African Words, African Voices: Critical Practices in Oral History (2001). A lively group of essays offer various perspectives on the uses of oral history in African research.

Chapter 6

From Republic to Empire

R. Baumann, Women and Politics in Ancient Rome (1995). A study of the role of women in Roman public life.

A.H. Bernstein, Tiberius Sempronius Gracchus: Tradition and Apostasy (1978). A new interpretation of Tiberius's place in Roman politics.

T.J. Cornell, The Beginnings of Rome: Italy and Rome from the Bronze Age to the Punic Wars, c. 1000–264 B.C. (1995). A consideration of the royal and early republican periods of Roman history.

T. Cornell and J. Matthews, Atlas of the Roman World (1982). Much more than the title indicates, this book presents a comprehensive view of the Roman world in its physical and cultural setting.

J-M. David, The Roman Conquest of Italy (1997). A good analysis of how Rome united Italy.

A. Goldsworthy, Roman Warfare (2002). A good military history of Rome.

A. Goldsworthy, In the Name of Rome: The Men Who Won the Roman Empire (2004). The story of Rome's greatest generals in the republican and imperial periods.

E.S. Gruen, Diaspora: Jews amidst Greeks and Romans (2002). A fine study of Jews in the Hellenistic and Roman world.

E.S. Gruen, The Hellenistic World and the Coming of Rome (1984). A new interpretation of Rome's conquest of the eastern Mediterranean.

W.V. Harris, War and Imperialism in Republican Rome, 327–70 B.C. (1975). An analysis of Roman attitudes and intentions concerning imperial expansion and war.

A. Keaveney, Rome and the Unification of Italy (1988). The story of how Rome organized its defeated opponents.

S. Lancel, Carthage, A History (1995). Includes a good account of Rome's dealings with Carthage.

J.F. Lazenby, Hannibal's War: A Military History of the Second Punic War (1978). A careful and thorough account.

F.G.B. Millar, The Crowd in Rome in the Late Republic (1999). A challenge to the view that only aristocrats counted in the late republic.

M. Pallottino, The Etruscans, 6th ed. (1974). Makes especially good use of archaeological evidence.

H.H. Scullard, A History of the Roman World, 753–146 B.C., 4th ed. (1980). An unusually fine narrative history with useful critical notes.

G. Williams, The Nature of Roman Poetry (1970). An unusually graceful and perceptive literary study.

Imperial Rome

W. Ball, Rome in the East: The Transformation of an Empire (2001). A thorough account of the influence of the East on Roman history.

T. Barnes, The New Empire of Diocletian and Constantine (1982).

K.R. Bradley, Slavery and Society at Rome (1994). A study of the role of slaves in Roman life.

P. Brown, The Rise of Western Christendom: Triumph and Diversity, 200–1000 (1996). A vivid picture of the spread of Christianity by a master of the field.

A. Ferrill, The Fall of the Roman Empire, The Military Explanation (1986). An interpretation that emphasizes the decline in the quality of the Roman army.

K. Galinsky, Augustan Culture (1996). A work that integrates art, literature, and politics.

A.H.M. Jones, The Later Roman Empire, 3 vols. (1964). A comprehensive study of the period.

D. Kagan, ed., The End of the Roman Empire: Decline or Transformation? 3rd ed. (1992). A collection of essays discussing the problem of the decline and fall of the Roman Empire.

J.E. Lendon, Empire of Honor, The Art of Government in the Roman World (1997). An original and path-breaking interpretation.

E.N. Luttwak, The Grand Strategy of the Roman Empire (1976). An original and fascinating analysis by a keen student of modern strategy.

R. MacMullen, Roman Social Relations, 50 B.C. to A.D. 284 (1981).

R. MacMullen, Corruption and the Decline of Rome (1988). A study that examines the importance of changes in ethical ideas and behavior.

R.W. Mathison, Roman Aristocrats in Barbarian Gaul: Strategies for Survival (1993). An unusual slant on the late empire.

J.F. Matthews, Laying Down the Law: A Study of the Theodosian Code (2000). A study of the importance of Roman law as a source for the understanding of Roman history and civilization.

W.A. Meeks, The Origins of Christian Morality: The First Two Centuries. An account of the shaping of Christianity in the Roman Empire.

F. Millar, The Emperor in the Roman World, 31 B.C.–A.D. 337 (1977). A study of Roman imperial government.

F. Millar, The Roman Empire and Its Neighbors, 2nd ed. (1981).

H.M.D. Parker, A History of the Roman World from A.D. 138 to 337 (1969). A good survey.

M.I. Rostovtzeff, Social and Economic History of the Roman Empire, 2nd ed. (1957). A masterpiece whose main thesis has been much disputed.

V. Rudich, Political Dissidence under Nero: The Price of Dissimulation (1993). A brilliant exposition of the lives and thoughts of political dissidents in the early empire.

E.T. Salmon, A History of the Roman World, 30 B.C. to A.D. 138 (1968). A good survey.

R. Syme, The Roman Revolution (1960). A brilliant study of Augustus, his supporters, and their rise to power.

R. Syme, The Augustan Aristocracy (1985). An examination of the new ruling class shaped by Augustus.

L.A. Thompson, Romans and Blacks (1989).

Chapter 7

D. Bodde, China's First Unifier (1938). A study of the Qin unification of China, viewed through the Legalist philosopher and statesman Li Si.

T.T. Ch'u, Law and Society in Traditional China (1961). Treats the sweep of Chinese history from 202 B.C.E. to 1911 C.E.

T.T. Ch'u, Han Social Structure (1972).

A. Cotterell, The First Emperor of China (1981). A study of the first Qin emperor.

R. Coulborn, Feudalism in History (1965). One chapter interestingly compares the quasi feudalism of the Zhou with that of the Six Dynasties period.

J.K. Fairbank, E.O. Reischauer, and A.M. Craig, East Asia: Tradition and Transformation (1989). A fairly detailed single-volume history covering China, Japan, and other countries in East Asia from antiquity to recent times.

J. Gernet, A History of Chinese Civilization (1982). A survey of Chinese history.

D.A. Graff and R. Higham, A Military History of China (2002).

C.Y. Hsu, Ancient China in Transition (1965). On social mobility during the Eastern Zhou era.

C.Y. Hsu, Han Agriculture (1980). A study of the agrarian economy of China during the Han Dynasty.

J. Levi, The Chinese Emperor (1987). A novel about the first Qin emperor based on scholarly sources.

M. Loewe, Everyday Life in Early Imperial China (1968). A social history of the Han Dynasty.

J. Needham, The Shorter Science and Civilization in China (1978). An abridgment of the multivolume work on the same subject with the same title—minus Shorter—by the same author.

S. Owen, ed., and Trans., An Anthology of Chinese Literature: Beginnings to 1911 (1996).

I. Robinet, Taoism: Growth of a Religion (1987).

M. Sullivan, The Arts of China (1967). An excellent survey history of Chinese art.

D. Twitchett and M. Loewe, eds., The Ch'in and Han Empires, 221 B.C.E.–C.E. 220 (1986). Vol. 1 of The Cambridge History of China.

Z. S. Wang, Han Civilization (1982).

B. Watson, Ssu-ma Ch'ien, Grand Historian of China (1958). A study of China's premier historian.

B. Watson, Records of the Grand Historian of China, Vols. 1 and 2 (1961). Selections from the Shiji by Sima Qian.

B. Watson, The Columbia Book of Chinese Poetry (1986).

F. Wood, The Silk Road: Two Thousand Years in the Heart of Asia (2003). A lively narrative combined with photographs and paintings.

A. Wright, Buddhism in Chinese History (1959).

Y.S. Yu, Trade and Expansion in Han China (1967). A study of economic relations between the Chinese and their neighbors.

Chapter 8

General

P. Bol, This Culture of Ours (1992). An insightful intellectual history of the Tang through the Song dynasties.

J. Cahill, Chinese Painting (1960). An excellent survey.

J.K. Fairbank and M. Goldman, China: A New History (1998). The summation of a lifetime engagement with Chinese history.

F.A. Kierman Jr., and J.K. Fairbank, eds., Chinese Ways in Warfare (1974). Chapters by different authors on the Chinese military experience from the Zhou to the Ming.

Sui and Tang

P.B. Ebrey, The Aristocratic Families of Early Imperial China (1978).

D. McMullen, State and Scholars in T'ang China (1988).

S. Owen, The Great Age of Chinese Poetry: The High T'ang (1980).

S. Owen, trans. and ed., An Anthology of Chinese Literature: Beginnings to 1911 (1996).

E.G. Pulleyblank, The Background of the Rebellion of An Lu-shan (1955). A study of the 755 rebellion that weakened the central authority of the Tang Dynasty.

E.O. Reischauer, Ennin's Travels in T'ang China (1955). China as seen through the eyes of a ninth-century Japanese Marco Polo.

E.H. Schafer, The Golden Peaches of Samarkand (1963). A study of Tang imagery.

So. Teiser, The Ghost Festival in Medieval China (1988). On Tang popular religion.

D. Twitchett, ed., The Cambridge History of China, Vol. III: Sui and T'ang China, 589–906 Part 1 (1979).

G. W. Wang, The Structure of Power in North China during the Five Dynasties (1963). A study of the interim period between the Tang and the Song dynasties.

A. F. Wright, The Sui Dynasty (1978).

Song

B. Birge, Women, Property, and Confucian Reaction in Song and Yuan China (960–1366) (2002). The rights of women to property—whether in the form of dowries or inheritances—were considerable during the Song but declined thereafter.

C.S. Chang and J. Smythe, South China in the Twelfth Century (1981). China as seen through the eyes of a twelfth-century Chinese poet, historian, and statesman.

E.L. Davis, Society and the Supernatural in Song China (2001).

J.W. Haeger, ed., Crisis and Prosperity in Song China (1975).

R. Hymes, Statesmen and Gentlemen (1987). On the transformation of officials into a local gentry elite during the twelfth and thirteenth centuries.

R. Hymes, Way and Byway: Taoism, Local Religion, and Models of Divinity in Sung and Modern China (2002).

M. Rossabi, China among Equals (1983). A study of the Liao, Qin, and Song empires and their relations.

W.M. Tu, Confucian Thought, Selfhood as Creative Transformation (1985).

K. Yoshikawa, An Introduction to Song Poetry, trans. by B. Watson (1967).

Yuan

T.T. Allsen, Mongol Imperialism (1987).

J.W. Dardess, Conquerors and Confucians: Aspects of Political Change in Late Yuan China (1973).

I. de Rachewiltz, Trans., The Secret History of the Mongols: A Mongolian Epic Chronicle of the Thirteenth Century (2003). A new translation of a key historical work on the life of Genghis.

H. Franke and D. Twitchett, eds., The Cambridge History of China, Vol. VI: Alien Regimes and Border States, 710–1368 (1994).

J.D. Langlois, China under Mongol Rule (1981).

R.Latham, trans., Travels of Marco Polo (1958).

H.D. Martin, The Rise of Chingis Khan and His Conquest of North China (1981).

D. Morgan, The Mongol Empire and Its Legacy (1999). Genghis, the several khanates, and the aftermath of empire.

P. Ratchnevsky, Genghis Khan, His Life and Legacy (1992). The rise to power of the Mongol leader, with a critical consideration of historical sources.

Chapter 9

M. Adolphson, The Gates of Power: Monks, Courtiers, and Warriors in Premodern Japan (2000). A new interpretation stressing the importance of temples in the political life of Heian and Kamakura Japan.

B.L. Batten, To the Ends of Japan: Premodern Frontiers, Boundaries, and Interactions. (2003). An interesting treatment of Heian Japan, topic by topic.

C. Blacker, The Catalpa Bow (1975). An insightful study of folk Shinto.

R. Borgen, Sugawara no Michizane and the Early Heian Court (1986). A study of a famous courtier and poet.

D.M. Brown, ed., The Cambridge History of Japan: Ancient Japan (1993). This series of six volumes sums up several decades of research on Japan.

D. Brown and E. Ishida, eds., The Future and the Past (1979). A translation of a history of Japan written in 1219.

The Cambridge History of Japan, D.M. Brown, ed.; Vol. 1, Ancient Japan, W. McCullough and D. H. Shively eds; Vol. 2, Heian Japan, K. Yamamura, ed. Vol. 3, Medieval Japan. Fine multi-author works.

M. Collcutt, Five Mountains (1980). A study of the monastic organization of medieval Zen.

T.D. Conlon, State of War: The Violent Order of Fourteenth Century Japan (2003). Compare Conlon's account with those of Souyri and Friday.

W.T. DeBary, D. Keene, G. Tanabe, and P. Varley, Comps., Sources of Japanese Tradition, 2nd ed. (2001).

P. Duus, Feudalism in Japan (1969). An easy survey of the subject.

W.W. Farris, Population, Disease, and Land in Early Japan, 645–900 (1985). An innovative reinterpretation of early history.

W.W. Farris, Heavenly Warriors: The Evolution of Japan's Military, 500–1300 (1992).

W.W. Farris, Sacred Texts and Buried Treasures (1998). Studies of Japan's prehistory and early history, based on recent Japanese research.

K.F. Friday, Samurai, Warfare and the State in Early Medieval Japan (2004). Weapons and warfare in Japan from the tenth to fourteenth centuries.

A.E. Goble, Go-Daigo's Revolution (1996). A provoking account of the 1331 revolt by an emperor who thought emperors should rule.

J.W. Hall, Government and Local Power in Japan, 500–1700: A Study Based on Bizen Province (1966). A splendid and insightful book.

J.W. Hall and T. Toyoda, Japan in the Muromachi Age (1977). Another collection of essays.

D. Keene, ed., Anthology of Japanese Literature from the Earliest Era to the Mid-Nineteenth Century (1955).

D. Keene, ed., Twenty Plays of the Nō Theatre (1970).

T. Lamarre, Uncovering Heian Japan: An Archeology of Sensation and Inscription (2000). The "archeology" in the title refers to digging into literature.

I.H. Levy, The Ten Thousand Leaves (1981). A fine translation of Japan's earliest collection of poetry.

J.P. Mass and W. Hauser, eds., The Bakufu in Japanese History (1985). Topics in Bakufu history from the twelfth to the nineteenth centuries.

I. Morris, trans., The Pillow Book of Sei Shōnagon (1967). Observations about the Heian court life by the Jane Austen of ancient Japan.

S. Murasaki, The Tale of Genji comparison of this translation with those of E. Seidensticker and R. Tyler.

S. Murasaki, The Tale of Genji, trans. by E.G. Seidensticker (1976). The world's first novel and the greatest work of Japanese fiction.

R.J. Pearson et al., eds., Windows on the Japanese Past: Studies in Archaeology and Prehistory (1986).

D.L. Philippi, trans., Kojiki (1968). Japan's ancient myths.

J. Piggot, The Emergence of Japanese Kingship (1997).

E.O. Reischauer, Ennin's Diary, the Record of a Pilgrimage to China in Search of the Law and Ennin's Travels in T'ang China (1955).

E.O. Reischauer and A.M. Craig, Japan: Tradition and Transformation (1989). A more detailed work covering the sweep of Japanese history from the early beginnings through the 1980s.

H. Sato, Legends of the Samurai (1995). Excerpts from various tales and writings.

D.H. Shively and W.H. McCullough, eds., The Cambridge History of Japan: Heian Japan (1999).

D.T. Suzuki, Zen and Japanese Culture (1959).

H. Tonomura, Community and Commerce in Late Medieval Japan (1992).

R. Tsunoda, W.T. de Bary, and D. Keene, comps., Sources of the Japanese Tradition (1958). A collection of original religious, political, and philosophical writings from each period of Japanese history. The best reader. A new edition was published in 2005.

H.P. Varley, Imperial Restoration in Medieval Japan (1971). A study of the 1331 attempt by an emperor to restore imperial power.

A. Waley, trans., The Nō Plays of Japan (1957). Medieval dramas.

K. Yamamura, ed., Cambridge History of Japan: Medieval Japan (1990).

Chapter 10

O. Grabar, The Formation of Islamic Art (1973). A critical and creative interpretation of major themes in the development of distinctively Islamic forms of art and architecture.

A. Hourani, A History of the Arab Peoples (1991). A masterly survey of the Arabs down through the centuries and a clear picture of many aspects of Islamic history and culture that extend beyond the Arab world.

H. Kennedy, The Prophet and the Age of the Caliphates: The Islamic Near East from the Sixth to the Eleventh Century (1986). The best survey of early Islamic history.

I. Lapidus, A History of Islamic Societies (1988). A comprehensive overview of the rise and development of Islam all over the world.

F.E. Peters, Muhammad and the Origins of Islam (1994). A balanced analysis of the life of Muhammad.

F. Rahman, Major Themes of the Qur'an (1980). The best introduction to the basic ideas of the Qur'an and Islam, seen through the eyes of a perceptive Muslim modernist scholar.

F. Schuon, Understanding Islam (1994). Compares the Islamic worldview with Catholic Christianity. A dense, but intellectually stimulating, discussion.

M. Sells, Approaching the Qur'an. The Early Revelations (1999). A fine introduction and new translations of some of the more common earlier Qur'anic revelations.

B. Stowasser, Women in the Qur'an, Traditions and Interpretation (1994). An outstanding systematic study of statements regarding women in the Qur'an.

Chapter 11

K. Armstrong, Muhammad: A Biography of the Prophet (1992). Strong on religion.

R. Bartlett, The Making of Europe, 950–1350 (1992). A study of the way immigration and colonial conquest shaped the Europe we know.

M. Bloch, Feudal Society, Vols. 1 and 2, trans. by L. A. Manyon (1971). A classic on the topic and as an example of historical study.

C.B. Brown, Singing the Gospel: Lutheran Hymns and the Success of the Reformation (2005). Outstanding study of Luther's hymns for children.

C.M. Brand, Byzantium Confronts the West, 1180–1204 (1968). Analyzes the internal and external pressures that Byzantium experienced during this quarter-century time period.

P. Brown, Augustine of Hippo: A Biography (1967). Late antiquity seen through the biography of its greatest Christian thinker.

J.H. Burns, The Cambridge History of Medieval Political Thought c. 350–c. 1450 (1991). The best scan.

R.H.C. Davis, A History of Medieval Europe: From Constantine to St. Louis (1972). Unsurpassed in clarity.

N.M. El-Cheikh, Byzantium Viewed by the Arabs (2004). Examines the Arabic-Islamic view of Byzantium.

R. Fletcher, The Barbarian Conversion: From Paganism to Christianity (1998). Up-to-date survey.

J.B. Glubb, The Great Arab Conquests (1995). Jihadists.

G. Guglielmo, ed., The Byzantines (1997). Updates key issues.

D. Gutas, Greek Thought, Arabic Culture (1998). A comparative intellectual history.

G. Holmes, ed., The Oxford History of Medieval Europe (1992). Overviews of Roman and northern Europe during the "Dark Ages."

B.J. Kaplan, Divided by Faith: Religious Conflict and the Practice of Toleration in Early Modern Europe (2007). How the Reformation created religious toleration and sowed the seeds of religious pluralism.

B. Lewis, The Middle East: A Brief History of the Last 2,000 Years (1995).

A.E. Laiou and H. Maguire, eds., Byzantium, a World Civilization (1992). Examines the centrality of Byzantium's role in world history.

C. Mango, Byzantium: The Empire of New Rome (1980).

J. Martin, Medieval Russia 980–1584 (1995). A concise narrative history.

R. Mckitterick, ed., Carolingian Culture: Emulation and Innovation (1994). Fresh essays.

J.J. Norwich, Byzantium: The Decline and Fall (1995).

J.J. Norwich, Byzantium: The Apogee (1997). The whole story in two volulmes.

G. Ostrogorsky, History of the Byzantine State (1999). Traces the thousand-year course of the Byzantine Empire.

R.I. Page, Chronicles of the Vikings: Records, Memorials, and Myths (1995). Sources galore.

F. Robinson, ed., The Cambridge Illustrated History of the Islamic World (1996). Spectacular.

S. Runciman, Byzantine Civilization (1970). Succinct, comprehensive account by a master.

P. Sawyer, The Age of the Vikings (1962). Old but solid account.

C. Stephenson, Medieval Feudalism (1969). Excellent short summary and introduction.

L. White Jr., Medieval Technology and Social Change (1962). Often fascinating account of how primitive technology changed life.

D. Whitford, Reformation and Early Modern Europe: A Guide to Research (2008). A goldmine of information on all aspects of the Reformation.

H. Wolfram, The Roman Empire and Its Germanic Peoples (1997). Challenging, but most rewarding.

Chapter 12

The Islamic Heartlands

L. Ahmed, Women and Gender in Islam: Historical Roots of a Modern Debate (1992). A good historical survey of the status of women in Middle Eastern societies.

J. Berkey, The Formation of Islam: Religion and Society in the Near East, 600–1800 (2002). An interesting new synthesis focusing on political and religious trends.

C.E. Bosworth, The Islamic Dynasties: A Chronological and Genealogical Handbook (1967). A handy reference work for dynasties and families important to Islamic history in all periods and places.

M.A. Cook, Commanding Right and Forbidding Wrong in Islamic Thought (2001). A masterful analysis of the development of Islamic law.

P.K. Hitti, History of the Arabs, 8th ed. (1964). Still a useful English resource, largely for factual detail. See especially Part IV, "The Arabs in Europe: Spain and Sicily."

A. Hourani, A History of the Arab Peoples (1991). The newest survey history and the best, at least for the Arab Islamic world.

S.K. Jayyusi, ed., The Legacy of Muslim Spain, 2 vols. (1994). A comprehensive survey of the arts, politics, literature, and society by experts in various fields.

B. Lewis, ed., Islam and the Arab World (1976). A large-format, heavily illustrated volume with many excellent articles on diverse aspects of Islamic (not simply Arab, as the misleading title indicates) civilization through the premodern period.

D. Morgan, The Mongols (1986). A recent and readable survey history.

J.J. Saunders, A History of Medieval Islam (1965). A brief and simple, if sketchy, introductory survey of Islamic history to the Mongol invasions.

India

W.T. de Bary et al., comp., Sources of Indian Tradition, 2nd ed. (1958), Vol. I, From the Beginning to 1800, ed. and rev. by Ainslie T. Embree (1988). Excellent selections from a wide variety of Indian texts, with good introductions to chapters and individual selections.

S.M. Ikram, Muslim Civilization in India (1964). The best short survey history, covering the period 711 to 1857.

R.C. Majumdar, gen. ed., The History and Culture of the Indian People, Vol. VI, The Delhi Sultanate, 3rd ed. (1980). A comprehensive political and cultural account of the period in India.

F. Robinson, ed., The Cambridge History of India, Pakistan, Bangladesh, Sri Lanka, Nepal, Bhutan, and the Maldives (1989). A very helpful quick reference source with brief but well-done survey essays on a wide range of topics relevant to South Asian history down to the present.

A. Wink, Al-Hind: The Making of the Indo-Islamic World, Vol. 1 (1991). The first of five promising volumes to be devoted to the Indo-Islamic world's history. This volume treats the seventh to eleventh centuries.

Southeast Asia

L. Andaya, The World of Maluku: Eastern Indonesia in the Early Modern Period (1993). A comprehensive view of the formation of what is now Indonesia.

B.W. Andaya and L. Andaya, A History of Malaysia (1982). A good overview of Indonesia's smaller but critical northern neighbor.

J. Siegel, Shadow and Sound: The Historical Thought of a Sumatran People (1979). An excellent analysis tracing the relation between foreign influences and local practice.

Chapter 13

B.S. Bauer, The Development of the Inca State (1992). Emphasizes archaeological evidence over the Spanish chronicles in accounting for the emergence of the Inca Empire.

B. S. Bauer, Ancient Cuzco: Heartland of the Inca (2004). Exploration of the ramifications of late-twentieth-century archaeological explorations of the ancient Inca capital

K.O. Bruhns, Ancient South America (1994). A clear discussion of the archaeology and civilization of the region with emphasis on the Andes.

E. M. Brumfiel, The Aztec World (2008). A well-illustrated work.

R.L. Burger, Chavín and the Origins of Andean Civilization (1992). A detailed study of early Andean prehistory by one of the leading authorities on Chavín.

R. L. Burger, Machu Picchu: Unveiling the Mystery of the Incas (2008). The best study of this famous site.

I. Clendinnen, Aztecs: An Interpretation (1995). A classic exploration of the Aztec world.

B. Cobo and R. Hamilton, History of the Inca Empire, rev. ed. (1983). A seventeenth-century account, with a modern translation and interpretation.

M.D. Coe, Breaking the Maya Code (1992). The story of the remarkable achievement of deciphering the ancient Maya language.

M.D. Coe, Mexico from the Olmecs to the Aztecs (2008). A wide-ranging introductory discussion.

G. Conrad and A.A. Demarest, Religion and Empire: The Dynamics of Aztec and Inca Expansionism (1984). An interesting comparative study.

T. N. D'Altroy, The Incas (2004). A major study of all aspects of Inca civilization

A. Demarest, Ancient Maya: The Rise and Fall of a Rainforest Civilization (2004). Lively and engaged in recent scholarly debates.

S. T. Evans, Ancient Mexico & Central America: Archaeology and Culture History (2008). Now the best wide-ranging introduction.

S. Freidel, L. Schele, and J. Parker, Maya Cosmos: Three Thousand Years on the Shaman's Path (1995). The best account of the subject.

S.D. Gillespie, The Aztec Kings (1989).

R. Hassig, Aztec Warfare: Imperial Expansion and Political Control (1995). Explores the achievement of the Aztec Empire.

J. Hyslop, Inka Settlement Planning (1990). A detailed study.

M. León-Portilla, Fifteen Poets of the Aztec World (1992). An anthology of translations of Aztec poetry.

G. M. McEwan, The Incas: New Perspectives (2006). An excellent overview with fine reading lists for further exploration.

H. McKillop, The Ancient May: New Perspectives (2004). Clear presentations of recent research and debates.

M.E. Miller, The Art of Mesoamerica from Olmec to Aztec (2006). Most recent edition of a pioneering work.

C. Morris and A. Von Hagen, The Inka Empire and Its Andean Origins (1993). A clear overview of Andean prehistory by a leading authority. Beautifully illustrated.

M.E. Mosely, The Incas and Their Ancestors: The Archaeology of Peru (2001). Readable and thorough.

J.A. Sabloff, The Cities of Ancient Mexico (1989). Capsule summaries of ancient Mesoamerican cultures.

L. Schele and M.E. Miller, The Blood of Kings (1986). A rich and beautifully illustrated study of ancient Maya art and society.

H. Silverman, Andean Archaeology (2004). Overview of various Andean peoples.

M.E. Smith, The Aztecs (2002). Emphasizes impact of late-twentieth-century archaeological research.

R. Stone-Miller, Art of the Andes: From Chavin to Inca (2002). A well-illustrated overview.

Chapter 14

J. Abun-Nasr, A History of the Maghrib in the Islamic Period (1987). The most recent North African survey. Pages 59–247 are relevant to this chapter.

E.K. Akyeampyong, ed., Themes in West Africa's History (2006). A wide-ranging collection of essays by leading scholars.

I. Battuta, N. King, and S. Hamdun, Ibn Battuta in Black Africa, rev. ed. (2005). Well-selected excerpts from Battuta's extensive journals.

P. Ben-Amos, Art, Innovation and Politics in Eighteenth-Century Benin (1999). Offers insights into the many levels of meaning and authority in Benin's artworks.

I. Berger, E.F. White, and C. Skidmore-Hess, Women in Sub-Saharan Africa: Restoring Women to History (1999). A valuable resource on the role of women in African history.

D. Birminham, Central Africa to 1870 (1981). Chapters from the Cambridge History of Africa that give a brief, lucid overview of developments in this region.

P. Bohannan and P. Curtin, Africa and Africans, rev. ed. (1995). Accessible, topical approach to African history, culture, society, politics, and economics.

P.D. Curtin, S. Feiermann, L. Thompson, and J. Vansina, African History, rev. ed. (1995). An older, but masterly survey. The relevant portions are Chapters 6–9.

B. Davidson, West Africa before the Colonial Era (1998). A typically readable survey by one of the great popularizers of African history.

R. Elphick, Kraal and Castle: Khoikhoi and the Founding of White South Africa (1977). An incisive, informative interpretation of the history of the Khoikhoi and their fateful interaction with European colonization.

R. Elphick and H. Giliomee, The Shaping of South African Society, 1652–1820 (1979). A superb, synthetic history of this crucial period.

J.D. Fage, A History of Africa, rev. ed., (2001). Still a readable survey history.

E. Gilbert and J. Reynolds, Africa in World History, 2nd ed. (2008). The best new survey of African history, placing it in a global context. See especially Chapters 6 and 7 on Islam, and Chapters 8 through 12 for the period leading to European colonization.

M. Hiskett, The Development of Islam in West Africa (1984). The standard survey study of the subject. Of the relevant sections (Chapters 1–10, 12, 15), that on Hausaland, which is treated only in passing in this text, is noteworthy.

M. Horton and J. Middleton, The Swahili (2000).

R.W. July, A History of the African People, 3rd ed. (1980). Chapters 3–6 treat Africa before about 1800 area by area; Chapter 7 deals with "The Coming of Europe."

N. Levtzion and R. Pouwels, eds. History of Islam in Africa (2000). A wide-ranging collection of essays.

N. Levtzion and D.T. Niani, eds., Africa from the Twelfth to the Sixteenth Century, UNESCO General History of Africa, Vol. IV (1984). Many survey articles cover the various regions and major states of Africa in the centuries noted in the title.

R. Oliver, The African Experience (1991). A masterly, balanced, and engaging survey, with outstanding syntheses and summaries of recent research.

C.A. Quinn and F. Quinn, Pride, Faith, and Fear: Islam in Sub-Saharan Africa (2005). A readable account of Islam in Africa, bringing the story almost to the present.

D. Robinson, Muslim Societies in African History (2004). A comprehensive overview.

A.F.C. Ryder, Benin and the Europeans: 1485–1897 (1969). A basic study.

John K. Thornton, The Kingdom of Kongo: Civil War and Transition, 1641–1718 (1983). A detailed and perceptive analysis for those who wish to delve into Kongo state and society in the seventeenth century.

M. Wilson and L. Thompson, eds., The Oxford History of South Africa, Vol. I., South Africa to 1870 (1969). Relatively detailed, if occasionally dated, treatment.

Chapter 15

M. Brecht, Martin Luther: His Road to Reformation, 1483–1521 (1985). Best on young Luther.

C. Brown et al., Rembrandt: The Master and His Workshop (1991). A great master's art and influence.

R. Briggs, Witches and Neighbors: A History of European Witchcraft (1996). A readable introduction.

E. Duffy, The Stripping of the Altars (1992). Strongest argument yet that there was no deep Reformation in England.

H.O. Evennett, The Spirit of the Counter Reformation (1968). The continuity and independence of Catholic reform.

Hans-Jürgen Goertz, The Anabaptists (1996). Best treatment of minority Protestants.

O.P. Grell and A. Cunningham, Health Care and Poor Relief in Protestant Europe (1997). The civic side of the Reformation.

M. Holt, The French Wars of Religion, 1562–1629 (1995). Scholarly appreciation of religious side of the story.

J.C. Hutchison, Albrecht Durer (1990). The life behind the art.

H. Jedin, A History of the Council of Trent, Vols. 1, 2 (1957–1961). Comprehensive, detailed, and authoritative.

M. Kitchen, The Cambridge Illustrated History of Germany (1996). Comprehensive and accessible.

A. Kors and E. Peters, eds., European Witchcraft, 1100–1700 (1972). Classics of witch belief.

W. Maccaffrey, Elizabeth I (1993). Magisterial study.

G. Mattingly, The Armada (1959). A masterpiece, novel-like in style.

D. Mccolloch, The Reformation (2004). No stone unturned, with English emphasis.

H.A. Oberman, Luther: Man between God and Devil (1989). Authoritative biography.

J.W. O'Malley, The First Jesuits (1993). Extremely detailed account of the creation of the Society of Jesus and its original purposes.

S. Ozment, The Age of Reform, 1250–1550: An Intellectual and Religious History of Late Medieval and Reformation Europe (1980). Broad, lucid survey.

S. Ozment, When Fathers Ruled: Family Life in Reformation Europe (1983). Effort to portray the constructive side of Protestant thinking about family relationships.

S. Ozment, The Bürgermeister's Daughter: Scandal in a Sixteenth-Century German Town (1996). What a woman could do at law in the sixteenth century.

G. Parker, The Thirty Years' War (1984). Large, lucid survey.

J.H. Parry, The Age of Reconnaissance (1964). A comprehensive account of explorations from 1450 to 1650.

W. Prinz, Durer (1998). Latest biography of Germany's greatest painter.

J.J. Scarisbrick, Henry VIII (1968). The best account of Henry's reign.

G. Strauss, ed. and trans., Manifestations of Discontent in Germany on the Eve of the Reformation (1971). A rich collection of sources for both rural and urban scenes.

H. Wunder, He Is the Sun, She Is the Moon: Women in Early Modern Germany (1998). Best study of early modern women.

Chapter 16

J. Abun-Nasr, A History of the Maghrib in the Islamic Period (1987). The essential North African survey. Pages 59–247 are relevant to this chapter.

D. Birmingham, Central Africa to 1870 (1981). Chapters from the Cambridge History of Africa that give a brief, lucid overview of developments in this region.

P. Bohannan and P. Curtin, Africa and Africans, rev. ed. (1971). Accessible, topical approach to African history, culture, society, politics, and economics.

P.D. Curtin, S. Feiermann, L. Thompson, and J. Vansina, African History (1978). An older, but masterly survey. The relevant portions are Chapters 6–9.

R. Elphick, Kraal and Castle: Khoikhoi and the Founding of White South Africa (1977). An incisive, informative interpretation of the history of the Khoikhoi and their fateful interaction with European colonization.

R. Elphick and H. Giliomee, The Shaping of South African Society, 1652–1820 (1979). A superb, synthetic history of this crucial period.

J.D. Fage, A History of Africa (1978). Still a readable survey history.

M. Hiskett, The Development of Islam in West Africa (1984). The standard survey study of the subject. Of the relevant sections (Chapters 1–10, 12, 15), that on Hausaland, which is treated only in passing in this text, is noteworthy.

R.W. July, Precolonial Africa: An Economic and Social History (1975). Chapter 10 gives an interesting overall picture of slaving in African history.

R.W. July, A History of the African People, 3rd ed. (1980). Chapters 3–6 treat Africa before about 1800 area by area; Chapter 7 deals with "The Coming of Europe."

I.M. Lewis, ed., Islam in Tropical Africa (1966), pp. 4–96. Lewis's introduction is one of the best brief summaries of the role of Islam in West Africa and the Sudan.

D.T. Niani, ed., Africa from the Twelfth to the Sixteenth Century, UNESCO General History of Africa, Vol. IV (1984). Many survey articles cover the various regions and major states of Africa in the centuries noted in the title.

R. Oliver, The African Experience (1991). A masterly, balanced, and engaging survey, with outstanding syntheses and summaries of recent research.

J.A. Rawley, The Transatlantic Slave Trade: A History (1981). Impressively documented, detailed, and well-presented survey history of the Atlantic trade; little focus on African dimensions.

A.F.C. Ryder, Benin and the Europeans: 1485–1897 (1969). A basic study.

John K. Thornton, The Kingdom of Kongo: Civil War and Transition, 1641–1718 (1983). A detailed and perceptive analysis for those who wish to delve into Kongo state and society in the seventeenth century.

M. Wilson and L. Thompson, eds., The Oxford History of South Africa, Vol. I., South Africa to 1870 (1969). Relatively detailed, if occasionally dated, treatment.

Chapter 17

R. Adorno, The Polemics of Possession in Spanish American Narrative (2008). An exploration of the rhetoric used by the Spanish to assure their holding of their American empire.

A.C. Bailey, African Voices of the Atlantic Slave Trade: Beyond the Silence and the Shame (2006). Delivers just what the title promises.

B. Bailyn, Atlantic History: Concepts and Contours (2005). An essential overview to this burgeoning area of historical inquiry, written by a leader in the field.

I. Berlin, Many Thousands Gone: The First Two Centuries of Slavery in North America (1998); Generations of Captivity: A History of African American Slaves (2003). Two volumes representing the most extensive and important recent treatment of slavery in North America; highlights the diversity of slave experiences.

R. Blackburn, The Making of New World Slavery from the Baroque to the Modern 1492–1800 (1997). An extraordinary work.

V. Carretta, Equiano, the African: The Biography of a Self-Made Man (reprint 2007). Provides context and analysis of the renowned accounts of one-time slave Olaudah Equiano.

N.D. Cook, Born to Die: Disease and New World Conquest, 1492–1650 (1998). A survey of the devastating impact of previously unknown diseases on the native populations of the Americas.

M.S. Creighton and L. Norling, eds. Iron Men, Wooden Women: Gender and Seafaring in the Atlantic World, 1700–1920 (2006). Eye-opening accounts of life at sea, and how gender roles were shaped and challenged on the Atlantic.

P.D. Curtin, The Atlantic Slave Trade: A Census (1969). Remains a basic work.

P.D. Curtin, The Rise and Fall of the Plantation Complex (1998). Places the plantation economy in the context of world history.

D.B. Davis, Inhuman Bondage: The Rise and Fall of Slavery in the New World (2006). A splendid overview by a leading scholar.

J.H. Elliot, Empires of the Atlantic World: Britain and Spain in America 1492–1830 (2006). A brilliant, accessible comparative history.

D. Eltis, The Rise of African Slavery in the Americas (1999). Detailed discussion of the size and scope of the Atlantic market, with attention to the role of Africans on both sides of the Atlantic.

H.L. Gates Jr. and W.L. Andrews, eds., Pioneers of the Black Atlantic: Five Slave Narratives from the Enlightenment, 1772–1815 (1998). An anthology of autobiographical accounts.

S. Gruzinski, The Conquest of Mexico: The Incorporation of Indian Societies into the Western World, 16th–18th Centuries (1993). Interprets the experience of Native Americans, from their own point of view, during the time of the Spanish conquest.

L. Hanke, All Mankind Is One: A Study of the Disputation between Bartolome De Las Casas and Juan Gines De Sepulveda in 1550 on the Intellectual and Religious (1994). A study of the Spanish debate over the humanity of Native Americans in the Spanish Empire.

R. Harms, The Diligent: A Voyage through the Worlds of the Slave Trade (2002). A powerful narrative of the voyage of a French slave trader.

J. Hemming, The Conquest of the Incas, rev. ed., (2003). A lucid account of the conquest of the Inca Empire and its aftermath.

J. Hemming, Red Gold: The Conquest of the Brazilian Native Americans, 1500–1760 (1978). A careful account with excellent bibliography.

H. Kamen, Empire: How Spain Became a World Power, 1492–1763 (2005). An excellent overview by a major scholar.

H. Klein, The Atlantic Slave Trade (1999). A synthesis of scholarly knowledge.

W. Klooster and A. Padula, The Atlantic World: Essays on Slavery, Migration, and Imagination (2004). Essays by leading scholars examine important aspects of the creation of a new way of living—and a new way of thinking about the world.

P.E. Lovejoy, Transformations in Slavery: A History of Slavery in Africa (2000). An important new evaluation of slavery as it was practiced within Africa, and its relation to the Islamic and transatlantic slave trades.

K. Macquarrie, The Last Days of the Incas (2007). A fast-moving popular account.

K. Mann, Rethinking the African Diaspora: The Making of a Black Atlantic World in the Bight of Benin and Brazil (2005). This analysis of the dynamics of human and cultural migration and exchange on the busiest route of the slave trade is a significant addition to Atlantic World scholarship.

P. Manning, Slavery and African Life: Occidental, Oriental, and African Slave Trades (1990). An admirably concise economic-historical synthesis of the evidence, with multiple tables and statistics to supplement the magisterial analysis.

A. Pagden, Lords of All the World: Ideologies of Empire in Spain, Britain, and France c. 1500–c. 1800 (1995). An effort to explain the imperial thinking of the major European powers.

S. Peabody and K. Grinberg, Slavery, Freedom, and the Law in the Atlantic World: A Brief History with Documents (2007). Examines the legal frameworks through which slavery was institutionalized, and documents the many ways people challenged slavery.

M. Rediker, The Slave Ship: A Human History (2007). A exploration of the harrowing experience of slave transportation across the Atlantic.

M. Rediker, Villains of all Nations: Atlantic Pirates in the Golden Age (2008). A serious historical treatment of the subject.

D.K. Richter, Facing East from Indian Country: A Native History of Early America, new ed. (2003). Uses the biographies of three Native Americans to offer a fresh perspective on North American history from the time of Columbus to the American Revolution.

M. Russell, Seven Myths of the Spanish Conquest (2003). Challenges many long-held views of the event.

S.B. Schwartz, All Can Be Saved: Religious Tolerance and Salvation in the Iberian Atlantic World (2009). The most important recent study of the social and religious life of the Spanish Empire.

S.B. Schwartz, ed., Tropical Babylons: Sugar and the Making of the Atlantic World, 1450–1680 (2003). A comprehensive examination of the role of sugar in the plantation economy.

S.E. Smallwood, Saltwater Slavery: A Middle Passage from Africa to American Diaspora (2008). An intimate examination of the experience and economy of the slave trade.

H. Thomas, Conquest: Montezuma, Cortés, and the Fall of Old Mexico (1993). A splendid modern narrative of the event, with careful attention to the character of the participants.

J. Thornton, Africa and Africans in the Making of the Atlantic World, 1400–1680 (1992). A discussion of the role of Africans in the emergence of the transatlantic economy.

N. Wachtel, The Vision of the Vanquished: The Spanish Conquest of Peru through Indian Eyes, 1530–1570 (1977). A presentation of the Incan experience of conquest.

C.A. Williams, Bridging the Early Modern Atlantic World (2009). Explores the cultural and ethnic diversity of the transatlantic economy.

Chapter 18

China

D. Bodde and C. Morris, Law in Imperial China (1967). Focuses on the Qing Dynasty (1644–1911).

T. Brook, The Confusions of Pleasure: Commerce and Culture in Ming China (1988).

C.S. Chang and S.L.H. Chang, Crisis and Transformation in Seventeenth-century China: Society, Culture, and Modernity (1992).

P. Crossley, Translucent Mirror: History and Identity in Qing Imperial Ideology (1999).

W.T. De Bary, Learning for One's Self: Essays on the Individual in Neo-Confucian Thought (1991). A useful corrective to the view that Confucianism is simply a social ideology.

M.C. Elliott, The Manchu Way: The Eight Banners and Ethnic Identity in Late Imperial China (2001). The latest word; compare to Crossley above.

M. Elvin, The Pattern of the Chinese Past: A Social and Economic Interpretation (1973). A controversial but stimulating interpretation of Chinese economic history in terms of technology. It brings in earlier periods as well as the Ming, Qing, and modern China.

J.K. Fairbank, ed., The Chinese World Order: Traditional China's Foreign Relations (1968). An examination of the Chinese tribute system and its varying applications.

H.L. Kahn, Monarchy in the Emperor's Eyes: Image and Reality in the Ch'ien-lung Reign (1971). A study of the Chinese court during the mid-Qing period.

P. Kuhn, Soulstealers: The Chinese Sorcery Scare of 1768 (1990).

Li Yu, The Carnal Prayer Mat, trans. by P. Hanan (1990).

F. Mote and D. Twitchett, eds., The Cambridge History of China: The Ming Dynasty 1368–1644, Vols. VI (1988) and VII (1998).

S. Naquin, Peking Temples and City Life, 1400–1900 (2000).

S. Naquin and E.S. Rawski, Chinese Society in the Eighteenth Century (1987).

J.B. Parsons, The Peasant Rebellions of the Late Ming Dynasty (1970).

P.C. Perdue, Exhausting the Earth, State and Peasant in Hunan, 1500–1850 (1987).

D.H. Perkins, Agricultural Development in China, 1368–1968 (1969).

E. Rawski, The Last Emperors: A Social History of Qing Imperial Institutions (1998).

M. Ricci, China in the Sixteenth Century: The Journals of Matthew Ricci, 1583–1610 (1953).

W. Rowe, Hankow (1984). A study of a city in late imperial China.

G.W. Skinner, The City in Late Imperial China (1977).

J.D. Spence, Ts'ao Yin and the K'ang-hsi Emperor: Bondservant and Master (1966). An excellent study of the early Qing court.

J.D. Spence, Emperor of China: A Self-Portrait of K'ang-hsi (1974). The title of this readable book does not adequately convey the extent of the author's contribution to the study of the early Qing emperor.

J.D. Spence, Treason by the Book (2001). An account of the legal workings of the authoritarian Qing state that reads like a detective story.

L.A. Struve, trans. and ed., Voices from the Ming-Qing Cataclysm (1993). A reader with translations of Chinese sources.

F. Wakeman, The Great Enterprise (1985). On the founding of the Manchu Dynasty.

Japan

M.E. Berry, Hideyoshi (1982). A study of the sixteenth-century unifier of Japan.

M.E. Berry, The Culture of Civil War in Kyoto (1994). On the Warring States era.

H. Bolitho, Treasures among Men: The Fudai Daimyo in Tokugawa Japan (1974). A study in depth.

H. Bolitho, Bereavement and Consolation: Testimonies from Tokugawa Japan (2003). Instances of how Tokugawa Japanese handled the death of a child.

C.R. Boxer, The Christian Century in Japan, 1549–1650 (1951).

The Cambridge History of Japan; Vol. 4, J.W. Hall, ed., Early Modern Japan (1991). A multi-author work.

M. Chikamatsu, Major Plays of Chikamatsu, trans. by D. Keene (1961).

R.P. Dore, Education in Tokugawa Japan (1965).

G.S. Elison, Deus Destroyed: The Image of Christianity in Early Modern Japan (1973). A brilliant study of the persecutions of Christianity during the early Tokugawa period.

J.W. Hall and M. Jansen, eds., Studies in the Institutional History of Early Modern Japan (1968). A collection of articles on Tokugawa institutions.

J.W. Hall, K. Nagahara, and K. Yamamura, eds., Japan before Tokugawa (1981).

S. Hanley, Everyday Things in Premodern Japan: The Hidden Legacy of Material Culture (1997).

H.S. Hibbett, The Floating World in Japanese Fiction (1959). An eminently readable study of early Tokugawa literature.

M. Jansen, ed., The Nineteenth Century, Vol. 5 in The Cambridge History of Japan (1989).

K. Katsu, Musui's Story, trans. by T. Craig (1988). The life and adventures of a boisterous, no-good samurai of the early nineteenth century. Eminently readable.

D. Keene, trans., Chushingura, the Treasury of Loyal Retainers (1971). The puppet play about the forty-seven men who took revenge on the enemy of their former lord.

O.G. Lidin, Tanegashima: The Arrival of Europe in Japan (2002). The impact of the musket and Europeans on sixteenth-century Japan.

M. Maruyama, Studies in the Intellectual History of Tokugawa Japan, trans. by M. Hane (1974). A seminal work in this field by one of modern Japan's greatest scholars.

J.L. McClain et al., Edo and Paris: Urban Life and the State in the Early Modern Era (1994). Comparison of city life and government role in the capitals of Tokugawa Japan and France.

K.W. Nakai, Shogunal Politics (1988). A brilliant study of Arai Hakuseki's conceptualization of Tokugawa government.

P. Nosco, ed., Confucianism and Tokugawa Culture (1984). A lively collection of essays.

H. Ooms, Tokugawa Village Practice: Class, Status, Power, Law (1996).

A. Ravina, Land and Lordship in Early Modern Japan (1999). A sociopolitical study of three Tokugawa domains.

I. Saikaku, The Japanese Family Storehouse, trans. by G.W. Sargent (1959). A lively novel about merchant life in seventeenth-century Japan.

G.B. Sansom, The Western World and Japan (1950).

J.A. Sawada, Confucian Values and Popular Zen (1993). A study of Shingaku, a popular Tokugawa religious sect.

C.D. Sheldon, The Rise of the Merchant Class in Tokugawa Japan (1958).

T.C. Smith, The Agrarian Origins of Modern Japan (1959). On the evolution of farming and rural social organization in Tokugawa Japan.

P.F. Souyri, The World Turned Upside Down: Medieval Japanese Society (2001). After a running start from the late Heian period, an analysis of the overthrow of lords by their vassals.

R.P. Toby, State and Diplomacy in Early Modern Japan: Asia in the Development of the Tokugawa Bakufu (1984).

C. Totman, Tokugawa Ieyasu: Shōgun (1983).

C. Totman, Green Archipelago, Forestry in Preindustrial Japan (1989).

H.P. Varley, The Ōnin War: History of Its Origins and Background with a Selective Translation of the Chronicle of Ōnin (1967).

K. Yamamura and S.B. Hanley, Economic and Demographic Change in Preindustrial Japan, 1600–1868 (1977).

Korea

T. Hatada, A History of Korea (1969).

W.E. Henthorn, A History of Korea (1971).

Ki-Baik Lee, A New History of Korea (1984).

P. Lee, Sourcebook of Korean Civilization, Vol. I (1993).

Vietnam

J. Buttinger, A Dragon Defiant, a Short History of Vietnam (1972).

Nguyen Du, The Tale of Kieu (1983).

N. Tarling, ed., The Cambridge History of Southeast Asia (1992).

K. Taylor, The Birth of Vietnam (1983).

A.B. Woodside, Vietnam and the Chinese Model (1988).

Chapter 19

R.C. Allen, The British Industrial Revolution in Global Perspective (2009). A much needed addition to the study of the industrial revolution.

F. Anderson, The Crucible of War: The Seven Years' War and the Fate of Empire in British North America, 1754–1766 (2000). A splendid narrative and analysis.

W. Beik, Louis XIV and Absolutism: A Brief Study with Documents (2000). An excellent collection by a major scholar of absolutism.

T. Blanning, The Pursuit of Glory: Europe l648–l815 (2007). The best recent synthesis of the emergence of the modern European state system.

J. Blum, Lord and Peasant in Russia from the Ninth to the Nineteenth Century (1961). Remains a thorough and wide-ranging discussion.

P. Burke, The Fabrication of Louis XIV (1992). Examines the manner in which the public image of Louis XIV was forged in art.

J. Burnet, Gender, Work and Wages in Industrial Revolution Britain (2008). A major revisionist study of the wage structure for work by men and women.

P. Bushkovitch, Peter the Great: The Struggle for Power, 1671–1725 (2001). Replaces previous studies.

C. Clark, The Rise and Downfall of Prussia l600-l947 (2006). A stunning survey.

L. Colley, Britons: Forging the Nation, 1707–1837 (1992) A major study of the making of British nationhood.

P. Deane, The First Industrial Revolution (1999). A well-balanced and systematic treatment.

J. De Vries, The Industrious Revolution: Consumer Behavior and the Household Economy, 1650 to the Present (2008). Discusses the rise of development through the psychology and actions of consumers, thus presenting an important new perspective.

W. Doyle, The Old European Order, 1660–1800 (1992). Remains a classic study.

D. Fraser, Frederick the Great: King of Prussia (2001) Excellent on both Frederick and eighteenth-century Prussia.

T. Harris, Restoration: Charles II and His Kingdom, 1660–1685 (2006). A major exploration of the tumultuous years of the restoration of the English monarchy after the civil war.

E. Hobsbawm, Industry and Empire: The Birth of the Industrial Revolution (1999). A survey by a major historian of the subject.

K. Honeyman, Women, Gender and Industrialization in England, 1700–1850 (2000). Emphasizes how certain work or economic roles became associated with either men or women.

O.H. Hufton, The Poor of Eighteenth-Century France, 1750–1789 (1975). A brilliant classic study of poverty and the family economy.

L. Hughes, Russia in the Age of Peter the Great (1998). An excellent account.

C.J. Ingrao, The Habsburg Monarchy, 1618–1815 (2000). The best recent survey.

D.I. Kertzer and M. Barbagli, The History of the European Family: Family Life in Early Modern Times, 1500–1709 (2001). A series of broad-ranging essays covering the entire Continent.

S. King and G. Timmons, Making Sense of the Industrial Revolution: English Economy and Society, 1700–1850 (2001). Examines the industrial revolution through the social institutions that brought it about and were changed by it.

M. Kishlansky, A Monarchy Transformed: Britain 1603–1714 (1996) An excellent synthesis.

A. Lossky, Louis XIV and the French Monarchy (1994). The most recent major analysis.

F.E. Manuel, The Broken Staff: Judaism through Christian Eyes (1992). An important discussion of Christian interpretations of Judaism.

M.A. Meyer, The Origins of the Modern Jew: Jewish Identity and European Culture in Germany, 1749–1824 (1967). A general introduction organized around individual case studies.

S. Pincus, 1688: The First Modern Revolution (2009). The most important recent study.

G. Treasure, *Louis XIV (2001). The best, most accessible recent study.*

D. Valenze, The First Industrial Woman (1995). An elegant work exploring the manner in which industrialization transformed the work of women.

J. West, Gunpower, Government, and War in the Mid-Eighteenth Century (1991). A study of how warfare touched much government of the day.

Chapter 20

S.S. Blair and J. Bloom, The Art and Architecture of Islam, 1250–1800 (1994). A fine survey of the period for all parts of the Islamic world.

R. Canfield, ed., Turko-Persia in Historical Perspctive (1991). A good general collection of essays.

K. Chelebi, The Balance of Truth (1957). A marvelous volume of essays and reflections by probably the major intellectual of Ottoman times.

W.T. de Bary et al., comp., Sources of Indian Tradition, 2nd ed. (1958), Vol. I, From the Beginning to 1800, ed. and rev. by Ainslie T. Embree (1988). Excellent selections from a wide variety of Indian texts, with good introductions to chapters and individual selections.

S. Faroqi, Towns and Townsmen of Ottoman Anatolia (1984). Examines the changing balances of economic power between the urban and rural areas.

C.H. Fleischer, Bureaucrat and Intellectual in the Ottoman Empire: The Historian Mustafa Ali (1541–1600) (1986). A major study of Ottoman intellectual history.

G. Hambly, Central Asia (1966). Excellent survey chapters (9–13) on the Chaghatay and Uzbek (Shaybanid) Turks.

R.S. Hattox, Coffee and Coffee-Houses: The Origins of a Social Beverage in the Medieval Near East (1985). A fascinating piece of social history.

M.G.S. Hodgson, The Gunpowder Empires and Modern Times, Vol. 3 of The Venture of Islam, 3 vols. (1974). Less ample than Vols. 1 and 2 of Hodgson's monumental history, but a thoughtful survey of the great post–1500 empires.

S.M. Ikram, Muslim Civilization in India (1964). Still the best short survey history, covering the period from 711 to 1857.

H. Inalcik, The Ottoman Empire: The Classical Age, 1300–1600 (1973). An excellent, if dated, survey with solid treatment of Ottoman social, religious, and political institutions.

H. Inalcik, An Economic and Social History of the Ottoman Empire, 1300–1914 (1994). A masterly survey by the dean of Ottoman studies today.

C. Kafadar, Between Two Worlds: The Construction of the Ottoman State (1995). A readable analysis of theories of Ottoman origins and early development.

N.R. Keddie, ed., Scholars, Saints, and Sufis: Muslim Religious Institutions in the Middle East since 1500 (1972). A collection of interesting articles well worth reading.

M. Mujeeb, The Indian Muslims (1967). The best cultural study of Islamic civilization in India as a whole, from its origins onward.

G. Necipoglu, Architecture, Ceremonial, and Power: The Topkapi Palace in the Fifteenth and Sixteenth Centuries (1991). A superb analysis of the symbolism of Ottoman power and authority.

L. Pierce, The Imperial Harem: Women and Sex in the Ottoman Empire (1993). Ground-breaking study on the role of women in the Ottoman Empire.

D. Quatarert, An Economic and Social History of the Ottoman Empire, 1300–1914 (1994). The authoritative account of Ottoman economy and society.

J. Richards, The Mughal Empire, Vol. 5 of The New Cambridge History of India (1993). A impressive synthesis of the varying interpretations of Mughal India.

S.A.A. Rizvi, The Wonder That Was India, Vol. II (1987). A sequel to Basham's original The Wonder That Was India; treats Mughal life, culture, and history from 1200 to 1700.

F. Robinson, Atlas of the Islamic World since 1500 (1982). Brief, excellent historical essays, color illustrations with detailed accompanying text, and chronological tables, as well as precise maps, make this a refreshing general reference work.

R. Savory, Iran under the Safavids (1980). A solid and readable survey.

S.J. Shaw, Empire of the Gazis: The Rise and Decline of the Ottoman Empire, 1280–1808, Vol. I of History of the Ottoman Empire and Modern Turkey (1976). A solid historical survey with excellent bibliographic essays for each chapter and a good index.

Chapter 21

D. Beales, Joseph II, 2 Vols. (1987, 2009). The best treatment in English of the life of Joseph II.

M. Biagioli, Galileo Courtier: The Practice of Science in the Culture of Absolutism (1993). A major revisionist work that emphasizes the role of the political setting in Galileo's career and thought.

D.D. Bien, The Calas Affair: Persecution, Toleration, and Heresy in Eighteenth-Century Toulouse (1960). Classic treatment of the famous case.

T.C.W. Blanning, The Culture of Power and the Power of Culture: Old Regime Europe 1660–1789 (2002). The strongest treatment of the relationship of eighteenth-century cultural changes and politics.

P. Blom, Enlightening the World: Encyclopedie, The Book That Changed the Course of History (2005). A lively, accessible introduction.

J. Buchan, Crowded with Genius: The Scottish Enlightenment (2003). A lively, accessible introduction.

J.A. Conner, Kepler's Witch: An Astronomer's Discovery of Cosmic Order amid Religious War, Political Intrigue, and the Heresy Trial of His Mother (2005). Fascinating account of Kepler's effort to vindicate his mother against charges of witchcraft.

L. Damrosch, Rousseau: Restless Genius (2007). The best recent biography.

R. Darnton, The Literary Underground of the Old Regime (1982). Classic essays on the world of printers, publishers, and booksellers.

P. Dear, Revolutionizing the Sciences: European Knowledge and Its Ambitions, 1500–1700 (2001). A broad-ranging study of both the ideas and institutions of the new science.

I. De Madariaga, Catherine the Great: A Short History (1990). A good brief biography.

M. Feingold, The Newtonian Moment: Isaac Newton and the Making of Modern Culture (2004). A superb, well-illustrated volume.

S. Gaukroger, The Emergence of a Scientific Culture: Science and the Shaping of Modernity (2007). A challenging book exploring the differing understanding of natural knowledge in early modern European culture.

S. Gaukroger, Francis Bacon and the Transformation of Early-Modern Philosophy (2001). An excellent, accessible introduction.

J. Gleixk, Isaac Newton (2003). The best brief biography.

D. Goodman, The Republic of Letters: A Cultural History of the French Enlightenment (1994). Concentrates on the role of salons.

J.L. Heilbron, The Sun in the Church: Cathedrals as Solar Observatories (2000). A remarkable study of the manner in which Roman Catholic cathedrals were used to make astsronomical observations and calculations.

C. Hesse, The Other Enlightenment: How French Women Became Modern (2004). Explores the manner in which French women authors created their own sphere of thought and cultural activity.

K.J. Howell, God's Two Books: Copernican Cosmology and Biblical Interpretation in Early Modern Science (2003). Best introduction to early modern issues of science and religion.

J. Melton, The Rise of the Public in Enlightenmen Europe (2001). A superb overview of the emergence of new institutions that made the expression of a broad public opinion possible in Europe.

C. A. Kors, Encyclopedia of the Enlightenment (2002). A major reference work on all of the chief intellectual themes of the era.

J. Marshall, John Locke, Toleration and Early Enlightenment Culture (2006). A magisterial, challenging survey of seventeenth-century arguments for and against toleration.

T. Munck, The Enlightenment: A Comparative Social History 1721–1794 (2000). A clear introduction to the social background that made possible the spread of Enlightenment thought.

S. Muthu, Enlightenment against Empire (2003) A study of philosophes who criticized the European empires of their day.

D. Outram, The Enlightenment (1995). An excellent brief introduction.

R. Peason, Voltaire Almighty: A Life in Pursuit of Freedom (2005). An accessible biography.

R. Porter, The Creation of the Modern World: The Untold Story of the British Enlightenment (2001). A superb, lively overview.

J. Repcheck, Copernicus' Secret: How the Scientific Revolution Began (2007). A highly accessible biography of Copernicus.

E. Rothchild, Economic Sentiments: Adam Smith, Condorcet, and the Enlightenment (2001). A sensitive account of Smith's thought and its relationship to the social questions of the day.

S. Shapin, The Scientific Revolution (1996). An important revisionist survey emphasizing social factors.

J. Sheehan, The Enlightenment Bible (2007). Explores the Enlightenment treatment of the Bible.

D. Sorkin, The Religious Enlightenment: Protestants, Jews, and Catholics from London to Vienna (2008). Argues that important Enlightenment figures sought to protect religion.

L. Steinbrügge, The Moral Sex: Woman's Nature in the French Enlightenment (1995). Emphasizes the conservative nature of Enlightenment thought on women.

P. Zagorin, How the Idea of Religious Toleration Came to the West (2003). An excellent exploration of the rise of toleration.

Chapter 22

D. Andress, The Terror: The Merciless War for Freedom in Revolutionary France (2006). The best recent survey of the reign of terror.

R. Anstey, The Atlantic Slave Trade and British Abolition, 1760–1810 (1975). A standard overview that emphasizes the role of religious factors.

B. Bailyn, The Ideological Origins of the American Revolution (1967). An important work illustrating the role of English radical thought in the perceptions of the American colonists.

K.M. Baker, Inventing the French Revolution: Essays on French Political Culture in the Eighteenth Century (1990). Important essays on political thought before and during the revolution.

K.M. Baker and C. Lucas, eds., The French Revolution and the Creation of Modern Political Culture, 3 vols. (1987). A splendid collection of important original articles on all aspects of politics during the revolution.

R.J. Barman, Brazil: The Forging of a Nation, 1798–1852 (1988). The best coverage of this period.

D. Bell, The First Total War: Napoleon's Europe and the Birth of Warfare as We Know It (2007). A consideration of the Napoleonic conflicts and the culture of warfare.

M. S. Bell, Toussaint Louverture: A Biography (2007). An outstanding new biography.

J.F. Bernard, Talleyrand: A Biography (1973). A useful account.

L. Bethell, The Cambridge History of Latin America, Vol. 3 (1985). Contains an extensive treatment of independence.

R. Blackburn, The Overthrow of Colonial Slavery, 1776–1848 (1988). A major discussion quite skeptical of the humanitarian interpretation.

J. Brooke, King George III (1972). The best biography.

R. Cobb, The People's Armies (1987). The major treatment in English of the revolutionary army.

O. Connelly, Napoleon's Satellite Kingdoms (1965). The rule of Napoleon and his family in Europe.

D.B. Davis, The Problem of Slavery in the Age of Revolution, 1770–1823 (1975). A transatlantic perspective on the issue.

W. Doyle, The Oxford History of the French Revolution (2003). A broad, complex narrative with an excellent bibliography.

L. Dubois, Avengers of the New World: The Story of the Haitian Revolution (2004). An analytic narrative likely to replace others.

P. Dwyer, Napoleon: The Path to Power, 1769–1799 (2008). A major study of the subject.

J. J. Ellis, His Excellency: George Washington (2004). A biography that explores the entire era of the American Revolution.

M. Glover, The Peninsular War, 1807–1814: A Concise Military History (1974). An interesting account of the military campaign that so drained Napoleon's resources in western Europe.

J. Godechot, The Counter-Revolution: Doctrine and Action, 1789–1804 (1971). An examination of opposition to the revolution.

A. Goodwin, The Friends of Liberty: The English Democratic Movement in the Age of the French Revolution (1979). A major work that explores the impact of the French Revolution on English radicalism.

L. Hunt, Politics, Culture, and Class in the French Revolution (1986). A series of essays that focus on the modes of expression of the revolutionary values and political ideas.

F. Kagan, The End of the old order: Napoleon and Europe, 1801–1805 (2006). A masterful narrative.

W.W. Kaufmann, British Policy and the Independence of Latin America, 1802–1828 (1951). A standard discussion of an important relationship.

E. Kennedy, A Cultural History of the French Revolution (1989). An important examination of the role of the arts, schools, clubs, and intellectual institutions.

M. Kennedy, The Jacobin Clubs in the French Revolution: The First Years (1982). A careful scrutiny of the organizations chiefly responsible for the radicalizing of the revolution.

M. Kennedy, The Jacobin Clubs in the French Revolution: The Middle Years (1988). A continuation of the previously listed study.

H. Kissinger, A World Restored: Metternich, Castlereagh and the Problems of Peace, 1812–1822 (1957). A provocative study by an author who became an American secretary of state.

G. Lefebvre, The Coming of the French Revolution (trans. 1947). A classic examination of the crisis of the French monarchy and the events of 1789.

G. Lefebvre, Napoleon, 2 vols., trans. by H. Stockhold (1969). The fullest and finest biography.

J. Lynch, Simon Bolivar: A Life (2006). Now the standard biography.

J. Lynch, The Spanish American Revolutions, 1808–1826 (1986). An excellent one-volume treatment.

P. Maier, American Scripture: Making the Declaration of Independence (1997). Stands as a major revision of our understanding of the Declaration.

S.E. Melzer and L.W. Rabine, eds., Rebel Daughters: Women and the French Revolution (1992). A collection of essays exploring various aspects of the role and image of women in the French Revolution.

M. Morris, The British Monarchy and the French Revolution (1998). Explores the manner in which the British monarchy saved itself from possible revolution.

R. Muir, Tactics and the Experience of Battle in the Age of Napoleon (1998). Examines the wars from the standpoint of the soldiers in combat.

H. Nicolson, The Congress of Vienna (1946). A good, readable account.

R.R. Palmer, Twelve Who Ruled: The Committee of Public Safety during the Terror (1941). A clear narrative and analysis of the policies and problems of the committee.

R.R. Palmer, The Age of the Democratic Revolution: A Political History of Europe and America, 1760–1800, 2 vols. (1959, 1964). An impressive survey of the political turmoil in the transatlantic world.

C. Proctor, Women, Equality, and the French Revolution (1990). An examination of how the ideas of the Enlightenment and the attitudes of revolutionaries affected the legal status of women.

A.J. Russell-Wood, ed., From Colony to Nation: Essays on the Independence of Brazil (1975). A series of important essays.

P. Schroeder, The Transformation of European Politics, 1763–1848 (1994). A fundamental treatment of the diplomacy of the era.

R. Scurr, Fatal Purity: Robespierre and the French Revolution (2007). A compelling analysis of a personality long difficult to understand.

A. Soboul, The Parisian Sans-Culottes and the French Revolution, 1793–94 (1964). The best work on the subject.

D.G. Sutherland, France, 1789–1825: Revolution and Counterrevolution (1986). A major synthesis based on recent scholarship in social history.

T. Tackett, Religion, Revolution, and Regional Culture in Eighteenth-Century France: The Ecclesiastical Oath of 1791 (1986). The most important study of this topic.

T. Tackett, Becoming a Revolutionary: The Deputies of the French National Assembly and the Emergence of a Revolutionary Culture (1789–1790) (1996). The best study of the early months of the revolution.

J.M. Thompson, Robespierre, 2 vols. (1935). The best biography.

D.K. Van Key, The Religious Origins of the French Revolution: From Calvin to the Civil Constitution, 1560–1791 (1996). Examines the manner in which debates within French Catholicism influenced the coming of the revolution.

M. Walzer, ed., Regicide and Revolution: Speeches at the Trial of Louis XVI (1974). An important and exceedingly interesting collection of documents with a useful introduction.

I. Woloch, The New Regime: Transformations of the French Civic Order, 1789–1820s (1994). An important overview of just what had and had not changed in France after the quarter century of revolution and war.

G. Wood, Empire of Liberty: A History of the Early Republic, 1789–1815 (2009) A major interpretation.

A. Zamoyski, Rites of Peace: The Fall of Napoleon and the Congress of Vienna (2007). A lively analysis and narrative.

Chapter 23

I. Berlin, Generations of Captivity: A History of African-American Slaves (2003). A major work.

P. Bew, Ireland: The Politics of Enmity 1789–2006 (2007). A major, new, outstanding survey of the sweep of modern Irish history.

D. Blackbourn, The Long Nineteenth Century: A History of Germany, 1780–1918 (1998). An outstanding survey.

D.G. Creighton, John A. MacDonald (1952, 1955). A major biography of the first Canadian prime minister.

D. Donald, Lincoln (1995). Now the standard biography.

R.B. Edgerton, Death or Glory: The Legacy of the Crimean War (2000). Multifaceted study of a badly mismanaged war that transformed many aspects of European domestic politics.

D.K. Goodwin, Team of Rivals: The Political Genius of Abraham Lincoln (2005). An accessible study of Lincoln's administration.

M. Holt, The Fate of Their Country: Politicians, Slavery Extension, and the Coming of the Civil War (2005). A brief introduction to the crucial decade of the 1850s in the United States.

M. Holt, The Rise and Fall of the American Whig Party: Jacksonian Politics and the Onset of the Civil War (2003). An extensive survey of the Jacksonian era.

R. Kee, The Green Flag: A History of Irish Nationalism (2001). A vast survey.

W. Lacquer, A History of Zionism (1989). The most extensive one-volume treatment.

M.B. Levinger, Enlightened Nationalism: The Transformation of Prussian Political Culture, 1806–1848 (2002). A major work.

J.M. McPherson, The Battle Cry of Freedom: The Civil War Era (1988). An excellent one-volume treatment.

D. Morton, A Short History of Canada (2001). Useful popular history.

J.P. Parry, The Rise and Fall of Liberal Government in Victorian Britain (1994). An outstanding study.

A. Plessis, The Rise and Fall of the Second Empire, 1852–1871 (1985). A useful survey of France under Napoleon III.

D.M. Potter, The Impending Crisis, 1848–1861 (1976) A penetrating study of the coming of the American Civil War.

L. Riall, Garibaldi: Invention of a Hero (2007). An exploration of a nationalist hero's reputation in his own day and later.

D. Shafer, The Paris Commune: French Politics, Culture, and Society at the Crossroads of the Revolutionary Tradition and Revolutionary Socialism (2005). Excellent in relating the Commune to previous and later revolutionary traditions.

A. Sked, Decline and Fall of the Habsburg Empire, 1815–1918 (2001). A major, accessible survey of a difficult subject.

A. Sked, Metternich and Austria: An Evaluation (2008). A thoughtful restoration of Metternich to the position of leading diplomat of his age.

D.M. Smith, Cavour (1984). An excellent biography.

C.P. Stacey, Canada and the Age of Conflict (1977, 1981). A study of Canadian foreign relations.

D. Wetzel, A Duel of Giants: Bismarck, Napoleon III, and the Origins of the Franco-Prussian War (2001). Broad study based on most recent scholarship.

Chapter 24

M. Adas, Machines as the Measure of Men: Science, Technology, and Ideologies of Western Dominance (1989). The best single volume on racial thinking and technological advances as forming ideologies of European colonial dominance.

A. Ascher and P.A. Stolypin, The Search for Stability in Late Imperial Russia (2000). A broad-ranging biography based on extensive research.

I. Berlin, Karl Marx: His Life and Environment, 4th ed. (1996). A classic volume that remains an excellent introduction.

P. Bowler, Evolution: The History of an Idea (2003). An outstanding survey.

Janet Browne, Charles Darwin, 2 vols. (2002). An eloquent, accessible biography.

J. Burrow, The Crisis of Reason: European Thought, 1848–1914 (2000). The best overview available.

A.D. Chandler Jr., The Visible Hand: Managerial Revolution in American Business (1977). Remains the best discussion of the innovative role of American business.

A. Clarke, The Struggle for the Breeches: Gender and the Making of the British Working Class (1995). An examination of the manner in which industrialization made problematical the relationships between men and women.

W. Cronin, Nature's Metropolis: Chicago and the Great West, 1848–1893 (1991). The best examination of any major American nineteenth-century city.

P. Gay, Freud: A Life for Our Time (1988). The new standard biography.

P. Gay, Modernism: The Lure of Heresy (2007). A broad interdisciplinary exploration.

R.F. Hamilton, Marxism, Revisionism, and Leninism: Explication, Assessment, and Commentary (2000). A contribution from the perspective of a historically minded sociologist.

S. Hahn, A Nation under Our Feet: Black Political Struggles in the Rural South from Slavery to the Great Migration (2003). A major synthesis.

A. Hourani, Arab Thought in the Liberal Age 1789–1939 (1967). A classic account, clearly written and accessible to the nonspecialist.

T. Hunt, Marx's General: The Revolutionary Life of Friedrich Engels (2009). A biography that also considers the general landscape of late nineteenth-century socialism.

D.I. Kertzer and M. Barbagli, eds., Family Life in the Long Nineteenth Century, 1789–1913: The History of the European Family (2002). Wide-ranging collection of essays.

J.T. Kloppenberg, Uncertain Victory: Social Democracy and Progressivism in European and American Thought (1986). An extremely important comparative study.

J. Köhler, Zarathustra's Secret: The Interior Life of Friedrich Nietzsche (2002). A controversial new biography.

L. Kolakowski, Main Currents of Marxism: Its Rise, Growth, and Dissolution, 3 vols. (1978). Especially good on the last years of the nineteenth century and the early years of the twentieth.

P. Krause, The Battle for Homestead, 1880–1892 (1992). Examines labor relations in the steel industry.

D. Landes, The Wealth and Poverty of Nations: Why Some Are So Rich and Some So Poor (1998). A major international discussion of the subject.

B. Lightman, Victorian Popularizers of Science: Designing Nature for New Audiences (2007). A study that adds numerous new dimensions to the subject.

G. Makari, Revolution in Mind: The Creation of Psychoanalysis (2008). A major, multidimensional survey.

M. McGerr, A Fierce Discontent: The Rise and Fall of the Progressive Moevement in America, 1870–1920 (2003). The best recent synthesis.

E. Morris, Theodore Rex (2002). Major survey of Theodore Roosevelt's presidency and personality.

A. Pais, Subtle Is the Lord: The Science and Life of Albert Einstein (1983). Remains the most accessible scientific biography.

J. Rendall, The Origins of Modern Feminism: Women in Britain, France and the United States, 1780–1860 (1985). A well-informed introduction.

R. Service, Lenin: A Biography (2002). Based on new sources and will no doubt become the standard biography.

R.M. Utley, The Indian Frontier and the American West, 1846–1890 (1984). A broad survey of the pressures of white civilization against Native Americans.

D. Vital, A People Apart: The Jews in Modern Europe, 1789–1939 (1999). A deeply informed survey.

Chapter 25

S. Arrom, The Women of Mexico City, 1790–1857 (1985). A pioneering study.

W. Baer, Brazilian Economy: Growth and Development (2007). An in-depth study of the subject.

L. Bethell, ed., The Cambridge History of Latin America, 8 vols. (1992). The single most authoritative coverage, with extensive bibliographical essays. This series has now been published in several smaller, nation-specific volumes edited by L. Bethell.

J.P. Brennan and M. Rougier, The Politics of National Capitalism: Peronism and the Argentine Bourgeoisie, 1946–1976 (2009). A challenging study of the relationship of Perón and business.

V. Bulmer-Thomas, The Economic History of Latin America since Independence (1994). Remains a major.

E.B. Burns, The Poverty of Progress: Latin America in the Nineteenth Century (1980). Remains a significant work arguing that the elites suppressed alternative modes of cultural and economic development.

D. Bushnell and N. Macaulay, The Emergence of Latin America in the Nineteenth Century (1994). A survey that examines the internal development of Latin America during the period.

R. Conrad, The Destruction of Brazilian Slavery, 1850–1889 (1971). Still a good survey of the most important problem in Brazil in the second half of the nineteenth century.

R. Conrad, World of Sorrow: The African Slave Trade to Brazil (1986). An excellent treatment of the subject.

N. Craske, Women and Politics in Latin America (1999). A useful overview.

E.V. Da Costa, The Brazilian Empire: Myths and Histories (1985). Essays that provide a thorough introduction to Brazil during the period of empire.

H.S. Ferns, Britain and Argentina in the Nineteenth Century (1968). Classic exploration of the intermeshing of the two economies.

M. Font, Coffee, Contention, and Change in the Making of Modern Brazil (1990). Extensive discussion of the problems of a single-commodity economy.

A. Gilly, The Mexican Revolution: A People's History (2005). Explores lesser known figures of the revolution.

R. Graham, Britain and the Onset of Modernization in Brazil (1968). Another study of British economic dominance.

S.H. Haber, Industry and Underdevelopment: The Industrialization of Mexico, 1890–1940 (1989). Examines the problem of industrialization before and after the revolution.

G. Hahner, Emancipating the Female Sex: The Struggle for Women's Rights in Brazil, 1850–1940 (1990). An extensive examination of a relatively understudied issue in Latin America.

C.H. Haring, Empire in Brazil: A New World Experiment with Monarchy (1958). Remains a useful overview.

J. Hemming, Amazon Frontier: The Defeat of the Brazilian Indians (1987). A brilliant survey of the experience of Native Americans in modern Brazil.

R.A. Humphreys, Latin America and the Second World War, 2 vols. (1981–1982). The standard work on the topic.

D. James, Resistance and Integration: Peronism and the Argentine Working Class, 1946–1976 (l994). Explores the complicated relationship of Perón and the working class over several decades.

M.B. Karush and O. Chamosa, The New Cultural History of Peronism: Power and Identity in Mid-Twentieth-Century Argentina (2010). Interdisciplinary collection of essays on the emergence of Peronism.

F. Katz, ed., Riot, Rebellion, and Revolution in Mexico: Social Base of Agrarian Violence, 1750–1940 (1988). Essays that put the violence of the revolution in a longer context.

F. Katz, The Life and Times of Pancho Villa (1998). An extensive critical biography

A. Knight, The Mexican Revolution, 2 vols. (1986). The best treatment of the subject.

C. M. MacLachlan, A History of Modern Brazil: The Past against the Future (2003). A basic brief introduction.

S. Mainwaring, The Catholic Church and Politics in Brazil, 1916–1985 (1986). An examination of a key institution in Brazilian life.

F. McLynn, Villa and Zapata: A History of the Mexican Revolution (2002). Examines the revolution through the lives and interrelationship of its two most important figures.

M. Morner, Adventurers and Proletarians: The Story of Migrants in Latin America (1985). Examines immigration to Latin America and migration within it.

A.D. Ortiz, Eva Perón: A Biography (1997) A biography of one of the most enigmatic figures of modern Latin America.

J. Page, Perón: A Biography (1983). The standard English treatment.

M. B. Plotkin, Manana Es San Perón: A Cultural History of Perón's Argentina (2003). Explores Argentina during the curious governance of Perón.

D. Rock, Politics in Argentina, 1890–1930: The Rise and Fall of Radicalism (2009). The major discussion of the Argentine Radical Party.

D. Rock, Argentina, 1516–1987: From Spanish Colonization to Alfonsin (1987). Now the standard survey.

D. Rock, ed., Latin America in the 1940s: War and Postwar Transitions (1994). Essays examining a very difficult decade for the continent.

R.M. Schneider, "Order and Progress": A Political History of Brazil (1991). A straightforward narrative with helpful notes for further reading.

R. Scott, The Abolition of Slavery and the Aftermath of Emancipation in Brazil (1988). A brief overview.

T.E. Skidmore, Black into White: Race and Nationality in Brazilian Thought (1993). Examines the role of racial theory in Brazil.

T.E. Skidmore, Politics in Brazil 1930–1964: An Experiment in Democracy (2007). An in-depth exploration of Brazilian politics before and after World War II.

S.J. Stein and B.H. Stein, The Colonial Heritage of Latin America: Essays on Economic Dependence in Perspective (1970). A classic statement of the dependence interpretation.

D. Tamarin, The Argentine Labor Movement, 1930–1945: A Study in the Origins of Perónism (1985). A useful introduction to a complex subject.

H.J. Wiarda, Politics and Social Change in Latin America: The Distinct Tradition (1974). Excellent essays that stress the ongoing role of Iberian traditions.

J.D. Wirth, ed., Latin American Oil Companies and the Politics of Energy (1985). A series of case studies.

J. Wolfe, Working Women, Working Men: São Paulo and the Rise of Brazil's Industrial Working Class, 1900–1955 (1993). Pays particular attention to the role of women.

J. Womack, Zapata and the Mexican Revolution (1968). A classic study.

Chapter 26

General Works

S. Cook, Colonial Encounters in the Age of High Imperialism (1996). A good introduction to the imperial enterprise in Africa and Asia.

D.K. Fieldhouse, The West and the Third World. Trade: Colonialism, Depedence and Development (1999). Addresses whether colonialism was detrimental or beneficial to colonized peoples.

D. Headrick, The Tentacles of Progress: Technology Transfer in the Age of Imperialism, 1850–1940 (1988). Discusses the roles of new methods of transportation (railroads, steamships), forms of expertise (doctors, botanists), and other types of "technology transfer" in European colonization, and post-independence development.

P. Hopkirk, The Great Game: The Struggle for Empire in Central Asia (1992). Focuses on the political and economic rivalries of the imperial powers.

India

A. Ahmad, Islamic Modernism in India and Pakistan, 1857–1964 (1967). The standard survey of Muslim thinkers and movements in India during the period.

C.A. Bayly, Indian Society and the Making of the British Empire, The New Cambridge History of India, II. 1 (1988). One of several major contributions of this author to the ongoing revision of our picture of modern Indian history since the eighteenth century.

A. Ghosh, In an Antique Land: History in the Guise of a Traveler's Tale (1992). An anthropologist traces the footsteps of a premodern slave traveling with his master from North Africa to India. A gripping tale of premodern life in the India Ocean basin and also of contemporary Egypt.

R. Guha, ed., Subaltern Studies: Writings on South Asian History and Society (1982). Essays on the colonial period that focus on the social, political, and economic history of "subaltern" groups and classes (hill tribes, peasants, etc.) rather than only the elites of India.

S.N. Hay, ed., "Modern India and Pakistan," Part VI of Wm. Theodore de Bary et al., eds., Sources of Indian Tradition, 2nd ed. (1988). A superb selection of primary-source documents, with brief introductions and helpful notes.

F. Robinson, ed., The Cambridge Encyclopedia of India, Pakistan, Bangladesh, Sri Lanka, Nepal, Bhutan, and the Maldives (1989). A fine collection of survey articles by various scholars, organized into topical chapters ranging from "Economies" to "Cultures."

Central Islamic Lands

W. Cleveland, A History of the Modern Middle East, 3rd ed. (2004). A balanced and well-organized overview of modern Middle Eastern history.

A. Dawisha, Arab Nationalism in the Twentieth Century, From Triumph to Despair (2003). A good overview of the development of Arab nationalism.

S. Deringil, The Well-Protected Domains: Ideology and the Legitimation of Power in the Ottoman Empire, 1876–1909 (1998). An impressive study on nationalism and reform in the Ottoman Empire.

J.J. Donahue and J.L. Esposito, eds., Islam in Transition: Muslim Perspectives (1982). An interesting selection of primary-source materials on Islamic thinking in this century.

D.F. Eickelman, Knowledge and Power in Morocco: The Education of a Twentieth-Century Notable (1985). A fascinating study of traditional Islamic education and society in the twentieth century through a social biography of a Moroccan religious scholar and judge.

A. Hourani, Arabic Thought in the Liberal Age, 1798–1939 (1967). The standard work, by which all subsequent scholarship on the topic is to be judged.

N.R. Keddie, An Islamic Response to Imperialism (1968). A brief study of al-Afghani, the great Muslim reformer, with translations of a number of his writings.

B. Lewis, The Emergence of Modern Turkey, 2nd ed. (1968). A concise but thorough history of the creation of the Turkish state, including nineteenth-century background.

J.O. Voll, Islam: Continuity and Change in the Modern World (1982). Chapters 1–6. An interpretive survey of the Islamic world since the eighteenth century. Its emphasis on eighteenth-century reform movements is especially noteworthy.

Africa

C. Achebe, Things Fall Apart (1959). Reading this classic novel may be the best way to get a profound sense of the ways African and European cultures interacted in the early colonial period.

D. Anderson, Histories of the Hanged: The Dirty War in Kenya and the End of Empire (2005). This account of the Kikuyu-led Mau Mau movement in Kenya emphasizes the way Mau Mau activities, and the British response, shaped and distorted Kenya's independence movement. (See also C. Elkins's Imperial Reckoning below.)

A.A. Boahen, Africa under Colonial Domination, 1880–1935 (1985). Vol. VII of the UNESCO General History of Africa. Excellent chapters on various regions of Africa in the period. Chapters 3–10 detail African resistance to European colonial intrusion in diverse regions.

W. Cartey and M. Kilson, eds., The Africa Reader: Colonial Africa (1970). Original source materials give a vivid picture of African resistance to colonial powers, adaptation to foreign rule, and the emergence of the African masses as a political force.

P. Curtin, S. Feiermann, L. Thompson, and J. Vansina, African History (1978). The relevant portions are Chapters 10–20.

B. Davidson, Modern Africa: A Social and Political History (1989). A very useful survey of African history.

C. Elkins, Imperial Reckoning: The Untold Story of Britain's Gulag in Kenya (2004). The Pulitzer Prize–winning account of Britain's appalling response to the Mau Mau movement in colonial Kenya; while Elkins focuses on the British, D. Anderson in Histories of the Hanged (see above) emphasizes the Kenyan side of the story.

J.D. Fage, A History of Africa (1978). The relevant chapters, which give a particularly clear overview of the colonial period, are 12–16.

B. Freund, The Making of Contemporary Africa: The Development of African Society since 1800 (1984). A refreshingly direct synthetic discussion and survey that take an avowedly, but not reductive, materialist approach to interpretation.

E. Gilbert and J.T. Reynolds, Africa in World History, 2nd ed. (2008). An engaging overview of the period, with attention to technology, economics, and ideologies, among other factors. See especially Chapters 13–15.

D. Headrick, Tools of Empire (1982). A provocative evaluation of the roles played by technology in the imperial venture.

A. Hochschild, King Leopold's Ghost: A Story of Greed, Terror, and Heroism in Colonial Africa (1998). A compelling, well-documented narrative of the atrocities committed in turn-of-the-twentieth-century Congo when it was held as the personal fiefdom of Belgium's monarch.

T. Pakenham, The Scramble for Africa (1991). An excellent analysis of the imperialist age in Africa.

A.D. Roberts, ed., The Colonial Moment in Africa: Essays on the Movement of Minds and Materials, 1900–1940 (1986). Chapters from The Cambridge History of Africa treating various aspects of the colonial period in Africa, including economics, politics, and religion.

Chapter 27

China

P.M. Coble, The Shanghai Capitalists and the Nationalist Government, 1927–1937 (1980).

L.E. Eastman, The Abortive Revolution: China under Nationalist Rule, 1927–1937 (1974).

L.E. Eastman, Seeds of Destruction: Nationalist China in War and Revolution, 1937–1949 (1984).

M. Elvin and G.W. Skinner, The Chinese City between Two Worlds (1974). A study of the late Qing and Republican eras.

J.W. Esherick, The Origins of the Boxer Rebellion (1987).

S. Et, China's Republican Revolution (1994).

J.K. Fairbank and M. Goldman, China, a New History (1998). A survey of the entire sweep of Chinese history; especially strong on the modern period.

J.K. Fairbank and D. Twitchett, eds., The Cambridge History of China. Like the premodern volumes in the same series, the volumes on modern China represent a survey of what is known. Volumes 10–15, which cover the history from the late Qing to the People's Republic, have been published, and the others will be available soon. The series is substantial. Each volume contains a comprehensive bibliography.

J. Fitzgerald, Awakening China: Politics, Culture, and Class in the Nationalist Revolution (1996).

C. Hao, Chinese Intellectuals in Crisis: Search for Order and Meaning, 1890–1911 (1987).

W.C. Kirby, ed., State and Economy in Republican China (2001).

P.A. Kuhn, Rebellion and Its Enemies in Late Imperial China: Militarization and Social Structure, 1796–1864 (1980). A study of how the Confucian gentry saved the Manchu Dynasty after the Taiping Rebellion.

P. Kuhn, Origins of the Modern Chinese State (2002).

J. Levenson, Liang Ch'i-ch'ao and the Mind of Modern China (1953). A classic study of a major Chinese reformer and thinker.

Lu Xun, Selected Works (1960). Novels, stories, and other writings by modern China's greatest writer.

S. Naquin, Peking: Temples and City Life, 1400–1900 (2000).

E.O. Reischauer, J.K. Fairbank, and A.M. Craig, East Asia: Tradition and Transformation (1989). A detailed text on East Asian history. Contains ample chapters on Japan and China and shorter chapters on Korea and Vietnam.

H.Z. Schiffrin, Sun Yat-sen, Reluctant Revolutionary (1980). A biography.

B.I. Schwartz, Chinese Communism and the Rise of Mao (1951). A classic study of Mao, his thought, and the Chinese Communist Party before 1949.

B.I. Schwartz, In Search of Wealth and Power: Yen Fu and the West (1964). A fine study of a late-nineteenth-century thinker who introduced Western ideas into China.

J.D. Spence, The Gate of Heavenly Peace: The Chinese and Their Revolution, 1895–1980 (1981). Historical reflections on twentieth-century China.

J.D. Spence, The Search for Modern China (1990). A thick text but well written.

M. Szonyi, Practicing Kinship: Lineage and Descent in Late Imperial China (2002).

S.Y. Teng and J.K. Fairbank, China's Response to the West (1954). A superb collection of translations from Chinese thinkers and political figures, with commentaries.

T.H. White and A. Jacoby, Thunder Out of China (1946). A view of China during World War II by two who were there.

Japan

G. Akita, Foundations of Constitutional Government in Modern Japan (1967). A study of Itō Hirobumi in the political process leading to the Meiji constitution.

G.C. Allen, A Short Economic History of Modern Japan (1958).

E. Barshay, The Social Sciences in Modern Japan: The Marxian and Modernist Traditions (2004). Different interpretations of history.

J.R. Bartholomew, The Formation of Science in Japan (1989). The pioneering English-language work on the subject.

W.G. Beasley, Japanese Imperialism, 1894–1945 (1987). Excellent short book on the subject.

G.M. Berger, Parties Out of Power in Japan, 1931–1941 (1977). An analysis of the condition of political parties during the militarist era.

G.L. Bernstein, ed., Recreating Japanese Women, 1600–1945 (1991).

The Cambridge History of Japan, The Nineteenth Century, M.B. Jansen, ed. (1989); The Twentieth Century, P. Duus, ed. (1988). Multi-author works.

A.M. Craig, Chōshū in the Meiji Restoration (2000). A study of the Chōshū domain, a Prussia of Japan, during the period 1840–1868.

A.M. Craig and D.H. Shively, eds., Personality in Japanese History (1970). An attempt to gauge the role of individuals and their personalities as factors explaining history.

P. Duus, Party Rivalry and Political Change in Taisho Japan (1968). A study of political change in Japan during the 1910s and 1920s.

P. Duus, The Abacus and the Sword: The Japanese Penetration of Korea, 1895–1910 (1995). A thoughtful analysis.

S. Ericson, The Sound of the Whistle: Railroads and the State in Meiji Japan (1996). An economic and social history of railroads, an engine of growth and popular symbol.

Y. Fukuzawa, Autobiography (1966). Japan's leading nineteenth-century thinker tells of his life and of the birth of modern Japan.

S. Garon, The State and Labor in Modern Japan (1987). A fine study of the subject.

C.N. Gluck, Japan's Modern Myths: Ideology in the Late Meiji Period (1988). A brilliant study of the complex weave of late Meiji thought.

A. Gordon, The Evolution of Labor Relations in Japan: Heavy Industry, 1853–1955 (1985). A seminal work.

B.R. Hackett, Yamagata Aritomo in the Rise of Modern Japan, 1932–1922 (1973). History as seen through the biography of a central figure.

I. Hall, Mori Arinori (1973). A biography of Japan's first minister of education.

T.R.H. Havens, The Valley of Darkness: The Japanese People and World War II (1978). Wartime society.

A. Iriye, After Imperialism: The Search for a New Order in the Far East, 1921–1931 (1965). (Also see other studies by this author.)

D.M.B. Jansen and G. Rozman, eds., Japan in Transition from Tokugawa to Meiji (1986). Contains fine essays.

W. Johnston, The Modern Epidemic: A History of Tuberculosis in Japan (1995). A social history of a disease.

D. Keene, ed., Modern Japanese Literature, An Anthology (1960). A collection of modern Japanese short stories and excerpts from novels.

Y.T. Matsusaka, The Making of Japanese Manchuria, 1904–1932 (2001). On railroad strategies in empire building.

J.W. Morley, ed., The China Quagmire (1983). A study of Japan's expansion on the continent between 1933 and 1941. (For diplomatic history, see also the many other works by this author.)

R.H. Myers and M.R. Peattie, eds., The Japanese Colonial Empire, 1895–1945 (1984).

T. Najita, Hara Kei in the Politics of Compromise, 1905–1915 (1967). A study of one of Japan's greatest party leaders.

K. Ohkawa and H. Rosovsky, Japanese Economic Growth: Trend Acceleration in the Twentieth Century (1973).

M. Ravina, The Last Samurai: The Life and Battles of Saigo Takamori (2004). Unlike the movie, this account of the Satsu-ma uprising is historical.

G. Shiba, Remembering Aizu (1999). A stirring autobiographical account of a samurai youth whose domain lost in the Meiji Restoration.

K. Smith, A Time of Crisis: The Great Depression and Rural Revitalization (2001). An intellectual history of village movements during the 1930s.

J.J. Stephan, Hawaii under the Rising Sun (1984). Japan's plans for rule in Hawaii.

R.H. Spector, Eagle against the Sun: The American War with Japan (1985). A narrative of World War II in the Pacific.

E.P. Tsurumi, Factory Girls: Women in the Thread Mills of Meiji Japan (1990). A sympathetic analysis of the key component of the Meiji labor force.

W. Wray, Mitsubishi and the N. Y. K., 1870–1914 (1984). The growth of a shipping zaibatsu, with analysis of business strategies, the role of government, and imperialist involvements.

Chapter 28

L. Albertini, The Origins of the War of 1914, 3 vols. (1952, 1957). Discursive but invaluable.

V.R. Berghahn, Germany and the Approach of War in 1914 (1973). A work similar in spirit to both of Fischer's (see below) but stressing the importance of Germany's naval program.

S.B. Fay, The Origins of the World War; 2 vols. (1928). The most influential of the revisionist accounts.

F. Fischer, Germany's Aims in the First World War (1967). An influential interpretation that stirred a great controversy in Germany and around the world by emphasizing Germany's role in bringing on the war.

D. Fromkin, Europe's Last Summer: Who Started the Great War in 1914? (2004). A lively account that fixes on the final crisis in July 1914.

J.N. Horne, Labour at War: France and Britain, 1914–1918 (1991). An examination of a major issue on the home fronts.

J. Keegan, The First World War (1999). A vivid and readable narrative.

P. Kennedy, The Rise of the Anglo-German Antagonism 1860–1914 (1980). An unusual and thorough analysis of the political, economic, and cultural roots of important diplomatic developments.

D.C.B. Lieven, Russia and the Origins of the First World War (1983). A good account of the forces that shaped Russian policy.

A. Mombauer, The Origins of the First World War. Controversies and Consensus (2002). A fascinating survey of the debate over the decades and the current state of the question.

R. Pipes, A Concise History of the Russian Revolution (1996). A one-volume version of a scholarly masterpiece.

Z. Steiner, Britain and the Origins of the First World War (1977). A perceptive and informed account of the way British foreign policy was made in the years before the war.

H. Strachan, The First World War (2004). A fine one-volume account of the war.

A.J.P. Taylor, The Struggle for Mastery in Europe, 1848–1918 (1954). Clever but controversial.

S.R. Williamson, Jr., Austria-Hungary and the Origins of the First World War (1991). A valuable study of a complex subject.

Chapter 29

W.S. Allen, The Nazi Seizure of Power: The Experience of a Single German Town, 1930–1935, rev. ed. (1984). A classic treatment of Nazism in a microcosmic setting.

A. Applebaum, Gulag: A History (2003). A superbly readable account of Stalin's system of persecution and resulting prison camps.

J. Barnard, Walter Reuther and the Rise of the Auto Workers (1983). A major introduction to the new American unions of the 1930s.

R.J. Bosworth, Mussolini (2002). A major new biography.

R.J.B. Bosworth, Mussolini's Italy: Life under the Fascist Dictatorship, 1915–1945 (2007) A broad-based study of both fascist politics and the impact of those politics on Italian life.

A. Brinkley, Voices of Protest: Huey Long, Father Coughlin, & the Great Depression (1983). An excellent study of Franklin Roosevelt's opponents.

M. Burleigh and W. Wipperman, The Racial State: Germany 1933–1945 (1991). Emphasizes the manner in which racial theory influenced numerous areas of policy.

R. Conquest, The Great Terror: Stalin's Purges of the Thirties (1968). Remains a major study.

B. Eichengreen, Golden Fetters: The Gold Standard and the Great Depression, 1919–1939 (1992). A remarkable study of the role of the gold standard in the economic policies of the interwar years.

R. Evans, The Coming of the Third Reich (2004) and The Third Reich in Power, l933–l939 (2005) A superb narrative.

M.S. Fausold, The Presidency of Herbert Hoover (1985). An important treatment.

G. Feldman, The Great Disorder: Politics, Economics, and Society in the German Inflation, 1914–1924 (1993). The best work on the subject.

S. Fitzpatrick, Stalin's Peasants: Resistance and Survival in the Russian Village after Collectivization (1994). A pioneering study.

J.K. Galbraith, The Great Crash (1979). A well-known account by a leading economist.

R. Gellately, The Gestapo and German Society: Enforcing Racial Policy, 1933–1945 (1990). A discussion of how the police state supported Nazi racial policies.

R. Gellately and N. Stoltzfus, Social Outsiders in Nazi Germany (2001). Important essays on Nazi treatment of groups the party regarded as undesirables.

H.J. Gordon, Hitler and the Beer Hall Putsch (1972). An excellent account of the event and the political situation in the early Weimar Republic.

R. Hamilton, Who Voted for Hitler? (1982). An examination of voting patterns and sources of Nazi support.

P. Kenez, The Birth of the Propaganda State: Soviet Methods of Mass Mobilization, 1917–1929 (1985). An examination of the manner in which the communist government inculcated popular support.

D. Kennedy, Freedom from Fear: The American People in Depression and War, 1929–1945 (2001). The best one-volume study of the era.

B. Kent, The Spoils of War: The Politics, Economics, and Diplomacy of Reparations, 1918–1932 (1993). A comprehensive account of the intricacies of the reparations problem of the 1920s.

I. Kershaw, Hitler, 2 vols. (2001) Replaces all previous biographies.

D. Landes, The Unbound Prometheus: Technological Change and Industrial Development in Western Europe from 1750 to the Present (1969). Includes an excellent analysis of both the Great Depression and the few areas of economic growth.

W.E. Leuchtenburg, Franklin D. Roosevelt and the New Deal: l932–l940 (2009). A superb one-volume treatment.

B. Lincoln, Red Victory: A History of the Russian Civil War (1989). An excellent narrative account.

D.J.K. Peukert, Inside Nazi Germany: Conformity, Opposition, and Racism in Everyday Life (1987). An excellent discussion of life under Nazi rule.

R. Pipes, The Unknown Lenin: From the Secret Archives (1996). A collection of previously unpublished documents that indicated the repressive character of Lenin's government.

P. Pulzer, Jews and the German State: The Political History of a Minority, 1848–1933 (1992). A detailed history by a major historian of European minorities.

L.J. Rupp, Mobilizing Women for War: German and America Propaganda, 1939–1945 (1978). Although concentrating on a later period, it includes an excellent discussion of general Nazi attitudes toward women.

R. Service, Stalin: A Biography (2005). The strongest of a host of recent biographical studies.

R. Service, Trotsky: A Biography (2009). A major new biography.

A. Solzhenitsyn, The Gulag Archipelago, 3 vols. (1974–1979). A major examination of the labor camps under Stalin by one of the most important late twentieth-century Russian writers.

A.J.P. Taylor, English History, 1914–1945 (1965). Lively and opinionated.

A. Tooze, The Wages of Destruction: The Making and Breaking of the Nazi Economy (2006). A wide-ranging, accessible study of the politics and ideology behind Nazi economic policy.

H.A. Turner Jr., German Big Business and the Rise of Hitler (1985). An important major study of the subject.

L. Yahil, The Holocaust: The Fate of European Jewry, 1932–1945 (1990). A major study of this fundamental subject in twentieth-century history.

Chapter 30

A. Adamthwaite, France and the Coming of the Second World War, 1936–1939 (1977). A careful account making good use of the French archives.

O. Bartov, Mirrors of Destruction: War, Genocide, and Modern Identity (2001). Remarkably penetrating essays.

E.R. Beck, Under the Bombs: The German Home Front, 1942–1945 (1986). An interesting examination of a generally unstudied subject.

P.M.H. Bell, The Origins of the Second World War in Europe, 3rd ed. (2007). A comprehensive study of the period and debates surrounding the European origins of World War II.

A. Beevor, The Spanish Civil War (2001). Particularly strong on the political issues.

C. Browning, The Origins of the Final Solution: The Evolution of the Nazi Jewish Policy (2004). The story of how Hitler's policy developed from discrimination to annihilation

A. Bullock, Hitler: A Study in Tyranny, rev. ed. (1964). A brilliant biography.

W.S. Churchill, The Second World War, 6 vols. (1948–1954). The memoirs of the great British leader.

A. Crozier, The Causes of the Second World War, 1997. An examination of what brought on the war.

R.B. Frank, Downfall: The End of the Imperial Japanese Empire (1998). A thorough, well-documented account of the last months of the Japanese Empire and the reasons for its surrender.

J.L. Gaddis, We Now Know: Rethinking Cold War History (1998). A fine account of the early years of the Cold War, making use of new evidence emerging since the collapse of the Soviet Union.

J.L. Gaddis, P.H. Gordon, E.May, eds., Cold War Statesmen Confront the Bomb: Nuclear Diplomacy since 1945 (1999). A collection of essays discussing the effect of atomic and nuclear weapons on diplomacy since World War II.

M. Gilbert, The Holocaust: A History of the Jews of Europe during the Second World War (1985). The best and most comprehensive treatment.

A. Iriye, Pearl Harbor and the Coming of the Pacific War (1999). Essays on how the Pacific war came about, including a selection of documents.

J. Keegan, The Second World War (1990). A lively and penetrating account by a master military historian.

I. Kershaw, Hitler: 1889–1936: Hubris (1999) and Hitler: 1936–1945: Nemesis (2001). An outstanding two-volume biography.

W.F. Kimball, Forged in War: Roosevelt, Churchill, and the Second World War (1998). A study of the collaboration between the two great leaders of the West based on a thorough knowledge of their correspondence.

W. Murray and A.R. Millett, A War to Be Won: Fighting the Second World War, (2000). A splendid account of the military operations in the war.

P. Neville, Hitler and Appeasement: The British Attempt to Prevent the Second World War (2005). A defense of the British appeasers of Hitler.

R. Overy, Why the Allies Won (1997). An anlysis of the reasons for the victory of the Allies, with special emphasis on technology.

N. Rich, Hitler War Aims, 2 vols. (1973–1974). The best study of the subject in English.

P. Wandycz, The Twilight of French Eastern Alliances, 1926–1936 (1988). A well-documented account of the diplomacy of central and eastern Europe in a crucial period.

G.L. Weinberg, A World at Arms: A Global History of World War II (1994). A thorough and excellent narrative account.

Chapter 31

B.S. Anderson and J.P. Pinsser, A History of Their Own: Women in Europe from Prehistory to the Present, Vol. 2 (1988). A broad-ranging survey.

R. Bernstein, Out of the Blue: The Story of September 11, 2001, from Jihad to Ground Zero (2002). An excellent account by a gifted journalist.

A. Brown, The Gorbachev Factor (1996). An important commentary by an English observer.

D. Calleo, Rethinking Europe's Future (2003). A daring book by an experienced commentator.

M. Cini, European Union Politics (2007). An authoritative guide.

J.F. Frieden, Global Capitalism: Its Fall and Rise in the Twentieth Century (2007). Background to the current financial crisis.

J.L. Gaddis, The Cold War: A New History (2006). An important overview.

D.J. Garrow, Bearing the Cross: Martin Luther King Jr. and the Southern Leadership Conference, 1955–1968 (1986). The best work on the subject.

M. I. Goldman, Petrostate: Putin, Power, and the New Russia (2008). A thoughtful, but critical analysis.

D. Halberstam, The Coldest Winter: America and the Korean War (2007). A superb narrative by a gifted journalist.

W. Hitchcock, Struggle for Europe: The Turbulent History of a Divided Continent, 1945–2002 (2003). The best overall narrative now available.

D. Kearns, Lyndon Johnson and the American Dream (1976). Remains a useful biography.

J. Keep, The Last of the Empires: A History of the Soviet Union, 1956–1991 (1995). A clear narrative.

M. Mandelbaum, The Ideas That Conquered the World: Peace, Democracy, and Free Markets (2002). An important analysis by a major commentator on international affairs.

J. Mann, The Rise of the Vulcans: The History of Bush's War Cabinet (2004). An account of the major foreign policy advisers behind the invasion of Iraq.

R. Mann, A Grand Delusion: America's Descent into Vietnam (2001). The best recent narrative.

J. McCormick, Understanding the European Union: A Concise Introduction (2002). Outlines the major features.

N. Naimark, Fires of Hatred: Ethnic Cleansing in Twentieth-Century Europe (2002). A remarkably sensitive treatment of a tragic subject.

T. R. Reid, The United States of Europe: The New Superpower and the End of American Supremacy (2004). A journalist's exploration of the impact of the European Union on American policy.

M.E. Sarotte, 1989: The Struggle to Create Post-Cold War Europe (2009). Explores paths taken and not taken at the time of the collapse of communism.

V. Sebestyen, Revolution 1989: The Fall of the Soviet Empire (2009). A masterful overview of the end of the Cold War Era.

L. Shevtsova, Russia—Lost in Transition: The Yelsin and Putin Legacies (2007). A major analysis and meditation on the past two decades.

R. Story, The Rise of Conservatism in America, 1945–2000: A Brief History with Documents (2007). A basic introductory overview.

M. Walker, The Cold War and the Making of the Modern World (1994). Remains a major survey.

Chapter 32

China

R. Baum, Burying Mao: Chinese Politics in the Age of Deng Xiaoping (1996).

A. Chan, R. Madsen, and J. Unger, Chen Village uunder Mao and Deng (1992).

J. Chang, Wild Swans: Three Daughters of China (1991). An intimate look at recent Chinese society through three generations of women. Immensely readable.

J. Feng, Ten Years of Madness: Oral Histories of China's Cultural Revolution (1996).

J. Fewsmith, China since Tiananmen: The Politics of Transition (2001). Focus is on the rise to power of Jiang Zemin and Chinese politics during the 1990s.

B.M. Frolic, Mao's People: Sixteen Portraits of Life in Revolutionary China (1987).

T. Gold, State and Society in the Taiwan Miracle (1986). The story of economic growth in postwar Taiwan.

M. Goldman, Sowing the Seeds of Democracy in China: Political Reform in the Deng Xiaoping Era (1994).

A. Iriye, China and Japan in the Global Setting (1992).

D.M. Lampton, Same Bed, Different Dreams: Managing U.S.–China Relations, 1989–2000 (2001).

H. Liang, Son of the Revolution (1983). An autobiographical account of a young man growing up in Mao's China.

K. Lieberthal, Governing China, from Revolution through Reform (2004).

B. Liu, People or Monsters? and Other Stories and Reportage from China After Mao (1983). Literary reflections on China.

R. MacFarquhar and J.K. Fairbank, eds., The Cambridge History of China, Vol. 14, Emergence of Revolutionary China (1987), and Vol. 15, Revolutions within the Chinese Revolution, 1966–1982 (1991).

L. Pan, Sons of the Yellow Emperor: A History of the Chinese Diaspora (1990). A pioneer study that treats not only Southeast Asia but the rest of the world as well.

M.R. Ristaino, Port of Last Resort: The Diaspora Communities of Shanghai (2001).

T. Saich, Governance and Politics of China (2004).

H. Wang, China's New Order (2003). Translation of a work by a Qinghua University professor, a liberal within the boundaries of what is permissible in China.

G. White, ed., In Search of Civil Society: Market Reform and Social Change in Contemporary China (1996).

M. Wolf, Revolution Postponed: Women in Contemporary China (1985).

Zhang X. and Sang Y., Chinese Lives: An Oral History of Contemporary China (1987).

Japan

A. Barshay, State and Intellectual in Imperial Japan (1988).

A. Barshay, The Social Sciences in Modern Japan (2007).

G.L. Bernstein, Haruko's World: A Japanese Farm Woman and Her Community (1983). A study of the changing life of a village woman in postwar Japan.

T. Bestor, Neighborhood Tokyo (1989). A portrait of contemporary urban life in Japan.

T. Bestor, Tsukiji (2003).

G.L. Curtis, The Logic of Japanese Politics: Leaders, Institutions, and the Limits of Change (1999).

G.L. Curtis, Policymaking in Japan: Defining the Role of Politicians (2002).

M.H. Cusumano, The Japanese Automobile Industry (1985). A neat study of the postwar business strategies of Toyota and Nissan.

W.T. DeBary, C. Gluck, and A. E. Tiedemann, Comps., Sources of the Japanese Tradition, 2nd ed. (2005).

R.P. Dore, Land Reform in Japan (1959). Another classic.

R.P. Dore, City Life in Japan (1999). A classic, reissued.

S. Garon, Molding Japanese Minds: The State in Everyday Life (1997).

S.M. Garon, The Evolution of Civil Society from Meiji to Heisei (2002). That is to say, from the mid-nineteenth century to the present day.

A. Gordon, ed., Postwar Japan as History (1993).

H. Hibbett, ed., Contemporary Japanese Literature: An Anthology of Fiction, Film, and Other Writing since 1945 (1977). Translations of postwar short stories.

Y. Kawabata, The Sound of the Mountain, trans. by E.G. Seidensticker (1970). Sensitive, moving novel by Nobel author.

J. Nathan, Sony, the Private Life (1999). A lively account of the human side of growth in the Sony Corporation.

D. Okimoto, Between MITI and the Market (1989). A discussion of the respective roles of government and private enterprise in Japan's postwar growth.

S. Pharr, Losing Face: Status Politics in Japan (1996).

E.F. Vogel, Japan as Number One: Lessons for America (1979). Though dated and somewhat sanguine, this remains an insightful classic.

Korea and Vietnam

B. Cumings, Korea: The Unknown War (1988).

B. Cumings, The Origins of the Korean War (Vol. 1, 1981; Vol. 2, 1991).

B. Cumings, The Two Koreas: On the Road to Reunification? (1990).

C.J. Eckert, Korea Old and New, A History (1990). The best short history of Korea, with extensive coverage of the postwar era.

C.J. Eckert, Offspring of Empire: The Koch'ang Kims and the Colonial Origins of Korean Capitalism, 1876–1945 (1991).

G.M.T. Kahin, Intervention: How America Became Involved in Vietnam (1986).

S. Karnow, Vietnam: A History, rev. ed., (1996).

L. Kendall, Shamans, Housewives, and Other Restless Spirits: Women in Korean Ritual and Life (1985).

K.B. Lee, A New History of Korea (1984). A translation by E. Wagner and others of an outstanding Korean work covering the full sweep of Korean history.

T. Li, Nguyen Cochinchina: South Vietnam in the Seventeenth and Eighteenth Centuries (1998).

D. Marr, Vietnam 1945: The Quest for Power (1995).

C.W. Sorensen, Over the Mountains Are Mountains (1988). How peasant households in Korea adapted to rapid industrialization.

A. Woodside, Vietnam and the Chinese Model (1988). Provides the background for Vietnam's relationship to China.

Chapter 33

General Works

P. Farmer, Pathologies of Power: Health, Human Rights, and the New War on the Poor (2003). Farmer, a physician, uses his experiences at Harvard and in the Caribbean to argue that inadequate health care in the Third World violates human rights and imperils us all.

J.H. Latham, Africa, Asia, and South America since 1800: A Bibliographic Guide (1995). A valuable tool for finding materials on the topics in this chapter.

S. Power, A Problem from Hell: America and the Age of Genocide (2002). A masterful analysis of genocides in the twentieth century (in Armenia, the Holocaust, the Khmer Rouge, Kurds, Rwanda, and Bosnia) and the U.S. response.

J.D. Sachs, The End of Poverty: Economic Possibilities for Our Time (2005). A renowned economist's plan to end extreme poverty around the world by 2025.

Latin America

S. Balfour, Castro (2008). A relatively brief survey of Castro's ability to hold power for half a century.

P. Brenner, A Contemporary Cuba Reader: Reinventing the Revolution (2007). A useful analysis of the developments in this century.

J. Dominguez and M. Shifter, Constructing Democratic Governance in Latin America (2008). Contains individual country studies.

G. W. Grayson, Mexico: Narco-Violence and a Failed State? (2009). Explores the impact of drug violence on Mexican politics.

G. Joseph et al., The Mexico Reader: History, Culture, Politics (2003). Excellent introduction to major issues.

P. Lowden, Moral Opposition to Authoritarian Rule in Chile (1996). A discussion of Chilean politics from the standpoint of human rights.

J. Preston and S. Dillon, Opening Mexico: The Making of a Democracy (2004). Excellent analysis of developments in Mexico prior to the outbreak of the drug wars.

H. Wiarda, Politics and Social Change in Latin America (2003). Attempts to examine the subject in light of long-standing historic trends in Latin America.

E. Williamson, The Penguin History of Latin America (2010). The best recent survey.

Africa

B. Davidson, Let Freedom Come (1978). Remains a thoughtful commentary of African independence.

P. Gourevitch, We Wish to Inform You that Tomorrow We Will Be Killed with Our Families (1999). An account of the Rwandan genocide that is beautifully written and almost unbearable to read.

J. Herbst, States and Power in Africa (2000). Relates current issues of African state-building to those before the colonial era.

R.W. July, A History of the African People, 5th ed. (1995). Provides a careful and clear survey of post–World War I history and consideration of nationalism.

N. Mandela, Long Walk to Freedom: The Autobiography of Nelson Mandela (1995). Autobiography of the African leader who transformed South Africa.

L. Thompson, A History of South Africa (2001). The best survey.

N. Van de Walle, African Economies and the Politics of Permanent Crisis, 1979–1999 (2001). Exploration of the difficulties of African economic development.

India and Pakistan

O.B. Jones, Pakistan: Eye of the Storm (2003). Best recent introduction.

R. Rashid, Taliban: Militant Islam, Oil and Fundamentalism in Central Asia (2001). Analysis of radical Isalmist regime in Afghanistan.

R.W. Stern, Changing India: Bourgeois Revolution on the Subcontinent (2003). Overview of forces now changing Indian society.

S. Wolpert, A New History of India (2003). The closing chapters of this fine survey history are particularly helpful in orienting the reader in postwar Indian history until the mid-1980s.

Islam and the Middle East

A. Ahmed, Discovering Islam: Making Sense of Muslim History and Society, rev. ed. (2003). An excellent and readable overview of Islamic–Western relations.

J. Esposito, The Islamic Threat: Myth or Reality, 2nd ed. (1992). A useful corrective to some of the polemics against Islam and Muslims today.

J.J. Esposito, ed., The Oxford Encyclopedia of Islam (1999). A thematic survey of Islamic history, particularly strong in the Modern Era.

D. Fromkin, A Peace to End All Peace: The Fall of the Ottoman Empire and the Creation of the Modern Middle East (2001). Very good on the impact of World War I on the region.

G. Fuller, The Future of Political Islam (2003). A very good overview of Islamist ideology by a former CIA staff member.

J. Keay, Sowing the Wind: The Seeds of Conflict in the Middle East (2003). A balanced account.

N.R. Keddie, Modern Iran: Roots and Results of Revolution (2003). Chapters 6–12 focus on Iran from 1941 through the first years of the 1978 revolution and provide a solid overview of history in this era.

G. Kepel, Jihad: The Trail of Political Islam (2002). An extensive treatment by a leading French scholar of the subject.

Credits

Cover: Erich Lessing/Art Resource, NY/Harpist playing and singing to Anhour Khaou, chief builder at Thebes, and to his wife. Wall painting in Anhour Khaou's tomb, carved 10 m below ground level, in the cemetery of Deir el-Medina, Tombs of the Nobles, Thebes, Egypt.

Chapter 1, page 1: De Agostini Editore Picture Library; **page 4:** Reconstruction credited to John Swogger; **page 7:** Victory stele of Naram-Sin, King of Akkad, over the mountain-dwelling Lullubi, Mesopotamian, Akkadian Period, c. 2230 B.C. (pink sandstone). Louvre, Paris, France/The Bridgeman Art Library International Ltd. **page 8:** Clay tablet from the Chaldean period (612 539 B.C.E.) Courtesy of the Trustees of the British Museum. © Copyright The British Museum; **page 11:** Kenneth Garrettings/National Geographic Image Collection; **page 12:** Jon Arnold/Alamy Images; **page 13:** "Seated Scribe" from Saqqara, Egypt. 5th Dynasty, c. 2510-2460 B.C.E. Painted limestone, height 21' (53 cm). Musée du Louvre, Paris. Bridgeman-Giraudon/Art Resource, NY; **page 14:** British Museum, London, UK/The Bridgeman Art Library International Ltd. **page 15:** Gilgamesh. Relief from the Temple of Saragon II, Khorsabad. Assyrian, 8th century B.C.E. Louvre, Paris, France. Copyright Giraudon/Art Resource, NY; **page 18:** Borromeo/Art Resource, NY; **page 19:** © Scala/Art Resource, NY; **page 24:** Lowell Georgia/CORBIS - NY; **page 26:** Freer Gallery of Art, Smithsonian Institution, Washington, D.C.: F1936.6; **page 28:** Werner Forman/Art Resource, NY.

Chapter 2, page 32: Courtesy of the Library of Congress; **page 36:** National Palace Museum, Taipei, Taiwan, Republic of China; **page 37:** Courtesy of the Freer Gallery of Art, Smithsonian Institution, Washington, D.C.; **page 42:** Mario Tama/Getty Images, Inc. **page 43:** Borromeo/EPA/Art Resource, NY; **page 45:** Courtesy of the Library of Congress; **page 46:** Relief, Israel, 10th-6th Century: Judean exiles carrying provisions. Detail of the Assyrian conquest of the Jewish fortified town of Lachish (battle 701 BC). Part of a relief from the palace of Sennacherib at Niniveh, Mesopotamia (Iraq). British Museum, London, Great Britain. Copyright Erich Lessing/Art Resource, NY; **page 47:** Courtesy of the Library of Congress. Gardiner Greene Hubbard Collection; **page 50:** © Scala/Art Resource; **page 56:** Courtesy of the Library of Congress; **page 57:** Minkowski, Maurycy (1881–1930). "After the Pogrom", c. 1910. The Jewish Museum, New York, NY, U.S.A. Photo Credit: Jewish Museum/Art Resource, NY.

Chapter 3, page 58: Picture Desk, Inc./Kobal Collection, NY; **page 61:** Scala/Art Resource, NY; **page 63:** Art Resource, NY; **page 68:** Courtesy of the Trustees of the British Museum; **page 69:** Bibliotheque Nationale de France; **page 70:** © Foto Marburg/Art Resource, NY; **page 72:** cAAAC/Topham/The Image Works; **page 79:** Meredith Pillon/Greek National Tourism Organization; **page 81:** David Lees/CORBIS; **page 84:** Laocoon, Vatican Museums, Vatican State. Copyright Giraudon/Art Resource, NY; **page 85:** © 2004 Christie's Images, Inc.

Chapter 4, page 90: Art Resource, NY; **page 94:** © Tim Page/CORBIS All Rights Reserved; **page 97:** © Ashmolean Museum, Oxford, England, U.K. **page 98:** Werner Forman Archive; **page 99:** Sculpted head of Buddha, from Gandhara, 2nd century B.C. Paris, Musée Guimet. RMN: Reunion Musées Nationaux. **page 100:** © CORBIS All Rights Reserved; **page 103:** A leaf from a Manichaean Book, Kocho, Temple K (MIK III 6368), 8th-9th century, manuscript painting, 17.2 × 11.2 cm. Bildarchiv Preussischer Kulturbesitz/Art Resource, NY; **page 106:** Borromeo/Art Resource, NY; **page 109:** Scala/Art Resource, NY; **page 111:** Rick Sherwin/Photolibrary.com; **page 116:** The Nelson-Atkins Museum of Art, Kansas City, Missouri. (Purchase: Nelson Trust) 50-20; **page 117:** argus/Schwarzbach/Photolibrary/Peter Arnold, Inc.

Chapter 5, page 118: Henri Lhote Collection. Musée de l'Homme, Paris, France. © Photograph by Erich Lessing/Art Resource, NY; **page 123:** John Warburton-Lee/Danita Delimont Photography; **page 126:** AKG Images/Jurgen Sorges; **page 129:** Nigeria, Nok head, 900BC-200AD, Rafin Kura, Nok. Prehistoric West African sculpture from the Nok culture. Terracotta, 36 cms high. © Werner Forman/Art Resource, NY; **page 130:** University of Pennsylvania Museum object E8183, image# 142043; **page 131:** Werner Forman/Art Resource, NY; **page 132:** © Michael S. Lewis/CORBIS; **page 135:** Getty Images Inc. - Hulton Archive Photos; **page 135:** © Michael & Patricia Fogden/CORBIS All Rights Reserved; **page 137:** © CORBIS All Rights Reserved; **page 138:** Anup Shah/Nature Picture Library.

Chapter 6, page 142: Fresco with seated woman playing a kithara (lyre). Roman, ca. 40-30 B.C. Paintings. Pompeian, Boscoreale. 1st Century B. C. Wall painting from the east wall of large room in the villa of Publius Fannius Synistor. Fresco on lime plaster. H. 6 ft. 1 1/2 in. W. 6 ft. 1 1/2 in. (187 × 187 cm.). The Metropolitan Museum of Art, Rogers Fund, 1903. (03.14.5) Photograph © 1986 The Metropolitan Museum of Art. Art Resource, NY; **page 145:** Sarcophagus of a Couple. Etruscan, 6th B.C.E. Terracotta. H: 114 cm. Louvre, Paris, France. Copyright Erich Lessing/Art Resource, NY; **page 147:** Alinari/Art Resource, NY; **page 149:** Getty Images/De Agostini Editore Picture Library; **page 151:** Rheinisches Landesmuseum, Trier, Germany. Alinari/Art Resource, NY; **page 155:** Simon James © Dorling Kindersley; **page 157:** Charitable Foundation, Gemeinnutzige Stiftung Leonard von Matt; **page 158:** Saturnia, Tellus, Goddess of Earth, Air and Water. Panel from the Ara Pacis. 13-9 B.C.E.. Museum of the Ara Pacis, Rome. Nimatallah/Art Resource, NY; **page 160:** Scala/Art Resource, NY; **page 161:** Sappho, idealized portrait of a girl posing as a poetess. Fresco from Pompeii, Insula Occidentale. Museo Archeologico Nazionale, Naples, Italy Erich Lessing/Art Resource, NY; **page 161:** Gismondi. Reconstruction of a large house and apartments at Ostia. Museo della Civilta Romana, Rome, Italy. Copyright Scala/Art Resource, NY; **page 163:** Courtesy of the Library of Congress.

Chapter 7, page 174: Erich Lessing/Art Resource, NY; **page 178:** Photo Researchers, Inc.; **page 179:** KEREN SU/Danita Delimont.com; **page 183:** Werner Forman/Art Resource, NY;

Chapter 15, page 358: Courtesy of the Library of Congress. Rare Book and Special Collections Division; **page 363:** Scala/Art Resource, NY; **page 364:** Fotomarburg/Art Resource, NY; **page 365:** Scala/Art Resource, NY; **page 367:** Cliche Bibliotheque Nationale de France - Paris; **page 368:** Copyright Scala/Art Resource, NY; **page 369:** William haranguing his troups for combat with the English army. Detail from the Bayeux tapestry, scene 51. Musée de la Tapisserie, Bayeux, France. Photograph copyright Bridgeman-Giraudon/Art Resource, NY; **page 373:** The Granger Collection, New York; **page 374:** Statue of Pope Boniface VIII. Museo Civico, Bologna. Scala/Art Resource, NY; **page 377:** St. Bavo, Ghent, Belgium/The Bridgeman Art Library; **page 377:** Embassy of Italy; **page 378:** Scala/Art Resource, NY.

Chapter 16, page 384: Courtesy of the Library of Congress; **page 387:** Sebastiano del Piombo (1485–1547). Portrait of a man, said to be Christopher Columbus (born about 1446, died 1506. 1519. Oil on canvas, 42 × 34 3/4 in. (106.7 × 88.3 cm). Gift of J. Pierpont Morgan, 1900 (00.18.2). The Metropolitan Museum of Art, New York, NY, USA. Image copyright © The Metropolitan Museum of Art/Art Resource, NY; **page 391:** Lawrence Pordes © Dorling Kindersley, Courtesy of The British Library; **page 391:** Art Resource, NY; **page 394:** Courtesy of the Library of Congress; **page 395:** "Suffer the Little Children to Come Unto Me," 1538 (oil on panel) by Lucas Cranach, the Elder (1472–1553) © Hamburger Kunsthalle, Hamburg, Germany/The Bridgeman Art Library; **page 398:** Peter Paul Rubens (1577–1640)/Art Resource, NY; **page 399:** "Holbein, Hans the Younger" (1497–1543) after: The Artist's Family. Photo: P. Bernard. Location: Musée des Beaux-Arts, Lille, France Photo Credit: Réunion des Musées Nationaux/Art Resource, NY; **page**

400: Hacker Art Books Inc.; **page 402:** The Art Archive/Musée des Beaux Arts Lausanne/Picture Desk, Inc./Kobal Collection; **page 403:** The "Milch Cow." Rijksmuseum, Amsterdam; **page 404:** Elizabeth I (1558–1603) standing on a map of England in 1592. An astute politician in both foreign and domestic policy, Elizabeth was perhaps the most successful ruler of the sixteenth century. By courtesy of the National Portrait Gallery, London; **page 406:** "The Weather Witches" 1523 Hans Baldung Grien (1484/85–1545 German) Oil on wood Städelsches Kunstinstitut, Frankfurt am Main, Germany/Superstock; **page 408:** Courtesy of the Library of Congress. Rare Book and Special Collection Divsion; **page 412:** The Pentecost, ca. 1150–1175. Made in Meuse Valley, South Netherlands, Champleve' enamel on copper gilt. Overall: 4 1/16 × 4 1/16 in. (10.3 × 10.3 cm). The Cloisters Collection, 1965 (65.105) The Metropolitan Museum of Art, New York, NY, USA. Image copyright © The Metropolitan Museum of Art/Art Resource, NY; **page 413:** Lee Marriner/AP Wide World Photos.

Chapter 17, page 414: The Granger Collection; **page 416:** Jeremy Horner/CORBIS - NY; **page 418:** Samuel Scott, "Old Custom House Quay" Collection. V&A Images, The Victoria and Albert Museum, London; **page 419:** © Bildarchiv Preussischer Kulturbesitz/Art Resource, NY; **page 420:** The Granger Collection, New York; **page 422:** Library of Congress; **page 424:** Fur traders and Indians: engraving, 1777. © The Granger Collection, New York; **page 426:** The Granger Collection; **page 426:** Photolibrary/Peter Arnold, Inc.; **page 430:** Abby Aldrich Rockefeller Folk Art Museum, The Colonial Williamsburg Foundation, Williamsburg, VA; **page 432:** Courtesy of the Library of Congress; **page 435:** Library of Congress; **page 436:** The New York Public Library/Art Resource, NY.

Index

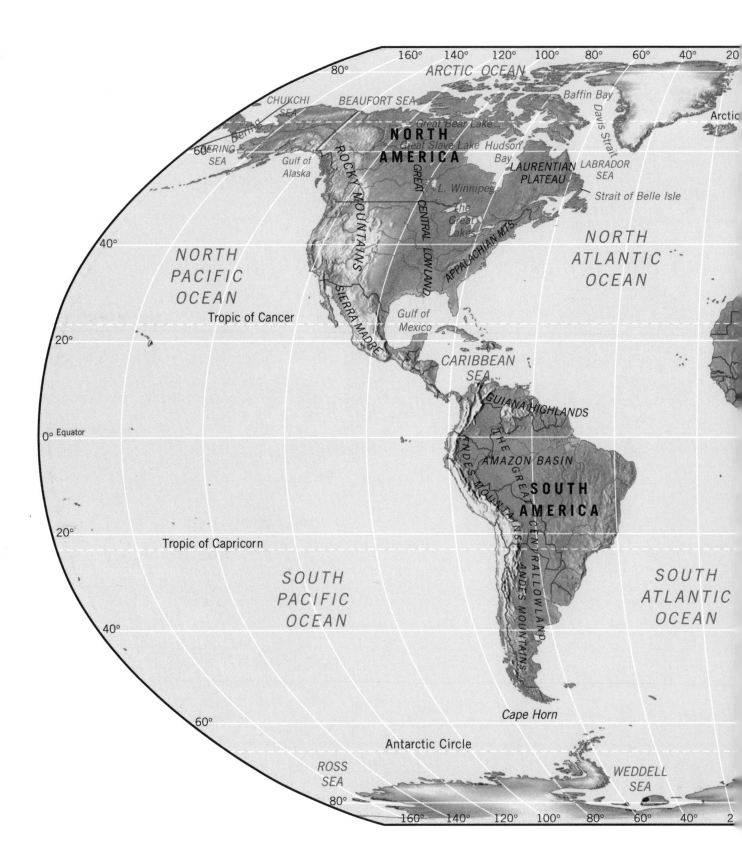

ARCTIC OCEAN

160° 140° 120° 100° 80° 60° 40° 20

80°

CHUKCHI
SEA

BEAUFORT SEA

Baffin Bay

Arctic

Bering

Great Bear Lake

NORTH
AMERICA

Davis Strait

60°

BERING
SEA

Great Slave Lake Hudson

Gulf of
Alaska

ROCKY MOUNTAINS

L. Winnipeg

Bay

LAURENTIAN
PLATEAU

LABRADOR
SEA

GREAT CENTRAL LOWLAND

the
Great
Lakes

Strait of Belle Isle

40°

NORTH
PACIFIC
OCEAN

APPALACHIAN MTS.

NORTH
ATLANTIC
OCEAN

Tropic of Cancer

SIERRA MADRE

Gulf of
Mexico

20°

CARIBBEAN
SEA

GUIANA HIGHLANDS

0° Equator

THE GREAT MOUNTAINS

ANDES MOUNTAINS

AMAZON BASIN

SOUTH
AMERICA

20°

Tropic of Capricorn

CENTRAL LOWLAND

SOUTH
PACIFIC
OCEAN

ANDES MOUNTAINS

SOUTH
ATLANTIC
OCEAN

40°

60°

Cape Horn

Antarctic Circle

ROSS
SEA

WEDDELL
SEA

80°

160° 140° 120° 100° 80° 60° 40° 2

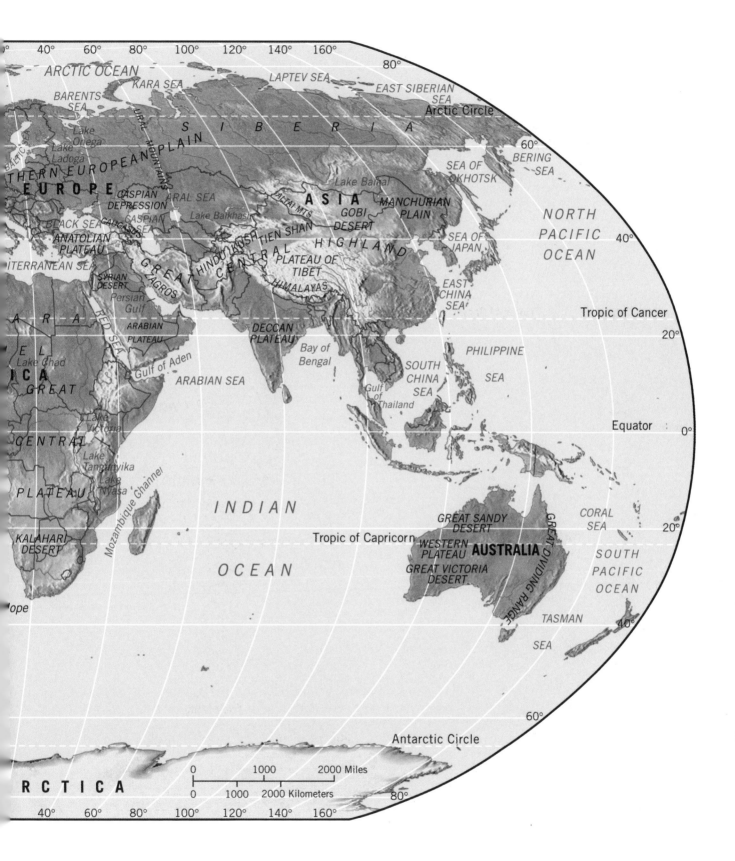

ARCTIC OCEAN

KARA SEA

LAPTEV SEA

EAST SIBERIAN SEA

BARENTS SEA

Arctic Circle

Lake Onega

URAL MOUNTAINS

S I B E R I A

60°

BERING SEA

Lake Ladoga

BALTIC

ORTHERN EUROPEAN PLAIN

Lake Baikal

SEA OF OKHOTSK

NORTH PACIFIC OCEAN

EUROPE

CASPIAN DEPRESSION

ARAL SEA

A S I A

MANCHURIAN PLAIN

40°

CASPIAN SEA

Lake Balkhash

ALTAI MTS

GOBI DESERT

BLACK SEA

CAUCASUS

ANATOLIAN PLATEAU

HINDU KUSH

TIEN SHAN

CENTRAL HIGHLAND

SEA OF JAPAN

ITERRANEAN SEA

GREAT

ZAGROS

PLATEAU OF TIBET

EAST CHINA SEA

SYRIAN DESERT

HIMALAYAS

Tropic of Cancer

A R A

Persian Gulf

ARABIAN PLATEAU

DECCAN PLATEAU

20°

E L

RED SEA

Lake Chad

Gulf of Aden

Bay of Bengal

PHILIPPINE

ICA

ARABIAN SEA

SOUTH CHINA SEA

SEA

GREAT

Gulf of Thailand

Lake Victoria

Equator

0°

CENTRAL

Lake Tanganyika

Lake Nyasa

Mozambique Channel

INDIAN

GREAT SANDY DESERT

CORAL SEA

PLATEAU

OCEAN

20°

KALAHARI DESERT

Tropic of Capricorn

WESTERN PLATEAU

AUSTRALIA

GREAT DIVIDING RANGE

SOUTH PACIFIC OCEAN

OCEAN

GREAT VICTORIA DESERT

ope

TASMAN

40°

SEA

60°

Antarctic Circle

0		1000		2000 Miles
0	1000	2000 Kilometers		

RCTICA

80°

40°   60°   80°   100°   120°   140°   160°